D1172851

Lessing's Dramatic Theory

CAMBRIDGE
UNIVERSITY PRESS
LONDON: BENTLEY HOUSE
NEW YORK, TORONTO, BOMBAY
CALCUTTA, MADRAS: MACMILLAN
TOKYO: MARUZEN COMPANY LTD

THE HAMBURG THEATRE OPENED BY ACKERMANN IN 1765

(*From a watercolour in the possession of the Museum für Hamburgische Geschichte*)

Lessing's Dramatic Theory

BEING AN
INTRODUCTION TO & COMMENTARY
ON HIS
HAMBURGISCHE DRAMATURGIE

by

J. G. ROBERTSON

*Late Professor of German Language and Literature
in the University of London*

CAMBRIDGE
AT THE UNIVERSITY PRESS
1939

26728

PRINTED IN GREAT BRITAIN

CONTENTS

Part Three

LESSING'S DRAMATIC THEORY

ILLUSTRATIONS

INTRODUCTORY NOTE

The present volume is the outcome of investigations pursued for many years by the late Professor J. G. Robertson. At his death in 1933 the work was almost complete, with the exception of Chapter xv, for which a series of memoranda and extracts existed showing the line of treatment which the author intended to follow, and of the *Conclusion*, for which a first draft was found. This draft has been printed here, since it embodies the author's personal view and has for that reason a special value, although it is almost certainly not wholly in the form which it would ultimately have taken. With these exceptions, the MS. only stood in need of final revision, and of the verifications involved in its preparation for the press. But since the author alone could be aware of the extent to which verification was needed, it has been necessary to carry out a much more comprehensive examination than is usually required at this stage. Professor Robertson had drawn information from many libraries and collections in different European countries, and over a long period of years. It has been my task to trace his materials to their source, even though this might often imply covering again ground which had already been covered. All references and quotations have been verified, and in some cases *lacunae* have been filled in accordance with what was clearly the intention of the author. Quotations have been given in the exact form in which they occur in the original, without standardisation in respect of spelling or accentuation. Both grammatical and orthographical peculiarities have thus been reproduced unchanged—the only exception to this being the indications of *Umlaut*.

I have avoided, as far as I have been able to do so, alterations in the text of the work; my guiding principle has been to present it in a form as near as possible to that which I believe it would have assumed under the author's hand. I am well aware that no labour of mine can take the place of the final revision which the author himself would have made. But it has been a privilege, which I have valued, to associate myself at his request with a work to which he gave so much labour and so many years.

It is impossible for me to express—as Professor Robertson would have expressed—the gratitude which is undoubtedly due to individuals and institutions with whose help the original researches were carried out. But for my own part I wish to acknowledge my particular indebtedness to the authorities of the Preussische Staatsbibliothek, Berlin, the Staats- und Universitäts-Bibliothek, Hamburg, the Herzogliche Bibliothek, Gotha, the Staatsbibliothek, München, and the Universitätsbibliothek, Leipzig, for much courtesy and kindness during my visits to these libraries, and to the Director of the Auskunftsbüro der Deutschen Bibliotheken for his helpful aid in enquiries for rare works; to the librarians of the University Library, Cambridge, the Bibliothèque Nationale, the Royal Library at The Hague, the Stadtbibliothek, Dresden, and the Universitätsbibliothek, Marburg, for their kindness in lending books and in answering enquiries; to Dr Lothar Gross, of the Haus-Hof- und Staatsarchiv, Vienna, for his good offices in obtaining books and information from other libraries, and to Dr L. W. Kahn (Rochester, U.S.A.) for his personal kindness in sending me photostat pages from a rare volume in the New York Public Library. I am indebted to the authorities of the *Museum für Hamburgische Geschichte* for permission to publish the picture of the Hamburg Theatre which appears as frontispiece.

I need hardly add that the work which I have carried out in connexion with this volume would have been impossible without the extensive resources of the British Museum Library and the great kindness of its custodians.

The publication of this book has been generously aided by a grant from the Publications Fund of the University of London.

EDNA PURDIE

London 1938

JOHN GEORGE ROBERTSON

Born January 18, 1867

Educated Glasgow University, M.A. 1886, B.Sc. 1889;

Leipzig University, Ph.D. 1892;

Lecturer in English (subsequently Professor Extraordinarius), Strassburg University, 1896–1903;

Professor of German Language and Literature, University of London, 1903–1933 (1920–1933 tenable at Bedford College);

Director of Scandinavian Studies, University College, London, 1924–1933;

Editor of *Modern Language Review*, 1905–1933;

Chairman of Council, English Goethe Society, 1923–1930, President, 1930–1933;

President of Modern Humanities Research Association, 1924–1925;

Hon. Litt.D., Manchester, 1928;

Hon. Litt.D., Dublin, 1928;

F.R.S.L.; F.B.A.;

Order of the Star of the North of Sweden;

Order of St Olaf of Norway;

Medal *Für Kunst und Wissenschaft.*

Died May 28, 1933.

LARGER WORKS

History of German Literature, 1902 (revised 1931).

Schiller after a Century, 1905.

The Literature of Germany (Home University Library).

Goethe and the Twentieth Century (Cambridge Manuals of Science and Literature), 1912.

Studies in the Genesis of Romantic Theory in the Eighteenth Century, 1923.

Goethe and Byron (Publications of the English Goethe Society, N.S. v), 1925.

Goethe (Republic of Letters), 1927.

The Life and Work of Goethe, 1932.

Essays and Addresses on Literature, 1935.

INTRODUCTION

The German drama was the last of the greater national dramas of Europe to free itself from the leading-strings of the Church, to emerge from that common matrix of dramatised liturgy and naïvely reproduced biblical story from which the drama sets out in all Christian lands. Apart from such plays, performed, or at least controlled, by servants of the Church, one can hardly point to any German dramatic literature before the sixteenth century; the instincts of the people for imitative representation, resting often on traditions which stretched back into pre-Christian times, took no shape which could be described as literary. The profession of the actor was correspondingly slower to disengage itself from that of the mediaeval mountebank who provided the favourite entertainment of the common crowd.

The sixteenth century was not without promise of a kind. Indeed, in the striving of the literature of that century to dissociate itself from the all-obsessing religious controversy the drama was not behindhand; it does reveal, in a dim, unconscious way, some effort to take upon itself aesthetic form. Slowly and with difficulty the humanistic drama of ancient pedigree found acceptance with the German people; but, Latin in form, technique and spirit, it long remained an exotic. For that matter, the highest dramatic achievement of Germany in the sixteenth century is to be sought in the plays written in the Latin language. This fact alone is testimony to the lack of a dramatic art that could be called national, or had root in the consciousness of the people. The movement for religious reform which filled the sixteenth century, however, provided the plays of that century with a serious content; and, difficult as their untutored authors found it to press their ardent Protestantism into the Procrustean bed of humanistic form—the resultant products were often grotesque enough—a certain progress as the century advanced is noticeable. More hopeful, in many ways, than the religious drama was the beginning of a genuinely autochthonous comedy which knew nothing of humanistic example, with the 'Fastnachtspiele' or shrovetide plays, which in the hands of the prolific cobbler poet of Nürnberg, Hans Sachs, often attained a high degree of excellence. Thus there was dramatic promise of a kind in the sixteenth century, and one likes to think that under more auspicious political and social conditions, the German people might have entered thus early upon a development such as that which in England led to such dizzy heights before the century was out.

Difficult as the Germans found it to throw a bridge from these stirrings of the popular dramatic instinct to the humanistic drama, it was much harder for them to acquire understanding for the real essence of dramatic poetry. Their plays, whatever may have been their promise, were still little more than narratives in dialogue form. They were first to learn what constituted the real nerve of the drama and distinguished it from other forms of imaginative creation, on the arrival of wandering companies of English actors towards the close of the sixteenth century. These troupes brought with them the English form of stage, on which they performed the more showy and sensational plays of the Elizabethan theatre—sadly garbled, it may be, for since they were playing to foreigners who did not understand their tongue, they were under no necessity to be careful about their words. Here was the opportunity of a great education for the German theatre, still hardly emerged from its infancy; and if the German imitators of these English plays—men such as the Nürnberg notary Jakob Ayrer and Duke Heinrich Julius of Brunswick—had not been so lacking in higher poetic talent, the German drama might have reaped immediate benefit from this invasion. Here was the moment to graft on the naïve native art of Hans Sachs a higher dramatic significance. As it was, however, these German imitators represent only the glimmer of better things; their attempts did not get beyond the adoption of the English mode of dramatic presentation. And they had hardly ceased to write when all progress was brought to a standstill by the devastation of the Thirty Years' War. But the war was not alone responsible for the check; in the seventeenth century Germany was exposed to the delayed influence of the Latin Renaissance, and the English example was forgotten in the desire to vie with the polite writers of Latin Europe. But how futile it all was! At a time when Corneille was already celebrating his triumphs in France, the Germans were still as far from a national dramatic art as ever; they could point to nothing better than the crude Senecan tragedy of Andreas Gryphius and Daniel Caspar von Lohenstein.

If the German tragedy of the seventeenth century was thus so hopelessly inferior to that of England or France—its comedy was, in isolated examples, not lacking in promise—the state of the German theatre was yet more deplorable. The German actor was still little more than a wandering vagabond, dependent on the caprice of town or village authorities as to whether he should be allowed to play at all; and of buildings set apart for the express purpose of performing dramas there was no question, at least not until late in the century. There is indeed no darker and more depressing chapter among the many dark chapters of European dramatic history than that which concerns the German theatre of the seventeenth century.

A faint hope of improvement came with the activities of Meister Johann Velthen (1640–92), the one German actor of the seventeenth century who stands out with some pre-eminence as a man inspired by higher ideals. With a certain pride the German literary histories record that Velthen actually played Corneille's *Polyeucte* in Leipzig in 1669, that he cultivated Molière and adapted the scenarios of Gherardi to German needs.[1] But when we look closely into Velthen's activities, we find that the version of *Polyeucte* by C. Cormarten (Christophorus Kormart) which he produced, was an outrage on Corneille —was, in fact, a mere collection of sensational horrors decked out with the naïve realism which had been made popular by the English actors; and that his imitations of Franco-Italian comedy were the crudest of buffooneries. What Velthen offered the Germans was only the empty shell of the new dramatic literature of Europe—indeed it was hardly recognisable as such. It is idle to claim that he made any attempt to bridge the yawning gulf that separated literature from the stage in Germany; and he probably cherished no ambitions beyond the daily toil to make ends meet. But even for such modest efforts as his there was no response from the German public; and broken and disappointed, he died in 1692 in Hamburg—that Hamburg which was to stand in the forefront of German theatrical enterprise in the next hundred years. Moreover, any germs of better things in the 'legitimate' theatre of the seventeenth century were killed by a new and insidious form of dramatic entertainment which appealed mightily to German tastes, the opera. On this opera, and not on the drama, was lavished the extravagance of later seventeenth-century minor potentates who wished to emulate at their courts the splendours of Versailles. The first German theatres were opera-houses. Velthen then was not the first of the moderns, but rather the last of the race of mediaeval vagabonds who carried over into a later age the traditions of histrionic entertainment which had come down from Roman times. 'The art of the theatre', says Devrient, 'did not die in the seventeenth

[1] Cp. E. Devrient, *Geschichte der deutschen Schauspielkunst,* new ed. by H. Devrient, Berlin, 1905, i, pp. 125 ff.

century; it was stunted, ran wild, had to pass through all the stages of decay...and do penance for all the extravagances to which rivalry with the opera and the abandonment of poetry had condemned it.'[1] Comedy meant crude and coarse improvisation, and tragedy still cruder and coarser 'Haupt- und Staatsaktionen'—in all, perhaps the lowest level to which the art of the theatre in Europe ever sank.

Velthen's widow continued the work of her husband, not without success, for some twenty-five years after his death; but there was still no hope of better things. A new foreign invasion—companies of extempore players from the south of Europe, at the head of which stood the harlequin—introduced another disturbing factor. For a time the old Hans Wurst and Pickelhäring of the native stage were forgotten, ousted by the Italian in his coat of many colours; the Italian masks enjoyed an enormous vogue. Still, as Lessing insisted,[2] the harlequin was not entirely a thing of evil, and with the Viennese comic actors Johann Anton Stranitzky (who had begun his career with Velthen) and Gottfried Prehauser, a fusion with native elements was effected: early in the eighteenth century[3] the Italian harlequin was converted into a German harlequin. Nothing is less international than humour, and the comic figure of the old German theatre never remained long an exotic figure, whatever his origins—English clown or Italian harlequin—had been. This is perhaps one drop of consolation in all the unhappy history of stagnancy and decay.

It is thus hardly possible to find a single encouraging moment in the history of the German theatre prior to the advent of Caroline Neuber in the eighteenth century; and even her activities set in when that century had already passed its first quarter. Friederike Caroline Neuber (*née* Weissenborn)[4] was a woman of remarkable acumen and character; but she, too, had had to pass through the apprenticeship of vagabondage and bear the brunt of the unhappy tradition. In no art are the links of tradition closer and more tenacious than in that of the theatre. But with her a new hope for the fraternisation of stage and literature was born. She came of something better than the strolling acting class, her father having been a doctor of laws. Born

[1] Cp. E. Devrient, *op. cit.* i, p. 159. Cp. also *Das deutsche Drama*, herausg. von R. F. Arnold, München, 1925, pp. 167 ff.

[2] *Dramaturgie*, XVIII, 36 ff.; see below, pp. 424 ff.

[3] Cp. W. Creizenach, *Die Entstehungsgeschichte des neueren deutschen Lustspiels*, Halle, 1879, p. 9.

[4] Cp. F. J. von Reden-Esbeck, *Caroline Neuber und ihre Zeitgenossen*, Leipzig, 1881; also Devrient, *op. cit.* i, pp. 263 ff.

in Reichenbach in 1697, she enjoyed a comparatively good education, and when her father settled as an advocate in Zwickau, she, weary of his galling tutelage, ran away from home. This was in 1717. She married Johann Neuber of Zwickau, and with him joined Spiegelberg's company of players at Weissenfels. Caroline Neuber—one always speaks of her, not of her husband, who was but an indifferent actor—passed then to the 'Polnisch-Sächsische' company of Madame Hoffmann, the best of its day. In the course of her wanderings she occasionally saw French troupes playing in Germany, and fell under the spell of their declamation of the alexandrine. Even before Gottsched stretched out a helping hand to her, she had appeared in dramas of literary distinction, such as Corneille's *Cid* and Pradon's *Regulus*, crudely adapted as they no doubt were. Her strength seems, however, to have lain rather in comedy rôles. Ultimately she formed a company of her own, and in 1727 played at the Leipzig Easter Fair. This was the significant moment when Gottsched took the step of inviting her to join forces with him and assist him to elevate and purify the German stage. For over ten years Leipzig was the headquarters of her company, and may thus fairly claim the honour of being the cradle of the modern German theatre. From Leipzig she paid periodical visits to Dresden, Brunswick, Hanover, Hamburg and Nürnberg. The honours in this partnership of the actress with the Leipzig professor, whereby a certain conciliation was effected between dramatic poetry and the entertainment of the stage, lay rather with Frau Neuber than with Gottsched. It was condescension on his part; but not a little heroism on hers. It was she who had to bear the brunt of that antagonism which, in matters of the theatre, always takes so brutal a form; she who had to face discouragement and failure.

Gottsched's action in enlisting Frau Neuber's co-operation was no mere sudden impulse or inspiration—Gottsched was not the man to be influenced by such—but was part of an important movement which originated in France. There is, indeed, no more decisive event in the history of the modern theatre than when the great Cardinal Richelieu condescended to extend a helping hand to the French theatre in 1630, and when, backed by his authority, Chapelain set up laws and norms for a French national drama and d'Aubignac devised his *Projet pour le rétablissement du théâtre français*, to be followed later by his famous *Pratique du Théâtre*. Thus the stage entered the service of the state as something more than a mere provider of entertainment— as a vehicle of education, an 'école de vertu'. In the course of time, after it had justified itself at home, this reform spread to other lands. Italy was the first country to welcome it; and it is possible that it did not reach Germany directly from France, but by way of Italy.[1] Many new literary ideas, not only French but even English, came to her through this channel in the early eighteenth century. Impressed by Richelieu's patronage of the theatre, the Italian churchman and scholar, Ludovico Muratori, pleaded for a similar reform of the Italian theatre; his plea was taken up and put into practice by Count Scipione Maffei, who attempted to establish in his native Verona a national Italian stage. Maffei enlisted the assistance of the actor Luigi Riccoboni or 'Lelio', and revived old Italian plays, while the encroachment of the harlequin on the serious drama was at least kept within bounds. Maffei's *Teatro scelto* was the forerunner and model of Gottsched's *Deutsche Schaubühne*. As Maffei, with Riccoboni's help, created a theatre to fulfil the functions of the re-organised theatre in France, so the 'Senior' of the Deutsche Gesellschaft in Leipzig won over Caroline Neuber and her company to bring about similar reforms in Germany. Following Maffei's lead, he declared war on the harlequin; and as Riccoboni won fame for his patron's *Merope*, so Gottsched, with the help of Caroline Neuber, gave Germany a tragedy, *Der sterbende Cato*, which was to point out the way she should go. Unfortunately *Der sterbende Cato*, a quite uninspired blending of the *Caton d'Utique* of F. M. C. Deschamps with Addison's *Cato*, was no masterpiece. All this happened just a hundred years after the reform of the theatre had been initiated in France.

Caroline Neuber's innovations were not restricted to the establishment of the regular alexandrine tragedy on the German stage; she also introduced order and punctuality into her company; she fought the old inborn tendencies of the actor class to loose living, she insisted on good morals and would not countenance unlicensed unions. The weak side of her management in Lessing's opinion (in 1754) was her excessive fondness for stage display:

Man müsste sehr unbillig seyn, wenn man dieser berühmten Schauspielerin eine vollkommne Kenntniss ihrer Kunst absprechen wollte. Sie hat männliche Einsichten; nur in einem Artikel verräth sie ihr Geschlecht. Sie tändelt ungemein gerne auf dem Theater. Alle Schauspiele von ihrer Erfindung sind voller Putz, voller Verkleidung, voller Festivitäten; wun-

---

[1] For the following see my *Studies in the Genesis of Romantic Theory in the Eighteenth Century*, Cambridge, 1923, pp. 282 ff.

derbar und schimmernd. Vielleicht zwar kannte sie ihre Herren Leipziger, und das war vielleicht eine List von ihr, was ich für eine Schwachheit an ihr halte.[1]

Her fight for the alexandrine tragedy was no easy one, and the rebuffs she received were many. Hamburg, an increasing lure for the wandering companies, would at first have none of it. To Gottsched her husband wrote in 1730:

Die Verse gefallen, aber man klagt über eine gewisse unbekannte versteckte Dunkelheit, welche verursachet, dass der Zuhörer nicht sogleich Alles verstehen kann, was gesaget wird; man muss Geduld haben, mit der Zeit wird sich's geben.

And again later:

Unsre Comödien und Tragödien haben noch so ziemlich Zuschauer. Die Mühe, so zu Verbesserung des Geschmackes angewendet wird, scheint nicht gar vergebens zu seyn. Es finden sich auch allhier verschiedene bekehrte Herzen. Leute, denen man es fast nicht hätte zutrauen können, sind nunmehr Liebhaber der Poesie geworden und Viele finden an den ordentlich gesetzten Stücken ein gutes Belieben.[2]

But the general mass of the public in Hamburg remained obdurate; they frankly preferred the old farces and the 'Haupt- und Staatsaktionen'. Hanover in the same year proved a little better; and in Nürnberg in 1731, *Cinna* had a considerable measure of success, thanks partly, no doubt, to the fact that the translator, Führer, was a 'Ratsherr' of that town.

Of the Gottsched-Neuber reforms none stirred up more dust and controversy than the banishment of the harlequin. This in fact involved a much more far-reaching reform than the mere exclusion of comic irrelevancies from serious poetic tragedies. It was a blow at the old extempore comedy with its fixed types; if the harlequin went, the doctor, the pantaloon and the other figures of the *commedia dell' arte* had to go too. It is interesting, even a little ironical, that this reform should have been advocated in Paris by the leader of the Théâtre italien, Riccoboni, who had served under Maffei. In October, 1737,

[1] Introduction to Mylius's *Vermischte Schriften* in G. E. Lessing, *Sämtliche Schriften*, herausgegeben von K. Lachmann, 3. Auflage [von] F. Muncker, Stuttgart, 1886–1924 (hereafter quoted as *Schriften*), vi, p. 403. (References to lines of sections of the *Dramaturgie* refer to this edition.) Caroline Neuber is mentioned in the *Dramaturgie*, XVIII, 22 and XXVI, 29.

[2] Cp. T. W. Danzel, *Gottsched und seine Zeit*, Leipzig, 1848, pp. 131 ff., and E. Devrient, *op. cit.* i, p. 270.

in a theatre-booth in Bose's garden in Leipzig, Frau Neuber performed a Prelude composed by herself, in which the harlequin was tried for his misdemeanours, condemned and banished. From this time on she fought resolutely against his reinstatement; but it was a losing battle: Germany was not yet prepared to relinquish the comic element in her tragedies. Perhaps—and in view of Lessing's subsequent defence of the harlequin, this may be the truer explanation—Frau Neuber did not sufficiently recognise that what was most urgently called for was not his complete banishment, but his transformation; that he should be set free, as it were, should be divested of his coat of many colours, and should become merged, like any other character, in the action of the plays in which he appeared. It is a truism that to attempt to tamper with tradition in the things of the theatre is always dangerous; and no doubt Frau Neuber was too uncompromising. The public showed its disapproval by deserting her theatre; and nowhere was this desertion more marked and the antagonism to this reform bitterer than in Hamburg. At last, in January, 1740, she was stung to retaliation, and closed her season there with a satiric epilogue which made her return to that city for ever impossible.

Meanwhile, troubles of another kind were brewing. The old alliance with Gottsched, which Frau Neuber's anti-harlequin zeal had helped to maintain, was beginning to show signs of breaking. The dictator was becoming more dictatorial; and a breach of some seriousness was caused when Gottsched demanded that the Neuber company should unlearn the translation of *Alzire* which they had hitherto performed, and substitute for it a new translation by his wife. The breach widened rapidly; finally, faced by defeat and ruin, Caroline Neuber left Germany and took her company for a year to Russia. When she returned, she found that Gottsched had transferred his patronage to a younger disciple of her own, who had joined her company in 1730 as a harlequin player—Johann Friedrich Schönemann.[1] She took a peculiar revenge; she discredited Gottsched in the eyes of the public by putting one of his own reforms into practice. She performed, as an 'experiment', the third act of *Der sterbende Cato* and (to the great amusement of the audience) made the characters appear, not in the conventional court costume of the eighteenth-century stage but in Roman costume, and speak their lines with an affected exaggeration of Gottsched's demands. This meant open warfare, and Gottsched

[1] Cp. H. Devrient, *J. F. Schönemann und seine Schauspielergesellschaft* (*Theatergeschichtliche Forschungen*, xi), Hamburg, 1895.

was the stronger. Frau Neuber, however, got in one more effective blow before she succumbed: on September 18, 1741, she produced a Prologue, written by herself, entitled *Der allerkostbarste Schatz*, in which Gottsched himself was brought on to the stage in a fantastic costume as the 'Tadler', searching for faults with a lantern. From now on Caroline Neuber's fortunes went gradually downhill; in 1750 she finally gave up the struggle and died some ten years later in penury and bitterness.

Her mantle fell on Schönemann's shoulders; he carried on the Leipzig tradition. As an actor, Schönemann may be largely discounted; he had acquired all the stiff traditions of the classic school, without being able to give them distinction. He had also in an aggravated degree a weakness common to so many actor-managers, a vanity that led him to show his versatility in rôles that lay beyond his physical capacity. And other outstanding members of his company followed his example. But Schönemann certainly possessed qualities that make for leadership in things theatrical. He had practical common sense, and his enterprise never transgressed, as Caroline Neuber's did, the bounds of expediency, so necessary if bankruptcy was to be avoided; above all, he seems to have had the power of attracting to his standard and retaining the best talent of his time. It was at Lüneburg in 1740 that Schönemann became formally 'Principal' of his company, and for more than ten years he advanced steadily to the position of acknowledged leader of the German theatre. His company, which included Sophie Schröder, Ackermann and Ekhof, played in all the towns of North Germany from Hamburg to Breslau, and with rising prestige and success. His repertory, without making much literary pretension, included the best plays that were available. He entered into the heritage of the alexandrine tragedy which Caroline Neuber had sought to establish; and the plays of the French masters afforded to Ekhof and himself a welcome opportunity to shine. Modern French comedy was equally favoured; and the local farce of Hamburg, as well as the popular adaptations of Holberg, had a place in his repertory.

No town has been more closely associated with the progress of the German theatre than Hamburg.[1] It was the chief centre of theatrical activity in German-speaking lands in the eighteenth century, eclipsing even Vienna; in the latter city the instinct for the theatre may have been more widespread and more deep-rooted in the popular con-

[1] Cp. J. F. Schütze, *Hamburgische Theater-Geschichte*, Hamburg, 1794.

sciousness; but the eighteenth century was nearly over before the Viennese were aware of the new literary spirit that was stirring in the north, and they took their theatre less seriously. And Hamburg had the advantage of being a large and wealthy city—the largest and wealthiest of Northern Germany. At the time of the 'National Theatre' in which we are interested, its population was about 97,000.[1] Moreover its people were in closer touch with the outside world, notably with England; its tastes were more cosmopolitan; its republican government gave it a freedom and democratic control which the Berlin of Frederick the Great did not know; and in the affairs of the theatre it was less hampered by petty police control. Thus everything pointed to its being the right place for the first attempt to create a serious national theatre.

The history of its theatre shows that it was always in the forefront of such progress as there was in the eighteenth century. Already at the close of the seventeenth it had been able to rival wealthy courts like that of Dresden by providing its citizens with a home for the Italian opera; and its opera house, associated with the early work of Händel, was opened in 1678, only to be demolished in 1765 to make room for the theatre which was to be the occasion of the *Hamburgische Dramaturgie*. This opera house may have had little literary significance; the baroque *libretti* of the operas it produced may have had no poetic value; but their fabrication or translation gave occupation to Hamburg poets, and their very extravagance provoked satiric antagonism and led to a reaction in taste.

For a time in the Gottsched-Neuber period, Leipzig had been a more important centre of theatrical activity; but between 1737 and 1740 the Neuber troupe played long and frequently in Hamburg, and from then onwards it became virtually the headquarters of the leading theatrical companies. It had been the main centre of Schönemann's activities ever since he first played there in 1741–42; Sophie Schröder, after her dissociation from Schönemann, gave performances, between 1742 and 1744, in the old opera house, and subsequently in the Hof von Holland in the Fuhlentwiete. We find Schönemann again in Hamburg in 1747, and in the early 'fifties, when his company reached the acme of its reputation, its triumphs were all intimately associated with that city. Between 1758 and 1763 the fortunes of Hamburg

---

[1] J. L. von Hess, *Topographisch-politisch-historische Beschreibung der Stadt Hamburg*, Hamburg, 1796, ii, p. 362 (cited also by B. Litzmann, *F. L. Schröder, ein Beitrag zur deutschen Litteratur- und Theatergeschichte*, i (Hamburg, 1890), p. 248).

theatrical enterprise were mainly in the hands of Gottfried Heinrich Koch (1703–75). This actor had begun as a student in Leipzig, but he was too poor to continue his studies there, and he joined Caroline Neuber in 1728, subsequently becoming a member of Schönemann's troupe. His years in Hamburg were prosperous, the more so perhaps as he was not overburdened with an artistic conscience, but studiously gave his public what it wanted. Lastly Konrad Ackermann, who had had a company of his own since 1753 and had frequently played in Hamburg, was, as will be seen, the 'Principal' of the troupe which immediately preceded the period of Hamburg theatrical history in which we are interested.

After the failure of the National Theatre in 1769, Ackermann again assumed control of Hamburg's theatre, this time with the help of his famous stepson, Friedrich Ludwig Schröder (1744–1816), the greatest German actor of the eighteenth century. In 1771 Schröder took over the sole control, and for nearly ten years gave Hamburg the most brilliant period of its theatrical history. The greatest of all his achievements was the acclimatisation of Shakespeare in Germany, the first performance of *Hamlet* on September 20, 1776, being a particularly memorable event. There was a break in Schröder's directorship of the Hamburg theatre between 1780 and 1785. This marked the close of the dominating part which the city had played in the development of the German stage. For in these years permanent theatres under state patronage and with state assistance were established in Gotha and Mannheim, the latter theatre becoming under August Wilhelm Iffland the particular focus for the new literary 'Sturm und Drang'; Berlin and Vienna were rapidly pushing to the front; and from now on Hamburg became only one of several centres of theatrical activity.

Part I

THE HAMBURG 'NATIONALTHEATER'

1767–1769

CHAPTER I

ORGANISATION AND STAFF OF THE THEATRE

The history of the Hamburg 'Enterprise' to which we owe the *Hamburgische Dramaturgie* begins, not with the opening of the theatre on April 22, 1767, but with that of the same theatre by the actor and 'Principal' Konrad Ackermann on July 31, 1765. It cannot be sufficiently emphasised that the new undertaking was virtually a continuation of the previous one, and the fact that it was described as 'national' and was nominally controlled by a 'Consortium' meant no essential break.

Konrad Ernst Ackermann[1] was born at Schwerin on February 1, 1710, and had a chequered enough career behind him before he became, in 1740, a member of Schönemann's company. He had served for a time in the army as a professional soldier. His first attempt at acting seems to have met with immediate success, and he rapidly advanced to a leading position in the company. In 1742 he joined the independent company of Sophie Schröder, the mother of Friedrich Ludwig Schröder, and he remained with her for two years. Then he went back for a time to Schönemann. In 1749, however, he married Sophie Schröder, and from then onwards his activity was bound up with hers, and later with that of her famous son. His strength as an actor lay on the comic rather than the tragic side; he was more at his ease in the realism of the 'tragedy of common life'

---

[1] Ackermann has not yet been made the subject of an adequate monograph. See, however, the biographies of his stepson Schröder: F. L. W. Meyer, *F. L. Schröder: Beitrag zur Kunde des Menschen und des Künstlers*, Hamburg, 1819, and B. Litzmann, *F. L. Schröder: ein Beitrag zur deutschen Litteratur- und Theatergeschichte*, Hamburg and Leipzig, 1890–94.

than in the artificial alexandrine tragedy.[1] It is thus not surprising that his repertory favoured plays of English origin, and was strengthened on the side of comedy by adaptations of Goldoni. It displays in consequence a variety which compares favourably with the more assiduous cultivation of the higher tragedy and the preference for French comedy of his predecessor Schönemann. It may have been that it was not so much Ackermann as G. H. Koch who imported the new realistic drama from England, but Ackermann, finding this drama congenial to his particular talent, reaped the benefit of Koch's initiative. In respect of variety, indeed, Ackermann's repertory compares favourably, not merely with Schönemann's, but also with that of his immediate successors.[2]

In 1764 Ackermann brought his company to play in the Hamburg theatre. The first difficulty which confronted him was the inadequacy of the old 'Komödienhaus' which had been originally a stable for riding horses. Not only was the building cramped and unsuitable, but Koch, from whom Ackermann took it on lease, refused to extend that lease to his rival beyond the beginning of December, 1764. Ackermann first thought of turning his back on Hamburg altogether, but he was dissuaded by his friends and patrons; and with the financial aid they offered him he resolved to build a new theatre. The old Opera House, which stood on the eastern side of the Gänsemarkt and had lent glamour to Hamburg theatrical life for eighty-seven years, was to be demolished, and the site was leased to Ackermann by its owner, Demoiselle Willers, on advantageous terms. Here, within the comparatively short period of six months, a simple theatre was erected at a cost of some 20,000 talers. The new building did not stand directly on the market-place, but was connected with it by two narrow, shop-lined courts. The site was cramped and the auditorium suffered on this account.[3] The main building was roughly fifty-five feet broad and

[1] F. L. W. Meyer, *op. cit.* i, p. 16, quotes Schröder's tribute to Ackermann's talent in his best years: 'Er glänzte im August, im Ulfo, im Cato, im Mithridat, im Oedip, im Oresman, im Polieuct, im Beverley....Freilich stand auch damals schon der komische Schauspieler weit über dem tragischen. Im ersten Fache gab es durchaus keine Rollen, die er nicht vollkommen darstellte. Ich erinnere mich nicht, in den langen Jahren meiner Beobachtung, eine einzige Übertreibung von ihm bemerkt zu haben.'

[2] B. Litzmann (*op. cit.* i, pp. 81 ff.) seems to me to underrate the merits of Ackermann's repertory.

[3] The dimensions are given by J. F. Schütze, *Hamburgische Theater-Geschichte*, Hamburg, 1794, pp. 322 ff., who had them from a description of the theatre published by Ekhof in the *Hamburgische Unterhaltungen*, ii, 2, August, 1766, pp.

a hundred and three feet long; the side-building which provided accommodation for the actors—the women's dressing-rooms were under the stage—approximately twenty feet by forty-five feet. The stage of the theatre was just over fifty-one feet wide and of the same depth, but so faultily constructed that the crossbeams at the top were visible from the auditorium.[1] Schröder relates how he himself helped to remove the worst of them before the opening of the theatre. The preliminary descriptions stated that the occupants of the back seats in the boxes had a full view of the stage, but Löwen was probably nearer the truth when he said that little could be seen from them.[2] The entrances were narrow, and the building was not adjudged safe from fire; permission to use it was at first refused, and a large sum had still to be expended to meet the objections of the town authorities. The proscenium was just over thirty-four feet wide and twenty-five feet high, and on each side stood two Corinthian pillars painted to resemble marble, with gilded plinths and capitals. Between each pair of pillars stood a gilded vase on a pedestal. At each side of the orchestral well was a stove by which the auditorium could be heated. The accommodation for the spectators consisted of a sloping parterre, which could be boarded over for the masquerade balls held from time to time in winter in the theatre, and two rows of boxes and a gallery. The ceiling was decorated with an allegorical painting, and Schütze speaks contemptuously of the two curtains, which were both, no doubt, still in use under the later régime. The first showed a picture of Liberty sitting under a baldachin and protecting Tragedy and Comedy, the second one of the Hamburg arms and arm-bearers, from which an ugly dancer was drawing back a curtain and smirking at the audience. These and the scenery had been hastily painted by an incompetent

164 ff. I have converted them into English feet, the Hamburg foot being a little under three-quarters of an inch shorter than ours. There is also an account of the theatre in L. Wollrabe, *Chronologie sämmtlicher Hamburger Bühnen*, Hamburg, 1847, p. 57. See also B. Litzmann, *op. cit.* i, pp. 316 ff. The theatre was not demolished until 1877. The picture of it which I reproduce as frontispiece to this volume, is from a water-colour in the possession of the Museum für Hamburgische Geschichte. It is also to be found in the edition of the *Dramaturgie* published by J. Petersen, Berlin [1915].

[1] F. L. W. Meyer, *op. cit.* i, p. 139: 'Wie erschrak Schröder als er das ganz verpfuschte neue Haus erblickte! Selbst die Suffiten mussten, um sie den Augen der Zuschauer einigermassen zu entziehn, als Gardinen gehandhabt werden, so viele Kreuzbände waren über der Bühne angebracht.'

[2] *Schreiben an einen Freund über die Ackermannsche Schaubühne zu Hamburg* (dated December 13, 1765), Hamburg and Leipzig, 1766, p. 5.

scene-painter, Kawall,[1] and the disabilities under which the new theatre laboured were thus increased.

The theatre was opened by Ackermann on July 31, 1765, with a 'Vorspiel', *Die Comödie im Tempel der Tugend*, written by J. F. Löwen, which was followed by a new French tragedy, *Zelmire*, by De Belloy. The entertainment concluded with a ballet, *Die Kornerndte*, in which Schröder, then a youth of twenty, displayed his remarkable choreographic talents. In the matter of his repertory Ackermann seems to have met, at least at first, the tastes of his patrons; in addition to the numerous plays of French origin there was a fair sprinkling of English and Italian works; and the native drama was represented mainly by Johann Elias Schlegel, Lessing and J. C. Krüger. Ackermann seems to have succeeded best in keeping his somewhat fickle public loyal to him by the unfortunately costly expedient of elaborate stage-mountings and costumes. Much money was squandered on the production of Favart's *Soliman II*, and on Corneille's *Rodogune*, and the ballets and pantomimes which were the most popular feature of his repertory made heavy inroads into his exchequer. He had begun his management deep in debt, and that debt went on growing. His staff does not seem to have been satisfactory from the standpoint of *ensemble*. He himself and his wife were too old to bear adequately the burden that lay upon their shoulders; she, in fact, played little, and Ackermann's memory frequently left him in the lurch; and his two daughters were still little more than children. He had too many inexperienced members in his company, and young Schröder was mainly utilised in the ballets. Konrad Ekhof, however, who returned to Hamburg to join him, was a tower of strength, although he did not, under Ackermann, have full opportunity for displaying his powers. Sophie Friederike Hensel, who had been playing in Vienna, where her success had not been conspicuous, was engaged to take the place of the manager's wife, and made her début on November 1 in Voltaire's *Zayre*.[2] She had already in two previous periods been a member of Ackermann's company, and it might have been thought that his former experience of her difficult temper would have made him wary of inviting her to return; but her attraction for the public was not to be gainsaid. The situation was aggravated by her finding, when she came to Hamburg, that her rival, Karoline Schulze, was in possession

---

[1] 'Dieser Kawall', says Schütze (*op. cit.* p. 324), 'war ein Sudler.'

[2] Cp. C. H. Schmid, *Chronologie des deutschen Theaters*, ed. P. Legband in *Schriften der Gesellschaft für Theatergeschichte*, i (Berlin, 1902), p. 151.

of many of her best rôles. From the first, therefore, she was a centre of intrigue and dissension. Outside the theatre she had friends, among whom the chief was Abel Seyler, the son of a Swiss clergyman who had established a business in Hamburg and brought it to the verge of bankruptcy. Seyler had a passion for the theatre, and more particularly for Madame Hensel, who became his mistress and ultimately, in 1772, his wife. Another admirer was Adolf Siegmund Bubbers, a tapestry manufacturer, who, stage-struck in early days, had run away from home and become an actor under Schönemann.

Apart from such difficulties with his company, the chief thorn in Ackermann's flesh was Johann Friedrich Löwen.[1] Born in Klaustal on September 13, 1727, Löwen had studied at Helmstedt and Göttingen, but owing to want of means was obliged to give up his academic career. The poet Hagedorn suggested that he should try his fortune in London and provided him with letters of introduction to friends there, but a Hamburg Legationsrat, Zink, induced him to settle in Hamburg, probably putting him in the way of congenial work as theatre critic for a local journal. In 1757 he obtained a miserably paid secretaryship in Schwerin. His theatrical interests had brought him into close touch with Schönemann; he assisted the latter in his business embarrassments and ultimately married his daughter. In spite of his official connexion with Schwerin, he appears to have spent the better part of each year in Hamburg, and when Ackermann assumed control of the theatre there Löwen was engaged as a kind of literary adviser. Soon, however, Ackermann—irritated no doubt by Löwen's frank criticism of his management—supplanted him by appointing a certain Ast as his 'house poet'. This slight drove Löwen into the ranks of Ackermann's enemies. Before the end of 1765 he wrote an outspoken criticism of the theatre, *Schreiben an einen Freund über die Ackermannsche Schaubühne zu Hamburg*, and in the following year an undisguised attack, *Schreiben an einen Marionetten-Spieler als eine Abfertigung des Schreibens an einen Freund über die Ackermannsche Schaubühne. Im Namen des Ackermannschen Lichtputzers*. His *Geschichte des deutschen Theaters*, also published in 1766,[2] culminates in a general arraignment of the German 'Principals' or actor-managers for their incompetency. Löwen's history, as history, is negligible, but what he has to say of contemporary conditions throws valuable light on the situation with

---

[1] Cp. O. D. Potkoff, *Johann Friedrich Löwen*, Heidelberg, 1904.

[2] A reprint, edited by H. Stümcke, is published in the *Neudrucke literarhistorischer Seltenheiten*, viii (Berlin, 1905).

which Lessing was faced. He suggests reforms which, a little later, were to be incorporated in the scheme for the 'National Theatre'; in particular, he proposes the abolition of the control of the theatre by the leading actor of a company. He says:

> Es würde demnach die Aufnahme unsrer Bühne sehr befördern, wenn man erstlich die Principalschaft ganz aufheben wollte; und wenn der Fürst, oder die Republik, die die Schauspiele schützen, selbst das Direktorium führen, das heisst, einen Mann wählen wollten, dem, da er selbst eine feine Kenntniss der schönen Künste und Wissenschaften besässe, die Annahme der Schauspieler, die Wahl der Stücke, und die ganze Policey des Theaters, ohne dass er selbst Schauspieler wäre, müsste überlassen werden.[1]

It was Löwen's attitude, combined with the growing dissension within the theatre, and not financial difficulties (for the receipts were by no means so unsatisfactory) which ultimately forced Ackermann to give up his directorship. The question now was: what next? No doubt it was Löwen who came forward with a scheme for re-organisation. A 'Consortium', consisting nominally of twelve Hamburg business-men, was formed to carry out Löwen's plans, and the financial control of the theatre was vested in them. By an agreement dated October 24, 1766, they took over the theatre with its scenery and properties for a period of ten years, from 1767 to 1777. They agreed to pay an annual rent of a thousand 'Speciesdukaten',[2] that is, about £500; the properties and garderobe were purchased for 20,000 Hamburg marks, about £1250, to be paid in instalments. A third of the proceeds from masquerades was to be handed to Ackermann, and suitable fines were arranged in case either party should break the contract.[3]

This was not the first time that Hamburg citizens had come to the rescue of their theatre—nine years before, in 1757, they had assisted Ekhof to keep the old Schönemann troupe above water in Hamburg;[4] but it was the first time that financial supporters had taken over the actual control of the undertaking. It seemed a step in the direction of an endowed and municipally controlled theatre; but the parallel does not extend very far. One's suspicions are awakened by the constitution of the Consortium. The leading spirits were Madame

---

[1] *Geschichte des deutschen Theaters* (Reprint, p. 68).
[2] F. L. Schmidt, *Geschichte des Hamburgischen Theaters* (Fortsetzung) in *Almanach fürs Theater*, Hamburg, 1810, p. 3.
[3] F. L. W. Meyer, *op. cit.* i, pp. 153 f.   [4] J. F. Schütze, *op. cit.* p. 302.

Hensel's admirers, Seyler and Bubbers. The latter, although he had no money to put into the enterprise, was actively associated with it because of his experience in theatrical matters; and he made himself useful by travelling through North Germany in search of talent for the theatre. A third member of the Consortium was Seyler's business partner Johann Martin Tillemann; he, however, took no active part at all, and this was also the case with the nine other Hamburg citizens whom these three apparently succeeded in interesting in their venture. Thus in practice the famous Consortium was a one-man affair—it consisted of Seyler and Seyler alone; and as far as he was concerned, there was little enough idealism in the scheme, he being mainly intent on furthering the interests of his mistress. The more staid members of the Hamburg plutocracy could not but look askance on the half bankrupt Seyler and his stage-struck friends.

Thus the Hamburg theatre of 1767 was in no essential sense an advance on the existing conditions of theatrical enterprise. Ackermann had found himself in difficulties; and Seyler had seized the opportunity —which has tempted the stage-struck amateur with money to spend in all ages—to become its manager. Löwen, who had quarrelled with Ackermann, was able to win Seyler's ear for his schemes of reform, and became director of the new undertaking, which was grandiloquently described as a 'Nationaltheater'.[1] These are the facts. There is little reason for believing that anyone but Löwen was really interested in seeing an essentially different theatre from that which Schönemann, Koch or Ackermann had conducted in the past. Something might indeed have been hoped for from Löwen, who had found valuable support, and possibly had drawn inspiration for his scheme in the recommendations (not published until 1764) of Johann Elias Schlegel

---

[1] The description 'Nationaltheater' seems to have been used in Vienna just before this. Cp. J. von Sonnenfels, *Der Mann ohne Vorurtheil*, III, xiii (*Gesammelte Schriften*, Wien, 1783–7, iii, p. 118): 'Ich bin aber auch der Meinung, eine Anleitung [für die Zuschauer]...könne zur Verbesserung und Reinigung eines Nationaltheaters mehr beitragen, als die feinsten Beobachtungen' (September, 1766), and J. H. F. Müller, *Genaue Nachrichten von beiden k. k. Schaubühnen in Wien*, Pressburg, 1772, p. 13, where the term 'Nationalbühne' is used to describe the German theatre in Vienna in 1766. Cp. also Nicolai's note to a letter, addressed to Lessing, of August 19, 1769 (*Lessing's sämmtliche Schriften*, xxvii (Berlin, 1794), p. 247; 2nd ed. Berlin, 1809, pp. 328 f.): 'Ich weiss nicht, was das Wort Nationaltheater bedeuten soll, das zuerst dem Theater in Wien zu einer Zeit beygelegt ward, da es kaum mittelmässig war, und das die Herren Schauspieler seitdem allenthalben zum Scherwenzel gebraucht haben; aber ein sehr vorzügliches Theater zu besitzen, ist Hamburg gewiss der erste Ort in Deutschland.'

for the theatre in Copenhagen;[1] but he was unfortunately unable to assert his authority as director. Now, as under Ackermann, the actor was in control: it was Ekhof, whose power had been enhanced by the retirement of Ackermann, and not the inexperienced Seyler or Löwen, who arranged the repertory and decided upon the distribution of the rôles; and things went on as before. The acting staff of the theatre was enlarged by the engagement of Elisabeth Löwen and Susanna Mecour among the principals, but otherwise it was not essentially changed; and there was no alteration at all in the quality of the repertory or in the manner in which plays were produced and acted. Indeed, if anything, the change was for the worse. The fact that Lessing was associated with the undertaking was purely adventitious and exerted no influence on the conduct of the theatre; and Lessing made no concealment of his powerlessness.

In October, 1766, immediately after the agreement was signed, the plans of the new management were given publicity in a printed statement,[2] of which Löwen was no doubt the author, in spite of the self-praise it contains. This statement is sufficiently important for an understanding of the conditions under which the *Hamburgische Dramaturgie* was written to justify its being reprinted here in full.[3]

VORLÄUFIGE NACHRICHT VON DER AUF OSTERN 1767 VORZUNEHMENDEN VERÄNDERUNG DES HAMBURGISCHEN THEATERS

> Amphora cœpit
> Institui; currente rota cur urceus exit?
>
> HORAT.

Wir kündigen dem Publico die vielleicht unerwartete Hoffnung an, das deutsche Schauspiel in Hamburg zu einer Würde zu erheben, wohin es unter andern Umständen niemals gelangen wird. So lange dieser vortreff-

---

[1] J. E. Schlegel, *Werke* (ed. J. H. Schlegel), iii (Copenhagen, 1764), pp. 251–98. Cp. J. F. Löwen, *Schriften*, Hamburg, 1765–6, iv, pp. 1–2.

[2] Cp. *Hamburgische Dramaturgie, Ankündigung* (5).

[3] This *Vorläufige Nachricht*, which was 'gedruckt und zu bekommen bey Michael Christian Bock' in Hamburg, was referred to in the *Hamburgische Unterhaltungen*, ii, 5, November, 1766, p. 440; it was discussed in Löwen's journal, *Freye Nachrichten aus dem Reiche der Wissenschaften und der schönen Künste* of November 7, 1766 (St. 45), and also (in less encouraging terms) in the *Hamburgische Correspondent* of November 8, 1766. (Cp. also O. D. Potkoff, *op. cit.* p. 89.) It was then reprinted by F. L. W. Meyer (*op. cit.* ii, 2, pp. 31 ff.), and in our time by H. Stümcke in his edition of Löwen's *Geschichte des deutschen Theaters* (pp. 83 ff.). Löwen's *Anrede an die sämtlichen Mitglieder des Hamburgischen Theaters* was also printed, Hamburg, 1767, and is to be found in Stümcke (pp. 91 ff.).

liche, angenehme und lehrreiche Zweig der schönen Künste noch in den Händen solcher Männer, auch der redlichsten Männer ist, die ihre Kunst lediglich zu einer Brodtwissenschaft zu machen gezwungen sind; so lange die Aufmunterung und der edle Stolz der Nachahmung unter den Schauspielern selbst fehlt; so lange man die Dichter der Nation nicht zu Nationalstücken anzufeuern gewohnt ist; und so lange vorzüglich die theatralische Policey, sowol auf der Bühne in der Wahl der Stücke, als auch bey den Sitten der Schauspieler selbst, eine ganz fremde Sache bleibt; so lange wird man umsonst das deutsche Schauspiel aus seiner Kindheit hervortreten sehen.

Wir setzen die grossen Vortheile zum voraus, die eine Nationalbühne dem ganzen Volke verschaffen kann; und wir dürfen sie auch heut zu Tage niemand mehr beweisen, als den Eigensinnigen, die sie nicht erwiesen haben wollen. Wenn es inzwischen wahr ist, und es ist längst ausgemacht, dass, ausser dem edelsten Zeitvertreib, den das Theater gewährt, auch der Sittenlehre durch ihn die herrlichsten Dienste geleistet werden; so verlohnt es sich gewiss der Mühe, nicht mit derjenigen Schläfrigkeit an die wahre Aufnahme der Bühne zu gedenken, mit der man bis auf den heutigen Tag die innerliche Vollkommenheit derselben bearbeitet hat. Und aus eben diesem wichtigen Grunde, dessen Folgen für eine ganze Nation interessant sind, und wovon sich die Vortheile, die aus der Verfeinerung des Geschmacks, und ihrer Sitten fliessen, auf den ganzen Staat und auf die Biegsamkeit seiner Bürger erstrecken; aus diesem wichtigen Grunde, sagen wir, freuen wir uns, dass wir die Mittel in Händen haben, unsern Mitbürgern, ausser dem edelsten Vergnügen, dessen der menschliche Verstand nur fähig seyn kann, auch die reichsten Schätze einer geläuterten Moral zu gewähren.

Wir wollen uns über die Möglichkeit und Gewissheit dieser Absicht näher erklären.

Eine kleine Gesellschaft gutdenkender Bürger hieselbst hat schon seit verschiedenen Jahren auf die Ausführung dieses Plans gedacht; und da sie gegenwärtig dahin arbeiten, eine hinlängliche Anzahl von gesitteten Leuten zu erhalten, und die zugleich die vortrefflichsten und besten unter den deutschen Schauspielern sind, so sind sie willens, das deutsche Theater zu derjenigen Zeit, die alsdann in den öffentlichen Blättern bekannt gemacht werden soll, mit aller der Vollkommenheit zu eröffnen, die man mit Recht von einer wohleingerichteten und lehrreichen Bühne fodert. Man hat zu dem Ende das Directorium derselben den Händen eines Mannes anvertrauet, dessen untadelhafte Sitten, und dessen bewusste Einsichten in die Geheimnisse dieser Kunst zu der Aufnahme des Theaters nothwendig sind. Da dieser Mann nichts mit der eigentlichen Arbeit als Acteur zu schaffen haben wird, sondern lediglich, ausser den bekannten Pflichten, die einem jeden Directeur obliegen, noch die so höchst nothwendige Verbindlichkeit über sich genommen hat, für die Bildung des Herzens, der Sitten und der Kunst junger, angehender Schauspieler zu sorgen; so kann man leicht denken, dass das Publicum sich in der Erwartung,

die man ihm macht, gewiss nicht betriegen wird. Man ist willens, dieser
Gesellschaft gesitteter und einsichtsvoller Leute alle die Vortheile zu ver-
schaffen, die man in einer theatralischen Akademie gewinnen kann.
Zu dem Ende wird der Directeur, ausser seinem übrigen Unterricht, der,
wie bereits gesagt, die Bildung des Herzens und des Geschmacks betrifft,
über kurze von ihm herauszugebende Grundsätze der körperlichen
Beredsamkeit,[1] und über des Dorat vortrefflichen Essai sur la Declamation
Tragique, der nächstens National gemacht werden soll, ordentliche Vorlesungen halten. Man wird sich hiebey der vortrefflichen theatralischen
Auszüge bedienen, welche Herr Lessing in seiner theatralischen Bibliothek,
und in den Beyträgen zur Historie des Theaters aus den besten Werken der
Ausländer gemacht hat. In diesen Vorlesungen sollen diejenigen, die sich
der Bühne widmen, von den ersten Anfangsgründen der Kunst an, durch
das ganze dramatische Feld geführt, und mit den Geheimnissen dieser
wichtigen Kunst bekannt gemacht werden. Den theoretischen Unterricht
wird man ihnen durch Beyspiele unsrer besten Acteurs erläutern lassen;
und da sie vornehmlich dereinst in dem Spiele der Leidenschaften die
Seele der ganzen Action setzen müssen, so wird es eins von den Haupt-
geschäften dieser theatralischen Vorlesungen seyn, sie mit der wichtigen
Lehre der Affecten bekannt zu machen, und überhaupt nichts vergessen,
was nur irgend zu den feinsten Nüancen dieser schweren Kunst gezählet
werden kann.

Da man den Schauspieler so vortrefflich zu bilden suchen wird; und er,
wenn zu diesem Unterricht Talente kommen, dem deutschen Theater
gewiss Ehre macht; so ist man auch darauf bedacht, die äusserlichen
Glücksumstände desselben vorzüglich bequem einzurichten. Man wird
daher den Stand dieser Leute so geehrt zu machen suchen, als es die Kunst
verdient, der sie sich gewidmet haben. Man wird einen, ihren Talenten
angemessenen, jährlichen Gehalt aussetzen: aber vorzüglich darauf bedacht
seyn, diejenigen Schauspieler anständig und Lebenslang zu versorgen, die
Altershalber dem Theater nicht mehr dienen können. Bey dergleichen
glänzenden Aussichten aber verlangt man durchaus die strengste, edelste
und untadelhafteste Aufführung, und die besten und liebenswürdigsten
Sitten, die Leute von gutem Denken, und einer feinen Lebensart unterscheiden müssen. Da der ganze Nutze des Theaters, der überdem immer
beschrieen wird, sogleich wegfällt, und die Sitten der Mitbürger umsonst
gebessert werden, wenn diejenigen, die der Spiegel dieser Sitten seyn sollen,
ihre eigene Handlungen beflecken; so wird die ungeheuchelte Gottesfurcht,
der Abscheu an allen, der bürgerlichen Gesellschaft so gefährlichen Lastern,
eine unverletzte, und von dem geringsten Verdacht befreyte Lebensart,
die erste Pflicht eines jeden Schauspielers seyn; und auch der Beste unter
ihnen wird sogleich alle Vortheile verlieren, so bald man ihn von dieser

---

[1] Löwen proposed to publish a new edition of this work, which appeared
originally in 1755.

Pflicht, und von allen den übrigen strengen Gesetzen, die man unter sich machen wird, nur im geringsten vorsetzlich abweichen siehet.

Da endlich selbst nach dem Ausspruch des Diderot, eines Philosophen, der selbst bey seinen wichtigen Arbeiten, so viel Zeit gefunden, zwo der grössten Meisterstücke für das Theater zu verfertigen, der theatralische Nutze nur alsdann erst beträchtlich für eine ganze Nation werden kann, wenn sie ihre eigene Bühne hat; so wird man sein wichtiges Augenmerk seyn lassen, das deutsche Theater mit der Zeit so national zu machen, als sich alle andere Nationen des ihrigen zu rühmen Ursache haben. Man weiss, dass dies das erste Geschäfte unserer dramatischen Dichter seyn muss: aber man kennt auch die Ursachen, die dieser Arbeit zum Theil noch immer im Wege gestanden sind; und man hofft, durch Aufmunterung und ausgesetzte Preise diese Absicht mit zu erreichen. Freylich wird man durch Belohnung keine eigentliche Genies für das Theater bilden können; aber die Talente dererjenigen, die bereits Genie haben, durch thätigen und belohnenden Beyfall der Nation anzufeuern, ist längst bey allen Nationen, von den Griechen und Römern an, von dem herrlichsten Nutzen gewesen. Man wird demnach jährlich einen Preis von funfzig Ducaten, auf das beste Trauerspiel, es sey heroisch oder bürgerlich; funfzig Ducaten auf das beste Lustspiel setzen; und es mit der Einsendung durch versiegelte Namen und Devisen eben so halten, als es bey allen gelehrten Gesellschaften, und noch zuletzt bey den erhabenen Kennern des Schönen, bey den Verfassern der Bibliothek der schönen Wissenschaften zum Ruhm des deutschen Geschmacks üblich gewesen ist. Die Entscheidung, welches von den eingesandten Stücken den Preis verdienet, wird man auf den Ausspruch der Leute von bekannten Talenten ankommen lassen. Die Ankündigung des erhaltenen Preises wird, so wie bey der Bibliothek der schönen Wissen-schaften,[1] jedesmal öffentlich, mit dem gekrönten Stücke zugleich, durch den Druck geschehen.

Eine solche Bühne, von deren nähern Einrichtung, Beschaffenheit und Fortgang man von Zeit zu Zeit fortfahren wird, dem Publico umständliche Nachricht zu ertheilen, darf allerdings des Beyfalls unserer gesitteten Mitbürger gewiss seyn. Und um das Antheil öffentlich zu rühmen, das diese gesegnete Stadt an der Verbesserung des Geschmacks, und der Verfeinerung der Sitten nimmt, wissen wir kein besseres Merkmaal einer unauslöschlichen Dankbarkeit, als wenn wir uns entschliessen, verschie-denemal, freywillig des Jahrs, an gewissen bestimmten Tagen, die ganze Einnahme den hiesigen öffentlichen frommen Stiftungen und Häusern zu widmen. Man hofft, im Stande zu seyn, bey der Eröffnung dieser Bühne die zwote Nachricht von der Einrichtung derselben dem Publico vorlegen zu können.[2]

[1] Cp. *Bibliothek der schönen Wissenschaften und der freyen Künste*, i (Leipzig, 1757), p. 15. The prize here was awarded to Cronegk's *Codrus*. See below, p. 147 (note 1).

[2] No 'zwote Nachricht' was issued; its place was presumably taken by Lessing's *Ankündigung*.

It was proposed then to eliminate the 'Principal'—a reform which Lessing endorses (*Ank.* 31)—and to institute fixed salaries; and old-age pensions were promised. Löwen had particularly at heart plans which would make the life of the acting profession less precarious. He warmly supported the claim which Johann Elias Schlegel had put forward, and which Lessing himself quoted in his *Ankündigung* (24):

Die Ursache, dass noch kein hiesiges Theater von Bestand gewesen ist, scheint diese zu seyn, dass man vorhin den Komödianten selbst die Sorge überlassen hat, für ihren Verlust und Gewinnst zu arbeiten. Entweder wird in diesem Falle alles durch den Neid verderbt, der leicht in eine solche Gesellschaft einschleichen kann; oder sie verzehren auf einmal die Einkünfte der fetten Zeiten, und in den magern machen sie Schulden. Sie müssen also unter einer gewissen Aufsicht stehen, und nach festgesetzten Regeln arbeiten.[1]

It was hoped to realise the scheme for the better training of actors which Ekhof had initiated in Schwerin, by the institution of a 'theatralische Akademie'; and Löwen was to give lectures on declamation and 'Mimik'. To encourage dramatic writers prizes were to be given for the best original tragedies and comedies. In all this Löwen, convinced that 'der Vorwurf, den uns die Ausländer machen, dass wir kein eigenes Theater haben, mehr als zu gegründet [ist]',[2] was inspired by the most admirable ideals, and he rightly believed that Hamburg was the best place in which to try the experiment.[3] It is unfair to stigmatise him as merely an ambitious journalist, intent on furthering purely personal ends; he was entirely sincere in his desire to give Hamburg an organised and efficiently equipped theatre. Between October, 1766 and the opening day, April 22, 1767, he put his best energies into the work of preparation, and his address to the staff of the theatre before the first performance is admirable.[4]

[1] The passage is not from the *Gedanken zur Aufnahme des dänischen Theaters*, as Lessing implies, but from the short essay, *Schreiben von Errichtung eines Theaters in Kopenhagen*, which precedes it in Schlegel's *Werke* (*ed. cit.* iii, p. 252).

[2] The reviewer of Nicolai's *Briefe über die schönen Wissenschaften* in the *Bibliothek der schönen Wissenschaften* (i, pp. 116 f.) had said: 'Hier stimmen wir den Herrn V. vollkommen bey, wann sie behaupten, dass es mit unserer Schaubühne gar ungemein schlecht bestellt sey, und dass eben die allgemeine gute Meynung, welche man davon zu haben pflegt, eine wichtige Verhinderung ihrer Verbesserung sey.'

[3] Cp. the dedication of vol. iv of Löwen's *Schriften* (Hamburg, 1766), p. [iii]: 'Es fehlt freylich noch viel, ehe wir so weit kommen, uns eines Nationaltheaters rühmen zu dürfen; allein, wenn wir nie den Anfang machen wollen, wie werden wir es erhalten? Kein Ort in ganz Deutschland ist hiezu geschickter, als eben Hamburg.'   [4] Reprinted by Stümcke, *op. cit.* pp. 91 ff.

He shared, however, the fate of every would-be reformer of the theatre; from the first he was met by the bitterest opposition, even on the part of those who were to benefit by his reforms. There were plenty of people in Hamburg who, as Lessing said (*Ank.* 11):

bey jedem guten Unternehmen nichts als Nebenabsichten erblicken. Man könnte ihnen diese Beruhigung ihrer selbst gern gönnen; aber, wenn die vermeinten Nebenabsichten sie wider die Sache selbst aufbringen; wenn ihr hämischer Neid, um jene zu vereiteln, auch diese scheitern zu lassen, bemüht ist: so müssen sie wissen, dass sie die verachtungswürdigsten Glieder der menschlichen Gesellschaft sind.

'Es regnete Pasquille der unflätigsten Art auf sie', writes F. L. W. Meyer;[1] and J. F. Schütze makes a similar statement:

Andre, aus Neid, Nebenabsichten und Neuerungshass, verhöhnten öffentlich die gute Sache. Ein Schöngeist (wahrscheinlich Dreyer) liess folgendes gegen Löwens Nachricht handschriftlich ins Publikum fliegen:

Klein ist der Bühne Ruhm, der Schade desto grösser,
der aus dem Zweck sie zu verändern fliesst,
wenn die Veränderung nicht besser,
als diese Nachricht ist.[2]

One must also be fair, however, to Löwen's opponents. The Hamburg public was, no doubt, quick to see that his innovations would not lead to any real improvement of the theatre. Löwen had neither enough personality nor sufficient experience to command the situation; he was at the mercy of Seyler, and still more, of the actors; they scorned his theories and laughed at his attempts to teach them their business. His lectures did not get beyond the first, and there was never any question of prizes for plays.[3] Before the opening of the theatre the promise of the *Vorläufige Nachricht* had been shorn of its best features; and it was not long before Ekhof took over in all practical matters of production Löwen's duties. The cardinal feature of the scheme, the abolition of the 'Principal', was tacitly allowed to lapse. Such a beginning was anything but promising, and only a month after the opening day, Lessing wrote to his brother Karl: 'Mit unserm

---

[1] *Op. cit.* i, p. 180.

[2] *Op. cit.* pp. 336 f. On Johann Matthias Dreyer see Stümcke, *op. cit.* pp. xxvi ff., and O. D. Potkoff, *op. cit.* pp. 78 f.

[3] Schröder sums him up very fairly (Meyer, *op. cit.* i, pp. 180 f.): 'Einsicht und guter Wille lassen sich ihm nicht absprechen, Kraft und Ansehn wurden ihm versagt.'

Theater (das im Vertrauen!) gehen eine Menge Dinge vor, die mir nicht anstehn. Es ist Uneinigkeit unter den Entrepreneurs, und keiner weiss, wer Koch oder Kellner ist.'[1] Both Schütze and Meyer[2] state that it was intended to dispense with the most popular feature of Ackermann's management, the ballets; but I am doubtful whether this was ever seriously contemplated. Far from regarding them as an offence against artistic taste, Löwen had nothing but praise for them.[3] In any case, if there had been any such intention, it was given up at a quite early stage of the preparations. As the attendance at the theatre fell off, it was found necessary to make much more objectionable concessions to the popular taste and have recourse to acrobats and jugglers to coax an unwilling public. Intrigue was rife behind the scenes—it could hardly be otherwise where Madame Hensel was concerned—and financial difficulties soon became pressing; by September Seyler's means were approaching exhaustion. After eight months the season was brought to a close on December 4, theatrical performances being forbidden in Hamburg in Advent; and the company betook itself to Hanover in the hope of retrieving their losses by a repetition there of the successful plays of the Hamburg season. On May 13, 1768, they returned to make a fresh start; but the public was not to be lured into the theatre in the heat of summer, and rival attractions, a circus and a French troupe, increased their embarrassments. Moreover, they found their creditors awaiting them, and only with the greatest difficulty could the actors be paid their weekly wage. The theatre had again to be closed for a time; by June or July even Löwen had deserted the sinking ship. One more attempt—not entirely without success—was made to court back fortune in Hanover at the beginning of December, 1768; but the situation was clearly hopeless. The actors had ultimately to use their fists to get paid at all; and on March 3, 1769, in Hanover, the great 'Enterprise' which had been begun with such high hopes was borne to its grave.

Löwen attributed the failure to extravagance in the management

---

[1] *Schriften*, xvii, p. 232.

[2] Schütze, *op. cit.* p. 337; Meyer, *op. cit.* i, p. 154.

[3] Cp. *Geschichte des deutschen Theaters* (Reprint, p. 58): 'Dass die vortrefflichen Ballette, mit welchen itzt vornehmlich Ackermann das Theater aufstützet, dem wahren Geschmack nachtheilig seyn sollten, wie einige behaupten, kann ich nicht sehen. Ich kann es ganz wol leiden, dass man auch unsern Augen ein reizendes Vergnügen gewährt, wenn man vorher unser Herz entzückt hat: und es verlohnt sich schon der Mühe, einige von Ackermanns vortrefflichen Balletten, die zwar nicht alle durchgehends pantomimisch sind, zu sehen.'

and to 'one great political mistake'—the retention of Ackermann.[1]
Still, Ackermann had never refused his co-operation, and his financial
interest in success must surely have tempered any slight malice that
he may have felt. Löwen died in poverty-stricken circumstances in
1771. We part from him with kindly feelings, for, after all, his ideas
were right ideas, and his intentions were of the best. We may like,
too, to remember that with his poem *Die Walpurgisnacht* he contributed
a stone to the great temple of German poetry, by bringing Dr Faustus
to take part in the witches' revelry on the Blocksberg.

Seyler's day was by no means over when his theatre came to grief.
He and Madame Hensel remained in Hanover, and he succeeded in
obtaining from George III an appointment as 'königlicher und
churfürstlicher teutscher Hof-schau-spieler' with various privileges
and subventions. The latter allowed him to deal a damaging blow
to any hopes that might have been entertained for a revival of the
theatre in Hamburg; for he was able to lure Ekhof back to his flag.
But this belongs to a later chapter in the history of the German stage.

The leading actor and the most commanding personality of the
Hamburg company was Hans Konrad Dieterich Ekhof[2]—he himself
always wrote his name so, not as Eckhof. He was born in Hamburg
on August 12, 1720, in the Opernhof where the theatre was to stand
in which he achieved his most memorable success. Although the son
of a blacksmith who subsequently did service as a city militiaman,
he had a comparatively good education; and his excellent hand-
writing obtained for him at about the age of fifteen a clerkship at the
Swedish postal agency in Hamburg. He threw up this position,
however, when the commissioner demanded that he should also do
service as lackey. He then found a similar post with an advocate in
Schwerin, where his interest in the theatre was awakened by the
books which his master permitted him to read from his library, as
well as by personal acquaintance with Frau Sophie Schröder.
Towards the end of 1739 he joined the company which Schönemann
was then forming—it was Schönemann's first independent step—in
Lüneburg. Early in 1740, he made his début as an actor in a barn
there in the rôle of Xipharès in Racine's *Mithridate*, playing with
Ackermann, who assumed the title-rôle, and Madame Schröder who

---

[1] *Hamburgische Unterhaltungen*, vi, 4, October, 1768, p. 348.
[2] Cp. H. Uhde, *Konrad Ekhof* in *Der neue Plutarch*, ed. R. Gottschall, iv (Leipzig,
1876), pp. 119 ff.

appeared as Monime. He made no phenomenal beginning, and success only came to him after long years of hard work.

Ekhof's association with Schönemann extended over seventeen years, and in a member of this company, Demoiselle Georgine Spiegelberg, he found his future wife. He married her in 1746; but it was not a happy marriage. She was fourteen years his senior; she outlived him nevertheless, and the later years of marriage were darkened by her mental derangement. In 1740 Ekhof seems to have been advanced to leading rôles; and as Schönemann had accepted Gottsched's reforms, Gottsched's *Deutsche Schaubühne* was liberally drawn upon for the repertory. He had also, however, invaluable experience in comedy. In particular, Johann Christian Krüger, a young student of theology who turned to the theatre and was employed by Schönemann as actor and 'theatre poet', provided him, in his *Herzog Michel* and in an adaptation of a play by Marivaux, *Der Bauer mit der Erbschaft*, with two of his most popular rôles. In 1741 he appeared in Leipzig, playing under the eye of the dictator Gottsched himself; but his first resounding success would seem to have been won in his native town, where the company opened their season on June 7 of the same year with *Le Cid*. The alexandrines gave him trouble at first, but his audience was quick to perceive the genuine feeling that lay behind his declamation; his fine voice carried conviction and made one forget his false accents and exaggerated emphasis. In 1749, in Leipzig, he made the acquaintance of the dramatist Christian Felix Weisse, who, from now on, always submitted his plays to Ekhof before printing them. Through Weisse he was later introduced to Lessing, and the acquaintance of actor and critic ripened in the 'fifties into genuine intimacy. For the seven years from 1749 onwards, Schönemann, with Ekhof as his chief supporter, oscillated between Hamburg and Mecklenburg, their repertory consisting mainly of works by Johann Elias Schlegel, Gellert and Lessing, together with Holberg's comedies and the established favourites of the French theatre. On October 25, 1754, Lillo's *Merchant of London* (*Der Kaufmann von London*) was successfully produced in Hamburg with Ekhof as the apprentice; on October 6, two years later, *Miss Sara Sampson* was played there for the first time with Ekhof in the part of Mellefont; and a few weeks later he added still another to his brilliant performances with Beverley in Moore's *Gamester* (*Der Spieler*). At no time had Ekhof's support of Schönemann been merely that of a prominent actor; and in the later years when Schönemann was growing old and was more interested in

horse-dealing and the tavern than in his theatre, Ekhof became
virtually manager. In some respects the most important period of
his career was in the early 'fifties, when the patronage of the Schwerin
court gave Schönemann's company something of the dignity of a
court company there; and it is perhaps not too much to claim that
this patronage did more towards furthering the establishment of a
German National Theatre than the experiment of more than ten
years later in which we are immediately interested. To Ekhof was due
in particular the idea of a dramatic academy at Schwerin, which, as
we have seen, was also to have been a feature of the Hamburg undertaking.

In 1757 Ekhof left Schönemann to join the company of Franz
Schuch, a popular harlequin-player, then in Danzig; but this connexion did not last long; before the end of the year he was back again
in Hamburg with his old company, Schönemann having meanwhile
withdrawn altogether from its management. Things did not go well
with the company, however, and Gottfried Heinrich Koch next came
to the rescue of the Hamburg theatre. Under Koch Ekhof played for
the next five years, mainly in Hamburg and Lübeck. The two actors
did not get on well together, Ekhof missing the freedom he had
enjoyed under Schönemann, and when, in 1764, Koch again opened
a season in Hamburg, Ekhof left him, going back to Ackermann who
was then playing in Hanover. With Ackermann he returned to
Hamburg and was the chief and indispensable prop of the company
during the season which preceded the inauguration of the National
Theatre. The Seyler régime no doubt suited Ekhof, for he had soon as
free a hand as he could have desired. And, as we have seen, he
remained faithful to Seyler after the latter's failure. Subsequently he
enjoyed the patronage of the Duke of Gotha, who inaugurated under
his directorship the first German Hoftheater, in the modern sense, in
his capital. In Gotha Ekhof passed the remainder of his days. His
death, hastened by an overdose of laudanum, occurred on June 16,
1778, his last rôle having been the Ghost in *Hamlet* on February 11
of that year.

Like our own Garrick, Ekhof suffered under physical disabilities;
he had a short, unprepossessing figure. But, again like Garrick, once
he was on the stage, he made his audience forget such disabilities.
His principal asset seems to have been his magnificent voice. Although
he had learned his art under Schönemann, he avoided the stiffness of
Schönemann's school, introducing into his delivery of tragic rôles a

natural tone which did a great deal towards counteracting the rant into which, on German lips, the alexandrine so readily degenerated. In comedy he avoided still more the conventional tone of the French theatre; but here at times he went to extremes of coarseness and vulgarity which distressed his admirers.

From the *Dramaturgie* it might be inferred that Lessing regarded Ekhof as little short of the ideal actor; he has only praise for him.[1] Obviously, however, one could hardly expect Lessing to be entirely honest here in the opinions he expresses about Ekhof. His first mention of him (II, 91) is to say that 'whatever rôle he plays, even if it be the smallest, one recognises in him the foremost actor, and can only regret that it is not possible to see him play all the others'. In St. III and IV he illustrates the art of delivering 'moral maxims' from Ekhof's part of Evander in *Olint und Sophronia*. Later, he singles out for particular praise his acting as the father in *Julie* (IX, 97), especially the 'way in which he brings down over his eyes the grey hair by which he conjures his daughter'. As Orosmann in *Zayre* (XVI, 147) Ekhof typifies 'everything that Sainte Albine will have us observe, in so perfect a way that one might think he alone had been the critic's model'. As Sidnei (XVII, 37) 'unquestionably one of his strongest rôles...what a wealth of expressive gestures!...what an impelling tone of conviction!' Lessing praises his convincing playing of Dorimond in *Cenie* (XX, 76): 'this mingling of gentleness and seriousness, of softheartedness and sternness, will actually exist in just such a man, or it will be found nowhere'; and he has particular praise for a gesture of Ekhof's at the close of the piece.[2] Again Ekhof's Graf Essex calls forth Lessing's

---

[1] The only passage where Lessing seems to reflect adversely on Ekhof is (XVII, 120) where he speaks of the farcical treatment of the rôle of Strabo in Regnard's *Democrit*; but this is mainly a translation from a French criticism of the rôle (see below, p. 194).

[2] F. L. W. Meyer (*op. cit.* i, p. 129) writes of a performance of *Cenie* in Hanover on May 9, 1764: 'Eckhof [spielte] den Mericourt in der Cenie, bei weitem nicht so gut als Kirchhof. Drei Jahr später übernahm er den Dorimond, der ganz für ihn gemacht war, und worin er sicherlich auf keiner Bühne der Welt übertroffen werden konnte, eben weil ihm der Körper nicht im Wege stand. Hier trafen Vortrag der Rede, Ausdruck des Gesichts und Bewegung der Hände meisterhaft zusammen; und Schröder war, so oft er dieser Rolle erwähnte, noch beredter in Eckhofs Lobe als Lessing selbst. Nur glaubte er, dass Lessing die Gebehrde, welche die grosse Welt bezeichnet, die Mericourts Vaterland ist, nicht so sehr herausstreichen, nicht sagen sollen wer sie dem Mann gelehrt: weil er dafür hielt, kein verständiger Schauspieler werde die Stelle anders bezeichnen, jedem müsse die Natur das Nämliche eingeben.' For the Latin quotation at the end of this criticism (XX, 86) see below, p. 479, note 2.

admiration (xxv, 44). In Schröder's judgment Ekhof's Masuren in *Der poetische Dorfjunker* was a caricature, and Karoline Schulze described it as 'ekelhaft', but Lessing does not mention his acting of this part at all; his Patelin again, which was notorious for its vulgarity, Lessing describes (xiv, 108) as 'quite excellent'.[1]

Ekhof's weak side was a growing vanity which led him to show his versatility by playing rôles for which he was physically unsuited. We find him assuming youthful parts—Franz in *Die Hausfranzösin*,[2] Von Kaltenborn in *Das Testament*, Lycast, the younger brother in Romanus's *Die Brüder*, while the young actor Böck played the older brother—when he was not far short of fifty.[3] At the first performance of *Minna von Barnhelm* in Hamburg he played Tellheim, and Schröder commented on his performance: 'Unübertreffl[ich], wenn der Körper gepasst hätte.'[4]

Ekhof had also literary ambitions and talent. He translated La Chaussée's *Die Mütterschule* in 1753, and Collet's *Die wüste Insel* in 1762;[5] he had a share in the version of Voltaire's *Der verlorene Sohn*, published in Hamburg in 1754 (in Schönemann's *Neue Sammlung von Schauspielen*, i) as well as in the verse translation of *Der verheyrathete Philosoph* by Destouches.[6] A rendering, published in 1780, of the chapter on the theatre in J. F. von Bielfeld's *Progrès des Allemands* was by him, and he had the intention of translating an English book on *The Art of Acting*[7] and of writing a history of the German theatre. His playbills and materials collected for this purpose, now preserved in the Herzogliche Bibliothek, Gotha, are of the greatest value for the theatrical history of his time. He is also said to have translated Diderot's *Père de Famille*, but to have withdrawn his translation when Lessing's version appeared.

Ekhof may be said to have combined a respect for the classical traditions of the art of acting in the eighteenth century with the

---

[1] Cp. Meyer, *op. cit.* i, pp. 128 f., 139; see also below, p. 69.

[2] But see below, p. 80.

[3] Meyer, *op. cit.* i, p. 151.

[4] *Ibid.* ii, 2, p. 20. The *Hamburgische Unterhaltungen*, vi, 6, December, 1768, while praising his acting of the part, wished 'er [möchte ihn] durchgehends mit mehr Würde spielen'.

[5] Cp. H. A. O. Reichard's *Theater-Kalender, oder Taschenbuch für die Schaubühne, auf das Jahr 1777*, Gotha, p. 177.

[6] See below, p. 62. Lessing's criticism of this translation is in St. xii (49).

[7] This may possibly have been *An Essay on the Art of Acting*, by Aaron Hill, London, 1746.

naturalism which had been introduced with the new 'tragedy of common life' and which was sponsored by Diderot; in other words his attitude was identical with that which Lessing maintained as a critic of the drama. This may well explain the wholehearted appreciation which Lessing expresses for Ekhof's art. In other respects Ekhof showed himself worthy of the sobriquet subsequently given him: 'der Vater der deutschen Schauspielkunst'. In an age when his profession was regarded as lying outside the pale of respectable citizenship, he won by his straight dealing, his upright life, his efforts to improve the moral and social standing of the actor, and his own intercourse with the intellectual élite of his time, general respect which redounded to the honour of the German theatre.

Beside Ekhof stood, as the two outstanding male players of the National Theatre, Böck and Borchers. Johann Michael Böck (1743–93), who had begun life as a barber, joined Ackermann's company in 1762 and came rapidly to the front. He seems to have been a serviceable actor with an unimposing figure and no very conspicuous genius; but he was a favourite with the public. An anecdote which Schröder tells of him has clung pertinaciously to his memory. On his return to Hamburg in 1768, Schröder asked him how he was getting on; his reply was to the effect that he had now learned the trick of winning applause—which was to let his voice drop before his exit and then suddenly burst out into loud tones.[1] It is possible that Lessing had this affectation in mind when in St. v (119) he deprecated the appeal of certain actors to the gallery by a noisy exit. Böck was better in youthful comedy parts—Schröder mentions Theophan in Lessing's *Freygeist* as his best[2]—than in tragedy, where his declamation tended to degenerate into rant. He remained faithful to Ekhof and became his successor in Gotha, where he had the reputation of being a good Hamlet. Subsequently he went to Mannheim where he played leading rôles with Iffland. He was the first Karl Moor. His death occurred in 1793.

David Borchers (1744–96) was much more talented than Böck. He was a native of Hamburg, and the son of a clergyman. He early gave up his theological studies at Göttingen to become an actor; and Ackermann took him into his company as a beginner at eight marks a week. He had an unmistakable talent for the stage; even as a novice he played with extraordinary sureness, and his versatility was greater

---

[1] F. L. W. Meyer, *op. cit.* i, p. 187.
[2] *Ibid.* p. 147.

than that of any other German actor of his time. He seems to have
been equally successful as a young lover and a comic 'charge'; and
he even shared with Ekhof quite elderly parts. The only time that
Lessing mentions him (xix, 120), it is to praise him for this versatility.
Had it not been for a lamentable instability of character which was
his ruin, he might have risen to be one of the great actors of his
time.

The new direction retained—perhaps as a kind of peace-offering—
the services of Ackermann and his two daughters; but Ackermann,
who had been through so much anxiety in the preceding year, was
not very willing to co-operate: he declined at first to let himself be
formally bound. He promised, however, to help the new company
should difficulties arise. He would accept no payment for such services
during the summer, which he spent mainly with relatives in Mecklenburg.[1] His name appeared only once on the playbills in Lessing's
time, in *Der verheyrathete Philosoph* by Destouches, and on that occasion
(April 30, 1767; xii, 59) Lessing described him as 'unexceptionable'
('unverbesserlich'); but he also acted during the month of May in
Das Caffeehaus, *Miss Sara Sampson*, *Das Gespenst mit der Trommel* (twice)
and *Die falschen Vertraulichkeiten*; on July 3 and again on August 24 he
played in *Solimann der Zweyte*; and in the performances of *Minna von
Barnhelm* on September 30[2] and October 1 he was the Wachtmeister.
From September on he accepted a regular engagement at eight talers
a week, the same sum being paid for the services of his daughters.[3]
The situation was, no doubt, a difficult one—the actual owner of the
theatre was a salaried actor of the company; and there may have
been some ground for Löwen's complaint that it was one of the
reasons for the ultimate disruption.

Of the other actors of the troupe little can or need be said. Lessing
has a word of commendation for Johann Gottlieb Hensel, the husband
of Madame Hensel; he and Merschy seem to have been capable
interpreters of lackeys and servants—Lessing praises them for this
(xviii, 69)—and such characters had a large share in the comedy of

---

[1] F. L. Schmidt, *Geschichte des Hamburgischen Theaters* (Fortsetzung) in *Almanach
fürs Theater*, Hamburg, 1810, p. 5 (quoted also by Litzmann, *op. cit.* i, p. 345).

[2] This date is uncertain. The *Hamburgische Address-Comtoir Nachrichten* of September 28, 1767, announced the first performance for September 30, and a
repetition for October 1. The playbill for September 30 is missing from Ekhof's
collection; the printed word 'nochmals' on the playbill for October 1 has been
crossed out in ink.

[3] F. L. Schmidt, *loc. cit.*

the time.[1] Christian Witthöft was engaged from Koch's company to take over Ackermann's rôles; he was a capable actor of comic old men and servants. Schmelz, Cludius, Garbrecht and Schulz are hardly more than names to us.

Of the women the most commanding personality was, needless to say, Sophie Friederike Hensel (*née* Sparmann). She was born in Dresden on May 23, 1738, and began her stage career in 1754, her début being in Voltaire's *Zayre*. A year later she married Hensel; but the bonds of matrimony did not lie heavily on either husband or wife. For the greater part of her stage career she had been associated with Ackermann; her reputation rapidly grew, and at the time of the National Theatre she was generally looked upon as one of the first actresses of her time. Lessing describes her (IV, 108) as 'unquestionably one of the best actresses the German theatre has ever had', and he gives us the impression that he regarded her as a worthy partner of Ekhof himself. But in the case of no member of the Hamburg staff was it more obviously necessary for him to express himself warily than in hers. She had an imposing stage presence and an impressive declamation. 'Sie weiss', he said, (IV, 110)

den verworrensten, holprichsten, dunkelsten Vers, mit einer Leichtigkeit, mit einer Präcision zu sagen, dass er durch ihre Stimme die deutlichste Erklärung, den vollständigsten Commentar erhält. Sie verbindet damit nicht selten ein Raffinement, welches entweder von einer sehr glücklichen Empfindung, oder von einer sehr richtigen Beurteilung zeuget.

And he proceeds to demonstrate these qualities by an analysis of her rendering of the love scene in Act iii, sc. 3 of *Olint und Sophronia*.[2] One cannot help thinking, however, that when Lessing reproves the poet for letting his Clorinde 'rave in the true tone of a drunken vivandière' (v, 39), he is also expressing disapproval of the interpreter of the rôle. He describes in detail and praises Madame Hensel's death scene in

---

[1] Schröder's opinion of them (Meyer, *op. cit.* i, pp. 147 f.) was: 'Hensel war fleissig, und in dummen schläfrigen Bedienten, und einigen komischen Alten, sehr brav. Er übertrieb nie. Zu ernsthaften Rollen konnte er nur aus Noth gebraucht werden. Merschy besass mehr Leben und eigentlich komische Kraft, aber es fehlte ihm an Kopf. Als Figurant war er brauchbar, und ein trefflicher Pierot.' Schröder is said to have taken Lessing to task for his praise of these two actors. Lessing's answer was: 'Wollen Sie auf eine Redensart Gewicht legen, die sich selbst widerspricht? Was kann man sich nicht besser wünschen?' (v. W. Cosack, *Materialien zur Hamburgischen Dramaturgie*, 2nd ed. Paderborn, 1891, p. 133.)

[2] This is an imitation of a similar analysis by Sainte Albine of a scene in *Phèdre* (see below, pp. 478 f.).

Miss Sara Sampson (XIII, 123): 'Nothing more can be demanded from art than what she achieves in the rôle of Sara.'[1] But in writing of her Cenie on May 22 he tempered high praise with a word of censure. He said (XX, 70): 'I only know of one defect, but it is a very rare defect, a very enviable defect: the actress is too big for the rôle. I seem to see a giant exercising with the gun of a cadet. I should not like to do everything that I am able to do excellently.' Madame Hensel resented this criticism as a reflection on her personal appearance, with the unfortunate consequence that, after the twenty-fifth part of the *Dramaturgie*, Lessing decided that it would be advisable not to criticise the players at all. Another ground for Madame Hensel's umbrage may have been that she felt Lessing was not doing her justice in his journal. Down to the beginning of June, when his criticism of the actors was suspended, she had played twelve leading parts, and of these only the three just mentioned had been noticed by him. He ignored her playing of Semiramis, Zayre and Henriette (in *Der poetische Dorfjunker*)—in the two latter of which at least she was famous—while he had criticised Madame Löwen on five occasions.

In his criticism of the acting of *Graf Essex*, in which Madame Hensel did not appear, Lessing makes a generalisation which seems to throw some light on his judgment of her. In speaking of the difficulties of an actress in impersonating a character such as Queen Elizabeth, who is both tender and proud, he asks (XXV, 66):

Wie kann eine Aktrice nun weiter gehen, als die Natur? Ist sie von einem majestätischen Wuchse, tönt ihre Stimme voller und männlicher, ist ihr Blick dreist, ist ihre Bewegung schnell und herzhaft: so werden ihr die stolzen Stellen vortrefflich gelingen; aber wie steht es mit den zärtlichen?

[1] Karoline Schulze, Madame Hensel's predecessor in Hamburg, asserted in her *Denkwürdigkeiten*, published by H. Uhde in Riehl's *Historisches Taschenbuch*, 5te. Folge, iii, Leipzig, 1873, p. 398 (referred to by Petersen, *Lessings Werke* (*Goldene Klassiker-Bibliothek*), Berlin [1925–29], *Anmerkungen zu Teil 1–7*, p. 193) that her rival had borrowed her 'business' from her: 'An jungen Actricen, welche neben ihr emporzukommen trachteten, versündigte sie sich geradezu; so auch an mir. Und doch lauschte sie mir mehr als eine Nuance meines Spieles ab; so zum Beispiel copirte sie mich völlig als Sarah Sampson, und wenn ihr der grosse Lessing in seiner "Dramaturgie" wegen der Sterbescene ein so bedeutendes Compliment macht, so gilt dasselbe eigentlich mir, denn die Hensel ahmte mir sklavisch nach. Leider hatte ich ja Gelegenheit gehabt, die Schauer des Todes an mehr als einem Sterbebette zu studiren!' Cp. for a fuller account *Lebenserinnerungen der Karoline Schulze-Kummerfeld*, ed. E. Benezé (*Schriften der Gesellschaft für Theatergeschichte*, XXIII and XXIV), Berlin, 1915, i, pp. 222, 224 ff.

Ist ihre Figur hingegen weniger imponirend; herrscht in ihren Minen Sanftmuth, in ihren Augen ein bescheidnes Feuer, in ihrer Stimme mehr Wohlklang, als Nachdruck; ist in ihrer Bewegung mehr Anstand und Würde, als Kraft und Geist: so wird sie den zärtlichen Stellen die völligste Genüge leisten; aber auch den stolzen? Sie wird sie nicht verderben, ganz gewiss nicht....

It is tempting to see in this contrast that between Madame Hensel and Madame Löwen; the more so as in the next paragraph he replies to the former's unwillingness to be criticised. Possibly, too, the penultimate sentence of this section (145) is again a reflexion on Madame Hensel:

Eine ernsthafte Königinn, mit gerunzelter Stirne, mit einem Blicke, der alles scheu und zitternd macht, mit einem Tone der Stimme, der allein ihr Gehorsam verschaffen könnte, wenn die zu verliebten Klagen gebracht wird, und nach den kleinen Bedürfnissen ihrer Leidenschaft seufzet, ist fast, fast lächerlich.

As far as we can now judge, Madame Hensel was at her best in pathetic and tragic parts, while her tragedy queens of a heroic mould were apt to degenerate into extravagance and rant. Schröder disliked her long drawn-out 'Zittertöne' but found her excellent in quiet rôles;[1] he was unable, however, to understand how Lessing could compare her with Ekhof. He commented once, too, on her dragoon-like stride, which suggests the criticism of Lessing's that gave offence.[2] She was endowed to the full with the vanity of her calling, and we have already seen how her jealousy of Karoline Schulze had contributed to the dissolution of Ackermann's management in 1765. After the close of the National Theatre she remained in Hanover with Seyler; later she played again in Vienna, where, however, she never enjoyed much favour. She died in 1789.

Löwen's wife, Elisabeth Lucia Dorothea—a daughter of Schönemann, born in 1732 and married in 1757—shared the honours with Madame Hensel as far as it was permitted for anyone to share them. But whether she was entitled to this honour by her gifts, or merely by her husband's position in the theatre, it is a little difficult to say. As Demoiselle Schönemann she had been a favourite with the Hamburg

[1] Meyer, *op. cit.* i, pp. 96, 141 f.

[2] Years later in a letter to Freiherr von Gebler (October 25, 1772; *Schriften*, xviii, p. 56) Lessing gave his personal opinion of Madame Hensel: 'Ich bin kein persönlicher Freund von Madame Hänselin. Aber ich muss ihr die Gerechtigkeit widerfahren lassen, dass ich noch keine Actrice gefunden, die das, was sie zu sagen hat, mehr versteht, und es mehr empfinden lässt, dass sie es versteht.'

public, but she had retired from the stage on her marriage. When she joined the company now, she had not acted for nine years (VIII, 44); and when the Hamburg enterprise came to an end she did not act again. Here again, Lessing's flattering tribute to her powers obviously cannot be taken too literally. Criticising her Melanide, he said (VIII, 47):

Madame Löwen verbindet mit dem silbernen Tone der sonoresten lieblichsten Stimme, mit dem offensten, ruhigsten und gleichwohl ausdruckfähigsten Gesichte von der Welt, das feinste schnellste Gefühl, die sicherste wärmste Empfindung, die sich, zwar nicht immer so lebhaft, als es viele wünschen, doch allezeit mit Anstand und Würde äussert.

In the part of Celiante (*Der verheyrathete Philosoph*, XII, 57) he said she was a 'Meisterinn'; in her performance as Orphise (*Cenie*, XX, 63) he again praised her 'Würde und Empfindung': 'Every mien speaks of the calm consciousness of her unrecognised worth; and gentle melancholy can only be successfully expressed by eyes and tone like hers.' He paid her a compliment when she appeared as Frau Praatgern in *Die stumme Schönheit* (XIII, 116), although he did not find the rôle suited to her talent. Finally, on one occasion only, he had the opportunity to which he had looked forward (VIII, 99) of criticising her in a tragic rôle, that of Elisabeth in *Graf Essex* (XXV, 85). He commended her, and justified her for representing the queen rather as 'the tender woman' than 'the proud monarch'. Her talent was obviously of a quieter and more subdued kind than Madame Hensel's; more than once Lessing uses the expression 'Anstand und Würde' in describing her acting.[1] She showed to the best advantage in comedy; in tragedy, Meyer tells us, she had the stiff declamatory style of her father's school.[2]

It is sometimes claimed that the real genius among the actresses of the Hamburg theatre was not Madame Hensel, but Madame Susanna Mecour (*née* Preissler). Born in Frankfurt am Main in 1738, she made her début in 1754, and had a varied and chequered career before the Hamburg days. Shortly before she came to Hamburg she had been playing with the Viennese company of Bernardon (J. F.

---

[1] VI, 9; VIII, 51; (for a further use of the expression 'Anstand und Würde' cp. LIV, 123).

[2] Meyer, *op. cit.* i, p. 182: '[Madam Löwen erhielt] den grossen und verdienten Beifall,...der jeder ihrer Darstellungen gebührte. Nur im hohen Trauerspiel waren Sprache und Anstand etwas geziert, und erinnerten an den allgemeinen Fehler der Schönemannschen Schule, von dem nur Eckhof sich rein erhielt.'

Kurz), which visited the chief middle German towns in 1765 and 1766; and she was, no doubt, the best of Löwen's new recruits. She brought with her several of the plays, new to Hamburg, in which she had been appearing, among them *Olint und Sophronia*; but she does not seem to have made much impression as Sophronia. Nor, indeed, was she suited to tragic rôles. Her particular province was soubrette parts, her best being Franziska in Lessing's *Minna von Barnhelm*. Unfortunately, either from vanity or from an unwillingness to cross Madame Hensel, she made it a condition that Lessing should not mention her, either favourably or unfavourably, in his *Dramaturgie*. This refusal, if it has deprived her of immortality, has also woven a nimbus of mystery round her head and has perhaps tempted critics to make exaggerated claims for her genius. It is difficult to form any clear estimate of her success; but personal charm she certainly had, as Schröder was to find later. She acted subsequently under Ekhof in Gotha, and then again in Vienna, where she died in 1784. A portrait of her as Franziska is to be found in Reichard's *Theater-Kalender auf das Jahr 1776*.[1]

Sophie Böck (*née* Schulz), wife of the actor Böck, played as her speciality coquette rôles, and in particular those in which she had to don male attire: 'she handled the hat', said Schröder, 'more easily than the fan'.[2] In parts in which she was not called upon to belie her sex she was stiff and affected, whereas in doublet and hose she possessed grace, self-assurance and freedom. Lessing commends her as Manley in Weisse's *Amalia*; she played the rôle, he says (xx, 92), 'with much charm and all the unforced ease without which we should find it rather improbable that a young woman should be so long unrecognised as such'. But her broad Hamburg accent seems to have been a serious disadvantage.

Ackermann's two daughters, Dorothea and Charlotte, were also, as we have seen, members of the company; but they did not take—or were not permitted to take—much active part in Lessing's time. But Dorothea was then only fifteen and her sister ten. They won warm praise from Meyer, but it is questionable whether they inherited much of their parents' talent. Dorothea retired from the stage when she married in 1778, and Charlotte died suddenly in 1775 at the age of

---

[1] On Susanna Mecour see particularly B. Litzmann, *op. cit.* ii, pp. 26 ff. and Reinecke, *Biographien einiger deutschen Schauspielerinnen*, i (Kopenhagen und Leipzig, 1787), pp. 177–90. For her performance of Sophronia in Hamburg see below, p. 55.   [2] Meyer, *op. cit.* i, p. 142.

Madame Mecour, Herr Böck, H. Brandes als
Francisca, Tellheim, u. Werner.

Madame Böck und Herr Eckhof im
Bauer mit der Erbschaft.

MADAME MECOUR, HERR BÖCK,
HERR BRANDES
as FRANCISCA, TELLHEIM and
WERNER in
Minna von Barnhelm

(Act III, Sc. 10)

MADAME BÖCK and HERR ECKHOF
as LISE and JÜRGE in
Der Bauer mit der Erbschaft

(Sc. 1)

Reproduced from Theater-Kalender auf das Jahr 1776, *Gotha*

eighteen. Therese Schulz, who was engaged from Breslau on Lessing's recommendation, does not seem to have justified expectations. But Cornelie Felbrich, a young actress for whom Lessing has a word of encouragement (x, 78) was a genuine loss to the company when she left Hamburg in November, 1767,[1] to join Karl Döbbelin in Berlin. The other women—the wives of the actors Schmelz, Merschy, Renouard, Garbrecht and Witthöft—played only unimportant minor rôles, and do not call for notice.

Regret has sometimes been expressed that one member of Ackermann's company, his afterwards famous stepson Friedrich Ludwig Schröder, should not have been retained and thus have been associated with the first 'National Theatre'. But in those early days it could hardly be realised that he was anything more than a capable dancer and a useful actor in minor (and particularly 'harlequin') rôles. Schröder himself was not disposed to submit himself to the stiffer discipline which was threatened, and to the critical eye of Ekhof. He preferred to try his fortune with the more easy-going Viennese company of Bernardon, which was then playing in Mannheim.

The management of the ballets, which would certainly have benefited by young Schröder's collaboration, was entrusted to an old balletmaster, Curioni, who had done useful service under Ackermann; but as Lessing did not share Löwen's approval of these, he never mentions them, and consequently they do not concern us here.

---

[1] Cp. Meyer, *op. cit.* i, p. 183: 'Unter allen ersten Erwartungen machte Demoiselle Felbrich, am 30sten April, in der neuen Agnes, das meiste Glück.'

CHAPTER II

THE REPERTORY OF THE THEATRE

The repertory of the 'National Theatre' of 1767–69—which the historian of the Hamburg stage described as 'unexceptionable'[1]—shows, in point of fact, hardly a trace of that purpose which Löwen had emphasised in his *Vorläufige Nachricht*, namely, to encourage and further the interests of German—or indeed, any other—dramatic literature. Not merely had the offer of prizes for new German plays to be eliminated from the scheme at an early stage, but also any pretence at all of serving literary ends. The plays which were performed were selected exclusively from the standpoint of theatrical expediency.

The new lessees had, it will be remembered, purchased, or undertaken to purchase, from Ackermann the properties and costumes which had accumulated under his management, and it was natural that they should wish to repeat the more elaborately and expensively staged productions of that management. This made the inclusion in the repertory of such pieces as *Rodogune*, *Zelmire* and *Solimann II* inevitable. But a much more cogent ground for choice lay in the interests and demands of the actors. Madame Hensel had to be provided, in the first instance, with an opportunity of appearing in the rôles with which she had won popularity, and especially those in which she believed she could demonstrate her superiority to the rival she displaced, Karoline Schulze. This was an immediate motive for the production of such works as *Miss Sara Sampson*, *Rodogune*, *Zayre*, *Merope*, *Semiramis*, *Der verheyrathete Philosoph*. The wife of the director, Madame Löwen, who was returning to the stage after a long absence, naturally desired to appear in parts with which she had won her earlier laurels: Elisabeth in *Graf Essex*, Melanide, Julie in *Das unvermuthete Hinderniss*, Frau Praatgern in *Die stumme Schönheit*, perhaps even Mlle La Fleche in *Die Hausfranzösin*. The principal newcomer, Madame Mecour, no doubt made it a condition of her engagement that she should appear in the rôles in which she had shone as a member of Kurz's troupe in the immediately preceding years. Hence the choice of *Olint und Sophronia*, *Julie*, and numerous other pieces in which soubrette parts were prominent—hence perhaps also the revival of Quinault's *Die coquette Mutter*.

[1] J. F. Schütze, *op. cit.* p. 342; cp. F. L. W. Meyer, *op. cit.* i, p. 184.

Of the men, Ekhof obviously had to be primarily considered—or at least, he so considered himself. But as the mainstay of the company he acted so frequently and had so many opportunities of displaying his talents that he could have no reason to complain. In any case, a season in which he did not show himself in *Cenie, Miss Sara Sampson, Sidnei, Graf Essex, Democrit, Amalia, Der Advokat Patelin, Der Mann nach der Uhr, Das Caffeehaus*, and, of course, *Der Bauer mit der Erbschaft*, was unthinkable. *Richard der Dritte* and *Der Hausvater* also gave him excellent opportunities. But there is more than a suspicion that his desire to show his versatility by appearing in absurdly juvenile parts was responsible for the revival of *Die stumme Schönheit, Die Frauenschule, Die Brüder* and Regnard's *Der Spieler*. The talents of the other members of the company had also to be shown to advantage; while for the frequent performances of Löwen's worthless after-pieces *Die neue Agnese* and *Das Räthsel* no explanation is necessary. Thus until the performance of *Minna von Barnhelm* some five months after the 'Enterprise' was inaugurated—and the delay, it must in fairness to the management be explained, was not due to neglect on their part, but to political scruples on the part of the official Prussian resident in Hamburg—it is difficult to point to a single play the choice of which was due to a desire to serve the ends of literature. And by the time *Minna von Barnhelm* was produced the theatre was in financial difficulties, and there could be less consideration than ever for literary interests. It is little wonder then that Lessing's execution of that part of his plan which was covered by the phrase 'critisches Register' was so often perfunctory. Nor is it surprising that students of the *Hamburgische Dramaturgie* have not given the repertory of the theatre the same critical attention which they have bestowed on the dramatic theory for which that repertory provided the materials.

The section of Hamburg theatre history which is covered by the new experiment extended, as we have seen, from April 22, 1767, to March 3, 1769. It falls into four periods: the first in Hamburg from April 22 to December 4, 1767; the second in Hanover from December 28, 1767 until May 6, 1768; the third again in Hamburg from May 13 to November 25, 1768; and a final season in Hanover from December 2, 1768 to March 3, 1769. The playbills for the entire period, with few exceptions, were kept by Ekhof, and are preserved in the Herzogliche Bibliothek at Gotha. Some of the few gaps can fortunately be filled by reference to the collection in the Hamburg Staats- und Universitätsbibliothek. There are two repertory lists among Lessing's

papers which supplement the playbills. The first of these, a record of
the performances in Hamburg from July 1 to December 4, 1767,
accompanied by a few notes and memoranda, must have been drafted
by him, as Muncker has shown,[1] about the middle of December 1767.
The second is a list of the performances of the second Hamburg period,
and was drawn up by Löwen at the end of November, 1768.[2]

While only a small section of this repertory concerns the reader of
the *Hamburgische Dramaturgie*, it will not be without interest to survey
the activity of the Hamburg theatre as a whole; its 'unexceptionable'
programme throws valuable light on the state of the German theatre
and the conditions of German theatrical enterprise in the eighteenth
century. It has also to be remembered that, although the latest
performance to be recorded in Lessing's journal was that of July 28,
1767, he had by that date only written about one-third of the work,
and while he was engaged on the remainder he witnessed, or had at
least the opportunity of witnessing, the continued activity of the
theatre far beyond July. This, as will be seen, is not entirely without
bearing on his criticism.

In accordance with a common practice of the eighteenth-century
theatre, the evening entertainment in Hamburg, which began at
half-past five (occasionally at five o'clock), consisted normally of two
items: a tragedy or comedy, for the most part of five acts, followed by
lighter fare, a one-act comedy or farce ('Nachspiel'), the latter being
varied by pantomimic representations given by the ballet of the
company, by musical divertissements, or even, as the theatre degenerated, by less reputable attractions. The theatre was only open
on five evenings of the week, there being no performances on Saturdays
and Sundays. In the following summary of its activities I do not deal
with the ballets—as has been seen, they were completely ignored by
Lessing, but some of them seem to have been elaborate choreographic
productions, and they were occasionally introduced by lengthy synopses
in the programme of the evening. Such were, in Lessing's time,
Admetus und Alceste, produced on June 2,[3] and *Armide*, on July 14.

---

[1] *Schriften*, xv, pp. 48 ff.   [2] *Ibid.* p. 55.

[3] The following is the description from the playbill (in Gotha) of this 'grosse
Heroisch-Pantomimische Ballet': 'Der Schauplatz stellt einen Tempel vor, in
dessen Mitte ein Altar ist. Alceste und Admetus stehen mit ihren Gefolge zur
Seiten. Amor führt den Admetus und Hymen die Alceste zum Altar, und die
Liebesgötter zünden ihre Fackeln an. Admetus verlangt, dass Alceste ihren
Schleyer abnehmen soll: sie weigert sich: Amor thut es an ihrer Statt, und sie
wirft sich in die Arme ihres Gemahls. Der Tempel wird unter dem Getöse des

And there were Turkish ballets, Chinese ballets, ballets of gipsies, huntsmen, gardeners, Flanders peasants and Strassburg market-folk.[1] Harlequin pantomimes were re-instated by the balletmaster Barzanti, who joined the company in September, 1767. They were particularly popular, *Harlekins Grabmal* being played thirteen times, *Die Geburt des Harlekins aus einem Ei* five, *Reise des Harlekin und Pierot* five, and *Arlekin ein Sklave in der Türkei* four. Later on, four Italian Intermezzi were produced, *La Serva padrona, Il Giocatore e la Bachettone, La Giardiniera Contessa* and *La Pace campestre*.

Leaving aside then such ingredients of the repertory, I append a synopsis of all the dramatic works performed by the 'National Theatre' in Hamburg and Hanover during the entire period of its existence.[2] Where the number of acts in the plays in my lists is not specified, it is five; in the case of the 'Nachspiele', one. I have added the original date of production of each play and the number of performances given.[3]

Donners durch ein finstres Gewölke bedeckt: Apollo erscheint in den Wolken, und wirft einen Dolch mitten unter das Volk, worauf der Altar auf einmal folgende feurige Schrift zeigt: Admetus. Peribit. Nisi. Quis. Cadat. Pro. Ipso. Das Volk weicht vor Angst zurück. Die Höflinge verlassen den Admetus, und niemand will sich für ihn zu sterben darbieten. Er empfindet hierauf die Würkung dieser schröcklichen Verkündigung: er erblasset, und ohngeachtet aller Hülfe der Alceste, sinkt er todt bey den Stufen des Altars nieder. Alceste nimt den Dolch; durchstösst sich, und fällt den Herumstehenden in die Arme. Sobald der Stoss geschehen, wird Admetus wieder lebendig: wie er aber Alcesten erblickt, fällt er seinen Leuten voll Raserey und sinnlos in die Arme. Das finstre Gewölke verschwindet; das Chor der Götter erscheint in den Wolken, und lässt sich über dem Tempel nieder. Durch Hülfe des Amors werden Admetus und Alceste wieder lebendig: die Freude wird allgemein, und eine von Geniis getragene Blumenkrone kömt aus den Wolken über dieses Paar.' (See also R. Schlösser, *Vom Hamburger Nationaltheater zur Gothaer Hofbühne, 1767–1779 (Theatergeschichtliche Forschungen,* xiii), Hamburg, 1895, p. 98.)

[1] Cp. the list of ballets performed under Ackermann and Schröder given by Meyer, *op. cit.* ii, 2, pp. 76 ff.

[2] The information in these lists is based mainly on Ekhof's collection of playbills preserved in the Herzogliche Bibliothek at Gotha; but I am also much indebted to the work of R. Schlösser quoted above. Schlösser's statistics contain, however, a number of inaccuracies.

[3] The statistics of performances are based on the information contained in Ekhof's collection of playbills. Where the evidence of these conflicts with that of the announcements in the *Hamburgische Address-Comtoir Nachrichten,* the playbills have been taken as authoritative, except in one instance (see below, p. 44 note 1); for the small number of performances for which the playbills are missing, the announcements in the *Hamburgische Address-Comtoir Nachrichten* have been used and figures including this evidence have been added in square brackets.

TRAGEDIES

GERMAN

J. E. Schlegel, *Canut* (1748), 1.

G. E. Lessing, *Miss Sara Sampson* (1755), 5.

C. F. Weisse, *Eduard III* (1758), 2; *Richard III* (1759), 4; *Rosemunde* (1761), 3; *Crispus* (1764), 4; *Romeo und Julie* (1767), 9.

J. F. von Cronegk, *Codrus* (1760), 1; *Olint und Sophronia* (1760), 4.

H. P. Sturz, *Julie und Belmont* (1767), 4.

C. H. von Ayrenhoff, *Hermann und Thusnelda* (1768), 1.

FRENCH

P. Corneille, *Rodogüne* (1644, printed 1647), 8.

Th. Corneille, *Der Graf von Essex* (1678), 2.

F. de Voltaire, *Zayre* (1732), 4; *Alzire* (1736), 3 [4]; *Mahomet* (1742), 4 [5]; *Merope* (1743), 4; *Semiramis* (1748), 7.

A. M. Lemierre, *Hypermnester* (1758), 5.

P. L. Buyrette de Belloy, *Zelmire* (1762), 4.

J. G. Dubois Fontanelle, *Ericia, oder die Vestalin* (1768), 6.

ENGLISH

G. Lillo, *Georg Barnwell* (1731), 3.

J. Thomson, *Eduard und Eleonora* (1739), 5.

E. Moore, *Der Spieler* (1753), 4.

COMEDIES (INCLUDING 'SERIOUS' COMEDIES)
OF MORE THAN ONE ACT

GERMAN

L. A. Gottsched, *Die Hausfranzösin* (1744), 1.

J. E. Schlegel, *Der Triumph der guten Frauen* (1748), 5.[1]

J. C. Krüger, *Die Candidaten* (1748), 4.

G. E. Lessing, *Der Misogyn* (3 acts) (1755), 5; *Der beschämte Freygeist* (1755), 5 [6]; *Minna von Barnhelm* (1767), 15 [16].[2]

K. F. Romanus, *Crispin als Vater* (3 acts) (1756), 4; *Die Brüder* (1761), 4.

C. F. Weisse, *Amalia* (1765), 6; *List über List* (1767), 6.

F. von Heufeld, *Julie* (3 acts) (1766), 7.

J. F. Löwen, *Ich habe es beschlossen* (3 acts) (1766), 3.

[1] The number of performances of this play for which playbills are to be found in Ekhof's collection in Gotha is 6. But this figure includes a playbill for June 10, 1768; and the *Hamburgische Address-Comtoir Nachrichten* of June 11 states that actually *Sidnei* and *Der Advocat Patelin* were given on the previous evening, owing to the indisposition of Madame Hensel. This evidence has been accepted and the number of performances of these three plays calculated accordingly.

[2] See above, p. 33, note 2.

J. C. Brandes, *Der Schein betrügt* (1767), 7; *Der Graf von Olsbach* (1768), 2.
J. L. Schlosser, *Der Zweykampf* (1767), 6.

FRENCH

J. B. P. Molière, *Die Männerschule* (3 acts) (1661), 1; *Die Frauenschule* (1662), 7; *Der Geitzige* (1667), 6; *Der Tartüffe* (1667), 1; *Amphitryon* (3 acts) (1668), 2; *Der Kranke in der Einbildung* (3 acts) (1673), 1 [2].
Ph. Quinault, *Die coquette Mutter* (1665), 1.
J. F. Regnard, *Der Spieler* (1696), 5; *Der Zerstreute* (1697), 5; *Democrit* (1700), 5.
D. A. de Brueys and J. Palaprat, *Der Stumme* (1691), 6; [de Brueys], *Der Advocat Patelin* (1706), 8.[1]
A. R. Lesage, *Turcaret* (1709), 1.
J. de Lafont, *Der Schiffbruch* (3 acts) (1710), 4.
Ph. N. Destouches, *Das unvermuthete Hinderniss* (1717), 4; *Der Philosoph, der sich der Heyrath schämet* (1727), 7; *Der Ruhmredige* (1732), 4; *Der Poet vom Lande* (1736, played 1759), 6; *Das Gespenst mit der Trommel* (1736, played 1762), 1.
P. C. de Chamblain de Marivaux, *Die Überraschung der Liebe* (3 acts) (1722), 7; *Das falsche Kammermädchen* (3 acts) (1724), 4; *Das Spiel der Liebe und des Zufalls* (3 acts) (1730), 5; *Die falschen Vertraulichkeiten* (1737), 4.
L. F. de la Drevetière Delisle, *Der Wilde* (3 acts) (1721), 1.
T. S. Gueullette, *Die Liebe als Lehrmeister* (3 acts) (1726), 2.
F. de Voltaire, *Der verlorene Sohn* (1736), 2; *Nanine* (3 acts) (1749), 6; *Die Frau, welche Recht hat* (3 acts) (played 1748 in one-act version, and 1758 in three-act version, printed in three-act version, 1759), 3; *Das Caffeehaus* (1760), 4; *Das Herrenrecht* (1762), 4.
P. C. Nivelle de la Chaussée, *Das Vorurtheil nach der Mode* (1735), 2; *Melanide* (1741), 6; *Die Mütterschule* (1744), 6.
J. B. L. Gresset, *Sidnei* (3 acts) (1745), 6.[2]
G. F. Poullain de Saint-Foix, *Die vollkommenen Verliebten* (4 acts) (1748), 1 [2].
C. S. Favart, *Solimann II* (3 acts) (1761), 9.
F. d'Happoncourt de Grafigny, *Cenie* (1750), 6.
L. de Boissy, *Der Mann nach der Welt* (1740), 2.
D. Diderot, *Der natürliche Sohn* (1757), 1; *Der Hausvater* (1758), 12.
M. J. Sedaine, *Der Philosoph, ohne es zu wissen* (1765), 6.
P. A. Caron de Beaumarchais, *Eugenie* (1767), 10.
C. G. Fenouillot de Falbaire, *Der Galeerensklave* (*L'honnête Criminel*) (1767), 7 [8].

ITALIAN

C. Goldoni, *Der Diener zweier Herren* (1749), 2; *Der Lügner* (1748), 6; *Die schlaue Wittwe* (1748), 4; *Der Vormund* (1753), 1; *Die verstellte Kranke* (1750), 7. (All these comedies are in 3 acts.)

---

[1] See above, p. 44, note 1.   [2] See above, p. 44, note 1.

ENGLISH

G. Colman, *Die eifersüchtige Ehefrau* (1761), 5.

DUTCH

P. Langendijk, *Claus Lustig* (*Krelis Louwen*, 3 acts) (1715), 1.

NACHSPIELE

GERMAN

K. C. Gärtner, *Die geprüfte Treue* (1744), 1.
J. E. Schlegel, *Die stumme Schönheit* (1748), 6.
C. Mylius, *Der Kuss* (1748), 1.
C. F. Gellert, *Die kranke Frau* (1747), 3.
J. C. Krüger, *Herzog Michel* (1750), 5.
G. E. Lessing, *Der Schatz* (1750, printed 1755), 2.
S. Gessner, *Erast* (1762), 2.
G. K. Pfeffel, *Der Schatz* (1761), 6.
F. A. Nuth, *Die Gouvernante* (1763, in revised form), 1.
Th. G. von Hippel, *Der Mann nach der Uhr* (1760), 9.
J. F. Löwen, *Die neue Agnese* (1767), 9; *Das Räthsel* (1767), 5.
D. Schiebeler, *Die Schule der Jünglinge* (1767), 4.

FRENCH

M. A. Le Grand, *Die ausschweifende Familie* (1709), 2; *Der sehende Blinde* (1716), 5; *Der Sieg der vergangenen Zeit* (1725), 2.
Ph. N. Destouches, *Die dreyfache Heyrath* (1716), 1.
P. C. de Chamblain de Marivaux, *Der unvermuthete Ausgang* (1724), 4; *Der Bauer mit der Erbschaft* (1725), 11.
G. F. Poullain de Saint-Foix, *Das Orakel* (1740), 2; *Deukalion und Pyrrha* (1741), 5; *Der Finanzpachter* (1761), 2.
— Cérou, *Der Liebhaber als Schriftsteller und Bediener* (1740), 4.
Th. L'Affichard, *Ist er von Familie?* (1736), 5.
F. A. de Chevrier, *Die Frau als Magd* (*L'Épouse suivante*) (1755), 2.
P. Rousseau, *Irrungen* (*Les Méprises*) (1754), 4 [5].
S. R. N. Chamfort, *Die junge Indianerin* (1764), 5.
B. J. Saurin, *Die Sitten der Zeit* (1760), 2 [3].
[J. B. Collet de Messine], *Die wüste Insel* (imitated from Metastasio, *L'isola disabitata*) (1758), 2.
Ph. Poisson, *Die Heyrath durch Wechselbriefe* (1735), 5.
A 'Festspiel', *Der Bürger*, was performed on two evenings.

This list may be conveniently summarised in respect of the country of origin of the plays. The figures in brackets are the number of performances.[1]

[1] These totals include the figures given in square brackets for the individual plays.

	German	French	English	Italian	Dutch
Tragedies	11 (38)	10 (49)	3 (12)	—	—
Comedies (of more than one act)	15 (82)	43 (194)	1 (5)	5 (20)	1 (1)
Nachspiele (comedies in one act)	13 (54)	17 (65)	—	—	—
Festspiele	1 (2)	—	—	—	—
Totals	40 (176)	70 (308)	4 (17)	5 (20)	1 (1)

The total number of dramatic works in the repertory was 120 and the number of performances 522. Thus there is an average of rather more than four for each piece.

As far as the German constituents of this repertory are concerned, the two authors who head the list are Lessing and Weisse. The former's *Misogyn*, *Der Freygeist* and *Miss Sara Sampson* have each performances in excess of the average, and *Minna von Barnhelm* with its sixteen[1] representations was much the most popular play in the entire repertory. In all, Lessing was played on thirty-four evenings. Weisse with seven plays—five tragedies and two comedies—has the same number of evenings to his credit, his 'bürgerliches Trauerspiel' *Romeo und Julie* proving the most popular of his plays with nine representations. Of the older generation, Johann Elias Schlegel alone maintained his hold on the German public with the two comedies *Der Triumph der guten Frauen* and *Die stumme Schönheit* (in all eleven performances); but the day of his tragedies was past, *Canut* being only played once. J. C. Krüger reached nine performances with two comedies, and K. F. Romanus, also with two comedies, eight. Of immediate contemporaries of the theatre, J. F. Löwen, perhaps for obvious reasons, comes first with three pieces and seventeen representations; Heufeld's *Julie* reached seven; Schlosser's *Der Zweykampf* six, but Sturz's *Julie und Belmont* only four. J. C. Brandes, who joined the company as an actor in 1768, and whose plays were subsequently to bulk so largely in German repertories, occupied nine evenings with two comedies.

The oldest constituent of the repertory is naturally the French drama of the seventeenth century; but here, too, as in the German repertory, it is noticeable that the older classic tragedy in alexandrines,

[1] This and the succeeding figure assume a performance of *Minna von Barnhelm* on September 30, 1767, in respect of which there is some uncertainty. See above, p. 33, note 2.

for the supremacy of which Gottsched had fought thirty years before, had ceased to attract. Racine is unrepresented in the repertory, and if Corneille's *Rodogune* reached the respectable number of eight performances, this was due partly to its being played in a new translation and partly to an elaborate *mise-en-scène*. Most significant of all for the change in taste is that *Der Graf von Essex*, by Thomas Corneille, the most popular historical tragedy of the earlier eighteenth century in Germany, could only be performed twice. Molière, however, remained in favour with six comedies and nineteen performances; but only *Die Frauenschule* and *Der Geitzige* had any real success. Regnard, a well-established favourite, could still register fifteen representations for three of his comedies.

But the dominating dramatist of the Hamburg theatre, as he is the dominating figure of the *Hamburgische Dramaturgie*, is Voltaire. Of no other dramatist were so many plays performed, namely ten; and the aggregate of the number of evenings devoted to him—forty-three—far exceeds that for the next most popular dramatists, Lessing and Weisse. But by 1767 Voltaire's day on the German stage was beginning to wane; he belonged to the old guard who had been the main props of the Schönemann period. *Alzire* and *Zayre*, in fact, go back to Caroline Neuber's time in Leipzig; and they stood at the height of their vogue in the early 'forties. Their revival now could not but have an antiquarian flavour. Next to Voltaire in popularity comes Marivaux with six comedies and thirty-five performances; thus he also is in advance of Lessing and Weisse. Then comes Destouches, with six plays and twenty-three performances. Nivelle de la Chaussée is represented by three plays performed fourteen times. De Brueys enjoyed considerable popularity with two comedies, one in collaboration with Palaprat (fourteen performances); but the most popular French comedy in the repertory, with the exception of Marivaux' *Der Bauer mit der Erbschaft*, was Favart's *Solimann der Zweyte*, with nine performances—a success, however, that was largely due to its being one of the show pieces not merely of this company, but of Ackermann's before it. As far as the work of quite contemporary French dramatists is concerned, it is interesting to note that Sedaine's *Der Philosoph, ohne es zu wissen* reached six performances, and Fontanelle's *Ericia* the same number; while the *Zelmire* of De Belloy, a writer who had won the high favour of the Paris public, only rose to four. The form of French play that appealed most to the new generation in Germany was the so-called 'drame'. Diderot had a success with his *Hausvater* (twelve performances) which could, comparatively speaking, hardly be paralleled in France; Beaumarchais' *Eugenie* was performed ten times, and Falbaire's *Galeerensklave* eight.

It is surprising that English drama should be so poorly represented in the repertory, for under Ackermann the English tragedy of common life was in favour; but even Edward Moore's *Der Spieler*, which had been one of Ackermann's favourites, was in these years only played four times. Italy is better represented by Goldoni, another of Ackermann's favourite authors, five of whose comedies were performed on twenty evenings.

Modern critics complain of the neglect of German plays in favour of those of French and other foreign origin; they are emphatic in their condemnation of the ballets and harlequinades with which the work of this 'National' Theatre was 'degraded'. But does the Hamburg theatre of 1767–69 compare in this respect so unfavourably with other theatrical undertakings of its time? There was not a theatre in Europe in the eighteenth century which did not eke out its serious entertainment and increase its attractiveness by the very means which the Hamburg theatre employed; our own Drury Lane, then and for many a year afterwards, thought nothing of softening the asperities of a Shakespearean tragedy by tacking on to it a roaring farce, or some other form of entertainment quite as repugnant to our modern sense of artistic decency as the kind of 'afterplay' provided in Hamburg. Native works, it is true, were neglected in favour of plays of foreign, and especially French, origin; as a matter of fact, the German plays of the Hamburg repertory do not exceed some thirty-three per cent. of the whole. But is this distressing feature to be laid at the door of the Hamburg management? Is it not simply a testimony to the poverty of German dramatic production? Moreover, it has to be noted in defence of the theatre that, as it progressed, the balance against the national literature was steadily redressed. After the first season in Hamburg, eleven new German plays were added to the repertory, as compared with thirteen French plays and one English play; and the number of performances of these novelties was not very unequal—namely, forty-five of the German productions, compared with sixty of the foreign.

Lessing himself gives us no reason to think that he was particularly dissatisfied with the repertory. While recognising (*Ank.* 72) that mediocre plays must form a part of it, he accepted the whole as quite reasonably satisfactory. Nor is there any hint, except in the fact that he does not criticise them, that he regarded the ballets as a degradation of the theatre. In respect of the quality of the repertory, I doubt much whether Lessing saw in it the defects which strike us to-day. He may have had hard enough things to say about the literary qualities of the works which came under his notice, but recognising the practical exigencies of the theatre (*Ank.* 24 ff.) he does not cavil at its choice of plays, nor does he offer any suggestion as to how the quality of the repertory might be improved. In fact, his equanimity here is a little disappointing. There are some modern critics who imagine that Lessing would have welcomed it, had his Hamburg theatre elected to produce Shakespeare's plays instead of Voltaire's, which he takes a particular delight in condemning by pointing to the superiority of the English poet. But I question very much whether Lessing or any one else on the continent in his time would have countenanced such an experiment, before Ducis, in a series of adaptations between 1769 and 1792, had pointed out how Shakespeare could be rendered practicable for the eighteenth-century theatre. Even when his association with the theatre had long been severed and the unhappy 'Enterprise' had failed, it did not occur to Lessing, in the last section of the *Dramaturgie*, to ascribe that failure to the bad selection of plays for performance.

The fatal defect of the Hamburg venture, then, was inherent from its inception: it was an actor-controlled theatre. Löwen may have had the best intentions of creating a living theatre in touch with the best literary ideals, but he was powerless against this weight of interest; and probably the theatre would have failed still more disastrously had he carried out his policy. Some of the plays produced under the new management were old favourites—and pretty threadbare favourites— that had come down from the days of Caroline Neuber. These had passed over into the repertory of her successor Schönemann; a few, not on Schönemann's list, had been played by other companies, notably Koch's. (The French pieces of this category, indeed, were still produced in the translations available in Gottsched's *Schaubühne* or in the eight volumes of Schönemann's.) This, the oldest constituent of the repertory of the National Theatre, includes about fifty-two pieces, that is to say, some forty-three per cent. of the whole. No less than thirty-eight other pieces were taken over by Löwen from Ackermann's repertory, that is, some thirty-two per cent. Of those which remain—most of which were anything but new plays—only a very few were performed under the new management for the first time. During the period when Lessing commented on the theatre, at least, not more than four of the plays—I exclude the ancient *Coquette Mutter* of Quinault, of which I have been able to find no trace in earlier theatrical records—were performed for the first time in Hamburg. These were Cronegk's *Olint und Sophronia* and Heufeld's *Julie*—both imported from Vienna—and the two quite inconsiderable trifles by the director of the theatre, Löwen—*Die neue Agnese* and *Das Räthsel*.

The *Hamburgische Dramaturgie* is only concerned with the activity of the Hamburg theatre during the first fourteen weeks of its existence, namely, from April 22 to July 28, 1767. In that period the theatre was open on fifty-two evenings, and its repertory was as follows:

REPERTORY OF THE HAMBURG THEATRE

APRIL 22–JULY 28, 1767

Wednesday, April 22   Cronegk, *Olint und Sophronia.*
Le Grand, *Der Sieg der vergangenen Zeit.*

Thursday, April 23   Cronegk, *Olint und Sophronia.*
Le Grand, *Der Sieg der vergangenen Zeit.*

Friday, April 24   La Chaussée, *Melanide.*
Ballet: *Der Wirth auf dem Berge.*

Monday, April 27   Heufeld, *Julie.*
Lessing, *Der Schatz.*

Tuesday, April 28   Destouches, *Das unvermuthete Hinderniss.*
Löwen, *Die neue Agnese.*

Wednesday, April 29 Voltaire, *Semiramis.*
Ballet: *Die verwandelten Zittern.*

Thursday, April 30   Destouches, *Der Philosoph, der sich der Heyrath schämet.*
Löwen, *Die neue Agnese.*

Friday, May 1   Voltaire, *Das Caffeehaus.*
Ballet: *Die verwandelten Zittern.*

Monday, May 4   Löwen, *Die neue Agnese.*
Nuth, *Die Gouvernante* (with a ballet).

Tuesday, May 5   Destouches, *Der Poet vom Lande.*
Schlegel, *Die stumme Schönheit.*

Wednesday, May 6   Lessing, *Miss Sara Sampson.*
Ballet: *Die Heu-Erndte.*

Thursday, May 7   Regnard, *Der Spieler.*
Ballet: *Der Wirth auf dem Berge.*

Friday, May 8   Destouches, *Der Philosoph, der sich der Heyrath schämet.*
Cerou, *Der Liebhaber, als ein Schriftsteller und Bedienter.*

Monday, May 11   Quinault, *Die coquette Mutter.*
De Brueys, *Der Advocat Patelin.*

4-2

Tuesday, May 12	Lessing, *Der beschämte Freygeist.*
	Pfeffel, *Der Schatz.*
Wednesday, May 13	Voltaire, *Zayre.*
	Ballet: *Ein serieuses Ballet.*
Thursday, May 14	Gresset, *Sidnei.*
	L'Affichard, *Ist er von Familie?*
Friday, May 15	Destouches, *Das Gespenst mit der Trommel.*
	Ballet: *Das neue serieuse Ballet.*
Monday, May 18[1]	Destouches, *Der Philosoph, der sich der Heyrath schämet.*
	Ballet: *Die Zigeuner in ihrem Lager.*
Tuesday, May 19	Regnard, *Democrit.*
	Ballet: *Die verwandelten Zittern.*
Wednesday, May 20	Marivaux, *Die falschen Vertraulichkeiten.*
	L'Affichard, *Ist er von Familie?*
Thursday, May 21	De Belloy, *Zelmire.*
	Ballet: *Ein serieuses Ballet.*
Friday, May 22	Grafigny, *Cenie.*
	Ballet: *Die Zigeuner in ihrem Lager.*
Monday, May 25	Weisse, *Amalia.*
	Saint-Foix, *Der Finanzpachter.*
Tuesday, May 26[2]	De Belloy, *Zelmire.*
	Ballet: *Der Wirth auf dem Berge.*
Friday, May 29	La Chaussée, *Die Mütter-Schule.*
	Ballet: *Ein neues Gärtner-Ballet.*
Monday, June 1	Voltaire, *Nanine.*
	Löwen, *Die neue Agnese.*
	Ballet.
Tuesday, June 2	De Brueys, *Der Advocat Patelin.*
	Gellert, *Die kranke Frau.*
	Ballet: *Admetus und Alceste.*
Wednesday, June 3	La Chaussée, *Melanide.*
	Hippel, *Der Mann nach der Uhr.*
Thursday, June 4[3]	Corneille, *Der Graf von Essex.*
	Ballet.
Wednesday, June 10[4]	Mad. Gottsched, *Die Hausfranzösin.*
	Ballet: *Die Zigeuner in ihrem Lager.*

[1] The programme of May 18 was given by request, in the presence of Princess Louise, sister of the King of Denmark, and her husband Prince Karl of Hesse (*Hamburgische Address-Comtoir Nachrichten*, May 21, 1767).

[2] The Feast of the Assumption of Our Lady fell on May 28; the theatre was closed on May 27 and 28.

[3] Whit-Sunday fell on June 7; the theatre was closed on June 5, 8 and 9.

[4] For Wednesday, June 10 'nach den Feyertagen', the *Hamburgische Address-Comtoir Nachrichten* of June 4 announced *Richard der Dritte*, but announced on June 11 that this play was not given 'weil die Direction für gut fand, einige Rollen anders zu besetzen'.

Thursday, June 11	Voltaire, *Semiramis.*
	Ballet: *Admetus und Alceste.*
Friday, June 12	Voltaire, *Nanine.*
	Ballet.
	Marivaux, *Der Bauer mit der Erbschaft.*
Monday, June 29[1]	Regnard, *Der Zerstreute.*
	Löwen, *Das Räthsel.*
Wednesday, July 1	Corneille, *Rodogüne.*
	Ballet: *Armide.*
Friday, July 3[2]	Favart, *Solimann der Zweyte.*
	Ballet.
Saturday, July 4[3]	Voltaire, *Nanine.*
	De Brueys, *Der Advocat Patelin.*
Tuesday, July 7	Voltaire, *Merope.*
	Ballet: *Ein serieuses Ballet.*
Wednesday, July 8	Destouches, *Der Philosoph, der sich der Heyrath schämet.*
	Löwen, *Die neue Agnese.*
Thursday, July 9	Schlegel, *Der Triumph der guten Frauen.*
	Ballet: *Die verwandelten Zittern.*
Friday, July 10	Grafigny, *Cenie.*
	Hippel, *Der Mann nach der Uhr.*
Monday, July 13	Molière, *Die Frauen-Schule.*
	Ballet.
Tuesday, July 14	La Chaussée, *Die Mütter-Schule.*
	Ballet: *Armide.*
Wednesday, July 15	Corneille, *Der Graf von Essex.*
	Ballet: *Die Zigeuner in ihrem Lager.*
Friday, July 17[4]	Romanus, *Die Brüder.*
	Saint-Foix, *Das Orakel.*
Monday, July 20	Lessing, *Miss Sara Sampson.*
	Ballet.
Tuesday, July 21	Schlosser, *Der Zweykampf.*
	[Collet de Messine], *Die wüste Insel.*[5]

[1] From June 13–28 the theatre was closed owing to mourning for the death of the Empress Maria Josepha, wife of Joseph II.

[2] There was no performance on July 2 owing to the Feast of the Visitation of Our Lady. The playbill for July 3 is missing from Ekhof's collection, but the *Hamburgische Address-Comtoir Nachrichten* confirm the programme stated above.

[3] This exceptional performance on a Saturday was due to the visit of the King of Denmark. There was none on Monday, July 6, as the theatre was used for a masked ball.

[4] On Thursday, July 16, the actors were apparently given a holiday. The *Hamburgische Address-Comtoir Nachrichten* for July 16 contains the notice 'Heute bleibt der Schauplatz geschlossen'.

[5] For the programme of July 21 Lessing substitutes that of July 28, possibly by an oversight. See p. 90, note 2. For July 28 Lessing inserts a performance of Romanus's *Brüder.*

Wednesday, July 22	Weisse, *Richard der Dritte*.
	Krüger, *Herzog Michel*.
Thursday, July 23	Voltaire, *Die Frau, welche Recht hat*.
	L'Affichard, *Ist er von Familie?*
Friday, July 24	Molière, *Die Frauen-Schule*.[1]
	Ballet: *Die Jäger*.
Monday, July 27	Diderot, *Der Hausvater*.
	Ballet.
Tuesday, July 28	Voltaire, *Nanine*.
	Ballet.
	Marivaux, *Der unvermuthete Ausgang*.[2]

Beyond giving a synopsis of all these plays the older commentaries on Lessing's work are sparing in their information about them. Notably, little attempt has been made to identify the translations of the French items of the repertory; and in fact, it is usually stated that in the great majority of instances it is impossible to attain certainty in this matter. This, however, is not the case; and, as will be seen from the data which I have collected in the following notes, it would be possible—were the undertaking not an entirely futile one—to provide in print, with rare exceptions, the actual versions of all the plays performed during the period of Lessing's association with the theatre.

The notes in the present chapter are concerned exclusively with the theatrical history of the plays in question, Lessing's criticism of them being reserved for the second part of this volume. Only in the case of plays where some knowledge of the plot and contents is necessary for the understanding of what Lessing has to say about them, have I added a brief synopsis.

1. *Olint und Sophronia*, a tragedy in five acts and in alexandrines by Johann Friedrich von Cronegk. Wednesday, April 22, 1767. [St. I–VII.] This play, in the unfinished form in which Cronegk left it, was published in his *Schriften*, Leipzig and Ansbach, 1760 (2nd ed. 1761–63, i, pp. 279 ff.). It was completed by Cassian Anton von Roschmann-Hörburg (1739–1806), and first performed in Vienna on January 14, 1764 (J. H. F. Müller, *Genaue Nachrichten von beyden k. k.*

---

[1] For the programme of July 24 Lessing substitutes that of July 31 (Gresset, *Sidnei* and Le Grand, *Der sehende Blinde*, followed by the ballet *Die verwandelten Zittern*).

[2] See above, p. 53, note 5.

Schaubühnen in Wien, Pressburg, 1772, p. 30). It was published as '*ein christliches Trauerspiel*' in the fourth volume of the *Neue Sammlung von Schauspielen* (Vienna, 1764); and in the 'Vorbericht' to volume iii (p. 6) it is stated that the play 'auf hiesiger Schaubühne ungemeinen Beyfall erhalten [hat]; und man wird ihm denselben—oder wir müssten sehr irren—auch an andern Orten nicht versagen'. There are reprints in *Theater der Deutschen*, v (1767), pp. 121 ff., and in *Lessings Jugend-freunde*, ed. by J. Minor (*Deutsche Nationalliteratur*, lxxii [1883], pp. 121 ff.). (See K. F. Kummer, *Cronegks Olint und Sophronia, fortgesetzt von Roschmann* in *Archiv für Litteraturgeschichte* (ed. F. Schnorr von Carols-feld), Leipzig, ix (1880), pp. 64 ff. Cp. also *Zeitschrift für die Österreich-ischen Gymnasien*, xxx (1879), p. 119.) Bernardon (J. F. von Kurz) included it in his repertory when his company played in Munich (1765), Nürnberg (1766) and Frankfurt (1767); in these performances, as originally in Vienna and now, Susanna Mecour played the rôle of Sophronia (see F. Raab, *J. J. F. von Kurz*, Frankfurt, 1899, pp. 135, 149 f.). The fact that this play had been selected by Kurz to open the 'Comödien-Haus im Fechthaus' in Nürnberg on June 24, 1766, may have been one reason for its being used to open the new Hamburg undertaking. In Kurz's flamboyant *Ankündigung* it had been pro-claimed a masterpiece: 'Wir machen damit den Anfang, da wir uns nun im Stande sehen, nach unseren Absichten, und der hegenden ehrfurchtsvollesten Achtung vor die hiesigen Kenner und Liebhaber einer reinen deutschen Schaubühne etwas vollkommenes zu zeigen...' (F. Raab, *J. J. F. von Kurz*, p. 149).

The cast of the play was; Aladin, Schmelz; Argant, Cludius; Ismenor, Borchers; Olint, Böck; Evander, Ekhof ('trefflich' was Schröder's comment, F. L. W. Meyer, *op. cit.* ii, 2, p. 19); Sophronia, Mad. Mecour; Serena, Mlle Ackermann; Clorinde, Mad. Hensel; Hernicie, Mad. Merschy. The choruses (of Christian virgins) were omitted. Lessing restricts his criticism of the actors to Ekhof and Madame Hensel (St. ii–v). From F. L. W. Meyer (*op. cit.* i, pp. 181 f.) we learn, however, that 'die Sophronia der Madam Mecour [gefiel] nicht sehr, vielleicht weil sie nicht zu sehr gefallen sollte....Auch Schmelz gefiel nicht als Aladin.' Lessing mentions the 'äussere Pracht' of the representation (ii, 79). Cp. J. F. Schütze, *Hamburgische Theater-geschichte*, p. 342: 'Die Dekorationen und Kleidungen waren schön und geschmackvoll. Man gieng nicht unbefriedigt aus der Vorstellung und kam mit Erwartung zur nächsten. Aber man fand oder glaubte nicht zu finden, was man erwartete.' F. L. W. Meyer (*op. cit.* i, p. 159) refers to a 'schönen Säulengang' which the Berlin scene-painter Rosenberg had supplied for the play; and, as Lessing tells us (XXVI, 152), J. W. Hertel had composed 'eigne Symphonien' for it. The programme of the first evening was repeated on the second, as had been the case when Ackermann opened the theatre in 1765. A third performance of *Olint und Sophronia* did not take place until August 12; the fourth and last was given in Hanover on May 4, 1768.

Evander learns from his son Olint that he has just stolen, from the mosque where it had been placed, the crucifix which had been carried off from the Christians by the priest Ismenor; he has restored it to Gottfried von Bouillon. Olint stands in high favour with King Aladin, but Evander fears for the consequences of his theft. Olint is not, as his father thinks, in love with the heathen Clorinde, but with the Christian Sophronia. Clorinde wishes Olint to lead the campaign against the crusaders. The theft of the crucifix is discovered, and Olint is entrusted by the king with the task of finding the thief. Ismenor has doubts of Olint; Clorinde loves him passionately. Sophronia now resolves to offer herself as a substitute for the Christians, who have been condemned to death unless the author of the theft is discovered; she loves Olint and hopes that he will protect the Christians. She declares herself to have been the thief of the crucifix, and is thrown into prison. The king informs Olint that, as the thief has been discovered, the Christians will be spared. Olint now resolves to save Sophronia and declares that he himself has committed the theft. He persists in his espousal of Christianity in spite of Ismenor's appeal to him and of Clorinde's wrath when she learns that he loves Sophronia. Aladin pleads with Olint and pretends that Sophronia has recanted her faith. Olint remains firm in his desire to sacrifice himself. Clorinde has now been converted, in an interview with Sophronia, and plans to save the lovers, fully resolved as they both are to be martyrs.—In Roschmann's conclusion, the priest Ismenor plans to poison Sophronia and accuses Olint of treason. Clorinde arrives with the Sultan's pardon, but too late; Sophronia dies, as does also the wounded Olint. The tragedy ends with a general conversion of the heathens to Christianity.

'Vor dem Anfange des Trauerspiels,' says the playbill, 'wird ein Prologus von Madame Löwen, und nach Endigung desselben ein Epilogus von Madame Hensel gehalten.' The authorship of the prologue and epilogue is uncertain. Schütze (*op. cit.* p. 341) claimed as the author of both Johann Jakob Dusch, who had been resident in Altona since 1756, and in this very year had been appointed Professor of German and English in the 'Gymnasium' there. (Cp. also *Jenaische Zeitungen von gelehrten Sachen* of December 18, 1767, quoted by J. W. Braun, *Lessing im Urtheile seiner Zeitgenossen*, Berlin, 1884–97, i,

p. 196: 'Diese Stücke sind von Hn. Dusch, dem ietzigen Freunde des Herrn Lessings. Man muss sie auswendig lernen. Es sind eine Menge Verse darinnen, die Sprichwörter werden können, wie die von Boileau.') This view is followed by Schmid (*Chronologie*, ed. by P. Legband, Berlin, 1902, p. 164), K. H. Jördens (*Lexikon deutscher Dichter*, Leipzig, 1806–11, vi, p. 28) and others; and among modern critics by C. C. Redlich (*Lessings Werke*, Berlin [1868–77], xix, p. 659).[1] Dusch would thus have been the 'deutsche(n) Dryden in der Nähe' (vii, 128). A difficulty in accepting this view is that in the preface to his *Fabeln* in 1759, Lessing had expressed himself about Dusch in very different terms; and in the *Literaturbriefe* (1759–60) he had written with particular acerbity: 'Herr Dusch hat nicht Witz und Erfindungskraft genug, ein Dichter zu seyn; und ein Philosoph zu seyn, nicht genug Scharfsinn und Gründlichkeit' (cp. *Schriften*, vii, p. 417; viii, pp. 93 ff., 101 ff., 110). The critic of the *Dramaturgie* in Klotz's *Deutsche Bibliothek der schönen Wissenschaften*, iii (Halle, 1769), pp. 55 f. commented on Lessing's inconsistency, he, too, being of the opinion that Dusch was the author of prologue and epilogue:

Dass auch grosse Kunstrichter sich in ihren Urtheilen nicht gleich bleiben, erweise ich aus dem Urtheile über Duschen. Hier heisst er ein Dichter, der es mehr als irgend ein andrer versteht, tiefsinnigen Verstand mit Witz aufzuheitern, und nachdenklichem Ernste die gefällige Mine des Scherzes zu geben, hier heisst er der Deutschen Dryden, der mehr als alle unsre Dichter so gut wie der Engelländer, Moral und Kritik mit attischen Salze zu würzen versteht. Dies schreibt Duschens Recensent in den Litteraturbriefen, zu den sich Herr Lessing in der allgemeinen Bibliothek hat bekennen lassen, so sehr er es ehemals in der Vorrede zu den Fabeln leugnete.

Mendelssohn, however, had published a respectful review of Dusch's poetry in the *Allgemeine deutsche Bibliothek*, v (1767), pp. 3 ff.—there is also a somewhat less favourable one in the *Bibliothek der schönen Wissenschaften*, iv (1758), pp. 532 ff.—and it is conceivable that Lessing might have been influenced by his friend's opinion here, as he was in so much else. The view that Löwen wrote both prologue and epilogue seems to have been first put forward by Adolf Stahr (*G. E. Lessings Leben*, Berlin, 1859, i, p. 282), and it is maintained by Cosack (*Materialien zu Lessings Hamburgischer Dramaturgie*, Paderborn,

---

[1] This edition, published by Gustav Hempel, is frequently referred to as the Hempel edition.

1891, pp. 43 f.), and by W. Oehlke (*Lessing und seine Zeit*, Munich, 1919, ii, p. 16). It would have been natural that he should be the author, especially as he had written the prologue with which the same theatre was opened by Ackermann in 1765. The question is dealt with at length by O. D. Potkoff (*op. cit.* pp. 114 ff.; cp. also p. 20) who decides in favour of Löwen's authorship. He mentions that as a student in Göttingen in 1748, Löwen had read a paper to the 'Deutsche Gesellschaft' on the theme: 'In einer wohleingerichteten Republik muss der Flor der Schaubühne nothwendig erhalten werden,' in which views on the relation of state and stage similar to those in this prologue were expressed. In spite of the readiness of contemporary opinion to ascribe the poems to Dusch, I confess that it is difficult for me to think that Löwen would have let himself be deprived of the privilege of writing prologue and epilogue to the first performance.

2. *Der Triumph der vergangenen Zeit*, a comedy in one act by Marc Antoine Le Grand. Wednesday, April 22, 1767. [St. v, 136.] *Le Tems passé* was one of three one-act plays published under the general title *Le Triomphe du tems* (1725). The German version was produced as *Der Sieg der vergangenen Zeit*—the title which it also bears on the present playbill—by Schönemann on April 6, 1747; and it remained a popular after-piece. Gottsched in his *Nöthiger Vorrath* (i, Leipzig, 1757, p. 325), under the year 1746, mentions a translation which appeared 'in einer Monathschrifft, ohne Titel und Ort, mit der Devise: Quantum est in rebus inane!' This journal was *Das Buch ohne Titel*, edited by the brothers Adolf and Elias Schlegel (E. Wolff, *Vierteljahresschrift für deutsche Literaturgeschichte*, iv (1891), p. 385). The cast on the present occasion was: Cleon, Garbrecht; Frau Roquentin, Mad. Garbrecht; Leander, Borchers; Isabelle, Mlle Ackermann; Drillot, Merschy; Dorinette, Mad. Schulz. F. L. W. Meyer (*op. cit.* i, p. 182) comments on the performance: 'Im Nachspiel, dem Siege der vergangenen Zeit, debutirte Madam Therese Schulz als Dorinette, und Garbrecht und seine Frau, die veraltet, und nur als Schutzbefohlne der Madam Hensel angenommen waren.' It was only repeated once, on the following evening.

3. *Melanide*, a comedy in five acts by Nivelle de la Chaussée. Friday, April 24, 1767. [St. viii, 3.] *Mélanide*, comédie en cinq actes et en vers (1741). The translation is in prose (viii, 27). Originally produced in Hamburg on October 4, 1742 (F. L. W. Meyer, *op. cit.*

ii, 2, p. 44), this play enjoyed a long popularity on the German stage. B. Litzmann (*F. L. Schröder*, i, Hamburg, 1890, p. 33) mentions B. H. Brockes as the author of the translation; but he does not give the source of his information. Gottsched again states (*Nöthiger Vorrath*, i, p. 324) that a translation appeared in a now undiscoverable *Sammlung einiger Schrifften zum Zeitvertreibe des Geschmacks*, St. IV, Leipzig, 1746; and C. H. Schmid adds (*Nekrolog*, Berlin, 1785, p. 247) that this collection was edited by J. Elias Schlegel and N. D. Giseke. Actually, however, the editor seems to have been J. Adolf Schlegel (J. von Antoniewicz, *J. E. Schlegels ästhetische und dramaturgische Schriften*, in *Deutsche Litteraturdenkmale des 18. und 19. Jahrhunderts*, 26, Heilbronn, 1887, p. cxxxiv). The translation played by Schönemann (and, no doubt, used now) was produced at Schwerin on August 6, 1753. It may have been new then. It is printed in Schönemann's *Schaubühne*,[1] vii (*Neue Sammlung von Schauspielen*, i, 1754; see H. Devrient, *J. F. Schönemann*, Hamburg, 1895, pp. 219, 233). Cast: Dorisee, Mad. Schmelz; Rosalie, Mad. Mecour; Theodon, Borchers; D'Orvigny, Ekhof ('trefflich' was Schröder's comment, Meyer, *op. cit.* ii, 2, p. 19); Melanide, Mad. Löwen; von Arviane, Böck. It was repeated on June 3 (XXII, 60), August 13, October 16, 1767, January 21, 1768 (in Hanover), and July 4, 1768. It was followed on the present occasion by 'ein pantomimisches Ballet, *Der Wirth auf dem Berge*, von der Erfindung des Herrn Balletmeisters Curioni', which was repeated four times.

4. *Julie, oder Wettstreit der Pflicht und Liebe*, a comedy in three acts by Franz Heufeld. Monday, April 27, 1767. [St. VIII, 101–IX, 101]. Goedeke (*Grundriss zur Geschichte der deutschen Dichtung* (3rd ed.), IV (1), p. 657), mentions two editions, one published at Vienna in 1766, and a 16mo edition without date. This 'neues deutsches Original' (VIII, 101) was new to Hamburg, but had been produced in Vienna on December 6, 1766 (J. H. F. Müller, *op. cit.* p. 35). On the author (1731–95) see Goedeke, *loc. cit.*, and also Schmid (*Chronologie, ed. cit.* pp. 159 f.) who criticises him adversely. Cast: Baron von Adelburg, Ekhof ('sehr gut', is Schröder's comment, Meyer, *op. cit.* ii, 2, p. 19);

---

[1] The first volume of Schönemann's *Schaubühne* is entitled *Sechs Schauspiele aus dem Französischen übersetzt*, Brunswick and Hamburg, 1748; volumes ii to vi, *Schauspiele, welche auf der...Schönemannischen Schaubühne aufgeführt werden*: they appeared respectively in 1748, 1749, 1749, 1751, and 1752; volumes vii and viii form the two volumes of *Neue Sammlung von Schauspielen*, i, ii, Hamburg, 1754 and 1757.

Baronessin, Mad. Garbrecht; Julie, Mad. Hensel; Clarisse, Mad. Mecour; Mylord Eduard, Borchers; Wolmar, Schmelz; Siegmund, Böck. *Julie* was not repeated until August 14; then on September 1, November 17, 1767, April 6 (in Hanover), July 26, and August 25, 1768.

Siegmund is tutor in the house of the Baron von Adelburg, and falls in love with his pupil, the Baron's daughter, Julie. He resolves, as his love is obviously hopeless, to leave the house; but at his parting from Julie he learns that she reciprocates his affection. Julie has, however, been promised to Wolmar, who has just returned from a business journey to England; he finds Julie and Siegmund together, and is suspicious; a duel is the consequence. The duel, however, is interrupted. Julie's father now learns of the affair with Siegmund, and reproaches his wife for having taken so low-born a fellow into the house. He beseeches his daughter on his knees not to disgrace the family. She yields to him; and Siegmund nobly renounces her. Then Wolmar announces that he can never love Julie, and induces the Baron, who is impressed by Siegmund's manly bearing, to make the lovers happy.

5. *Der Schatz*, a comedy in one act by Lessing. Monday, April 27, 1767. [St. IX, 102.] 'Verfertiget im Jahre 1750', this play was first published in the fifth part of Lessing's *Schrifften* (Berlin, 1755, pp. 189 ff.). The earliest representation in Hamburg seems to have taken place under Ackermann in 1757 (Meyer, *op. cit.* ii, 2, p. 53); but it is difficult to obtain reliable information concerning the theatrical history of Lessing's minor plays. Cast: Leander, Schmelz; Staleno, Garbrecht; Philto, Borchers; Anselmus, Ekhof; Lelio, Böck; Mascarill, Hensel; Raps, Merschy. Under the present management it was only played on one other occasion, on May 20, 1768.

6. *Das unvermuthete Hinderniss, oder das Hinderniss ohne Hinderniss*, a comedy in five acts by Ph. Néricault Destouches. Tuesday, April 28, 1767. [St. X, 1.] *L'Obstacle imprévu, ou l'Obstacle sans obstacle*, comédie en cinq actes en prose (1717). Although a favourite with the German public in the time of Caroline Neuber, who produced it in 1735 (Reden-Esbeck, *op. cit.* p. 108), this comedy did not appear in Schönemann's repertory until August 6, 1755 (H. Devrient, *op. cit.* p. 252). The translation, the author of which is unknown, was published in Schönemann's *Neue Sammlung von Schauspielen*, ii (Schwerin), in 1757. Cast: Lisimon, Garbrecht; Licander, Ekhof; Julie, Mad. Löwen; Gräfin de la Pepiniere, Mad. Garbrecht; Angelique, Mad. Schulz;

Leander, Böck; Valer, Borchers; Nerine, Mad. Mecour; Crispin, Merschy; Pasquin, Hensel. It was played again on November 24, 1767, and on April 15 (in Hanover), and May 25, 1768.

7. *Die neue Agnese*, a comedy in one act by J. F. Löwen. Tuesday, April 28, 1767. [St. x, 40.] This 'Nachspiel' was first printed in the *Hamburgische Unterhaltungen*, vi, 5, November, 1768, pp. 364 ff. On the playbill it is described as a 'neue Comödie', without the author's name; this was first mentioned on the occasion of the third performance on May 4: 'Eine Comödie des Herrn Löwen in einem Aufzuge. Nach einer französischen Operette [by Favart]: Isabelle und Gerdrut.' Lessing had evidently the original manuscript before him (x, 74). Cast: Gerdrut, Mad. Schulz; Agnese, Mlle Felbrich; Mangold, Ekhof; Richard, Garbrecht; Valentin, Böck. The piece was repeated on April 30, May 4 (xiii, 5), June 1, July 8 (li, 2), August 11, 1767, March 4, April 12 (in Hanover), and June 3, 1768.

8. *Semiramis*, a tragedy in five acts by Voltaire. Wednesday, April 29, 1767. [St. x, 86–xii, 44.] *Sémiramis*, Tragédie en cinq actes en vers (1748). The translation, in alexandrines, was by J. F. Löwen: '*Semiramis, ein Trauerspiel in Versen und fünf Aufzügen*, vom Herrn Sekretär Löwen, aus den Werken des Herrn von Voltaire übersetzt.'[1] It was included in Schönemann's *Neue Sammlung von Schauspielen*, ii (1757), and first played by Schönemann's company, probably early in 1755 (cp. H. Devrient, *op. cit.* p. 276). There is also a reprint (dated 1763) in the Viennese *Neue Sammlung von Schauspielen*, iii (1764), and a separate reprint, of which there is a copy in the British Museum (xvi and 80 pp.), appeared in Vienna in 1765. Löwen's preface is dated 'Rostock am 6. des Jan. 1755'. (See K. Gröschl, *Die deutschen Übersetzungen Voltaire'scher Tragödien* (*Prager deutsche Studien*, xxi), Prague, 1912, pp. 58 ff.) 'Löwens Übersetzung', said J. von Sonnenfels (*Briefe über die Wiener Schaubühne*, Vienna, 1768, p. 309; reprint in *Wiener Neudrucke*, vii, Vienna, 1884, p. 128; cp. also pp. 208 ff.), 'erreicht natürlich den Schwung des Originals nicht; aber welche Übersetzung kann den jemals erreichen? Für eine Menge schieler, und hartläufiger Verse halten uns eine Menge sehr wohlklingende

---

[1] The *Hamburgische Address-Comtoir Nachrichten* of April 27 contained the information that '...Herr Director Löwen hat die ehemals wider seinen Willen gedruckte Übersetzung, aufs neue durchgesehen, sehr stark verändert und verbessert; und nach dieser Veränderung wird die Semiramis künftig auf dem hiesigen Theater aufgeführt werden'.

und ausdrucksvolle schadlos.' In a letter to Klotz from Rostock on October 22, 1769, Löwen says: (*Briefe deutscher Gelehrten an Klotz*, herausg. von J. J. A. von Hagen, ii, Halle, 1773, p. 8, quoted in *Lessing und Hamburg*, Festgabe der Staats- und Universitätsbibliothek, Hamburg, 1929, p. 25):

> Dem Herrn von Sonnenfels verdenke ich es, dass er der lahmen Über-setzung der Semiramis Erwehnung thut. Da er doch weiss, dass ich sie in meinen Jünglingsjahren gemacht, dass sie ganz wider meinen Willen vor vielen Jahren von Schönemann, und noch dazu sehr fehlerhaft, gedruckt, dass sie nachher von mir ganz umgeschmolzen, und auch nur nach dieser Verbesserung auf dem Hamburgischen Theater gespielt ist. Allein ich habe sie nie mögen drucken lassen, weil ich immer noch nicht selbst damit zufrieden bin.

There is a note on the playbill: 'Das Mausoläum und die übrigen Verzierungen in dieser Tragödie, die, selbst nach dem Geständniss des Herrn von Voltaire, von einer ganz besondern Art ist, und wo das Schrecken und das Wunderbare auf das Höchste getrieben, sind von dem Herrn Rosenberg verfertiget' (cp. XII, 42). For this note another was substituted on the playbill at the second performance on June 11: 'Die Symphonie zu dieser Tragödie, wie auch die Musik zwischen jedem Aufzuge, ist von dem Herrn Agricola in Berlin componirt.' The cast was: Semiramis, Mad. Hensel; Arsatz, Böck; Azema, Mad. Mecour (she had played this rôle in Vienna); Assur, Borchers; Oroes, Ekhof ('meisterhaft,' said Schröder, Meyer, *op. cit.* ii, 2, p. 19); Otan, Hensel; Mitran, Schmelz; Cedar, Cludius. Repetitions took place on June 11 (XXVI, 16–XXVII), September 2, 1767, March 11, April 20, September 13, 1768, and February 2, 1769. At the first performance it was followed by 'ein pantomimisches Ballet: *Die verwandelten Zittern*, von der Erfindung des Herrn Balletmeisters Curioni', which was repeated seven times.

9. *Der verheyrathete Philosoph*—on the playbill *Der Philosoph, der sich der Heyrath schämet*—a comedy in five acts by Ph. Néricault Destouches. Thursday, April 30, 1767. [St. XII, 45.] *Le Philosophe marié, ou le Mari honteux de l'être*, comédie en cinq actes en vers (1727). The translation was in alexandrines, and was by J. C. Krüger with the help of Ekhof (see above, p. 31, and H. Devrient, *op. cit.* p. 145); it originally bore the title *Der verehelichte Philosoph* (Schönemann's *Schaubühne*, i, 1748), later that of *Der verheyrathete Philosoph, oder der Ehemann der sich schämet, es zu seyn*, and in the Viennese *Neue Sammlung von Schauspielen*, ix, 1767,

it was entitled *Der verehlichte Philosoph, oder der Mann, der sich schämet, einer zu seyn* (1765). Devrient (*op. cit.* p. 145), who gives no date for the incorporation of the play in Schönemann's repertory, quotes from a criticism in the *Hamburgische Beyträge* (1752): 'Mich deucht, wenn der verehelichte Philosoph unter die Hände eines bessern Übersetzers geraten wäre, man würde ihn lieber sehen, aber itzt sieht er über die massen verunstaltet aus.' It reappears in Ackermann's repertory from 1754 on. Madame Hensel had played her present rôle in Vienna in 1765. The cast at the first performance now was: Arist, Ekhof; Damon, Böck; Marquis von Lauret, Borchers; Lisimon, Hensel; Geront, Ackermann (XII, 59); Melite, Mad. Hensel; Celiante, Mad. Löwen; Finette, Mad. Mecour. Repetitions took place on May 8 (XIV, 80), May 18 (XVII, 92), July 8 (LI, 2), August 31, December 29, 1767, and February 17, 1768. On this last occasion, the title on the playbill was *Der verheyrathete Philosoph oder: Der Mann, der sich der Heyrath schämt*. It was followed on April 30 by Löwen's *Die neue Agnese*.

10. *Das Caffeehaus, oder die Schottländerinn*, a comedy in five acts by Voltaire. Friday, May 1, 1767. [St. XII, 63.] *L'Écossaise*, comédie en cinq actes en prose, par M. Hume, traduite en François [par Jérôme Carré] (1760). 'Imprimée', says Léris (*Dictionnaire portatif historique et littéraire des Théâtres*, 2nd ed. Paris, 1763, p. 159), 'au commencement de l'année 1760, et donnée au Thé[âtre] Fran[çais] le 27 Juillet[1] suivant, avec le plus grand concours.' The translation was by J. J. C. Bode: *Das Caffeehaus, ein rührendes Lustspiel*. Aus dem Französischen übersetzt von B..., Hamburg, 1760. (A copy is in the Hamburg Staats- und Universitätsbibliothek.) It was also published as *Das Caffee-Haus, oder die Schottländerinn*, Ein Lustspiel, Berlin, Stettin and Leipzig, 1760 (a copy is in the Preussische Staatsbibliothek); and under the same title, with the addition 'aufgeführet in dem K. K. privilegirten Stadttheater', Vienna, 1761 (a copy of this is in the Hamburg Staats- und Universitätsbibliothek). This same translation appears also in the Viennese *Neue Sammlung von Schauspielen*, i, 1764. It was produced in Hamburg in 1760 (Meyer, *op. cit.* ii, 2, p. 54). In the Preface to Bode's translation (Hamburg, 1760) mention is made of a previous translation by a Madame Z..., already printed; the present one, it

---

[1] The date of representation is given as July 26, 1760, by J. M. Quérard, *Bibliographie Voltairienne*, Paris, 1842, p. 42, and by G. Bengesco, *Voltaire. Bibliographie de ses œuvres*, Paris, 1882–90, i, p. 55.

is stated, was offered to Koch's company and accepted. Cast: Lindane, Mad. Hensel; Polly, Mlle Ackermann; Lady Alton, Mad. Schulz; Fabriz, Borchers; Monrose, Ekhof; Lord Murray, Böck; Frelon, Hensel; Friport, Ackermann (not mentioned on the playbill, but see Meyer, *op. cit.* i, p. 183; Ackermann had formerly played Murray). It was not repeated until April 8, 1768 in Hanover; then on September 23, 1768, and on January 25, 1769. It was followed now by the second performance of *Die verwandelten Zittern*.

The scene of the play is an inn in London. Lord Monrose, a Scottish nobleman, who as a result of the intrigues of a family called Murray has long been exiled and condemned to death, comes to seek the help of his friend Lord Fallbridge. At the same inn is living the scurrilous journalist Frelon, who hopes to make capital out of the misfortunes of Monrose, and of a poor young lady, Lindane, who is also resident at the inn. We learn that Lindane is the daughter of Monrose, and is in love with Lord Murray, a son of the house which has ruined her family. This Lord Murray, however, has had as mistress a Lady Alton, who is now resolved, with the help of Frelon, to avenge herself on him and on Lindane. Friport, the good genius of the play, saves Lindane from imprisonment on a charge of treason; Monrose recognises his daughter, and Lord Murray makes amends to him for all the wrongs he has suffered.

11. On the ninth evening, Monday, May 4, Madame de Grafigny's *Cenie* was to have been played, but, owing to an epidemic of influenza, the programme had to be altered (XIII, 1), *Cenie* not being given until the 22nd (xx, 1). *Die neue Agnese* was repeated and followed by '*Die Gouvernante, eine comische Operette in einem Aufzuge. Nebst einem Ballet. In dieser Operette wird Madame Curioni eine Rolle spielen.*' This, according to C. H. Schmid (*Chronologie, ed. cit.* p. 140), was an operetta by Franz Anton Nuth, who had been harlequin with Prehauser in Vienna in the later 'thirties. Nuth was still living in 1782 (*Gallerie von Teutschen Schauspielern*, ed. R. M. Werner, *Schriften der Gesellschaft für Theatergeschichte*, xiii, Berlin, 1910, pp. 107, 342). *Die Gouvernante* is mentioned by Schmid (*l.c.*) as having been performed in Leipzig at Easter, 1763, by a Dresden company formed by an Italian, Moretti; in the following year it appears in Ackermann's repertory (Meyer, *op. cit.* ii, 2, p. 54). Both Dorothea and Charlotte Ackermann are mentioned (*ibid.* ii, 2, pp. 123, 133) as playing at different times 'ein Kind'; and in 1765 Dorothea played 'Fiametta' (p. 124). Kurz seems to have made the operetta a diverting farce, he himself playing the 'governess'; in his hands it became *Bernardon*

die Guvernante, or *Die versoffene Guvernante*, and was produced by him as a 'neues Singspiel'. The piece as played by Bernardon is described by Raab (*op. cit.* pp. 130, 166 ff.). The earliest performance mentioned by Raab was at Pressburg on July 12, 1764. The cast now was not stated on the playbill, and the operetta was not repeated. It was printed as *Die Gouvernante*, eine ganz neue Opera comique mit einem pantomimischen Ballet. Aufgeführet unter der Direction des Hrn. J. J. Br., Brünn, 1763. It is mentioned in Goethe's *Wilhelm Meisters theatralische Sendung* (*Werke*, Weimar ed. li (1911), p. 211).

12. *Der poetische Dorfjunker* (or, as on the playbill for this performance, *Der Poet vom Lande*, and on subsequent playbills, *Der poetische Landjunker*), a comedy in five acts by Ph. Néricault Destouches. Tuesday, May 5, 1767. [St. XIII, 6.] *La fausse Agnès, ou le Poète campagnard*, comédie en trois actes en prose (printed 1736, first played 1759). The translation was by Gottsched's wife, and was published in the *Deutsche Schaubühne*, iii (1741), pp. 443 ff. Schönemann had intended to perform it in Hamburg in 1741, but Sophie Schröder was not satisfied with her rôle, and the first performance by his company was deferred until May 6, 1743, when it was given in Berlin; from that date on it occupied a prominent place in his repertory (H. Devrient, *op. cit.* p. 74). Meanwhile Sophie Schröder introduced the play to Hamburg on September 14, 1742, playing it eight times in this and the following year. Henriette was one of her best rôles (B. Litzmann, *F. L. Schröder*, i, p. 33). Cast: Baron von Altholz, Garbrecht; Baronessin, Mad. Schmelz; Henriette, Mad. Hensel; Charlotte, Mlle Ackermann; Treuendorf, Böck; Masuren, Ekhof (see above, p. 31); Michel, Hensel; Jagdhausen, Schulz; Frau von Jagdhausen, Mad. Curioni; Amtshauptmann, Borchers; Amtshauptmannin, Mad. Merschy. Repetitions took place on August 28, October 20, 1767, March 4 (in Hanover), September 6, 1768, and (in Hanover) January 24, 1769.

13. *Die stumme Schönheit*, a comedy in one act by J. Elias Schlegel (in alexandrines). Tuesday, May 5, 1767. [St. XIII, 46.] Published in 1747 and 1752, and in Schlegel's *Werke, ed. cit.* ii (1762), pp. 469 ff.; also in the Viennese *Neue Sammlung von Schauspielen*, ii (1762) and in *Theater der Deutschen*, iv (1767), pp. 197 ff. The first performance was by Schönemann, on July 14, 1752 (H. Devrient, *op. cit.* p. 198). Cast: Richard, Borchers; Jungwitz, Ekhof; Jacob, Hensel; Laconius, Garbrecht; Frau Praatgern, Mad. Löwen; Charlotte, Mlle Felbrich; Leonore, Mad. Hensel; Cathrine, Mad. Schulz. Repetitions took

place on August 14 and October 29, 1767, and then not until January 2, January 5, and February 13, 1769, in Hanover.

Richard, a gentleman of means, who has entrusted the upbringing of his daughter Charlotte to Frau Praatgern, introduces a suitor to her, Jungwitz. Instead of the charming girl they expect, they find a stupid and affected young person who can only answer yes or no. Jungwitz much prefers Frau Praatgern's daughter Leonore. It turns out ultimately that Leonore is really Richard's daughter. A husband is, however, also found for Charlotte, in the person of the philosopher Laconius, who decides to marry her because she cannot converse.

14. *Miss Sara Sampson*, a tragedy in five acts by G. E. Lessing. Wednesday, May 6, 1767. [St. XIII, 121–XIV, 63.] First produced by Ackermann's company at Frankfurt a/d. Oder on July 10, 1755 (B. Litzmann, *F. L. Schröder, ed. cit.* i, p. 91); and in Hamburg by Schönemann on October 6, 1756, with great success (J. F. Schütze, *op. cit.* p. 293). Published in Lessing's *Schrifften*, vi (1755), pp. 1 ff. Cast: Sir Sampson, no name on the playbill, but Ackermann, who took over the rôle in 1764 (Meyer, *op. cit.* ii, 2, p. 115); Miss Sara, Mad. Hensel;[1] Mellefont, Ekhof; Marwood, Mad. Schulz; Arabella, Mlle Ackermann; Waitwell, Borchers; Norton, Hensel; Betty, Mlle Felbrich; Hannah, Mad. Merschy. On Ekhof's Mellefont Meyer reports the comment (*op. cit.* i, p. 131): 'stellenweise vortrefflich, im Ganzen eine seiner schwächsten Rollen, weil ihn der Körper zu sehr im Stich liess'. The play was repeated on July 20, 1767 (LXXIII, 15), February 22 (in Hanover), September 12, 1768, and February 23, 1769 (in Hanover). On the present occasion it was followed by *Die Heu-Erndte*, 'ein pantomimisches Ballet von der Erfindung des Herrn Balletmeisters Curioni', which was repeated twice at the beginning of 1768.

15. *Der Spieler*, a comedy in five acts by J. F. Regnard. Thursday, May 7, 1767. [St. XIV, 64.] *Le Joueur*, comédie en cinq actes en vers (1696). This had been an extraordinarily popular play since the time of Caroline Neuber, for whom Lessing and Weisse translated it in 1748 (Weisse, *Selbstbiographie*, Leipzig, 1806, p. 13; J. Minor, *C. F. Weisse und seine Beziehungen zur deutschen Literatur des 18. Jahrhunderts*, Innsbruck, 1880, p. 8). Schönemann produced it in Hamburg on

---

[1] Mad. Hensel had played Sara with Schuch in Berlin in 1756. Cp. letter of Nicolai to Lessing, November 3, 1756 (*Schriften*, xix, p. 45; quoted by Petersen, *ed. cit.* p. 193).

April 11, 1747; the translation, which is in prose, was printed in Schönemann's *Schaubühne*, i, 1748 (H. Devrient, *op. cit.* p. 126), the author being probably J. C. Krüger (cp. W. Wittekindt, *J. C. Krüger*, Berlin, 1898, pp. 101 ff.). It was reprinted in the Viennese *Neue Sammlung von Schauspielen*, xi, 1766. There was another translation in Part I of *Des Herrn Regnards sämtliche theatralische Werke*, 2 vols, Berlin, 1757 (cp. Lessing's notice in the *Bibliothek der schönen Wissenschaften*, *Schriften*, vii, p. 76); but no doubt Schönemann's was used now. Cast: Geront, Garbrecht; Valer, Ekhof; Angelique, Mad. Löwen; Die Gräfin, Mad. Schmelz; Der Marquis, Böck; Dorant, Borchers; Nerine, Mad. Schulz; Hector, Hensel. Of Ekhof Schröder said: 'Valer, der jung seyn soll, nicht gut' (Meyer, *op. cit.* ii, 2, p. 14). It was repeated on September 24, November 27, 1767, and on March 1 (in Hanover), and August 10, 1768. On the present occasion it was followed by the ballet, *Der Wirth auf dem Berge*.

16. *Der Liebhaber, als ein Schriftsteller und Bedienter*, a comedy in one act by Cérou. Friday, May 8, 1767. [St. xiv, 81.] *L'Amant auteur et valet*, jolie Com[édie] en un Acte en prose, par M. Cérou, lors étudiant en Droit, jouée aux Italiens le 8 Fév[rier] 1740, avec succès (Léris, *op. cit.* p. 21). The popularity of the play is vouched for by the large number of editions—in the Bibliothèque nationale there are nine between 1740 and 1801. There seems to have been some uncertainty about the author's name. The *Mercure de France* (1740, p. 765), which noticed the play at some length on its production (February, 1740, pp. 330 ff.), states that the author was not Cérou, but ' M. Seron, étudiant en droit'. The German translation and the playbills of May 8, September 1, 1767 and January 21, 1768, call him 'Ceron'; but the playbill of September 19, 1768, has ' Cerou'. The play was produced on July 11, 1752, as *Der Liebhaber, ein Schriftsteller und ein Lackey*, in a version by Bierling, the translator of Molière (H. Devrient, *op. cit.* p. 198), and published anonymously in 1755—there is a copy of this version in the British Museum—and it was also included in Schönemann's *Schaubühne*, viii (*Neue Sammlung von Schauspielen*, ii, 1757). (Cp. also *Lessing und Hamburg, ed. cit.* p. 23.) There was another version by C. L. Martini, who was a member of Schönemann's company from 1750 to 1754; and this translation—*Der Liebhaber, als ein Schriftsteller und Bedienter*, Frankfurt and Leipzig, 1750 (also Altona and Leipzig, 1755), seems to have been subsequently substituted by the company for Bierling's. The title on the playbill suggests that it was

used now.[1] (A copy of the 1755 edition is in the Hamburg Staats- und Universitätsbibliothek.) Cast: Erast, Böck; Mangold, Garbrecht; Lucinde, Mad. Hensel; Frontin, Hensel; Lisette, Mad. Mecour. The play was repeated three times, on September 1, 1767, January 21 (in Hanover), and September 19, 1768.

17. *Die coquette Mutter, oder: Die veruneinigten Verliebten*, a comedy in five acts by Philippe Quinault. Monday, May 11, 1767. [St. xiv, 86.] *Les Amans brouillés, ou la Mère coquette*, comédie en cinq actes en vers (1665). This very old play was obviously no novelty; but I have been unable to find a German translation later than *Die bulhafftige Mutter*, included in the *Schau-Bühne englischer und frantzösischer Comödianten*, Frankfurt, 1670, i, pp. 431 ff.[2] Perhaps, as I have suggested, Susanna Mecour, who played the prominent rôle of Laurette, was responsible for its revival. Cast: Ismene, Mad. Löwen; Isabelle, Mlle Ackermann; Laurette, Mad. Mecour; Acant, Böck; Cremant, Garbrecht; Der Baron, Borchers; Christian, Hensel. This was the only performance.

18. *Der Advocat Patelin*, a comedy in three acts by D. A. de Brueys. Monday, May 11, 1767. [St. xiv, 87.] *L'Avocat Patelin*, comédie en trois actes en prose (1706). According to Litzmann (*F. L. Schröder*, i, p. 32) this comedy had been performed by Sophie Schröder's company on four evenings in 1742 under the title *Der betrogene Lackenhändler*. In Schönemann's repertory it first appears as a 'Nachspiel' on December 1, 1755. Petersen states (*ed. cit.* p. 195) that it was translated by 'J.C.S.', Danzig, 1762. Heinsius, *Allgemeines Bücherlexicon*, i, Leipzig, 1793, p. 297, mentions besides this translation one published at Lübeck in the same year. Cast: Patelin, Ekhof; Frau Patelin, Mad. Merschy; Henriette, Mlle Ackermann; Colette, Mad. Schulz; Wilhelm, Hensel; Valer, Borchers; Agnelet, Merschy. Meyer (*op. cit.* i,

---

[1] The *Hamburgische Address-Comtoir Nachrichten*, however, announced the play on May 8 as *Der Liebhaber ein Schriftsteller und Lakey*, while the announcement of the performance on September 1, 1767, printed the title as *Der Liebhaber als ein Schriftsteller und Bedienter* (by Ceron). On Monday, September 19, 1768, the earlier title appears in the announcement, and the author's name is given as Cerou; the playbill of September 19 has *Der Liebhaber als ein Schriftsteller und Lakey*, by Cerou.

[2] In Reichard's *Theater-Kalender, oder Taschenbuch für die Schaubühne auf das Jahr 1775*, Gotha, p. 143, a translation published in 1771 is mentioned: '*Die verbuhlte Mutter oder die veruneinigten Liebhaber*...Wezlar, 1771. Von Quinault 1665 übers. von H. Pfeufer, aber nicht nach der Verbess[erung] die H. Colle darinn für die französische Bühne gemacht hat.'

p. 139) says: 'Den Patelin gab Eckhof mit allen Zoten, die seine Gebehrden verstärkten, Hensel den Tuchhändler neben ihm gut und wahr.' Schröder's criticism of Ekhof was (*ibid.* ii, 2, pp. 16 f.): 'Hier wetteiferte er mit dem zotenvollesten Hanswurst (Lessing ward nicht dadurch beleidigt).' (Cp. xiv, 107.) Repetitions took place on June 2 (xxii, 2), July 4 (xxxvi, 58), August 21, November 2, 1767, January 22 (in Hanover), June 10,[1] 1768, and on February 7, 1769 (in Hanover).

19. *Der Freygeist*—on the playbill *Der beschämte Freygeist*—a comedy in five acts by G. E. Lessing. Tuesday, May 12, 1767. [St. xiv, 109.] 'Verfertiget im Jahre 1749,' this play was first printed in Lessing's *Schrifften*, v (Berlin, 1755), pp. 1 ff.; a second edition appeared in his *Lustspiele*, ii (Berlin, 1767), pp. 1 ff. It had doubtless been played in Leipzig under Koch, and was given in Hamburg under Ackermann in 1757. 'Stl.' in the *Deutsche Bibliothek* (iii, 1769, p. 57) implies that the title *Der beschämte Freygeist*, to distinguish it from Brawe's tragedy of the same name[2] (xiv, 112), was given to Lessing's play in Hamburg. Cast: Adrast, Ekhof; Theophan, Böck; Lisidor, not named on the playbill, but no doubt Ackermann; Juliane, Mad. Hensel; Henriette, Mad. Schulz; Frau Philane, Mad. Merschy; Araspe, Borchers; Johann, Merschy; Martin, Hensel; Lisette, Mlle Ackermann. Schröder's comment (Meyer, *op. cit.* ii, 2, p. 16) was: 'Adrast, sehr gut, nur fehlte der Körper des Liebhabers,' and he said that Theophan was Böck's best rôle (*ibid.* i, p. 147). The play was repeated on October 27, 1767, February 23, June 27, August 16, and October 20, 1768.

20. *Der Schatz*, a pastoral comedy in one act by G. K. Pfeffel. Tuesday, May 12, 1767. [St. xiv, 126.] This play is in alexandrines; it was published in Frankfurt in 1761. (A copy is in the Hamburg Staats- und Universitätsbibliothek. Cp. also E. Schmidt's account of it in his review of Cosack's *Materialien* in *Anzeiger für deutsches Altertum*, v (1879), pp. 138 ff.) It had been produced in Hamburg by Ackermann in 1765. Cast: Chrysant, Ekhof; Hylas, Böck; Palämon, Borchers; Margaris, Mlle Ackermann; Myrtha, Mad. Schulz. There were five repetitions; on September 8, 1767, February 5 and April 14 (in Hanover), September 26, 1768, and (in Hanover) January 25, 1769.

21. *Zayre*, a tragedy in five acts by Voltaire. Wednesday, May 13, 1767. [St. xv, xvi.] *Zayre*, tragédie en cinq actes, 'donnée au Thé[âtre] Fran[çais] le 13 Août 1732' (Léris, *op. cit.* p. 457); it was

---

[1] See above, p. 44, note 1.   [2] See below, p. 139.

published in 1733. The translation (in alexandrines) was that of J. J. Schwabe, published in Gottsched's *Deutsche Schaubühne*, ii (1741), pp. 359 ff.; also in *Deutsche Schauspiele, welche in Wien auf dem k. k. Hoftheater aufgeführet worden*, x, Vienna, 1750 (see K. Gröschl, *op. cit.* pp. 37 ff.). It had always been popular in Germany, from Frau Neuber's time onwards (1741), and it had an established place in Schönemann's repertory. Cast: Orosmann, Ekhof (who in 1766 had played Lusignan); Lusignan, Borchers; Zayre, Mad. Hensel; Fatime, Mad. Curioni; Nerestan, Böck; Chatillon, Hensel; Corasmin, Cludius. Repetitions took place on September 7, 1767, January 27 (in Hanover), and November 3, 1768. It was followed on the present occasion by 'ein serieuses Ballet von der Erfindung des Herrn Balletmeisters Curioni', which was repeated under this title five times.

Orosmann, the Sultan of Jerusalem, loves his slave Zayre, who, although born of Christian parents, has been brought up in the Mohammedan faith. She loves him in return, and Orosmann makes preparations for their marriage. The former king of Jerusalem, Lusignan, with other Christian prisoners, is in the hands of Orosmann; and the young French knight Nerestan has been permitted to return to France to obtain a ransom for them. The ransom he brings is not sufficient, and Nerestan offers to remain himself a prisoner that the others may go free. This sacrifice Orosmann will not accept; he magnanimously refuses the ransom and sets them all free except Lusignan and Zayre. The latter, however, induces Orosmann in his love for her to liberate the aged Lusignan, who discovers before he dies that she is his daughter, and Nerestan his son. Horror-struck at the discovery that Zayre has been brought up as a Mohammedan, he exacts an oath from her that she will become a Christian, and adjures her to keep the secret of her parentage. Zayre is now involved in a conflict between her love for Orosmann and her promise to her father. Her sudden reluctance to enter on the marriage rouses the sultan's suspicions, and a letter from Nerestan, asking her to meet him secretly, awakens his jealousy. He waylays her as she is on her way to the meeting-place and stabs her; Nerestan then reveals himself as her brother. In his despair Orosmann kills himself, giving orders that all the Christians are to be set free.

22. *Sidnei, oder: der Schwermüthige*, a comedy in three acts, by J. B. L. Gresset. Thursday, May 14, 1767. [St. xvii, 1.] *Sidnei*, comédie en vers et en trois actes (1745). This was a popular play in Schönemann's repertory from 1750 on (H. Devrient, *op. cit.* p. 168). It was published in Schönemann's *Schaubühne*, v, 1751. The translator is unknown. Cast: Sidnei, Ekhof ('trefflich', said Schröder, Meyer, *op. cit.* ii, 2, p. 16); Rosalie, Mad. Löwen; Hamilton, Böck; Dümont, Hensel;

Kätchen, Mlle Felbrich. Repetitions took place on July 31, October 29, 1767, February 4 (in Hanover), June 10,[1] and October 14, 1768.

Sidnei, a rich young Englishman, has fallen a prey to melancholy and remorse, and has retired to the country, accompanied by his faithful servant Dümont. His friend Hamilton does all he can to cure him, but to no purpose; Sidnei is resolved to commit suicide. Hamilton arranges a meeting with Sidnei's old love Rosalie, who has been living in seclusion since Sidnei abandoned her four years previously. But when she arrives, it is apparently too late: Sidnei has taken poison. Dümont, however, has saved his master by substituting another glass for that containing the poison, and a tragedy is avoided; Sidnei and Rosalie are re-united.

23. *Ist er von Familie?* a comedy in one act by T. L'Affichard. Thursday, May 14, 1767. [St. xvii, 46.] *La Famille*, comédie en un acte et en prose (1736). A German translation, *Die Familie*, had been in Schönemann's repertory since its publication; it is included in Schönemann's *Schaubühne*, iv, 1749 (H. Devrient, *op. cit.* pp. 157 f.). But to judge by the present playbill, where it is described as 'eine neue Comödie', and by the differing title, the version now presented may have been a new one. Cast: Der Graf, Borchers; Dorant, Ekhof; Die Gräfin, Mad. Löwen; Melite, Mlle Ackermann; Licast, Böck; Röschen, Mad. Mecour; Hännschen, Merschy. Repetitions took place on May 20, July 23 (lxxxiii, 92), September 24, 1767, and March 8, 1768 (in Hanover).

24. *Das Gespenst mit der Trommel, oder: Der wahrsagende Ehemann*, 'eine Comödie aus dem Französischen des Destouches in fünf Aufzügen, nach einem englischen Stücke des Addison'. Friday, May 15, 1767. [St. xvii, 72.] *Le Tambour nocturne, ou le Mari devin*, comédie en cinq actes et en prose (1736, but not played until 1762). The translation was by Frau Gottsched and was published in the *Deutsche Schaubühne*, ii (1741), pp. 231 ff. (*Das Gespenste mit der Trummel, oder der wahrsagende Ehemann*. Ein Lustspiel des Herrn Addisons, nach dem Französischen des Herrn Destouches übersetzt); also in the Viennese *Neue Sammlung von Schauspielen*, v, 1765. The play appeared in Schönemann's repertory from 1741 onwards (H. Devrient, *op. cit.* p. 360). Cast: Der Baron, Ekhof (he had formerly played the youthful Windhausen, 'abscheulich', said Schröder, 'hernach den Baron, gut', Meyer, *op. cit.* ii, 2, p. 14); Die Baronessin, Mad. Hensel; Windhausen, Borchers; Liebhold, Böck; Salome, Mad. Schmelz; Schulwitz, not named, but Ackermann (Meyer, *op. cit.* i, p. 183, ii, 2, p. 113);

---

[1] See above, p. 44, note 1.

Gotthard, Hensel; Peter, Garbrecht; Michel, Merschy. The present performance was the only one; it was followed by the 'serieuses Ballet' of May 13.

The performance of *Der verheyrathete Philosoph* by Destouches on Monday, May 18, 1767, was followed by 'ein neues pantomimisches Ballet von der Erfindung des Herrn Balletmeisters Curioni, *Die Zigeuner in ihrem Lager*'. The scene is described on the playbill: 'Das Theater stellet einen Wald vor, woselbst aus einem Baum, der in der Geschwindigkeit sich öfnet, eine Bande Zigeuner kommen; und Bauern, welche Holz fällen, bezaubern.'

25. *Democrit, oder: Der lachende Philosoph*, a comedy in five acts by Regnard. Tuesday, May 19, 1767. [St. xvii, 94.] *Démocrite amoureux*, comédie en cinq actes en vers (1700). Like Regnard's other two popular plays, this was an old favourite in Germany; it was played in Leipzig in 1742 (Schmid, *Chronologie, ed. cit.* p. 66) and by Sophie Schröder on April 27, 1744, in Hamburg (where it was repeated three times). A translation of *Democrit* had appeared in Part ii of Regnard's *Theatralische Werke*, Berlin, 1757. The translation used by Schöne-mann, and now, was in alexandrines and was by the actor H. G. Koch. It was published in Schönemann's *Schaubühne*, iv, 1749, and reprinted in the Viennese *Neue Sammlung von Schauspielen*, i, 1764. Cast: Democrit, Hensel; Agelas, Böck; Agenor, Merschy; Ismene, Mlle Felbrich; Strabo, Ekhof; Cleanthis, Mad. Hensel; Criseis, Mad. Mecour; Thaler, Borchers. Schröder noted (Meyer, *op. cit.* ii, 2, pp. 15 f.) that Ekhof played Strabo as a 'Caricatur, und auch Lessing zu arg' (but see below, p. 194). *Democrit* was repeated on January 28 (in Hanover), August 15, October 25, 1768, and (in Hanover) on January 10, 1769. It was followed on the present occasion by the ballet *Die verwandelten Zittern*.

Democrit has retired with his servant Strabo to the solitude of a cave in the desert. Their only friend is a peasant, Thaler, with whose daughter Criseis Democrit, against all his principles, is in love. Agelas, king of Athens, comes upon them in the course of a hunting expedition and persuades them all to come to his court. Here we learn that the Princess Ismene is intended to be Agelas' wife and that to remove all obstacles a stepsister has been given as a child to be brought up as a peasant. Agelas, however, is charmed by Criseis, and Prince Agenor, being in love with Ismene, encourages the king's new passion. Criseis, of course, turns out to be the lost stepsister and marries Agelas; Ismene and Agenor are be-trothed. Meanwhile Strabo has fallen in love with Ismene's waiting-woman Cleanthis, who is eventually discovered to be his own long forsaken wife.

26. *Die falschen Vertraulichkeiten,* a comedy in three acts by Marivaux. Wednesday, May 20, 1767. [St. xviii, 1.] *Les fausses confidences,* comédie en trois actes en prose (1737). This piece probably belonged to an earlier period, but I have not been able to trace any mention of it in repertory lists before it was produced in Hamburg in 1761 (Meyer, *op. cit.* ii, 2, p. 54). Nor have I been able to find the German translation. Later a new version was made by Gotter under the title *Die falschen Entdeckungen* (cp. V. Golubew, *Marivaux Lustspiele in deutschen Übersetzungen des 18. Jahrhunderts,* Heidelberg, 1904, pp. 89 ff.). There is a copy (*Die falschen Entdeckungen.* Ein Lustspiel in drey Aufzügen. Nach Marivaux. Für das Hoftheater zu Weimar. Gotha, 1774) in the Herzogliche Bibliothek, Gotha. A comedy bearing the title *Das falsche Vertrauen,* published at Augsburg in 1764, I have not seen (Kayser, *Vollständiges Bücher-Lexikon,* vi, Schauspiele, p. 105). Cast: Araminte, Mad. Hensel; Remy, unnamed. but played by Ackermann—it was a rôle in which, according to Schröder (Meyer, *op. cit.* i, p. 145 and ii, 2, p. 114), he won, from 1761 onwards, 'ungetheilte[n] Beyfall'; Dorant, Böck; Argante, Mad. Schmelz; Dorimont, Borchers; Peter, Merschy; Pasquin ('ein anderer Bedienter', xviii, 67), Hensel; Marton, Mad. Curioni. Repetitions took place in Hanover on March 10 and May 3, 1768, and again in Hamburg on July 21, 1768. It was followed on the present occasion by *Ist er von Familie?,* a fact which Lessing omits to mention.

27. *Zelmire,* a tragedy in five acts by P. L. Buyrette de Belloy. Thursday, May 21, 1767. [St. xviii, 72–xix.] *Zelmire,* tragédie en cinq actes et en vers (1762). Lessing, following the playbill, wrongly calls the author 'Du Belloy'. The drama was played 'nach einer hier in Hamburg verfertigten Übersetzung' (Playbill); and Lessing notes that the version was in prose (xix, 76). The article in *Lessing und Hamburg* (*ed. cit.* p. 31) on translators of French plays mentioned in the *Dramaturgie* suggests that the author was Lessing's friend Johann Friedrich Schmidt, on the ground that an unprinted translation by him of *Zelmire* is mentioned by Reichard in his *Theaterkalender auf das Jahr 1778* (p. 118); but the translation used now seems to have been printed. Löwen might occur to one, but Löwen would probably have translated into verse. Schmid's *Chronologie* (*ed. cit.* p. 162) mentions another translation, in verse, printed in Pfeffel's *Theatralische Belustigungen,* ii (1766) and separately (Frankfurt and Leipzig, 1766). (Cp. also Kayser, *Vollständiges Bücher-Lexicon,* vi (Leipzig, 1836), *Schauspiele,* p. 10.) The present version had been first produced in Hamburg as

an inauguration of Ackermann's season on July 31, 1765 (Schütze, *op. cit.* pp. 325 f.). Cast: Polidor, Ekhof (at the first performance he had played the youthful Ilus, Meyer, *op. cit.* ii, 2, p. 17); Zelmire, Mad. Hensel; Ilus, Böck; Antenor, Borchers; Rhamnes, Schmelz; Philaide, Mad. Schmelz. The play was repeated on May 26 (xx, 146), September 14, 1767, and on June 30, 1768. It was followed now by a 'serieuses Ballet'.

Zelmire, the daughter of Polidore, late King of Lesbos, is supposed to have aided her brother Azor to compass the death of their father; Azor himself has since died at the hand of an unknown assassin. Zelmire reveals to Philaide that she has saved Polidore and that he is concealed in a vault near by. Meanwhile Antenor, a prince of the blood, has assumed command of the Thracian army, but has declined the throne in favour of Zelmire's infant son, of whom he thus becomes the guardian; he entrusts Rhamnes with the command of the army, and discloses to him his plan of eventually destroying the young prince and thus securing undisputed sovereignty. A Thracian soldier has just revealed to Zelmire and Polidore that Antenor, while pretending to avenge the death of Azor, was himself the author of it, when Antenor appears; he informs Zelmire that the people have denounced her for the crime of parricide and have decreed that she is to be banished, and is to leave her son under his guardianship. At this moment Zelmire's husband Ilus arrives after a long absence. Antenor repeats the accusation of parricide, which Zelmire does not dare to deny, lest Polidore's presence should be revealed to Antenor. The latter subsequently finds Ilus alone and raises his dagger to murder him, but is prevented by the timely arrival of Zelmire; the dagger remains in her hands, but this enables Antenor to accuse her of intended crime, and to have her arrested by his soldiers. Ilus remains alone, horrified and uncertain; but is enlightened by Polidore, who emerges from the vault. Ilus decides to call his Trojan followers to fight the Thracian soldiers, and Polidore is determined to fight also, disguised as a Trojan. The battle goes against Ilus and his men; Zelmire, her father and husband are all taken prisoner, and Antenor condemns Zelmire and Polidore to death. But at the altar Rhamnes, turning on Antenor, strikes him down in place of Polidore. Azor's last written words, accusing Antenor of his death, have come into the hands of Rhamnes, who thus avenges Azor and saves Zelmire and her whole family.

The following 'Nachricht aus Frankreich', taken from the *Bibliothek der schönen Wissenschaften*, ix, (i), 1763, pp. 135 f., was printed, with slight alterations, on the playbill:

Wir erinnern uns kaum seit etlichen Jahren eines Stücks, das mit mehr Beyfall aufgenommen worden: es giebt wenig dramatische Werke unter uns, wo mehr Feuer in der Handlung so wohl als in dem Styl hervorleuchtet. Durch und durch herrschen die grössten tragischen Bewegungen: und das Interesse steiget bis zum höchsten Gipfel. Die Seele der Handlung beruhet auf der Zärtlichkeit einer Tochter, die ihren Vater nicht nur mit ihrer eignen Brust ernähret, sondern ihm auch ihre Ehre auf die schimpflichste und schmerzhafteste Art aufopfert, indem sie sich für die Mörderinn desselben halten lässt, um ihn zu retten. Die Situationen sind so heftig, dass sie das ganze Herz erschüttern; die Charaktere contrastiren so wohl, dass einer den andern hebt. Man hat uns bisher nur Tyrannen vorgestellet, die ihre Verbrechen ungescheut und ungeschickt begehen. Hier ist aber einer, der seine Ränke auf das geschickteste und listigste ausführet, und seine Schändlichkeit entdecket sich erst in dem letzten Augenblick.

28. *Cenie, oder: Die Grossmuth im Unglücke*, a drama in five acts and in prose by Madame Françoise de Grafigny. Friday, May 22, 1767. [St. xx, 2.] *Cénie*, pièce en cinq actes et en prose (1750). The translation was by Gottsched's wife, and was published as *Cenie, oder die Grossmuth im Unglücke*, ein moralisches Stück, Vienna, 1753; but possibly also in the previous year at Leipzig (cp. Gottsched, *Nöthiger Vorrath*, ii, Leipzig, 1765, p. 280); also in *Deutsche Schaubühne zu Wienn*, iv (1753). It had had a place in Schönemann's repertory since 1753 (H. Devrient, *op. cit.* pp. 218, 224), and was included in volume vii of his *Schaubühne* (*Neue Sammlung von Schauspielen*, i, 1754). Cast: Dorimond, Ekhof (originally he played Mericourt, 'nicht so gut als Kirchhof, später Dorimond, vortrefflich', Schröder said, Meyer, *op. cit.* ii, 2, p. 14); Mericourt, Schmelz; Clerval, Böck; Cenie, Mad. Hensel; Orphise, Mad. Löwen; Lisette, Mad. Mecour; Dorsainville, Borchers. *Cenie* was repeated on July 10 (LIII, 2), August 5, November 30, 1767, and on January 25 and February 24, 1768 in Hanover. It was followed on the present occasion by the ballet *Die Zigeuner in ihrem Lager*.

The drama turns round the intrigues of the dissolute Mericourt to win the hand and fortune of his uncle Dorimond's daughter Cenie. The latter, who loves Mericourt's brother Clerval, refuses to accept Mericourt. She has a staunch friend in her governess Orphise, who mourns a lost husband, Dorsainville. Mericourt proves by means of letters that Cenie is not Dorimond's daughter, but Orphise's. Clerval comes to the rescue of the women; he has aided Dorsainville to gain pardon for having engaged in an affair of honour, and brings him to the house, thus restoring to Orphise her lost husband and Cenie's real father.

29. *Amalia*, a comedy in five acts (1765) by C. F. Weisse. Monday, May 25, 1767. [St. xx, 88.] Published in *Beytrag zum deutschen Theater*, iv, Leipzig, 1766, pp. 113 ff.; reprinted in *Theater der Deutschen*, viii (1769), pp. 103 ff., and again separately at Vienna in 1783. It was first produced in Hamburg under Ackermann in 1766. Cast: Freemann,

Ekhof; Lady Freemann, Mad. Hensel; Manley, Mad. Böck (see above, p. 38); Hearty, Borchers; Triks, Hensel; Frau Triks, Mad. Schulz; Betty, Mlle Ackermann. Schröder commented on Ekhof's playing (Meyer, *op. cit.* ii, 2, pp. 18 f.): 'zu grob'; and Meyer adds (*ibid.*): 'Diesen wiederholten Vorwurf verschuldete Eckhofs Ansicht. Er glaubte den Engländer so bezeichnen zu müssen, und gab, ganz im Gegensatz von Ackermann und Schröder, auch im Leben, der Freimüthigkeit immer einen Anstrich von Härte.' Repetitions took place on August 4, September 8, December 1, and (in Hanover) December 31, 1767; then in Hanover on December 28, 1768.

Freemann, a wealthy young man, has abandoned Amalia some five years before the drama opens, and is living an extravagant life with Sophie in an inn at Bristol. They are ultimately reduced to penury, while Amalia has inherited great wealth. She hears of Freemann's plight, and disguised as a man (Manley), goes to Bristol to help him. Sophie falls in love with Manley; but loses her jewelry to him in play. Manley is resolved to test Sophie, and to help her and Freemann if she resists temptation; he therefore offers to return the jewels to her on dishonouring conditions. Sophie refuses to accept these, and her lover Freemann, who has been concealed in a cabinet during the final interview between Manley and Sophie, challenges Manley, whereupon the latter reveals herself as Amalia. Freemann is now anxious to marry Amalia, but she will have nothing to do with him and marries another.

30. *Der Finanzpachter*, a comedy in one act by Saint-Foix. Monday, May 25, 1767. [St. xx, 139.] *Le Financier*, comédie en un acte en prose (1761). The translation was *Der Finanzpachter*, ein Lustspiel in einem Aufzuge, von den französischen Comödianten zu Paris im Jahr 1761 zu verschiedenenmalen aufgeführt, und aus dem Französischen ins Deutsche übersetzt, Leipzig, 1762. (There is a copy in the British Museum.) It was produced in Hamburg by Ackermann in 1765. *Des Herrn von Saint-Foix Theatralische Werke* had appeared in Leipzig, 1750–68. Petersen (*ed. cit.* p. 203) notes that C. A. Wichmann was reputed to be the author of the translation. A version by Weisker[n], entitled *Die Wirkung der Rechtschaffenheit*, was performed in Vienna on August 13, 1766 (cp. *Repertoire des deutschen Schauspieles in Wien*, MS. in the Stadtbibliothek, Vienna, JC 40428, p. 200). Cast: Alcimon, Böck; Der Marquis, Borchers; Chevalier, Schmelz; Geront, Ekhof; Henriette, Mlle Ackermann. It was only repeated once, on August 4, 1767.

31. *Die Mütter-Schule*, a comedy in five acts by Nivelle de la Chaussée. Friday, May 29, 1767. [St. xxi, 2.] *L'École des mères*,

comédie en vers et en cinq actes (1744). The German translation, probably by Ekhof (cp. H. Uhde, *op. cit.* p. 151), is printed in Schönemann's *Schaubühne,* viii (*Neue Sammlung von Schauspielen,* ii, 1757). In the repertory lists there is some confusion with Marivaux' play of the same name (see below, pp. 228 f.);[1] but La Chaussée's appears to have been added to Schönemann's repertory on February 5, 1756 (H. Devrient, *op. cit.* p. 253). Cast: Argant, Ekhof ('sehr gut', Schröder said, Meyer, *op. cit.* ii, 2, p. 14); Frau Argant, Mad. Löwen; Der Marquis, Mad. Böck; Mariane, Mlle Ackermann; Doligni, Borchers; Valer, Böck; Rosette, Mad. Schulz; La Fleur, Hensel. Repetitions took place on July 14 (LIV, 2), August 20, 1767; on February 29 (in Hanover), June 29, 1768, and (in Hanover) on February 9, 1769. It was followed on the present occasion by 'ein neues Gärtner-Ballet von der Erfindung des Herrn Balletmeisters Curioni', which seems to have been repeated twice.

32. *Nanine, oder: Das besiegte Vorurtheil,* a comedy in three acts by Voltaire. Monday, June 1, 1767. [St. XXI, 21.] *Nanine, ou le Préjugé vaincu,* comédie en trois actes, en vers de dix syllabes (1749). Schönemann opened the renovated 'Comödienhaus beym Dragonerstall' in Hamburg on June 5, 1754 (Schütze, *op. cit.* p. 280), with this comedy, in the verse translation of B. G. Straube, Leipzig, 1750;[2] but possibly he had already produced it in the previous year. H. Devrient (*op. cit.* p. 221) mentions a version by a Herr Pistorius, which may have been the one used on the present occasion.[3] Cast: Olban, Ekhof (Schröder commented on Ekhof's Graf Olban, that he was 'nicht vornehm genug', Meyer, *op. cit.* ii, 2, p. 20); Marquisin von Olban, Mad. Schmelz; Nanine, Mlle Felbrich; Baronessin von Orme, Mad. Böck; Bläse, Böck; Hombert, Borchers; Germon, Hensel; Marin, Merschy. Repetitions took place on June 12 (XXVIII, 2),

---

[1] E.g. the *Repertoire des deutschen Schauspieles in Wien* (p. 127) records the performance on January 26, 1765, of *Die Mütterschule* aus dem Französ[ischen] des Marivaux... übersetzt von Conrad Eckhof (Die eingelegten Couplets von Hagedorn).

[2] C. H. Schmid (*Chronologie, ed. cit.* p. 97) mentions this translation in disparaging terms. There is a copy of it in the Hamburg Staats- und Universitätsbibliothek.

[3] I have not been able to trace this version. J. G. Meusel (*Lexikon der vom Jahr 1750 bis 1800 verstorbenen Teutschen Schriftsteller,* x (Leipzig, 1810), pp. 438 ff.) gives an account of Hermann Andreas Pistorius (1730–98) who was active in translating for Hamburg periodicals in 1753 and 1754 and contributed to the *Allgemeine Deutsche Bibliothek,* but there is no mention of a translation of *Nanine* by him. In the *Repertoire des deutschen Schauspieles in Wien* (p. 129) a performance of *Nanine* in a translation by [J. W.] Mayberg in 1754 is listed, also one 'in einer andern Übersetzung' on April 17, 1769.

July 4 (xxxvi, 58), July 28, 1767; in Hanover on April 18, 1768, and in Hamburg again on June 9, 1768. It was followed on the present occasion by *Die neue Agnese* and a ballet.

Count Olban, a widower, is involved in a long-standing legal process with his relative, the Baroness de l'Orme; and the latter suggests as a settlement that they should marry. The count, however, knowing the baroness's temper, reveals his preference for the girl Nanine, whom she has brought up in her service; whereupon the baroness offers Nanine the choice of marrying her gardener Blaise or taking the veil. She chooses the latter, but the count finds means to prevent her departure. The baroness now succeeds in intercepting a letter of Nanine's to her father, who unknown to all is staying near by, and arouses the count's suspicions to such an extent that he dismisses Nanine from the house and agrees to marry the baroness herself. Ultimately, however, Nanine's innocence is proved, the baroness leaves in anger, and Nanine becomes the count's wife.

33. *Die kranke Frau*, a comedy in one act by C. F. Gellert. Tuesday, June 2, 1767. [St. xxii, 2.] This comedy was published in Gellert's *Lustspiele*, Leipzig, 1748 (pp. 399 ff.). It had been in Schönemann's repertory since 1749 (H. Devrient, *op. cit.* p. 168). Cast: Frau Stephan, Mad. Löwen; Stephan, Ekhof; Philippine, Mad. Böck; Henriette, Mlle Ackermann; Wahrmund, Hensel; Richard, Borchers. Repeated on August 21, 1767, and in Hanover on January 4, 1768. It was preceded on the present occasion by *Der Advocat Patelin*, and followed by 'ein neues grosses Heroisch-Pantomimisches Ballet, von der Erfindung des Herrn Balletmeisters Curioni', *Admetus und Alceste*,[1] which was repeated on June 11 and August 21, 1767.

Die kranke Frau turns round the illness of Frau Stephan, which is induced by envy because her sister-in-law, Frau Richard, possesses an 'Adrienne'.[2] Her husband consults a chiromantist who prophesies her a short life. Nothing avails to restore her to health but the possession of the coveted garment.

---

[1] See above, pp. 42 f.

[2] An 'Adrienne' (xxii, 33), or more correctly, 'Andrienne', was a robe with a long skirt which the actress Mlle Dancourt had worn in Baron's comedy *L'Andrienne*, produced on November 16, 1703. 'Bey Gelegenheit dieses Lustspiels, erdachte die Schauspielerinn Mad. Dancourt die ältere welche die Rolle der Andrierin spielte, eine neue Kleidertracht, welche hernach unter dem Namen der Andriennen bekannt genug geworden ist' ('Nachricht aus Paris' in *Bibliothek der schönen Wissenschaften*, iii (1758), p. 177). Cosack notes (*op. cit.* p. 165) the occurrence of the word in Schlegel's *Die stumme Schönheit* (Sc. xii, 'Andrienne'). The form 'Adrienne' seems to have been the normal one in Germany. It occurs in Mylius's first essay in Lessing's *Beyträge zur Historie und Aufnahme des Theaters* (Stuttgart, 1750, i, i, p. 3).

34. *Der Mann nach der Uhr, oder der ordentliche Mann*, a comedy in one act by Th. G. von Hippel. Wednesday, June 3, 1767. [St. xxii, 60.] Published in Königsberg, 1760, and in 1765; also in *Theater der Deutschen*, i (1768), and in Hippel's *Sämmtliche Werke*, Berlin, 1827–38, x, pp. 371 ff. It was first produced in Hamburg by Ackermann in 1766, and was very popular. Cast: Orbil, Ekhof (Schütze, *op. cit.* p. 330, called his performance 'meisterhaft', Schröder (Meyer, *op. cit.* ii, 2, p. 18) 'vortrefflich'); Wilhelmine, Mlle Felbrich; Valer, Borchers; Magister, Hensel; Lisette, Mad. Schulz; Johann, Merschy. Repetitions took place on July 10 (liii, 2), August 13, November 10, 1767; in Hanover on April 18, 1768, and again in Hamburg on May 17, August 22, September 20, 1768, and in Hanover on February 7, 1769.

35. *Der Graf von Essex*, a tragedy in five acts by Thomas Corneille. Thursday, June 4, 1767. [St. xxii, 77–xxv.] *Le Comte d'Essex*, tragédie en cinq actes en vers (1678). The translation (in alexandrines) was by Peter Stüven, licentiate in law in Hamburg (cp. F. Heitmüller, *Hamburgische Dramatiker zur Zeit Gottscheds*, Dresden, 1891, pp. 34 ff.). It was published in Hamburg in 1747 (a copy of this edition is in the Preussische Staatsbibliothek) and reprinted in the *Deutsche Schaubühne zu Wienn*, i (1749), pp. 1 ff. It had already been a popular piece when Caroline Neuber's company played in Hamburg in 1735 (cp. F. J. von Reden-Esbeck, *Caroline Neuber*, Leipzig, 1881, pp. 107 ff.). Schönemann, who played the title rôle, revived it at Breslau in 1744 and Hamburg in 1747 (H. Devrient, *op. cit.* pp. 91, 360, cp. also Schütze, *op. cit.* p. 247). C. H. Schmid (*Chronologie, ed. cit.* p. 62) says: 'Auch führte sie [die Neuberin] von dem Gottscheden so verhassten Herrn von Stüven eine Übersetzung von dem Essex des Thomas Corneille auf, welche sich unerachtet ihrer Mattigkeit fast bis auf den heutigen Tag [1775] auf den Bühnen erhalten hat'; and H. Devrient (*op. cit.* p. 91, note) states that it was 'eines der beliebtesten Stücke der Wanderbühnen von der Neuber bis zur Hamb[urger] Entreprise'. Schönemann had in his time been particularly fond of the rôle of Essex, and refused to relinquish it to Ekhof (cp. H. Devrient, *op. cit.* p. 249, and Schütze, *op. cit.* pp. 247 f.); Ackermann had also played it, but, according to Schütze (*op. cit.* p. 317), had spoiled it. Cast: Elisabeth, Mad. Löwen; Henriette, Fürstin von Irton, Mad. Mecour; Graf von Essex, Ekhof; Cecile, Borchers; Salsbury, Böck; Tilney, Mlle Felbrich; Crommer, Hensel. The tragedy was only

repeated once, on July 15 (LIV, 3 ff.). It was followed now by a ballet.

The Earl of Essex has forfeited the confidence of Queen Elisabeth by an armed advance upon the royal palace. The queen's advisers and Essex's enemies, Raleg [*sic*], Coban [*sic*] and Cecile [*sic*], persuade her that Essex is in collusion with the Irish rebels, whereas the real reason for Essex's attempt was to prevent the marriage of the Countess of Irton, with whom he is in love, and for whose sake he wishes to free himself from the now irksome passion which the queen herself still cherishes for him. Elisabeth offers Essex her pardon and her love if he will admit his guilt. This he refuses to do. Thereupon she has him arrested for high treason and condemned to death. Preparations are made for his execution. When the queen learns the true state of the case, she is at first still more incensed, but eventually makes efforts to force the earl to yield and ask for pardon. She endeavours to move him through the Countess of Irton, then through his friend Earl Salsbury. In vain: Essex maintains his innocence and refuses to countenance the charge by asking for grace. Essex's enemies, meanwhile, on the pretext of the queen's orders, hasten his execution, and prevent his friends from gaining access to Elisabeth. Too late she repents her own pride, and her only hope is to be freed from her grief by an early death.

36. *Die Hausfranzösin, oder: Die Mammsell*, a comedy in five acts by Luise V. A. Gottsched. Wednesday, June 10, 1767. [St. XXVI, 2.] This comedy was published in the *Deutsche Schaubühne*, v (1744), pp. 67 ff.,[1] and was probably played by Schönemann's company in the same year; he brought it to Hamburg in 1747 (H. Devrient, *op. cit.* pp. 123, 349). Cast: Germann, Borchers; Wahrmund, Schulz; Luischen, Mlle Ackermann; Hannchen, Mlle Ackermann; Franz, Mad. Böck; Der junge Wahrmund, Böck; De Sotenville, Ekhof; Mlle La Fleche, Mad. Löwen; Erhard, Hensel; La Fleur, Merschy. Schröder is evidently in error when in his list of Ekhof's rôles (Meyer, *op. cit.* ii, 2, p. 19), he states that he played on this occasion 'Franz, den Gelbschnabel! der sieben und vierzigjährige!' The comedy was followed by the ballet *Die Zigeuner in ihrem Lager*, and was not repeated.

37. *Der Bauer mit der Erbschaft*, a comedy in one act by Pierre Carlet de Chamblain de Marivaux. Friday, June 12, 1767. [St. XXVIII, 2.] *L'héritier de village*, comédie en un acte en prose (1725). The translation, by J. C. Krüger, was published in the *Sammlung einiger Lustspiele aus*

---

[1] The other plays in the volume (XXVI, 4) were *Panthea*, Trauerspiel; *Dido*, Trauerspiel von J. E. Schlegel; *Der Bock im Processe*, Lustspiel von Th. J. Quistorp; *Mahomed IV*, Trauerspiel von B. E. Krüger; *Elisie*, Schäferspiel von A. G. Uhlich.

dem Französischen des Herrn von Marivaux, Hanover, 1747–49. *Der Bauer mit der Erbschaft* had also appeared separately (without place or date; see Goedeke, *Grundriss*, iii (2nd ed.) p. 373). It had enjoyed great popularity in Hamburg since its production in 1747, and shared with Borkenstein's *Der Bookesbeutel* the reputation of being the most popular local play (cp. V. Golubew, *op. cit.* p. 32). Cast: Frau Damis, Mad. Merschy; Baron, Böck; Jürge, Ekhof; Lise, Mad. Böck; Hans, Borchers; Grete, Mlle Ackermann; Valentin, Hensel. Ekhof was particularly famous as 'Jürge'—'unübertrefflich in d[er] plattdeutschen Sprache', said Schröder (Meyer, *op. cit.* ii, 2, p. 17). It is of this play that the story is told of the peasant in the audience who was so deceived by Ekhof's acting that he asked his neighbour: 'Wo to'm Düwel hewwt de Lüde den Buern herrenohmen?' (H. Uhde, *K. Ekhof*, *ed. cit.* p. 133; V. Golubew, *op. cit.* p. 33). Reichard's *Theater-Kalender* for 1776 (Gotha) contains an engraving of Mad. Böck and Ekhof in this play which is reproduced in Golubew's dissertation and here.[1] *Der Bauer mit der Erbschaft* was one of the most popular plays of the repertory and was repeated ten times: on August 25 and November 19, 1767, in Hanover on January 7, January 22, February 23, April 21, again in Hamburg on May 31, July 15, October 3, and in Hanover on December 28, 1768. It was preceded on this first occasion by *Nanine* and a ballet.

38. *Der Zerstreute*, a comedy in five acts by J. F. Regnard. Monday, June 29, 1767. [St. xxviii, 69.] *Le Distrait*, comédie en cinq actes en vers (1697). This play was originally produced in Hamburg by Caroline Neuber in 1735 under the title, *Der Zerstreute, oder der seine Gedanken nicht beysammen hat* (Reden-Esbeck, *op. cit.* pp. 108, 304), the translation being probably by Lessing and Weisse. H. Devrient (*op. cit.* p. 192) records a performance in Hamburg under Schönemann on August 9, 1751: 'ein aus dem Französischen des Herrn Renard in Schlesswig von einer vornehmen Standesperson übersetztes Lustspiel, in fünf Aufzügen, *le Distrait, Der Unachtsinnende.*' *Der Zerstreuete, ein Lust-Spiel in fünf Aufzügen*; aus dem Französischen des Herrn Regnard übersetzt, was published in Dresden in 1752 (cp. Gottsched, *Nöthiger Vorrath*, ii, p. 278). (A copy of this edition is in the Hamburg Staats- und Universitätsbibliothek.) The translation now used may have been the Dresden one, or, perhaps, that in the first Part of Regnard's *Sämmtliche theatralische Werke*, Berlin, 1757, where the play is also

---

[1] See plate facing p. 38.

entitled *Der Zerstreute*. The British Museum possesses a translation
(in alexandrines), *Der Zerstreute des Herrn Regnard*, übersetzt von C.L.R.,
Frankfurt and Leipzig, 1761; but its description of the 'Personen'
does not tally with that on the present playbill. Cast: Leander,
Ekhof; Clarice, Mad. Böck; Madame Grognac, Mad. Schmelz;
Isabelle, Mlle Ackermann; Chevalier, Schmelz; Valer, Borchers;
Lisette, Mad. Mecour; Carlin, Hensel. Ekhof played Leander (according to Schröder 'gut bis auf den Liebhaber', Meyer, *op. cit.* ii,
2, p. 17). *Der Zerstreute* was repeated four times, on August 18, 1767,
on April 7 (in Hanover), July 12, 1768, and (in Hanover) on January
11, 1769.

39. *Das Räthsel, oder: Was dem Frauenzimmer am meisten gefällt*, a
comedy in one act, with a *divertissement*, by J. F. Löwen. Monday,
June 29, 1767. [St. xxix, 22.] This after-piece was published in
Löwen's *Schriften*, Hamburg, 1765–66, iv, pp. 339 ff. Goedeke (*Grundriss* (3rd ed.), iv (1), p. 46) refers to criticisms in the *Allgemeine deutsche
Bibliothek*, iii (1769), pp. 235 ff. and in the *Hamburgische Correspondent*,
No. 191 (December 2, 1766). The present performance, in spite of
the fact that the word 'neue' does not appear on the playbill (cp.
those for April 27, April 28 and May 14) would appear to have been
the first. For the 'Divertissement' which followed Hertel wrote the
music. Cosack (*op. cit.* p. 192) quotes a critic in the *Neue Bibliothek
der schönen Wissenschaften*, iv (1767), p. [290], to the effect that the
'Divertissement', which consisted of arias, duets and choruses, 'zu
Ehren des Dichters wegfallen könnte'. Cast: Bertha, Mad. Böck;
Robert, Böck; Die Fee Radiante, Mad. Mecour; Pedrillo, Hensel;
eine Alte, Mlle Ackermann; Magotnie, Mad. Schulz. Repetitions
took place on August 5, 1767, and in Hanover on February 16,
February 24, and April 25, 1768.

40. *Rodogüne*, a tragedy in five acts by Corneille. Wednesday, July
1, 1767. [St. xxix, 53–xxxii.] *Rodogune, Princesse des Parthes*, tragédie
en cinq actes en vers (1644, printed 1647). There had been an older
translation by F. C. Bressand (Wolfenbüttel, 1691); this new translation, which was not published until 1769, was also in alexandrines and
entitled: *Rodogüne, Prinzessin der Parther*, ein Trauerspiel in fünf Ackten
des Herrn von Corneille (zum Behuf des Hamburgischen Theaters),
Hamburg and Bremen, 1769. (A copy is in the Hamburg Staats- und
Universitätsbibliothek.) According to Klotz's *Deutsche Bibliothek*, iv
(1770), p. 724, the translator's name was Meyer; the writer of the

article in *Lessing und Hamburg* already quoted suggests (p. 30) the actor Wilhelm Christian Dieterich Meyer, adding 'who played the rôle of Oront'—which he did not. The following passage is from the preface to the translation:

Ich übersetzte Rodogüne zu einer Zeit, da noch beynahe alle Welt mit P. Corneillen glaubte, dass es eines seiner besten Stücke, wo nicht gar das beste wäre....Die Hamburgische Dramaturgie hat es mich eben so wohl als andere Leute kennen gelehrt, und nun ist es leicht einzusehen, warum ich nicht nach der Zeit in die Versuchung gerathen bin, meine Übersetzung in Absicht auf die Reinigkeit der Verse und des Dialogs einer genauern Prüfung und Verbesserung zu unterwerfen. Und überdem, warum sollte ich etwas zu verbessern suchen, das man vielleicht nicht mehr liest, und das man sich schon müde gesehn hat?

Rodogüne had been one of the most spectacular productions under Ackermann's management (in 1766), and its choice on the present occasion was in honour of the visit of King Christian VII of Denmark. The cast was as follows: Cleopatra, Mad. Hensel; Seleucus, Böck; Antiochus, Ekhof ('junger Prinz und Liebhaber' Schröder notes, Meyer, *op. cit.* ii, 2, p. 18); Rodogüne, Mad. Mecour; Timagen, Borchers; Oront, Hensel; Laonice, Mad. Schmelz. Repetitions took place on August 26, 1767, in Hanover on January 11, February 8, February 19, 1768, again in Hamburg on June 16, 1768, and in Hanover on January 26 and February 21, 1769.

At the opening of the drama, we learn the previous history of the chief characters. The king of Syria, Nicanor, has been taken prisoner by the Parthians, and he and his wife Cleopatra are threatened by a usurper Tryphon. It is reported that Nicanor has died in captivity, and Cleopatra, to save herself, marries Nicanor's brother Antiochus, who overthrows Tryphon, but himself dies in battle. Cleopatra's two sons, Antiochus and Seleucus, are meanwhile being brought up in Egypt by Timagen. The news comes that Nicanor is not dead, but is marching on Syria with the Parthian army, and that in order to avenge himself on his faithless wife, he intends to marry Rodogüne, sister of the Parthian king. The Syrians however, defeat the invaders; Cleopatra kills her husband with her own hand, and makes Rodogüne prisoner. In the first scene, Timagen, returning with the two young princes from Egypt, learns of the death of their father from his sister, the queen's confidante Laonice. He also hears that Cleopatra is about to reveal which of the two princes is the elder, in order that he may be crowned king and receive Rodogüne as his bride. Rodogüne is loved by both the young men, and she herself confesses that she loves one of them. Cleopatra, on learning this, reveals her plan. She announces to her confidante and to her sons that she will bestow the throne on whichever of the latter avenges her on Rodogüne. Neither will consent to do this. Rodogüne, informed by Laonice of Cleopatra's hatred, also cherishes thoughts of vengeance; at the instigation of her brother, she resolves to give her hand to the prince who avenges on Cleopatra the murdered Nicanor and her own imprisonment. Both princes are terror-stricken by this fresh complication. But Antiochus has the courage to act, on learning that it is he whom Rodogüne loves. Rodogüne, however, cannot maintain her resolve when she has confessed her love for Antiochus, and the latter endeavours to placate his mother; but in vain. Cleopatra appears to yield to his entreaties; but after attempting unsuccessfully to win Seleucus to her side, resolves on a more terrible revenge. She murders Seleucus and proposes to poison Antiochus and Rodogüne at their wedding ceremony. Before they drink the poisoned cup, however, Timagen arrives to announce the death of Seleucus; but he cannot say who is the murderer. Cleopatra, suspected by Antiochus, endeavours to throw suspicion on Rodogüne; Antiochus completes the marriage ceremony, but when he is about to drink from the poisoned cup, Rodogüne insists that Cleopatra herself should taste the wine. She does so, and is led away to die, pronouncing a final malediction on their union.

Rodogüne was followed on this occasion by *Armide*, 'ein Heroisch-Pantomimisches Ballet, mit Auszierungen und Verwandlungen', which was repeated twice.

41. *Solimann der Zweyte, oder: Die drey Sultaninnen*, a comedy in three acts by C. S. Favart. Friday, July 3, 1767. [St. xxxiii, 2–xxxvi, 56.] *Soliman II, ou les Sultanes*, comédie en trois actes en vers (1761). According to Schmid (*Chronologie, ed. cit.* p. 162), the translation was by Rudolf Erich Raspe and Starke; it was published in 1765.[1] There was another translation in the first volume of a *Sammlung einiger französischen Lustspiele für das deutsche Theater*, published by the brothers Walz (2 vols. Bremen, 1766–68). A separate reprint of this: *Die drey Sultanninnen*, Bremen [N.D.] is in the British Museum.[2] The choice

---

[1] A copy of *Solimann der Zweyte oder die drey Sultaninnen.* Aus dem Französischen des Herrn Favart übersetzt von St. [N.P.], 1765, is in the Hamburg Staats- und Universitätsbibliothek. The second translator may have been Johann Ludwig Starke (1723–69), an actor of considerable repute, who is stated to have made a number of translations for the stage (cp. *Gallerie von Teutschen Schauspielern, ed. cit.* pp. 140 f.). The playbill for a performance of this play in Vienna on July 26, 1778 (preserved in the Theatersammlung of the Nationalbibliothek, Vienna) states that the translation was by 'Herr Starke'.

[2] There is a slight difference in the spelling of Solimann's name between the 1765 translation and the reprint of the one published at Bremen: the form of the 1765 translation corresponds to that on the playbill and in Lessing's criticisms. But the playbill (see below, p. 85, note 1) does not correspond to either translation in its spellings Delie and Roxolane.

of the play for performance on the occasion of the visit of the King of Denmark was again due to the fact that it was one of the show-pieces inherited from Ackermann. The latter had produced it on September 6, 1765, 'mit opermässige[m] Prunk' (Schütze, *op. cit.* p. 326); the ballets were arranged by Schröder. On that occasion Madame Hensel's rôle of Roxolane fell to Karoline Schulze, other-wise the cast was the same as now (*ibid.*; cp. also Meyer, *op. cit.* i, p. 141).[1] This was: Solimann, Ekhof; Osmin Kisslar Aga, name not given, but Ackermann; Elmire, Mad. Böck; Delie, Mlle Dorothea Ackermann; Roxolane, Mad. Hensel. On Ekhof as Solimann, Schröder commented: 'der Körper schadete dem Spiel' (Meyer, *op. cit.* ii, 2, p. 17). Repetitions of the play took place on August 24, November 11, 1767, in Hanover on January 8, January 19, February 25, in Hamburg on July 20, November 18, and in Hanover on December 12, 1768. On the playbill was the following statement:

'Nach Endigung des dritten Aufzuges wird bey der Krönung der Roxolane in fränkischer Sprache gesungen:

> Vivir, Vivir Sultana,
> Vivir, Vivir Roxolana.

Und in Türkischer:	Verstand der türkischen Worte:
Eyuvallah, Eyuvallah,	Ruhm, Ruhm, Glückseligkeit,
Salem alekin,	Heil und Ehre,
Sultan Zillulah	Unserm erhabenen Kaiser,
Solimann Padichaïm.	Dem Solimann, dem Spiegel der Gottheit.
Eyuvallah, Eyuvallah.	Ruhm, Ruhm, Glückseligkeit.[2]

---

[1] The playbill for July 3 is missing from Ekhof's collection in Gotha; but that for the next performance, on August 24, is available there, and has been used for the quotations and the cast.

[2] In the reprint published at Bremen, the passage is as follows (p. 95):

> Es leb, es lebe die Sultane!
> Es leb, es lebe Roxelane!
> (und die Türken)
> Heil, Ehre, Ruhm, Glückseligkeit,
> Sey dir Erhabener! geweyht.
> Mit Wonne sey dein Herz erfüllt,
> O Soliman! der Gottheit Bild.*

* Im Originale werden die vier letzten Zeilen türkisch ausgedruckt:

> Eyuvallah, Eyuvallah,
> Salem alekim,
> Sultan zilullah,
> Soliman Padichaïm,
> Eyuvallah, Eyuvallah.

42. *Merope*, a tragedy in five acts by Voltaire. Tuesday, July 7, 1767. [St. xxxvi, 60–L.] *Mérope*, tragédie en cinq actes en vers (1743). A *Merope* was produced in Frankfurt as early as 1748 (E. Mentzel, *Geschichte der Schauspielkunst in Frankfurt*, Frankfurt, 1882, p. 212); but this may have been Maffei's, which was early translated—according to Gottsched (*Neuer Büchersaal der schönen Wissenschaften und freyen Künste*, i (1745), p. 329) in the 'thirties by 'Herr Prof. Stähelin' (cp. also C. Stählin, *Aus den Papieren Jacob von Stählins*, Berlin, 1926, p. 26). Goedeke (*Grundriss*, iii (2nd ed.), p. 365) mentions two translations of Voltaire's tragedy, one by a 'Liebhaber der deutschen Dichtkunst' (in alexandrines), Dresden, 1754 (a copy of which is in the Hamburg Staats- und Universitätsbibliothek); the other by J. F. Gries, an advocate in Glückstadt, Glückstadt, 1754 (see K. Gröschl, *op. cit.* pp. 50 f. and Gottsched, *Nöthiger Vorrath*, ii, p. 283). The playbill corresponds to the Dresden translation in respect of the 'Personen des Trauerspiels'. *Merope* seems to have been first performed in Hamburg in 1755 (Meyer, *op. cit.* ii, 2, p. 52); and Ackermann's company also played it in Frankfurt in 1757. Cast: Merope, Mad. Hensel; Egist, Böck; Poli[fo]nt,[1] Ekhof; Narbas, Borchers; Eurikles, Schmelz; Erop [Erox], Hensel; Ismene, Mad. Böck. There were repetitions on August 3, 1767, on January 4 (in Hanover), and August 18, 1768. It was followed on this occasion by 'ein serieuses Ballet'.

Since the murder of Cresfont fifteen years before, no successor has been chosen for him in Messene. The queen, Merope, his widow, sees in her son Egist (whom she had saved from the blood bath by entrusting him to Narbas, an old servant, to bring up in Elis) the rightful heir to the throne. She now learns that Narbas and the youth have disappeared from Elis; but there is still hope that they may be on the way to Messene. The tyrant Polifont lays claim to the vacant throne, and demands that Merope shall become his wife. He has secretly given orders that Narbas and Egist are to be slain if they attempt to come to Messene. A young man is now brought before the queen accused of murder, and he relates how he has slain one of his two assailants in self-defence. Merope is led to believe that the victim of this act is her son Egist, a proof being that he wears a coat of mail which had belonged to Cresfont. Polifont presses for the execution of the stranger; but Merope desires to take her revenge by slaying him herself. Narbas arrives at Messene and bewails the loss of Egist and the tyranny of Polifont. At the critical moment when Merope raises the dagger to slay the stranger, Narbas reveals to her that he is her son. The only way she sees to save his

---

[1] 'Polisant' on the playbill for this performance; but the name appears correctly on the playbills for January 4 and August 18, 1768.

life is for her to agree to marry Polifont, but now she learns from Narbas that Polifont is the assassin of her husband and children. Although Egist affirms to Polifont that he is the murderer of the heir to the throne, the tyrant is resolved to have him executed in any case. His suspicions are awakened by the sympathy which Merope shows for the young man; he orders his immediate execution, whereupon Merope declares him to be her son. The tyrant then offers her the alternative of marrying him or seeing her son die. The marriage is arranged with the approval of the people. Egist is induced to bow to the inevitable and pay his homage to the tyrant, but at the marriage ceremony he slays Polifont and is proclaimed the rightful king of Messene.

43. *Der Triumph der guten Frauen*, a comedy in five acts by Johann Elias Schlegel. Thursday, July 9, 1767. [St. LII, 1.] This play was published in *Beyträge zum dänischen Theater*, Copenhagen, 1748, and in Schlegel's *Werke, ed. cit.* ii (1762), pp. 323 ff. It was produced as a novelty by Schönemann in Hamburg on August 3, 1751 (H. Devrient, *op. cit.* p. 191). Cast: Agenor, Böck; Juliane, Mad. Hensel; Nicander, Ekhof ('einen Liebhaber, einen Wüstling!', Schröder commented, Meyer, *op. cit.* ii, 2, p. 17); Hilarie, Mad. Böck; Agathe, Mad. Schmelz; Catharine, Mad. Mecour; Heinrich, Merschy. It was repeated on October 22, 1767, and on January 26 (in Hanover), on November 16, and (in Hanover) on December 7, 1768.[1] It was followed now by the ballet, *Die verwandelten Zittern*.

Hilaria, disguised as a man and passing under the name of Philinte, is seeking her husband Nicander, who has deserted her ten years previously (soon after their marriage) and is now trying to make love to Juliane, the wife of his friend Agenor. Philinte enters the field as Nicander's rival for Juliane's favour. Agenor is induced by Nicander to tyrannise over Juliane and to deprive her of all society except Nicander's and his own. Hilaria, meanwhile, resuming her woman's dress and giving herself out to be Philinte's sister, gains Nicander's favour, upholding the idea of liberty in marriage; and Nicander now endeavours to pacify Agenor and to bring him and Juliane together again. In the guise of Philinte, Hilaria urges Juliane to place herself under her protection; Juliane's refusal is overheard by Agenor (according to a plan made by Hilaria and Catharine). Agenor is about to draw on the supposed lover of his wife, when Philinte discloses her identity; Nicander greets her revelation with delight, and Agenor is convinced of his injustice towards Juliane.

---

[1] There is also a playbill for June 10, 1768; but the *Hamburgische Address-Comtoir Nachrichten* of June 11 states that owing to the indisposition of Madame Hensel, *Sidnei* and *Der Advokat Patelin* were actually performed on the previous evening. See above, p. 44, note 1.

44. *Die Frauen-Schule*, a comedy in five acts by Molière. Monday, July 13, 1767. [St. LIII, 71.] *L'École des femmes*, comédie en cinq actes en vers (1662). It is difficult to obtain reliable information concerning Molière's plays in the German repertories of the eighteenth century. *Die Frauen-Schule*, or *Weiberschule*, had long been familiar; Schönemann had produced it, describing it as a novelty, in Hamburg on August 20, 1753 (H. Devrient, *op. cit.* p. 221). On the present playbill it is stated: 'Dieses Stück wird heute zum erstenmale aufgeführt'; but presumably this means under the present management (see also above, p. 41). A translation (*Die Schule des Frauenzimmers*) had appeared in 1752 at Berlin; that used by Schönemann and now was by F. J. Bierling, *Des Herrn Molieres sämmtliche Lustspiele*, nach einer freyen und sorgfältigen Übersetzung, 3 vols. Hamburg, 1752 (2nd edition, 4 vols. 1769). The Hamburg Staats- und Universitätsbibliothek possesses Ekhof's copy of his part, with Ekhof's note that it was taken from Bierling's translation. Cast: Arnolph, Ekhof ('Caricatur' Schröder comments, Meyer, *op. cit.* ii, 2, p. 20); Heinrich, Schmelz; Agnes, Mlle Felbrich; Chrisaldes, Borchers; Horaz, Böck; Orontes, Hensel; Claus, Merschy; Catharine, Mad. Schulz. Repetitions took place on July 24, December 2, 1767, and February 3 (in Hanover), July 15, October 17, and (in Hanover) December 30, 1768. It was followed on the present occasion by 'ein Ballet'.

45. *Die Brüder, oder: Die Früchte der Erziehung*, a comedy in five acts by K. F. Romanus. Friday, July 17, 1767. [St. LXX, 101–LXXIII, 11, and XCVI, 2–C.] This play was first printed in Romanus's *Komödien*, Dresden and Warsaw, 1761; then reprinted in *Theater der Deutschen*, vi (1768), pp. 283 ff., and in the Viennese *Neue Sammlung von Schauspielen*, iv, 1763, as *Die Brüder, oder die Schule der Väter*. Michel Baron, or Boyron, had written an imitation of Terence, entitled *L'École des Pères*, not published until 1736, after Baron's death, but performed in 1705.[1] Romanus's play was performed for the first time in Hamburg under Ackermann in 1766. Cast: Philidor, Borchers; Lisimon, Witthöft; Leander, Böck; Lycast, Ekhof; Lucinde, Mlle Felbrich; Cidalise, Mad. Böck; Nerine, Mad. Schulz; Frontin, Hensel. Schröder says (Meyer, *op. cit.* ii, 2, p. 18; cp. also i, p. 183) that Ekhof played 'den jüngeren ausgelassenen Bruder; Boek den älteren'. Repetitions took place on August 11, October 7, 1767, and in Hanover on

---

[1] Cp. B. E. Young, *Michel Baron*, Paris, 1905, pp. 284, 315.

January 5, 1768. It was followed on the present occasion by Saint-Foix' *Orakel*.

The brothers of Romanus's comedy are Philidor and Lysimon. Philidor lives in the town and, being of a gentle and kindly nature, has brought up his son Leander by gentle means; Lysimon, on the other hand, is violent and quarrelsome and has employed such severity in bringing up his son Lycast that the latter has fallen into extravagant and dissolute ways. Philidor plans a marriage between Leander and Lucinde, the ward of an old friend Orgon. Leander, out of kindness to his cousin and with the object of keeping him from worse courses, allows him to arrange a party in his father's house. At this party Cidalise, Lycast's mistress, is expected but does not at first appear; they hear that she has transferred her favours to a baron. Lycast, in spite of Leander's protests, goes to seek her and throws the baron out of her house. Lucinde meets Cidalise in Leander's house, and is led to believe that Leander is faithless to her and in love with Cidalise. To shield his cousin from his father's anger, Leander does not contradict the accusation. Frontin, Leander's valet, takes advantage of the misunderstanding between Leander and Lucinde, and confirms it to Lucinde's maid; he then assures Lysimon that Lycast is a model of propriety, while Leander is really dissolute; the valet leads Lysimon to do various things which will discredit Leander in the eyes of his father, such as paying Leander's alleged debts, the debts being actually those of his own son. Finally when Lysimon reveals to his brother Leander's supposed misdemeanours, Philidor, who has investigated the facts of the case, turns upon him and convinces him of the bad results of his way of bringing up Lycast. With some difficulty Lysimon is persuaded to forgive his son, and promises to give Philidor's methods a trial.

46. *Das Orakel*, a comedy in one act by Saint-Foix. July 17, 1767. [St. LXX, 101 and LXXIII, 12.] '*L'Oracle, com[édie]* en un Ac[te] en pro[se] par M. de Saint-Foix, donnée pour la premiere fois sur le Théatre Fran[çais] le 22 Mars 1740, avec beaucoup de succès, et souvent revue depuis avec plaisir' (Léris, *op. cit.* p. 325). Produced on May 17, 1742 in Hamburg by Sophie Schröder, it was played fifteen times in that year, the translation being probably published at Hamburg in 1745 (cp. Gottsched, *Nöthiger Vorrath*, i, p. 322). There is also a version in *Des Herrn von Saint-Foix Theatralische Werke*, i, Leipzig, 1750, which Lessing mentions with commendation in his *Theatralische Bibliothek* (*Schriften*, vi, p. 345). This translation is ascribed to Johann Elias Schlegel by Schmid (*Chronologie, ed. cit.* p. 97)[1] but was probably by C. A. Wichmann (cp. Petersen, *ed. cit.* p. 203). *Das Orakel* appears for the first time in Schönemann's repertory on April 17, 1747, and

[1] Cp. also the review in Klotz's *Deutsche Bibliothek*, ii (Halle, 1768), p. 350.

is published in his *Schaubühne*, vi, 1752 (cp. also H. Devrient, *op. cit.*
p. 128). J. C. Krüger was the author of another version in the manner
of a 'Singspiel', produced on October 28, 1751 (H. Devrient, *op. cit.*
p. 194; cp. W. Wittekindt, *op. cit.* p. 13); Gellert also wrote an
operetta *Das Orakel*, performed in Vienna in 1755,[1] and there was an
adaptation of Saint-Foix' play by Löwen (1756). Lastly, the British
Museum possesses an undated translation (according to Gottsched,
Nöthiger Vorrath, i, p. 335, there was one belonging to the year 1750),
'wie solches auf der Schuchischen Schaubühne vorgestellet wird'; and
there is a reprint in *Deutsche Schauspiele*, Vienna, 1750 (Goedeke,
Grundriss, iii (2nd ed.), p. 370). The version used now was probably
Schönemann's. Cast: [Die Fee] Souveraine, Mad. Löwen; Alcindor,
Böck; Lucinde, Mlle Felbrich. There was only one repetition, on
August 27.

47. *Der unvermuthete Ausgang*, a comedy in one act by Marivaux.
Tuesday, July 21,[2] 1767. [St. LXXIII, 16.] *Le Dénouement imprévu*,
com[édie] en un Ac[te] en prose, 'qui n'eut pas grand succès au
Thé[âtre] Fran[çais] où elle parut pour la premiere fois le 2 Décembre
1724' (Léris, *op. cit.* p. 139). On the playbill is stated: 'Dies Stück
wird heute zum erstenmal aufgeführt'; but this can only refer to the
present and Ackermann's management, for it had been a favourite
'Nachspiel' under Schönemann since 1749 (H. Devrient, *op. cit.* pp.
168, 352, 353, 355). The translation was by J. C. Krüger (*Sammlung
einiger Lustspiele aus dem Französischen des Herrn von Marivaux*, 2 vols.
Hanover, 1747–49). Cast: Argant, Witthöft; Jungfer Argante, Mad.
Löwen; Dorant, Borchers; Erast, Böck; Peter, Hensel; Lisette, Mad.
Mecour; Crispin, Merschy. Schröder notes (Meyer, *op. cit.* ii, 2, p. 20)
that Ekhof played the rôle of Argant, but this does not agree with the
playbill. Meyer states (*op. cit.* i, pp. 182 f.) that ['Madam Löwens]
Liebhaberin in Marivaux unvermuthetem Ausgange...Schrödern
unvergesslich [blieb]'. Repetitions took place on August 10, 1767,
March 1 (in Hanover), and June 15, 1768.

[1] *Repertoire des deutschen Schauspieles in Wien*, MS. Stadtbibliothek, Vienna, p. 136.
[2] The programme of July 21 consisted actually of Schlosser's *Der Zweykampf*
and *Die wüste Insel*, a one-act comedy translated (by Ekhof) from the French of
J. B. Collet de Messine. *Nanine* and *Der unvermuthete Ausgang* were not performed
until a week later, July 28, a date on which Lessing sets the repetition of Romanus's
Die Brüder. That play was actually not repeated until August 11. The first error
may have been no more than an oversight, but the insertion of a performance of
Die Brüder was made, no doubt, in order to give an opportunity of continuing his
discussion of that play.

48. *Richard der Dritte*, a tragedy in five acts by C. F. Weisse. Wednesday, July 22, 1767. [St. LXXIII, 67–LXXIII, 75.] It was published in *Beytrag zum deutschen Theater*, i, Leipzig, 1759, and in this form was played by Koch and received with great favour in Hamburg in 1761 (cp. Ekhof's letter of July 6, 1761, to Weisse, published by J. Minor, *Briefe aus Weisses Nachlass* in Schnorr's *Archiv für Litteraturgeschichte*, ix, 1880, p. 475). Ekhof, however, was not satisfied with the last act and Weisse remodelled it in 1761. Cp. the preface to the second edition (Leipzig, 1765): 'Richard den Dritten hat er [der Verfasser] in den leztern Akten gänzlich umgeschmolzen: der Vorwurf war gegründet, dass sich die Haupthandlung im dritten Akte schloss; da sie nach der neuern Veränderung bis ans Ende fortläuft.' The new form appeared in the second edition of the *Beytrag*, i, Leipzig, 1765; also in *Theater der Deutschen*, iii, 1766, pp. 193 ff.; it is reprinted by D. Jacoby and A. Sauer in *Deutsche Literaturdenkmale des 18. und 19. Jahrhunderts*, No. 130, Berlin, 1904. The revised version was produced in Leipzig in 1767, and in Hamburg on the present occasion. Cast: Richard, Ekhof; Eduard, Mad. Böck; Herzog von York, Mlle Ackermann; Richmond, Schmelz; Stanley, Borchers; Catesby, Hensel; Königin Elisabeth, Mad. Löwen; Prinzessin Elisabeth, Mad. Hensel; Tyrel, Böck. On the performance Schröder commented (Meyer, *op. cit.* ii, 2, p. 20): '[Ekhof spielte] Richard, gut, bis auf die körperliche Kraft'; and the *Hamburgische Unterhaltungen* was eloquent in praise of his rendering of 'O hätt' es nur Ein Haupt!' (H. Uhde, *op. cit.* p. 169). There were repetitions on August 6, October 6, 1767, and (in Hanover) on January 3, 1769.

49. *Herzog Michel*, a comedy in one act by J. C. Krüger. Wednesday, July 22, 1767. [St. LXXIII, 76.] In Krüger's works this play was described as 'ein Lustspiel von einer Handlung, nach dem ausgerechneten Glücke in den neuen Beyträgen zum Vergnügen des Verstandes und Witzes, im ersten Stücke des vierten Bandes. Zum ersten Male den 19. Januar 1750 in Leipzig aufgeführet' (*J. C. Krügers poetische und theatralische Schriften*, herausg. von J. F. Löwen, Leipzig, 1763, p. 447). *Das ausgerechnete Glück* was by J. Adolf Schlegel and is based on Lafontaine's *La laitière et le pot au lait* (*Fables*, vii, 10). The first performance of Krüger's play in Hamburg took place under Schönemann on July 24, 1750 (H. Devrient, *op. cit.* p. 177) and it is included in the latter's *Schaubühne*, v, 1751. On its long popularity—it was the most popular 'Nachspiel' of its time—see Wittekindt, *op.*

cit. pp. 81 ff., 123 ff. It will be remembered that Goethe played in it
as a student in Leipzig (*Dichtung und Wahrheit*, vii, *Werke* (Weimar ed.),
xxvii (1889), pp. 110 f.). Cast: Andreas, Borchers; Hannchen, Mad.
Löwen; Michel, Ekhof. Of Ekhof Schröder said (Meyer, *op. cit.* ii, 2,
p. 14) 'Michel, nicht so gut als Ackermann.' Repetitions were given
on January 1 (in Hanover) and October 5, 1768, and (in Hanover)
on January 17 and February 17, 1769.

50. *Die Frau, welche Recht hat*, a comedy in three acts by Voltaire.
Thursday, July 23, 1767. [St. LXXXIII, 91.] *La Femme qui a raison*,
comédie en trois actes en vers (1758). The comedy was originally
written in one act, and was played in 1748; the three-act version was
performed in 1758, and printed in 1759 (G. Bengesco, *Voltaire.
Bibliographie de ses œuvres*, Paris, 1882–90, i, pp. 47 f.). It was produced
by Ackermann in Hamburg in 1764; it had been printed at Berlin in
1762. It is in three acts; the name of the translator is not known.
There is a copy of this edition in the Hamburg Staats- und Universitätsbibliothek, and a copy of the second impression (Berlin, 1764)
in the Preussische Staatsbibliothek. Petersen (*ed. cit.* p. 254) mentions
another anonymous translation which appeared in Berlin in 1756;
this must have been of the one-act version. Cast: Hart, Ekhof; Frau
Hart, Mad. Böck; Berg, Borchers; Damis, Böck; Erise, Mad. Schulz;
Raspe, Hensel; Marthe, Mad. Mecour. Repetitions took place on
October 2, 1767, and (in Hanover) January 29, 1768. It was followed
now by 'ein Tanz' and *Ist er von Familie?*

51. *Der sehende Blinde*, a comedy in one act by Le Grand. Friday,
July 24, 1767.[1] [St. LXXXIII, 110.] *L'Aveugle clair-voyant*, comédie en
un acte et en vers (1716). The translator was 'Hr. Secretair Carl
August Suabe' (Gottsched, *Nöthiger Vorrath*, ii, p. 279)[2]; the translation
(which is in alexandrines) was published at Dresden in 1752 and at
Hamburg in 1756. A copy of each edition is in the Hamburg Staats-
und Universitätsbibliothek. In Schönemann's repertory the play
appears on June 10, 1756 (H. Devrient, *op. cit.* p. 265), but it was
possibly performed two years earlier (Meyer, ii, 2, p. 51). There is a
later version in prose (Dresden, 1777), of which a copy is also in the
Hamburg Staats- und Universitätsbibliothek. Cast: Leonore, Mad.

---

[1] For the actual programme of July 24 Lessing substitutes that of July 31. See
above, p. 54, note 1.

[2] The *Hamburgische Address-Comtoir Nachrichten* of August 3, however, states that
it was 'übersetzt von Herrn Krüger'.

Mecour; Leonore, ihre Tante, Mad. Merschy; Damon, Borchers; Leander, Böck; Doctor Saft, Merschy; Lisette, Mlle Ackermann; Caspar, Witthöft; Notarius, Hensel. It was repeated on January 28 (in Hanover), August 19, October 12, 1768, and (in Hanover) on January 20, 1769 (on the last three occasions with the title *Der hellsehende Blinde*). It was preceded on the present occasion by *Sidnei*.

52. *Der Hausvater*, a comedy in five acts by Diderot. Monday, July 27, 1767. [St. LXXXIV–XCI.] *Le Père de famille*, comédie en cinq actes en prose (1758, first played 1761). This play was translated by Lessing (*Das Theater des Herrn Diderot*, Berlin, 1760, ii, pp. 1 ff.). According to Meyer (*op. cit.* ii, 2, p. 53) it was first played in Hamburg in 1759; if so, presumably in another translation than Lessing's. A version also appeared in 1761 at Nürnberg: *Der Hausvater*, Ein Lustspiel, in fünf Aufzügen, und in ungebundener Rede. Aus dem Französischen übersetzet. Nürnberg, 1761. A copy of this version is in the Hamburg Staats- und Universitätsbibliothek. (The Preface to this translation mentions a criticism in the *Göttinger gelehrte Nachrichten*, St. 18 and 89 (1759); and the anonymous translator alleges that he received encouragement from Herr Ludewig Jakob Heyde in Nürnberg.) Assézat (*Œuvres Complètes de Diderot*, Paris, 1875–7, vii, p. 178) also mentions a later translation by Anton von Riegger, Vienna, 1777.[1] Cast: D'Orbesson, Ekhof; D'Aulnoi, Witthöft; Saint Albin, Böck; Caecilia, Mad. Löwen; Sophia, Mlle Felbrich; Germeuil, Borchers; Le Bon, Schmelz; Clairet, Mlle Ackermann; Hebert, Mad. Schmelz; La Brie, Hensel; Philipp, Merschy; Frau Papillon, Mad. Merschy. Ekhof now played the rôle—formerly Ackermann's— of D'Orbesson. Schröder (who himself played D'Orbesson for the first time in 1779) commented on Ekhof's performance (Meyer, *op. cit.* ii, 2, p. 20): 'Vollkommen. Ich hätte mich nicht mit ihm messen mögen' while the *Hamburgische Unterhaltungen*, vii, i (Jan. 1769), p. 89, said that 'Herr Eckhof spielte den Hausvater mit einer Einsicht und mit einem Gefühl, das Kenner und Nichtkenner bewundern'. Repetitions took place on July 30, October 19, November 13, 1767, in Hanover on February 11, February 18, and May 5, in Hamburg on June 2, August 9, August 24, October 26, 1768, and in Hanover on January 27, 1769.

[1] This translation, however, is mentioned in a letter from J. G. von Laudes to A. von Riegger printed at the end of the latter's adaptation *Pamela als Mutter* (Wien, 1771, pp. [84–5]). The letter is dated May 6, 1764 and refers to von Riegger's translation of *Der Hausvater* 'schon vor einigen Jahren' (p. [84]).

CHAPTER III

LESSING'S EARLIER DRAMATURGIC JOURNALS

In view of Lessing's future activity as a critic, theorist and reformer of the drama, critics have liked to underline his fondness for Terence and Plautus in his St Afra schooldays and his active interest in the theatre of Caroline Neuber during his student years in Leipzig. It is questionable, however, whether these were more than generally symptomatic of a young man of genius, whose bent was towards plastic artistic expression in contrast to the abstractions of learning and scholarship. Lessing was, indeed, already trying his hand at writing plays, aspiring in his heart to be a 'German Molière'.

THE 'BEYTRÄGE ZUR HISTORIE UND AUFNAHME DES THEATERS'

To find a starting-point for the author of the *Hamburgische Dramaturgie* it is hardly necessary to go back beyond his *Beyträge zur Historie und Aufnahme des Theaters*, the preface of which is dated October 1749. His journalistic activity had, however, begun about a year earlier in the *Berlinische privilegirte Zeitung*, when he was nineteen. Accepting the articles which Muncker prints in his edition of Lessing[1] as his contributions to that newspaper, it is interesting to see to what extent they are devoted to drama and the theatre, and thus foreshadow the journal which Lessing and his friend Christlob Mylius launched in 1750.

In these reviews we find Lessing interesting himself in pantomime: he discusses Samuel Geissler's *Abhandlung von den Pantomimen* (1749); he recalls the performances of Nicolini's company of juvenile actors, who in the summer of 1748 in Leipzig had 'die Bewunderung vieler tausend Zuschauer auf sich gezogen, daselbst mehr als einen Freund des Theaters angereizet, etwas von den Pantomimen der Alten aufzusetzen und herauszugeben', and in his criticism of Geissler's book he shows that he had been actively inquiring into the nature of pantomime.[2] There is a notice of the latest French tragedy, Crébillon's *Catilina*, which is commended for containing 'keinen tragischen Helden nach der gewöhnlichen Mechanik des Theaters',[3] and of a volume of the

---

[1] *Schriften*, iv, pp. 5 ff.   [2] *Ibid.* pp. 13 f.   [3] *Ibid.* pp. 15 ff.

Deutsche Schaubühne zu Wienn, published in 1749;[1] while the extracts given from the French journal *La Bigarure*—the 'recht angenehmes Blatt' which was also drawn upon in the *Beyträge*—deal with Crébillon and Voltaire.[2] Perhaps the most interesting thing about these early reviews is to see how the young writer who had made his début under the ægis of Gottsched, was gradually—with the encouragement, no doubt, of the attacks on the latter made by Bodmer and Georg Friedrich Meier—sharpening his weapons against his master.

In the *Beyträge*,[3] however, Lessing plainly indicates that his object is to prepare the way for Gottsched's promised 'Historie des Theaters'; he desired to supplement the materials which Gottsched had been accumulating in his *Deutsche Schaubühne*.[4] That critic's periodicals, the *Beyträge zur critischen Historie der deutschen Sprache, Poesie und Beredsamkeit* (1732–44), and more particularly its successor, *Neuer Büchersaal der schönen Wissenschaften und freyen Künste* (1745–50)[5]—both in large measure modelled on the *Journal des Sçavans*—defined more or less the form of Lessing's journal. It is true, Lessing reproached his

---

[1] *Ibid.* pp. 37 f. Muncker considers Lessing's authorship to be doubtful.

[2] *Ibid.* pp. 39 f., 42 f. Cp. Th. W. Danzel and G. E. Guhrauer, *G. E. Lessing. Sein Leben und seine Werke*, 2nd ed. Berlin, 1880–81, i, pp. 509, 513 f.; Muncker regards Lessing's authorship of the reviews as doubtful.

[3] See my 'Notes on Lessing's *Beiträge zur Historie und Aufnahme des Theaters*' in the *Modern Language Review*, viii, 1913, pp. 511 ff. and ix, 1914, pp. 213 ff. The present section is a revised summary of the results there arrived at. The title of Lessing's journal was perhaps suggested by Bodmer's anti-Gottschedian *Critische Betrachtungen und freye Untersuchungen zum Aufnehmen und zur Verbesserung der deutschen Schau-Bühne*, Bern, 1743 (Goedeke, *Grundriss*, iv (1) (3rd ed.), p. 11).

[4] *Schriften*, iv, pp. 54 ff. In the preface to the last (sixth) volume of the *Schaubühne* (1745) Gottsched had said: 'Künftig erwarte der geneigte Leser von mir eine Historie der Schaubühne überhaupt, und unsrer deutschen insbesondre. Mein Vorrath deutscher Schauspiele von allen Gattungen, ist nun schon über anderthalb-tausend Stücke angewachsen: und ich würde auch hier eine ziemliche Nachlese zu dem Verzeichnisse derselben mittheilen können, wenn es der Raum der Bogen zuliesse. Sie sollen aber künftig in ihrer Stelle erscheinen: nur ersuche ich die Liebhaber und Besitzer theatralischer Stücke hiermit nochmals, mir mit denjenigen Nachrichten an die Hand zu gehen, die mir etwa noch fehlen möchten'. Cp. also *Neuer Büchersaal*, i (iii), Sept. 1745, p. 287.

[5] The date 1754, given by Goedeke (*Grundriss*, iii (2nd ed.), p. 359) and others, would appear to be an error for 1750. The note "Ende des ganzen Werks" appears at the end of the third 'Register' of vol. x (1750). Moreover, the books of Messrs Breitkopf und Härtel do not show any payments to Gottsched for the *Neuer Büchersaal* after 1750, while payments for the new periodical, *Das Neueste aus der anmuthigen Gelehrsamkeit*, begin in 1751. This information was obtained through the kindness of Dr W. Schmieder, of Leipzig, who examined the ledgers of the firm.

predecessors for having reduced the German theatre to monotony by drawing their materials too exclusively from France; and he complained that the existing 'Monatsschriften' were inclined to neglect the drama.[1] This was certainly noticeable in the case of the *Neuer Büchersaal*, which had at first devoted much space to the drama, but ultimately ignored it almost entirely.

A comparison of the 'Vorrede' of Gottsched's second journal with that of Lessing's corroborates what I have said of the relations between them. Gottsched opens with an apology for adding one more to the many existing 'deutschen Monatschriften', but justifies himself on the ground of the increase of specialisation. 'Die schönen Wissenschaften und freyen Künste sind bisher noch mit keinem besondern Tagebuche versehen gewesen; und diesem augenscheinlichen Mangel, bin ich willens hierdurch einigermassen abzuhelfen' (*Neuer Büchersaal*, i, p. 7). Lessing feels a similar need of justifying his periodical; and he specifies his field as 'nur den dramatischen Theil'. Neither journal proposes to restrict itself to Germany. 'Nicht nur deutsche', says Gottsched, 'sondern auch englische, französische und italienische Sachen werden hier ihren Platz finden' (i, p. 8), and Lessing desires that his *Beyträge* shall be a contribution to the universal history of the theatre; he will not only deal with the ancient drama, but with French, Italian, English, Spanish and Dutch drama, besides, of course, that in his own tongue. Here he had clearly in view that first 'comparative' history of the theatre, Luigi Riccoboni's *Réflexions historiques et critiques sur les différens Théâtres de l'Europe*, Paris, 1738. At the same time, Greek and Latin drama was to have the chief share of attention; and the plan which Lessing lays down in this respect may have been suggested by Brumoy's *Théâtre des Grecs* (Paris, 1730).[2] Of the modern drama he goes on to say: 'Wir werden besonders unser Augenmerk auf das englische und spanische Theater richten.'[3] At this time he had no particular knowledge of, or even interest in, either of these literatures; he knew, indeed, little more than was to be gleaned from Voltaire's *Lettres Philosophiques*, where the English theatre is compared with that of Spain.[4] From Voltaire he obviously drew his list of

[1] *Schriften*, iv, p. 50.

[2] Cp. Danzel and Guhrauer, *op. cit.* i, p. 179; J. Kont, *Lessing et l'Antiquité*, Paris, 1894–9, i, pp. 63 f.

[3] *Schriften*, iv, p. 52.

[4] 'Die Engländer hatten, sowohl wie die Spanier, schon ihre Schaubühne, als die Franzosen noch auf Brettern spielten. Shakespear, der der Engländer Corneille war, blühte mit dem Lopez de Vega beynahe zu einer Zeit.' *Des Herrn von Voltaire*

English dramatists, omitting only Addison;[1] and his knowledge of Spanish drama was even hazier. With regard to Italian and Dutch drama he makes a particular reservation: 'Von den Italiänern und Holländern aber werden wir nur das, was sie regelmässiges und eigenthümliches haben, aufsuchen' (*Beyträge*, Vorrede). And the general conclusion to which this translating, criticising and comparing lead is one towards which Johann Elias Schlegel had been moving when he compared Gryphius with Shakespeare, and which Lessing himself was ultimately so brilliantly to establish: 'Das ist gewiss, wollte der Deutsche in der dramatischen Poesie seinem eignen Naturelle folgen, so würde unsre Schaubühne mehr der englischen als französischen gleichen' (*Beyträge*, Vorrede).

Lessing's partner in the editorship of the *Beyträge*, although his name is not mentioned, was his friend Christlob Mylius; but there is still uncertainty concerning the authorship of a number of items in the journal. In 1754, when Lessing replaced the *Beyträge* by the *Theatralische Bibliothek*, he wrote:

Von mir nehmlich schrieb sich nicht nur der gantze Plan jener periodischen Schrift her, so wie er in der Vorrede entworfen wird; sondern auch der grösste Theil der darinn enthaltenen Aufsätze ist aus meiner Feder geflossen.[2]

Of the contents, the *Abhandlung* on Plautus and the translation of *Die Gefangnen* are by Lessing. This has never been questioned. The editorial notes to the *Critik über die Gefangnen des Plautus* and the criticism of that *Critik* in the third and fourth parts are obviously by the translator of the *Gefangnen*; and in a letter to his father Lessing claimed the authorship of the review of Gregorius's translation of Werenfels.[3] On the other hand, we have to attribute to Mylius the translation of Machiavelli's *Clitia* and the *Untersuchung, ob man in Lustspielen die Charaktere übertreiben solle*; and the opening article, *Versuch eines Beweises, dass die Schauspielkunst eine freye Kunst sey* was also doubtless by him.[4]

Gedanken über die Trauer- und Lustspiele der Engländer, translated from Voltaire's Lettres sur les Anglois in the Beyträge zur Historie und Aufnahme des Theaters, Stuttgart, 1750, I, p. 96.

[1] Lessing mentions Shakespeare, Dryden, Wycherley, Vanbrugh, Cibber and Congreve (*Beyträge*, Vorrede). Cp. Voltaire's *Lettres sur les Anglois*, Nos. xviii and xix (where the same authors, together with Otway and Addison, are discussed).

[2] *Schriften*, vi, p. 3. [3] November 2, 1750 (*Schriften*, xvii, p. 23).

[4] Cp. preface to the *Theatralische Bibliothek* and note to the first article in that journal (*Schriften*, vi, pp. 3, 47); also preface to Mylius's *Vermischte Schriften* by Lessing (*ibid.* p. 405). Jördens, *Lexikon deutscher Dichter und Prosaisten*, iii (Leipzig, 1808), p. 774, claims for Mylius 'unter andern' the three items mentioned.

This is the most that can be said with complete certainty. The present opinion with regard to Lessing's share in the periodical depends on a categorical statement by his brother Karl Lessing in the preface to Part XXII of the first collected edition of Lessing's works (Berlin, 1794; p. iii):

> Das meiste darin sind Übersetzungen, Theils aus dem Französischen, Theils aus dem Italiänischen. Diese könnten aber, und wenn es auch wirklich ausgemacht wäre, dass sie von Lessing herrührten, keinen Platz in der gegenwärtigen Sammlung finden. Von eignen Aufsätzen hat Lessing in den Beyträgen etc. gewiss weiter nichts, als was hier daraus abgedruckt worden ist, obgleich in den so genannten Analekten etc. auch noch die Abhandlung: Versuch eines Beweises, dass die Schauspielkunst eine freye Kunst sey, ihm zugeschrieben wird.

And the works which Karl Lessing reprints are: *Das Leben des Plautus, Die Gefangnen, Critik über die Gefangnen*, and *Werenfels' Rede*. This canon has been accepted by subsequent editors; but the second Lachmann edition added the 'Vorrede',[1] and the Hempel edition the translation of François Riccoboni's *Art du Théâtre*, an ascription which Muncker has also accepted.[2]

Lessing's most substantial contribution to his first periodical is thus concerned with Plautus. He had, as we have seen, a predilection for Roman comedy in his school days;[3] and his continued interest is to be seen not merely in his contributions to the *Beyträge*, but also in his adaptation from Plautus, *Der Schatz* (1750). Further, the sketch of a drama preserved in his 'Nachlass'—*Weiber sind Weiber*—is built on motives from *Stichus*: it borrows the name 'Labrax' from the *Rudens*, and, like *Die alte Jungfer*, it is provided with a motto from Plautus. Another play, *Justin*, was planned as a version of *Pseudolus*, a drama which probably also influenced in part *Der junge Gelehrte*.[4]

Das Leben des Plautus is not a very original compilation, although it shows extensive reading. Lessing discusses the Latin poet in much the same way as he had been discussed in J. A. Fabricius's *Bibliotheca Latina* (Hamburg, 1697), or in G. E. Müller's *Historisch-critische Einleitung zu nöthiger Kenntniss und nützlichem Gebrauche der alten lateinischen Schriftsteller* (Dresden, 1747 ff.). That is to say, an account of the poet's life is followed by brief notes on the individual plays, and a list of

---

[1] On the advocacy of Danzel; cp. Danzel and Guhrauer, *op. cit.* i, pp. 177 f.
[2] *Schriften*, iv, pp. viii, 180.   [3] Cp. *Schriften*, v, p. 268.
[4] Cp. Danzel and Guhrauer, *op. cit.* i, p. 143; E. Schmidt, *Lessing*, 4th ed. (Berlin, 1923), i, p. 137.

editions of Plautus. The sources of Lessing's information are the editions of Plautus of F. Taubmann (Wittenberg, 1605), of J. Gruter (Wittenberg, 1621) and of J. Operarius, 'in usum Delphini' (Paris, 1679). His main indebtedness is, however, to the 'Dissertation préliminaire sur la vie et les œuvres de Plaute' which is prefixed to H. P. de Limiers' *Les Œuvres de Plaute en Latin et en François*, 10 vols. Amsterdam, 1719. After giving a list of editions of Plautus, Lessing passes on to discuss the modern translations of this 'Vater aller Comödienschreiber', notably Madame Dacier's (included in Limiers' collection), that of Gueudeville (also 1719, Leyden), and Coste's translation of *Les Captifs* (Amsterdam, 1716).

The *Abhandlung* is followed by a translation of the *Captivi* which apparently belongs to an earlier date. Judged by modern standards, it has no great merit; it is often awkward and crude, and inaccuracies are frequent. It is, however, more literal than the French translation by Coste, and is not disfigured by those perversions of the original in the interests of polite French taste of which Coste is guilty; and it is much more literal than Gueudeville's. Lessing's notes on the text, for the most part suggested by those to Coste's translation and by Taubmann's commentary, are meagre; but he apologises for them and promises a more detailed discussion in 'einer besondren Abhandlung'. Some of this, no doubt, passed into the reply to the *Critik*.

It has hitherto been accepted, as we have seen, that the *Critik über die Gefangnen des Plautus* is not what it professes to be, the contribution of an outsider, but that it was written by Lessing himself. Lessing, it is urged, adopted a device familiar in the journalism of the time from the *Spectator* onwards, in order to give variety to the contents of his journal; instead of publishing the promised criticism of Plautus's comedy, he introduced an element of piquancy by throwing his ideas into a form of criticism ostensibly hostile to himself. But a careful scrutiny of the *Critik* shows that it could not be from Lessing's pen. Even external characteristics of language and style point against Lessing's authorship. Danzel, who recognised the difference of style,[1] admired the skill with which Lessing converted himself for the occasion into a good Gottschedian; although, as a matter of fact, the Lessing of the *Beyträge* was more orthodox in this respect than his co-editor Mylius. Danzel quotes a single phrase that reminds him of Gottsched; but there are many expressions and stylistic turns that are foreign to Lessing at this time. Further, the whole criticism is put together so

[1] Cp. Danzel and Guhrauer, *op. cit.* i, p. 181.

clumsily and with so little of that logical method which was characteristic of Lessing, even in his beginnings, that this alone speaks against
his authorship.[1] The same writer could not have written both the
Critik and the reply to it. Apparently Karl Lessing, seeing that his
brother had promised a 'besondre Abhandlung', hastily assumed that
the *Critik* was the fulfilment of that promise.

The author of the *Critik*—and I am unable to offer any conjecture
as to his identity—makes no pretence to classical scholarship, and
does not venture to criticise Lessing on this ground; but he had a wide
knowledge of French literature on the theatre—wider, no doubt, than
Lessing as yet possessed—and his mode of attack is to confront Lessing
with arguments mainly drawn from French sources. He assumes that
Lessing only knew Coste's translation by repute, being clearly unaware
that the second edition (which he regrets Coste has never published)
had actually appeared in Limiers' work.[2] The critic was evidently
not acquainted with the latter.

The reply which Lessing makes to the *Critik*[3] is distinctly the best
piece of critical writing in the volume; here Lessing begins already
to emerge as a master of his craft. He sums up his opponent's attack
on Plautus as being concerned with three things: 'Kunst, Witz und
Moral'; and he considers each of these in turn. Beginning with the
last, he takes his stand on the opinion maintained by Brumoy,[4] that
an author's morality must be judged by the standard of his own time
and contemporaries. Turning to the second point, Lessing states that
he shares the abhorrence of the classical critics for the 'Wortspiel'—
condemned by Boileau, for instance, and by Gottsched in his *Critische
Dichtkunst*—and he exonerates Plautus, as Gottsched had exonerated
Virgil for a pun in his *Eclogues*: 'Allein der Poet kann leicht damit
entschuldiget werden, dass er sein Räthsel in den Mund eines einfältigen Schäfers leget, der auf dem Dorfe leicht etwas für schön halten

---

[1] Iti s perhaps worth noting that C. H. Schmid in his life of Plautus in *Biographie
der Dichter*, i (Leipzig, 1769), pp. 220 f., has no suspicion that the *Critik* might be by
Lessing; he says the volume of the *Beyträge* contains a criticism, 'die sehr* viele
Kleinigkeiten tadelt, das beleidigte Costüme, und die verschwiegne Ursache von
Stalagmus Ankunft ausgenommen, und eine Widerlegung dieser Kritik, die desto
leichter fiel, je seichter die Kritik selbst war'.

* (selbst die schleunige Zurückkunft des Philokrates rechne ich dahin).

[2] *Schriften*, iv, pp. 138 f.; *Beyträge, ed. cit.* iii, pp. 379 f.

[3] *Schriften*, iv, pp. 171 ff., 180 ff.; *Beyträge*, iii, pp. 429 ff., 573 ff.

[4] *Discours sur la Comédie grecque* in Brumoy, *Théâtre des Grecs*, Paris, 1730, iii,
pp. xxxvi ff.

konnte, was doch Virgil selbst für was schlechtes hielte.'[1] Lessing takes the opportunity of making an appeal for realism in the theatre, which was coming into favour with the importation of English tragedies of common life; and he appears still more as an advocate of this type of drama when he claims it as a merit (*Schriften*, iv, p. 191) that the 'empfindliche Seele' will say with Hegio: 'Was für grossmüthige Seelen! Sie pressen mir Thränen aus.'

Lessing deals also with the arguments concerning the 'mechanische Einrichtung' (*ibid.* pp. 185 ff.)—arguments which had been so damaging to his claim for the superlative excellence of the *Captivi*. He calls in Houdart de la Motte's 'unité de l'intérêt',[2] to meet the criticism that Plautus had unnecessarily complicated the action by making Tyndarus a son of Hegio; and to mitigate the offence against the unity of time, he falls back on Coste's own defence[3] that the two places in Aetolia and Elis might be thought of as lying not far from the boundary between the two provinces. Further, he maintains that a certain latitude must be allowed to a poet in the matter of the time-unity, especially when he is skilful enough to arrange his plot so that the audience do not easily perceive it.[4] From all of this it may be inferred that Lessing had not yet progressed beyond the classical attitude to the unity of time and that he was in agreement with Corneille. After defending the use of asides on the ground of the spaciousness of the Roman stage—an argument set forth and dealt with by Ménardière[5]—Lessing concludes by once more asserting 'dass dieses Stück das schönste sey, welches jemals auf das Theater gekommen ist', on the ground that it conforms most closely to the purpose of comedy (*ibid.* p. 191). As a subsidiary virtue he claims one which Voltaire—and also Luigi Riccoboni and Calepio—had extolled in tragedy, namely, that Plautus 'die gereinigte Moral, welche durch das ganze Stück herrscht, nicht durch den allzuzärtlichen Affect der Liebe geschwächt hat' (*ibid.* p. 192).

The translations from the French and Italian in the *Beyträge* may be

---

[1] *Critische Dichtkunst*, i, chap. vii, ed. of 1737, p. 238.

[2] *Premier Discours sur la Tragédie* (see Houdart de la Motte, *Oeuvres*, Paris, 1754, iv, p. 37).

[3] In Limiers' edition, vol. ii (Amsterdam, 1719), p. 204 (Dissertation sur la Durée de l'action des *Captifs*).

[4] Cp. D'Aubignac, *La Pratique du Théâtre*, Amsterdam, 1715, ii, chap. vii, i, pp. 113 f.

[5] *La Poëtique de Jules de la Mesnardiere* (Pilet de la Mesnardiere), Paris, 1640, chap. ix, pp. 269 ff.

summarily disposed of. That of two of Voltaire's *Lettres philosophiques*
is almost certainly by Mylius.[1] That of Corneille's *Trois Discours*
(which had also been previously translated into German[2]) I have, in
an article already cited,[3] claimed for Lessing—or if not the entire
translation, at least some share in it. For there is a noticeable improvement in quality between the translation of the first *Discours* and
that of the other two; and this difference is further emphasised by the
fact that the first was evidently translated from the 1663 [1664] Paris
edition of the *Théâtre de Corneille* (or a Dutch reprint of this). The
translator reproduces here the phrase of the earlier editions (1660
and 1663): 'Je hasarderai quelque chose sur trente ans de travail
pour la scène'; whereas a later edition (1668) has 'quarante', and
the final editions have 'cinquante'.[4] For the last *Discours*, as will be
seen from a comparison of the textual variants, a later edition was
used.[5] If Lessing is not responsible for the whole translation, may not
Mylius and he have shared it? Perhaps the best argument in favour
of Lessing's authorship is the fact that, seventeen years later, when he
had occasion to discuss Corneille in the *Hamburgische Dramaturgie*, he
turned to this old translation and quoted it often quite literally, or at
most with very little alteration or improvement.[6]

Boxberger's plea for Lessing's authorship of the translation of

---

[1] It was not the first translation. Cp. the criticism of Lessing's periodical in the
Berlinische Bibliothek, iv, i, 1750, p. 138: 'Man hat zwar schon eine Übersetzung
dieser Gedanken in der *Samlung verschiedener Briefe des H. von Voltair, die Engelländer
und andere Sachen betreffend*. Aus dem französischen übersetzt und mit einigen
Anmerkungen begleitet von N**. Jena, 1747. 8. S. 273–300. Allein jene hat den
Vorzug vor dieser und ist mit einer Critick begleitet.'

[2] *Herrn P. Corneilles Gedancken von den Schauspielen*, Hamburg, without date.
The translator was Friedrich Georg Behrmann, a native of Hamburg, and author
of *Timoleon* and *Die Horatier*, which were performed in Hamburg by Caroline
Neuber's company. (See F. Heitmüller, *Hamburgische Dramatiker zur Zeit Gottscheds*,
ed. cit. p. 34, and Schütze, *Hamburgische Theatergeschichte*, ed. cit. pp. 221 ff., 225 ff.)

[3] *Modern Language Review*, ix, pp. 214 ff.

[4] See *Œuvres de Corneille*, ed. Marty-Laveaux (in Régnier, *Les Grands Écrivains de
la France*), Paris, 1862, i, p. 16. (But cp. also *Hamburgische Dramaturgie*, LXXV, 101
'funfzig Jahre'; see below, p. 364, note 1.) Other variants exclude the edition of
1660: *Beyträge*, p. 59: 'befürchten', translating 'craindre' (1660: 'prendre garde'
Œuvres, ed. cit. i, p. 18); *Beyträge*, p. 64: 'ersetzen', translating 'suppléer' (1660:
'réparer', *Œuvres*, i, p. 23).

[5] Cp. *Beyträge*, p. 551: 'Ammon' (in the earlier eds. of Corneille, including that
of 1668, 'Timante', *Œuvres, ed. cit.* i, p. 103). Cp. also *Beyträge*, p. 556 and *Œuvres*,
i, p. 107.

[6] Cp. particularly the Corneille quotations in St. LXXV, LXXXII and LXXXIII of
the *Dramaturgie* with the *Beyträge*, pp. 221 f., 215, 74. See also below, p. 377.

François Riccoboni's *L'Art du Théâtre*, Paris, 1750,[1] is convincing. The version is quite on a level with that of the last *Discours* of Corneille. Lessing wrote to his father on November 2, 1750 (*Schriften*, xvii, p. 20):

> Ich habe...das ganze vierte Stück der theatr. Beyträge besorgen müssen, was eigentlich schon diese Messe hätte sollen fertig werden, und diese Arbeit hat mich bis an vergangnen Sonnabend nicht über eine Stunde Herr seyn lassen.

The translation of Machiavelli's *Clitia* in St. III is by Mylius. In the 'Vorbericht des Übersetzers' he apologised for offering this translation (*Beyträge, ed. cit.* III, p. 298):

> Fragt man mich, warum ich nicht lieber ein gutes, als ein mittelmässiges Stück, gewählet habe? so bitte ich, mir erst ein gutes Stück von dem italienischen Theater zu nennen. Ich weis die Antwort hierauf, ohne sie zu hören. Man wird sagen: so hätte ich ja das Übersetzen aus dem italienischen Theater gar können bleiben lassen.

Mylius was here merely expressing an opinion that was generally held by the French critics—an echo, no doubt, of the anti-Italian trend in the 'Querelle des anciens et des modernes'. D'Aubignac, for instance, had said:

> Il ne faut pas dire non plus que la Comédie des Italiens ait pris la place de celles de Plaute et de Terence, car ils n'en ont gardé ni la matiere ni la forme....Et je m'étonne comment il est arrivé que les enfans des Latins soient si peu sçavans en l'Art de leurs Peres.[2]

Lessing, however, was indignant at this depreciation of the Italians, with the result that their partnership was dissolved. But at this time he knew little more about Italian comedy than Mylius, and had been moved to anger by the fact that Luigi Riccoboni wrote his *Histoire du Théâtre italien* (Paris, 1728–31) to refute just such opinions. In that work Riccoboni says (*ed. cit.* i, pp. 149 f.):

> La *Clitia* est prise de la *Casina* de Plaute, mais la *Mandragola* est toute de l'invention de l'Auteur: c'est une des bonnes Comédies que nous aïons, mais je ne voudrois pas dire qu'elle fut la meilleure. Parmi un nombre de

---

[1] See the Hempel edition of Lessing's *Werke*, xi (i), pp. xv f.

[2] *Pratique du Théâtre*, ii, chap. x, *ed. cit.* i, p. 132; or, for that matter, Mylius may be only re-echoing Gottsched's views, *Critische Dichtkunst*, ii, chap. xi, ed. of 1737, p. 695: 'Und in der That hat man aus der Erfahrung gesehen, dass das italienische Theater seit etlichen Jahrhunderten gar nichts kluges hervorgebracht hat. Ihre beste Comödien enthalten nichts, als Romanstreiche, Betrügereyen der Diener, und unendlich viel abgeschmackte Narrenpossen.'

très-bonnes Comédies qui sont dans mon Catalogue, il y en a plusieurs qui pourroient lui disputer cet avantage et même l'emporter. Un Auteur François s'est hazardé de dire dans un Livre imprimé depuis quelques années, que les Italiens n'ont d'autre Comédies que la *Mandragola*: il seroit à souhaiter qu'il eût lû les bonnes Pièces de ce Catalogue, il n'auroit pas dit que la *Mandragola* est la seule Pièce ni même la meilleure Pièce que nous aïons.

Danzel hazarded the opinion that the reports on the theatre in Paris might have been sent in by Melchior Grimm, with whom Mylius had come into personal contact in Leipzig.[1] Footnotes to the first two articles explain that they are 'nicht von uns'—that is to say, not by Lessing or Mylius.[2] As a matter of fact, they are merely translations from a new journal published by Pierre Gosse at the Hague, entitled: *La Bigarure, ou Meslange curieux, instructif et amusant de Nouvelles, de Critique, de Morale, de Poèsies, et autres matières de Littérature, d'Evénements singuliers et extraordinaires, d'Avantures galantes, d'Histoires secrettes, et de plusieurs autres Nouveautés amusantes, avec des Réflexions Critiques sur chaque Sujet*, La Haye, 1749. The extracts in the *Beyträge* are from 'Lettres d'une Dame de Paris, à une Dame de ses Amies', that in the first number being from *La Bigarure*, i, pp. 8–16 and iii, pp. 26 f. and 29 ff. The corresponding article in the second part comes mainly from Nos. vi and ix of the French journal.[3] The fact that Lessing was familiar with the *Bigarure* gives some ground for inferring that these articles were translated by him. In a review of Gottsched's new journal, *Das Neueste aus der anmuthigen Gelehrsamkeit*,[4] in the *Critische Nachrichten aus dem Reiche der Gelehrsamkeit*, Lessing—and I think there is no reason to doubt his authorship of this review—mentions the French journal; and as we have seen, two reviews of the *Bigarure* in the *Berlinische privilegirte Zeitung* in 1749 may have also been written by him.[5] The second of these, containing the story of the quarrel

[1] Danzel and Guhrauer, *op. cit.* i, p. 177, note 1.

[2] 'Wir haben diese Nachrichten von guter Hand. Die darinne gefällten Urtheile kommen nicht von uns, sondern selbst aus Paris' (*Beyträge*, 1, p. 110); 'Wir erinnern nochmals, dass die unter dieser Aufschrift befindlichen Urtheile nicht von uns herrühren, sondern aus Paris kommen' (*ibid.* 11, p. 287).

[3] The critic of the *Berlinische Bibliothek* remarked ironically (iv, i, p. 138): 'Theatralische Neuigkeiten aus Paris; von welchen die H. Verf. versichern, dass sie solche von guter Hand haben; vielleicht haben sie solche hernach auch dem Verleger der Bigarrure mitgetheilet?'

[4] *Schriften*, iv, p. 219. Cp. also B. A. Wagner, *Lessing-Forschungen*, Berlin, 1881, p. 157.

[5] See above, p. 95.

between admirers of Voltaire and Crébillon, passed over into the *Beyträge*. As will be seen, the *Bigarure* was still put under contribution in the *Hamburgische Dramaturgie*.[1]

The third article on the Paris theatres, which does not profess to come from Paris, consists almost exclusively of statistics.[2] Muncker thinks that the notices on 'Das Theater in Berlin' may have been sent in, if not contributed, by Mylius, but were probably retouched or added to by Lessing; and he quotes a number of passages in support of this view.[3] The reports of the theatres in Dresden are similar and of equally uncertain authorship. Lastly, the final item in the *Beyträge*, 'Nachricht von einem in Freyberg aufgeführten Schulschauspiel', was, according to Karl Lessing's conjecture,[4] inserted by Mylius without Lessing's knowledge; but this seems improbable. In 1754, Lessing stated that he had borne increasing responsibility for the last part of the journal.[5]

THEATRALISCHE BIBLIOTHEK

Lessing's second dramaturgic journal is more liberally represented in modern editions of his complete works than the first one. The first editor, Karl Lessing, was sparing in his selection of items for reproduction. He said:

> Man hat hier alles abdrucken lassen, was darin von Lessing selbst ist, auch das kurze Leben Jakob Thomsons, und die flüchtig hingeworfene Geschichte der englischen Schaubühne nicht ausgenommen, weil er selbst des ersteren bei anderer Gelegenheit erwähnt, und weil die letztere für den blossen Liebhaber der Litteratur noch immer brauchbar ist.[6]

He omitted everything that appeared to him to be translation—the essays by Chassiron and Gellert, and the analysis of Montiano's

---

[1] See below, pp. 467 f.

[2] I have not been able to discover a source, but the information about the 'Théâtre italien' probably came directly or indirectly from L. Riccoboni's *Nouveau Théâtre italien*, Paris, 1733 ff.

[3] *Schriften*, iv, p. 82.

[4] *G. E. Lessings Leben*, Berlin, 1793–5, i, p. 107.

[5] Cp. the passage already quoted in part (see above, p. 97) from the *Theatralische Bibliothek* (i, Berlin 1754, Vorrede): 'Von mir nehmlich schrieb sich nicht nur der gantze Plan jener periodischen Schrift [*Beyträge*] her, so wie er in der Vorrede entworfen wird; sondern auch der grösste Theil der darinn enthaltenen Aufsätze ist aus meiner Feder geflossen. Ja ich kann sagen, dass die fernere Fortsetzung nur dadurch wegfiel, weil ich länger keinen Theil daran nehmen wollte.'

[6] *Sämmtliche Schriften* (1771–94), xxii (Berlin, 1794), pp. iv f.

Virginia (but he printed the introductions to both these items); Sainte Albine's *Comédien* was excluded, as well as the translations from Riccoboni—in the case of the latter he retained only the 'Nachricht vom Verfasser'. Of the remainder of the journal he only published the 'Geschichte der englischen Schaubühne'. Lachmann omitted the *Virginia* analysis, and the translations from Riccoboni, Du Bos and Dryden. Maltzahn in his new edition of Lachmann (1854) was more liberal, restoring the *Virginia*, as well as the analyses of the three Italian plays from Riccoboni; but he omitted the article on the English stage. The third Lachmann edition by Muncker (vol. vi, 1890) reprints the *Bibliothek* in full to the end of the article on Seneca, then omits the Riccoboni and Du Bos translations, and the English article. The Hempel edition (vol. xi, i [1875]) had omitted nothing, and Boxberger in Kürschner's *Deutsche Nationalliteratur* (vol. lxii [1885]) only the translation of Du Bos. These variations in selection are largely due to the uncertainty that has hitherto prevailed as to how much in the journal may be claimed as Lessing's original composition. In point of fact, if everything is to be omitted that is merely translation, very little will be left at all.

Lessing was sole editor of the new undertaking. His difficulties with his co-editor Mylius had made the continuance of the *Beyträge* impossible; but on March 6, 1754, Mylius died in London[1]—he was on his way to America on a scientific expedition—and Lessing felt himself free to continue in his own way. The continuation of the *Beyträge* was entitled *Theatralische Bibliothek*, and its publication was transferred to the firm of C. F. Voss in Berlin—a firm with which Lessing's journalistic activity had brought him into contact.

The 'Vorrede' of eleven widely printed pages makes it clear that the new venture is a continuation of the old, but with certain modifications of the earlier programme. The plan of the *Beyträge* had been too ambitious; and Lessing is now less liberal in his promises. In his notice of the journal in the *Berlinische privilegirte Zeitung* of October 17, 1754, he wrote:

Man wird sich der Beyträge zur Historie und Aufnahme des Theaters erinnern, von welchen vor einigen Jahren vier Stück an das Licht traten. Gegenwärtige Bibliothek ist eine Fortsetzung jener Beyträge, nach einem in etwas veränderten und eingeschränkten Plane. Sie soll nehmlich kein

---

[1] See Lessing's notice in the *Berlinische privilegirte Zeitung*, March 26, 1754 (*Schriften*, v, pp. 395 f.). Cp. also E. Thyssen, *Christlob Mylius: sein Leben und Wirken*, Diss. Marburg, 1912.

Werk ohn Ende und kein blosser theatralischer Mischmasch werden, sondern wirklich eine kritische Geschichte des Theaters zu allen Zeiten und bey allen Völkern enthalten, obgleich ohne Ordnung weder nach den einen, noch nach den andern.[1]

He also proposes to give the continuation a more scholarly flavour by eliminating matter of merely ephemeral or contemporary interest; he will avoid drawing upon himself the ill-will of his colleagues either by expressing adverse opinions concerning their work, or by discriminating in his praise. Similarly, he will have nothing to say about living actors or the state of the theatre, fearing to raise jealousies and hostility—a policy he may have remembered in after years, when he was obliged to modify his third dramaturgic journal in this very respect.

Although he was chary of promises in his preface, it was not for lack of material. He had a good deal of matter in hand which had been collected or prepared for the *Beyträge*; and he repeatedly held out the promise of continuations of articles. He proposed, for instance, to come back to Thomson's dramas; to give some account of Montiano's 'Abhandlung von der spanischen Tragödie'; to discuss in detail the works of Destouches; to follow up the Seneca articles with similar articles on the Roman poet's other tragedies; to publish the lists of Italian plays in Riccoboni's *Histoire du Théâtre italien*, and discuss other works by that writer; to continue the article on Dryden.[2] In addition, we hear of his intention to print in Part IV extracts from the comedies of Goldoni, and possibly also translations of tragedies on the theme of Medea.[3]

The first number of the *Theatralische Bibliothek*, which was adorned with a portrait of James Thomson as frontispiece, appeared at the Michaelmas fair of 1754; the second number, completing Volume i, at Easter, 1755 (with the date 1754). Part III, to which a portrait of Destouches, who had been discussed in the first part, served as frontispiece, appeared at Michaelmas, 1755: but the fourth and last part not until the Easter fair of 1759 (with the date 1758).

The statement has been made, on the strength of the first article in the journal, that the *Theatralische Bibliothek* forms the theoretical background to *Miss Sara Sampson*.[4] But the *Abhandlung von dem weinerlichen*

---

[1] *Schriften*, v, p. 437.   [2] *Schriften*, vi, pp. 70, 72, 153, 167, 245, 294.

[3] Cp. letter to Mendelssohn of December 8, 1755 and letter to K. W. Ramler of December 11, 1755 (*Schriften*, xvii, pp. 46, 49).

[4] Cp. W. Oehlke, *Lessing und seine Zeit, ed. cit.* i, p. 226.

und rührenden Lustspiele stands merely on the threshold of Lessing's interest in the new type of drama; it is rather his introduction to it than a critical judgment of it. In fact, in the summer of 1756, two years after the publication of this article, and a year after *Miss Sara* had been played, Lessing was only just coming to clearness on the theoretical aspects of the 'bürgerliches Trauerspiel'.[1]

Lessing's attention was probably drawn to Chassiron's tract by Voltaire's preface to *Nanine*[2]; that by Gellert is a translation of his Leipzig inaugural address, *Pro Comoedia commovente commentatio orationi aditiali a C. F. Gellerto*, Lipsiae, 1751.[3] Apart from the material which Lessing draws from Chassiron and Gellert, his views are hardly in advance of those expressed by Voltaire in his prefaces to *Nanine* and *L'Enfant prodigue*.

The *Leben des Herrn Jacob Thomson* is Lessing's first published translation from English.[4] The original he found in Theophilus Cibber's *Lives of the Poets of Great Britain and Ireland*, London, 1753, v, pp. 190–218.[5] As a translation, this is much freer than Lessing's renderings from the French; it is often, if not exactly inaccurate, at least loose, and disfigured by Anglicisms. He shows a tendency to shirk difficulties; he also abbreviates by omitting the leisurely generalisations of the original, as well as several pages describing and criticising *The Seasons* and *The Castle of Indolence*. When, in discussing Thomson's dramas, Lessing arrives at *Agamemnon*, he takes the opportunity of citing the

---

[1] See below, p. 397.

[2] To Voltaire as to Lessing the author is only 'M.D.C.', but the name had already been revealed in the *Mercure de France*, May, 1749 (p. 125), and in Fréron's *Lettres sur quelques écrits de ce tems*, iv, London [Paris], 1752 (Lettre i, p. 5).

[3] Gellert himself published a translation in the first edition of his *Sammlung vermischter Schriften*, Leipzig, 1756. It is interesting to see how Lessing translates the Greek phrases in Gellert's oration: '$\dot{\epsilon}\nu$ $\tau\hat{\eta}$ $\dot{\epsilon}\pi\iota\tau\acute{a}\sigma\epsilon\iota$ fabulae', 'wann sich die Fabel am meisten verwirret', and '$\dot{\epsilon}\nu$ $\tau\hat{\eta}$ $\kappa\alpha\tau\alpha\sigma\tau\rho o\phi\hat{\eta}$, inueniri solet', 'wann sie sich entwickelt'.

[4] Lessing's translation of *An Impartial Foreigner's Remarks upon the Present Dispute between England and Prussia* (1753) was, as R. Koser has shown (*Preussische Staatsschriften aus der Regierungszeit Friedrichs II*, ii, Berlin, 1885, pp. 474 ff.), translated at least with the aid of a French text. The only portions of the *Leben Jacob Thomsons* which are not translation are *Schriften* vi, p. 53, l. 29 to p. 54, l. 15, p. 65, l. 27 to p. 67, l. 4 and p. 70, ll. 6–9.

[5] A *Life of Thomson* appeared in the *Brittische Bibliothek*, vi, 3 (Leipzig, with the date 1767), pp. 268 ff. J. F. von Palthen, who had prefaced his prose translation of *The Seasons* with Lessing's translation of Thomson's Life, combined with this in his second edition of 1766 the Life published in the *Brittische Bibliothek* (cp. *Jakob Thomsons Jahreszeiten*, 2te Auflage, Rostock, 1766, Vorrede).

passage from that play quoted in Cibber's essay, in the words of the anonymous German translation of 1750;[1] he also offers some criticism of the quality of this translation. But it is in fact a poor piece of work, and Lessing's encomium of it as 'treu, fliessend und stark' may be taken as further evidence of the meagreness of his knowledge of our language. The remainder of the article comes direct from Cibber with frequent abbreviations.[2] The portrait which forms the frontispiece of the volume is taken from the first volume of the edition of Thomson's *Works* published at London in 1752. Prior to this article Lessing, it might be noted, had himself begun translations of *Agamemnon* and *Tancred and Sigismunda*; and in 1756 he provided a preface for *Des Herrn Jacob Thomsons Sämtliche Trauerspiele*, Leipzig, 1756, an indifferent translation published by a learned society, 'einer gelehrten Gesellschaft zu Stralsund...die unter dem Namen der englischen noch [1780] daselbst existirt'.[3]

The *Auszug aus dem Trauerspiele Virginia des Don Augustino de Montiano y Luyando* is a translation from D'Hermilly's *Dissertation sur les Tragédies espagnoles*.[4] It is characteristic of Lessing's small interest at this time in dramatic theory that he leaves the *Dissertation* to be translated in a subsequent number of his journal and presents his readers first with the main contents of D'Hermilly's second volume, the *Exposition de Virginie, Tragédie avec la Traduction de plusieurs endroits de cette Pièce*. He implies (*Schriften*, vi, p. 72) that he has drawn his biographical materials from the 'historisches Register' appended by D'Hermilly to his volumes; but, as a matter of fact, the biography of Montiano (*ibid.* pp. 70 ff.) is a direct translation from D'Hermilly's preface (pp. xxv–xxxii).

[1] *Agamemnon, ein Trauer-Spiel*, aus dem Englischen übersetzt, Göttingen, 1750. (A copy of this translation, which was probably by J. D. Michaelis (see Holzmann und Bohatta, *Deutsches Anonymen-Lexikon 1501–1850*, i, Weimar, 1902, p. 33, No. 999) is in the Hamburg Staats- und Universitätsbibliothek.) In his *Laokoon*, chap. iv (*Schriften*, ix, p. 26) Lessing cites in English a few lines from the same speech which he quotes in the *Leben des Herrn Jacob Thomson*.

[2] Occasional errors in the transcription of English names have been perpetuated by Lessing's editors without comment. 'Wilk' (*Schriften* vi, p. 62, l. 28) should be 'Wilks'; 'Herrn Weffington' (p. 68, l. 23) 'Mrs Woffington'. Lessing corrects Cibber's 'Masinessa' (p. 62, l. 26) to 'Masinissa', but not 'Seffredi' (p. 67, l. 14) which ought to be 'Siffredi'. He writes most frequently the French form 'Sopho-nisbe'; also in translating Riccoboni and in the preface to the *Sämtliche Trauerspiele* of Thomson (*Schriften*, vii, p. 69).

[3] *Theater-Kalender auf das Jahr 1780*, Gotha, pp. 131 f. (referred to by Muncker, *Schriften*, vii, p. 66).   [4] Paris, 1754, ii, pp. 1 ff. See below, pp. 293 f.

In a note to the *Critik über die Gefangnen des Plautus* in the *Beyträge*, the author had referred to 'das ganz neue Werk, le comédien', by Sainte Albine, as one of the best books on the actor's art;[1] here Lessing says: 'Ich habe lange Zeit vorgehabt, dieses Werk des Herrn von Sainte Albine zu übersetzen.'[2] His attention was probably drawn to the book by a review in Gottsched's *Neuer Büchersaal* (vi (iv), pp. 330 ff.), in April, 1748. This article begins:

Dieser Schriftsteller, welcher der Welt bereits aus einem Memoire composé sur le Laminage bekannt ist, liefert allhier ein Werk, welches allen Schauspielern, die theils schon gegenwärtig der Bühne dienen, theils sich noch künftig derselben widmen wollen, überaus nützlich seyn wird. Es ist zu verwundern, dass uns Frankreich nicht bereits lange dergleichen Werk geliefert; und dass in einem Lande, wo man von den Schauspielern fast mehrere Vollkommenheiten fordert, als in irgend einem andern, sich noch kein Schriftsteller gefunden, der ihnen die Mittel angezeiget hätte, zu denselben zu gelangen. Wir reden hier von französischen Schriftstellern; denn des Herrn Riccoboni Tractat dell' arte rappresentativa ist der Welt schon längst bekannt. Unser gegenwärtiger Schriftsteller hat diesem Mangel glücklich abgeholfen, und wir wollen sein Werk näher betrachten.

Then follows a summary of the contents of the work similar to that which Lessing offers here, but briefer and without direct quotation. The reviewer concludes (pp. 349 f.)

Herr von St. Albine hat der Welt ein schönes Werk, und den Schauspielern ein Buch geschrieben, welches ihnen künftig unentbehrlich seyn wird. Wir freuen uns, dass ein geschicktes Mitglied der röm. kaiserl. deutschen Schaubühne in Wien, die Übersetzung desselben übernehmen, und es mit noch andern wichtigen Zusätzen, seinen deutschen Mitgehülfen zu gute bekannt machen wird.

Although the *Leben des Herrn Nericault Destouches*, which forms the fifth article of the *Theatralische Bibliothek*, cannot be described as merely a translation, like the life of Thomson, it is in point of fact little more. It is an ingenious compilation from the prefaces and other matter to be found in the edition of the works of Destouches which was published in four volumes at the Hague in 1752; and from this edition comes the portrait which adorns as frontispiece the second volume of the periodical. Dates of first performances of the plays Lessing found, no doubt, in a work such as Léris' *Dictionnaire des Théâtres*.

As in the *Beyträge* the weightiest contribution—Lessing's reply to

---

[1] *Schriften*, iv, p. 135, note.   [2] *Schriften*, vi, p. 120.

the criticism of the *Captivi*—had dealt with a classical author, so in the present periodical the most original article—one might say the only really original article—is that *Von den lateinischen Trauerspielen, welche unter dem Namen des Seneca bekannt sind*. It is to be regarded as a polemic against Brumoy's depreciation of Latin drama as compared with Greek. Lessing's method of treating his theme is accordingly similar to that of the *Théâtre des Grecs*: summaries of the plays, interspersed with translations of striking passages, are followed by 'Beurtheilungen' ('Examens') and discussions of versions of the same theme by other poets. Lessing regards Seneca as a great tragic poet in spite of his excesses and exaggerations:

Er ist mit den poetischen Farben allzuverschwenderisch gewesen; er ist oft in seiner Zeichnung zu kühn; er treibt die Grösse hier und da bis zur Schwulst; und die Natur scheinet bey ihm allzuviel von der Kunst zu haben. Lauter Fehler, in die ein schlechtes Genie niemals fallen wird![1]

He shows that Seneca is superior in certain aspects to the Greeks. He repeats the opinion which he had already expressed in discussing Plautus, that a poet must always be judged by the conditions of his own and not of a later time. Finally, he commends Seneca for his faithful observance of the unities.

It was Lessing's intention to discuss all ten plays in their accepted order, and he begins in the present article with *Hercules furens* and *Thyestes*. Setting out from Brumoy's summary of the former play, he gives a fuller and more sympathetic account of it. He does not hesitate to say of the scene in which Cerberus appears in the third act—a scene which Brumoy had brushed aside as 'rodomontades':

Die gantze deutsche Sprache—wenigstens so wie ich derselben mächtig bin,—ist zu schwach und zu arm, die meisterhaften Züge des Römers mit eben der kühnen und glücklichen Kürze auszudrücken.[2]

Apart from this, however, Lessing's critical comments are sparing. His comparison of Seneca with Euripides shows no knowledge of Euripides other than he could obtain from Brumoy; but in the section 'Unbilliges Urtheil des Pater Brumoy' he defends Seneca, with not a little of the skill of maturer years, against the French Jesuit. The section 'Von neuern Trauerspielen auf den rasenden Herkules' is

[1] *Theatralische Bibliothek*, ii, p. 39; *Schriften*, vi, p. 188.
[2] *Theatralische Bibliothek*, ii, p. 24; *Schriften*, vi, p. 179.

based on notices which Lessing found in Léris' dictionary and on Riccoboni's list of Italian plays. More curious than valuable is his 'Vorschlag für einen heutigen Dichter' of the manner in which an opera might be constructed out of Seneca's play. But it bears witness to the fresh outlook of the practical dramatist, who was not content merely to see the literature of antiquity through the eyes of the scholar. More important is the section which follows on 'Die Moral des rasenden Herkules'. Here he discusses not merely the moral which lies in the play but also that which can be read into it.

The part of Lessing's article dealing with *Thyestes* is largely taken up with a discussion of the unity of time in the spirit of the Ménage-D'Aubignac controversy concerning Terence's alleged shortcomings. The authorship of Seneca's tragedies is discussed on the basis of Brumoy, and modern versions of the *Thyestes* theme with the aid of the sources already mentioned. A last section treats of 'dem Atreus und Thyestes des ältern Hrn. von Crebillon'. Lessing's general remarks on Crébillon point partly to Léris as a source of information, partly to the introduction to the works of Crébillon. From the latter comes the characterisation of Corneille, Racine, Voltaire and Crébillon ('der Schreckliche', *Schriften*, vi, p. 233) to which Lessing comes back in the *Dramaturgie* (LXXIV, 44). His chief criticism of Crébillon's play is that it is 'too new-fashioned':

...dass er die Haupthandlung mit einer unnöthigen Episode, und zwar mit einer verliebten Episode, geschwächt, und das Ganze durch die Einführung so vieler Vertrauten, welches immer nichts anders als sehr frostige Personen sind, die bloss die Monologen müssen vermeiden helfen, matt gemacht habe.[1]

The article concludes with a translation of a couple of pages from Crébillon's own preface.

The eighth article of the *Theatralische Bibliothek*—probably a heritage from the *Beyträge*—is a virtually complete translation of volume 1 of Luigi Riccoboni's *Histoire du Théâtre italien depuis la décadence de la Comédie latine*, Paris, 1728. Lessing prefaces his translation with a 'Nachricht vom Verfasser' which is compiled partly from information obtained from the book itself and partly from Léris' article on Riccoboni. The extracts from the three Italian dramas which follow are translated—with the abbreviation of occasional sentences—from the second volume of Riccoboni's *Histoire*, Paris, 1731. The entire third

---

[1] *Theatralische Bibliothek*, ii, p. 129; *Schriften*, vi, p. 240.

part of the *Bibliothek* is occupied with a translation of the seventeen chapters which constitute the third volume of Du Bos' *Réflexions critiques sur la Poésie et sur la Peinture*.[1]

The opening article of the fourth part, which, however, did not appear until 1758, is a *Geschichte der englischen Schaubühne*. It is not now-a-days disputed that this contribution was written by Nicolai. The last attempt to claim it, or part of it, for Lessing was made in the Hempel edition, but on quite inadequate grounds; and although Boxberger reprinted it in his edition in Kürschner's *Deutsche National-literatur*, he did not dispute Nicolai's authorship. In point of fact, Nicolai himself inserted the following note in a letter written by himself to Lessing on August 31, 1756 (*Lessings Sämmtliche Schriften*, xxvii (Berlin, 1794), p. 415):

Dieser mein Entwurf blieb ungedruckt. Lessing rückte ihn nachher in seine theatralische Bibliothek (Th. iv, S. 3) ein, woraus er in Lessings sämmtlichen Schriften (Th. xxiii, S. 269) [*als ein Aufsatz von Lessing*—these five words do not appear in the 1794 edition, but are inserted in the 2nd edition, xxvii (Berlin, 1809), p. 99] wieder abgedruckt worden ist.

It must not be forgotten, however, that the conditions of journalistic collaboration in the eighteenth century, especially where unsigned articles were concerned, were such that it would be rash to deny Lessing all share in putting Nicolai's article into shape. It is possible that Lessing made some additions to the article out of his own know-ledge—in particular, information (probably gleaned from the *Monthly Review*) about the latest period. For the rest, Nicolai's essay is virtually a translation from Dodsley's *Select Collection of Old Plays*, 12 vols, London, 1744, and Theophilus Cibber's *Lives of the Poets of Great Britain and Ireland*, 5 vols, London, 1753.

The second item in the fourth part also concerns the English drama; it is the first instalment of what was apparently intended to be a series of studies *Von Johann Dryden und dessen dramatischen Werken*. In 1753 Gottsched had made an appeal for a translation of Dryden's *Essay of Dramatic Poesy*.[2] On December 18, 1756, we find Lessing writing to

---

[1] Lessing's translation was reprinted in the *Historisch-kritische Beyträge zur Aufnahme der Musik*, edited by F. W. Marpurg, vol. ii (Berlin, 1756), v, vi; iii (1757), i, iii, iv, v; iv (1758), ii, iv, vi; v (1760), i, iii, iv. A German translation of Du Bos' entire work (of which this third volume was added in the second edition, 1733) appeared at Copenhagen in 1760–61. The translator was G. Funcke.

[2] Cp. *Das Neueste aus der anmuthigen Gelehrsamkeit*, Leipzig, 1753, ii, pp. 134 f.; also iii, pp. 212 ff. (*Drydens Gedanken von der englischen und französischen Schaubühne,*

Mendelssohn: 'Bitten Sie doch den Hrn. Nicolai in meinem Nahmen, mir mit ehestem denjenigen Theil von Cibbers Lebensbeschreibung der englischen Dichter zu schicken, in welchem Drydens Leben steht. Ich brauche ihn.'[1] For all that Lessing seems to have drawn from Cibber, however—the sparse biographical items in his opening paragraph—he might never have consulted the book. He passes at once to the essay, of which he used the edition: '*Of Dramatick Poesie, an Essay*. By John Dryden. London, 1693.' In his translation Lessing abbreviates considerably the earlier pages of the essay; but when he reaches his discussion of the drama, his text becomes an almost unbroken reproduction of the original. Occasional sentences and references are omitted which deal too specially with English poets (Ben Jonson, Cleveland, etc.), or discuss in detail English plays. Dryden's 'Examen of the Silent Woman' (ed. of 1693, pp. 33 ff.) is in great part omitted or reserved for discussion on another occasion (*Schriften*, vi, p. 291), only a few paragraphs dealing with humour and the use of rhyme being retained. The translation is accurate and shows an advance over that of Thomson's life; only occasionally do slips occur where Lessing has not understood literary references. The importance of this translation, as marking a stage in the development of Lessing's understanding for the English drama and its greater freedom in comparison with that of France, cannot be over-emphasised. Dryden, in fact, may have provided the immediate inspiration for the bold plea for Shakespeare in the seventeenth *Litteraturbrief*.

The last hundred and seventy pages of the *Theatralische Bibliothek* are occupied with a translation of *Entwürfe ungedruckter Lustspiele des italiänischen Theaters* from the *Dictionnaire des Théâtres de Paris*, by the brothers Claude and Frédéric Parfaict (7 vols, Paris, 1756).

This examination of Lessing's first two dramaturgic journals has led to more negative conclusions than have hitherto been accepted, in respect of Lessing's interest in dramatic theory. The *Beyträge* and the *Theatralische Bibliothek* show that he was mainly interested in the outward history of the drama, in Plautus and Seneca—and as has been seen, his criticism of these two authors outweighs in original value all the other contributions contained in either part—in the

---

aus einer Vorrede). A 'Leben Johann Drydens' formed part of the contents of the *Neue Erweiterungen der Erkenntniss und des Vergnügens*, which Lessing noticed in the *Berlinische privilegirte Zeitung* of May 26, 1753 (*Schriften*, v, p. 169), and there is a 'Vie de Dryden' in the *Journal étranger* of August, 1755, pp. 112 ff.

[1] *Schriften*, xvii, p. 86.

history of the Italian theatre, in the dramatists Thomson, Destouches, Montiano. His critical interests, such as they were, were directed rather to the art of acting, as elucidated by François Riccoboni and Sainte Albine, or the theatrical representations of the ancients (as treated in Du Bos' third volume). Dramatic theory thus occupies a very subordinate place. His interest in the new form of tragedy which he himself with *Miss Sara Sampson* had established on the German stage is particularly meagre. Aristotle's name does not occur except in the *Critik über die Gefangnen des Plautus*—of which Lessing was not the author—and in translations in the second periodical—notably, of course, in that of Dryden's *Essay*.

Nor do Lessing's writings, other than those contained in the two journals, materially supplement these. Of the many notices and reviews of books which he contributed to the *Berlinische privilegirte Zeitung* and other journals down to the year 1756, a negligible proportion—not more than three per cent.—deals with literary aesthetics, the drama, or the theatre. He had occasion to review briefly Voltaire's *Amélie*, translations of Crébillon's *Idomenée* and Mme de Grafigny's *Cénie*, Marivaux' *Théâtre*, and a few indifferent German plays;[1] in 1753 he noticed briefly a translation of Le Bossu's *Sur le poème épique* and Curtius's version of Aristotle's *Poetics*;[2] and in 1756, as we have seen, he provided an introduction to Thomson's tragedies.[3] Of greater interest for his subsequent development is his discussion of Batteux' *Beaux Arts réduits à un même principe* in German translation and Diderot's *Lettre sur les sourds et muets*.[4] The significance of these two critics for Lessing's dramatic theories I shall have occasion to discuss in my third part.

---

[1] *Schriften*, v, pp. 14 f., 17 f., 168 f., 403 f.
[2] *Ibid*. pp. 193 ff.   [3] *Schriften*, vii, pp. 66 ff.
[4] *Schriften*, iv, pp. 413 ff.

CHAPTER IV

LESSING'S ASSOCIATION WITH
THE NATIONAL THEATRE

Essential to the scheme of the Hamburg organisers was an official 'theatre poet', a man of letters who could be depended upon to supply the theatre with new pieces, provide translations or adaptations of desirable foreign works, lend a helping hand with prologues and epilogues on formal occasions and generally advise on the choice of the repertory. The German theatre did not forget the advantage it had gained from the co-operation of Gottsched in Leipzig; and the 'Principals' of the intervening period had usually had some man of literary pretensions attached to their companies. Thus with Schönemann was associated Johann Christian Krüger; while Löwen himself, and, after his dismissal, Ast, had filled this post for Ackermann in the period immediately preceding the National Theatre.

That the Consortium with its ambitious plans should have thought of securing Lessing's co-operation is not difficult to understand; his name had wide resonance in the literary world; and his reputation as a dramatist, even before *Minna von Barnhelm*, was high. Of his contemporaries, Weisse would have been a more satisfactory theatre poet; he was much more prolific. But Lessing had the advantage that in his two earlier journals he had shown himself eager to further the interests of the theatre in other ways besides writing plays. It was resolved then that he should be invited. Wessely, a Jewish merchant in Hamburg, was apparently commissioned in November to sound him in the matter in Berlin. Lessing was in a mood to be approached. He had been relieved of his secretaryship in Breslau and had returned to Berlin in January, 1765, by way of Kamenz and Leipzig; and in Berlin he had resolved to settle until he had completed his *Laokoon* and *Minna von Barnhelm*. He then seems to have harboured some vague plans of travel; he thought of Vienna, Italy, perhaps even Greece, for whose art the *Laokoon* had awakened in him a warm interest. These plans were not realised, however, although in the autumn he did accompany a young nobleman, Leopold von Brenkenhof, to Pyrmont, returning by way of Göttingen, Kassel and Halberstadt. Meanwhile, two prospects of future employment came to nought. He was invited

to a chair in the University of Königsberg, but declined it, as he would
have been obliged every year to deliver a eulogy on the king of Prussia;
and a librarianship in the Royal Library of Berlin—a post that would
have been very much to his taste—was refused him in 1766 by
Frederick the Great, who naturally preferred a Frenchman and had
possibly not forgotten Lessing's undiplomatic quarrel with Voltaire
fifteen years before. This rejection was a bitter disappointment to
Lessing, and made him particularly ready to consider an invitation
that came from outside Berlin. His interest in the practical side of
the theatre, it is true, had been temporarily eclipsed by the aesthetic
studies to which *Laokoon* had led him;[1] but now, when he had a new
play practically complete, this interest was not difficult to reawaken.
Indeed, the prospect of close association with a stage of such serious
intention as that of Hamburg must have been alluring. 'Ich stand
eben am Markte und war müssig; niemand wollte mich dingen: ohne
Zweifel, weil mich niemand zu brauchen wusste; bis gerade auf diese
Freunde!' (CI–CIV, 28.)

The negotiations progressed favourably, and early in December
Lessing went for a few weeks to Hamburg to investigate the matter
on the spot. He had been there once before, in May, 1756, when he
visited Klopstock and made the acquaintance of Ekhof. This acquaintance was, no doubt, an additional inducement to accept the
engagement now. To his brother Karl he wrote on December 22:

Ich kann Dir nur erst so viel melden, dass die bewusste Sache, derentwegen ich hauptsächlich hier bin, einen sehr guten Gang nimmt, und dass
es nur auf mich ankömmt, sie mit den vortheilhaftesten Bedingungen zu
schliessen. Allein Du kennst mich, dass der klingende Vortheil bey mir
eben nicht der vornehmste ist; und solchemnach äussern sich andre
Bedenklichkeiten, derentwegen ich erst beruhigt seyn muss, ehe ich mich
völlig bestimme.[2]

The main difficulty which made Lessing hesitate to accept the
invitation was one for which he felt it necessary to apologise at some
length at the close of his journal. He could not bind himself to turn
out plays regularly: 'no one in the world', he said (CI–CIV, 68), 'is
less suited than I to be a workman who has to supply a theatre with
novelties.' The Lessing who could not be a Prussian professor because
he felt unable to eulogise officially the king of Prussia, was nothing if
not conscientious. But the Consortium does not seem to have laid

---

[1] To Gleim he wrote on February 1, 1767, of his 'fast erloschene Liebe zum
Theater' (*Schriften*, xvii, p. 228).   [2] *Schriften*, xvii, p. 226.

weight on this objection; they rightly decided that his name would lend prestige to their undertaking. And so, without apparently any very clear formulation of his duties, Lessing was engaged at a salary of 800 talers (about £180). To Gleim he wrote, in the letter which has just been quoted, that the Hamburg theatre had made a kind of agreement with him 'welches mir auf einige Jahre ein ruhiges und angenehmes Leben verspricht.... Ich will meine theatralischen Werke, welche längst auf die letzte Hand gewartet haben, daselbst vollenden, und aufführen lassen.' Thus, without having it definitely in his contract, he did hope to satisfy his employers' wishes and contribute to their repertory. *Minna von Barnhelm* was immediately available, although its performance, through no fault of the theatre, was delayed for five months, the official Prussian resident in Hamburg having raised political difficulties. He resolved to finish *Der Schlaftrunk*, which had been sketched in the preceding year, and he set to work in Hamburg on a new drama, *Die Matrone von Ephesus*.[1]

What then were Lessing's official functions in Hamburg to be? If he were not under contract to produce plays, how could he be effectively employed? There could be no question of his taking a hand in the management of the theatre, for that was Löwen's province. At most, perhaps, he could help in engaging actors and advise on the choice of plays, for he was given a seat on the managing committee. But this was vague, and hardly sufficient to justify the outlay of 800 talers a year. 'Endlich,' he tells us, 'fiel man darauf, selbst das, was mich zu einem so langsamen, oder, wie es meinen rüstigern Freunden scheinet, so faulen Arbeiter macht, selbst das, an mir nutzen zu wollen: die Critik. Und so entsprang die Idee zu diesem Blatte.' (CI–CIV, 94.) The suggestion of this way out of the difficulty was, no doubt, Löwen's. He himself in 1752 had written 'Bemerkungen', which were not, however, published, on the performances of Schönemann's company in Hamburg;[2] and since then he had been largely concerned as an active journalist with theatre criticism. It says a good deal for the sincerity of purpose with which Löwen undertook his directorship that he courted criticism, and had no fear that difficulties might arise, such as had led to his own quarrel with Ackermann. The employment of a critic to conduct a journal published at the expense of the theatre he was to criticise was indeed a curious innovation. 'Theatre poets' were already familiar both in

[1] *Schriften*, iii, pp. 414 ff., 439 ff.; cp. *Dramaturgie*, xxxvi, 15.
[2] Cp. O. D. Potkoff, *op. cit.* pp. 34 ff.

Germany and elsewhere; Lessing himself refers (CI–CIV, 70) to Goldoni's work in this capacity in Italy.[1] But no theatre in Europe had yet ventured to appoint an official whose function lay in criticising itself. Criticism did not, however, necessarily mean discouraging and unfriendly condemnation, and the Consortium probably found Lessing willing to agree to be helpful. Seyler may have been dubious about Löwen's idea, yet he could not but see the advertising value of such a periodical, if properly conducted; it would help to attract the public to the theatre. The advantages of theatrical criticism, as it had been developed in the French and English press, and (in imitation) in the German periodicals, were beginning to be realised—in Hamburg itself the *Hamburgische Unterhaltungen*, since its inception in 1766, had devoted much space to the doings of the theatre. Moreover, there was room in the proposed journal for helpful information apart from criticism of the performances—information about the dramas themselves and their authors. Since Gottsched's *Critische Dichtkunst*, too, there had been a growing interest in Germany in the theory of the drama; Lessing himself had contributed to it, and the important writings of Johann Elias Schlegel on the organisation of the theatre had not long been published. Schlegel was firmly convinced that the progress ('Aufnahme') of the theatre was dependent on a thorough study of the aesthetic foundations of dramatic art. There were also precedents for a running commentary on the activity of a particular theatre, in such publications as the *Schildereyen der Gottfried H. Kochschen Bühne*, or the *Kritische Nachricht von der Schuchischen Schauspielergesellschaft* which appeared at Danzig in 1758.

The nature and scope of the journal which the National Theatre proposed to publish seem to have been left largely to Lessing himself. It could not, of course, be planned on the lines of his own earlier periodicals, for these had no relation to the daily routine of a theatre. Indeed, he seems to have started without any very definite plan; but it was evident that it went as much against the grain in him to bind himself down to a regular and punctual chronicle of the performances, as it had to undertake to provide the theatre with new plays at prescribed intervals. His own somewhat wayward intellectual temperament required freedom.

The first purpose of the publication was obviously to provide a

---

[1] See below, p. 280. The quotation from *Tristram Shandy* with which Lessing supports his statement here that first thoughts are not always best (CI–CIV, 80) is from vol. v, ch. xvi of Sterne's novel (2nd ed. London, 1760–67, v, p. 74).

'critisches Register' (*Ank.* 67) of the plays performed by the company, a running commentary on the work of the theatre. Lessing tells us that this suggested to him the 'Didaskalien' of the Greeks, that is, the short notes which Aristotle made on the plays of the Greek theatre (CI–CIV, 98). Dacier had spoken of these in his commentary on the last words of the sixteenth chapter of the *Poetics*:

Il parle sans doute des Traitez qu'il avoit faits sur les sujets des Poëmes dramatiques, et qu'il avoit intitulez *Didascalies*. Aristote y avoit expliqué non seulement les sujets des pieces; mais en quel temps, comment, pour quelle occasion, et avec quel succez ces pieces avoient été joüées, de sorte que cet ouvrage étoit, et une Histoire exacte des Poëtes anciens, et une méthode seure pour bien démêler les difficultez des temps dans l'Histoire Grecque. Les Didascalies qui sont encore aujourd'huy à la tête des Comedies de Terence, peuvent en donner une legere idée, c'est un fort grand dommage que ces Traitez soient perdus.[1]

But the word 'Didaskalie', Lessing goes on to say, has a strange sound (113); moreover, he adds, modern scholars are agreed about the narrow scope of such a catalogue. So in preference to 'Didaskalien', he chose 'Dramaturgie' as the title of his journal.

In many respects, however, the word 'Dramaturgie' had quite as unusual a sound as 'Didaskalien', and as far as its use and definition were concerned, it also was originally restricted to a mere catalogue of plays.[2] In his next sentence Lessing refers to the first use of the word in a modern tongue: in 1666 Leone Allacci (1586–1669) published his catalogue of plays under the title *La Drammaturgia*; brought

---

[1] *La Poétique d'Aristote…traduite en François, avec des Remarques critiques sur tout l'ouvrage*, Paris, 1692, pp. 270 f. The passage quoted in Lessing's note (CI–CIV, 122) is from Isaac Casaubonus, *Animadversiones in Dipnosophistas libri xv*, Lyons, 1600, bk. VI, cap. vii, pp. 260 f. In English the passage is: '$\Delta\iota\delta\alpha\sigma\kappa\alpha\lambda\acute{\iota}\alpha$ is used for that writing in which is explained where, when, how and with what success a certain piece has been played…. How much the critics with their diligence assisted the old chroniclers, they alone will be able to estimate who know how weak and meagre are the aids of those who first felt themselves impelled to fix the fleeting time. I do not doubt that Aristotle had primarily this in view when he composed his $\Delta\iota\delta\alpha\sigma\kappa\alpha\lambda\acute{\iota}\alpha$.' The further reference to Casaubonus (119) describing the 'didaskalia' of Terence as 'breviter et eleganter scriptæ' is from the same chapter of this work (p. 261). Lessing gives evidence of his familiarity with the writings of Casaubonus in his *Leben Sophocles* (cp. *Schriften*, viii, pp. 309, 344, 350). The Olympiads (109) were periods of five years in the Greek reckoning of time; the Archon was the chief magistrate of Athens.

[2] The word seems to have owed its currency, in the first instance, to a passage in Lucian's *De Saltatione*, where $\delta\rho\alpha\mu\alpha\tau\upsilon\rho\gamma\acute{\iota}\alpha$ is employed in the sense of 'dramatic composition'.

up-to-date, this work appeared in a second edition at Venice in 1755. Lessing probably had this edition; but in any case the character and scope of the work were familiar to him from Riccoboni's *Histoire du théâtre italien*.

Lessing, then, had probably in view, when planning his journal, brief items of information—not perhaps quite so catalogue-like and unreadable as those in Allacci's work, or the lists of a similar kind which Gottsched appended to his *Deutsche Schaubühne* and afterwards collected in his *Nöthiger Vorrath zur Geschichte der deutschen dramatischen Dichtkunst* (Leipzig, 1757–65). He may possibly have known the French *Almanach historique et chronologique de tous les spectacles de Paris* of 1752, or its German imitations, or even the English theatrical journal *The Prompter* (1734 ff.); in any case we know that he possessed Léris' *Dictionnaire portatif des Théâtres* and the *Histoire du Théâtre françois* (Paris, 1745–49) and *Dictionnaire des Théâtres de Paris* (Paris, 1756) by the brothers Parfaict.[1] For that matter, he had already printed notes on the theatre, of a similar kind, in his *Beyträge zur Historie und Aufnahme des Theaters*.

The *Hamburgische Dramaturgie* is, however, much more than a 'critisches Register'. From the first, as one might expect from his earlier experiments in theatrical journalism, Lessing had something in view which was not covered either by the word 'Didaskalien' or by the word 'Drammaturgia' in Allacci's usage. In fact, he expressly declined to be bound by Allacci's precedent (CI–CIV, 114 ff.):

Was ich in eine Dramaturgie bringen oder nicht bringen wollte, das stand bey mir: wenigstens hatte mir Lione Allacci desfalls nichts vorzuschreiben.

His journal was not merely to record the performances of the Hamburg playhouse; it was also to discuss the nature of the drama; and it was to be of practical aid to poet and actor, and help to educate the taste of the public by stimulating an appreciation for what was good—thus contributing to the ultimate aim of the Hamburg undertaking, the creation of a national theatre. In other words, what Lessing wished to produce was a German 'pratique du théâtre'. And just here he had a predecessor, in a countryman of his own, Johann Elias Schlegel, who prepared the way for such a national theatre—for Denmark, it is true, not for Germany—with his *Schreiben von Errichtung eines*

---

[1] See below, p. 164. Lessing was obviously thinking of such works in St. CI–CIV (132): 'In welchem Jahre Ludewigs des Vierzehnten...dieses oder jenes französische Meisterstück zuerst aufgeführet worden...' etc.

Theaters in Kopenhagen and *Gedanken zur Aufnahme des dänischen Theaters.*
These had only been published three years before Lessing inaugurated
his *Dramaturgie*.

Such plans obviously went very far beyond the aims of Allacci in
his *Drammaturgia.* It has not been observed, however, that the word
had been used before Lessing's time in a much less restricted sense
than that of a mere catalogue of plays. Lessing had in his possession
in Hamburg another Italian work, the *Biblioteca teatrale italiana*,
scelta e disposta da Ottaviano Diodati, patrizio lucchese (12 vols.,
Lucca, 1762–65). This is a collection of Italian plays; but in each of
the volumes there is a chapter in verse 'correlativo alle cose teatrali,
per servire di tratto completo di Drammaturgia'. The subjects of
these chapters are: i. Introduzione alla Drammaturgia sopra l'utilità
della presente Raccolta; ii. Sopra l'utilità delle rappresentazioni
teatrali; iii. Da che dipenda l'esito delle rappresentazioni teatrali;
iv. Della declamazione e del recitare in generale; v. Delle diverse
maniere del declamare e del recitare; vi, vii. Del ben recitar; viii,
ix. Del gesto; x. Sopra la scena muta; xi, xii. Sopra l'opportuna
scelta. Here then, in these discussions of dramatic representation,
declamation, recitation and gesture, Lessing found, if it was necessary
for him to find, a precedent for his own extension of the use of the
word to dramatic theory and practice in general.[1]

The form of the word, 'Dramaturgie', suggests also the possibility
of a French precedent. According to the *Dictionnaire général* of Hatzfeld
and Darmesteter, the word first makes its entry into the French
language as a translation by Chapelain [in 1668] of Allacci's title.
Before the appearance of Lessing's work, both 'dramaturgie' and
'dramaturge'—the latter in the still accepted sense of a dramatic
writer—had been in use by French writers, notably by those of anti-
classical views. Diderot, it is true, does not seem to have used either;
but Marmontel, a critic who is quoted by Lessing, writes 'dramaturge'.[2] This, too, may have carried weight with Lessing.[3]

---

[1] Lessing's attention may have been drawn to Diodati's work by the notices in
the *Bibliothek der schönen Wissenschaften*, ix (1763), pp. 123, 277; xii (1765), pp. 167 f.
It is not unlikely, however, that these were contributed by Lessing himself.

[2] See Bescherelle, *Nouveau Dictionnaire National* (ii, 1278, s. 'dramaturge') where
Marmontel and Desroches are cited; Littré, *Dictionnaire de la langue française* (i, ii,
1239) where Mercier is cited. For allusions to Marmontel in Lessing's work see
below, pp. 355 f., 398.

[3] After the publication of Lessing's journal, the word was extensively used, and
always in his sense, in Germany; cp. *Theater-Kalender für das Jahr 1776*, Gotha,

After being distributed gratis on the day of the opening of the theatre, April 22, 1767, the *Ankündigung* of the *Hamburgische Dramaturgie* was re-issued with St. I–III on May 8. Each number was priced at a schilling (about a penny); but the journal could be subscribed for at five Hamburg marks (about 6s. 3d.) a year. The printing was undertaken by the printing-house of Johann Joachim Christoph Bode, with whom Lessing had become associated as a partner. The publication proceeded regularly for several weeks, a number appearing every Tuesday and Friday. But then trouble began, owing to the lack of copyright protection in the German states. A piratical reprint was issued in Leipzig by printers who masqueraded under an English name as 'Dodsley und Compagnie' (CI–CIV, 381)—Dodsley being taken from the well-known London publishing house established in 1735. The German firm consisted of a widowed Frau Dyk and her assistant Engelhard Benjamin Schwickert.[1] They existed by pirating and publishing all kinds of worthless literature. In refusing to have his *Dramaturgie* put upon the market at the Leipzig fairs—a procedure which would have provided some kind of protection—Lessing laid himself open to piracy.[2]

Lessing was apparently informed of Dodsley and Co.'s activities by Nicolai. He wrote to the latter on August 14, 1767, in reply to a letter now lost (*Schriften*, xvii, p. 236):

Ich danke Ihnen für die Nachricht von dem Nachdrucke der Dramaturgie, und für Ihren guten Rath dem Nachtheile desselben, so viel noch möglich, abzuhelffen. Ich kann eigentlich freylich nichts dabey verlieren; ich bin aber sonst nur in der Verfassung, dass es mir äusserst unangenehm seyn würde, wenn andere dabey verlören. Seyn Sie doch so gütig und schicken mir ein Exemplar von dem Nachdrucke, und zwar mit eben der Gelegenheit, mit welcher Sie diesen Brief erhalten.

What Nicolai's good advice had been we do not know. Possibly to abandon periodical publication and issue the work in volumes at the fairs, or perhaps to arrange for publication by private subscription,

p. 232, where a *Wienerische Dramaturgie*, Vienna, 1775, is mentioned; also O. H. v. Gemmingen, *Mannheimer Dramaturgie* (1779); J. F. Schink, *Dramaturgische Fragmente* (1781–4); A. v. Knigge, *Dramaturgische Blätter* (1788–9); H. C. Albrecht, *Neue Hamburgische Dramaturgie* (1791). An anonymous volume, published in Leipzig in 1796, combined the two titles which Lessing had considered: *Didaskalien, oder Streifereyen im Gebiete der Dramaturgie.*

[1] Cp. G. Wustmann, *Aus Leipzigs Vergangenheit*, Leipzig, 1885, pp. 236 ff.; also E. Schmidt, *Lessing, ed. cit.* i, pp. 649 f.

[2] Cp. E. Kundt, *Lessing und der Buchhandel*, Heidelberg, 1907, pp. 50 ff. (Cp. also Petersen, *ed. cit.* p. 268.)

although it is not clear how the latter plan would have counteracted the evil. Years later Lessing wrote an article of which a fragment has been preserved in his 'Nachlass', *Leben und leben lassen, ein Projekt für Schriftsteller und Buchhändler*, in which private subscription is recommended as a remedy for piracy;[1] and in the last words of the *Dramaturgie* (CI–CIV, 475) he refers to the project which Leibniz had set forth in 1668 of a 'Societas eruditorum Germaniæ' (*De vera ratione reformandi rem literariam*).[2]

However that may be, the course which was now decided upon was to abandon publication in serial numbers. The following notice was inserted in the *Kaiserlich-privilegirte Hamburgische Neue Zeitung*, St. 131, on August 21, 1767:

NACHRICHT AN DAS PUBLIKUM

Da man der Hamburgischen Dramaturgie, von welcher heute das zwey und dreyssigste Stück erscheinen sollte, auswärts die unverlangte Ehre erweiset, sie nachzudrucken; so sieht sich der Verfasser, um dem für den hiesigen Verlag daraus erwachsenden Nachtheile einigermassen auszuweichen, gedrungen, die Ausgabe derselben in einzelnen Blättern einzustellen; und die Interessenten werden sich gefallen lassen, das Rückständige des ersten Bandes, von dem 32sten. Stück an, auf instehende Michaelismesse, zusammen zu erhalten.

In spite of this promise that the first volume should be issued at Michaelmas, nothing more happened until December 8. On the previous day there appeared another notice in the same Hamburg newspaper (St. 192):

NACHRICHT WEGEN DER HAMBURGISCHEN DRAMATURGIE

Da man zu Fortsetzung der Hamburgischen Dramaturgie (welche vor einiger Zeit durch einen auswärtigen Nachdruck unterbrochen ward, und durch einen zweyten, der selbst hiesigen Orts dazukam,[3] noch mehr

---

[1] Lessing offered the essay, which could not have been written earlier than 1772, to Lichtenberg for his *Göttingisches Magazin der Wissenschaft und Litteratur* in a letter of January 23, 1780 (*Schriften*, xvi, pp. 464 ff.). The fragment was published in 1800 by G. G. Fülleborn in his journal *Nebenstunden*, Breslau, pp. 37 ff. (*ibid.* and cp. also Redlich, *Lessing's Werke* (Hempel ed.), xix, p. 732). Lessing published his *Nathan der Weise* by subscription.

[2] Cp. A. Harnack, *Geschichte der Königlich Preussischen Akademie der Wissenschaften zu Berlin*, Berlin, 1900, i, pp. 27 ff., ii, p. 7.

[3] For the Hamburg reprint a certain Bock was responsible. See J. W. Braun, *Lessing im Urtheile seiner Zeitgenossen*, Berlin, 1884–97, i, p. 190; F. von Biedermann, *Lessings Gespräche*, Berlin, 1924, p. 123.

beeinträchtigt zu werden Gefahr lief, so dass die versprochne gesamte Ausgabe des ersten Bandes unterbleiben musste) nunmehr die erforderliche Vorkehr, in Ansehung der Privilegien und andrer Umstände getroffen zu haben glaubet: so macht man dem Publico hiermit bekannt, dass von Morgen an, mit der einzelnen Austheilung derselben wiederum der Anfang gemacht werden soll; und zwar sollen wöchentlich vier Stücke davon erscheinen, bis die versäumte Zeit eingebracht worden. Die auswärtigen Leser, welche die Fortsetzung dieser Schrift wünschen, ersucht man ergebenst, sie auch dadurch befördern zu helfen, dass sie sich keine andre als die Original-Ausgabe anschaffen. Sie können sie dreist von den Buchhändlern ihres Orts verlangen, indem sie allen mit den billigsten Bedingungen ange-bothen werden. Man kann zwar weder diesen, noch ihnen, verbiethen, dem Nachdruck zu favorisiren; aber man giebt ihnen zu überlegen, dass sie sich nothwendig dadurch um das Werk selbst bringen müssen. Denn wenn die Anzahl von Exemplaren, welche zur Bestreitung der Unkosten erforderlich ist, nicht abgesetzt werden kann, so bleibt es unfehlbar liegen.

St. XXXII–XXXV appeared on December 8; St. XXXVI–XXXIX followed on the 15th; St. XL–XLIII on the 22nd; St. XLIV–LI at the end of December and in the beginning of January, 1768. From this time on the publication was again continued in single numbers, two or three a week, to St. LXXXII. Again a suspension was decided upon and the *Neue Zeitung* contained in its issue of April 25 (St. 66) the following notice:

NACHRICHT WEGEN DER HAMBURGISCHEN DRAMATURGIE

Eine nöthige Vorsicht, wegen des noch fortdauernden Nachdrucks der Hamburgischen Dramaturgie, erfordert, die Ausgabe derselben in einzelnen Blättern nochmals abzubrechen. Es soll aber gegen die Mitte des künftigen Monats, als um welche Zeit vorigen Jahres das Werk seinen Anfang genommen, der Rest des zweiten Bandes, nemlich die Stücke 83 bis 104, nebst den Titeln zu beiden Bänden, mit eins geliefert werden.

Some six weeks later, on June 9, 1768, Lessing wrote to his brother Karl:

Hier habe ich alle Hände voll zu thun, und vornehmlich beschäftigt mich noch die Dramaturgie. Sie ist nicht weiter heraus, als bis Nro. 82. Der Rest des zweyten Bandes wird in einigen Wochen zusammen erscheinen. Wenn ich das Werk noch weiter fortsetze, so soll es Bandweise, und nicht Bogenweise geschehen. Du sollst ein complettes Exemplar haben, sobald eins fertig ist.[1]

[1] *Schriften*, xvii, pp. 253 f.

St. LXXXIII–CIV did not appear until Easter, 1769; and at the same time the entire work was published in two volumes by the firm of J. H. Cramer in Bremen.

The *Ankündigung*—of the separate publication of which on April 22 no copy appears to be extant[1]—fulfils a twofold purpose. The first part, in which the public is invited to give its best support to the new undertaking, takes the place of that later announcement which Löwen had promised in his *Vorläufige Nachricht*; the latter half is an introduction to the journal itself. Lessing makes clear his independence of the management of the theatre; and by way of warning his readers that they will not find in his pages untempered praise, anticipates the mediocrity of the repertory which the theatre will offer; the choice of good plays is very limited, and even with the best will, a practical theatre cannot always choose only the best; it must cater for the tastes of its public and provide its actors with parts in which they can display their talents. Nor must the public cherish too high hopes of the acting: a theatre in which even the 'Lichtputzer' is a Garrick (II, 89) is an impossible ideal. Before the undertaking had proceeded very far he saw that he was on dangerous ground here; as we have seen, the actors resented being criticised, and after the twenty-fifth number the *Dramaturgie* as a 'critisches Register' was shorn of one of its important features: Lessing ceased to comment on their performances at all.[2]

But changes of plan set in from the beginning. In the first place, Lessing did not keep pace with the performances; he began a week late, and when he had completed what he had to say about the first evening, the theatre had been open for twenty-two evenings. In St. XXXII, which is dated August 18, he was still only discussing the performance of July 1. The suspension of serial publication with St. XXXII robbed the *Dramaturgie* of all pretension to be a journalistic commentary on the work of the theatre; and Lessing himself felt still

[1] Cp. C. C. Redlich, *Lessing-Bibliothek* (*Lessings Werke*, Hempel ed., xix, p. 701); also F. Muncker (*Schriften*, ix, p. vi): 'Die paar Blätter, wahrscheinlich ein Unikum, befanden sich einst im Besitze Dr F. A. Cropps in Hamburg, nach dessen Tode sie in die Hamburger Stadtbibliothek gelangten. Hier aber waren sie augenblicklich nicht aufzufinden. Indes scheint die Texteskritik dadurch nichts verloren zu haben. Wenigstens kann Redlich...sich keiner textlichen Varianten dieses Einzeldrucks erinnern; nur der äussere Satz des Druckes war von dem im ersten Bande der "Dramaturgie" verschieden.'

[2] Mad. Hensel insinuated that Lessing paid insufficient attention to the performances of the actors; that he walked restlessly about, or stayed at the buffet while whole acts were being played, only looking now and then through the open door of the parterre. (Cp. W. Oehlke, *Lessing und seine Zeit, ed. cit.* ii, p. 20.)

less under compulsion to maintain touch with it. Accordingly St.
XXXIII to XXXV are devoted to Favart's *Solimann II*, and St. XXXVI to L
to discussions prompted by Voltaire's *Mérope*. When he had finished
with the latter play, nominally on October 20, the theatre had been
playing nearly six months.

The first season of the company came to a close on December 4,
and they betook themselves to Hanover, where they played for four
and a half months in the small Schlosstheater. Lessing was under no
obligation to accompany them, the more so as they were only to
repeat their Hamburg repertory; in any case, his interest in Bode's
printing business made his presence in Hamburg desirable. It fell
to him in these months to keep the *Dramaturgie* going until the company
returned.[1] But as at their departure he was only in the midst of
discussing—nominally, at least—the forty-fourth evening, July 15, he
had obviously plenty of material to go on with. By this time, however,
his breach with the activity of the theatre was complete, and all
pretension of offering a 'critisches Register' was abandoned; and
after St. LXII, which is dated December 4, he only discusses—and
hardly even discusses—seven plays, the last being that given at the
performance of July 28, 1767.

All this will be made clear by the following table:

No.	Nominal date 1767	Actual date of publication 1767	Date of performance discussed 1767
Ank.	April 22	April 22	—
I	May 1 ⎫		
II	5 ⎬ May 8		
III	8 ⎭		
IV	12 ⎫		I (April 22)
V	15 ⎪		
VI	19 ⎬		
VII	22 ⎭		
VIII	26		II–IV (April 23–27)
IX	29		IV (April 27)
X	June 2		V–VI (April 28–29)
XI	5		VI (April 29)
XII	9		VI–VIII (April 29–May 1)
XIII	12		IX–XI (May 4–6)
XIV	16	As dated	XI–XV (May 6–12)

[1] See Lessing's letter to Nicolai of February 2, 1768 (*Schriften*, xvii, p. 243):
'Ich muss um mich greifen, um die Materie zu meiner Dramaturgie so lange zu
dehnen, bis die Gesellschaft wieder nach Hamburg kömmt.'

No.	Nominal date 1767	Actual date of publication 1767	Date of performance discussed 1767
XV	June 19	As dated ⎫	
XVI	23	⎬	XVI (May 13)
XVII	26		XVII–XX (May 14–19)
XVIII	30		XXI–XXII (May 20–21)
XIX	July 3		XXII (May 21)
XX	7		XXIII–XXV (May 22–26)
XXI	10		XXVI–XXVII (May 29–June 1)
XXII	14		XXVIII–XXX (June 2–4)
XXIII	17	⎫	
XXIV	21	⎬	XXX (June 4)
XXV	24	⎭	
XXVI	28		XXXI–XXXII (June 10–11)
XXVII	31		XXXII (June 11)
XXVIII	August 4		XXXIII–XXXIV (June 12–29)
XXIX	7		XXXIV–XXXV (June 29–July 1)
XXX	11		⎫
XXXI	14		⎬ XXXV (July 1)
XXXII	18		⎭
XXXIII	21	December 8	
XXXIV	25		XXXVI (July 3)
XXXV	28		
XXXVI	September 1		XXXVI–XXXVIII (July 3–7)
XXXVII	4	December 15	
XXXVIII	8		
XXXIX	11		
XL	15		
XLI	18	December 22	
XLII	22		
XLIII	25		
XLIV	29		XXXVIII (July 7)
XLV	October 2	December 29	
XLVI	6		
XLVII	9		
XLVIII	13		
XLIX	16	1768	
L	20	January 5	
LI	23		XXXIX (July 8)
LII	27		XL (July 9)
LIII	November 3		XLI–XLII (July 10–13)
LIV	6		XLIII–XLIV (July 14–15)
LV	10		
LVI	13		
LVII	17		

No.	Nominal date 1767	Actual date of publication 1768	Date of performance discussed 1767
LVIII	November 20	Serial publi-	
LIX	24	cation con-	
LX	27	tinued, but	
LXI	December 1	irregularly,	
LXII	4	one or two ⎫	XLIV (July 15)
LXIII	8	parts each	
LXIV	11	week, until	
LXV	15	June 9	
LXVI	18		
LXVII	22		
LXVIII	25 ⎫		
LXIX	29 ⎭		
	1768		
LXX	January 1		XLIV–XLV (July 15–17)
LXXI	5	⎫	
LXXII	8	⎭	XLV (July 17)
LXXIII	12		XLV–XLVIII (July 17–22)
LXXIV	15		
LXXV	19		
LXXVI	22		
LXXVII	26		
LXXVIII	29		XLVIII (July 22)
LXXIX	February 2		
LXXX	5		
LXXXI	9		
LXXXII	12 ⎭		
LXXXIII	16 ⎫		XLVIII–L (July 22–24)
LXXXIV	19		LI (July 27)
LXXXV	23		
LXXXVI	26	⎫	
LXXXVII–LXXXVIII	March 4		
LXXXIX	8		
XC	11		LI (July 27)
XCI	15		
XCII	18	1769	
XCIII	22	Easter	
XCIV	25		
XCV	29	⎫	
XCVI	April 1		
XCVII	5		
XCVIII	8		LII (July 28)
XCIX	12		
C	15		
C–CIV	19 ⎭	⎭	

R L

9

Lessing himself was fully aware of the shortcomings of his journal and of its failure to meet the expectations of the public. In St. L (9 ff.), after devoting fourteen numbers to a single play, he apologises to his readers for not giving them the 'theatralische Zeitung' they had hoped for, full of 'kurzweiliger, auch wohl ein wenig skandalöser Anekdoten von Schauspielern und besonders Schauspielerinnen', but only 'lange, ernsthafte, trockne Kritiken über alte bekannte Stücke; schwerfällige Untersuchungen über das, was in einer Tragödie seyn sollte und nicht seyn sollte... wie gesagt, ich betauere sie: sie sind gewaltig angeführt!—Doch im Vertrauen; besser, dass sie es sind, als ich.' And in St. xcv, after a tedious discussion of characters in drama, he says (138): 'Ich erinnere hier meine Leser, dass diese Blätter nichts weniger als ein dramatisches System enthalten sollen. Ich bin also nicht verpflichtet, alle die Schwierigkeiten aufzulösen, die ich mache. Meine Gedanken mögen immer sich weniger zu verbinden, ja wohl gar sich zu widersprechen scheinen: wenn es denn nur Gedanken sind, bey welchen sie Stoff finden, selbst zu denken. Hier will ich nichts als Fermenta cognitionis ausstreuen.'[1]

In the closing section of the *Dramaturgie*, he reviews the disastrous course of the undertaking and voices his bitter disappointment at its failure. The hopeful tone in which he had welcomed it in his *Ankündigung* (22: 'So glücklich sey Hamburg in allem, woran seinem Wohlstande und seiner Freyheit gelegen: denn es verdienet, so glücklich zu seyn') gives place to the melancholy plaint at the close (CI–CIV, 362):

Der süsse Traum, ein Nationaltheater hier in Hamburg zu gründen, ist schon wieder verschwunden: und so viel ich diesen Ort nun habe kennen lernen, dürfte er auch wohl gerade der seyn, wo ein solcher Traum am spätesten in Erfüllung gehen wird.[2]

This epilogue, or 'Nachspiel' as he calls it, to the *Hamburgische*

[1] In his *Collectanea* (*Schriften*, xv, p. 422) Lessing had extracted, with a view to utilising it in his *Laokoon*, the following passage from Solinus's prefatory chapter to his *Collectanea rerum memorabilium* (Praefatio, cap. 1.): 'Cui si animum propius intenderis, velut fermentum cognitionis magis ei inesse, quam bracteas eloquentiæ deprehendes.' (Cp. Schröter and Thiele, *Lessings Hamburgische Dramaturgie*, Halle, 1878, p. 561.) He used the work of Solinus in his *Antiquarische Briefe* (xxiv, *Schriften*, x, p. 305).

[2] To Klotz Löwen wrote on December 29, 1768 (*Briefe Deutscher Gelehrten an Klotz*, herausg. von J. J. A. von Hagen, ii (Halle, 1773), p. 5, quoted by Petersen, *ed. cit.* p. 265), that he had resigned his directorship, 'da, aller Versuche ohngeachtet, Deutschland nie die Hoffnung zu einem National-Theater wird erfüllt sehen. Auch Hr. Lessing hat sich von allen Theatralischen Verbindlichkeiten losgemacht und geht im Monat März nach Italien'.

Dramaturgie will remain always memorable as containing one of the few personal confessions which Lessing, a man at no time given to wearing his heart on his sleeve, has left us.

Denn warum [he asks (CI–CIV, 20)] sollte nicht auch ein Nachspiel einen Prolog haben dürfen, der sich mit einem Poeta, cum primum animum ad scribendum appulit, anfinge?[1]

Als, vor Jahr und Tag, [he continues] einige gute Leute hier den Einfall bekamen, einen Versuch zu machen, ob nicht für das deutsche Theater sich etwas mehr thun lasse, als unter der Verwaltung eines sogenannten Principals geschehen könne: so weiss ich nicht, wie man auf mich dabey fiel, und sich träumen liess, dass ich bey diesem Unternehmen wohl nützlich seyn könnte?—Ich stand eben am Markte und war müssig; niemand wollte mich dingen: ohne Zweifel, weil mich niemand zu brauchen wusste; bis gerade auf diese Freunde!...Ich bin weder Schauspieler, noch Dichter. Man erweiset mir zwar manchmal die Ehre, mich für den letztern zu erkennen. Aber nur, weil man mich verkennt. Aus einigen dramatischen Versuchen, die ich gewagt habe, sollte man nicht so freygebig folgern. Nicht jeder, der den Pinsel in die Hand nimt, und Farben verquistet, ist ein Mahler. Die ältesten von jenen Versuchen sind in den Jahren hingeschrieben, in welchen man Lust und Leichtigkeit so gern für Genie hält. Was in den neuerern erträgliches ist, davon bin ich mir sehr bewusst, dass ich es einzig und allein der Critik zu verdanken habe. Ich fühle die lebendige Quelle nicht in mir, die durch eigene Kraft sich empor arbeitet, durch eigene Kraft in so reichen, so frischen, so reinen Strahlen aufschiesst: ich muss alles durch Druckwerk und Röhren aus mir herauf pressen. Ich würde so arm, so kalt, so kurzsichtig seyn, wenn ich nicht einigermaassen gelernt hätte, fremde Schätze bescheiden zu borgen, an fremdem Feuer mich zu wärmen, und durch die Gläser der Kunst mein Auge zu stärken. Ich bin daher immer beschämt oder verdrüsslich geworden, wenn ich zum Nachtheil der Critik etwas las oder hörte. Sie soll das Genie ersticken: und ich schmeichelte mir, etwas von ihr zu erhalten, was dem Genie sehr nahe kömmt. Ich bin ein Lahmer, den eine Schmähschrift auf die Krücke unmöglich erbauen kann.[2]

---

[1] This quotation from Terence is from the opening of the prologue to the *Andria*.

[2] Cp. Lessing's letter to Ramler of April 21, 1772, after the appearance of *Emilia Galotti* (*Schriften*, xviii, pp. 32 f.): 'Kritik, will ich Ihnen nur vertrauen, ist das einzige Mittel, mich zu mehrerem aufzufrischen, oder vielmehr aufzuhetzen. Denn da ich die Kritik nicht zu dem kritisirten Stücke anzuwenden im Stande bin; da ich zum Verbessern überhaupt ganz verdorben bin, und das Verbessern eines dramatischen Stücks insbesondere fast für unmöglich halte, wenn es einmal zu einem gewissen Grade der Vollendung gebracht ist, und die Verbesserung mehr als Kleinigkeiten betreffen soll: so nutze ich die Kritik zuverlässig zu etwas Neuem. —Also, liebster Freund, wenn auch Sie es wollen, dass ich wieder einmal etwas Neues in dieser Art machen soll; so sehen Sie, worauf es dabey mit ankömmt:— mich durch Tadel zu reitzen, nicht dieses Nehmliche besser zu machen, sondern

überhaupt etwas Besseres zu machen. Und wenn auch dieses Bessere sodann nothwendig noch seine Mängel haben muss: so ist dieses allein der Ring durch die Nase, an dem man mich in immerwährendem Tanze erhalten kann'(quoted by Petersen, *ed. cit.* p. 264).

The phrase 'Ich bin ein Lahmer', etc. (57) is possibly an allusion to a passage in Edward Young's *Conjectures on Original Composition* (translated by "G." (Hamburg, 1760) and by v. T[eubern] (Leipzig, 1760)). The passage runs in German (v. Teubern's translation, 2nd ed. 1761, p. 29): 'Denn Schönheiten, die man noch nie in Regeln vorgeschrieben, und etwas Vortrefliches, von dem man noch kein Exempel hatte, (und diess ist die Charakteristik des Genies) diese liegen weit ausser den Gränzzeichen der Herrschaft der Gelehrsamkeit und ihrer Gesetze. Diese Gränzzeichen muss das Genie überspringen, um zu jenen zu gelangen. Aber bey diesem Sprunge, wenn das Genie fehlt, brechen wir den Hals, und verlieren das kleine Ansehen, in dessen Besitz wir vielleicht vorher waren. Denn Regeln sind wie Krücken, eine nothwendige Hülfe für den Lahmen, aber ein Hinderniss für den Gesunden.' ('For Rules, like Crutches, are a needful aid to the Lame, tho' an Impediment to the Strong.' *Conjectures on original Composition, in a Letter to the Author of Sir Charles Grandison*, London, 1759, p. 28.) Reference to the quotation is made also in the *Litteraturbriefe (Briefe, die neueste Litteratur betreffend)*, Berlin, 1759–65, xii, p. 327, No. cciv (December 17, 1761). For another reference to Young, cp. *Dramaturgie*, xxxvi, 107, where Lessing refers to a phrase from *The Last Day* (Bk. i, l. 60) which is also quoted by Mendelssohn in *Bibliothek der schönen Wissenschaften*, i (i), 1757, p. 95.

Part II

LESSING'S CRITICISM OF THE DRAMA

CHAPTER V

THE GERMAN PLAYS OF THE REPERTORY

Lessing was, as we have seen, under no illusions as to the poverty of the repertory in plays of German origin. In 1760, reviewing a volume of Weisse's dramas, he had frankly admitted 'dass es mit dem deutschen Drama noch so gar elend aussiehet';[1] and in the *Dramaturgie* (LXXX, 30) he endorses Löwen's plaint: 'Wir Deutsche bekennen es treuherzig genug, dass wir noch kein Theater haben.' He welcomed the undertaking in Hamburg as the possible beginning of a better state of things (*Ank.* 37); but he had grave doubts about the quality of the dramas which were available; the choice was small, and 'wenn nicht immer Meisterstücke aufgeführet werden sollten, so sieht man wohl, woran die Schuld liegt' (*Ank.* 71). Lessing understood the situation too well to reproach Hamburg—as some of his modern critics would like to see him do—with the fact that the plays of French origin performed in its National Theatre so seriously outnumbered the native productions.

In the present chapter I bring together what Lessing has to say in his journal concerning German dramas and German dramatists. I discuss in particular the sources of his knowledge and the grounds on which his own judgments are based. It will be convenient to deal with the dramas here, not in the order in which they are reviewed in the *Dramaturgie*, but under their authors, arranged in an approximately chronological sequence.

J. C. GOTTSCHED

When the 'Enterprise' opened in 1767, Gottsched had only been a little over four months dead; but he had long ceased to be a vital or even a respected power in the literary world over which he had once

---

[1] *Litteraturbriefe*, No. lxxxi (February 7, 1760); *Schriften*, viii, p. 218.

ruled dictatorially. *Der sterbende Cato*, that production of 'scissors and paste',[1] had not been a playable tragedy since about 1750. In a certain sense, however, the Gottschedian era was not yet a thing of the past; of the plays in the Hamburg repertory no less than five came from Gottsched's *Deutsche Schaubühne*: *Das Gespenst mit der Trommel*, *Zayre*, *Alzire*, *Der poetische Dorfjunker* and *Die Hausfranzösinn*; and of these, all but *Alzire* were performed during the period of Lessing's criticism. He had the six volumes of Gottsched's collection at hand, and he turned, as will be seen, to Gottsched's introductions when the plays from it were performed. The affair of the banishment of the Harlequin by Gottsched and Caroline Neuber is recalled (XVIII, 22);[2] and even echoes of the *Critische Dichtkunst* are not lacking.[3] In St. LXXXI (24) Lessing pronounces his final word on the old dictator of German taste, as one of whose disciples he no doubt regarded himself when he began his literary career in Leipzig. In his youth, he says, Gottsched had been hailed as a poet, because in those days people did not know how to distinguish between the poetaster and the poet; he clung in his vanity to the belief that he *was* a poet, whereas he was merely a verse-maker. 'Er konnte unmöglich erlangen, was er schon zu besitzen glaubte: und je älter er ward, desto hartnäckiger und unverschämter ward er, sich in diesem traümerischen Besitze zu behaupten.'

FRAU L. A. V. GOTTSCHED

In the *Dramaturgie* the old antagonism to Gottsched is transferred to his spouse, 'seine gelehrte Freundinn' (XIII, 11).[4] Against her, indeed, is directed the most negative and bitter criticism which falls to any German writer. The repertory included in Lessing's time, besides Frau Gottsched's translations of Destouches' *Das Gespenst mit der Trommel* and *Der poetische Dorfjunker*, and Madame de Grafigny's *Cénie*, one original play by her, *Die Hausfranzösin* (XXVI, 1).[5] Lessing

---

[1] *Litteraturbriefe*, No. xvii (February 16, 1759); *Schriften*, viii, p. 42.

[2] See below, pp. 424 ff.

[3] See below, pp. 458 f. Cp. also p. 441.

[4] Gottsched alludes to his wife in the prefaces to the *Deutsche Schaubühne* as 'die geschickte Übersetzerinn' (i, p. 16), 'meine fleissige Freundinn' (ii, p. 37), and 'meiner fleissigen Gehülfinn' (iii, p. vi).

[5] He also mentions *Das Testament* (XXVI, 9); it is in vol. vi of the *Deutsche Schaubühne* (1745).

found in Gottsched's recommendation of this piece the following (*Deutsche Schaubühne*, v, 1744, p. 11):

Mehr glaube ich zu ihrem Ruhme nicht sagen zu dörfen: da jene [*Die Hausfranzösinn*] schon sehr vielfältig, sowohl hier, als in Berlin, und auf verschiedenen Schulen, und zwar mit grossem Beyfalle, auf die Schaubühne gebracht worden.

But the play finds no mercy at Lessing's hands; it is 'nicht allein niedrig, und platt, und kalt, sondern noch oben darein schmutzig, eckel, und im höchsten Grade beleidigend'. How could a lady write such stuff! Little can be said now-a-days in Frau Gottsched's defence, but it is difficult to see that her play is so much worse than other comedies which Lessing treats with indulgence. His old feud with Gottsched was not yet dead.

C. F. GELLERT

Lessing has occasion to speak of two representatives of the early 'Saxon comedy', Gellert and Johann Elias Schlegel. Only Gellert's longest-lived piece, *Die kranke Frau* (a one-act 'Nachspiel'), was in the repertory; and it calls forth some warmth of appreciation (XXII, 4). Lessing regards Gellert as the comedy-writer whose plays are most intimately German; they are true pictures of domestic life—'Familien-gemählde'. Löwen had said of them (*Geschichte des deutschen Theaters*, ed. cit. p. 47):

Hier erblickt man lauter deutsche Familiengemählde, wovon die Anlagen und Auszeichnungen vortrefflich gerathen sind....Für das Theater ist ohnstreitig die kranke Frau sein schönstes Stück; ohne die unerheblichen Critiken zu gedenken, die man vielleicht bey dem alten Wahrmund machen könnte.

These plays, Lessing adds, hold the mirror up to the follies of everyday life; but the author's excessive realism leads to a monotonous flatness which leaves us cold. His fools, in particular, need some polishing and heightening of their colours to make them acceptable. *Die kranke Frau*, moreover, had aged by 1767; and the Hamburg audience must have found it difficult to interest itself in so old-fashioned an article of dress as the 'Adrienne' (XXII, 33)[1] on which the plot turns.

[1] See above, p. 78, note 2.

J. E. SCHLEGEL

Of Johann Elias Schlegel's two comedies, *Die stumme Schönheit* and *Der Triumph der guten Frauen*, Lessing speaks with great appreciation: the former is in his view (XIII, 51) 'unstreitig unser bestes komisches Original, das in Versen geschrieben ist'; the latter (LII, 3) 'unstreitig eines der besten deutschen Originale'; indeed, it is not merely Schlegel's best work, but 'die beste deutsche Komödie' (LII, 105).[1] Lessing possessed the edition of Schlegel's *Werke* edited by his brother J. H. Schlegel (vols. i–iv, Copenhagen and Leipzig, 1761–66 [vol. v, 1770]). His information concerning *Die stumme Schönheit* (XIII, 48) is drawn from the 'Vorbericht' prefixed by the editor (ii, p. 471):

Die stumme Schönheit ward für das neuerrichtete Kopenhagensche Theater geschrieben, um auf demselben in einer dänischen Uebersetzung aufgeführt zu werden. Die Uebersetzung ist meines Wissens nie zu Stande gekommen, und daher ist auch die erste Bestimmung dieses kleinen Lust-spiels weggefallen. Es ist 1747 gedruckt, und in eine Sammlung mit dem Triumphe der guten Frauen und der Langenweile gebracht worden.

Schlegel's brother also makes the suggestion (*Werke, ed. cit.* v, p. xxxxiv), which it is impossible now-a-days—and was impossible even in Lessing's time[2]—to verify, that the manners of the play are specifically Danish rather than German (cp. XIII, 50); but here the editor may be only echoing Lessing. The criticism of the play[3] is mainly concerned with the acting of the parts of Frau Praatgern and Charlotte; with this, as well as with the controversy concerning the use of verse or prose, I deal elsewhere.[4]

In discussing *Der Triumph der guten Frauen* in St. LII, Lessing turned to Mendelssohn's article in the *Litteraturbriefe* of January 31, 1765.[5]

[1] In the *Litteraturbriefe*, No. xvi (February 8, 1759; *Schriften*, viii, p. 40) Lessing had described Schlegel as the writer 'der doch bis itzt dem deutschen Theater die meiste Ehre gemacht hat'.

[2] 'Stl.' in Klotz's *Deutsche Bibliothek*, iii (ix), 1769, p. 49, commented: 'Warum die Sitten in der Stummen Schönheit mehr dänisch, als deutsch, seyn sollen, sehe ich in der That nicht ein.'

[3] The passages quoted are from scenes v and viii (*Werke, ed. cit.* ii, pp. 485, 492); for 'dass sie nichts spricht, kömmt daher, weil sie nichts denkt' (XIII, 77), see the last line but two of the play.

[4] See pp. 37, 461 ff.

[5] *Litteraturbriefe*, No. cccxii (*ed. cit.* xxi, pp. 129 ff.); *Mendelssohns Gesammelte Schriften*, Leipzig, 1843–5, iv, 2, pp. 455 ff.

There he read: 'Dieses Lustspiel wird, wie ich höre, auf alle deutsche Bühnen mit Beyfall aufgeführt, und auch vom Lesen zu urtheilen, möchte ich wenig deutsche Lustspiele ihm gleich schätzen.' Lessing then proceeds (50) to quote his friend's article on the essentially French characteristics of the persons in the play.[1]

But Lessing has more to say of Schlegel's comedies. In the first paragraph of St. LII he speaks of two earlier pieces, *Der geschäftige Müssiggänger* and *Der Geheimnissvolle*. The former play, which was first published in the *Deutsche Schaubühne* (iv, 1743, pp. 263 ff.), with a most laudatory recommendation by Gottsched,[2] is described by J. H. Schlegel as his 'erste Arbeit fürs komische Theater, wenn man einige kleinere Versuche ausnimmt, die er selbst unterdrückt oder doch zurück gehalten hat'.[3] Lessing's criticism of Schlegel's wit (8) is suggested by the following remarks of J. H. Schlegel:

Niemand wird es so leicht eines Mangels am Witze beschuldigen, aber ein entgegengesetzter Vorwurf wird schwerlich abzulehnen seyn; dass es nämlich bisweilen zu viel Witz hat, einen solchen, der zu lange bey einem Einfalle stehen bleibt, der den Situationen, in denen man ihn anbringt, nicht angemessen ist, und also der Natur, die er nachahmen will, ungetreu wird....Es könnte seyn...dass diese Malerey der Sitten sich zu oft und zu lange auf Kleinigkeiten erstreckte, die immer das meiste im täglichen Umgange ausmachen, und dass daher in gewissen Scenen, zumal einzeln betrachtet, das Stück matt und langweilig scheinen möchte. Aber wie könnte wohl ein geschäfftiger Müssiggänger anders gezeigt werden, als mit Kleinigkeiten umgeben?[4]

With regard to *Der Geheimnissvolle*[5] (written in 1746, published in 1747) Johann Elias Schlegel had himself suggested the comparison with Molière (14):

Dieses Lustspiel stellt einen von denenjenigen Charakteren vor, die Moliere denen zurückgelassen hat, die in seine Fusstapfen zu treten

---

[1] The quoted passages will be found in the *Litteraturbriefe, ed. cit.* xxi, pp. 133 ff.; *Gesammelte Schriften, ed. cit.* iv, 2, pp. 456 f.

[2] Vorrede, p. 12: 'Wie sich Scudery, und beyde Corneillen in Frankreich, Schakespear in England, und Andreas Gryphius im Deutschen, sowohl in comischen als tragischen Stücken versuchet haben: so hat sich auch dieser geschickte Poet an beyde Arten der theatralischen Dichtkunst wagen, und von der Welt den Ausspruch erwarten wollen: ob er zu der ernsthaften oder lustigen Bühne geschickter sey.'

[3] *J. E. Schlegels Werke, ed. cit.* ii, p. 47.

[4] *Ibid.* pp. 48 f.; also referred to by Cosack, *op. cit.* p. 283.

[5] Schönemann selected Schlegel's *Der Geheimnissvolle* to open his season in Rostock on May 11, 1751; and it was performed subsequently, in the same year, in Hamburg (H. Devrient, *op. cit.* pp. 188, 351).

suchen wollen. Er macht in seinem Menschenfeinde, im vierten Auf-
[t]ritte des zweyten Aufzugs, folgenden Entwurf davon:...[here follow the
lines quoted in Lessing's note]...Ich hatte vorher zu verschiedenen malen
versucht, diesen Charakter aufs Theater zu bringen; aber dasjenige, was
ich ausgearbeitet hatte, allemal so beschaffen gefunden, dass ich für das
Beste hielt, es wieder zu unterdrücken. Die grösste Schwierigkeit hierbey
war diese, dass ich den Charakter des Geheimnissvollen dadurch umge-
stossen haben würde, wenn ich ihm einen Vertrauten geben wollen, dem
er sich völlig eröffnet hätte; und dass es mir gleichwohl anfangs schien, als
würde ohne dieses Mittel die ganze Handlung vieler Dunkelheit unter-
worfen seyn.[1]

The comparison with Cronegk's *Der Misstrauische* (20) is suggested
by J. H. Schlegel:

Der Charakter eines Geheimnissvollen kann nichts anders zum Grunde
haben, als ein Mistrauen, beydes gegen sich selbst und gegen andre. Man
darf sich also über die Verwandtschaft nicht wundern, die sich zwischen
ihm und dem Charakter eines Mistrauischen zeigt, der nach der Zeit
gleichfalls durch den seligen Baron von Cronegk auf die deutsche Bühne
gebracht worden.[2]

And Mendelssohn had criticised Cronegk's comedy as follows:

Sein Lustspiel, der Misstrauische, ist zwar meines Erachtens kaum mehr
als mittelmässig. Vielleicht ist der Hauptcharakter keiner glücklichern
Ausführung fähig. Wer Argwohn, Mistrauen und Menschenfurcht so
weit treibet, erreget Widerwillen, und beynahe Mitleiden, denn man ist
geneigt, seine Schwachheit für einen Fehler des Gehirns zu halten.[3]

J. C. KRÜGER

The very popular 'Nachspiel' *Herzog Michel*, by Johann Christian
Krüger,[4] was inevitably in the Hamburg repertory. Lessing, however,
has little to say of it (LXXXIII, 76), except to comment on its popularity.
He also mentions Krüger's comedies, *Die Candidaten*, which, although
it was not played within the period covered by the *Dramaturgie*, he

[1] *Werke*, ed. *cit.* ii, pp. 185 f.
[2] *Ibid.* p. 188.
[3] *Litteraturbriefe*, No. cxci (October 15, 1761), ed. *cit.* xi, p. 187; *Gesammelte
Schriften*, ed. *cit.* iv, 2, pp. 310 f.
[4] In St. XXVIII, 21 Lessing spells his name 'Krieger', as he wrote 'betriegen';
in LXXXIII, 78, 82, 83, 88, however, 'Krüger'. Löwen said of this writer (*Geschichte
des deutschen Theaters*, ed. *cit.* p. 49): 'Er hatte alle Anlagen, ein deutscher Moliere
zu werden; aber er starb zu frühe, und sein Verlust war für die deutsche Bühne
gross.' He was born in 1723 and died in 1750.

may have seen in November, 1767, and *Die Geistlichen auf dem Lande*.[1] Krüger was, in addition, represented in the repertory by translations of several French plays: Destouches' *Der verheyrathete Philosoph*, probably Regnard's *Der Spieler*, and two by Marivaux, *Der unvermuthete Ausgang* and *Der Bauer mit der Erbschaft*.

G. E. LESSING

Of his own plays it was obviously impossible for Lessing to say much. When *Der Schatz*, his adaptation of Plautus's *Trinummus*, was performed, he referred (IX, 102) to its concentration in one act, and to the difficulty of the absence of female interest (113). C. H. Schmid commented in his *Chronologie des deutschen Theaters* (*ed. cit.* p. 96):

> So sehr es der Leser auch von der Seite bewundert, dass es ohne alle weibliche Rollen ausgearbeitet ist, so hat es doch eben deswegen auf den niedersächsischen Bühnen keinen grossen Beyfall finden wollen.

I refer later to the French and Italian versions of Plautus's comedy mentioned by Lessing.[2]

Der Freygeist gives occasion (XIV, 111) for a protest against the alteration of its title[3] to *Der beschämte Freygeist* in Hamburg,[4] since the 'Freygeisterey' of the play, Lessing argues, is not confined to Adrast. In discussing his *Miss Sara Sampson*—the oldest German tragedy in the repertory except *Canut*—Lessing admits (XIII, 125) that it is too

---

[1] Cp. Lessing's 'Vorrede' to the *Vermischte Schriften* of Ch. Mylius (*Schriften*, vi, p. 402): 'Kurz vorher waren die Geistlichen auf dem Lande zum Vorschein gekommen. Sie kennen dieses Stück; es hatte einen jungen Menschen zum Verfasser, der hier in Berlin noch auf Schulen war, der aber nach der Zeit bessere Ansprüche auf den Ruhm eines guten komischen Dichters der Welt vorlegte, und selbst aus Liebe zur Bühne ein Schauspieler ward, nämlich den verstorbenen Hrn. Krieger.' W. Wittekindt (*J. C. Krüger*, Berlin, 1898, p. 33) questions the statement that *Die Geistlichen auf dem Lande* was written while Krüger was in the Graue Kloster.

[2] See below, pp. 197 and 278. On the Plautine original see pp. 330 f.

[3] The titles of plays were a matter in which Lessing was particularly interested. See below, pp. 467 f.

[4] The critic in the *Deutsche Bibliothek* (iii (ix), 1769, p. 57) asserts that the title *Der beschämte Freygeist* was given to Lessing's comedy in Hamburg in order to distinguish it from Brawe's play of the same name (published as a supplement to the *Bibliothek der schönen Wissenschaften*, 1758). The earliest representations of the latter noted by A. Sauer (*J. W. von Brawe*, Strassburg, 1878, pp. 49 f.), were in Berlin in 1767; in Hamburg not until 1772. But Kurz (Bernardon) had played it in Nürnberg in 1766 (cp. F. Raab, *J. J. F. von Kurz*, ed. cit. p. 154).

long;[1] but he does not approve of the Hamburg method of curtailing it. He turns then (XIV, 1) to the review of his play in the *Journal étranger* of December 1761 (pp. 5 ff.),[2] which consists, for the most part, of a detailed analysis with extracts from a French translation.[3]

[1] Cp. Löwen, *Geschichte des deutschen Theaters, ed. cit.* p. 49: 'Die Comödianten beschweren sich, dass die letzten Scenen im letzten Aufzuge zu lang sind, und sie haben vielleicht nicht ganz unrecht. Inzwischen sind sie doch nicht langweilig und ermüdend.' The first performance, at Frankfurt a/d. Oder, had taken from three and a half to four hours. Litzmann (*F. L. Schröder, ed. cit.* i, p. 93) gives a note of the usual curtailments in the theatres of this time; and Weisse seems to have been responsible for those made in Leipzig in 1756. (Cp. Danzel and Guhrauer, *G. E. Lessing, ed. cit.* i, p. 324.) On the playbill for the performance of *Miss Sara Sampson* in Hanover on February 23, 1769, a note was added, explaining the absence of a ballet or after-piece: 'Wegen Länge des Stücks wird zum Beschluss Mlle Ackermann eine italienische Arie singen.'

[2] Lessing's attention was drawn to the article by the *Litteraturbriefe*, No. cclvi (January 27, 1763), *ed. cit.* xvi, p. 51: 'Im December wird aus Herrn Lessings Miss Sara Sampson ein ausführlicher Auszug geliefert und die schönsten Auftritte ganz übersetzt. Es werden auch verschiedene Einwürfe wider einzelne Scenen gemacht, die wohl einer näheren Beleuchtung werth wären. Da man aber so zu sagen immer das Buch bey der Hand haben müste, so würde mich dieses hier alzuweit führen. Im ganzen lassen die Verfasser diesem Stüke alle Gerechtigkeit wiederfahren. Ich weiss von guter Hand, dass dieses Trauerspiel vielleicht noch diesen Winter auf dem französischen Theater zu Paris wird aufgeführet werden; Eine Ehre, die vielleicht noch keinem Stüke, das nicht ursprünglich französisch ist, wiederfahren seyn mag. Herr Diderot wird auch nächstens die Uebersetzung dieses Trauerspiels und des engländischen Spielers mit vielen Anmerkungen herausgeben.' (Petersen, *ed. cit.* p. 194, assigns this letter to Resewitz.) On May 6, 1764, Lessing wrote to Weisse: 'Er [Professor Straube] hat von mir den Auftrag, mir die Theile von dem Journal etranger zu kauffen, in welchen, nach den Briefen über die neueste Litteratur, einige von meinen Geburthen recensiret sind. Haben Sie die Gütigkeit, ihm solche nachzuweisen' (*Schriften*, xvii, p. 207). Much of the review is reprinted by Danzel (Danzel and Guhrauer, *op. cit.* i, pp. 467 ff.), who, on the strength of what was said in the *Litteraturbriefe*, attributes it to Diderot himself. This too may have suggested Lessing's own reference (immediately following) to Diderot (XIV, 42).

[3] The French translation of *Miss Sara Sampson* appeared in Bielfeld's *Progrès des Allemands* (3rd ed. Leyden, 1767, ii, pp. 343 ff.). The French critic in the *Journal étranger* attributed the translation to a man 'qui donne à la culture des Sciences, des Lettres et des Arts (car il sacrifie au chœur entier des Muses) tous les intervalles que lui laissent ses importantes occupations' (p. 41). A translation of the play had been made by Trudaine de Montigny, and was played in the private theatre of the Duc d'Ayen at St Germain-en-Laye, producing so deep an impression that it was repeated several times. According to Grimm, *Correspondance littéraire* (December 1, 1764) this translation was not printed. Cp. Hans Kinkel, *Lessings Dramen in Frankreich* (Diss. Heidelberg), Darmstadt, 1908, p. 4; cp. also T. Süpfle: *Geschichte des deutschen Kultureinflusses auf Frankreich*, Gotha, 1886–8, ii (i), pp. 6 f., 184.

Lessing's quotation, however, concerns rather the 'bürgerliches Trauerspiel' as a form of drama[1] than *Miss Sara Sampson* itself. The French critic had much praise for the play, but he had objected (XIV, 55) to several scenes and situations as being exaggerated or inconsistent; he had said (pp. 39 f.):

Du reste on ne peut disputer à M. Lessing le vrai génie de la Poésie dramatique, c'est à dire, le don de se pénétrer des sentimens les plus intimes de la nature, et de les exprimer avec beaucoup de chaleur, d'énergie et de vérité. Nous ne desirons dans sa Piece que plus de précision et de rapidité dans le dialogue, des scenes moins alongées et par conséquent plus vives, en un mot un tissu plus serré dans l'intrigue et dans l'action, mais surtout moins de négligence dans la maniere de préparer et d'amener les événemens.

To this Lessing replies (XIV, 59) by quoting Voltaire's retort to the critics of his *Enfant prodigue*:

Je recevrai avec résignation toutes les critiques de Mr. d'Argental; mais on ne peut pas toujours exécuter ce que nos amis nous conseillent. Il y a d'ailleurs des défauts nécessaires. Vous ne pouvés guérir un bossu de sa bosse, qu'en lui ôtant la vie. Mon enfant est bossu; mais il se porte bien.[2]

Amongst Lessing's papers is the following which may have been intended for use when *Miss Sara Sampson* was repeated on July 20 (LXXIII, 15):

Den—ward Miss Sara Sampson wiederhohlt.
Auch der H. Baron von Bielefeld hat in der neuen Ausgabe seines Progrès des Allemands etc. [à Leide, 1767. 8. T. II. p. 343] dieses Stück durch einen umständlichen Auszug den Ausländern bekannt machen wollen. Der Verfasser muss ihm für diese Ehre verbunden seyn; aber sollte er nicht eines und das andre gegen das Urtheil des H. Barons einzuwenden haben?
'Sara Sampson,' sagt H. v. Bielefeld, 'ist zwar ein ursprünglich deutsches Stück; gleichwohl scheint der Stoff aus englischen Romanen genommen

---

[1] See below, pp. 397 ff.
[2] The passage comes from a letter to Berger of October 24, 1736; cp. C. B. Boxberger (*Einzelheiten über Voltaire bei Lessing*, Dresden, 1879, p. 17), who refers the anecdote to *Alzire*, and comments that he does not know how Lessing came to be aware of this letter. Lessing found it in the *Lettres secretes de Mr. de Voltaire*, publiées par Mr. L. B. [J. B. R. Robinet], Geneva, 1765, Lettre xix, p. 71. This collection of letters was included in the *Recueil de nouvelles pièces*, supplementary to the Geneva edition of Voltaire's works, viii (1765), reprinted at 'Francfort et Leipzig' in the same year. There was also a German translation (cp. G. Bengesco, *Bibliographie de Voltaire*, Paris, 1882–90, iii, p. 81) which may have been Lessing's immediate source.

oder nachgeahmt zu seyn, und der Geist, so wie der Geschmak dieser Nation, darinn zu herrschen.'

Was soll dieses eigentlich sagen? Der Stoff scheint aus englischen Romanen genommen zu seyn? Einem die Erfindung von etwas abzustreiten, ist dazu ein 'es scheint' genug? Welches ist der englische Roman?[1]

The first performance of *Minna von Barnhelm* on the Hamburg stage did not take place until September 30, 1767,[2] too late to be recorded by Lessing himself. But it is just possible that it has left some trace on the *Dramaturgie*. May not the words at the close of St. xxxvi (142), in which Lessing refers to his own refusal ('mein Beyspiel') to appear on the stage in answer to a call, relate to the first performance of *Minna*? Although St. xxxvi bears the date September 1, it was not published until December 15.[3] Apart from *Minna von Barnhelm* the plays by Lessing which had hitherto been performed were *Der Schatz* (April 27), *Miss Sara Sampson* (May 6) and *Der Freygeist* (May 12).

J. C. CRONEGK

In the *Litteraturbriefe* (No. lxxxi, February 7, 1760) Lessing had bracketed together the two rivals for the prize of the *Bibliothek der schönen Wissenschaften*, J. F. von Cronegk and J. W. von Brawe, 'von welchen beyden ohne Zweifel der letztere das grössere tragische Genie war'. But the Hamburg theatre gave him no opportunity of discussing Brawe; his name is only once mentioned in the *Dramaturgie* (xiv, 112).[4]

To Cronegk fell the honour of opening the 'Enterprise'. In criticising *Olint und Sophronia* Lessing probably had before him the edition of Cronegk's *Schriften*, published in two volumes by J. P. Uz

[1] *Schriften*, xv, pp. 38 f.

[2] This date is not certain; the first performance may possibly have been on October 1. See above, p. 33, note 2.

[3] For evidence of addition subsequent to the nominal date see above, p. 90, note 2, and below, p. 172, note 1. Lessing's mode of addressing himself in the third person is illustrated in his letter to Mendelssohn of October 22, 1757 (*Schriften*, xvii, p. 126): 'Es arbeitet hier noch ein junger Mensch an einem Trauerspiele' and in his letter to Nicolai of January 21, 1758 (*ibid.* p. 133): 'mein junger Tragikus'.

[4] Lessing's spelling here, 'Brave', may be merely a misprint; but cp. also *Litteraturbriefe*, No. lxxxi (February 7, 1760; *ed. cit.* v, p. 83). For Lessing's opinion of him, see especially his letters to Nicolai of February 19, 1757, and to Mendelssohn of February 18, 1758 (*Schriften*, xvii, pp. 94, 138).

at Leipzig in 1760–61 (or possibly the 'neue rechtmäsige und verbesserte Auflage' of 1765–66); but Roschmann's conclusion of the
play he probably only heard from the stage, although it had been
printed in Vienna in 1764. The modern reader is hardly likely to
cavil at Lessing's estimate of *Olint und Sophronia*; but it is not wholly
fair to the poet. Lessing was under some compulsion, when the theatre
opened, to pay tribute to its two leading actors, Ekhof and Madame
Hensel; thus he singled out their rôles for particular consideration.
Now that of Evander, which Ekhof played, is an exceedingly small
one, consisting only of some hundred and eighty lines in all; although
Olint's father, he is little more than his confidant (II, 90). Indeed,
after letting him appear in the two opening scenes and in three brief
scenes in Act II, Cronegk seems to have lost sight of him altogether.
Roschmann, however, finds a place for him in his fifth act. Olint is
naturally much the more important personage. For a similar reason
Lessing discusses Clorinde, played by Madame Hensel, and not
Sophronia, the central female figure of the play, whose part is about
twice the length of Clorinde's; but Sophronia was played by Madame
Mecour, and Lessing, it will be remembered, was debarred from
mentioning her. Unfortunately these considerations have distorted
the literary criticism of the play, for most of the small modicum of
poetry it contains is to be found in the lines that fall—especially in
Act IV—to Sophronia. Her rôle—in Tasso that of 'einer lieben,
ruhigen, ganz geistigen Schwärmerinn' (I, 81)[1]—was, at the best, not
much to Lessing's taste; but it was at least free from the extravagant
inconsistencies which he condemns a little too emphatically in Clorinde
(V, 14): 'ein sehr abgeschmacktes, widerwärtiges, hässliches Ding',
he calls her, who rants 'in dem wahren Tone einer besoffenen Marque-
tenderinn' (39). Nor is Lessing's proof of the absurdity of her 'so
zittre' (28) convincing; he was always a little intolerant of a poet's
right to overstep the limits of the conventional. When he says with
Mendelssohn (see below, p. 146) that Cronegk's characters are 'ausser
aller Natur' (V, 19) it is surely too sweeping a condemnation; Mendelssohn failed to see that once or twice, and precisely in the part of
Sophronia, Cronegk does rise above the dull rant of the German
alexandrine—as he also does occasionally in his choruses.

---

[1] Mendelssohn, in a review of Cronegk's works in the *Litteraturbriefe* (see below,
pp. 145 ff.), describes Sophronia as 'eine liebenswürdige Schwärmerinn' (*Litteraturbriefe*, No. cxci, *ed. cit.* xi, p. 179; *Gesammelte Schriften, ed. cit.* iv, 2, p. 305). Cp. my
edition of *Nathan der Weise*, Cambridge, 1912, p. xxvi.

Cronegk is arraigned for his ignorance of Mohammedanism, and in particular for representing it as a polytheistic belief (I, 53):[1] a Mohammedan priest—in Tasso, Lessing notes, it is a magician—could never have counselled the transference of the image of the Virgin—which Cronegk converts into a crucifix—from the temple to the mosque (50).[2] In making Olint steal the crucifix and thus jeopardise his people for so trivial a cause, Cronegk, Lessing points out (67), gives the character of the hero a very contemptible side.[3] In Tasso, moreover, it is his love for Sophronia alone which leads him to accuse himself. When the king has the two lovers bound to the same stake, Olindo says (canto ii, strophes xxxiii–xxxv—I quote from the translation of J. F. Koppe, Leipzig, 1744 (pp. 44 f.) which had, no doubt, been used by Cronegk):

> Ist dieses nun das Band, womit die Zärtlichkeit,
> Uns zu vereinigen, bisher mir prophezeiht?
> Soll das das Feuer seyn, das, wie ich hoffen wollte,
> Dereinst mit gleicher Brunst uns noch entzünden sollte?...
>
> Mein Trost ist, dass das Glück, das mir dein Bette raubt,
> Mir deinen Holzstoss noch zum wenigsten erlaubt!
> Wir sterben; doch nur dich, nur dich beklag' ich heute,
> Mein Schicksal aber nicht! ich sterb' an deiner Seite!
>
> Und o wie würde mir doch Tod und Schmerz und Pein
> So süss, so angenehm, so höchsterfreulich seyn,
> Erlangt' ich nur das Glück, in meinen letzten Zügen,
> Mit dir noch Brust an Brust und Mund an Mund zu fügen!
> Damit alsdenn mein Geist aus meinen Lippen flög,
> Und aus den deinigen die letzten Seufzer zög!

Lessing resents the allocation of all the virtues to the Christians, and all the vices to the heathens (VII, 25 ff.); he also criticises—strangely, in view of what he himself was to do some years later—Cronegk's

---

[1] The passages which Lessing quotes (55 ff.) are from Act I, sc. i and iii.

[2] In Mercier's *Olinde et Sophronie*, Paris, 1771, which was based on a French translation of Cronegk's play, the author makes the priest, Ismen, tear a manuscript of the *Koran* instead, the image of the Virgin or the crucifix being, in Mercier's opinion, too sacred to bring on to the stage (cp. W. Gensel, *J. F. von Cronegk*, Leipzig, 1894, p. 101). In the English play by A. Portal, *Olindo and Sophronia*, London, 1758 (see below, p. 150), the image of the Virgin is retained.

[3] Similarly Mercier had said in the Preface to his own play: 'ce qui, selon moi, détruit toute la noblesse du caractère de son Héros.' But might not Mercier have read the *Dramaturgie*? Cp. Lessing's defence of Mohammedanism in his 'Rettung' of Cardanus (*Schriften*, v, pp. 315 ff.).

choice of Jerusalem at the time of the Crusades as the scene of a drama preaching tolerance. His condemnation of the play is largely based on the fact that he sees in it, with the *Journal encyclopédique* (see below, p. 149), a 'Christian' tragedy after the manner of Corneille's *Polyeucte* (I, 105); whereas in Tasso's treatment of the story (I, 35) the erotic theme is given more prominence than the religious one. Cronegk might have been allowed more credit, however, for his efforts to weld a recalcitrant epic story into a play.

The general character of Cronegk's adaptation will be seen from a comparison of its plot (see above, p. 56) with the following account of the episode as it appears in Tasso's epic:

Aladin, king of Jerusalem, is persuaded by Ismeno, a renegade Christian who has not entirely forgotten his old faith, to place an image of the Virgin, taken from a Christian church, in the mosque; he believes that by this means Jerusalem will be rendered impregnable against the crusaders. In the night it mysteriously disappears and the king, convinced that it has been stolen by some Christian, resolves to kill every Christian in the city, if the thief does not give himself up. Hereupon the beautiful Christian maiden, Sofronia, to save her people, takes the responsibility for the theft on her own shoulders. Then Olindo, who has long loved her, claims to have done the deed in order to save her. As both maintain their guilt, both are condemned to die at the stake. Clorinda, a Persian queen, saves their lives by inducing the king to exercise clemency. They marry, but are obliged to leave Jerusalem.

Lessing rightly criticises (II, 2) the suddenness of Clorinde's conversion to Christianity in Cronegk's play, and its lack of adequate motive in her character; Sophronia's words to her (17) in Act IV (Lessing by a slip writes 'des dritten Akts'), sc. iv, are not of a kind to effect such a conversion. Tasso manages this much better by reserving the conversion for Clorinde's last hour; and Lessing also adduces the parallel of Zamore in Voltaire's *Alzire*.

On the whole, the influence of Mendelssohn's review of Cronegk's works, which appeared in the *Litteraturbriefe* of October 8 and 15, 1761,[1] is plainly to be seen in Lessing's criticism here. Mendelssohn was of opinion that *Olint und Sophronia* was superior to *Codrus*,[2] of which

---

[1] Nos. cxc, cxci, *ed. cit.* xi, pp. 167 ff.; *Gesammelte Schriften, ed. cit.* iv, 2, pp. 299 ff. See also above, p. 138, for Mendelssohn's criticism of Cronegk's comedy *Der Misstrauische*.

[2] No. cxci, *ed. cit.* xi, pp. 175 f.; *Gesammelte Schriften, ed. cit.* iv, 2, pp. 303 f.

he had said: 'Es gehöret freylich zu den besten deutschen Trauerspielen; aber leider! die besten deutschen Trauerspiele würden in
Frankreich und England kaum gute Trauerspiele seyn.'[1] Mendelssohn
also compares—as Lessing does (i, 16 ff.)—Cronegk's treatment of the
subject with Tasso's, to the advantage of the latter.[2] And although
he does not deal with the excessive emphasis on martyrdom in the
play, his criticism of Cronegk's *Codrus* was clearly present, as Cosack
has shown (*op. cit.* p. 24), to Lessing's mind. For his 'beide haben
nichts als das Märterthum im Kopfe', etc. (i, 84) the following passage
from Mendelssohn may be compared:[3]

Die vollkommenen Charaktere müssen dem Dichter ungemein gefallen
haben. Alle seine Charaktere überschreiten die Natur. Codrus, Medon,
Elisinde[4] und Philaide sind höchst tugendhaft, und Artander höchst
lasterhaft. Jene sind vollkommene Engel, dieser ein vollkommener Teufel.
Es herrscht daher eine unerträgliche Einförmigkeit in den Gesinnungen
der handelnden Personen....Aus dieser Häufung der vollkommenen
Charaktere ist noch eine andere Unbequemlichkeit entsprungen. Der
Hauptvorwurf des Trauerspiels ist der Tod des Codrus fürs Vaterland,
Codrus pro patria non timidus mori. Die Bereitwilligkeit sich dem Wohl
des Vaterlandes aufzuopfern, sollte also in dem Charakter des Codrus
hervorleuchten, und ihn von allen übrigen handelnden Personen unterscheiden. Allein Medon, Elisinde und Philaide sind alle Augenblick bereit, für Athen, für den König und einer für den andern zu sterben.
Wenn unter diesen grossmüthigen Seelen irgend eine Uneinigkeit entstehet;
so ist es immer um den Vorzug zu sterben; so sehr entfernt sind sie, von
der feigen Liebe zum Leben, und also auch von der Befremdung, mit
welcher gemeine Seelen einen willigen Tod betrachten. Der Zuschauer,
den diese Heroische Gesinnungen beständig vor den Ohren gehen [gellen],
muss zuletzt das Betragen des *Codrus* eben nicht ausserordentlich finden.
Er wird sich vielmehr verwundern, dass der grosse Codrus den Tod fürs
Vaterland nicht so entschlossen, nicht so freudig stirbt, als jede andere
von den handelnden Personen thun würde. In der That, der Entschluss
für Athen zu sterben, macht den König bekümmert, unruhig und nieder-
geschlagen, indessen dass die übrigen handelnden Personen nichts sehnlicher
wünschen, als für Athen, oder auch einer für den andern zu sterben. Der

---

[1] *Litteraturbriefe*, No. cxc, *ed. cit.* xi, p. 167; *Gesammelte Schriften, ed. cit.* iv, 2,
pp. 299 f.

[2] The suggestion (i, 29) that Tasso modelled his episode on Virgil's Nisus and
Euryalus (*Aeneid*, v, 294–361; ix, 176–439) had not escaped the notice of the older
commentators of Tasso, *e.g.* G. Guastavini (*Il Goffredo, ovvero Gerusalemme liberata di
Torquato*, annotated by S. Gentili and G. Guastavini, Venice, 1760–1, i, p. 323).

[3] *Litteraturbriefe*, No. cxc, *ed. cit.* xi, pp. 169 ff.; *Gesammelte Schriften, ed. cit.* iv, 2,
p. 301.

[4] Lessing's 'Elesinde' (97) is obviously a misprint.

Dichter hätte sich die hohen heroischen Gesinnungen ausspahren [auf-sparen] sollen, damit sie in dem Charakter des Helden desto stärker in die Augen leuchten mögen.[1]

In asserting that the 'scattered moral sentiments' ('die eingestreuten Moralen') form the best side of Cronegk's work (II, 100) Lessing was again repeating an opinion of Mendelssohn's. Of *Codrus* the latter had said (p. 170 [301]):

Es ist wahr, die Sittensprüche des Herrn von C. sind vortreflich; es ist wahr, er schildert die Tugend erhaben, und das Laster kriechend und abscheulich; Allein je mehr dieses die Absicht des tragischen Dichters ist, desto sorgfältiger muss er sie verbergen. Wenn er gerade zu moralisiret; so wird er frostig.[2]

And it would almost seem as if Lessing had been prepared for the parterre's approval of such sentiments (II, 111) by Mendelssohn's anticipation that it would applaud (pp. 167 f. [300]):

...Der Beyfall des deutschen Parterre ist noch weit unzuverlässiger [than the praise of the critics]....Eine glückliche Tirade, einige spitzfindige Sittensprüche bringen ihre Hände in Bewegung; sie klatschen, das Volk gähnet, und die wahren Kenner schweigen. Wie wenig kann sich ein Dichter auf einen solchen Beyfall zu Gute thun![3]

Exception can hardly be taken to Lessing's statement at the outset of his criticism (I, 9) that Cronegk had died too early, and that his fame rested more 'auf das, was er, nach dem Urtheile seiner Freunde,[4]

---

[1] 'Der Codrus', wrote Lessing to Mendelssohn on October 22, 1757 (*Schriften*, xvii, p. 126; cp. also pp. 138 f.), 'hat nichts weniger, als meinen Beyfall. Doch wünschte ich, dass Herr Nicolai dem Verfasser nicht alle Wahrheiten sagte, die man ihm sagen könnte.' As has been seen, Nicolai had offered in 1756 a prize for the best German tragedy submitted to the *Bibliothek der schönen Wissenschaften*, and *Codrus*, not Brawe's *Freygeist*—surely a much better play—was awarded the prize. 'Dass die Verf. der Bibl[iothek] der schönen Wissenschaften', said Mendelssohn in his review just quoted (p. 168 [300]), 'dem Codrus den Preis zu erkant, wird Ihnen wohl der geringste Beweis für seine Vortreflichkeit seyn'. Cp. *Dramaturgie*, VII, 54.

[2] Quoted also by L. Goldstein, *Moses Mendelssohn und die deutsche Ästhetik*, Königsberg, 1904, p. 211. Cp. Löwen's opinion of *Codrus* (*Geschichte des deutschen Theaters*, ed. cit. pp. 49 f.): 'Dem Codrus hat man schon lange vorgeworfen, dass er zu Sentenzenreich sey. Es ist wahr, Cronegk sagt diese Sentenzen allemal schön; aber nur Schade, am unrechten Ort. Diese Art zu schreiben ist verführerisch, und blendet sehr.'   [3] Cp. also Goldstein, *op. cit.* p. 211.

[4] In the 'Vorrede' to Cronegk's *Schriften*: 'Was konnte man sich nicht von einem Genie versprechen, das schon so viel geleistet, und noch weit mehr versprach! Sein früher Tod ist ein wahrer Verlust für ganz Deutschland.' This passage is also quoted in the review in the *Bibliothek der schönen Wissenschaften*, vi (i), 1760,

für [die Bühne] noch hätte leisten könne, als was er wirklich geleistet hat'. But contemporary opinion held that Lessing had been unduly harsh to this play.[1] He was surprised by this disapproval and a little apologetic (VII, 43); and he intended to return on a later occasion to 'dem vermeinten Unrechte, welches ich dem H. v. C. als dramatischen Dichter erwiesen haben soll'.[2] But his opinion of *Olint und Sophronia* was essentially in agreement with Mendelssohn's.

If Lessing is severe on Cronegk, he is still more so on Roschmann, the completer of the play (II, 62), who is described in the preface to the Vienna edition as 'ein junger Dichter aus Tyrol, der viel tragisches Genie blicken lässt'.[3] Lessing was indeed inclined to be severe on

p. 107. When Cronegk died, at the age of twenty-six, on December 31, 1757, Lessing wrote to Nicolai (*Schriften*, xvii, p. 132): 'Er war ein Genie, dem bloss das fehlte, wozu er nun ewig nicht gelangen wird: die Reife.' Cp. VII, 53.

[1] The critic of the Leipzig *Neue Zeitungen von gelehrten Sachen* had said (September 24, 1767): 'Man vermisst [die Strenge] gewiss auch nicht bey...Olint und Sophronia'. Cp. also J. W. Braun, *op. cit.* i, p. 190: 'bey unseren Originalstücken, unter welchen *Olint und Sophronia* hier den Anfang macht...'; and W. Gensel, *op. cit.* p. 103, refers to a letter from Weisse to Uz of October 16, 1767 (published in the *Morgenblatt* of November 26, 1840, No. 283): 'Die Art, die man ietzt zu kritisiren einführet, gefällt mir gar nicht und ich sehe nicht, was man für Beruf hat, sich lächerlich machen zu lassen. Ich verehre Lessingen, als meinen Freund und einen scharfsinnigen Kunstrichter; aber die Art, wie er mit unserm ewig geliebten Cronegk umgeht, missfällt mir; er spricht ihm alle Fähigkeit, alles Genie ab, und chicaniret bisweilen über Kleinigkeiten, die höchstens beweisen, dass er ein Mensch und noch nicht das war, was er noch gewiss werden konnte.' On the other hand, Herder wrote on September 15, 1767 to Scheffner: 'Wir haben noch keine so gründliche Beurtheilung eines deutschen Trauerspiels, als er über Olint und Sophronia liefert' (cp. also Petersen, *ed. cit.* p. 178).

[2] *Entwürfe zu Besprechungen* (*Schriften*, xv, p. 42).

[3] Cp. the article by K. F. Kummer already cited (p. 55) for a detailed account of Roschmann's conclusion. Sonnenfels in his *Briefe über die Wienerische Schaubühne* under the date January 20, 1769, defended Roschmann against Lessing (ed. A. Sauer, *Wiener Neudrucke*, vii, Vienna, 1884, p. 322): 'Roschmannen kennen Sie als den Ergänzer von Olynth und Sophronia, dem Lessing in seiner Drammaturgie, wenn jemals einem Dichter, zu hart gethan, und wenn ich sagen darf, mit einem so hämischen Tone beurtheilt hat. Sein fünfter Aufzug hat nicht wenige, ich möchte sagen voltärische Verse; der Kühnheit; dem Wohlklange nach, *Croneghs* nicht unwürdig. Vielleicht hat Lessing recht, dass die Handlung ein wenig lau ist: aber setze sich der Kunstrichter hin an des Dichters Stelle, und ergänze er an einem Plane, dazu, wie die Verfasser der Briefe ü. d. N. Liter: sprachen, der Stoff schon ganz verschnitten ist! und er wird die Schwierigkeiten kennen lernen, die dem Ergänzer aufstossen....ich will die roschmannsche Ergänzung nicht mangelfrey finden; aber erträglich, mehr als erträglich.' Cp. W. Gensel, *op. cit.* p. 100. F. W. Gotter also supplied Cronegk's drama with a continuation in 1768 (cp. R. Schlösser, *F. W. Gotter*, Hamburg, 1894, p. 194) but this was not published.

completers, adapters and imitators.[1] In the present case the condemnation is not undeserved: the fifth act is definitely inferior to Cronegk's work.[2] Lessing appears to object particularly to Roschmann's tragic conclusion, contrasting it in this respect with the episode in Tasso (64); but Cronegk called his unfinished play a 'Trauerspiel', and the whole action points to such an end.[3]

Had the next performance of the play fallen within the period covered by the *Dramaturgie*, Lessing would, no doubt, have defended his standpoint in respect of both Cronegk and Roschmann. For his subsequent purpose he made some notes:[4]

Warum wollen wir mit Schätzen gegen Ausländer prahlen, die wir nicht haben? So sagt z. E. das Journal Encycl. [September 1, 1761], dass sein Misstrauischer, auf unserm Theater Beyfall gehabt, und allezeit gern gesehen würde. Nichts weniger als das. Es ist ein ausstehliches Stück, und der Dialog desselben äusserst platt.

And he then translated the following passage from the article concerning the present play in the *Journal encyclopédique* of September, 1761 (pp. 91 f.):

Encouragé par ce succès [*Codrus*], l'Auteur entreprit une autre Tragédie, où il avoit dessein d'introduire des chœurs, selon l'usage des Grecs. Il vouloit essayer si ce que Racine a fait en France avec succès dans *Athalie*, pourroit réussir en Allemagne; mais après avoir surmonté les plus grands obstacles, et son travail étant très avancé, il y renonça tout à coup, croyant que son projet ne pouvoit réussir, attendu la nature de la Musique allemande. Il crut appercevoir qu'elle n'étoit nullement propre à rendre la beauté des sentimens et la noblesse des pensées qu'il vouloit exprimer; mais il nous semble qu'il auroit pu se passer de musique, comme M. de Voltaire dans la Tragédie de *Brutus*, où il a mis des chœurs. Quoiqu'il en soit, il abandonna sa pièce; les fragmens qui en restent, où l'on trouve de grandes beautés, font regretter qu'il n'ait pas mis la derniere main à son projet. L'Allemagne pourroit se vanter d'avoir une Tragédie Chrétienne qui feroit honneur à son Théâtre. Le sujet est tiré de la *Jérusalem délivrée*....

[1] Cp. the criticisms referred to below, pp. 154 f., 157 f., 327 ff.

[2] I cannot throw any light on the origin or occasion of Lessing's anecdote (II, 71) of the heroine of a still worse tragedy, who was said to have died of the fifth act.

[3] It might be noted that neither the English dramatist Portal nor the French writer Mercier, who based his play on a French translation of Cronegk's, ends his piece tragically. Mendelssohn was of opinion (*loc. cit.* p. 176 [304]) that Cronegk had difficulty in finishing his play: 'Wo ich nicht irre, so hat der Ausgang den Dichter zu früh übereilt; der Stof war in den ersten vier Aufzügen verschnitten, und der Rest wollte zum fünften nicht hinreichen. Doch dieses sind Muthmassungen!'

[4] *Entwürfe zu Besprechungen* (*Schriften*, xv, pp. 42 f.).

Lessing's comment is:

Wie abgeschmakt ist das! Die deutsche Musik! Wenn man noch gesagt hätte die deutsche Poesie wär zur Musik ungeschikt! Und die ganze Sache ist nicht wahr. Cronegk hat seine Arbeit nicht aufgegeben, sondern er ist drüber gestorben. Was der Journalist am Ende dazu setzt, ist allem Ansehen nach auch eine Lügen: Un Ecrivain Anglois qui a senti le merite de cette Tragedie, se l'est appropriée. Sa piece a paru sous ce titre: *Olindo and Sophronia a Tragedy taken from Tasso, by Abraham Portal, Esq.* London. 1758. Da wird der gute Portal zum Plagiario, der vielleicht den Namen Cronegk, nie gehört hat. A[nn]o 1758 war Cronegks Olint noch nicht gedruckt.[1]

Further indication of what Lessing proposed to discuss when he returned to the play is to be found in his list of the repertory (*Schriften*, xv, p. 50):

Von Portlands [Portals] Sophronia. *Month. Review*, Vol. xix, p. 94. Von der WiederEinführung des Chors. Hord [Hurd] p. 116. N. 190. Von Mason's Chören. *Month. R.* Vol. xx p. 507. Von Stirlings Tragödien mit Chören. s. Cibb. Lif. Vol. i. p. 315. Auch Daniels seine ibid. p. 147.

C. F. WEISSE

Lessing's attitude to the friend of his youth, Christian Felix Weisse, whom, for some inexplicable reason, he persists in calling 'Weiss',[2] is still more lacking in warmth and charity, even in reasonable fairness. It has been suggested that Lessing was jealous of Weisse's popular success as a dramatist, so much greater than his own; but it is perhaps enough explanation to say that Lessing, judging Weisse's popularity out of proportion to his literary merit, felt that words should not be spared. Weisse, on his part, accepted meekly, even generously, his friend's trouncings. He did not allow them to interfere with the old friendship.[3]

---

[1] See *Journal encyclopédique*, September, 1761, p. 96. Mendelssohn also mentions the English play in his review already quoted (*Bibliothek der schönen Wissenschaften*, vi (i), 1760, p. 123): 'Da wir das englische Trauerspiel nicht gesehen haben, so können wir nicht entscheiden, welches den Vorzug verdient.'

[2] XXXIX, 127; LXXIII, 67, 75. In the *Litteraturbriefe* (No. lxxxi, *ed. cit.* v, pp. 82, 88; *Schriften*, viii, pp. 215, 218) he wrote 'Weise'. 'Stl.' in the *Deutsche Bibliothek*, iv (xv), 1769, p. 498, said: 'Ich kann nicht sagen, warum Lessing immer Weiss zu schreiben affectirt.'

[3] See Weisse, *Selbstbiographie*, Leipzig, 1806, pp. 137 ff. for Weisse's subsequent account of his later relations with Lessing.

Lessing had occasion to criticise two of his plays, *Amalia* and *Richard der Dritte*.[1] The former, he says (xx, 89), has been regarded by the critics as Weisse's best comedy;[2] a view which he appears to endorse. He does not altogether disapprove of the 'romanenhafte' element—the fact that Manley's sex is not recognised (97)—but suggests the modification of 'some all too bold strokes' in the last act.[3] He proposes another and more natural way of bringing about the dénouement: why should not Manley (Amalia) take advantage of her knowledge that Freemann is not really the husband of Sophie, and make serious love to Sophie with a view to bringing about the breach between her and Freemann? It is, however, difficult to see how the plot, unnatural at best, would be much improved by this. Lessing evidently did not like the frivolous tone of the whole, a feeling with which the modern reader will be apt to agree.[4] That the criticism was generally resented —if not by Weisse himself—is to be seen from C. H. Schmid's *Zusätze zur Theorie der Poesie nach den neuesten Grundsätzen und Nachrichten von den besten Dichtern*, i, Leipzig, 1767, pp. 44 f. (a book to which Lessing refers in St. LXXIII, 147):

Die liebenswürdige Weissische Amalia wird auf Unkosten seiner übrigen Lustspiele gelobt. „Sie hat", heisst es, „mehr Interesse, ausgeführtere Charactere, einen lebhaftern gedankenreichern Dialog als seine übrigen komischen Stücke." Besonders wird die fünfte Scene des letzten Acts getadelt. Ich weiss es zwar auch nicht, ob man wirklich mit dem Frauenzimmer in diesem zudringlichen Tone spricht, aber das weiss ich, dass in den französischen Lustspielen die Marquis ziemlich zudringlich sprechen, und wie spricht Tartuff? Marivaux in der fausse suivante und Steele im tender Husband haben in ähnlichen Fällen das Frauenzimmer eben so unbescheiden seyn lassen. Amalia kennt die Freemann als sie ihren Plan entwirft, nur als ein eitles Frauenzimmer, sie konnte also nicht hoffen, dass ein ernsthafter Antrag bey ihr gute Wirkung habe. Auf den Argwohn

---

[1] In the *Litteraturbriefe* (*ed. cit.* v, pp. 88 ff.) he had discussed *Eduard der Dritte*; and in xxxix, 127 he refers to Weisse's iambic tragedy *Atreus und Thyest*, which was published in the *Beytrag zum deutschen Theater*, iv, Leipzig, 1766, and produced at Leipzig on January 28, 1767. (Cp. J. Minor, *C. F. Weisse und seine Beziehungen zur deutschen Literatur des 18. Jahrhunderts*, Innsbruck, 1880, p. 230; also C. H. Schmid, *Chronologie des deutschen Theaters*, *ed. cit.* pp. 161 f.)

[2] There is an echo of this opinion in the *Deutsche Bibliothek*, iii (xii), 1769, p. 622: 'bis jetzo das beste rührende Lustspiel in unsrer Sprache.'

[3] Weisse followed Lessing's advice in revising the play (Act v, sc. 5) for the edition of his *Lustspiele*, Leipzig, 1783 (vol. ii). Cp. J. Minor, *op. cit.* p. 110.

[4] 'Stl.' asked bluntly (*Deutsche Bibliothek*, iii (ix), 1769, p. 53): 'So ist Amalia gar schlüpfrig?'

von der Eitelkeit der Freemann gründet sich das ganze Stück; und wenn
die Voraussetzung des Dichters interessante Scenen erzeigt, warum wollen
wir die Voraussetzung missbilligen?

The production of Weisse's *Richard der Dritte* on July 22 gave Lessing
an opportunity for a comparison of that play with Shakespeare's, and
for an important section of his Aristotelian criticism. Thus almost all
the eleven parts of the *Dramaturgie* nominally dealing with *Richard der
Dritte* (LXXIII–LXXXIII) fall to be discussed elsewhere in the present
volume.[1] Lessing has, in fact, little actual criticism to offer of Weisse's
play. He regards it (LXXIII, 69) as 'ohnstreitig eines von unsern
beträchtlichsten Originalen; reich an grossen Schönheiten, die ge-
nugsam zeigen, dass die Fehler, mit welchen sie verwebt sind, zu
vermeiden, im geringsten nicht über die Kräfte des Dichters gewesen
wäre, wenn er sich diese Kräfte nur selbst hätte zutrauen wollen'.
The comparison with Shakespeare (74) had been initiated by
Weisse's own prefatory note:

Shäkespear, der grösste englische Dichter nach dem allgemeinen Geständ-
nisse seiner eigenen Nation, hat auch aus dem Leben Richard des dritten
ein historisches Trauerspiel verfertigt. Der Verfasser des gegenwärtigen
würde es niemals gewagt haben, diesem grossen Meister nachzuarbeiten,
und den schrecklichen Zug aus dieses Königs Geschichte zum Innhalte
eines neuen Trauerspiels zu machen, wenn er sich nicht zu spät daran
erinnert hätte. Sollte er aber ja bey der Vergleichung zu viel verliehren,
so wird man wenigstens finden, dass er keinen Plagiat begangen, indem
das Seinige fertig war, ehe er das Englische gelesen; aber vielleicht wäre
es ein Verdienst gewesen, beym Shäkspear einen Plagiat zu begehen!?[2]

Lessing's comment on this is (81) that Shakespeare cannot be plagi-
arised: there is not a line in him that does not bear the stamp of his
genius and proclaim to the whole world that it is Shakespeare's;
there is not a scene or speech in *Richard the Third* which Weisse could
have used as it stands; Shakespeare must be studied, not plundered.
It is a pity, he continues (113), that the German poet had not known
Shakespeare earlier, and used him as a corrective to his own work.[3]

---

[1] See below, pp. 249 f., 353, 415 f.

[2] *Beitrag zum deutschen Theater* I, 2nd (revised) ed. Leipzig, 1765, p. 123.

[3] I deal more fully with this in my chapter on the English drama (see below,
pp. 249 f.). On the genesis of Weisse's play see W. Hüttemann, *C. F. Weisse und
seine Zeit in ihrem Verhältnis zu Shakespeare* (Diss. Bonn), Duisburg, 1912, pp. 64 ff.
It seems incredible that Weisse should have been in ignorance of Shakespeare when
he first wrote his *Richard der Dritte*. (This statement is made by R. Dohse, *Colley*

Lessing's condemnation of Weisse's tragedy rests mainly on the fact that, contrary to Aristotle's warning, he chooses an unmitigated villain as his hero. His Richard awakens as little terror as pity; in fact, he awakens neither. He is (LXXIV, 17) 'das grösste, abscheulichste Ungeheuer, das jemals die Bühne getragen', a devil incarnate (LXXIX, 11), and we could only feel the deepest satisfaction in seeing him handed over to the tortures of hell. And what does happen? He is allowed to die fighting, to die on the field of honour! Such a villain cannot awaken pity or terror (or rather fear, as Lessing now corrects himself)[1] of the right kind. It is only an evasion, too, to say that pity is awakened for the queen and the princes. Pity, yes! but not the kind of pity that has anything to do with tragedy. But Lessing admits that the play interests the public (LXXIX, 89). It has 'Poesie des Ausdrucks; Bilder; Tiraden; kühne Gesinnungen; einen feurigen hinreissenden Dialog; glückliche Veranlassungen für den Akteur, den ganzen Umfang seiner Stimme mit den mannichfaltigsten Abwechslungen zu durchlaufen'; it may have many of the attractive qualities of a 'dramatic poem', but it has not the true beauties of tragedy. Lessing reproaches Weisse for not having learned from Shakespeare; but in point of fact, much of his criticism here is equally applicable to Shakespeare's *Richard III*.[2] The questions which are raised, however, concern not so much Weisse's tragedy as the definition of tragedy itself.[3]

When Lessing enlarges (LXXIII, 132) on the duty of a poet to pay more attention to the fault-finding of his critics than to their praise, this is less a reproach to Weisse than an underlining of the latter's own assurance in his preface to *Richard der Dritte*: 'Er [der Verfasser] hat also den Tadel über dieselben [Versuche in der dramatischen

Cibbers Bühnenbearbeitung von Shakespeares Richard III, Bonner Beiträge zur Anglistik, ed. M. Trautmann, ii, p. 6.) It has been suggested that his denial of knowledge rested on a quibble, namely, that he knew only Colley Cibber's adaptation of Shakespeare's tragedy, published in 1700 (cp. W. Oehlke, *Lessing und seine Zeit*, ed. cit. ii, p. 106; F. W. Meisnest, *Die Quellen zu Christian Felix Weisses Richard III*, in *Euphorion*, xvii (1910), pp. 538 ff. (especially pp. 542 ff.)).

[1] See below, p. 353.

[2] 'Stl.' the critic of the *Dramaturgie* in Klotz's *Deutsche Bibliothek*, commented thus (iv (xv), 1769, p. 500): 'Weisse hätte, nach Lessings Meinung, den Richard von Shakspear als einen Spiegel nutzen sollen, um seinem Werke alle Flecken abzuwischen. Erscheint denn Richard beym Shakspear weniger als Tyrann?' Cp. G. Witkowski, *Aristoteles und Shakespeare in Lessings Hamburgischer Dramaturgie*, in *Euphorion*, ii (1895), pp. 517 ff.

[3] See below, pp. 353 ff., 357.

Dichtkunst] sorgfältiger, als die Lobsprüche gesammelt.' Among the eulogists was C. H. Schmid, to whose *Zusätze zur Theorie der Poesie* Lessing refers, as we have just seen, at the close of St. LXXIII. In his *Theorie der Poesie*, Leipzig, 1767, p. 495, Schmid had written extravagantly of Weisse:

Warum hat sich noch kein theatralischer Schriftsteller unter uns der Empfindung der Nation bemeistert? fragen irgendwo die Litteraturbriefe. Will sich anders die Nation bemeistern lassen: so ist die Frage durch Weissen vernichtet! Patriotischer nimmt sich niemand des deutschen Theaters an. O Nation! danke ihn mit patriotischem Enthusiasmus!....

K. F. ROMANUS

The comedy of *Die Brüder, oder eine Schule der Väter* by Karl Franz Romanus was discussed by Lessing (LXX, 101–LXXIII, 11) at a time when the Hamburg Enterprise was a thing of the past; and he was more interested in the playwright's ultimate source, Terence, than in the play itself. Of the latter he had, at first, nothing to say at all; but he promised some criticism when the play was repeated (LXXIII, 10); and by substituting one playbill for another,[1] he fulfilled in some small measure that promise (XCVI–XCIX).

Romanus, he tells us (XCVI, 9), published his plays anonymously, and it was these that recommended his name to the public, not his name his plays.[2] Lessing's criticism, however, still turns on Terence, that is, on the alterations which Romanus believed necessary to make the Latin play palatable to a modern audience. He first raises the question as to whether Greek or Roman customs cannot be reproduced just as well in comedy as in tragedy. He is not prepared to recognise any real distinction in this respect, but suggests that native customs are in fact more appropriate to both. But although on this principle Romanus would appear to be justified, Lessing states that he cannot approve of the liberties which he has actually taken with his original. He does not see (XCVII, 69) why the German playwright should have destroyed the double meaning of Terence's title by making the two

---

[1] See above, p. 90, note 2.

[2] Nicolai, in reviewing Romanus's *Komödien* in the *Litteraturbriefe*, No. cccxxix (June 20, 1765), *ed. cit.* xxiii, p. 51, had said: 'Ich habe hier eben einen Schriftsteller vor mir, der eine sehr gute Anlage zu einem komischen Dichter zu haben scheint. Er verdienet wohl, dass man ihn unter der Menge elender dramatischen Schriftsteller womit Deutschland überschwemmet ist, hervorziehe, und etwas näher betrachte.'

young men, Leander and Lycast (Aeschinus and Ktesipho in Terence)
cousins instead of brothers. The piece may be a 'Schule der Väter'
—its second title; but without the link by which Terence connects
Aeschinus and Ktesipho, and both with their father Demea, the whole
plot is loosened. If Aeschinus were the actual son of Micio, why should
Demea be so indignant? There is no adequate reason for Lysimon's
excessive indignation with Philidor, in the German play, over the
misdeeds of his own son. Again (xcviii, 1), solicitous interest for the
reform of a brother may be justified; but when he is only a cousin,
the cogent reason for Leander's action disappears. The German
Ktesipho (Lycast) is unnaturally depraved (xcviii, 77); he is 'ein
abgefeumter Bube, dem Lügen und Betrug sehr geläuffig sind' (125).
This compels the German author to involve his Lycast in an exposure
at the close (xcix, 29), which is unnecessary in Terence, and difficult
to make convincing to a modern audience. His ending is the conventional reconciliation of the comedy of the day; while Terence's
is not to be thus foreseen, but is naturally developed from his characters.
The whole criticism is a defence of Terence; and may be dealt with
better in connexion with the Latin author.[1] Meanwhile, it is but fair
to note that some of the strictures which Lessing makes on Romanus
really apply to the French *École des pères* by Michel Baron, or Boyron,
of which Romanus's play is a free adaptation. In Baron's play the
two cousins are brought up together, one having been adopted by the
father of the other.

G. K. PFEFFEL

In *Der Schatz*, by Gottlieb Konrad Pfeffel, Lessing finds more
interest than is usually to be met with in 'Schäferspiele' (xiv, 129);
but the style is 'öfters ein wenig zu gesucht und kostbar'. He drew his
information concerning the author's *Der Eremit* (135) from the *Schreiben
an einen Freund*, appended to the edition of Pfeffel's play published at
Frankfurt in 1761:

> Das Nachspiel, Der Einsiedler, das nach der Aufführung ernster Dramen
> nicht plötzlich die süssen Thränen durch Komik verjagen soll, wie die
> bisherigen lustigen Nachspiele, sondern das Gemüthe in seiner melancholi-
> schen Wollust erhalten.

The author expresses the hope that his *Einsiedler* 'einem Herzen,

[1] See below, pp. 318 ff.

welches noch um den Polyeuckt trauret, keine so widerwärtige Empfindungen aufbringet, als der Herzog Michel, oder die Liebe durch
Wechselbriefe'.[1]

T. G. VON HIPPEL

Theodor Gottlieb von Hippel's popular satire on pedantic people who
regulate their lives by the clock, *Der Mann nach der Uhr*, seems to have
irritated Lessing by its provincialism (XXII, 65). The allusion here to
'grüner Kohl' concerns Act I, sc. ii of the piece, where the reason
which the 'Mann nach der Uhr' gives for not allowing his daughter
to marry her lover Valer is that the latter does not eat 'braunen Kohl'
on Sundays: 'Ich glaube, dass mancher Sonntag vorbeigeht, ohne
dass er braunen Kohl isst'. Lessing has nothing more to say about
the piece. His statement that Hippel is in Danzig would appear to
be an error; he is probably confusing Danzig with Königsberg, where
Hippel had a legal appointment and ultimately rose to be Bürger-
meister. He was born in 1741 and died in 1796.[2]

F. VON HEUFELD

From the Preface to Heufeld's *Julie* (Vienna, 1766) Lessing obtained
the information that Heufeld was the author of other pieces (VIII, 104):
'Ich kann für den Beyfall, womit das hiesige Publikum meine zwey
ersten Stücke zu gütig beehret, meine Erkenntlichkeit nicht besser an
Tag legen, als wenn ich meine müssigen Stunden zu seinem Vergnügen
zu verwenden fortfahre.'[3] From this Preface (p. [4]) he also draws the
passage to which he refers at the beginning of St. IX (12): 'Einem
andern Einwurfe: dass Siegmund nicht in genugsamer Handlung
erscheine, glaube ich dadurch vorzubeugen, wenn ich zu erwägen
gebe: dass ein Mensch seines gleichen...nicht wie ein König...grosse
Handlungen verrichten kann.'

[1] See E. Schmidt's review of Cosack's *Materialien zur Hamburgischen Dramaturgie*
in *Anzeiger für deutsches Altertum*, v (1879), pp. 138 ff.

[2] Cp. F. J. Schneider, *T. G. von Hippel*, Prague, 1911, p. 147. In a review of his
own play (*ibid.* Anhang, p. 19) Hippel admitted the justice of Lessing's criticism that
the title of the play betrays too much.

[3] The two pieces were *Die Haushaltung nach der Mode* and *Die Liebhaber nach der
Mode*, both comedies in three acts, reprinted in the Viennese *Neue Sammlung von
Schauspielen*, vi and x (1765, 1767). See Goedeke, *Grundriss* (3rd ed.) iv (1), p. 657.
Schmid in his *Chronologie* (*ed. cit.* pp. 159 ff.) criticises Heufeld adversely. Heufeld
was born at Meinau in 1731 and died in 1795.

The theme of *Julie* is from Rousseau's *La nouvelle Héloïse* (1761); and this affords Lessing an opportunity of returning to the discussion of the relation between drama and narrative which he had touched upon in St. 1 (16).[1] Somewhat apologetically Heufeld had written (*ibid.*):

Diejenigen, welche dafür halten: es wäre etwas Leichtes einen ziemlich zugeschnittenen Stoff zu bearbeiten, lade ich ein, selbst einen Versuch dieser Art zu wagen. Es ist wahr! ich habe mir die Auftritte, die sich in meinen Plan schickten, zu Nutzen gemacht. Allein bey allem dem muss ich bekennen, dass es mir bey so vielen einzeln schönen Stellen, womit Juliens Geschichte ausgefüllet ist, schwerer fiel, wegzulassen, als heraus-zunehmen. Ich habe es erfahren, und meine Freunde—denen ich für ihren kritischen Beystand mit Vergnügen öffentlich danke—haben es auch erkennet: zu geschweigen, dass durch diesen Vortheil die Arbeit auf einer andern Seite erschweret wird, wenn man nämlich einem so starken Urbilde, als der Verfasser dieser Geschichte ist, nacharbeiten, und seinen Ton zu erreichen sich bestreben muss. Ich werde sehr zufrieden seyn, wenn ich nicht zu tief unter ihm stehen geblieben bin.

It has been pointed out by the commentators that Lessing's memory of the novel was not vivid enough to prevent him from making some slips in his comparison. The harshness of Julie's father towards her is far from being hardly touched upon in the novel (IX, 52); it is fully described in letter 63 of Part I, from Julie to her friend Claire. From this letter also comes what Lessing describes (IX, 68) as the best scene in the piece. 'Das Bürschchen will sich schlagen und erstechen' (IX, 8) is also true of Rousseau's hero (cp. Part I, letter 56, and III, 21).[2] Lessing's criticism of the weak points of the German plot are, however, entirely reasonable—the conversion of Rousseau's tragedy into a comedy with a happy ending (VIII, 121), the 'uninteresting' character of Julie (126), the inferiority of Heufeld's 'Siegmund'[3] to St Preux (157); indeed Siegmund, Lessing continues, is nothing but a petty conceited 'Pedant' (IX, 4), whose good qualities we learn from hearsay (31). The scene—the best in the play—where Julie's father beseeches her on bended knee, may be justified in the novel, Lessing says; but not here (69), where it outrages our better feelings. He quotes largely

---

[1] See below, pp. 460 f.

[2] See Cosack, *op. cit.* p. 57; also Petersen, *ed. cit.* p. 187.

[3] I am unable to substantiate Lessing's objection to the name Siegmund (VIII, 141), as being a name for domestics. It is the name of Lottchen's lover in Gellert's *Die zärtlichen Schwestern* (1747). Heufeld altered the name and made other changes in deference to Lessing's criticism (cp. L. Geiger in *Vierteljahrschrift für Litteratur-geschichte*, iii (3), 1890, pp. 502 f.; also Petersen, *ed. cit.* p. 186).

from Mendelssohn's article on Rousseau's novel in the *Litteraturbriefe* of June 4–18, 1761.[1] In addition the following passage from the same article might be adduced as illustrative of Lessing's words 'Der Werth der Neuen Heloise ist, von der Seite der Erfindung, sehr gering.... Die Situationen sind alltäglich oder unnatürlich' (VIII, 114 ff.):

Was er von der guten Absicht eines Romanenschreibers, und von der Lauterkeit der Moral sagt, die in seinen Briefen gepredigt wird; das lasse ich dahingestellt seyn. Aber die magern Erfindungen und der unnatürliche Vortrag lassen sich durch keine gute Absichten entschuldigen.... Was die Erfindung betrift? Urtheilen Sie selbst, ob folgender Plan eine sonderliche Fruchtbarkeit verräth!... Sie sehen, dass in dieser Anlage keine ausserordentliche Situationen Platz finden, und Rousseau selbst macht keinen Anspruch auf Situationen. Nehmen Sie diesen geringen Vorrath von Begebenheiten, dehnen Sie ihn aus, so weit Sie können, und füllen Sie die Lücken mit langen moralischen Predigten, und verliebten Spitzfindigkeiten aus; so haben Sie ohngefähr die Geschichte der neuen Heloise....[2]

Lessing subsequently read Heufeld's *Der Geburtstag*, and proposed to discuss it when *Julie* was repeated (*Entwürfe zu Besprechungen, Schriften*, xv, pp. 43 f.):

Den fünfundsechzigsten Abend (Freytags den 14tn August) ward die Julie des H. Heufeld, und Schlegels stumme Schönheit wiederhohlt.

Die zwey Stücke, mit welchen sich H. Heufeld, vor seiner Julie, in Wien bekannt gemacht hatte, heissen die Haushaltung, und der Liebhaber nach der Mode. Ich kenne sie noch nicht weiter, als ihren Titeln nach. Aber sein viertes Stück, welches er auf die Julie folgen lassen, habe ich gelesen.

Es heisst der Geburtstag, und ist in drey Aufzügen. Es gehört, seiner Einrichtung nach, unter die Pieces à tiroir, wie sie die Franzosen nennen; und seinem Haupttone nach, ist es ein Possenspiel, ob schon die Personen desselben bey weitem nicht aus der niedrigsten Klasse der Menschen sind. Er schildert verschiedne lächerliche Charaktere, die bey Gelegenheit eines Geburtstags auftreten, der in einer adlichen Familie auf die zu Wien gewöhnliche Art, gefeyert wird. Der erste Akt enthält eine Reihe von Morgenvisiten, die bey der Frau von Ehrenwerth, in der Absicht ihr zu diesem ihrem Feste Glück zu wünschen, gemacht werden. Der dritte Akt zeiget eine Abendbewirthung ungefehr der nehmlichen Personen, bey welcher gespielt wird. Der mittelste Akt besteht aus einem kleinen Lustspiele, genannt die Schwester des Bruder Philipps.[3]

---

[1] *Litteraturbriefe*, Nos. clxvi–clxx, *ed. cit.* x, pp. 255 ff.; *Gesammelte Schriften, ed. cit.* iv, 2, pp. 260 ff.

[2] *Litteraturbriefe*, x, pp. 259, 260, 266; *Gesammelte Schriften*, iv, 2, pp. 262, 264 f.

[3] According to Goedeke (3rd ed., iv (1), p. 657), *Der Geburtstag*, Lustspiel von drei Akten, appeared at Vienna in 1767, and *Die Tochter des Bruders Philipps*, Lustspiel in einem Akt, at Frankfurt and Leipzig in 1771: 'mit Zusätzen nachgedruckt' in *Theater der Deutschen*, Frankfurt, 1775.

J. F. LÖWEN

Finally, Lessing had occasion to notice two small plays by Johann Friedrich Löwen, the director of the theatre. Obviously there could be no question of serious criticism. They were inconsiderable after-pieces in one act, both based on verse tales by Voltaire, the first, *Die neue Agnese*[1] (x, 41) through the intermediary of Favart. It was played from manuscript, which Lessing evidently had the opportunity of reading (73); it was first printed in the *Hamburgische Unterhaltungen*, vi, 5, November, 1768, pp. 364–393. A review of Favart's operetta, *Isabelle et Gertrude, ou les Sylphes supposés* (1765), in the *Journal encyclo-pédique* of September, 1765 (pp. 106 f.) had made Favart's indebtedness to Voltaire (x, 60) clear: 'Il n'y a personne en France qui ne connoisse l'*Education des filles*, Conte charmant, par M. de Voltaire, publié l'année dernière et inséré dans l'ingénieux recueil des *Contes de Guillaume Vadé*.'[2] In scene x of the French operetta, to which Lessing particularly refers (42 ff.), Madame Gertrude tries to make her daughter believe that the voice she has heard 'est celle de Monsieur Dupré, sans être la sienne'.

Isabelle. Je ne comprens pas.
Mad. Gertrude. N'avez vous pas lû le livre que je vous ai donné?
Isabelle. Ah! oui; le Comte de Gabalis qui dit qu'il y a des Sylphes, des Esprits Aëriens, des intelligences,[3] cela m'a amusée; mais est-ce que tout cela est vrai?

Lessing's Bernard and Hilar (Löwen's Mangold and Richard) appear to correspond to Voltaire's André and Denis, and Favart's Dupré and Dorlis.

The second comedy by Löwen, *Das Räthsel, oder, Was den Damen am meisten gefällt* (XXIX, 22), had been printed in volume iv of Löwen's *Schriften* (Hamburg, 1766, pp. 339 ff.). In his Preface Löwen describes the origin of the piece as follows:

Das letzte Lustspiel: Das Räthsel, oder: Was den Damen am meisten gefällt? ward eigentlich auf Ersuchen des Herrn Ackermanns von mir

---

[1] It is hardly necessary to recall that Agnès is the 'naïve' of Molière's *École des femmes*.

[2] *L'éducation d'une fille*, in *Contes de Guillaume Vadé* [Geneva], 1764, pp. 28–32.

[3] In 1670 the Abbé Montfaucon Villars published *Le Comte de Gabalis, ou Entretiens sur les sciences secrètes*, in which the supernatural is treated with rationalistic irony. Here he speaks of 'Sylphes...qui sont une espèce de Substances Aëriennes, qui viennent quelquefois consulter les Sages sur les livres d'Averroës, qu'elles n'entendent pas trop bien' (Amsterdam ed. of 1715, p. 13).

verfertiget. Der Stoff ist aus der, auch vom Voltaire nachgeahmten Erzählung: Ce qui plait aux Dames genommen. Man hatte dem Herrn Ackermann ein kleines Nachspiel von wenigen Auftritten über diese Materie gegeben. Es war aber zu kurz, und hatte nicht die komische, muntre, und zugleich satyrische Miene, die man so gern in dergleichen kleinen Stücken sieht. Ich ward um die Aenderung dieses Stücks ersucht; fand aber, dass es leichter sey, ein ganz neues Stück zu verfertigen, als in die Arbeit eines andern mehr Lebhaftigkeit zu bringen; und auf die Art entstand diese kleine Plaisanterie, die vermuthlich auf dem Theater gefallen wird, wenn Herr Ackermann, wie er willens ist, die Rolle des Pedrillo spielt: denn die komischen Rollen gerathen ihm allemal vortrefflich.[1]

Löwen's comedy is thus based on Voltaire's tale in verse, *Ce qui plaît aux dames*, but he may possibly also have been influenced by Favart's *La Fée Urgèle, ou ce qui plaît aux dames* (1765), an operetta based also on Voltaire's tale.[2] The resemblances to Favart's piece are not, however, very conspicuous. Löwen's comedy was unfavourably reviewed in the *Neue Bibliothek der schönen Wissenschaften* (iv (1767), pp. 289 f.).

It was inevitable that through Lessing's criticism of the drama of his own land there should run a regretful sense of broken achievement. But, as we have seen, he had set out on his task as a critic of the Hamburg theatre with no illusions in respect of the value of the fare likely to be offered. Many masterpieces were not to be hoped for; but a critical standard could be maintained: 'Indess ist es gut, wenn das Mittelmässige für nichts mehr ausgegeben wird, als es ist' (*Ank.* 73). Nevertheless one could sometimes wish that he had been a little less harsh and acid in proclaiming that mediocrity, more especially in respect of his own contemporaries; that he had been readier to see those glimpses of hope and promise which were surely not absent. He complains bitterly, for example (xviii, 85), that Germany has no De Belloy—after all, no genius of a high order; that the Germans are not, like the French, jealous of their national fame: 'ein Volk, auf das die grossen Thaten seiner Vorfahren den Eindruck nicht verloren haben'. But Lessing might here have had a word for the *Hermanns-Schlacht* of Klopstock, even if that drama were as unsuitable for the

---

[1] *Schriften*, Hamburg, 1765–66, iv, pp. [xix f.]. The title of Löwen's piece in this passage (and in the *Dramaturgie* (xxix, 22)), varies from that in the volume (p. 339), where it appears as *Was dem Frauenzimmer am meisten gefällt.*

[2] *Ce qui plaît aux Dames* in *Contes de Guillaume Vadé, ed. cit.* pp. 1–18. Petersen (*ed. cit.* p. 210) notes that Schiebeler's operetta *Lisuart und Dariolette* (1766) was an adaptation of Favart's *La Fée Urgèle.* (Schmid, *Chronologie, ed. cit.* p. 161, notes the resemblance of *Lisuart und Dariolette* to *Ce qui plaît aux Dames.*)

theatre as no doubt, in his view, Shakespeare's plays were. Klopstock had visited Hamburg in June, 1767, and had allowed Lessing to read his play in manuscript; and the latter wrote to Nicolai on August 4, 1767:

> Klopstock ist hier gewesen, und ich hätte manche angenehme Stunde mit ihm haben können, wenn ich sie zu geniessen gewusst. Ich fand, dass er mir besser gefallen müsste, als jemals. Er ist sehr fleissig gewesen. Er hat eine neue Tragödie gemacht, Hermanns Schlacht; ein Stük völlig in dem alten deutschen Costume, häuffig mit Bardengesängen untermengt. Es ist ein vortreffliches Werk, wenn es auch schon etwa keine Tragödie seyn sollte.... Ich betaure nur, dass weder durch diese [Gerstenberg's tragedy *Ugolino*], noch durch Klopstocks Tragödie, das deutsche Theater im geringsten reicher geworden. Denn beide können schwerlich, oder gar nicht aufgeführt werden.[1]

Thus Lessing, so far from overlooking Klopstock, had, in writing of De Belloy's play, the *Hermanns Schlacht* quite definitely in his mind.[2] It is strange, too, that he should have seen no significance in *Ugolino* for the development of the German drama.[3]

What Lessing finds to praise in his own literature—and the comedies of Schlegel are almost alone in receiving this distinction—lies fairly far back in time; no German play subsequent to 1750 finds real favour in his eyes. It is a pity that he had not an opportunity to speak of Brawe's work, although I doubt whether he would have shown the warmth with which he had greeted Brawe ten years before. The judgment meted out to Cronegk and Weisse may not be wrong, viewed *sub specie æternitatis*—and it was the good right of the author of *Minna von Barnhelm* to look down on such mediocre rivals—but Lessing was inclined to be unduly hard on the writers of his own generation. To his admirers it was a proof of his critical integrity. But with less severity—one might even say with less intellectual arrogance, with a more charitable appreciation of such merits as his contemporaries undoubtedly possessed, Lessing might have been more helpful to the progress of his own literature. In the case of Weisse there was no doubt, mingled with Lessing's judgment, a sense of personal grievance

[1] *Schriften*, xvii, pp. 234 f.
[2] Cp. R. Hamel's edition of Klopstock's works, iv, in Kürschner's *Deutsche Nationalliteratur*, xlviii [1884], pp. 6 f.
[3] Cp., however, Lessing's letter to Gerstenberg of February 25, 1768 (*Schriften*, xvii, pp. 244 ff.), for a more detailed explanation of his views on *Ugolino*; cp. also his letter to J. A. Ebert of October 18, 1768 (*Schriften*, xvii, p. 264).

that Weisse enjoyed a favour at the hands of the public which seemed to him undeserved and disproportionate to his own.

German literature, Lessing generalises in St. xcvi (32), is distinguished disadvantageously from other modern literatures by its juvenility; it lacks maturer talents to give it stability. He regards it as a grave fault that the literature of his time has passed into the hands of young men (xcvi, 18); the older men turn to the serious occupations of state and church, and regard verses and comedies as trivial things to be put aside after their twenty-fifth year. What nourishment, he asks, can a seriously thinking man draw from the very trivial comedies that are produced? They contain puns and jests to amuse the parterre, but for the man who would laugh with understanding, nothing. A young man cannot possibly know and depict the world. The ancients could say of Menander that, had he lived longer, he might have achieved greater things; and yet Menander wrote a hundred and five comedies and did not die until his fifty-second year. None of the German comedy writers of the past reached such an age; and not one of those still living has yet reached it. One might again be tempted to see here a reflection of disappointment in the man of fifty who sees the theatre invaded by young talents, were it not that, more than ten years before, in December 1757, Lessing had written to Mendelssohn:

Denn Sie haben in der That Recht: den schönen Wissenschaften sollte nur ein Theil unsrer Jugend gehören; wir haben uns in wichtigern Dingen zu üben, ehe wir sterben. Ein Alter, der seine ganze Lebenszeit über nichts als gereimt hat, und ein Alter, der seine ganze Lebenszeit über nichts gethan, als dass er seinen Athem in ein Holz mit Löchern gelassen; von solchen Alten zweifle ich sehr, ob sie ihre Bestimmung erreicht haben.[1]

Lessing follows up his pessimistic estimate of the state of the drama with an attack on the contemporary critics, 'whose best criticism consists in making all criticism suspect' (xcvi, 68). They preach the supremacy of genius; the uselessness of rules which only hamper genius; and as a last consequence, the uselessness of criticism itself. It has been too readily assumed that Lessing is here making a stand against the new critics who ushered in the 'Sturm und Drang', such as Gerstenberg or Herder. The ideas which are here expressed are in fact little more than an echo of Trublet's *Essais sur divers sujets de littérature et de morale* (Paris, ed. of 1754, iii, pp. 138 f.):

[1] *Schriften*, xvii, pp. 130 f.

Les règles qui sont un secours pour les esprits médiocres, sont quelquefois un obstacle pour les génies supérieurs. Nous devons les règles aux premiers ouvrages, et ceux-ci au génie seul. Nous devons les seconds ouvrages, en partie, aux premiers, en partie aux règles, mais en plus grande partie encore au génie. Un homme ordinaire fait un ouvrage conforme aux règles connues. Un grand homme en fait un qui donne lieu à de nouvelles règles.

The critic whose words are quoted (xcvi, 99 ff.), is not one of these modern pioneers, but the redoubtable 'Stl.' of Klotz's *Deutsche Bibliothek*. The passage is from his review of the first volume of the *Dramaturgie*,[1] and is in full:

So viel auch die Theorie des Dramas verloren hätte, so wünschte ich doch fast lieber, man hätte Lessingen nicht die Kritik, sondern die Direction der Hamburger Bühne übertragen. Unser Theater, glaube ich, ist noch in einem viel zu zarten Alter, als dass es den monarchischen Scepter der Lessingischen Kritik ertragen könnte. Ist es nicht jetzt fast noch nöthiger, die Mittel zu zeigen, wie das Ideal erreicht werden kann, als darzuthun, wie weit wir noch von dem Ideal entfernt sind? Muss ein periodisches Blatt, wie die Dramaturgie ist, nicht auch einen periodischen Nutzen haben?...Nun wir eine Dramaturgie haben, nun werden wir doch eine Bühne bekommen? Eine Originalbühne? Ich zweifle sehr. Wir lernen daraus, was uns fehlt, aber durch sie können wir den Mangel nicht ersetzen. Die Bühne muss durch Beyspiele, nicht durch Regeln reformirt werden. Den Aesthetikern wird die Dramaturgie eine reiche Quelle seyn: unsere Dichter wird sie eher niederschlagen als ermuntern. Es wird Mode werden, ein Trauerspiel nicht nach der Empfindung, nicht nach den Thränen die es dem Zuschauer kostet, sondern nach ästhetischen Kunstwörtern zu beurtheilen. Die wenige Empfindung, die in unserm Publico zu erwachen angefangen hat, wird von philosophischer Kälte erstickt werden. Nichts schmeichelt unserm Stolz mehr, als jedem unsrer Raisonnemens einen philosophischen Anstrich zu geben, und raisonniren ist leichter als selbst erfinden.[2]

---

[1] *Deutsche Bibliothek*, iii (ix), 1769, pp. 42 f.

[2] Also quoted by Petersen, *ed. cit.* p. 261. The metaphor of the 'Grillen am Wege' with which Lessing winds up his attack (121) is, as C. B. Boxberger has pointed out (*Einzelheiten über Voltaire bei Lessing*, Dresden, 1879, pp. 31 f.), a memory of Voltaire's *Discours préliminaire* to *Alzire* (*Œuvres* [Geneva], 1756–7, viii, pp. 131 f.): 'Souvenons nous de la fable du *Boccalini*. "Un voyageur", dit-il, "était importuné dans son chemin du bruit des cigales; il s'arrêta pour les tuer; il n'en vint pas à bout, et ne fit que s'écarter de sa route. Il n'avait qu'à continuer paisiblement son voyage; les cigales seraient mortes d'elles-mêmes au bout de huit jours."'

CHAPTER VI

THE FRENCH PLAYS OF THE REPERTORY

Lessing's knowledge of the drama of France and its history was wide and intimate; from his early days he had been familiar with it, and it profoundly influenced his own dramatic work. This knowledge, coupled with the fact that dramas of French origin dominated the Hamburg repertory, makes the present section of this volume bulkier than all the others together which are concerned with the *Hamburgische Dramaturgie* as a critical 'Register'.

Lessing usually opens his discussion of a French play with some information about the original; its date, its sources, or facts about its author. For these things he drew, for the most part, on what he called the 'Annales des französichen Theaters' (x, 4)—two compendia which he had also at hand in editing his *Beyträge zur Historie und Aufnahme des Theaters* and *Theatralische Bibliothek*: the *Dictionnaire portatif historique et littéraire des Théâtres* by A. de Léris, Paris, 1754 (2nd ed., which he may now have possessed, 1763) and the *Histoire du Théâtre françois* by the brothers Claude and Frédéric Parfaict, 15 vols. Paris, 1745–49.[1] He also found a good deal of information about French plays in the great French reviews. Sets of the *Journal des Sçavans* and the *Mercure de France* we know him to have possessed;[2] but these had been left in Berlin to be sold with his library there; and I find no indication of his having had access to the current numbers of either of these periodicals in Hamburg. Nor does he seem to have read the *Année littéraire*. On the other hand, he made considerable use of two more recently established reviews, the *Journal étranger* and the *Journal encyclopédique*.[3] He had also a copy of the short-lived *Observateur*

---

[1] There is a reference in the *Beyträge* to vol. i of this work in the original Amsterdam edition of 1735 (*Schriften*, iv, p. 132). Another work by the brothers, the *Dictionnaire des Théâtres de Paris*, 7 vols. Paris, 1756, from which Lessing had translated large sections for his *Theatralische Bibliothek*, he does not appear to have had with him in Hamburg. I have summarised briefly Lessing's use of sources in his criticism of the French drama in a contribution to *Mélanges d'histoire littéraire générale et comparée offerts à F. Baldensperger*, Paris, 1930, ii, pp. 200 ff.

[2] Cp. letter to Gleim, February 1, 1767 (*Schriften*, xvii, p. 229; also pp. 238, 251, 253, 268, 311). Lessing refers repeatedly to the *Mercure* in his *Collectanea*; also in *Laokoon*, iv (*Schriften*, ix, p. 28).

[3] See below, pp. 173, 235 ff., 240 f., 277 f.

des Spectacles, ou Anecdotes théatrales, ouvrage périodique par M. de Chevrier, La Haye, 1762–63.[1] These were what might be called Lessing's general sources. More particular and specific sources of information and criticism will be dealt with as they come into question.

PIERRE CORNEILLE

Of the pre-Cornelian drama in France Lessing had little occasion to speak in the *Dramaturgie*; at most we find an occasional glance back into earlier history, and that usually in quotations. The most definite of these is a note on Garnier and tragi-comedy in St. LV (131) which he drew from D'Aubignac and Parfaict.[2] But even the French classical drama of the seventeenth century receives no kind of systematic consideration. The repertory of the Hamburg theatre did not, of course, give him much opportunity for such. No play of Racine was performed; and Lessing does little more than occasionally mention his name,[3] usually in conjunction with that of Corneille. Corneille alone comes in for detailed discussion, and that owing to the fact that *Rodogune* was played in Hamburg (in a new translation). Lessing's criticism of *Rodogune*, which occupies St. XXIX to XXXII, gives him the opportunity for his most trenchant attack on the *tragédie classique*. It is thus of paramount importance.

Lessing begins (XXIX, 63) by discussing the sources of Corneille's drama. Corneille himself supplies the information in his *Examen*; but Lessing took the trouble to compare the 'Examen' with the earlier 'Argument',[4] which differs in some details, a fact which raises a point

---

[1] See below, pp. 198, 231. This periodical was published 'aux depens de l'auteur' (title-page) from January to June, 1762, semi-monthly (vols. i and ii), and from January to March, 1763, in weekly numbers, which were published as vol. iii (*Suite de l'Observateur des Spectacles*) in 1764.

[2] For Lessing's views on Tragi-comedy see below, pp. 392 ff.

[3] Cp. [XXIV, 96]; XXVI, 27, [55, 63]; XLVIII, 141; [LIX, 84, 85]; [LXXIV, 118]; LXXXI, 41, 44, 52, 138; [LXXXII, 136]; CI–CIV, 243. (References in square brackets occur in quotations.)

[4] 'Argument' is the term used by Voltaire in his edition of Corneille's plays (*Théâtre de Pierre Corneille, avec des Commentaires*, Paris, 1764, iv, p. 289); in the original edition of *Rodogune* (Paris, 1647) the summary bears no heading except '*Appian Alexandrin*. Au Livre des Guerres de Syrie, sur la fin'. (The modern edition by Marty-Laveaux (Paris, 1862) uses the term 'Avertissement' to distinguish the earlier introduction from the later 'Examen'.) For the passages quoted from the 'Argument' in the following pages I use the original edition of *Rodogune*, for those from the 'Examen' the *Théâtre de Corneille*, Paris, 1660. The 'Examen' to *Rodogune* is quoted in part by Parfaict, *Histoire du Théâtre françois, ed. cit.* vi, pp. 312 ff.

of some slight bibliographical interest. The first edition of Corneille which printed both the 'Arguments' and the 'Examens' substituted for them by the poet in 1660 was that of Voltaire, *Théâtre de Pierre Corneille, avec des Commentaires*, 12 vols. Paris, 1764. As Lessing makes extensive use of these commentaries, especially when he deals with Thomas Corneille's *Le Comte d'Essex* (XXIII, 1 ff.),[1] and, of course, with *Rodogune*, it is possible that he possessed this costly edition; but he may only have had a Dutch reprint of the *Commentaires* without Corneille's text, such as that in three volumes mentioned in the *Bibliothek der schönen Wissenschaften* (xii (i), 1765, p. 183). In any case, he does not quote Corneille from Voltaire's text, with its characteristically Voltairean spelling, but from an older edition.

From the 'Examen' comes Lessing's statement (XXIX, 55 ff.): 'Corneille bekannte...ein wachsendes Interesse', and Corneille's summary (63 ff.) of the historical facts from Appianus Alexandrinus (*Théâtre*, Paris, 1660, iii, pp. xl ff.):

On m'a souuent fait une question dans la Cour, quel estoit celuy de mes Poëmes 'que j'estimois le plus, et j'ay trouué tous ceux qui me l'ont faite si préuenus en faueur de Cinna, ou du Cid, que je n'ay jamais osé déclarer toute la tendresse que j'ay tousjours euë pour celuy-cy....Ie veux bien laisser chacun en liberté de ses sentimens, mais certainement on peut dire que mes autres Pieces ont peu d'auantages, qui ne se rencontrent en celle-cy. Elle a tout ensemble la beauté du Sujet, la nouueauté des fictions, la force des Vers, la facilité de l'expression, la solidité du raisonnement, la chaleur des passions, les tendresses de l'amour et de l'amitié, et cet heureux assemblage est ménagé de sorte, qu'elle s'éleue d'Acte en Acte....

Corneille states at the outset the facts on which his drama is based:

Le Sujet de cette Tragedie est tiré d'Appian Alexandrin, dont voicy les paroles sur la fin du Liure qu'il a fait des guerres de Syrie. 'Demetrius surnommé Nicanor,[2] entreprit la guerre contre les Parthes, et vescut quelque temps prisonnier dans la Cour de leur Roy Phraates, dont il épousa la sœur nommée Rodogune. Cependant Diodotus, Domestique des Rois precedens, s'empara du Trosne de Syrie, et y fit asseoir un Alexandre encor enfant, fils d'Alexandre le bastard, et d'une fille de Ptolomée. Ayant gouuerné quelque temps comme Tuteur sous le nom de ce Pupille, il s'en deffit, et prit luy-mesme la Couronne, sous un nouueau nom de Tryphon qu'il se donna. Antiochus frere du Roy prisonnier ayant appris sa captiuité à Rhodes, et les troubles qui l'auoient suiuie, reuint dans la Syrie,

---

[1] See below, pp. 183 ff.
[2] Petersen (*ed. cit.* p. 211) points out that this should be Nikator; Lessing quotes the form used by Corneille.

où ayant deffait Tryphon, il le fit mourir. De là il porta ses armes contre Phraates, et vaincu dans une bataille, il se tua luy-mesme. Demetrius retournant en son Royaume fut tué par sa femme Cleopatre, qui luy dressa des embusches sur le chemin, en haine de cette Rodogune qu'il auoit épousée, dont elle auoit conceu une telle indignation, qu'il auoit épousé ce mesme Antiochus frere de son mary. Elle auoit deux fils de Demetrius, dont elle tua Seleucus l'aisné d'un coup de fléche, si-tost qu'il eust pris le Diadéme aprés la mort de son pere, soit qu'elle craignist qu'il ne la voulust vanger sur elle, soit que la mesme fureur l'emportast à ce nouueau parricide. Antiochus son frere luy succeda, et contraignit cette mere dénaturée de prendre le poison qu'elle luy auoit préparé (*ibid.* pp. xxxviii ff.).

But Lessing—noticing the slight variations in the versions given by Corneille in his 'Argument' and in his 'Examen'—also turned to the text of Appianus—no doubt in the edition of Stephanus.[1] Here he found for 'Alexandre le Bastard', the Latin translation 'Alexander Nothus'; he added to 'überwand den Tryphon', 'mit vieler Mühe' (σὺν πόνῳ πολλῷ; *Argument*: 'avec beaucoup de peine'), and expanded Corneille's 'De là il porta ses armes contre Phraates (*Argument*: 'luy redemandant son frere') et vaincu dans une bataille...' into 'Hierauf wandte er seine Waffen gegen den Phraates, und foderte die Befreyung seines Bruders. Phraates, der sich des Schlimmsten besorgte, gab den Demetrius auch wirklich los; aber nichts desto weniger kam es zwischen ihm und dem Antiochus zum Treffen.' The Greek text is: 'ὁ μὲν δὴ Φραάτης αὐτὸν ἔδεισε, καὶ τὸν Δημήτριον ἐξέπεμψεν· ὁ δ' Ἀντίοχος καὶ ὡς συνέβαλέ τε τοῖς Παρθυαίοις, καὶ ἡσσώμενος, ἑαυτὸν ἔκτεινεν.'[2]

This story, Lessing points out (xxix, 94), contains material for more than one tragedy; but Corneille was chiefly attracted by the problem of the avenging wife. This being so, however, the piece should have been called 'Cléopâtre'. Corneille had said in his 'Argument' (*Rodogune, ed. cit.* pp. [x f.]):

Pour le premier, ie confesse ingenuëment que ce Poëme deuoit plustost porter le nom de Cleopatre, que de Rodogune: mais ce qui m'a fait en user ainsi, a esté la peur que i'ay euë qu'à ce nom le peuple ne se laissast preoccuper des idées de cette fameuse et derniere Reyne d'Egypte, et ne confondist cette Reyne de Syrie auec elle, s'il l'entendoit prononcer. C'est pour cette mesme raison que i'ay euité de le mesler dans mes Vers, n'ayant

---

[1] H. Stephanus, Ἀππιάνου Ἀλεξανδρέως Ῥωμαϊκά. *Appiani Alexandrini Rom. historiarum Punica...Annibalica, Celticæ et Illyricæ fragmenta quædam. Item, de bellis civilibus libri V,* [Geneva], 1592.

[2] Stephanus, *op. cit. De Bellis Syriacis,* p. 132.

iamais fait parler de cette seconde Medée que sous celuy de la Reyne; et ie me suis enhardy à cette licence dautant plus librement que i'ay remarqué parmi nos anciens Maistres, qu'ils se sont fort peu mis en peine de donner à leurs Poëmes le nom des Heros qu'ils y faisoient paroistre, et leur ont souuent fait porter celuy des Chœurs, qui ont encore bien moins de part dans l'action que les personnages Episodiques comme Rodogune, tesmoin les Trachiniennes de Sophocle, que nous n'aurions iamais voulu nommer autrement que la Mort d'Hercule.

Lessing is in agreement with these views;[1] but he also endorses Voltaire's suggestion that the name of Cléopâtre should have been mentioned (*Commentaires, ed. cit.* iv, pp. 303 f.):

Le spectateur a besoin qu'on lui débrouille cette histoire. *Cléopatre* n'est pas nommée une seule fois dans la piéce. *Corneille* en donne pour raison, qu'on aurait pû la confondre avec la *Cléopatre* de *César*; mais il n'y a guère d'aparence que les spectateurs instruits, qui instruisent bientôt les autres, eussent pris cette reine de Syrie pour la maîtresse de *César*.

As Lessing notes (130), the translation remedied this defect, Cleopatra's name being mentioned twice in the opening speech of Laonice in the German play.

In St. xxx, after recapitulating the historical facts concerning Cléopâtre, Lessing proceeds (35) to show, in what are perhaps the most brilliant and incisive pages of literary criticism in the *Dramaturgie*, that Corneille had dealt with them not as a genius, but merely as a 'witziger Kopf'. Instead of adhering to the natural course of events —instead of preferring simplicity—the dramatist invents artificial complications.[2] It is not enough for him that Cléopâtre should slay her husband from jealousy; he introduces the motive of ambition. It is not the loss of her husband that stirs her, but the fact that Rodogune occupies her throne. As in his discussion of *Der Graf von Essex* (xxv, 112 ff.), so here (xxx, 77) Lessing regards pride as more unnatural in a woman than in a man. A woman's sphere is love and tenderness; and a heroine such as Corneille's Cléopâtre is an unnatural exception, compared with whom Medea is virtuous and amiable. All the art of the poet cannot make a woman interesting who commits crimes

[1] He returns repeatedly in the *Dramaturgie* to the matter of titles of plays; see below, pp. 467 f.

[2] Cp. Voltaire, *Commentaires, ed. cit.* iv, p. 469: 'On trouvera peut-être que j'ai examiné cette piéce avec des yeux trop sévères. Mais ma réponse sera toujours que je n'ai entrepris ce commentaire que pour être utile....Admirons le génie mâle et fécond de *Corneille*; mais pour la perfection de l'art connaissons ses fautes ainsi que ses beautés.'

from cold pride and ambition. Cléopâtre is only a monster (xxx, 92).
Voltaire, too, had described her as such (*Commentaires, ed. cit.* iv,
p. 443):

J'avoue que son atrocité me révolte, et quelque méchant que soit le
genre humain, je ne crois pas qu'une telle résolution soit dans la nature.
Si ses deux enfans avaient comploté de la faire enfermer, comme ils le
devaient, peut-être la fureur pouvait rendre *Cléopatre* un peu excusable;
mais une femme, qui de sang froid se résout à assassiner un de ses fils, et
à empoisonner l'autre, n'est pour moi qu'un monstre qui me dégoute.

Even the greatest villain (117) endeavours to exculpate himself by
arguing that his crime is not so great as it seems; but Cléopâtre revels
in tirades glorifying her viciousness. One should not speak of 'le
grand Corneille', but the 'monstrous', the 'gigantic' Corneille. What
Lessing says is more than an echo of Voltaire; it expresses a view of
his own on the limitations of women as tragic figures, which must have
made it difficult for him to accept, if not Medea, at least Lady
Macbeth.[1]

In history (xxxi, 1) Cléopâtre avenges herself on her husband, not
on Rodogune: in the play the murder of Demetrius is only narrated;
the action is concerned with Rodogune. Vengeance upon a rival
would be natural in a jealous woman; but Cléopâtre is not jealous,
only ambitious. Jealousy here might have been a great tragic passion:
ambition reduces Cléopâtre to a merely abominable criminal, who
deserves to be put in a madhouse. But even this is not enough for
Corneille: he invents still further complications. The marriage with
Rodogune had not been consummated when Demetrius was killed;
his two sons are in love with her; the mother has not revealed which
of the two is the rightful possessor of the throne, and she makes it a
condition that he in whose favour she decides must kill Rodogune.
Voltaire had condemned this theatrical complication in his note to
'Si vous voulez régner, le trône est à ce prix' (Act ii, sc. iii, 122; cp.
Commentaires, ed. cit. iv, pp. 361 f.):

La proposition de donner le trône à qui assassinera *Rodogune* est-elle
raisonnable? Tout doit être vraisemblable dans une tragédie. Est-il

---

[1] Lessing's 'die mit nichts als mit machiavellischen Maximen um sich wirft'
(xxx, 91) is also an echo of Voltaire's 'toutes ces sentences dans le goût de
Machiavel, ne préparent point aux tendresses de l'amour et à ce caractère d'innocence
timide que Rodogune prendra bientôt' (*Commentaires, ed. cit.* iv, p. 333). Cp. also
'Medea ist gegen ihr tugendhaft und liebenswürdig' (92); Corneille had called her
'cette seconde Medée' (*Commentaires, ed. cit.* iv, p. 292).

possible que *Cléopatre,* qui doit connaître les hommes, ne sache pas qu'on ne fait point de telles propositions sans avoir de très-fortes raisons de croire qu'elles seront acceptées? Je dis plus; il faut que ces choses horribles soient absolument nécessaires. Mais *Cléopatre* n'est point réduite à faire assassiner *Rodogune,* et encor moins à la faire assassiner par ses fils. Elle vient de dire que le *Parthe* est éloigné, qu'elle est sans aucun danger. *Rodogune* est en sa puissance. Il paraît donc absolument contre la raison que *Cléopatre* invite à ce crime ses deux enfans dont elle doit vouloir être respectée. Si elle a tant d'envie de tuer *Rodogune,* elle le peut sans recourir à ses enfans. Cependant cette proposition si peu préparée, si extraordinaire, prépare des événemens d'un si grand tragique, que le spectateur a toujours pardonné cette atrocité, quoiqu'elle ne soit ni dans la vérité historique, ni dans la vraisemblance. La situation est théatrale, elle atache malgré la réflexion. Une invention purement raisonable peut être très-mauvaise. Une invention théatrale, que la raison condamne dans l'examen, peut faire un très-grand effet.

Furthermore (xxxi, 69), Rodogune knows of Cléopâtre's plans. She is in love with one of the brothers, but does not confess it. Rather is she determined to marry the one who proves himself most worthy of her, whether he be the heir to the throne or not: her condition is that her future husband shall avenge her on Cléopâtre. With biting wit Lessing depicts the ludicrousness of the situation which is thus created. And then he quotes (xxxi, 110) Corneille's appeal, in self-justification, to the practice of the ancients. The passage which he translates occurs in the 'Argument' and runs as follows (*Rodogune, ed. cit.* pp. [x f.]):

On s'estonnera peut-estre de ce que i'ay donné à cette Tragedie le nom de Rodogune, plustost que celuy de Cleopatre sur qui tombe toute l'action Tragique; et mesme on pourra douter si la liberté de la Poësie peut s'estendre iusqu'à feindre un sujet entier sous des noms veritables, comme i'ay fait icy, où depuis la narration du premier Acte qui sert de fondement au reste, iusques aux effets qui paroissent dans le cinquiesme, il n'y a rien que l'Histoire auouë....[1] [Here follows the passage already quoted above, pp. 167 f.] ... Pour le second point ie le tiens un peu plus difficile à resoudre, et n'en voudrois pas donner mon opinion pour bonne, i'ay creu que pourueu

---

[1] Lessing notes (xxxii, 25) that Corneille boasted of his invention: 'L'ordre de leur naissance incertain, Rodogune prisonniere...ne sont que des embellissemens de l'inuention, et des acheminemens vray-semblables à l'effet desnaturé que me presentoit l'Histoire, et que les loix du Poëme ne me permettoient pas de changer' (*Rodogune, ed. cit.* [p. x] (quoted by Schröter and Thiele, *Lessings Hamburgische Dramaturgie,* Halle, 1878, p. 196)). But he points out that it is not 'das blosse Erdichten', but 'das zweckmässige Erdichten', that is the mark of creative genius (xxxii, 27).

que nous conseruassions les effets de l'Histoire, toutes les circonstances, ou comme ie viens de les nommer, les acheminements, estoient en nostre pouuoir, au moins ie ne pense point auoir veu de regle qui restreigne cette liberté que i'ay prise. Ie m'en suis assez bien trouué en cette Tragedie, mais comme ie l'ay poussée encore plus loin dans Heraclius que ie viens de mettre sur le Theatre, ce sera en le donnant au public que je tascheray de la justifier si ie voy que les sçavants s'en offencent, ou que le peuple en murmure. Cependant ceux qui en auront quelque scrupule m'obligeront de considerer les deux Electres de Sophocle et d'Euripide, qui conseruant le mesme effet, y paruiennent par des voyes si differentes, qu'il faut necessairement conclurre que l'une des deux est tout à fait de l'inuention de son Autheur. Ils pourront encore jetter l'œil sur l'Iphigenie *in Tauris*,[1] que nostre Aristote nous donne pour exemple d'une parfaite Tragedie, et qui a bien la mine d'estre toute de mesme nature, veu qu'elle n'est fondée que sur cette feinte que Diane enleua Iphigenie du sacrifice dans une nuée, et supposa une Biche en sa place. Enfin ils pourront prendre garde à l'Helene d'Euripide, où la principale action et les Episodes, le nœud et le desnouëment sont entierement inuentez sous des noms veritables.

And as previously in connexion with *Der Graf von Essex*,[2] Lessing accuses Voltaire (XXXI, 138) of futility in calculating that Corneille had made his Rodogune too young (*Commentaires, ed. cit.* iv, pp. 337 f.):

Cependant *Rodogune* n'est point jeune; elle épousa *Nicanor* lorsque les deux frères étaient en bas âge; ils ont au moins vingt ans. Cette rougeur, cette timidité, cette innocence semblent donc un peu outrées pour son âge; elles s'acordent peu avec tant de maximes de politique; elles conviennent encor moins à une femme qui bientôt demandera la tête de sa belle-mère aux enfans même de cette belle-mère.

How far had this brilliant condemnation of a play which, for more than a hundred years, was regarded as 'the greatest masterpiece of the greatest dramatist of France and Europe' (XXXII, 99), been fore-shadowed or prepared by previous critics? Dacier, to whom Lessing was indebted in his treatment of *Polyeucte*, has little to say of *Rodogune*;[3] but at the close of St. XXXII Lessing mentions three predecessors. The first of these, 'an honest Huron in the Bastille', is the hero of the story *L'Ingénu*, which was by Voltaire, although Lessing was obviously not

[1] In writing 'Iphigenia in Taurika' (XXXI, 127), Lessing would appear to be following Dacier, *Poétique d'Aristote, ed. cit.* pp. 154, 237, 283, 300, etc.: 'Iphigenie Taurique' (Curtius, 'taurische Iphigenia', *Aristoteles Dichtkunst*, Hanover, 1753, pp. 273, 276). [2] See below, p. 183.
[3] The few references are unfavourable (cp. *Poétique d'Aristote, ed. cit.* pp. 229, 234, 235, 254).

aware of his authorship at the time of writing.[1] Brought up among the Hurons of North America, 'l'Ingénu' comes to Europe and is thrown into prison. Here, in chapter xii, Gordon, a Jansenist, attempts to mould his taste in French literature:

Lisez *Rodogune*, lui dit Gordon, on dit que c'est le chef-d'œuvre du théatre; les autres piéces qui vous ont fait tant de plaisir sont peu de chose en comparison [*sic*]....Après avoir lu très attentivement la piéce, sans autre dessein que celui d'avoir du plaisir, il regardait son ami avec des yeux secs et étonnés, et ne savait que dire. Enfin, pressé de rendre compte de ce qu'il avait senti, voici ce qu'il répondit: Je n'ai guères entendu le commencement, j'ai été revolté du milieu; la derniére scène m'a beaucoup ému, quoiqu'elle me paraisse peu vraisemblable; je ne me suis intéressé pour personne, et je n'ai pas retenu vingt vers, moi qui les retiens tous quand ils me plaisent.

Cette piéce passe pourtant pour la meilleure que nous ayons.[2]

The second predecessor is 'ein Pedant' in Italy. Former commentators have referred this to Scipione Maffei (1675–1755), but the reference is to the anonymous author (Pietro di Calepio) of the *Paragone della Poesia tragica d'Italia con quella di Francia*, published by Bodmer at Zürich in 1732.[3] In the fourth article of chapter ii (*ed. cit.* pp. 39 f.), Calepio discusses the shortcomings of *Rodogune*; but, as far as I can see, Lessing owed nothing definite to his criticism. Lastly, there was Voltaire's criticism of the play in his edition of Corneille.[4]

Had *Rodogune* been repeated within Lessing's period—as a matter of fact, the next performance took place on August 26, a few days after the nominal date of St. xxxii—he proposed to say more of his predecessors (xxxii, 132). With a view to this, he made notes[5] from

---

[1] *Le Huron, ou l'Ingénu, histoire véritable, tirée des manuscrits du P. Quesnel* was published without Voltaire's name in September, 1767, and was confiscated eight or ten days after publication; consequently it could not have been known to Lessing on the nominal date of this part, August 18; but St. xxxii–xxxv were not published until December. An edition was published at Dresden in 1767; the edition from which I quote above was published with Voltaire's name [at London] in 1767. Cp. *Œuvres Complètes*, Paris, 1877–85, vol. l, p. 526.

[2] *L'Ingénu, histoire véritable*, Tirée de Manuscrits du Père Quesnel. Par M. de Voltaire. Genève [London], 1767, pp. 76 f.

[3] See below, pp. 291 f.

[4] In connexion with the statement 'denn es ist doch gemeiniglich ein Franzose, der den Ausländern über die Fehler eines Franzosen die Augen eröffnet' (xxxii, 125), Petersen (*ed. cit.* p. 212) refers to a similar statement in Lessing's preface to *Das Theater des Herrn Diderot* (*Schriften*, viii, pp. 286 f.).

[5] *Entwürfe zu Besprechungen, Schriften*, xv, p. 46.

an article in the *Journal encyclopédique* of October, 1761,[1] where an account is given of Voltaire's generous efforts on behalf of Corneille's granddaughter. He writes in the *Entwürfe zu Besprechungen*:

Die Komödianten waren die ersten, welche sich des Enkels des grossen Corneille öffentlich annahmen. Sie spielten zu seinem Besten die Rodogune, und man lief mit Hauffen hinzu den Schöpfer des Französischen Theaters in seinen Nachkommen zu belohnen. Dem H. v. Voltaire ward die Mademoiselle Corneille von le Brün empfohlen; er liess sie zu sich kommen, übernahm ihre Erziehung, und verschafte ihr durch die Ausgabe der Werke ihres Urvaters eine Art von Aussteuer. Man hat die That des H. von Voltaire ganz ausserordentlich gefunden; man hat sie in Prosa und in Versen erhoben; man hat die ganze Geschichte in einen besondern griechischen Roman verkleidet (La Petite Niece d'Eschyle 1761):

Sie ist auch wirklich rühmlich; aber sie wird dadurch nichts rühmlicher, weil es die Enkelin des Corneille war, an der sie Voltaire ausübte. Vielmehr war die Ehre, von der er voraussehen konnte, dass sie ihm nothwendig daraus zuwachsen müsste, eine Art von Belohnung; und der Schimpf der dadurch gewissermaassen auf Fontenelle zurückfiel, war vielleicht für Voltairen auch eine kleine Reitzung.

Auch das Unternehmen, den Corneille zu commentiren, schrieb man dem H. von Voltaire als eine ausserordentlich uneigennützige und grossmüthige That an. (*Journal encycl.* Oct. 1761.) L'exemple qu'il donne, est unique; il abandonne pour ainsi dire son propre fonds, pour travailler au champ de son voisin et lui donner plus de valeur. Que ceux qui calomnient son cœur, admirent au moins la noblesse d'un procedé si rare. Il est ordinaire que les grands hommes s'etudient, mais ils n'ont pas coutume de se commenter. Dans le nombre presque infini des Editeurs, des Commentateurs, des Compilateurs, on peut en citer beaucoup qui ont marqué de l'erudition; quelques-uns ont eu de l'esprit; tres peu du gout: voici le premier qui a du genie, et plus de gout, d'esprit et même d'erudition, qu'aucun d'eux. Nous admirerons d'avantage l'Auteur de Rodogune, de Polieucte, de Cinna, quand nous verrons toutes ses pieces enrichies des Commentaires que prepare l'Auteur de Mahomet, d'Alzire et de Merope; ils vont fortifier l'idee que nous nous formons de Corneille et le rendre, s'il est possible, encore plus grand à nos yeux; ils feront lire [*Journal encycl.* relire] le texte avec plus de plaisir et plus d'utilité.

Wie viel ist von dieser schmeichlerischen Prophezeyung abgegangen. Wie sehr ist dieser Commentar anders ausgefallen! Wie leicht wäre es zu glauben, dass Voltaire auch hierbey sehr eigennützige Absichten gehabt hätte.[2]

---

[1] *Journal encyclopédique*, vii, i, October 1, 1761, pp. 113 ff. A letter from Voltaire concerning the enterprise of preparing the *Commentaires sur Corneille* is printed here, with a preliminary account from which Lessing quotes. See note 2 below.

[2] *Schriften*, xv, pp. 45 ff. The passage quoted here from the *Journal encyclopédique* is in the first of the two October numbers of 1761, pp. 114 f. Voltaire's edition of

On the translation used at the Hamburg production Lessing comments favourably. It was not the old one by Bressand (Wolfenbüttel, 1691) but a new one completed in Hamburg and not yet printed.[1]

Corneille's name naturally appears with considerable frequency in the *Hamburgische Dramaturgie*, in those sections which are concerned with dramatic theory.[2] Many of his plays are mentioned; but no other work receives the special consideration accorded to *Rodogune*, that being the only one of his tragedies which was performed in Hamburg. *Polyeucte* is considered (II, 35, LXXV, 116) as the chief example of a kind of play which meets with no favour at Lessing's hands, the 'Christian tragedy';[3] he arraigns it for the lack of naturalness in its character-drawing and for its dependence on the untragic motive of martyrdom. *Le Cid*, again, is mentioned as an example of tragi-comedy (LV, 120);[4] Lessing deals, however, mainly with a specific matter (LV, 94), the famous box on the ear in Act I, scene 3, which creates the tragic situation in that drama by bringing about a quarrel between Don Diègue, father of Rodrigue and the Comte de Gormas, father of Chimène, who administers the 'soufflet'. Voltaire had insisted on its impropriety; he had said (*Commentaires, ed. cit.* i, p. 190):

On ne donnerait pas aujourd'hui un souflet sur la joue d'un héros. Les acteurs mêmes sont très-embarrassés à donner ce souflet, ils font le semblant. Cela n'est plus même soufert dans la comédie; et c'est le seul exemple qu'on en ait sur le théatre tragique. Il est à croire que c'est une des raisons qui firent intituler le *Cid* tragi-comédie.

Corneille brought in, says Beuchot in his preface to the *Commentaires*, a profit of 100,000 francs which was shared between the publisher and Mademoiselle Corneille (*Œuvres de Voltaire*, ed. M. Beuchot, XXXV (*Commentaires* I), Paris (1829), p. v). That Voltaire was not unaware of Lessing's strictures is apparent from a letter published in *Die Gegenwart* (No. 42), October 19, 1878, XIV, p. 251 (J. Duboc, *Ein Beitrag zur Voltaire-Literatur*). Voltaire, writing to W. Grossmann, theatre director in Hanover, on August 14, 1767, refers to Lessing's writings in Hamburg, and adds: 'Mon grand age et ma mauvaise santé ne me permettent guères de revenir sur l'édition de Pierre et de Thomas Corneille. J'ai chez moi leur nièce, qui me console dans la décrépitude, où je suis tombé. Les gens de Lettres éclairés augmentent encore cette consolation....'

[1] Cp. R. Raab, *Pierre Corneille in deutschen Übersetzungen und auf der deutschen Bühne bis Lessing*. Diss. Heidelberg, 1910, pp. 150 ff., 157 ff. See also above, pp. 82 f.

[2] See below, esp. pp. 355, 364 f., 377 f., 382 f., 384, 415 ff., 421 ff., 467.

[3] Cp. XV, 12; LXXXII, 67; see below, pp. 421 ff.; and cp. also Dacier's criticism quoted on p. 423. *Polyeucte* was the most popular of Corneille's plays in Germany (cp. R. Raab, *op. cit.* pp. 103 ff.).

[4] See below, p. 393.

'Die Schauspieler, sagt der Herr von Voltaire, wissen nicht, wie sie sich dabey anstellen sollen' (LVI, 14). Voltaire does not however mean, as is here assumed, that the actor is embarrassed by having to receive the insult, but rather because he has to give it. More reasonable is Lessing's objection to the argument that the audience is pained by the introduction of a farce-situation into tragedy. With some justice Lessing contends that, on the contrary, he would see the box on the ear banished from comedy rather than from tragedy. He defends the tragic effect—and with this defence the modern reader will be in sympathy—of the situation in *Le Cid*. What other form of insult could be substituted for it in Corneille's drama (87)? It is the only one where the 'Pundonor' cannot be satisfied by excuses or apologies.[1]

Lessing's commentary on the situation in *Le Cid* (LVI, 87 ff.) is based on information obtained from Parfaict (*op. cit.* v, p. 259): 'Le Cid reçut encore quelques altérations. Il parut après l'Edit contre les duels. Dans la Tragédie D. Arias pressoit le Comte de Gormas de la part du Roy de faire des réparations à Dom Diegue: le Comte répondoit:... [here follow the four lines which Lessing quotes]. On trouva ces maximes dangereuses, et peu convenables aux circonstances du tems. M. Corneille fut obligé de réformer ces quatres vers.' Parfaict gives as his authority the 'Avertissement' of the edition of Corneille by Jolly (Paris, 1738). In his *Commentaires* (*ed. cit.* i, pp. 204 f.) Voltaire gives another version of these lines:

> Les satisfactions n'apaisent point une ame;
> Qui les reçoit a tort, qui les fait se difame;
> Et de pareils acords, l'effet le plus comun
> Est de deshonorer deux hommes au lieu d'un

and adds: 'Ces vers parurent trop dangereux dans un tems où l'on punissait les duels qu'on ne pouvait arêter, et *Corneille* les supprima.'

J. B. P. MOLIÈRE

It is regrettable that in the *Dramaturgie* Lessing has so little opinion of his own to express about Molière. I doubt, however, whether he had at any time a very warm personal interest in the master of French

---

[1] On the *pundonor* of Spanish drama cp. D. Antonio Rubió y Lluch, *El Sentimento del honor en el Teatro de Calderón*, Barcelona, 1882; cp. also E. Martinenche, *La Comedia espagnole en France de Hardy à Racine*, Paris, 1900, pp. 91 ff., 99 ff., 130 f.

comedy.[1] There is little more to be done here than to put on record the sources which he used.

Molière's *Die Frauenschule* is discussed in St. LIII. The information contained in the two paragraphs beginning: ' Moliere hatte bereits...' (72) and 'Wenn indess, nach der Meinung...' (100), is based on two criticisms quoted by Parfaict (ix (1746), pp. 170 ff.). The first of these is from a *'Mémoire sur la Vie et les Ouvrages de Molière'*:

...La ressemblance que l'on pourroit trouver entre *l'École des Maris* et *l'École des Femmes*, sur ce qu'Arnolphe et Sganarelle sont tous deux trompés par les mesures qu'ils prennent pour assurer leur tranquillité, ne peut tourner qu'à la gloire de Moliere, qui a trouvé le secret de varier ce qui paroît uniforme. Les traits naïfs d'Agnès ingénue et spirituelle, qui ne pêche contre les bienséances, que parce qu'Arnolphe les lui a laissé ignorer, ne sont pas les mêmes que ceux d'Isabelle fine et déliée, qui n'ont d'autre principe que la contrainte où la tient son Tuteur.

The second is from De Visé, *Nouvelles nouvelles*, Troisième Partie:[2]

...Cette Piéce a cinq Actes: tous ceux qui l'ont vûe sont demeurez d'accord qu'elle est mal nommée, et que c'est plûtôt *l'École des Maris*, que *l'École des Femmes*: mais comme il y en a déjà [*de Visé*: il en a déja fait] une sous ce titre, il n'a pû lui donner le même nom. Elles ont beaucoup de raport ensemble; et dans la premiere, il garde une femme, dont il veut faire son épouse, qui, bien qu'il la croye ignorante, en sçait plus qu'il ne croit, ainsi que l'Agnès de la derniere, qui joue, aussi-bien que lui, le même personnage, et dans *l'École des Maris*, et dans *l'École des Femmes*: et toute la différence que l'on y trouve, c'est que *l'Agnès* de *l'Ecole des Femmes*, est un peu plus sotte, et plus ignorante que *l'Isabelle* de *l'Ecole des Maris*. Le sujet des [*de Visé*: de ces] deux Piéces n'est point de son invention, il est tiré de divers endroits, à sçavoir, de Boccace, des Contes d'Ouville [*de Visé*: de Douuille], de la Précaution inutile de Scarron, et ce qu'il y a de plus beau dans la derniere, est tiré d'un livre intitulé: *Les Nuits facétieuses du Seigneur Straparolle*, dans une Histoire duquel, un Rival vient tous les jours faire confidence à son ami, sans sçavoir qu'il est son Rival, des faveurs qu'il obtient de sa Maîtresse, ce qui fait tout le sujet et la beauté de *l'Ecole des Femmes*.[3]

[1] See, however, A. Ehrhard, *Les Comédies de Molière en Allemagne*, Paris, 1888, pp. 202 ff. (and especially pp. 234 ff.).

[2] The original passage is to be found (with slight orthographical and verbal differences) in *Nouvelles nouvelles* par Monsieur de .... [Jean Donneau de Visé], Paris, 1663, Troisesme Partie, p. 231.

[3] *La Précaution inutile* is the first of the *Nouvelles tragi-comiques* (Paris, 1655) of Paul Scarron (1610–60). *Le piacevoli Notti* of Giovanni Francesco Straparola appeared in 2 vols. at Venice, 1550–55, and was frequently reprinted. A French translation appeared in 1585. The story of this collection to which Molière is here probably indebted is that of Night iv, No. 4.

The passage translated from Trublet (LIII, 88 ff.) is in his essay 'De la Tragédie et de la Comédie' in *Essais sur divers sujets de littérature et de morale*, Paris, 1754–60, iv, p. 372:

Les deux sujets les plus heureux de Tragédie et de Comédie, c'est le *Cid* et l'*Ecole des femmes*. Mais l'un et l'autre ont été traités par *Corneille* et par *Moliere*, lorsque ces Auteurs n'étoient pas encore dans toute leur force. Je tiens cette observation de M. de *Fontenelle*.

In Lessing's *Entwürfe zu Besprechungen* (*Schriften*, xv, p. 40) is also the following extract translated from 'Trüblet', which was probably intended for use in commenting on the next performance of *l'École des femmes*:

Man nimt es mit den Komödien weit genauer, als mit den Tragödien. Man kann einen verständigen Mann weit leichter rühren, weit leichter so gar weinen machen, als belustigen, und zum lachen bringen. Das Herz lässt sich immer zu den Regungen willig finden, die man in ihm erwecken will: der Witz hingegen verweigert sich gewissermassen dem Scherzhaften. Es scheint, dass es unsere Eitelkeit weit mehr kränken würde, am unrechten Orte gelacht, als ohne Ursache geweint zu haben. Das erste zeiget von Dummheit, und das andre nur von Schwachheit, und diese Schwachheit selbst setzt eine Art von Güte voraus.

This is a translation of the following passage (*Essais, ed. cit.* iv, pp. 363 f.):

On est plus dificile sur les Comédies que sur les Tragédies. Il est plus aisé de toucher un homme d'esprit, et même de le faire pleurer, que de le réjouir et de le faire rire. Le cœur se prête volontiers aux mouvemens qu'on veut exciter en lui; mais l'esprit résiste en quelque sorte à la plaisanterie. Il semble que notre vanité seroit plus blessée d'avoir ri mal à propos, que d'avoir pleuré sans sujet. Le premier marque de la sotise. Le second ne marque que de la foiblesse, et cette foiblesse même suppose une sorte de bonté.

Lessing also quotes (LIII, 110) from Voltaire's account of *l'École des femmes*, in his *Vie de Molière, avec de petits Sommaires de ses Pièces*;[1] to this might be added a longer excerpt, which Lessing proposed to use in criticising the second performance of the play on July 24 (which did not, however, take place):

Moliere sahe in der letzten Helfte des Jahres 1661, und das ganze Jahr 62, sein Theater ziemlich verlassen. Denn die ganze Stadt lief zu den Italienern, um den Scaramouche zu sehen, der wieder nach Paris gekommen

---

[1] Cp. *Contes de Guillaume Vadé*, [Geneva], 1764, pp. 340 f.

war. Wollte Moliere nicht den leeren Logen spielen: so musste er das Publikum durch etwas Neues zu locken suchen, so ungefehr von dem Schlage der welschen Schnurren. Er gab also seine Frauenschule: aber das nehmliche Publicum, welches dort die abgeschmaktesten Possen, die eckelsten Zoten, in einem Gemengsel von Sprache ausgeschüttet, auf das unbändigste belachte und beklatschte, erwies sich gegen ihn so streng, als ob es nichts als die lauterste Moral, die allerfeinsten Scherze mit anzuhören gewohnt sey. Indess zog er es doch wieder an sich; und er liess sich gern kritisiren, wenn man ihn nur fleissig besuchte.

Die meisten von diesen Kritiken zu Schanden zu machen, hatte er ohnedem alle Augenblicke in seiner Gewalt, die er denn auch endlich auf eine ganz neue Art übte. Er sammelte nehmlich die abgeschmaktesten, legte sie verschiedenen lächerlichen Originalen in den Mund, mengte unter diese ein paar Leute von gesundem Geschmake, und machte aus ihren Gesprächen für und wider sein Stück, eine Art von kleinem Stücke, das er die Critik des erstern nannte (La Critique de l'Ecole des Femmes) und nach demselben aufführte. Diese Erfindung ist ihm in den folgenden Zeiten von mehr als einem Dichter nachgebraucht worden, aber nie mit besondrem Erfolge. Denn ein mittelmässiges Stück kann durch eine solche apologetische Leibwache, das Ansehen eines guten doch nicht erlangen; und ein gutes wandelt auch ohne sie, durch alle hämische Anfechtungen, auf dem Wege zur billigern Nachwelt sicher und getrost fort.[1]

One might compare with this a passage from Voltaire's *Vie de Molière* (*ed. cit.* p. 340):

Le théâtre de Moliére, qui avait donné naissance à la bonne comédie, fut abandonné la moitié de l'année 1661, et toute l'année 1662, pour certaines farces moitié Italiennes, moitié Françaises, qui furent alors accréditées par le retour d'un fameux Pantomime Italien, connu sous le nom de Scaramouche. Les mêmes spectateurs qui applaudissaient sans réserve à ces farces monstrueuses, se rendirent difficiles pour l'Ecole des femmes, piéce d'un genre tout nouveau, laquelle, quoique toute en récits, est ménagée avec tant d'art, que tout paraît être en action. Elle fut très suivie et très critiquée, comme le dit la gazette de Loret:

> Pièce qu'en plusieurs lieux on fronde,
> Mais où pourtant va tant de monde,
> Que jamais sujet important
> Pour le voir n'en attira tant.

In connexion with the references to Molière's play in Lessing's criticism of it, the following notes may be appended. 'Die Ehestandsregeln' (LIII, 85) are the 'maximes du mariage ou les devoirs de la femme mariée, avec son exercice journalier' which Agnès has to read in Act

---

[1] *Entwürfe zu Besprechungen, Schriften*, xv, pp. 41 f.

III, sc. ii. When Voltaire praised Molière for having given his piece the effect of action, although it is only narration, he might have remembered, Lessing comments (121), what Molière himself had said in *La Critique de l'École des femmes*. The passage to which Lessing alludes is in sc. vii:

Dorante. Premièrement, il n'est pas vrai de dire que toute la pièce n'est qu'en récits. On y voit beaucoup d'actions qui se passent sur la scène; et les récits eux-mêmes y sont des actions, suivant la constitution du sujet; d'autant qu'ils sont tous faits innocemment, ces récits, à la personne intéressée, qui, par là, entre à tous coups dans une confusion à réjouir les spectateurs, et prend, à chaque nouvelle, toutes les mesures qu'il peut, pour se parer du malheur qu'il craint.

In the *Entwürfe* (*Schriften*, xv, pp. 39 f.) is to be found the following translation by Lessing from the same scene:

Dorante. Sie glauben also, mein Herr, dass nur die ernsthaften Gedichte sinnreich und schön sind, und dass die komischen Stücke Armseligkeiten sind, die nicht das geringste Lob verdienen?
Urania. Ich wenigstens, denke so nicht. Die Tragödie ist unstreitig etwas schönes, wenn sie wohl behandelt ist: aber die Komödie hat ihren Nutzen gleichfalls, und ich halte dafür, dass die eine eben so schwer ist, als die andere.
Dorante. Sicherlich, Madame, und vielleicht würden Sie sich nicht irren, wenn Sie sagten, dass die Komödie noch ein wenig schwerer sey. Denn kurz, grosssprecherische Gesinnungen auszukramen, dem Glück in Versen Trotz zu bieten, das Schicksal anzuklagen, Lästerungen gegen die Götter auszustossen, finde ich weit leichter, als das Lächerliche der Menschen in sein gehöriges Licht zu setzen, und uns ihre Fehler auf eine angenehme Weise auf dem Theater vor Augen zu bringen. Wenn Sie Helden schildern, so machen Sie was Sie wollen; es sind Gesichter nach Gutdünken, von welchen man keine Ähnlichkeit verlanget; Sie brauchen nur die Züge auszudrücken, auf die Sie eine angespannte Einbildungskraft bringet, die nicht selten mit Fleiss das Wahre verlässt, um das Wunderbahre zu erhaschen. Aber wenn Sie Menschen mahlen: so will man, dass diese Gemählde gleichen sollen; und Sie haben schlechterdings nichts geleistet, wenn wir nicht unsere Zeitverwandten, so wie sie wirklich sind, darinn erkennen. Mit einem Worte, in einem ernsthaften Stücke ist es genug, um allen Tadel zu vermeiden, wenn man nur etwas vernünftiges sagt, und es gut ausdrückt. Hiermit aber ist es in den andern Stücken nicht gethan; da soll man scherzhaft seyn, und was für ein kitzliches Unternehmen ist es, vernünftige Leute zu lachen zu machen.

In elucidation of Lessing's criticism of Voltaire, it may be recalled that Arnolphe in Molière's play intends to marry Agnès, a country

12-2

girl whom he has had brought up in a convent in ignorance and innocence. He learns to his dismay that Horace, the son of his best friend, is in love with Agnès, and in Act III, sc. iv, he has to listen to the account given him by Horace (who does not know of the real state of affairs) of his 'progrès'—Lessing's 'Progressen' (LIII, 138).

In St. LXX (133) Lessing again quotes from Voltaire's *Vie de Molière* (*ed. cit.* pp. 335 ff.) on *l'École des maris*:

On a dit que l'Ecole des Maris était une copie des Adelphes de Térence: si cela était, Molière eût plus mérité l'éloge d'avoir fait passer en France le bon goût de l'ancienne Rome, que le reproche d'avoir dérobé sa piéce. Mais les Adelphes ont fourni tout au plus l'idée de l'Ecole des Maris. Il y a dans les Adelphes deux vieillards de différente humeur, qui donnent chacun une éducation différente aux enfans qu'ils élèvent; il y a de même dans l'Ecole des Maris deux tuteurs, dont l'un est sévère, et l'autre indulgent: voilà toute la ressemblance. Il n'y a presque point d'intrigue dans les Adelphes; celle de l'Ecole des Maris est fine, intéressante et comique. Une des femmes de la piéce de Térence, qui devrait faire le personnage le plus intéressant, ne paraît sur le théâtre que pour accoucher. L'Isabelle de Molière occupe presque toujours la scène avec esprit et avec grace, et mêle quelquefois de la bienséance, même dans les tours qu'elle joue à son tuteur. Le dénouement des Adelphes n'a nulle vraisemblance; il n'est point dans la nature, qu'un vieillard qui a été soixante ans chagrin, sévère et avare, devienne tout-à-coup gai, complaisant et libéral. Le dénouement de l'Ecole des Maris est le meilleur de toutes les piéces de Molière. Il est vraisemblable, naturel, tiré du fond de l'intrigue; et, ce qui vaut bien autant, il est extrêmement comique.

For the rest, Lessing's references to Molière in the *Dramaturgie* are sporadic and unimportant. I refer elsewhere to his claim (X, 18) that Destouches practised a higher form of comic writing than Molière.[1] In St. XXVIII (142) he defends Molière's *Misanthrope* against Rousseau;[2] and from that play, which Schlegel had suggested as a source of his own *Triumph der guten Frauen*, he quotes a passage (LII, 38). After Molière's death, Lessing says (XIII, 65) the actors had his prose plays turned into verse.[3] Lastly, in discussing Palissot's views on character in drama (LXXXVI, 23 ff.) he quotes the *Impromptu de Versailles*.[4]

---

[1] See below, p. 202.   [2] See below, pp. 390 f.
[3] See below, p. 463.
[4] Further mention of Molière or references to him are to be found in XIV, 91; XXI, 66; [XXVI, 75]; XXIX, 9; LXX, 105; [XCII, 37 ff.]. (References in square brackets occur in quotations.)

PH. QUINAULT

What Lessing has to say of Philippe Quinault's *Die coquette Mutter* (XIV, 87) is drawn exclusively from Parfaict (IX (1746), pp. 369 ff.):

> Cette Comédie est mise par les Connoisseurs au rang des meilleures qui sont restées au Théatre François....Le caractere du Marquis, (qui pour le dire en passant, est le premier qu'on ait mis au Théatre) a paru très-défectueux à l'Auteur de la Critique....[Parfaict then quotes from this criticism, which had appeared in the *Mercure de France* (March, 1729, pp. 588 ff.). He quotes again from it a little further on (pp. 373 f.).]...'Je ne m'arrêterai pas beaucoup à éxaminer le cinquiéme Acte, tout le monde convient qu'il pouvoit être mieux; le vieil Esclave annoncé dans les Actes précédens, ne paroît point, et l'on n'est pas trop satisfait de voir dénouer la Piéce par un récit, quand on a été preparé à une action plus Théatrale. Cela n'empêche pas que ce dénouement ne soit régulier, mais on s'attendoit à quelque chose de plus piquant...le titre de *Mere rivale*, lui conviendroit mieux que celui de *Mere coquette*, ou plûtôt on feroit mieux de s'en tenir à celui des *Amans brouillés*, que l'Auteur ne lui a donné qu'en second. Au reste, le succès de cette Piéce a été plus éclatant en cette derniere reprise qu'à toutes les précédentes, aussi n'a-t-elle été jamais mieux représentée qu'aujourd'hui. Je ne prétends rien lui dérober par-là de son propre mérite, et je crois que Moliere n'auroit pas rougi de l'avoir faite.'

THOMAS CORNEILLE

The play which nominally occupies the largest place in the *Hamburgische Dramaturgie* (XXII, 77–XXV and LIV–LXX, 99) is *Le Comte d'Essex* by Pierre Corneille's younger brother Thomas. In the articles in his second volume, however, Lessing is hardly concerned at all with the work of Corneille, but with English and Spanish dramas on the Earl of Essex. And indeed, even in his first articles, he has virtually little independent criticism of the French play to offer; he accepts and repeats Voltaire's estimate.

The information which Lessing supplies about the tragedy when it was first performed (XXII, 78 ff.) appears to have come from Parfaict (xii (1747), pp. 75 ff.). A reference to La Calprenède's play on the same theme, forty years previously, is to be found there:

> Il y a trente ou quarante ans que feu M. de la Calprenéde traita le sujet du *Comte d'Essex* [Marginal note: 'Le Comte d'Essex, de la Calprenede, parut en 1638. ainsi c'est 40 ans juste.'], et le traita avec beaucoup de succès.

On the later occasion[1] when he discussed the play, he turned (LIV, 9) to Léris (*Dictionnaire, ed. cit.* pp. 120 f.), where he found:

Le Comte d'Essex. Le malheur de cet infortuné Seigneur, qui eut la tête tranchée à Londres le 25 Février 1601, a fourni le sujet de trois *Tra*[gédies]. La premiere, par La Calprenede, laquelle eut un grand succès, à l'Hôtel de Bourgogne en 1638. La deuxieme, de Claude Boyer, donnée sur le Thé[âtre] de Guénégaud en 1672, ou, selon d'autres Auteurs, le 25 Fév[rier] 1678, un mois environ après le *Comte d'Essex*, de Corneille; et la troisieme de Thomas Corneille, qui est celle qui est restée en possession du Thé[âtre]. Elle fut représentée à l'Hôtel de Bourgogne au commencement de Janvier 1678, et fut d'abord critiquée.....

Lessing quotes (XXII, 84) Corneille's own *Avis*, which he found reprinted in Parfaict (xii, p. 76):

Il est certain que le Comte d'Essex eut grande part aux bonnes graces d'Elizabeth. Il étoit naturellement ambitieux, les services qu'il avoit rendus à l'Angleterre, lui enflerent le courage. Ses ennemis l'accuserent d'intelligence avec le Comte de Tiron, que les Rebelles d'Irlande avoient pris pour chef. Les soupçons qu'on en eut lui firent ôter le commandement de l'armée. Ce changement le piqua, il vint à Londres, révolta le Peuple, fut pris, condamné, et ayant toujours refusé de demander grace, il eut la tête coupée le 25. Février 1601. Voilà ce que l'Histoire m'a fourni. J'ai été surpris qu'on m'ait imputé de l'avoir falcifiée, parce que je ne me suis point servi de l'incident d'une bague qu'on prétend que la Reine avoit donnée au Comte d'Essex pour gage d'un pardon certain, quelque crime qu'il pût jamais commettre contre l'état; mais je suis persuadé que cette bague est de l'invention de M. de la Calprenéde, du moins je n'en ai rien lû dans aucun Historien.

Corneille is wrong, however (103), in calling the ring an invention of his predecessor; in proof of this Lessing turns to the *History of Scotland* by William Robertson, London, 1759 (ii, pp. 242 ff.):[2]

The most common opinion, at that time, and perhaps the most probable, was that it [the Queen's melancholy] flowed from grief for the Earl of Essex. She retained an extraordinary regard for the memory of that

[1] Lessing witnessed the second performance of *Der Graf von Essex* (July 15) while he was writing his first criticism.

[2] Lessing's quotation comes, with only a few slight verbal differences, from the German translation by M. Th. Chr. Mittelstedt, Braunschweig, 1762, ii, pp. 300 ff. On the other hand, his translations from Hume's *History of England* are apparently his own; for although a German version of that work had begun to appear at Breslau and Leipzig in 1762, the volume dealing with Elizabeth's reign (Pt. IV) did not appear until 1771.

unfortunate nobleman; and though she often complained of his obstinacy, seldom mentioned his name without tears. An accident happened soon after her retiring to Richmond which revived her affection with new tenderness, and imbittered her sorrows. The Countess of Nottingham, being on her death-bed, desired to see the Queen, in order to reveal something to her, without discovering which, she could not die in peace. When the Queen came into her chamber, she told her, that while Essex lay under sentence of death, he was desirous of imploring pardon in the manner which the Queen herself had prescribed, by returning a ring, which during the height of his favour she had given him, with a promise that, if in any future distress, he sent that back to her as a token, it should intitle him to her protection; that Lady Scroop was the person he intended to imploy in order to present it; that by a mistake, it was put into her hands instead of Lady Scroop's; and that she having communicated the matter to her husband, one of Essex's most implacable enemies, he had forbid her either to carry the ring to the Queen, or to return it to the Earl. The Countess, having thus disclosed her secret, begged the Queen's forgiveness; but Elizabeth, who now saw both the malice of the Earl's enemies, and how unjustly she had suspected him of inflexible obstinacy, replied, 'God may forgive you, but I never can'; and left the room in great emotion. From that moment, her spirit sunk entirely; she would scarce taste food; she refused all the medecines prescribed her by her physicians; declaring that she wished to die, and would live no longer. No intreaty could prevail on her to go to bed; she sat on cushions, during ten days and nights, pensive, and silent, holding her finger almost continually in her mouth, with her eyes open, and fixed on the ground. The only thing to which she seemed to give any attention, were the acts of devotion, performed in her apartment, by the Archbishop of Canterbury; and in these she joined with great appearance of fervour. Wasted, at last, as well by anguish of mind, as by long abstinence, she expired without a struggle, on Thursday the 24th day of March in the 70th year of her age, and the 45th of her reign.

Lessing's first concern is not with the poetic merit of Corneille's tragedy, but with Voltaire's peculiar method of criticising it by arraigning Corneille, history book in hand, for his historical errors. With the help of Hume and Robertson, Lessing has no difficulty in effectually convicting Voltaire himself of error.

In a note to Act I, sc. i, Voltaire tells us that 'presque personne en France du tems de *Thomas Corneille* n'était instruit de l'histoire d'Angleterre: aujourd'hui un poëte devrait être plus circonspect'.[1] And again, in a note to Act v, sc. viii: 'Rien ne prouve mieux l'ignorance où le public était alors de l'histoire de ses voisins.'[2]

Voltaire finds it ridiculous, Lessing recalls (XXIII, 18), that Elizabeth

---

[1] *Commentaires, ed. cit.* x, p. 263.　　　　[2] *Ibid.* p. 369.

should be represented as being in love in her sixty-eighth year: 'Elle avait alors soixante et huit ans. Il est ridicule d'imaginer que l'amour pût avoir la moindre part dans cette avanture.'[1] And on another occasion (XXIV, 26) he had jeered: 'Il falait qu'il entendît par là quelque autre dame que la reine *Elisabeth*, dont l'âge et le grand nez n'avaient pas de puissans charmes.'[2] But why should it be ridiculous, Lessing asks; do ridiculous things not sometimes happen in the world? Moreover (XXIII, 24), he turned to Hume's *History of England*, where he found:

> But the present situation of Essex called forth all her tender affections, and kept her in the most real agitation and irresolution. She felt a perpetual combat between resentment and inclination, pride and compassion, the care of her own safety and concern for her favourite; and her situation, during this interval, was perhaps more an object of pity, than that to which Essex himself was reduced. She signed the warrant for his execution; she countermanded it; she again resolved on his death; she felt a new return of tenderness. Essex's enemies told her, that he himself desired to die, and had assured her, that she could never be in safety while he lived: It is likely, that this proof of penitence and of concern for her, would operate a contrary effect to what they intended, and would revive all that fond affection, which she had so long indulged to the unhappy prisoner. But what chiefly hardened her heart against him was his supposed obstinacy, in never making, as she hourly expected, any application to her for mercy and forgiveness; and she finally gave her consent to his execution.[3]

And again (XXIII, 50–59), he refers to Hume:

> Most of Queen Elizabeth's courtiers feigned love and desire towards her, and addressed themselves to her in the stile of passion and gallantry. Sir Walter Raleigh, having fallen into disgrace, wrote the following letter to his friend Sir Robert Cecil, with a view, no doubt, of having it shewn to the Queen. '...I, that was wont to behold her riding like *Alexander*, hunting like *Diana*, walking like *Venus*, the gentle wind blowing her fair hair about her pure cheeks....' It is to be remarked that this nymph, Venus, Goddess, Angel, was then about sixty. Yet five or six years after, she allowed the same language to be used to her. Sir Henry Unton, her ambassador in France, relates to her a conversation which he had with Henry the fourth....[4]

Voltaire, Lessing says (63), attacks Corneille's presentation of the character of his hero; he states: 'Il y eut quelque tems le premier

---

[1] *Commentaires, ed. cit.* x, pp. 250 f.   [2] *Ibid.* p. 249.
[3] David Hume, *History of England from the Invasion of Julius Cæsar to the Revolution in 1688*, London, 1763, v, chap. xliv, p. 447.   [4] *Ibid.* p. 436 (note).

crédit: mais il ne fit jamais rien de mémorable.'[1] But Hume had shown (66) that Essex had claimed credit for the destruction of the Spanish ships:

In the preamble of the patent it was said, that the new dignity was conferred on him, on account of his good services in taking Cadiz, and destroying the Spanish ships; a merit which Essex pretended to belong solely to himself: And he offered to maintain this plea by single combat against the earl of Nottingham, or his sons, or any of his kindred.[2]

In his subsequent criticism of the play, Lessing again draws on Hume (LVI, 136), in stating the historical facts—and notably on the following passage:

Yet notwithstanding this additional provocation, the Queen's partiality was so prevalent, that she reinstated him in his former favour; and her kindness to him appeared to have acquired new force from that short interruption of anger and resentment.[3]

And the following extract may be adduced as an illustration of Lessing's statement (LVI, 141 ff.):

The earl of Essex possessed a monopoly of sweet wines; and as his patent was near expiring, he patiently expected that the Queen would renew it....She therefore refused his demand; and even added, in a contemptuous stile, that an ungovernable beast must be stinted in his provender. This rigour, pushed one step too far, proved the final ruin of this young nobleman, and was the source of infinite sorrow and vexation to the Queen herself.... Being now reduced to despair, he gave entire reins to his violent disposition, and threw off all appearance of duty and respect.[4]

Again, Lessing adds (XXIII, 73), Corneille had made his Essex speak contemptuously of his enemies (Act I, sc. i, ll. 57 ff.):

> Comme il hait les méchans, il ne serait utile
> A chasser un Coban, un Raleig, un Cécile,
> Un tas d'hommes sans nom....

on which Voltaire had commented:

Il n'y eut jamais de *Coban*, mais bien un lord *Cobham*, d'une des plus illustres maisons du pays, qui sous le roi *Jaques premier* fut mis en prison

---

[1] *Commentaires, ed. cit.* x, p. 250.
[2] *History of England, ed. cit.* v, chap. xliii, pp. 395 f.
[3] *Ibid.* p. 408.
[4] *History of England, ed. cit.* v, chap. xliv, p. 434.

pour une conspiration vraie ou prétendue. Il n'est pas permis de falsifier à ce point une histoire si récente, et de traiter avec tant d'indignité des hommes de la plus grande naissance et du plus grand mérite.[1]

It was not historically true, Lessing admits (XXIII, 81), when Corneille's Essex said (Act II, sc. vi, ll. 43 f.):

> C'est au trône, où peut-être on m'eût laissé monter,
> Que je me fusse mis en pouvoir d'éclater.

But this does not justify Voltaire's exclamation: 'Le lord *Essex* au trône! de quel droit? comment? sur quelle aparence? par quels moyens?'[2] Lessing draws again (86) on Hume, who writes:

Essex was descended by females from the royal family; and some of his sanguine partizans had been so imprudent as to mention his name among those of other pretenders to the crown; but the earl took care, by means of Henry Lee, whom he secretly sent into Scotland, to assure James, that, so far from entertaining such ambitious views, he was determined to use every expedient for extorting an immediate declaration in favour of that monarch's right of succession.[3]

It is with real satisfaction that Lessing finds (97) his 'profunder Historikus' tripping, when he says: 'Le comte de *Leicester* succéda dans la faveur à *Dudley*';[4] since these were one and the same person. Horace Walpole in the preface to his *Castle of Otranto* had already noted this error, and in a footnote Lessing refers to the French translation of this work. The relevant passage in this translation is as follows:

M. de Voltaire avoue dans sa Préface sur le Comte d'Essex de Thomas Corneille, qu'on s'est étrangement écarté de l'Histoire dans cette Pièce. L'excuse qu'il en donne est, que lorsque Corneille la composa, la Noblesse Françoise étoit très-peu versée dans l'Histoire d'Angleterre, mais qu'aujourd'hui qu'elle la sait, on ne pardonneroit point une pareille faute. Cependant, oubliant que ce siècle d'ignorance est passé et qu'il est inutile d'instruire les personnes versées dans l'Histoire, il s'avise pour faire parade de son érudition, d'apprendre à la Noblesse Françoise, les noms des Favoris de la Reine Elisabeth, qui étoient, suivant lui, *Robert Dudley*, et le Comte de *Leicester*. Croiroit-on qu'il fût besoin d'apprendre à M. de *Voltaire* lui-même que *Robert Dudley* et le Comte de *Leicester* étoit une seule et même personne?[5]

---

[1] *Commentaires, ed. cit.* x, pp. 258 f.

[2] *Ibid.* p. 294.

[3] *History of England, ed. cit.* v, chap. xliv, p. 438.

[4] *Commentaires, ed. cit.* x, p. 246.

[5] *Le Château d'Otrante, histoire gothique,* traduite sur la seconde édition angloise, par M. E., Amsterdam, 1767, i, pp. xiii f. (note).

And finally, Lessing states, Voltaire is wrong (102) when he says (in a note to Act III, sc. iv, l. 20):

Elle lui avait ôté précédemment toutes ses charges après sa mauvaise conduite en Irlande. Elle avait même poussé l'emportement honteux de la colére jusqu'à lui donner un souflet. Le comte s'était retiré à la campagne; il avait demandé humblement pardon par écrit, et il disait dans sa lettre, *qu'il était pénitent comme Nabucodonosor et qu'il mangeait du foin.* La reine alors n'avait voulu que l'humilier, et il pouvait espérer son rétablissement.[1]

Hume gives an account of the episode in the following passage, from which Lessing drew his facts:

Being once engaged in a dispute with her about the choice of a governor for Ireland, he was so heated in the argument, that he entirely forgot the rules both of duty and civility; and turned his back upon her in a contemptuous manner. Her anger, which was naturally prompt and violent, rose at this provocation; and she instantly gave him a box on the ear; adding a passionate expression, suited to his impertinence. Instead of recollecting himself, and making the submissions due to her sex and station, he clapped his hand to his sword, and swore he would not bear such usage, were it from Henry the eighth himself; and, in a great passion, he immediately withdrew from court. Egerton, the chancellor, who loved Essex, exhorted him to repair his indiscretion by proper acknowledgements.[2]

But what, after all, Lessing argues, do these questions of historical inaccuracy matter, whether the inaccuracy be Corneille's or Voltaire's? The tragedy (115), as Voltaire had admitted, is only a romance:

L'intrigue de la tragédie n'est qu'un roman; le grand point est que ce roman puisse intéresser. On demande jusqu'à quel point il est permis de falsifier l'histoire dans un poëme? Je ne crois pas qu'on puisse changer sans déplaire, les faits ni même les caractères connus du public.[3]

But of this latter limitation Lessing will not hear; we do not read Corneille's tragedy with the history of Rapin de Thoyras (XXIV, 9,

---

[1] *Commentaires, ed. cit.* x, p. 323.

[2] *History of England, ed. cit.* v, chap. xliii, p. 405. The incident is related by Hume under the date 1598; but Thomas Egerton was at that time Lord Keeper, and did not become Chancellor until 1603, under James I. Essex's letter to Egerton is quoted in full by Hume in a footnote (*ibid.* pp. 406 f.). But Hume also gives an account (*ibid.* p. 433) of a letter written by Essex to the Queen after his examination by the privy-council, which contains an allusion to Nebuchadnezzar similar to that given by Voltaire. Hume refers to this letter under the date 1600, but it seems to have been written in 1599. To this passage Lessing does not refer.

[3] *Commentaires, ed. cit.* x, p. 262 (note to Act I, sc. i).

38) at our elbow.[1] The poet has the right to deal with his materials as he chooses. This leads Lessing to the theoretical consideration of the attitude of the poet to history.[2]

Apart from the question of the relations of the *Comte d'Essex* to historical fact, Lessing is prepared (XXIV, 66) to endorse Voltaire's estimate of the play as mediocre in intrigue and style:

> Tout ce qu'on peut dire de l'*Essex* de *Thomas Corneille*, c'est que la piéce est médiocre, et par l'intrigue, et par le stile; mais il y a quelque intérêt, quelques vers heureux....Les acteurs, et surtout ceux de province, aimaient à faire le rôle du comte d'*Essex*, à paraître avec une jarretière brodée au-dessous du genou, et un grand ruban bleu en bandolière. Le comte d'*Essex* donné pour un héros du premier ordre, persécuté par l'envie, ne laisse pas d'en imposer. Enfin le nombre des bonnes tragédies est si petit chez toutes les nations du monde, que celles qui ne sont pas absolument mauvaises, atirent toujours des spectateurs quand de bons acteurs les font valoir.[3]

It was inherent in Corneille's French temperament, Lessing adds, to degrade his earl to the sighing lover of the Countess Irton,[4] and to make his despair, and not his pride, the motive that brings him to the scaffold.

To his criticism Lessing appends in translation (XXIV–XXV) a number of Voltaire's notes, which meet with his approval. They are in the original as follows:

[XXIV, 94]: Note to Act II, sc. iii (*Commentaires, ed. cit.* x, pp. 288 f.): Mais le rôle de *Cécil* est plus mauvais que ce stile; il est froid, il est subalterne. Quand on veut peindre de tels hommes, il faut employer les couleurs dont *Racine* a peint *Narcisse*.

[XXIV, 98]: Note to Act II, sc. vi (*ibid.* pp. 300 f.): La duchesse prétendue d'*Irton* est une femme vertueuse et sage, qui n'a voulu ni se perdre auprès

---

[1] The *Histoire d'Angleterre* by Rapin de Thoyras (La Haye, 1724–36), was a principal source of Voltaire's historical knowledge. Cp. Voltaire, *Œuvres*, Geneva, 1756–57, xvii, p. 284 (*Écrivains du Tems de Louis XIV*): 'L'Angleterre lui doit la meilleure histoire qu'on ait de ce Royaume, et la seule impartiale, dans un pays où l'on n'écrit guères que par esprit de parti.' The work was translated into German in 1758 (v. W. Hüttemann, *C. F. Weisse und seine Zeit im Verhältnis zu Shakespeare*, Diss. Bonn, 1912, p. 67).

[2] See below, pp. 437 ff.

[3] *Commentaires, ed. cit.* x, pp. 361 f. (note to Act v, sc. iv).

[4] This is not Voltaire's view, but possibly a reminiscence of Calepio's criticism in his *Paragone*, cap. v, art. iv, *ed. cit.* p. 104: 'Tomaso Cornelio deprava il costume del Co. d'Essec col renderlo pazzo d' amore, e farlo morire più per disperazione, che per la grandezza dell' animo.'

d'*Elisabeth* en aimant le comte, ni épouser son amant. Ce caractère serait beau s'il était animé, s'il servait au nœud de la piéce; elle ne fait là qu'ofice d'ami. Ce n'est pas assez pour le théatre.

[xxiv, 105]: Note to Act iii, sc. ii (*ibid*. pp. 314 f.): Il me semble qu'il y a toujours quelque chose de louche, de confus, de vague, dans tout ce que les personages de cette tragédie disent et font. Que toute action soit claire, toute intrigue bien connue, tout sentiment bien dévelopé; ce sont là des règles inviolables. Mais ici que veut le comte d'*Essex*? que veut *Elisabeth*? quel est le crime du comte? est-il acusé faussement? est-il coupable? Si la reine le croit innocent, elle doit prendre sa défense; s'il est reconu criminel, est-il raisonable que la confidente dise qu'il n'implorera jamais sa grace, qu'il est trop fier? La fierté est très convenable à un guerrier vertueux et innocent, non à un homme convaincu de haute trahison. *Qu'il fléchisse*, dit la reine. Est-ce bien-là le sentiment qui doit l'ocuper si elle l'aime? Quand il aura fléchi, quand il aura obtenu sa grace, *Elisabeth* en sera-t-elle plus aimée? *Je l'aime*, dit la reine, *cent fois plus que moi-même*. Ah, madame, si vous avez la tête tournée à ce point, si votre passion est si grande, examinez donc l'afaire de votre amant, et ne soufrez pas que ses ennemis l'acablent et le persécutent injustement sous votre nom, comme il est dit, quoique faussement, dans toute la piéce.

[xxiv, 127]: Note to Act iii, sc. iii (*ibid*. pp. 316 f.)—(but this is not closely translated): La scène du prétendu comte de *Salsbury* avec la reine.... On ne sait pas précisément de quoi il s'agit. *Le crime ne suit pas toujours l'aparence. Craignez les injustices de ceux qui de sa mort se rendent les complices*.... Mais après que ce *Salsbury* a dit que les injustices rendent complices les juges du comte d'*Essex*, il parle à la reine de clémence.... Il avoue donc que le comte d'*Essex* est criminel. A laquelle de ces deux idées faudra-t-il s'arrêter? A quoi faudra-t-il se fixer? La reine répond qu'*Essex* est trop fier, que *c'est l'ordinaire écueil des ambitieux*, qu'*il s'est fait un outrage des soins qu'elle a pris pour détourner l'orage*, et que *si la tête du comte fait raison à la reine de sa fierté, c'est sa faute*. Le spectateur a pu passer de tels discours; le lecteur est moins indulgent.

[xxiv, 136]: Note to Act iii, sc. iii (*ibid*. pp. 320 f.): Il est bien étrange que *Salsbury* dise qu'on a contrefait l'écriture du comte d'*Essex*, et que la reine ne songe pas à examiner une chose si importante. Elle doit assurément s'en éclaircir, et comme amante, et comme reine. Elle ne répond pas seulement à cette ouverture qu'elle devait saisir, et qui demandait l'examen le plus promt et le plus exact; elle répète encor en d'autres mots, que le comte est trop fier.

There is nothing in Voltaire's notes corresponding exactly to the last sentence of St. xxiv (144); but this expresses the queen's attitude to Essex.

[xxv, 1]: Note to Act iv, sc. iii (*ibid*. pp. 342 f.): On ne voit pas non plus pourquoi le comte veut mourir sans être justifié, lui qui se croit entiérement

innocent. On ne voit pas pourquoi étant calomnié par les prétendus faussaires, *Cécil* et *Raleig*, qu'il déteste, il n'instruit pas la reine du crime de faux qu'il leur impute. Comment se peut-il qu'un homme si fier, pouvant d'un mot se venger des ennemis qui l'écrasent, néglige de dire ce mot? Cela n'est pas dans la nature. Aime-t-il assez la duchesse d'*Irton*? est-il assez furieux, assez enyvré de sa passion, pour déclarer qu'il aime mieux être décapité que de vivre sans elle? Il aurait donc falu lui donner dans la piéce toutes les fureurs de l'amour qu'il n'a pas euës.

[xxv, 9]: Note to Act IV, sc. iii (*ibid.* p. 339): Cette fierté de la reine qui lutte sans cesse contre la fierté d'*Essex*, est toujours le sujet de la tragédie. C'est une illusion qui ne laisse pas de plaire au public. Cependant si cette fierté seule agit, c'est un pur caprice de la part d'*Elisabeth* et du comte d'*Essex*. Je veux qu'il me demande pardon; je ne veux pas demander pardon. Voilà la piéce. Il semble qu'alors le spectateur oublie qu'*Elisabeth* est extravagante, si elle veut qu'on lui demande pardon d'un crime imaginaire, qu'elle est injuste et barbare de ne pas examiner ce crime, avant d'exiger qu'on lui demande pardon. On oublie l'essentiel pour ne s'ocuper que de ces sentimens de fierté qui séduisent presque toujours.

[xxv, 20]: Note to Act IV, sc. i (*ibid.* p. 333): Tous les rôles paraissent manqués dans cette tragédie, et cependant elle a eu du succès. Quelle en est la raison? Je le répète, la situation des personages atendrissante par elle-même, et l'ignorance où le parterre a été longtems. Also Note to Act IV, sc. ii (*ibid.* p. 337): Un grand seigneur qu'on va mener à l'échafaut intéresse toujours le public; et la représentation de ces avantures sans aucun secours de la poësie, fait le même effet à peu près que la vérité même.

As will be seen, the translation which Lessing offers of the last passages is not literal.

Later, in comparing Banks's Elizabeth with Corneille's, Lessing says of the latter (LVII, 24): 'Seine Elisabeth klagt nicht, wie die Elisabeth des Corneille, über Kälte und Verachtung, über Gluth und Schicksal....' Here again he has in mind Voltaire's commentary on the lines in question:[1]

Je n'examine point si ces vers sont mauvais. Une reine telle qu'*Elisabeth*, presque décrépite, qui parle du poison qui dévore son cœur, et de ce que

---

[1] Act II, sc. i (*Commentaires, ed. cit.* x, p. 277):

> *Elisabeth.* En vain tu crois tromper la douleur qui m'acable;
> C'est parcequ'il me hait, qu'il s'est rendu coupable;
> Et la belle Suffolk refusée à ses vœux,
> Lui fait joindre le crime au mépris de mes feux.
> Pour le justifier, ne dis point qu'il ignore
> Jusqu'où va le poison dont l'ardeur me dévore.
> Il a trop de ma bouche, il a trop de mes yeux,
> Apris qu'il est, l'ingrat, ce que j'aime le mieux.

ses yeux et sa bouche ont dit à son ingrat, est un personage comique. C'est là peut-être un des plus grands exemples du défaut qu'on a si souvent reproché à notre nation, de changer la tragédie en roman amoureux. S'il s'agissait d'une jeune reine, ce roman serait tolérable; et on ne peut atribuer le succès de cette piéce qu'à l'ignorance où était le parterre de l'âge d'*Elisabeth.* Tout ce qu'elle pouvait raisonnablement dire, c'est qu'autrefois elle avait eu de l'inclination pour *Essex*: mais alors il n'y aurait eu rien d'intéressant. L'intérêt ne peut donc subsister qu'aux dépens de la vraisemblance. Qu'en doit-on conclure? Que l'avanture du comte d'*Essex* est un sujet mal choisi.

J. F. REGNARD

Of the three plays of the still popular Jean François Regnard which were performed in Hamburg, *Der Spieler, Democrit* and *Der Zerstreute,* Lessing has no original criticism to offer. At most, the last of these gives him an opportunity to discuss the suitability of the character of a 'distrait' for comedy.[1] The sources of his information are as follows. Of *Der Spieler* (xiv, 66), which Lessing considers 'without doubt his best play', Léris says (*op. cit.* pp. 254 f.):

On peut dire que c'est, à la versification près, ce que cet Auteur a fait de meilleur, cette piece pouvant aller de pair avec quelques-unes de Moliere.... Dufrény revendiquoit le fond de cette Com[édie] qu'il prétendoit que Regnard lui avoit pris, et l'avoit mis en vers. [Note: Regnard abusa effectivement de la confiance que Dufrény lui témoigna....] Regnard, au contraire, se plaint dans sa Préface d'une cabale suscitée contre son Ouvrage, par les injustes plaintes d'un Plagiaire, qui produisoit une autre piece en pro[se] sous le même titre. Quoi qu'il en soit, le *Chevalier Joueur,* de Dufrény, en 5 Ac[tes] en pro[se] avec un Prol[ogue] fut joué le 27 Fév. 1697; sur le même Thé[âtre] Fran[çais] où celle de Regnard avoit paru près de quatre mois auparavant; mais leur succès fut fort différent, car la piece de Regnard est restée en possession de la scene, où elle paroît encore souvent, et celle de Dufrény n'eut que cette représentation.

Lessing also looked up the account of the quarrel in Léris' source, the *Histoire du Théâtre françois* of Parfaict (xiv, 1748), where he found (p. 43): 'Il n'est pas aisé de décider qui des deux avoit tort; mais il est très certain que l'un a pris dans la Piéce de l'autre le fonds du sujet, les principaux caracteres, et plusieurs situations remarquables'; and on Du Fresny's play Parfaict comments (p. 52): 'En supposant,

---

[1] See below, pp. 389 f.

(comme il est très probable) que M. Regnard a profité des idées de M. Du Fresny, îl est toujours certain qu'il les a employées avec beaucoup plus d'art, et d'une maniere à lui faire honneur.'

Lessing's source of information concerning *Der Zerstreute* (XXVIII, 70)[1] was also Parfaict (xiv, pp. 71 ff.):

Le Distrait, Comédie en cinq Actes, et en vers, de M. Regnard, représentée pour la premiére fois le Lundi, 2. Décembre [1697]. (Quatre représentations.) Monsieur Regnard auroit été fort consolé de sa disgrace, s'il avoit pû se flatter que cette Comédie, que le Public avoit si mal accueillie, et qu'il sembloit avoir condamnée à ne plus reparoître au Théatre, dût au bout de trente-quatre ans y recevoir beaucoup d'applaudissemens....

This passage is followed by a quotation of a criticism of the play from the *Mercure de France* of July, 1731 (pp. 1788 ff.):

On ne sçauroit justifier le jugement qu'on semble aujourd'hui porter du *Distrait*, sans condamner en quelque maniere celui qu'on en porta autrefois; on peut cependant prendre un tempérament entre deux décisions si opposées, en disant que la Piéce n'est pas trouvée meilleure qu'elle l'a parû dans sa naissance, mais qu'on s'y divertit davantage, parce qu'on ne la revoit que comme une Farce pleine de gayeté;[2] au lieu que l'Auteur avoit, sans doute, prétendu la donner comme une Comédie dans les formes: ainsi la critique ayant déja prononcé sur la maniere dont les connoisseurs devoient la recevoir, nous n'y apportons plus cette sévérité qui l'avoit proscrite....

And in a note to p. 73 of Parfaict's *Histoire* Lessing read:

L'Auteur des *Lettres d'un François*, Tome 1, page 88. n'a fait autre chose qu'allonger cette réfléxion [*viz.*, 'qu'il ne dépend non plus de nous de n'être point distraits, qu'il est au pouvoir d'un aveugle de jouir de la lumiere'], qu'il donne cependant pour nouvelle. Voici le passage. 'La Comédie du *Distrait*.... Le fond, si je ne me trompe, est vicieux. Des gens raisonnables ne riront non plus d'un homme qui a le malheur d'être entraîné par des distractions involontaires, que d'un autre qui a celui d'être

---

[1] Schlegel's translation of the title, 'Träumer', is to be found in his *Demokrit* (*Werke, ed. cit.* iii, p. 188): '*Aristophanes*: Ey! ich kenne ihn; ist es nicht Regnard, dessen Buchführer versichert, dass seine Werke sehr nahe an des Moliere seine kämen? Moliere hat mir seinen Spieler und seinen Träumer gelobt.' Scheibe, quoted by Lessing (XXVI, 76) calls it der *Unschlüssige* [*Unentschlüssige*] oder *Zerstreute*. On the title see also W. Creizenach, *Zur Entstehungsgeschichte des neueren deutschen Lustspiels*, Halle, 1879, p. 37 (note 70).

[2] Lessing adds (XXVIII, 86) a quotation from Horace, *Satires*, i, x, 7 f.: 'Ergo non satis est' etc.: 'Therefore it is not enough to stretch the mouth of the listener with laughter; although there is also some merit in this.'

sujet à la migraine. La Comédie ne doit jouer que les défauts qu'elle peut corriger. Les plaisanteries que l'on fera sur un boiteux, lui aideront aussitôt à marcher droit, que la Piéce de Regnard corrigera un homme qui est né distrait.... nous aimons à voir plaisanter un homme de ses défauts, il y a de la barbarie à rire de ses infirmités.'

Lastly, he read in Parfaict (xiv, p. 81):

M. l'Abbé Pellegrin, Auteur des réfléxions qu'on vient de lire [this is the criticism from the *Mercure de France* from which extracts are given above], auroit pû ajoûter que M. Regnard a eu d'autant plus de facilité, qu'il a trouvé son principal personnage tout tracé dans les caracteres de M. de la Bruyere. [*Note*: Les Caracteres, ou les mœurs de ce siécle, par M. de la Bruyere, Chapitre XI.] Ce morceau est extrêmement comique, et très-susceptible de plaisanteries. M. Regnard n'a donc fait autre chose que de le mettre partie en action, et partie en récit: ce qu'il a ajouté est, comme on l'a déja dit, très-foiblement imaginé. Au reste, on sent aisément que l'Auteur ne s'est pas donné la peine de mettre la derniere main à cette Piéce, car la versification en est plus défectueuse, et plus négligée qu'aucune autre qu'il ait faite.

In the case of *Democrit* (XVII, 95 ff.), Lessing's debt to Parfaict is indicated in his foot-note, and has consequently not been overlooked by his commentators; but as none of these indicates the extent and nature of the indebtedness, I quote the French source in full (*op. cit.* xiv, pp. 164 ff.):

La réputation de cette Piéce est parfaitement établie; il en est peu qu'on voye plus fréquemment au Théatre, et qui y soit reçûe avec plus de plaisir. Les Connoisseurs mêmes, en y remarquant de très-grands défauts, ne sçauroient se dispenser de rire avec la multitude: ainsi ce que nous allons dire à ce sujet, n'est point pour lui porter aucun préjudice. On ne peut d'abord nier que la régle de l'unité de lieu ne soit extrêmement violée. Le premier Acte se passe dans un désert à la vûe de la caverne que Démocrite a choisi pour sa demeure: et les suivans dans le Palais des Rois d'Athênes. Ce défaut est un des moindres de l'Ouvrage; nous ne chicanons point non plus l'Auteur sur la liberté qu'il a prise de faire revivre à Athênes l'état Monarchique qui y étoit éteint plus de sept cens ans avant Démocrite: ce sont de légeres minuties pour lui, et qui ne méritent pas qu'on les reléve: mais ce qu'on ne sçauroit lui passer, est la maniere dont il a traité son principal Personnage. Qui n'eut crû que M. Regnard, qui, par sa façon de penser, avoit tant de conformité avec Démocrite, n'eut dû rendre au mieux ce caractere. Loin de cela, il est absolument méconnoissable. A la place du Philosophe dont il usurpe le nom, on ne voit qu'un ennuyeux Pédant, qui le contrefait fort mal, et n'a pas le sens commun. S'il se mêle de faire l'amour, c'est sans esprit, et sans sentiment: c'est encore bien pis, lorsqu'il veut raisonner, le jargon qu'il affecte alors est inintelligible à tout le monde, et à lui-même: il est sur cette matiere au-dessous de son Valet, dont le galimathias est au moins plus aisé à entendre....Passons au sujet de la Comédie, qui est des plus minces....Ce plan, comme on le voit, n'est pas fort difficile à imaginer; cependant tout foible et tout trivial qu'il est, on peut dire encore qu'il n'est ni bien conçu, ni clairement développé, ni conduit raisonnablement: que le dénouement est des plus romanesques, et l'épisode d'Ismene et d'Agénor tout-à-fait inutile. Il y a même quelque chose de trop bas, et de messéant dans le personnage de ce dernier. A franchement parler, il n'y en a que trois qui peuvent mériter qu'on les éxamine....Ces trois personnages dont nous allons parler sont, Strabon, Cléanthis, et Thaler. Le caractere du premier n'est pas aisé à définir: il change trop souvent, et suivant les personnes ausquelles il parle. Avec Démocrite, il est spirituel, fin, et railleur: mauvais plaisant vis-à-vis de Thaler. Dans ses deux conversations avec Cléanthis, il débute en cuistre, et poursuit sur le ton de Mascarille. Il faut avouer que l'idée des deux Scenes de Strabon et de Cléanthis, est véritablement neuve, et comique, mais l'Auteur l'a un peu chargée....Ce jeu de Théatre, inventé par Mademoiselle *Beauval* et par le Sieur de *la Thorilliere*, qui jouerent ces rôles d'original, et observé religieusement par les Acteurs et Actrices qui leur ont succédé, n'en est pas moins ridicule: les noms de ces fameux Acteurs, et celui même de M. Regnard, qui leur en avoit peut-être donné l'idée, ne doivent jamais faire passer une bouffonnerie qui choque le bon sens....Il ne reste plus que Thaler, c'est le seul Païsan que M. Regnard ait introduit sur la Scene: son rôle est très-comique, et soutenu d'un bout à l'autre. Les plaisanteries, si naturelles à l'Auteur, se trouvent admirablement placées dans la bouche de ce manant, qui conserve toujours cette rusticité, et cette malignité qui semblent de l'essence des gens de son état. Nous le répétons, c'est un des meilleurs personnages de la Piéce, des plus nécessaires à l'intrigue, et peut-être celui qui y paroît le plus à propos.

Lessing had also in mind, no doubt (XVII, 103), J. E. Schlegel's *Demokrit, ein Todtengespräch*. Demokrit there says:

So hatte ich mich also in eine Wüste bey Athen begeben, wo Bäre und Tiger waren? Du beschreibst mich als einen verwegenen Menschen.—Aber hatte ich denn diese Tiger und Bäre ausdrücklich in die Wüste kommen lassen, damit sie bey mir wohnen möchten? Denn man war zu Athen von Tigern eben nicht geplagt....Du krönest selber einen König in deinem Gehirne, zu der Zeit, da alle Welt weis, dass es eine freye Stadt war.[1]

---

[1] *Werke*, ed. cit. iii (1764), pp. 184 f. Cp. also Gottsched, *Deutsche Schaubühne*, iii (1741), p. xi, where Gottsched refers to the setting of Regnard's *Démocrite* in Athens, and to the contrast of such a setting with the modern details in the portrayal of the personages.

D. A. BRUEYS [AND J. PALAPRAT]

Der Advokat Patelin of de Brueys (xiv, 102) is not criticised. Lessing had found it stated both by Léris (*op. cit.* p. 67) and by Parfaict (*op. cit.* xiv, pp. 414 ff.) that this comedy was based on an old French farce, played in Paris about 1470, *Les tromperies, finesses et subtilités de Maistre Pierre Patelin*. The theme of Patelin was used in Reuchlin's Latin drama, *Henno* (1497); and Brueys' modern version in 1700 incorporated traits derived from *Henno* as well as new elements in the plot. The play was staged by Jean Palaprat in 1706 (see Parfaict, xiv, pp. 417 f.); a German translation, by J. C. S., appeared in Danzig in 1762 (cp. Petersen, *ed. cit.* p. 195).

M. A. LE GRAND

Lessing's information about the two one-act plays of Marc Antoine Le Grand (1673–1728), *Der Sieg der vergangenen Zeit* (v, 136) and *Der sehende Blinde* (LXXXIII, 110), again comes from his French 'Annales'. On the former play he found in Léris (*op. cit.* p. 439):

Le Triomphe du Tems, Com[édie] de Le Grand, représentée au Thé[âtre] Fran[çais] avec succès, le 18 Octo[bre] 1725 [Lessing's '1724' is evidently a slip], et imprimée tome troisieme de ses Œuvres. Cette Com[édie] est composée d'un Prolog[ue] et de trois petites pieces en un Ac[te] en pro[se] avec des Divertissemens, dont la musique étoit de Quinault. Le *Tems Passé* le *Tems Présent* et le *Tems Futur*, sont les titres des trois petites pieces. *Voyez* les *Amans ridicules*.

And under the latter title we read (*ibid.* p. 20):

Les *Amans ridicules*, Com[édie] en 5 Ac[tes] en vers, par Le Grand, donnée au Théatre Fran[çais] le premier Juin 1711. L'Auteur n'ayant pas fait imprimer cette piece, s'en servit dans la suite pour en composer le premier Acte du *Triomphe du Tems*.

Lessing has little to say about the piece except that, in spite of amusing situations, he found the victory of time over youth and beauty too unpleasant a subject for comic treatment (v, 145 ff.).

On *Der sehende Blinde*—the translation of which by Suabe[1] Lessing commends (LXXXIII, 141) as 'perhaps one of the best we have'—his information came from Parfaict. He found the play mentioned in

---

[1] See above, p. 92.

vol. xv (1749), with a reference to *L'Aveugle clair-voyant* by De Brosse, which is described in vol. vii (1746), pp. 226 ff., as follows:

L'aveugle Clair-voyant, Comédie de M. de Brosse [1649]. Un Officier, d'un certain âge, prêt d'épouser une jeune Veuve dont il est amoureux, reçoit un ordre de partir pour l'armée; il quitte sa prétendue avec des assurances réciproques de la plus sincere tendresse. Il est à peine parti, que la Veuve se rend aux soins du fils de cet Officier. La fille de ce même Officier, profite de l'absence de son pere, et reçoit dans sa maison un jeune homme qu'elle aime; cette double intrigue est mandée au pere, qui pour s'en assurer, fait écrire qu'il a perdu la vue. Ce stratagême produit tout l'effet qu'il s'en est promis: il revient à Paris. (C'est où l'action de la Piéce commence.) Et secondé de son Valet, qui aide à sa tromperie, il voit tout ce qui se passe dans sa maison. On peut assurer que les Scenes de la Veuve, et du fils de l'Officier, en présence de ce dernier, sont d'un bon comique: la Veuve feint de s'affliger de l'accident de l'Officier, et l'assure qu'elle ne l'aime pas moins: et en même temps elle donne un coup d'œil, ou fait un geste de tendresse à son amant, la fille de l'Officier, persuadée de l'aveugle-ment de son pere, continue à recevoir les visites du jeune homme qu'elle aime. On devine le dénouement de cette Comédie: l'Officier convaincu de l'inconstance de la Veuve, consent que son fils s'unisse avec elle; il donne une pareille permission à sa fille, qui épouse le jeune homme. Cette Comédie est une des plus passables du temps; le Sieur le Grand s'est servi du sujet, et d'une partie des Scenes de cette Piéce; pour en composer une en un Acte et en vers, sous le même titre, il a seulement changé le personnage du pere, et a mis à la place celui d'un oncle.

After referring to this account, Parfaict adds concerning Le Grand's play (xv, p. 242): 'et nous avons ajouté, en terminant son extrait, que M. le Grand en avoit employé tout le fond, mais qu'il s'en était servi en homme de goût et d'esprit. En effet, cette Piéce-ci est très-bien conduite, les rôles soutenus, l'intrigue heureuse et plaisante, et le dénouement très-naturel.'

PH. N. DESTOUCHES

In the first line of the French comedy-writers of the early eighteenth century who had dominated, and still continued to dominate, the German stage stand Destouches and Marivaux.[1] Considering that these dramatists had a considerable share in moulding Lessing's own

[1] For some details of the popularity of these writers in Germany cp. P. Ahrend, *Einiges über Destouches in Deutschland* (in *Neuphilologisches Centralblatt*, xii (1898), pp. 97 ff., 131 ff., 161 ff., 218 ff., 289 ff., 321 ff.) and V. Golubew, *Marivaux Lustspiele in deutschen Übersetzungen des 18. Jahrhunderts*, Heidelberg, 1904.

early dramatic work, what he has to say of them in his *Dramaturgie* is disappointingly meagre.

Four plays by Destouches were performed within the period of the *Dramaturgie*: *Das unvermuthete Hinderniss*, *Der verheyrathete Philosoph*, *Der poetische Dorfjunker* and *Das Gespenst mit der Trommel*. Lessing is for the most part, however, more concerned with the translations of these plays than with the plays themselves.

He had, it will be remembered, compiled a life of Destouches, out of the prefatory matter which he found in the latter's works, for the *Theatralische Bibliothek*.[1] Apparently he now had also at hand the 'zu Berlin übersetzten sämtlichen Werke des Destouches' (XII, 50); this was *Des Herrn von Destouches sämtliche theatralische Werke aus dem Französischen übersetzt*, 4 vols. Leipzig and Göttingen, 1756.[2] (A fifth volume appeared subsequently, in 1772.) This was briefly noticed—in all probability by Lessing himself—in the *Bibliothek der schönen Wissenschaften*;[3] and in St. LI (135) he speaks of the 'prächtige Ausgabe' in quarto, edited by the poet's son (*Œuvres dramatiques*, 4 vols. Paris, 1757), which was also reviewed in the *Bibliothek*.[4]

Concerning *L'Obstacle imprévu* (x, 4) Lessing found in Léris (*op. cit.* p. 321) the information that: 'Le Public fit à cette piece un accueil moins favorable qu'à la plûpart des autres de cet Auteur, n'ayant eu que six représentations la premiere fois, et cinq la seconde.' Similarly, Léris reported on the lack of success of the other comedies, which Lessing mentions (6). In the same source he found the following (*op. cit.* pp. 434 f.) on *Le Trésor caché*, which he mentions (IX, 127) in connexion with his own *Der Schatz*:

Le *Trésor Caché*, Com[édie] en 5 Ac[tes] en pro[se], donnée une seule fois au Thé[âtre] Ital[ien] le 17 Mai 1745, et qu'on ne finit pas même de jouer. On l'a attribuée à Nericault Destouches, et elle n'a pas été imprimée.[5]

And of *Le Philosophe marié*, which Lessing describes (XII, 61) as a 'masterpiece of the French stage', Léris said (*op. cit.* p. 348):

Cette piece, qui est tout-à-fait dans le goût de la bonne Coméd[ie] fut universellement applaudie, et eut 36 représentations dans le cours de l'année: on la revoit assez souvent.

---

[1] *Schriften*, vi, pp. 153 ff. See above, p. 110.
[2] The preface to the first volume of this edition ends with the words 'Berlin. den 1. des Mertzmonaths 1755'. The translation is in prose.
[3] *Bibliothek der schönen Wissenschaften*, i (ii) (1757), p. 403; *Schriften*, vii, p. 76.
[4] v (i) (1759), pp. 200 ff.
[5] It was first printed in *Œuvres dramatiques*, Paris, 1757, iv, pp. 259 ff. (*Der vergrabene Schatz* did not appear until vol. v of the German translation (1772).)

On the occasion of a repetition of *Der verheyrathete Philosoph* on July 8, Lessing refers (LI, 139) to Destouches' own matrimonial adventure in England, mentioned in the 'Avertissement' to the first volume of the edition published by the poet's son in 1757:

Il [Destouches] s'étoit marié en Angleterre; le secret important que cette alliance exigeoit alors, n'ayant point été gardé par une personne de la famille à laquelle il s'étoit uni, a donné lieu à la Comédie du *Philosophe marié*.[1]

This statement is translated in the review of the *Œuvres dramatiques* of Destouches in the *Bibliothek der schönen Wissenschaften* (v (i) (1759), p. 201). In this section Lessing also refers (LI, 3) to a statement by Chevrier in his *Observateur des Spectacles*, ii (1762), p. 135:

Lundi 10, on a donné *le Jaloux Desabusé* de *Campistron*, nous ne parlerons de cette Piéce, que pour observer que sans elle nous n'aurions eu n'y *le Philosophe Marié* le vrai chef-d'œuvre de *Destouches*, malgré les entousiastes du *Glorieux*, n'y *le Préjugé à la Mode*; Ces deux piéces ont été puisées dans celle de Campistron....

To Campistron's *Jaloux Désabusé*, which according to Léris (*op. cit.* pp. 238 f.) was produced on December 13, 1709, Lessing now turns. He summarises its plot and fails to find any similarity with that of *Le Philosophe marié*. One scene, however, the second of the second act, may, he thinks, have provided the suggestion for Chevrier's remark;[2] and he translates it in full. I quote the original from the edition of Campistron's *Œuvres*, published at Paris in 1750 (iii, pp. 129 ff.). It will be observed that Lessing's version is far from literal.

Dubois à part. Que diable est tout ceci?
Dorante.   Tu vois que ma tristesse
A changé mon humeur et m'accable sans cesse.
Rien de ce que j'aimois ne flatte mes desirs,
Et le ciel m'a donné, pour finir mes plaisirs,
Un bourreau de mes jours, un tyran de mon ame.
Dubois. Quel est-il, ce tyran, ou ce bourreau?
Dorante.   Ma femme.
Dubois. Votre femme, Monsieur?

---

[1] *Œuvres dramatiques de Nericault Destouches*, Paris, 1757, i, pp. ix f.
[2] The reluctance of the philosopher in *Le Philosophe marié* to acknowledge his marriage, because he had formerly ridiculed the married state, is compared with the reluctance of Campistron's jealous husband to admit his jealousy because of his previous diatribes against such husbands. Cp. also Act I, sc. ii of *Le Philosophe marié*, where Ariste expresses dislike of his wife's fashionable visitors, with the scene translated by Lessing from Campistron's play.

Dorante.   Tu n'en dois plus douter.
Elle me cause un mal que je ne puis dompter.
Je suis désespéré.
   Dubois.   Vous est-elle odieuse?
   Dorante. Ah! plut au ciel, ma vie en seroit plus heureuse.
Mon cœur pour mon malheur s'en est laissé charmer,
Et je ne souffre, hélas! que pour la trop aimer.
   Dubois. En seriez-vous jaloux?
   Dorante.   Jusqu'à la frénésie.
   Dubois. Vous, Monsieur, vous, frappé de cette fantaisie?
Vous contre les jaloux déclaré hautement.
   Dorante. Et c'est de-là que vient mon plus cruel tourment.
Quand j'entrai dans le monde une pente fatale
M'entraîna dans le cours de la grande cabale:
Ceux qui la composoient m'instruisant tous les jours,
J'eus bientôt attrapé leurs airs et leurs discours.
J'occupai mon esprit de leurs vaines pensées;
Et blâmant du vieux temps les maximes sensées,
J'en plaisantois sans cesse, et traitois de bourgeois
Ceux qui suivoient encor les anciennes loix.
Quel est l'homme, disois-je, en faisant l'agréable,
Qui garde pour sa femme un amour véritable?
C'est aux petites gens à nourrir de tels feux.
Ah! si l'hymen jamais m'enchaîne de ses nœuds,
Loin que l'on me reproche une pareille flamme,
Que je voudrai de bien aux Amans de ma femme!
Que ne croirai-je point devoir à leur amour,
S'ils peuvent loin de moi l'amuser tout le jour!
   Dubois. Et pourquoi teniez-vous cet imprudent langage?
   Dorante. Morbleu! pour imiter les gens du haut étage,
De qui les sentimens ou faux ou trop outrés,
De la droite raison sont toujours égarés.
Connu sur ce pied-là, pour plaire à ma Famille,
Je m'engage, j'épouse une petite fille,
De qui l'air enfantin et l'ingénuité
Ne prenoient sur mon cœur aucune autorité.
Je cru la voir toujours avec indifférence:
Malheureux! De ses traits j'ignorois la puissance.
Sa beauté s'est accruë; et sa possession,
Loin de me dégouter a fait ma passion.
   Dubois. Vous y voilà donc pris?
   Dorante.   Je n'ai comme ma flâme,
Qu'aux mouvemens jaloux qui déchirent mon ame.
De ce trouble secret je me suis allarmé,
Et j'ai douté long-temps que mon cœur fût charmé:
Mais enfin, j'ai senti toute mon infortune.

Je crains tous mes amis, leur aspect m'importune.
Je n'aspirois jadis qu'à les avoir chez moi,
Leur présence aujourd'hui m'y donne de l'effroi.
Pourquoi faut-il aussi qu'un ridicule usage
Souffre des étrangers au milieu d'un ménage?
Sages Italiens, que vous avez raison!
Vingt fainéans sans cesse assiégent ma maison:
Ils content devant moi des douceurs à Célie.
L'un dit qu'elle a bon air, l'autre qu'elle est polie;
Celui-ci, que ses yeux sont faits pour tout charmer,
Que sa grace jamais ne se peut exprimer;
Celui-là, de ses dents vante l'ordre agréable.
Enfin tous à l'envi la trouvent adorable;
Et la fin d'un discours qui me percent [sic] le cœur,
Est toujours employée à louer mon bonheur.
    Dubois. Il est vrai. C'est ainsi que la chose se passe.
    Dorante. Ils portent bien plus loin leur indiscrete audace:
Ils viennent la chercher au sortir de son lit;
Chacun fait là briller ses soins et son esprit;
Ce ne sont que bons mots, que jeux, que raillerie,
Que signes, que coups d'œil, et que minauderie.
Ma femme reçoit tout d'un esprit fort humain,
Et je vois quelquefois qu'on lui baise la main.
    Dubois. On a tort.
    Dorante.   Cependant il faut que je l'endure,
Et le public rira si ma bouche en murmure;
Si je montre l'ennui que mon cœur en reçoit,
Les enfans dans Paris me montreront au doigt,
Et traité de bizarre et d'Epoux indocile,
Je serai le sujet d'un heureux Vaudeville.

In his *Theatralische Bibliothek* Lessing had made the following statement concerning *Das Gespenst mit der Trommel* (cp. XVII, 72):

Es ist eigentlich nicht von der Erfindung des Herrn Destouches, sondern eine Nachahmung eines englischen Stückes des Herrn Addisons, welches in seiner Sprache The Drummer heisst, und auch in Deutschland bekannt genug ist. Unser Dichter war in England gewesen, und hatte den Herrn Addison persönlich kennen lernen.[1]

He suggests that the translator, Frau Gottsched, had availed herself of the English original; but Gottsched himself says in the preface to vol. ii of his *Deutsche Schaubühne* (p. 39):

Herr Destouches hat zweifelsfrey, in seiner französischen Uebersetzung, das englische Original in vielen Stücken verlassen, oder verändert; um

---

[1] *Theatralische Bibliothek*, i, pp. 273 f.; *Schriften*, vi, p. 156.

demselben die Ordnung und Regelmässigkeit zu geben, der die Engländer in ihren Schauspielen nicht gewohnt sind. Die Uebersetzerinn hat sich also lieber nach dieser Verbesserung, als nach dem Grundtexte richten wollen; da es ihr sonst eben so leicht gefallen wäre, diesen als jene zu übersetzen. Nur in den Namen hat sie sich eben der Freyheit bedienet, die sich Herr Destouches genommen, dass sie dieselben nach deutscher Art eingerichtet; um dem Stücke dadurch eine desto mehrere Anmuth bey uns zu geben.

Of *Der poetische Dorfjunker* (XIII, 6) Lessing has no criticism to offer; but he is witty over Frau Gottsched's expansion of it from three to five acts, to secure its admission into her husband's *Deutsche Schaubühne*.[1] In his preface to vol. iii of that work Gottsched had said (p. xiii):

Der Verfasser hatte sein Stücke nur in drey Aufzüge getheilet: Die Übersetzerinn aber hat geglaubt, dass es besser wäre, auch hier die Regel des Horaz zu beobachten.

> Neue minor, neu sit quinto productior actu
> Fabula, quae vult spectari, et spectata reponi.[2]
> *Art. Poet.* [ll. 189–90].

Der letzte Aufzug war auch im Französischen so ungeheuer lang, dass er sich ganz gern in die zwey letzten Aufzüge des Deutschen zertheilen liess. Aus den beyden erstern aber sind gleichfalls, mit einer ganz geringen Veränderung und Einschaltung eines kurzen Auftrittes, sehr leicht drey Aufzüge geworden.

Lessing does not find Frau Gottsched's translation bad, especially in respect of the 'Knittelverse' put into the mouth of Masuren. Her Germanisation of 'virtuose' by 'Wunder' (35) gives him, however, an excellent opportunity for irony. The passages in the original and in Frau Gottsched's translation are as follows:

Acte II, sc. 6	III. Aufzug, 2. Auftritt
M. des Mazures. . . . Mademoiselle, vous me surprenez à mon tour, je vous croyois une virtuose.	*Masuren*. . . . Gnädiges Fräulein, Sie machen mich ganz bestürzt. Ich dachte, Sie wären ein Wunder.
Angélique. Fi donc, Monsieur, Pour qui me preniez vous! je suis une honnête fille, afin que vous le sachiez.	*Henriette.* Ey Pfuy! Herr von Masuren! für wen halten Sie mich? Ich bin ein ehrlich Mädchen, dass Sie es wissen!

[1] P. Schlenther, *Frau Gottsched und die bürgerliche Komödie*, Berlin, 1886, pp. 173 ff., gives details of the changes involved by this expansion. (Cp. Petersen, *ed. cit.* p. 192.)

[2] Gottsched quotes the second line thus; the usual form is now
'fabula, quæ posci vult et spectata (*vel* spectanda) reponi'.

M. des Mazures. Mais on peut être une honnête fille, et être une virtuose.	*Masuren.* Je! man kann wohl ein ehrlich Frauenzimmer, und doch ein Wunder seyn.
Angélique. Et moi je vous soûtiens que cela ne se peut pas. Moi, une virtuose![1]	*Henriette.* Und ich sage, dass das gar nicht möglich ist! Ich? ein Wunder![1]

Only once (x, 16) does Lessing speak in general terms of the art of Destouches as a dramatist; he says that he has given examples of a 'höheres Komisches' than is usually to be found in Molière. Such an opinion strikes a modern reader as strange and misplaced; but it was a view held by Gottsched, who, in the preface to vol. iv of his *Deutsche Schaubühne*, had said of his wife (p. 10): 'Sie hat sich darinn [in *Die ungleiche Heyrath*] mehr die edle Art der Lustspiele des Herrn Destouches, als die niedrigen molierischen Comödien zum Muster genommen.' And again, in introducing *Das Testament* (*Deutsche Schaubühne*, vi, p. [x]):

Ein feiner Umgang in adelichen Häusern, ein artiger Scherz, das Spiel der Leidenschaften bey jungen Leuten, mislungene Absichten, die belohnte Tugend, und die Verspottung des Lasters sind die Vorzüge, die man darinn antreffen wird. Auf diesen Schlag sind die meisten von des Destouches Lustspielen verfertiget, der gewiss in solcher Absicht dem Moliere weit vorzuziehen ist.

Lessing at least offers (x, 26) some defence of Molière.

P. C. DE CHAMBLAIN DE MARIVAUX

Three plays by Marivaux were performed in the Hamburg theatre in Lessing's time. The most popular of these, *Der Bauer mit der Erbschaft*, is chiefly discussed (xxviii, 4) with reference to the translation.[2] Concerning *Der unvermuthete Ausgang* Lessing suggests (lxxiii, 18) that it ought to have been called 'Die unvermuthete Entwicklung'. Indeed, his notice of *Die falschen Vertraulichkeiten* (xviii, 4) alone throws a little

---

[1] Destouches, *Œuvres*, Paris, 1757, ii, p. 394; *Deutsche Schaubühne*, iii, p. 498.

[2] The passage which Lessing quotes (26 ff.) will be found in Marivaux, *Théâtre*, Amsterdam and Leipzig, 1754, ii, pp. 4 f.; but Lessing had apparently an earlier edition before him. Cosack (*op. cit.* p. 185) draws attention to the defects of the translation: 'ai-je fait' and 'ce m'a-t-on fait' are rendered by 'so veel is dat' and 'hed se mie dahn' (38–9) instead of 'sagte ich' and 'hat man mir gesagt'. (Cp. also K. Th. Gaedertz, *Das niederdeutsche Schauspiel*, Berlin, 1884, i, pp. 192 ff.) The old Hamburg Mark and Schilling (52)—the former here exceptionally as a neuter—represented approximately 1s. 3d. and a penny.

light on his opinion of Marivaux. From Léris (*op. cit.* p. 185) he learned that *Les fausses Confidences* was performed in 1736 'avec un médiocre succès, mais remise en Juillet 1738, avec applaudissemens'. And again (*ibid.* pp. 632 f.):

Marivaux...commença à travailler pour le Théatre en 1712...et mourut à Paris le 12 Février 1763, âgé de soixante-douze ans [actually 'soixante-quinze', as Marivaux was born in 1688]. Il a donné vingt-une pieces en prose au Théatre Italien depuis 1720....Le Théatre François a de lui la Trag[édie] d'*Annibal*, et les Comédies suivantes, au nombre de huit....Il a encore composé plusieurs pieces qui n'ont pas été représentées sur des Théatres publics.[1]

In his characterisation of Marivaux (XVIII, 12) Lessing may have had in mind the necrologue of this author in Palissot's *Nécrologe des hommes célèbres de France*, Paris, 1767, ii, p. 12:

On remarque d'ailleurs, dans les pièces de M. de Marivaux, une monotonie qui suffirait seule pour justifier ce que nous avons dit ailleurs du cercle étroit de ses idées. Presque toutes ses pièces sont des surprises de l'amour. Il semble avoir épuisé cette situation favorite à laquelle il revient sans cesse, et qui est l'ame de la plupart des comédies qu'il a données aux deux théâtres.[2]

Reviewing Marivaux' *Théâtre* (Amsterdam, 1754) in the *Berlinische privilegirte Zeitung* of May 23, 1754, Lessing had written:

Man lobt an ihm besonders seine Kenntniss des menschlichen Herzens und die Kunst seiner kritischen Schilderungen; man nennt ihn einen zweyten la Bruyere, welcher ehedem so vielen Personen die Larve abriss, und ihre Eitelkeit beschämte. Nicht weniger rühmt man an ihm die blühende Schreibart, welche voll kühner Metaphern und unerwarteter Wendungen ist. Allein man tadelt auch an eben derselben die allzu grosse Kühnheit, und die zu übertriebene Begierde, überall seinen Witz schimmern zu lassen.[3]

---

[1] Besides the plays mentioned Lessing refers to *La double inconstance* in a quotation (XXVI, 73) and to *L'École des mères* in his discussion (XXI, 5) of Nivelle de Chaussée's play of that name (see below, pp. 228 f.).

[2] This criticism would appear to have been made originally by D'Argens, *Réflexions historiques et critiques sur le goût*, Amsterdam, 1743, p. 322. Lessing's reference to Callipides (17) was suggested by Dacier, *Poétique d'Aristote, ed. cit.* p. 510: 'Muniscus...reprochoit à Callippide qu'il gesticuloit trop, et par cette raison il l'appelloit le singe; car il imitoit jusqu'à la moindre chose, et se demenoit si fort que sans bouger de sa place, il faisoit beaucoup de chemin. On avoit fait de son nom un proverbe, pour dire, un homme qui travailloit beaucoup pour ne rien faire.' The Latin source is Cicero's letters (Book xiii, ep. 12): 'Biennium praeteriit, cum ille Callipides adsiduo cursu cubitum nullum processerit.'

[3] *Schriften*, v, p. 403.

The fact that 'Peter' in the comedy *Die falschen Vertraulichkeiten* is virtually a harlequin (xviii, 33) leads Lessing to a discussion on the harlequin which I deal with elsewhere.[1] He has no further criticism to offer of this play.

F. A. DE VOLTAIRE

The question of Lessing's relations to Voltaire is the most vital of all those which concern foreign influence on his intellectual development. No other foreign writer played so decisive a rôle in his life. From Berlin, whither he had fled from Leipzig in 1748 to evade the creditors of his Leipzig friends, he had defended his play-writing to his father, it may be remembered, by pleading that it was no unworthy ambition to aspire to be a German Molière;[2] but it would have been truer—if no recommendation in the Kamenz pastor's eyes—had he described his ambition as that of becoming Germany's Voltaire. No writer at this time loomed larger in the European view than Voltaire, whom Frederick the Great was to receive, not long after Lessing's arrival in Berlin, with princely honours which could not but fill the young German aspirants to literary fame there with envy.

Lessing stood for a time in close personal contact with Voltaire. He had been introduced to him by Richier de Louvain, a French teacher in Berlin who in 1750 became Voltaire's secretary; and Lessing was employed in preparing translations of documents bearing on the unsavoury lawsuit between Voltaire and Abraham Hirsch over the former's speculations in Saxon bonds. Damaging as this notorious affair was, there is hardly a discordant note to be found in Lessing's journalism of the 'fifties when he has occasion to mention the illustrious Frenchman; even that very weak drama, *Amélie ou le Duc de Foix*, is treated with the respect due to a masterpiece.[3] At the same time, too much weight should not be attached to these book notices of Lessing's in the *Berlinische privilegirte Zeitung*, for many of them were little more than advertisements for the bookseller. Nor need it, on the other hand, be put seriously in the scales that in the *Beyträge zur Historie und Aufnahme des Theaters* (in a footnote to Mylius's translation of the *Lettres philosophiques*) Voltaire is reproached for his attitude to the drama of antiquity, and that in the reports on the theatre in Paris Lessing allowed to pass a scathing comment on *Sémiramis*.[4]

Until practically the end of the 'fifties Lessing's respect for Voltaire

---

[1] See below, pp. 424 ff. [2] *Schriften*, xvii, p. 16.
[3] *Schriften*, v, pp. 14 f. [4] *Beyträge*, i, pp. 108, 111.

as a man of letters continued unshaken; even in the correspondence on tragedy with Mendelssohn and Nicolai in 1756 and 1757, Voltaire's tragedies are freely cited by the three friends as eminent examples of dramatic composition.[1] And Lessing himself translated Voltaire.[2] Indeed, it was just in connexion with a projected translation of one of Voltaire's works that Lessing found himself in serious trouble with the French poet. The latter had had his *Siècle de Louis XIV* printed in a few copies for private circulation; and Lessing (who was anxious to translate the work) had succeeded in obtaining one of these on loan. He carelessly let it out of his hands, however, and forgot to return it when he left Berlin for Wittenberg in December 1751; and Voltaire sharply accused him of dishonest intentions. Lessing's indignation at such insinuations cast its shadow—for he was not a good forgetter— over his subsequent attitude to Voltaire, even perhaps as late as the *Dramaturgie*. How long his outward respect for Voltaire's dramatic genius continued, however, it is difficult to say. His ideas on the scope of dramatic poetry were rapidly widening in these years; the new wave of democratic realism that had spread from England to the continent appealed strongly to him; the tragedy of common life which he acclimatised in Germany with his *Miss Sara Sampson* in 1755, convinced him that there were other and better ways of tragic excellence than those laid down by Corneille, Racine and Voltaire. His *Theatralische Bibliothek* of 1754–58 revealed, moreover, a wide catholicity of dramatic interest; and it will be remembered that he offered his readers here a translation of a considerable slice of Dryden's *Essay of Dramatic Poesy*, including its praise of Shakespeare, a poet to whom Voltaire had directed the attention of the continent in his *Lettres philosophiques*.

The turning-point is usually held to be that remarkable and surprising contribution of Lessing's to the *Briefe, die neueste Litteratur betreffend*, No. xvii, of February, 1759, in which he launched his first unambiguous attack on the *tragédie classique*, and boldy proclaimed its inferiority to the drama of Shakespeare. This marked the beginning of Lessing's intensive war not merely against his first master Gottsched, but also against Voltaire and all that Voltaire represented:

Hat Corneille ein einziges Trauerspiel, das Sie nur halb so gerühret hätte, als die Zayre des Voltaire? Und die Zayre des Voltaire, wie

---

[1] *Schriften*, xvii, p. 71; xix, pp. 42, 50, 53, 56.
[2] *G. E. Lessings Übersetzungen aus dem Französischen Friedrichs des Grossen und Voltaires*, herausg. von E. Schmidt, Berlin, 1892. The preface to *Des Herrn von Voltaires kleinere historische Schriften*, Rostock, 1752, will be found in *Schriften*, v, pp. 1 ff.

weit ist sie unter dem Mohren von Venedig, dessen schwache Copie sie ist, und von welchem der ganze Charakter des Orosmans entlehnet worden?[1]

H. A. Korff would definitely associate the decline of Voltaire's authority in Germany with the growth of an understanding for Shakespeare.[2] This is true, but only with qualifications; for the way to Shakespeare was a long and difficult progress, even for Lessing. The English poet may have been an excellent example to pit against the artificial regularity of classic tragedy; but the cooling-off towards Voltairean drama was more immediately due to the growing demand for truth to nature, a demand of which the tragedy of common life was the expression.

From 1759 to the publication of the *Hamburgische Dramaturgie* we are left in the dark as to the progress of Lessing's disillusionment with Voltaire; the latter is hardly mentioned in his writings and correspondence. There is no doubt, however, that Diderot was in the main responsible for finally divesting Voltaire of authority in his eyes. Lessing was entirely won over to the new conception of drama, Diderot's examples and defence of which he had translated. Again, however, we must be cautious in attributing too much weight to his repudiation, even in the *Dramaturgie*, of Voltaire's authority. It must not be forgotten that, if Diderot's influence is paramount in the form and plan of Lessing's last great drama, *Nathan der Weise*, that play also owed a very considerable debt to the poet of *Zayre*. To Shakespeare it owed practically nothing.

Voltaire receives a very large share of attention in the *Hamburgische Dramaturgie*; of no other dramatist are the plays so assiduously discussed. For this the Hamburg repertory was largely responsible, as we have seen; no less than ten of Voltaire's dramas were represented during the régime of the Consortium, and six of these during the brief period of Lessing's chronicle of the work of the theatre. But Lessing is not content to destroy Voltaire's position as a playwright; he attacks and undermines his authority as a literary critic and especially as a historian (XXIII, 7 ff.). He loses no opportunity of showing us his ignorance of the Greek drama (XXXIX, 29), his lack of understanding for Terence (LXXI, 1; see note to p. 319 below); his wrong ideas about tragi-comedy (LV, 118) and his misunderstanding of the famous box

---

[1] *Schriften*, viii, p. 43.
[2] *Voltaire im literarischen Deutschland des 18. Jahrhunderts*, Heidelberg, 1918, p. 76.

on the ear in *Le Cid* (LVI, 14); his misconceptions concerning English drama (xv, 111). Again, Lessing tells us, Voltaire plumes himself on being a 'profunder Historikus' (XXIII, 8); and he seizes with alacrity on the attacks, then being bruited in the French press, on Voltaire's accuracy as a historian.[1] He gleefully ridicules his mistake in regarding the Earl of Leicester and Robert Dudley as two different people: 'mit eben dem Rechte [könnte man] den Poeten Arouet und den Kammerherrn von Voltaire zu zwey verschiedenen Personen machen' (XXIII, 100). Voltaire, he says, is 'intolerable' with his historical control of *Rodogune* (XXXI, 145); and again he quotes a statement which 'contains not less than three errors, not much for Voltaire (xv, 110)'. There is, it must be admitted, a certain triviality in all this petty fault-finding. It would not be difficult for an enemy of Lessing to discover plenty of similar slips in *his* writings; indeed, for this it would not be necessary to go beyond the *Dramaturgie* itself. Voltaire's personal character, where he was admittedly vulnerable, is vigorously impugned: his vanity at the first performance of *Mérope* (XXXVI, 99); his 'Verkleinerungssucht' (XLI, 48); his love of 'Chicane' (XXIV, 14, 16, 19)—is this word not equally applicable to his critic?—the meanness of his underhand attack on Maffei under a pseudonym (XLI, 32 ff.). 'Besonders ist Voltaire ein Meister, sich die Fesseln der Kunst so leicht, so weit zu machen, dass er alle Freyheit behält, sich zu bewegen, wie er will; und doch bewegt er sich oft so plump und schwer, und macht so ängstliche Verdrehungen, dass man meinen sollte, jedes Glied von ihm sey an ein besonderes Klotz geschmiedet' (XLIV, 61 ff.).

In St. LXX (110) Lessing sums up Voltaire's intellectual character and his own attitude towards him:

Primus sapientiae gradus est, falsa intelligere; (wo dieses Sprüchelchen steht, will mir nicht gleich beyfallen)[2] und ich wüsste keinen Schriftsteller in der Welt, an dem man es so gut versuchen könnte, ob man auf dieser ersten Stuffe der Weisheit stehe, als an dem Herrn von Voltaire: aber daher auch keinen, der uns die zweyte zu ersteigen, weniger behülflich seyn

---

[1] In the *Journal encyclopédique* for April, 1761 (ii, pp. 128 ff.), Lessing had, no doubt, read a 'Lettre...concernant quelques faits à rectifier dans la nouvelle édition de l'Essai sur l'Histoire Universelle que Mr. de Voltaire vient d'annoncer.' In 1759 a reviewer in the *Litteraturbriefe*, No. lxviii, November 15, 1759, *ed. cit.* iv, pp. 301 ff., had pointed out the inaccuracies in Voltaire's *Charles XII*, and in 1762 an anonymous writer published at Avignon and Paris two volumes on *Les erreurs de Voltaire*. Cp. *Année Littéraire*, vi (1762), pp. 217 ff.

[2] It is from *Lactantius Firmianus, Divinarum Institutionum Libri Septem* i (Venice ed. of 1535, 39a). (Cp. Petersen, *ed. cit.* p. 240.)

könnte; secundus, vera cognoscere. Ein kritischer Schriftsteller, dünkt mich, richtet seine Methode auch am besten nach diesem Sprüchelchen ein. Er suche sich nur erst jemanden, mit dem er streiten kann: so kömmt er nach und nach in die Materie, und das übrige findet sich. Hierzu habe ich mir in diesem Werke, ich bekenne es aufrichtig, nun einmal die französischen Scribenten vornehmlich erwählet, und unter diesen besonders den Hrn. von Voltaire.

But there is something to be said on the other side, too, although Lessing does not say it. Voltaire's *Commentaires sur Corneille* had an appreciable influence on Lessing's method of handling the dramas which he had to criticise and on the combative tone of much of his criticism; indeed, the full extent of his debt to Voltaire in the matter of his prose style—that brilliant, witty, sharply antithetic clearness which lends glitter and piquancy to the pages of the *Dramaturgie*— has not yet been estimated. Lessing learnt the art of writing from none more than from Voltaire and Bayle, the two men who, in the 'fifties, did most to emancipate him to intellectual freedom.

Voltaire's career and reputation were so familiar to Lessing's age that it is superfluous to seek for literary sources of his knowledge of such things.[1] Nor is it of much moment to determine which edition of Voltaire's works he had at hand in Hamburg; and indeed, the texts of the editions then available vary little.[2] The standard edition was that published at Geneva in 18 volumes in 1756–57—and from this, as far as Voltaire's older work is concerned, I take my quotations. But it may have been that he had the older Dresden edition (1752 ff.), which he used in earlier years,[3] completed by supplementary volumes. In any case, Voltaire's most recent writings, the *Commentaires sur Corneille*, the *Contes de Guillaume Vadé* and *L'Ingénu*, were in his hands.

In his criticism of Voltaire's dramas Lessing almost invariably takes his starting-point from the information supplied by the author himself in his prefatory matter. Thus what he has to say about *Zayre* in St. xv and xvi is largely drawn from the 'Avertissement' and the

---

[1] A biography of 119 pp. had appeared in E. L. Rathlef's *Geschichte Jetztlebender Gelehrten*, vii (Zelle, 1743). (Cp. H. A. Korff, *op. cit.* pp. 665 f.)

[2] In criticising *Nanine*, Lessing speaks of that play as having two title-pages in his edition (xxi, 78); but this affords little clue, as the original edition of 1749 and the Amsterdam edition of 1750 both show this feature. (Cp. Bengesco, *Voltaire. Bibliographie de ses œuvres, ed. cit.* i, pp. 48 ff.)

[3] Cp. *Theatralische Bibliothek*, i, p. 48; *Schriften*, vi, p. 32.

two 'Épitres dédicatoires' to Falkener.[1] The passage which he translates in his second paragraph (xv, 3) is from the former:

Ceux qui aiment l'Histoire littéraire seront bien-aises de savoir comment
cette Piéce fut faite. Plusieurs Dames avaient reproché à l'Auteur, qu'il
n'y avait pas assez d'amour dans ses Tragédies. Il leur répondit, qu'il ne
croyait pas que ce fût la véritable place de l'amour; mais que puisqu'il
leur fallait absolument des Héros amoureux, il en ferait tout comme un
autre. La Piéce fut achevée en dix-huit jours: elle eut un grand succès.
On l'appelle à Paris, *Tragédie Chrêtienne*, et on l'a jouée fort souvent à la
place de *Polyeucte*.[2]

Lessing's famous retort that Voltaire should not have said 'love' but
'gallantry'[3] (27) may have been provoked by the first 'Épitre à M.
Fakener':

Si vous n'avez pas la réputation d'être tendres, ce n'est pas que vos
Héros de Théâtre ne soient amoureux; mais c'est qu'ils expriment rarement
leur passion d'une manière naturelle. Nos amans parlent en amans, et les
vôtres ne parlent encor qu'en Poëtes.[4]

The critic who remarked that love itself had dictated *Zayre* to Voltaire
(26) was Rémond de Sainte Albine, who described it in *Le Comédien*
as 'une Piece que l'amour lui-même semble avoir dictée'.[5] 'Ich kenne
nur eine Tragödie', Lessing says (27 ff.), 'an der die Liebe selbst
arbeiten helfen; und das ist Romeo und Juliet...Voltaire verstehet,
wenn ich so sagen darf, den Kanzeleystyl der Liebe vortrefflich;...
oder hat gleichwohl Voltaire in das Wesen der Liebe eben die tiefe
Einsicht, die Shakespear gehabt, so hat er sie wenigstens hier nicht
zeigen wollen....'[6] This and the disparaging comparison of Orosmann—'eine sehr kahle Figur'—with Othello—'wir hören in dem

---

[1] In Voltaire's first editions 'Fakener' (cp. *Œuvres*, [Geneva], 1756–7, viii, p. 3),
hence Lessing's 'Fackener'.

[2] *Œuvres, ed. cit.* viii, p. 2. The substance of the passage is repeated, however,
by Léris (*op. cit.* p. 457). Voltaire subsequently substituted 'vingt-deux jours' for
'dix-huit jours'.

[3] Voltaire himself had said in the *Discours sur la Tragédie* prefixed to his *Brutus*
(*Œuvres, ed. cit.* vii, p. 208): 'Le mal est que l'amour n'est souvent chez nos Héros
de Théâtre que de la galanterie.'

[4] *Œuvres, ed. cit.* viii, p. 9.

[5] *Le Comédien*, Paris, 1747, ii, chap. x, p. 208.

[6] W. Wetz (*Studien zur Hamburgischen Dramaturgie* I, in *Zeitschrift für vergleichende
Literaturgeschichte*, N.F. ix (1896), pp. 145 ff.) points out that Lessing's praise of
'jenes lebendige Gemälde aller der kleinsten, geheimsten Ränke, durch die sich
die Liebe in unsere Seele einschleicht...' is hardly applicable to Shakespeare's
picture of sudden overwhelming passion (p. 168). (Cp. Petersen, *ed. cit.* p. 196.)

Orosmann einen Eifersüchtigen reden, wir sehen ihn die rasche That eines Eifersüchtigen begehen; aber von der Eifersucht selbst lernen wir nicht mehr und nicht weniger, als wir vorher wussten' (xv, 54 ff.)[1] —constitute practically the only criticism which Lessing offers us of Voltaire's tragedy. It would be interesting to discover how the quite unjustified suggestion that *Zayre* was an imitation of *Othello* arose; Voltaire himself gives no hint of it, as he would have been likely to do in dedicating the play to an Englishman.[2] Lessing's immediate authority, as he indicates, is Cibber's Prologue to the English translation of the French play (xv, 50, 81 ff.).[3]

Lessing's interest now turns from *Zayre* itself to the translation in question by Aaron Hill. Voltaire had informed Falkener in the 'Seconde Lettre':

Elle y a été traduite et jouée avec tant de succès, on a parlé de moi sur votre Théâtre avec tant de politesse et de bonté, que j'en dois ici un remerciment public à votre Nation.... Monsieur *Hille*, homme de Lettres, qui paraît connaître le Théâtre mieux qu'aucun Auteur Anglais, me fit l'honneur de traduire la Piéce....[4]

And Lessing proceeds to quote and discuss the views expressed by Voltaire to Falkener on the English theatre. These will be more appropriately considered in connexion with Lessing's criticism of English drama.[5]

He now passes to a comparative criticism of the German, Italian, English and Dutch translations of *Zayre*. Those by Hill and Gasparo Gozzi I discuss elsewhere;[6] and in respect of his observation on German taste as illustrated by the brevity of the German version of the scene of Orosmann's death (xvi, 51) I need only add that his inference is

---

[1] Petersen (*ibid.*) refers to a quotation in Mendelssohn's review of Lowth's lectures on the poetry of the Hebrews (*Bibliothek der schönen Wissenschaften*, i (i), p. 125; *Gesammelte Schriften, ed. cit.* iv, i, p. 173): 'Ein Shakespeare hat die Ursachen, Folgen und Wirkungen der Eifersucht in einem prächtigen Schauspiele besser, richtiger und vollständiger ausgeführt, als in allen Schulen der Weltweisheit jemals von einer solchen Materie ist gehandelt worden.'

[2] Cp. H. Morf, *Aus Dichtung und Sprache der Romanen*, i (Berlin, 1922), p. 287; R. Arndt, *Zur Entstehung von Voltaires Zaire*, Diss. Marburg, 1906 (especially pp. 15 ff.); A. H. Krappe, *The Source of Voltaire's 'Zaïre'*, in *Modern Language Review*, xx (1925), pp. 305 ff. See also below, p. 254. Hill, however, pointed out in *The Prompter* (No. 114) that Voltaire had been 'nobly warming himself at the fire of our English *Othello*' (cp. D. Brewster, *Aaron Hill*, New York, 1913, p. 144).

[3] See also below, pp. 258 f.   [4] *Œuvres, ed. cit.* viii, p. 19.

[5] See below, pp. 256 f.   [6] See below, pp. 258 f., 280.

hardly justified; the translator made as close a translation as he could, but possibly the stage version was abbreviated.[1] The discussion of the Dutch translation by Frederik Duim which he had before him (93) is Lessing's only incursion into the field of Dutch literature. Duim (born in 1674)[2] was the author of numerous dramas in the French classic style, and the adaptation of *Zayre* dates from 1732. He was the father of the famous Dutch actor Izaak Duim.[3]

Alzire Lessing mentions only in passing (II, 28 ff.);[4] he approves of the art with which Voltaire at the close of the tragedy allows Zamore 'to conjecture rather than believe the truth of the religion in whose adherents he sees so much that is great':

> Je demeure immobile, égaré, confondu;
> Quoi donc, les vrais Chrêtiens auraient tant de vertu!
> Ah! la Loi qui t'oblige à cet effort suprême,
> Je commence à le croire, est la Loi d'un Dieu même.[5]

The production of Voltaire's *Mérope* on July 7 gave Lessing occasion for the most elaborate piece of comparative criticism which the *Dramaturgie* contains; it occupies no less than fifteen numbers (XXXVI, 60–L). It covers, however, a very wide range of themes, which, in accordance with the arrangement of the present volume, will be found discussed in different sections. In the present chapter I restrict myself as far as possible to Lessing's criticism of Voltaire's tragedy; but some overlapping is inevitable.

With regard to the genesis and history of the French *Mérope*, Lessing tells us (XXXVI, 61) that Voltaire probably wrote it in 1737 at Cirey, where the learned Marquise du Châtelet, his 'Uranie',[6] afforded him

---

[1] Cp. Petersen, *ed. cit.* pp. 197 f.

[2] No date for Duim's death is given in Huberts's *Biographisch Woordenboek der Noord-en-Zuidnederlandsche Letterkunde*, Deventer, 1878. He was still living in 1751 (*ibid.* p. 131).

[3] Cp. J. A. Worp, *Geschiedenis van het drama en van het tooneel in Nederland*, ii, Groningen, 1908, pp. 141 ff. The critic in the *Deutsche Bibliothek* (iii (ix) 1769, pp. 48 f.) commented: 'Wozu gab sich der Verfasser mit dem einfältigen Holländer ab, der die Zaire hat verbessern wollen? Gewiss entweder um zu zeigen, dass er auch Holländisch versteht, oder um einige niedrige Spöttereyen anzubringen, die so sehr nach seinem Geschmack sind.'

[4] *L'Enfant prodigue* (*Der verlorene Sohn*) is referred to, but only in a quotation (XXVI, 74); *Brutus* and *La Mort de César* (*Cäsar*) are also mentioned (X, 90).

[5] *Œuvres, ed. cit.* viii, p. 209.

[6] Among Voltaire's occasional poems there is one addressed to this lady (*Etrennes à la même* [Madame du Châtelet]), which begins: 'Une Etrenne frivole à la docte Uranie, Peut-on la présenter?...' (*Le Porte-Feuille Trouvé*, Geneva, 1757, p. 40).

an idyllic asylum between 1736 and her death in 1749. In Léris (*op. cit.* p. 295) Lessing found (84) that *Mérope* was received in Paris with extraordinary favour:

Nous avions déja trois traductions de cette piece [Maffei's *Merope*], quand M. de Voltaire donna sa *Mérope Française*; elle fut représentée pour la premiere fois le 20 Février, 1743, avec un succès qui a peu d'exemples. Le Parterre fit même à l'Auteur un honneur inusité jusqu'à ce tems; il demanda à le voir à la fin de la représentation, et lorsqu'il parut, il reçut les applaudissemens les plus flateurs. C'est presque la seule piece profane qui soit dénuée d'amour, chose remarquable![1]

Lessing compares Voltaire's acceptance of this 'call' unfavourably with the dignified entry of Corneille (XXXVI, 86), who was, at least, the recognised master of his own theatre.[2] His criticism of the childish curiosity of the audience and the vanity of the poet (XXXVI, 99) is perhaps unnecessarily harsh. Voltaire's call need scarcely be ascribed to either motive; but it gives Lessing the opportunity for the excellent dictum (104): 'The true masterpiece, it seems to me, so engrosses us that it makes us forget the author.' He attributes the persistence of the objectionable practice of receiving calls before the curtain partly to Voltaire's complaisance (132); it continued 'von Voltairen bis zum Marmontel, und vom Marmontel bis tief herab zum Cordier';[3] until

---

[1] It has been suggested, however, that the applause at the first performance was really evoked by the actress Mlle Dumesnil, who, as Mérope, outstepped the rules of classic propriety by running across the stage to save her son's life (cp. *Œuvres Complètes de Voltaire*, Paris (Garnier Frères), 1877–85, iv, p. 175).

[2] On Corneille's reception (XXXVI, 90) cp. Voltaire, *Essay sur l'Histoire Générale VII* (*Écrivains du Tems de Louis XIV*; *Œuvres*, [Geneva], 1756–7, xvii, pp. 215 f.): 'On a imprimé dans plusieurs recueils d'anecdotes, qu'il avait sa place marquée toutes les fois qu'il allait au spectacle, qu'on se levait pour lui, qu'on battait des mains. Malheureusement les hommes ne rendent pas tant de justice. Le fait est que les Comédiens du Roi refusèrent de jouer ses huit dernières piéces, et qu'il fut obligé de les donner à une autre troupe.' Again, in the *Supplément au Siècle de Louis XIV*, ii (*Œuvres Complètes de Voltaire, ed. cit.* xv, p. 129): 'On nous répète tous les jours que, quand le grand Corneille, sur la fin de sa vie, venait au théâtre, tout le monde se levait pour lui faire honneur. Cela n'est pas...vrai....'

[3] Cp. an article 'Theatralische Neuigkeiten aus Paris' in the *Bibliothek der schönen Wissenschaften*, iii (i) (1758), pp. 177 f., where the writer, discussing the success of De la Touche's *Iphigénie en Tauride*, says: 'Der Beyfall war ganz ausserordentlich; das Parterre verlangte mit grossem Geschrey den Verfasser zu sehen. (Diese Ehre, welcher [*sic*] dem Hrn. von Voltaire zuerst bey der ersten Vorstellung der Merope wiederfuhr, hat hernach auch Hr. Marmontel bey der ersten Vorstellung seines Aristomene [April 30, 1749] gehabt, und vielleicht nach ihm, verschiedene andere.) Als er erschien, so vermehrte sich der beyfallgebende Zuruf dergestalt, dass...er ganz bleich hinter die Scenen eilte, wo er in Ohnmacht fiel.' I have not been able

the good taste of the nation revolted. He recalls 'the ingenious idea of Polichinell' (141); this would appear to be a reference to a parody on *Mérope* by Panard, Gallet and Pontan, entitled *Marotte* when it was played in 1743 and *L'Enfant retrouvé* at a performance in 1744—or it may be perhaps to another version, *La Pétarade ou Polichinel auteur*, en un acte, en prose et en vers (2nd ed. 1750). Petersen, to whose commentary I owe this reference, quotes (*ed. cit.* p. 216) the following from Moland's edition of Voltaire;[1]

> Polichinelle s'entretenant avec son compère: 'Eh bien,' lui dit celui-ci, 'vas-tu nous donner quelque pièce nouvelle?'—'Si elle est nouvelle, elle ne vaudra pas grand'chose,' répond Polichinelle; 'tu sais que je suis épuisé.'—'Bon, tu es inépuisable,' répond l'autre; 'donne toujours.'—'Tu le veux donc? Je le veux bien aussi,' dit Polichinelle, 'et je t'avouerai que j'en mourais d'envie. Mais...tous nos amis sont-ils là-bas?' Alors, déboutonnant sa culotte (ne l'oublions pas, la chose se passe aux Marionettes) et faisant la révérence *a posteriori*, il lâche une pétarade au parterre; et tout de suite on entend crier: 'L'auteur, l'auteur, l'auteur!'

The possible occasion of Lessing's own refusal to come before the curtain I have already discussed.[2]

In a letter (dated December 23, 1738, but written in October, and published, with *Mérope*, in 1746)[3] from the Père de Tournemine to Brumoy, the writer speaks of 'l'amitié paternelle, qui m'attache à lui [Voltaire] depuis son enfance'[4]—Tournemine had been one of Voltaire's teachers (xxxvi, 70). He writes of *Mérope*:

> Quelques succès que lui donne le goût inconstant de Paris, elle passera jusqu'à la postérité, comme une de nos Tragédies les plus parfaites, comme un modèle de tragédie. *Aristote*, ce sage législateur du Théâtre, a mis ce sujet au premier rang des sujets tragiques. *Euripide* l'avait traité, et nous apprenons d'*Aristote*, que toutes les fois qu'on représentait sur le Théâtre de l'ingénieuse *Athènes* le *Cresfonte* d'*Euripide*, ce peuple, accoûtumé aux chefs-d'œuvres tragiques, était frappé, saisi, transporté d'une émotion extraordinaire. Si le goût de Paris ne s'accorde pas avec celui d'Athènes, Paris aura tort sans doute. Le *Cresfonte* d'*Euripide* est perdu: Monsieur *de Voltaire* nous le rend.[5]

to assign a definite source for the reference to Cordier. But the *Mercure de France*, April, 1762 (i), p. 155, discussing the first performance of Cordier's *Zaruckma*, says: 'L'Auteur fut demandé par une acclamation unanime; il parut et reçut le prix flatteur et mérité du plaisir que son Ouvrage venoit de faire.'

[1] *Œuvres Complètes de Voltaire*, Paris, 1877–85, iv, p. 174.
[2] See above, p. 142.
[3] Cp. *Œuvres Complètes de Voltaire*, Paris, 1877–85, iv, p. 177 (note 1).
[4] Voltaire, *Œuvres*, [Geneva], 1756–57, viii, p. 216. [5] *Ibid.* pp. 213 f.

Before Lessing comes to an examination of *Mérope* and a comparison of it with the Italian tragedy, however, this statement in Tournemine's letter leads him to a consideration of matters concerning Aristotle and the Greek dramatists, which I deal with elsewhere.[1] He then continues (XXXIX, 16) by asking why we should attribute such importance to Tournemine?[2] Let us rather, says Lessing, substitute for him Voltaire himself, who has the same wrong idea of Euripides.

Lessing states his thesis at the beginning of St. XXXVII:

Ich habe gesagt, dass Voltairens Merope durch die Merope des Maffei veranlasset worden. Aber veranlasset, sagt wohl zu wenig: denn jene ist ganz aus dieser entstanden; Fabel und Plan und Sitten gehören dem Maffei; Voltaire würde ohne ihn gar keine, oder doch sicherlich eine ganz andere Merope geschrieben haben.[3]

To prove this thesis he considers first the 'historical facts' on which the story rests, then Euripides's handling of the theme, and finally the Italian play.[4] In this chapter I am only concerned with the part of this discussion which has direct bearing on the French tragedy.

In a previous section I have given a brief outline of the plot of Voltaire's *Mérope*.[5] Here it will be convenient to recapitulate first the points wherein it differs from Maffei's. Voltaire fills out the Italian plot in many ways. He begins by initiating his audience into the state of things in Messenia, whereas Maffei opens with Polifonte's demand that Merope shall marry him. In Voltaire's play, Mérope then learns that Narbas, to whom she had entrusted her surviving son, has disappeared from Elis with the child; but she is consoled by the hope that they may be on their way to Messenia. In Maffei Merope mourns

---

[1] See below, pp. 311 ff.

[2] The quotation concerning Tournemine is from a note to Montesquieu's letter to the Abbé Comte de Guasco of December 5, 1750. This letter was first published in the edition of the *Lettres familières* which appeared at Paris in 1767, and the words quoted by Lessing are in a note on p. 208 of this edition (cp. Montesquieu, *Œuvres Complètes*, Paris, 1875–79, vii, p. 361). In the letter Montesquieu complains of Tournemine's 'despotisme' and 'tracasseries'. The note adds: 'On a entendu conter à Montesquieu que, pour s'en venger, il ne fit jamais autre chose que de demander à ceux qui lui en parloient: *Qui est-ce que le P. Tournemine? je n'en ai jamais entendu parler*: ce qui piquoit beaucoup ce jésuite, qui aimoit passionémment la célébrité.'

[3] Lessing's conviction had probably been strengthened by reading De la Grange Chancel's emphatic statement in his letter on *Mérope* to the *Journal étranger* of August, 1756 (p. 238): '...le Poëte Italien (le Marquis Maffei) dont M. de Voltaire est le fidèle traducteur....'

[4] See below, pp. 310 ff., 281 ff.   [5] See above, pp. 86 f.

for her son Egisto as dead. Voltaire reveals Polifonte's intention to have Égiste and Narbas murdered, should they be on the way to Messenia. It is not until the second act in Voltaire that we learn of the arrest of a young man for murder; Maffei reaches this incident in the second scene of his play. In both plays the young man impresses the queen favourably; Maffei makes more of this than Voltaire, thus providing a more effective dramatic contrast when Merope, full of grief at the disquieting news of her son's disappearance, begins to suspect that the stranger may have been his murderer; to her mind, Polifonte's kindness to the young man is suspicious, and especially when he again insists that Merope should become his wife, promising that, if she does so, he will pardon the murderer. Voltaire does not emphasise these sentimental possibilities of the plot. His tyrant is elected king; and it is definitely stated that the young stranger has murdered Égiste, the proof being that he is in possession of a coat of mail—in the Italian play it is a costly ring—known to have belonged to Égiste. In both plays Merope decides to take her own revenge. In Maffei's drama, as she is about to slay the prisoner, she is momentarily softened by his protestations of innocence, when Polifonte enters and sets him free. In Voltaire's version, more dramatically, Mérope is determined to torture the victim, and is about to stab him when Narbas brings the news that he is her son, the lost Égiste. The recognition is brought about more circumstantially in the Italian play. Polidoro, introduced unrecognised into the palace, finds the young man asleep in a marble chair. When Merope arrives with an axe to slay him, Polidoro reveals to her that he is her son. The dénouement is similarly worked out by both poets: the marriage of Polifonte is about to be celebrated when Égiste behind the scenes slays the tyrant. Both dramas end with the triumphant acclamations of the citizens.[1]

In the first edition of 1744 Voltaire's tragedy was prefaced by a dedicatory letter 'A M. le Marquis Scipion Maffei', in which, with excessive politeness, he expressed his indebtedness to the Italian nobleman, and excused the faults of the latter's play on the ground that he had to appeal to an Italian taste much less polished than that of Paris (XLI, 53 ff.). He says:

...vous êtes le premier, Monsieur, qui dans ce siècle où l'Art des *Sophocles* commençait à être amolli par des intrigues d'amour, souvent

---

[1] Cosack (*op. cit.* pp. 225 ff.) provides a detailed and useful analysis of the two plays in parallel columns.

étrangères au sujet, ou avili par d'indignes bouffonneries qui deshonoraient le goût de votre ingénieuse Nation; vous êtes le premier, dis-je, qui avez eu le courage et le talent de donner une Tragédie sans galanterie, une Tragédie digne des beaux jours d'Athènes, dans laquelle l'amour d'une mère fait toute l'intrigue, et où le plus tendre intérêt naît de la vertu la plus pure.[1]

Voltaire was genuine in his admiration of Maffei's boldness in writing a tragedy devoid of sexual love. Such tragedies (*e.g. Julius Caesar*) had his warm approval—in theory, if not in practice.[2] He would have translated the Italian play, had he not found it unsuited for the French stage (cp. XLI, 23 ff., 57 ff.). His words are:

Notre délicatesse est devenuë excessive: nous sommes peut-être des *Sibarites* plongés dans le luxe, qui ne pouvons supporter cet air naïf et rustique, ces détails de la vie champêtre, que vous avez imités du Théâtre Grec....Ces entretiens sont naturels; mais notre Parterre, quelquefois si indulgent, et d'autres fois si délicat, pourrait les trouver trop familiers, et voir même de la coquetterie où il n'y a au fond que de la raison....Ce n'est pas, encor une fois, que tout cela ne soit dans la Nature; mais il faut que vous pardonniez à notre Nation, qui exige que la Nature soit toujours présentée avec certains traits de l'art; et ces traits sont bien différens à Paris et à Verone.[3]

The Paris parterre would not have tolerated the hackneyed device of a ring as a means of recognition; he, Voltaire, could not have risked the danger of having his hero taken for a thief. In these matters, says Lessing (XLI, 80), the taste of the Paris parterre is wrong. On the other hand, he asks, why does Voltaire, in cases where it certainly is not wrong, find fault with that taste rather than with Maffei?

Maffei replied point for point to the criticisms in Voltaire's dedication in the edition of his *Merope* which was published in 1745. It is to be regretted that this reply is not included in modern editions of Voltaire.[4] In a reference which is perhaps intentionally somewhat ambiguous (XLII, 143) Lessing expresses regret that Maffei's answer to Voltaire is not published in the correspondence; it would be, he

---

[1] *Œuvres, ed. cit.* viii, pp. 217 f.

[2] See, for instance, the *Dissertation sur la Tragédie ancienne et moderne* prefixed to *Sémiramis* (*Œuvres, ed. cit.* ix, pp. 19 f.) and also *Discours sur la Tragédie* prefixed to *Brutus* (*Œuvres, ed. cit.* vii, pp. 197 ff., 207 f.).

[3] *Œuvres, ed. cit.* viii, pp. 226 f.

[4] Cp. however, *Œuvres Complètes de Voltaire*, Paris, 1877–85, iv, p. 197 (note 2), where reference is made to a translation of Maffei's reply in a French translation of the *Dramaturgie*.

points out, the most interesting part of it.[1] What he no doubt wished
to see was the Italian poet's reply, not merely to Voltaire's dedication,
but to Lindelle's strictures as well. For when Voltaire read what
Maffei had to say, he felt, no doubt, that something more emphatic
was called for to put the Italian in his place; but since he could not
very well throw off the mask of politeness which he had assumed in
the dedication, he deputed to a fictitious 'M. de la Lindelle' the task
of bluntly demolishing the arguments of the Italian marquis. M. de
la Lindelle's letter to M. de Voltaire appeared in the edition of the
French *Mérope* which was published in 1748.[2] It is obviously solely
concerned with Maffei's play, and I deal with it in my chapter on the
Italian drama.[3] Here we need consider only the inferences which
Lessing drew from that controversy in support of his thesis that the
French *Mérope* was merely an adaptation of Maffei's. In St. XLIV he
turns to points in Voltaire's criticism of Maffei which are equally
applicable to Voltaire's own tragedy. He discusses (4 ff.) the question
whether Maffei's ring or Voltaire's suit of armour is the better means
of recognition. Voltaire had written:

Je ne vous le dissimulerai pas. Je trouve que Mr. *Maffei* a mis plus d'art
que moi dans la manière dont il s'y prend pour faire penser à Mérope que
son fils est l'assassin de son fils même. Je n'ai pu me servir comme lui d'un
anneau, parce que depuis l'*anneau* royal dont *Boileau* se moque dans ses
Satyres, cela semblerait trop petit sur notre Théâtre.[4]

The modern reader will be likely to agree that Voltaire's improvement
here is not conspicuous. Again (33 ff.) Lessing quotes Voltaire's response to the objection which Lindelle had raised concerning the
tyrant's suddenly awakened eagerness to marry Mérope:

Ni Mr. *Maffei* ni moi n'exposons des motifs bien nécessaires pour que le
Tyran *Polifonte* veuille absolument épouser *Mérope*. C'est peut-être là un
défaut du sujet; mais je vous avouë, que je crois, qu'un tel défaut est fort
léger, quand l'intérêt qu'il produit est considérable.[5]

---

[1] The reply of Maffei was in fact printed in the 1763 edition of the Italian *Merope*
(pp. 438 ff.).

[2] In *Œuvres de Voltaire*, Dresden, 1748–54, v, pp. 481 ff. Cp. *Œuvres Complètes*,
ed. cit. iv, p. 192 (note 1).

[3] See below, pp. 289 ff.

[4] *Œuvres, ed. cit.* viii, p. 242; the passage in Boileau (*Satires*, iii, 196): 'Surtout
"l'anneau royal" me semble bien trouvé' was directed against Quinault's *Astrate,
roi de Tyr* (cp. Schröter and Thiele, *ed. cit.* p. 246).

[5] *Œuvres, ed. cit.* viii, pp. 242 f.

Voltaire's excuse that the fault is inherent in the subject is hardly valid. Lessing points out (39) that Maffei had altered the original story, and Voltaire need not have accepted this alteration, had he not approved of it.

Lessing has naturally only contempt for Lindelle's pedantic objection to the Italian poet's laxity in matters of *liaison* and in providing motives for exits and entrances (XLV, 86 ff.) Voltaire had written:

> Les scènes souvent ne sont point liées, et le Théâtre se trouve vuide; défaut qui ne se pardonne pas aujourd'hui aux moindres Poëtes....Les Acteurs arrivent, et partent souvent sans raison; défaut non moins essentiel.[1]

This leads Lessing (XLVI, 1) to a vigorous attack on the artificiality of the French theatre, and especially on its practice in regard to the unities of place and time. His argument, as far as *Mérope* is concerned, is that Voltaire, in his observance of these rules, has no compunction in introducing the most patent absurdities into his play, crowding together in one place and within the prescribed time-unity impossible and incongruous things (XLIV, 61 ff.). Far from regarding the laxity of Maffei in respect of the rules as blameworthy, Lessing considers that Voltaire's own observance of them leads to far greater absurdities.[2]

'Regularity' cannot compensate for the smallest errors in character-drawing (XLVI, 61). Voltaire's condemnation of Maffei's Polifonte with his 'heillosen Maximen' is, Lessing admits, entirely justified:

> Autre puérilité de Collége. Le Tyran dit à son confident: *Je sai l'art de régner; je ferai mourir les audacieux; je lâcherai la bride à tous les vices; j'inviterai mes sujets à commettre les plus grands crimes, en pardonnant aux plus coupables; j'exposerai les gens de bien à la fureur des scélérats, etc.* Quel homme a jamais pensé et prononcé de telles sottises? Cette déclamation de Régent de sixiéme ne donne-t-elle pas une jolie idée d'un homme qui sait gouverner?[3]

But Voltaire's own tyrant, Lessing points out, indulges in sentiments such as the following (Act I, sc. iv):

> Et des Dieux quelquefois la longue patience
> Fait sur nous à pas lents descendre la venge[a]nce,

which a Polifonte would not be likely to express, especially when screwing up his courage to new crimes. Then there is his unconsidered and aimless behaviour towards Mérope; and his attitude to Égiste is

---

[1] *Œuvres, ed. cit.* viii, p. 236.   [2] See below, pp. 384 f.
[3] *Œuvres, ed. cit.* viii, p. 240.

inconsistent with the poet's initial picture of him as a cunning and resolute man. Égiste, Lessing continues, should not have been introduced into the scene of the sacrifice. For him to swear obedience to Polifonte before the people, and to the sound of his despairing mother's cries, would merely bring about what the tyrant fears—the loss of his power. He may expect anything from Égiste, who only demands the return of his sword in order to settle their quarrel once and for all; and yet Polifonte permits him to come quite close to him at the altar. Maffei's Polifonte is free from this absurdity; for the identity of Egisto has not yet been revealed to him. Lindelle accuses the Italian Merope of speaking like a cannibal:

> J'ajouterai encor, que quand la Reine, croyant son fils mort, dit, qu'elle veut arracher le cœur au meurtrier, et le déchirer avec les dents, elle parle en *Cannibale* plus encor qu'en mère affligée, et qu'il faut de la décence partout.[1]

But is the French Mérope, Lessing asks (XLVI, 130), in spite of her greater delicacy, any less of a cannibal? Surely (XLVII, 12 ff.) the Italian Merope, who acts impulsively, and thinks, in the passion of the moment, of a wild and cruel vengeance, is more of a mother than the French heroine who deliberately plans her revenge, proposing not to kill, but to torture her victim. Again (26), Voltaire might blame the traditional story, of which Mérope's wish to kill Égiste with her own hand is an integral part. But she need not do it deliberately; and neither Euripides nor Maffei makes it a matter of deliberation. Thus they retain the audience's sympathy for Merope, which Voltaire forfeits.

That Polifonte does not insist that Mérope should become his wife until after the lapse of fifteen years is not a fault of the original theme: in the fable of Hyginus, and presumably in the lost play of Euripides, the marriage takes place immediately after the murder of Cresphontes. Such an act was not so repugnant to Greek women when they saw it would bring advantage to their children; and Lessing recalls (79) 'de[n] griechischen Roman des Charitons, den d'Orville herausgegeben', in support of this.[2] Such a device would have obviated the cold scenes of a political love, and could have been made interesting in more ways than one. But Voltaire took this situation from Maffei, as he took the motive of Égiste's chance journey to Messenia, in ignorance of his own identity, and the suspicion which there falls on him of being his own

---

[1] *Œuvres, ed. cit.* viii, p. 238.   [2] See below, pp. 317 f.

murderer. In other words, both dramatists indulge in 'das armselige Vergnügen' (xlviii, 3) of surprise.[1]

Voltaire cannot employ a prologue in the manner of the ancients; but he feels the need of informing his audience that the young stranger is Égiste (xlix, 102). How does he achieve this? Simply by calling him Égiste in his printed book; so that we have the absurdity of a character named Égiste denying all knowledge of persons of that name. This is surely an unreasonable attack on Voltaire. More cogent is Lessing's objection that Égiste names his reputed father to Mérope, but does not give his own name, or the name by which he knows himself. In Maffei the young hero has two names (l, 1), Egisto and Cresfonte, but in the list of persons he appears only as the former.

There is no reason to doubt, with Lessing, the honesty of Voltaire's statement that he began with the intention of translating Maffei's *Merope*, but that the obstacles offered by the conventions of the French theatre—and even if Lessing could not approve of these, it was surely still his duty as an impartial critic to accept their existence—proved insuperable, with the consequence that his own play, in the course of several remodellings, ceased to be a translation or even an adaptation. In particular, Voltaire's fourth act is very different from Maffei's. There is a material change, too, in the characters and relations to each other of Mérope and Polifonte, on account of the fact that when the drama opens, Mérope is still the ruler of Messenia, not Polifonte, who is only proclaimed king in the third act; and that Mérope is ignorant of his crimes against her family. In Maffei Merope is withstanding not merely an overbearing soldier whom she cannot trust, but also the known murderer of her husband.[2] In several of the features which Lessing selects it may be that Voltaire is seen at a disadvantage in comparison with Maffei, but it surely cannot be denied that he has given a finer and deeper psychological presentation of a mother's love—it may be under fantastically exceptional conditions—than his model; and that even his minor characters have a little less of the conventional and the schematic. Lessing is certainly unjust to Voltaire; his antagonism to the French type of classic tragedy has weighed the scales heavily in Maffei's favour. And, after all, the

---

[1] See also below, p. 465.

[2] Cp. also H. Lion, *Les Tragédies et les Théories dramatiques de Voltaire*, Paris, 1895, pp. 157 f. La Harpe in his championship of Voltaire went so far as to insist that Voltaire owed no real debt to Maffei and that all that was good in his drama was his own. (*Lycée*, Paris [N.D.], An. vii, vol. x, pp. 35, 40, 43, 51.)

Italian *Merope* is no masterpiece. What Lessing's arguments do not prove is that Voltaire's tragedy is merely an adaptation of Maffei's (L, 29) and that there is only one alteration made by Voltaire in Maffei's plan which deserves to be called an improvement (L, 128). He is too intent on challenging the often merely trivial points adduced by Lindelle, and does not make the larger and unbiassed attempt we might have looked for to estimate the general character of the two plays.

For his discussion of *Sémiramis* (x, 86–xII, 44) Lessing found ample materials in the *Dissertation sur la Tragédie* which forms a preface to that play. Voltaire kindles his wrath (x, 89) by asserting the superiority of French tragedy to that of the Greeks:

Je ne prétends pas que la Scène Française l'ait emporté en tout sur celle des Grecs, et doive la faire oublier. Les inventeurs ont toujours la première place dans la mémoire des hommes; mais quelque respect qu'on ait pour ces premiers génies, cela n'empêche pas que ceux qui les ont suivis ne fassent souvent beaucoup plus de plaisir....On admire *Sophocle*; mais combien de nos bons Auteurs tragiques ont-ils de traits de Maître que *Sophocle* eût fait gloire d'imiter, s'il fût venu après eux? Les Grecs auraient appris de nos grands Modernes à faire des expositions plus adroites, à lier les scènes les unes aux autres, par cet art imperceptible qui ne laisse jamais le Théâtre vuide, et qui fait venir et sortir avec raison les personnages.... Le choc des passions, ces combats de sentimens opposés, ces discours animés de rivaux et de rivales, ces querelles, ces bravades, ces plaintes réciproques, ces contestations intéressantes, où l'on dit ce que l'on doit dire, ces situations si bien ménagées les auraient étonnés....Les Grecs auraient surtout été surpris de cette foule de traits sublimes qui étincellent de toutes parts dans nos Modernes.[1]

With brilliant wit Lessing turns on Voltaire (100): 'O freylich; was ist von den Franzosen nicht alles zu lernen! Hier und da möchte zwar ein Ausländer, der die Alten auch ein wenig gelesen hat, demüthig um Erlaubniss bitten, anderer Meinung seyn zu dürfen.' All these merits (103) have little to do with the essentials of tragedy. But it is of no avail to contradict Voltaire: 'er spricht, und man glaubt.'

And again (108) he turns to the *Dissertation*:

On a voulu donner dans *Sémiramis* un spectacle encor plus pathétique que dans *Mérope*; on y a déployé tout l'appareil de l'ancien Théâtre Grec. Il serait triste, après que nos grands Maîtres ont surpassé les Grecs en tant de choses dans la Tragédie, que notre Nation ne pût les égaler dans la dignité de leurs représentations. Un des grands obstacles qui s'opposent,

[1] *Œuvres, ed. cit.* ix, pp. 13 ff.

sur notre Théâtre, à toute action grande et pathétique, est la foule des spectateurs, confondue sur la Scène avec les Acteurs; cette indécence se fit sentir particuliérement à la première représentation de *Sémiramis*....Cet abus a été corrigé dans la suite aux représentations de *Sémiramis*, et il pourrait aisément être supprimé pour jamais....[1]

Mais ce grand défaut n'est pas assurément le seul qui doive être corrigé. Je ne peux assez m'étonner ni me plaindre du peu de soin qu'on a en France de rendre les Théâtres dignes des excellens ouvrages qu'on y représente, et de la Nation qui en fait ses délices. *Cinna, Athalie*, méritaient d'être re-présentés ailleurs que dans un jeu de paume, au bout duquel on a élevé quelques décorations du plus mauvais goût, et dans lequel les spectateurs sont placés, contre tout ordre et contre toute raison, les uns debout sur le Théâtre même, les autres debout dans ce qu'on appelle parterre, où ils sont gênés et pressés indécemment, et où ils se précipitent quelquefois en tumulte les uns sur les autres, comme dans une sédition populaire....vous voyez que c'était une entreprise assez hardie de représenter *Sémiramis* assemblant les Ordres de l'Etat pour leur annoncer son mariage; l'ombre de *Ninus*, sortant de son tombeau, pour prévenir un inceste, et pour venger sa mort; *Sémiramis* entrant dans ce Mausolée, et en sortant expirante, et percée de la main de son fils. Il était à craindre que ce spectacle ne revoltât:[2] et d'abord, en effet, la plûpart de ceux qui fréquentent les spectacles, accoûtumés à des élégies amoureuses, se liguèrent contre ce nouveau genre de Tragédie.[3]

The scene in question is the sixth of Act III. Sémiramis assembles the notables of her kingdom to announce to them the name of the man whom she has chosen to marry. Her choice falls, not on the intriguer Assur, but on Arzace, who, all unknown to her, is her own son, whose father Ninus she has murdered. At this announcement 'le tonnerre gronde, et le tombeau paraît s'ébranler'. I quote the scene (it is the final scene of Act III) in the version played in the Hamburg theatre (Vienna, 1765, pp. 47 ff.):

(*Der Donner brüllt, und das Grab scheint sich zu erschüttern.*)

SEMIRAMIS. Was hör ich? Himmel! ach!
OROES.   Ihr Götter! schützt uns doch!

[1] The bad custom to which Voltaire refers was not abolished at the Théâtre Français until later (1759). Cp. Adolphe Jullier, *Les Spectateurs sur le Théâtre*, Paris, 1875, pp. 17 ff. Marmontel in the fourth book of his *Mémoires* (Paris, ed. of 1891, i, p. 289) writes: 'Sémiramis éperdue et l'ombre de Ninus sortant de son tombeau étoient obligées de traverser une épaisse haie de petits-maîtres.'

[2] Léris, however, remarks (*op. cit.* p. 402): 'L'ombre de *Ninus* paroissant sur le théâtre dans cette piece, fut une nouveauté qui ne révolta pas tant le Public qu'on l'auroit cru.'

[3] *Œuvres, ed. cit.* ix, pp. 21 ff., 25.

SEMIRAMIS. Der Himmel donnert. Ach! ist's Güte oder Rache!
Ach Gnade! Götter! Ach! Arsaz für meine Sache.
Welch klägliches Geschrey vermehrt die Furcht! Ich seh
Das offne Grab. Er kömmt.... Ihr Götter!...ich vergeh.

(Der Schatte des Ninus kommt aus dem Grabe.)

ASSUR. Des Ninus Schatte selbst? Ist's möglich?
ARSAZ.   Gott der Schrecken!
Wohl, rede! was will uns dein Anblick hier entdecken?
ASSUR. Ja, rede!
SEMIRAMIS.   Willst du mir hold oder grausam seyn?
Der Zepter und das Bett, die ich verschenkt, sind dein.
Urtheil: soll dieser Held nicht deinen Zepter führen?
Sprich, ich gehorche dir.
DER SCHATTE (*zu dem* ARSAZ.)   Arsaz! du wirst regieren.
Doch es sind Laster da, die auszusühnen seyn.
Du musst in meiner Gruft mir erst ein Opfer weihn.
Dien meinem Sohn und mir. Denk an den Vater. Höre
Den Oberpriester.
ARSAZ.   Ja, du Schatte, den ich ehre,
Du Halbgott, dessen Geist dies Clima itzt beseelt,
Wiss, dass mir nicht der Muth bey deinem Anblick fehlt.
Ich will in deine Gruft, trotz meinem Leben steigen;
Doch sprich, was wird man mir dort für ein Opfer zeigen?

(Der Schatte kehrt sich von seiner Stelle zur Thüre des Grabes.)

Er flieht.
SEMIRAMIS.   Vergönn', da du des Ninus Schatte bist,
Dass diese Hand dein Knie in deiner Gruft umschliesst;
Dass meine Reue....
DER SCHATTE (*an der Thür des Grabes*). Halt! Scheu meine Asche. Gehe
Bis es erst Zeit wird seyn, dass ich dich wieder sehe.

(Der Schatte geht wieder hinein, und das Grabmahl schliesst sich zu.)

ASSUR. Welch schrecklich Wunderwerk!
SEMIRAMIS.   O folgt mir. Jedes Herz
Still in dem Tempel hier das Schrecken und den Schmerz.
Es wird des Ninus Geist sich schon versöhnen lassen.
Beschützt er den Arsaz: so kann er mich nicht hassen.
Der Himmel ists, der euch Monarchen geben kann.
Kommt, rufet ihn für mich und für Arsazen an.

Arzace learns in the following act from the High Priest the mystery
of his birth and the reason for the appearance of Ninus's ghost.
    Lessing scoffs at Voltaire's ghost which appears in the bright light

of day (XI, 85 ff.).[1] The *Journal encyclopédique* for September, 1756 (pp. 102 f.), recorded that 'De nos jours au[x] premieres Représentations de Sémiramis, le spectre de Ninus sortant de son tombeau lui parut moins digne de foi, que de risée. . . . Le succès de Sémiramis qui n'auroit pas été douteux à Londres, ne l'est plus aujourd'hui à Paris.'

Voltaire himself, in the *Dissertation sur la Tragédie ancienne et moderne* prefixed to *Sémiramis*, suggested the comparison with *Hamlet* which Lessing uses against him; in comparing the ghost in *Hamlet* with that of Ninus, he takes the opportunity of censuring Shakespeare's play as 'une piéce grossière et barbare', irregular and often absurd: 'On croirait que cet ouvrage est le fruit de l'imagination d'un Sauvage yvre.'[2]

But nevertheless Voltaire finds also sublime touches, worthy of the greatest genius: '. . . parmi les beautés qui étincellent au milieu de ces horribles extravagances, l'ombre du père d'*Hamlet* est un des coups de Théâtre des plus frappans';[3] and he proceeds to justify the apparition of Ninus in his own tragedy.

I deal elsewhere with the general principle of the use of the supernatural, and with the comparison with *Hamlet*.[4] But it may be said at once that here again Lessing is not quite fair to Voltaire: he denies him the right to introduce the supernatural, and then justifies Shakespeare, without making it clear that it is not Voltaire's right to use it, but his way of using it to which he objects. (There is a similarly unfair condemnation of Weisse when he is compared with Shakespeare in the treatment of *Richard III* (St. LXXIII).) The ghost in Voltaire's *Sémiramis* is in Lessing's view nothing but 'eine poetische Maschine, die nur des Knotens wegen da ist' (XII, 3). Here again he has Voltaire's own words in mind:

Si le nœud d'un Poëme tragique est tellement embrouillé, qu'on ne puisse se tirer d'embarras que par le secours d'un prodige, le spectateur sent la gêne où l'Auteur s'est mis, et la faiblesse de la ressource. Il ne voit qu'un Ecrivain qui se tire mal-adroitement d'un mauvais pas. Plus d'illusion,

[1] But according to the commentators on Voltaire, this was not the case. See *Œuvres Complètes de Voltaire*, Paris, 1877–85, iv, p. 543: 'A ce moment, on faisait la nuit sur le théâtre, les éclairs brillaient, et l'ombre blanche de Ninus apparaissait enveloppée d'une gaze noire.—Voltaire réclamait, à la reprise de *Sémiramis*, "une grande diable de porte qui se brise et une trappe qui fasse sortir l'Ombre du fond des abîmes".'

[2] *Œuvres*, [Geneva], 1756–57, ix, p. 27.

[3] *Ibid.*

[4] See below, pp. 445 ff., 251 ff.

plus d'intérêt. *Quodcunque ostendis mihi, sic incredulus odi.* Mais je suppose que l'Auteur d'une Tragédie se fût proposé pour but d'avertir les hommes, que Dieu punit quelquefois de grands crimes par des voies extraordinaires...je dis qu'alors ce prodige, bien ménagé, ferait un très-grand effet en toute langue, en tout tems et en tout pays.[1]

This may be more philosophical than Shakespeare, Lessing comments, but Shakespeare thought more poetically. To Voltaire the apparition of Ninus is a 'miracle';[2] the ghost of Hamlet's father is a great natural happening (xii, 1 ff.).

Voltaire had claimed as a merit of *Sémiramis* that, like the tragedy of the ancients, it was built upon a moral truth: 'Les Anciens avaient souvent dans leurs ouvrages le but d'établir quelque grande maxime; ainsi *Sophocle* finit son *Oedipe*, en disant, qu'il ne faut jamais appeller un homme heureux avant sa mort.'[3] So, too, *Sémiramis* ends with the lines:

> Par ce terrible exemple, apprenez tous, du moins,
> Que les crimes secrets ont les Dieux pour témoins.

Such a conclusion may be no defect in a poet; but it is by no means necessary; and if *Sémiramis* had no other merit, it would be, in Lessing's eyes, 'nur ein sehr mittelmässiges Stück' (xii, 32)—especially as Voltaire's moral is not a particularly lofty one.

Voltaire's *Nanine* is discussed in St. xxi. Lessing's objection to its title (22) I discuss later.[4] The statement that 'die Geschichte der Nanine ist die Geschichte der Pamela' (83) is from Léris (*op. cit.* p. 313): 'Le sujet de cette piece est tiré du Roman de *Pamela*.'[5] And under '*Pamela*' in Léris (*ibid.* pp. 330 f.) Lessing found the following: "Il y a deux *Com*[édies] de ce nom; la premiere, par Boissy, en 3 Ac[tes] en vers: elle a pour second titre la Vertu Mieux Éprouvée, et fut donnée avec succès au Thé[âtre] Ital[ien] le 4 Mars 1743. La

---

[1] *Œuvres, ed. cit.* ix, p. 29.
[2] Cp. the words of Oroès in Act iii, sc. ii:

> 'Du Ciel, quand il le faut, la justice suprême
> Suspend l'ordre éternel établi par lui-même:
> Il permet à la mort d'interrompre ses loix,
> Pour l'effroi de la Terre, et l'exemple des Rois.'

[3] *Œuvres, ed. cit.* ix, p. 30.   [4] See below, pp. 467 f.
[5] An account of *Nanine* in Gottsched's *Neuer Büchersaal* (x (i), 1750, pp. 72 ff.) contains the statement: 'Es ist nämlich die Geschichte der *Pamela*; doch so sehr ins Kurze gebracht, als es der sehr eingeschränkte Raum von dreyen Aufzügen erheischet hat' (p. 72). But Voltaire's play has little in common with *Pamela* apart from the difference in rank between Nanine and the Comte d'Olban.

seconde, de Nivelle de la Chaussée, en 5 Ac[tes] en vers, représentée une seule fois à la Comédie Fran[çaise] le 6 Déce[mbre] 1743, et qui n'est pas imprimée."[1] The remainder of St. xxi, which is derived from Voltaire himself, concerns, not *Nanine*, but the 'comédie larmoyante' in general; its place is consequently in another section of this volume.[2] Lessing has no criticism of his own to offer of the play, nor does he mention the translation.

Voltaire's comedy, *Die Frau, welche Recht hat*, was played late in the period covered by the *Dramaturgie*; and Lessing dismisses it briefly (LXXXIII, 103) as a play without characters and interest, but with comic situations arising from false recognitions and misunderstandings. In view of the foreignness of the customs and the wretchedness of the translation, Lessing finds Voltaire's 'mot pour rire' for the most part incomprehensible. In Léris (*op. cit.* p. 189) Lessing found only the meagre statement: '*Com*[édie] en pro[se] par M. de Voltaire, imprimée en 1760.'

The most modern of Voltaire's plays to be produced in Hamburg was *Das Caffeehaus* (XII, 64). The author had endeavoured to hoodwink the public about the origin of the play; in the original preface to *L'Écossaise*[3] he had informed his readers: 'La Comédie dont nous présentons la traduction aux amateurs de la littérature, est de Monsieur Hume, pasteur de l'Eglise d'Edimbourg, déjà connu par deux belles tragédies, jouées à Londres.' And in the introductory letter to 'Messieurs les Parisiens' he quotes a letter from 'Mr. Hume' and cites the *Journal encyclopédique* of April, 1758 (iii, p. 137) to the effect that 'L'auteur de Douglas est le ministre Hume, parent du fameux David Hume, si célèbre [par son esprit et] par son impiété.'[4] The author of *Douglas* was, of course, John Home, and he was not related to David Hume.[5]

---

[1] Lessing makes a casual reference to La Chaussée's *Pamela* in St. xxi (87); see below, p. 229.   [2] See below, pp. 395 ff.

[3] *Seconde Suite des Mélanges de Littérature, d'Histoire, de Philosophie*, etc. [Geneva], 1761, pp. 15 f. (*Œuvres, ed. cit.* v (ii), pp. 15 f.)

[4] *Œuvres, ed. cit.* v (ii), p. 8.

[5] On February 11, 1761, Mendelssohn wrote to Lessing (*Schriften*, xix, p. 167): 'Das Publikum bestehet noch immer darauf, Voltaire sey der Verfasser des *Coffé*, so wenig die Anlage des Stücks auch Voltairen ähnlich siehet. Meine Freunde melden mir aus Hamburg, es hätten verschiedene Kaufleute von da, nach England geschrieben, und die Urschrift verlangt, man hätte ihnen aber geantwortet, es sey kein englisches Stück unter diesem Nahmen bekannt. Ist das Stück anders von Voltairen; so muss die Luft der republikanischen Freyheit, die er itzt athmet, seine ganze Denkungsart verändert haben.'

Voltaire himself in his preface suggested a similarity (70) with Goldoni:

La Comédie intitulée *l'Ecossaise* nous parut un de ces ouvrages qui peuvent réussir dans toutes les langues, parce que l'auteur peint la nature, qui est partout la même: il a la naïveté et la vérité de l'estimable Goldoni, avec peut-être plus d'intrigue, de force, et d'intérêt.[1]

But there appears to be no ground for Lessing's suggestion (71) that Don Marzio in *La Bottega del Caffè* was the model of Frélon, in whom Voltaire attacked the editor of the *Année littéraire*, E. C. Fréron. French critics point out that Voltaire had already sketched a similar figure in his comedy *L'Envieux* (1738, but not printed until 1834).[2] It is not the character of Frélon, however, Lessing says (83), but that of Free-port with his 'plumpe Edelmüthigkeit', which would commend the play to German audiences. Partly in order to disprove Voltaire's statement in his preface, quoted above, Lessing now turns to George Colman's English version of his play and the English criticisms of it.[3] This I deal with in my next chapter, as being of greater interest for Lessing's estimate of the translator.[4] He also mentions here (137) the Italian translation which he found in the *Biblioteca teatrale italiana* of Ottaviano Diodati.[5] It is literal, apart from the fact that the ending is altered in the interests of poetic justice, Frélon receiving the punishment which Voltaire pretends he had received in his 'English original':

Nous avoüons en même temps que nous avons crû, par le conseil des hommes les plus éclairés, devoir retrancher quelque chose du rolle de Frélon, qui paraissait encor dans les derniers Actes: il était puni, comme de raison, à la fin de la piéce; mais cette justice qu'on lui rendait, semblait mêler un peu de froideur au vif intérêt qui entraine l'esprit vers le dénoüement.[6]

Voltaire's chief rival in the theatre, Prosper Jolyot de Crébillon, whom Lessing had treated with great respect in his *Theatralische*

---

[1] *Œuvres, ed. cit.* v (ii), p. 15.
[2] See Bengesco, *op. cit.* i, pp. 32 f.
[3] Schröter and Thiele (*Lessings Hamburgische Dramaturgie, ed. cit.* p. 74) point out that Lessing is wrong (XII, 107) in asserting that it is Lord Falbridge to whom Monrose owes his pardon; it is Murray.
[4] See below, pp. 257 f.
[5] Vol. i (1762), pp. 180 ff. See below, p. 279.
[6] *Œuvres, ed. cit.* v (ii), p. 16.

Bibliothek, is only mentioned twice in the *Dramaturgie* (LXXIV, 44— 'Crebillon der Schreckliche'[1]—and LXXXI, 138). The Crébillon mentioned in XX (120) is the son, Claude Prosper Jolyot de Crébillon, the author of *Le Sopha* (1745) and other novels.

C. F. P. DE SAINT-FOIX, CÉROU AND TH. L'AFFICHARD

Lessing has naturally little or no criticism to offer of the two one-act pieces by Saint-Foix, *Der Finanzpachter* (XX, 139)—'Nie hat ein Dichter ein kleineres niedlicheres Ganze zu machen gewusst' (143)—and *Das Orakel* (LXXIII, 12); for both had long been familiar on the German stage. The little play by Cérou (or Séron), *Der Liebhaber als Schriftsteller und Bedienter* (XIV, 83), is described by Léris (*op. cit.* p. 21) as a 'jolie *Com*[édie] en un Acte en prose, par M. Cérou[2] lors étudiant en Droit, jouée aux Italiens le 8 Fév[rier] 1740, avec succès'. Lessing praises its high comic merit, both in situation and action. L'Affichard's *Ist er von Familie?* (XVII, 46) is only criticised in respect of its title, which Lessing finds somewhat misleading.

P. C. NIVELLE DE LA CHAUSSÉE

Concerning Nivelle de la Chaussée's *Mélanide* (VIII, 4) Lessing found in Léris, besides the date (*op. cit.* p. 290) the comment: 'On prétend qu'elle est tirée du Roman intitulé *Mademoiselle de Bontems*.'[3] What he has to say, however, does not concern the play itself, but 'weinerliche Komödie' in general.[4] That the situation of Act III, sc. ii, where Rosalie endeavours to convince her lover, Darviane, of her want of love for him, should appeal especially to the author of *Minna von Barnhelm* (VIII, 19), might be expected. For the rest, Lessing discusses the translation, which he considers infinitely better than the Italian one in Diodati's *Biblioteca teatrale*.[5] The comparison which he institutes between *Die Mütterschule* of Nivelle de la Chaussée, performed on

---

[1] Cp. *Theatralische Bibliothek*, ii, p. 117; *Schriften*, vi, p. 233: 'So wie ihnen Corneille der grosse [cp. XXXVI, 86; LXXXI, 76]...Voltaire der prächtige heisst: so heisst ihnen Crebillon der schreckliche.'

[2] For the variant forms of the author's name see above, p. 67.

[3] The novel was by T. S. Gueullette (Paris, 1736); but it does not appear to have been La Chaussée's source. (Cp. Schröter and Thiele, *ed. cit.* p. 47.)

[4] See below, pp. 395 ff.   [5] See below, p. 279.

May 29, and the play of the same title by Marivaux (XXI, 5) was suggested in the comment of Léris (*op. cit.* p. 158):

L'Ecole des Meres. Nous avons deux *Com*[édies] sous ce titre; la premiere, de M. de Marivaux, en un Ac[te] en pro[se] suivie d'un Div[ertissement] jouée au Thé[âtre] Ital[ien] le 26 Juillet 1732; et la seconde en 5 Ac[tes] en vers libres, par Nivelle de La Chaussée, représentée pour la premiere fois à la Comédie Fran[çaise] le 27 Avril 1744, et continuée avec beaucoup de succès.

Lessing refers also, but only in passing, to La Chaussée's *Paméla* (XXI, 87).

J. B. L. GRESSET

On Gresset's *Sidnei* (XVII, 2) Lessing had again recourse to the work of Léris, where he found (*op. cit.* p. 405):

Sidney, Com[édie] de M. Gresset, en vers et en 3 Ac[tes], donnée au Thé[âtre] Fran[çais] le 3 Mai 1745. Cette piece, malgré le sublime qu'on y trouve, et sa versification coulante et châtiée, n'eut pas à Paris tout le succès qu'elle eût pu avoir à Londres; le héros de la piece étant un Seigneur Anglois dégoûté de la vie, et qui veut y renoncer volontairement.

Lessing, however, rightly thinks that the English would find the play un-English. The Germans are not so sensitive; but he takes exception to Gresset's concession to etiquette (in Act III, sc. v) in not mentioning first the servant who has saved his hero's life. The latter, he considers, philosophises too much before he takes the poison, and too little after. His penitence is cowardice, and he is altogether too much at the mercy of his servant (10).

F. H. DE GRAFIGNY

In the case of the first performance of Madame de Grafigny's *Cénie* (XX, 2)—'dieses vortreffliche Stück'—Lessing is concerned with the merit, or lack of merit, of the translation. Fourteen years before, he had reviewed Frau Gottsched's version in the *Berlinische privilegirte Zeitung* (May 24, 1753), and on that occasion favourably:[1]

Cenie ist ein Meisterstück in dem Geschmacke der weinerlichen Lustspiele. Die Kunstrichter mögen wider diese Art dramatischer Stücke einwenden was sie wollen; das Gefühl der Leser und Zuschauer wird sie

[1] *Schriften*, v, pp. 168 f. Petersen (*ed. cit.* p. 202) expresses doubts as to Lessing's authorship of this review.

allezeit vertheidigen, wenn ihre Verfasser anders das sanftere Mitleiden eben so geschickt zu erwecken wissen, als die Frau von Grafigny. Sie hat an der Frau Gottschedin die würdigste Übersetzerinn gefunden, weil nur diejenigen zärtliche Gedanken zärtlich verdollmetschen können, welche sie selbst gedacht zu haben fähig sind. Ihre Übersetzung war in Wien sehr fehlerhaft abgedruckt worden, und es ist ein Glück, dass die Fr. Professorin böse werden kann, sonst würden wir diesen richtigern Abdruck nicht erhalten haben.

But between 1753 and 1767 Lessing's attitude to Gottsched changed from discipleship to open hostility, and he could now afford to be critical of the 'gelehrte Freundinn'. He withdraws the very moderate praise he had bestowed on her translation of Destouches (XIII, 20), and condemns unsparingly that of *Cénie* (xx, 9 ff.).[1]

He shows how in her prosaic literalness she misses entirely the feeling of the original; as for example when she translates 'J'en jouirai, je vous rendrai tous heureux' (Act I, sc. iii) by 'Alsdenn werde ich meiner Güter erst recht geniessen, wenn ich euch beide dadurch werde glücklich gemacht haben', when it should have been: 'Ich will ihrer geniessen, ich will euch alle glücklich machen.' The language of the heart which is to be heard in the original is drowned in Frau Gottsched's deluge of words. Particularly witty is his sally against her 'ugly ceremonial tone': her translation of 'ma mère' by 'Frau Mutter', of 'son père' by 'sein gnädiger Herr Vater'. '„Frau Mutter! o welch ein süsser Name!"' ['Ma mère! que ce nom est doux!' Act IV, sc. iii.] Der Name Mutter ist süss; aber Frau Mutter ist wahrer Honig mit Citronensaft!' (54).[2] On the occasion of the second performance (July 10) Lessing discusses the question of Madame de Grafigny's

---

[1] A criticism of an English version of *Cénie* appeared in the *Journal étranger* for May, 1755. The critic there says of the original (pp. 142 f.): 'On y a fort admiré l'élégance et la pureté du stile... le sentiment, la diction, l'action excellente... ont assuré et soutenu le succès de la Pièce.' But he adds: 'On ne voit, dans l'original, ni le genre d'esprit, ni l'espèce de ridicule, ni la varieté de caractères qui constitue [une Comédie].'

[2] This sally of Lessing's was perhaps a reminiscence of a passage in Diderot's *De la poésie dramatique* (*Œuvres Complètes*, ed. J. Assézat, Paris, 1875–77, vii, p. 372; in Lessing's translation, ii, p. 420): 'Quelle sera donc la ressource d'un poëte, chez un peuple dont les mœurs sont faibles, petites et maniérées; où l'imitation rigoureuse des conversations ne formerait qu'un tissu d'expressions fausses, insensées et basses; où il n'y a plus ni franchise, ni bonhomie; où un père appelle son fils monsieur, et où une mère appelle sa fille mademoiselle; où les cérémonies publiques n'ont rien d'auguste; la conduite domestique, rien de touchant et d'honnête; les actes solennels, rien de vrai?'

authorship of the play (LIII, 3 ff.). This had been denied in Chevrier's *Observateur des Spectacles*, in a passage which Lessing quotes from vol. i, p. 211. The original is as follows:

Cenie annoncé sous le nom de Madame de *Graffigni* est de l'Abbé de V****, elle fut d'abord faitte en vers, mais comme Madame de Graffigny qui ne s'avisa qu'a 54 ans[1] de vouloir jouer l'Auteur, n'avoit jamais fait un vers, on mit Cenie en Prose mais l'Auteur y a laissé 81 vers qui y existent dans leur entier.

Again, the statement 'Chevrier hat mehr solche verkleinerliche geheime Nachrichten', etc. (LIII, 51) is based on the following passage:

Avant de donner les Couplets que nous annonçons, il est a propos de remarquer que la Demoiselle *Favart*[2] qui sait a peine lire, a la manie de vouloir tenir un rang parmi nos femmes Auteurs, l'Abbé *de Voisenon* digne prétre qui joüit d'une abbaye considerable, se dispense de dire la messe et fait de jolis vers, s'est offert pour être le teinturier de la Demoiselle *Favart* et même de son sombre mari sur les pièces duquel il jette la *polissoire*, l'Opera Comique d'Annette et Lubin[3] partant de la même manufacture, un plaisant a fait les cinq couplets suivans qui courent manuscrits dans tout Paris.[4]

What characteristics has *Cénie* that would tempt us to regard it as not the work of a woman? Here Lessing quotes from two notes to Rousseau's *Lettre à M. d'Alembert* (Amsterdam, 1758, pp. 193 and 78 of the first edition). The first of these is:

Les femmes, en général, n'aiment aucun art, ne se connoissent à aucun, et n'ont aucun génie. Elles peuvent réussir aux petits ouvrages qui ne demandent que de la légereté d'esprit, du goût, et de la grace, quelquefois même de la philosophie et du raisonnement. Elles peuvent acquérir de la science, de l'érudition, des talens, et tout ce qui s'acquiert à force de travail. Mais ce feu céleste qui échauffe et embrase l'ame, ce génie qui consume

---

[1] Mad. de Grafigny, born in 1695, published *Cénie* in 1750 (cp. G. Noël, *Madame de Grafigny* (1695–1758), Paris, 1913, pp. 7, 243 ff.); Lessing repeats Chevrier's statement.

[2] Marie Justine Benoîte La Favart, the wife of the dramatist (1727–72).

[3] *Annette et Lubin* was produced on February 15, 1762 (Léris, *op. cit.* p. 43). Chevrier discusses this work at the beginning of the second volume, criticising its style as being too elegant and mentioning the Abbé de Voisenon as its author (ii, p. 8).

[4] Vol. ii, p. 91. The couplets are entitled *Chanson sur les Auteur* [sic] *d'ANNETTE ET LUBIN* (pp. 92 f.). Lessing's reference to 'die Gassenhauer in der französischen Geschichte' (LIII, 56) may be compared to the statement in the 'Rettung' of Cochlæus: '...er sagte, die Reformation sey...in dem liederreichen Frankreich das Werk eines Gassenhauers gewesen' (*Schriften*, v, p. 366).

et dévore, cette brulante éloquence, ces transports sublimes qui portent leurs ravissemens jusqu'au fond des cœurs, manqueront toujours aux écrits des femmes....

And the second:

Ce n'est point par étourderie que je cite *Cénie* en cet endroit, quoique cette charmante Piece soit l'ouvrage d'une femme; car, cherchant la vérité de bonne foi, je ne sais point déguiser ce qui fait contre mon sentiment; et ce n'est pas à une femme, mais aux femmes que je refuse les talens des hommes. J'honore d'autant plus volontiers ceux de l'auteur de *Cénie* en particulier, qu'ayant à me plaindre de ses discours, je lui rends un hommage pur et désintéressé, comme tous les éloges sortis de ma plume.

DENIS DIDEROT

None of the many gaps in the dramatic criticism of the *Hamburgische Dramaturgie* is more to be regretted than the omission of any estimate of Diderot as a dramatic writer; for no German critic was better qualified than Lessing, who had virtually introduced him to his countrymen, to speak of him with sympathy and understanding. But *Der Hausvater* was produced at a time when Lessing had been long alienated from the Hamburg theatre; and he employs the occasion provided by the performance of that play (LXXXIV, 1) to discuss mainly questions of dramatic theory.

As in the preface to the second edition of his translation of Diderot Lessing had said: 'Diderot scheint überhaupt auf das deutsche Theater weit mehr Einfluss gehabt zu haben, als auf das Theater seines eigenen Volks',[1] so now (LXXXIV, 4) he repeats that *Le Père de famille* had been played 'kaum ein oder zweymal' in France. As a matter of fact, however, it had not been quite so unsuccessful. After being produced at Marseilles in 1760, it was played at the Comédie française on February 18, 1761, and repeated seven times, the performance being only interrupted by the Easter vacation.[2]

Lessing has more to say in criticism of *Le Fils naturel*, which was not performed in Hamburg in his time, than of *Le Père de famille*. He considers that Diderot's demand for naturalism in the drama is by

---

[1] *Schriften*, viii, p. 288.

[2] Diderot, *Œuvres complètes, ed. cit.* vii, pp. 171 f. Lessing wrote on January 13, 1771, to Eva König in Vienna (*Schriften*, xvii, p. 369): 'Versäumen Sie es doch aber ja nicht, ihm [Sonnenfels] seinen Willen zu thun und den Hausvater zu sehen. Ich bin sehr begierig zu wissen, ob er in Wien besser gespielt wird, als wir ihn in Hamburg gesehen haben.'

no means fulfilled in *Le Fils naturel*; there is (LXXXV, 126) too much uniformity in the characters, too much 'Romantische'; the dialogue is stiff and affected, a pedantic jumble of new-fangled philosophical sentences. Especially the solemn Theresia (or Constantia as she is called in the original),[1] who goes about even her wooing so philosophically, and speaks so wisely of virtuous children with the man who does not care for her, gives the critics ample scope for mockery. This scene (Act IV, sc. iii) had indeed been held up to ridicule by Palissot de Montenoy:

Où sommes-nous, Madame? Que deviennent les bienséances? Voilà donc le langage philosophique que doit parler l'amour sur nos Théatres. C'est l'amour envisagé comme le besoin de multiplier l'espéce, mis sur la Scène, comme il est peint dans le *Tableau de l'Amour conjugal*. Oui, Madame, et c'est encore une des singularités brillantes de cet Ouvrage.[2]

With this might be compared a criticism of *Le Fils naturel* which appeared in the *Bibliothek der schönen Wissenschaften* (but which is largely drawn from Palissot):

Die Charaktere sind alle von einer Art. Alle sind die ehrlichsten Leute von der Welt. Alle, so gar die Bedienten, sind Philosophen, und die Frauenzimmer sind so metaphysisch, als die Mannspersonen.... C o n s t a n c e ist vollends auf dem Theater unleidlich. Ihre lange metaphysische Liebeserklärung macht sie lächerlich. Ihr Streit mit dem D o r v a l, den sie nicht heirathen will, macht sie verächtlich: und welche Comödiantinn würde auf dem Theater, ohne ausgelacht zu werden, ihren Geliebten mit der Hoffnung unterhalten können, dass die Kinder, die sie bald mit einander zeugen würden, allerliebst seyn würden? Alles hat in diesem Stücke den metaphysischen Ton, den Ton der Zeit, die Schreibart ist oft gekünstelt, die Gedanken, so schön und fein sie oft sind, sind eben so monotonisch, als die Charakter.[3]

---

[1] Why Lessing changed the name of the heroine from Constantia to Theresia is not clear.

[2] *Petites lettres sur de grands philosophes*, Paris, 1757, p. 54 (*Théâtre et Œuvres diverses*, London (Paris), 1763, ii, p. 141; on Lessing's use of this edition see below, p. 411.) In *Le Fils naturel*, Act IV, sc. iii, Constance says: 'Dorval, vos enfants ne sont point destinés à tomber dans le chaos que vous redoutez. Ils passeront sous vos yeux les premières années de leur vie; et c'en est assez pour vous répondre de celles qui suivront. Ils apprendront de vous à penser comme vous. Vos passions, vos goûts, vos idées passeront en eux. Ils tiendront de vous ces notions si justes que vous avez de la grandeur et de la bassesse réelles; du bonheur véritable et de la misère apparente. Il ne dépendra que de vous, qu'ils aient une conscience toute semblable à la vôtre. Ils vous verront agir; ils m'entendront parler quelquefois. Dorval, vos filles seront honnêtes et décentes; vos fils seront nobles et fiers. Tous vos enfants seront charmants.'

[3] *Bibliothek der schönen Wissenschaften*, v (ii) (1759), pp. 253 f.

A further criticism by Palissot on which Lessing draws (LXXXVII–LXXXVIII, 5) is the following (*Théâtre et Œuvres diverses, ed. cit.* ii, p. 135):

Une des singularités de ce chef-d'œuvre; c'est son titre. Cela s'appelle *le Fils Naturel*, on ne sait pourquoi. Vous connaissez la marche de la piece. La condition de *Dorval* influe-t-elle en rien dans l'ouvrage? Y fait-elle un événement? Amene-t-elle une situation? Fournit-elle, seulement, un remplissage? Non. Quel peut donc avoir été le but de l'Auteur? De renouveler des Grecs deux ou trois réflexions sur l'injustice des préjugés de naissance? Mais, qui ne sait que l'homme sage ne compte point parmi les vrais biens les hazards de la fortune?[1]

Lessing leaves the play in St. LXXXVI and turns to Diderot's views on the nature of dramatic characters: how far they should be typical or individual; and how those of tragedy should differ from those of comedy.[2]

A note may here be inserted on an anonymous French play, *L'Humanité ou le Tableau de l'Indigence*, to which Lessing refers in St. XIV (51). It had been produced under Ackermann in 1764 as *Die Menschlichkeit, oder Schilderung der Dürftigkeit*, translated by J. H. Steffens. It was published under this title at Celle in 1764; also as *Die Menschlichkeit oder das Gemälde der Dürftigkeit*. Aus dem Französischen übersetzt [N.P.], in 1762, and as *Die Menschlichkeit, oder das Gemählde der Armuth. Ein bürgerliches Trauerspiel in fünf Aufzügen*, at Hamburg in 1764. A copy of the 1762 edition, and one of the Hamburg edition of 1764, which is a different translation, are in the Hamburg Staats- und Universitätsbibliothek. The French original was described by Léris (*op. cit.* p. 728 (Supplément)) as 'Piece singuliere... remplie de beautés et de situations attendrissantes: elle a été imprimée en 1761, avec des réflexions sur les spectacles et sur les mœurs; quelque tems après on la joua à Lyon avec de légers changemens, et elle eut un grand succès: on n'en connoît pas l'Auteur.' Lessing may have read a letter on the French original in the *Journal encyclopédique* of July 1761.[3] It was possibly the description of the play here—'un ouvrage anonyme, mais fait, si mon cœur ne me trompe, pour être avoué par nos plus grands Écrivains'—which induced the editor of the London edition

---

[1] The review in the *Bibliothek der schönen Wissenschaften* had repeated (p. 253) this criticism: 'Aber wir wissen nicht, warum es der natürliche Sohn genennt werde: Dorvals unächte Geburt hat nicht den geringsten Einfluss in die Begebenheiten der Handlung.'   [2] See below, pp. 400 ff.

[3] *Journal Encyclopédique*, July 15, 1761, pp. 138 ff.

of Diderot's works (1773) to attribute it to that writer (vol. v, pp. 344 ff.). It cannot, however, be by him. Crouslé says (*Dramaturgie de Hambourg*, trad. de E. de Suckau, Paris, 1869, p. 70): 'L'auteur de cette pièce est Randon, qui a donné, dans la même année (1761), *Zamir*, "tragédie bourgeoise". Randon est un disciple de Diderot.'[1]

C. S. FAVART

The performance of Favart's *Solimann der Zweyte* on July 3 (XXXIII, 2) gives Lessing an opportunity to return to a theme which more than once had claimed his attention in the *Dramaturgie*: the distinctive character of dramatic as compared with narrative presentation.[2] Favart's comedy is, as Léris had mentioned (*op. cit.* p. 408), a dramatisation of the second of Marmontel's *Contes Moraux*, which it follows closely. That story, Lessing says (14 ff.), is told with wit, elegance and charm; but it is difficult to say why it should be called 'moral'. It is only so in the sense that it is less immoral than the stories of La Fontaine or Grécourt. After giving us a lively summary of the tale (24 ff.) Lessing points out (63) that Marmontel introduces it with the reflection: 'C'est un plaisir de voir les graves Historiens se creuser la tête pour trouver de grandes causes aux grands événemens';[3] and closes it with the statement: 'Soliman transporté de joie et d'amour, vint prendre Roxelane pour la mener à la Mosquée, et il disoit tout bas en l'y conduisant: Est-il possible qu'un petit nez retroussé renverse les loix d'un Empire?'[4] He had, however (70), a more specific moral in view than merely to illustrate the disproportion between cause and effect. Lessing quotes from the preface, where Marmontel says (p. ii):

Je me proposai d'y faire sentir la folie de ceux qui employent l'autorité pour mettre une femme à la raison; et je pris pour exemple un Sultan et son Esclave, commes [*sic*] les deux extremités de la domination et de la dépendance.

Lessing found an incentive to make a comparison of Favart's play with its source in an article in the *Journal encyclopédique*, January 15,

[1] Cp. Quérard, *La France Littéraire*, vii (Paris, 1835), p. 451, where Randon is stated to be the author of both plays (editions dated 1761); but cp. also *Œuvres complètes de Diderot*, ed. cit. vii, pp. 5 f. and Petersen, *ed. cit.* p. 195.

[2] See below, pp. 460 f.

[3] *Contes Moraux*, Paris, 1765, i, p. 51.

[4] *Ibid.* p. 84.

1762—from which he quotes in condensed form (XXXIII, 107 ff.). The original is as follows (pp. 79 ff.):

Soliman II fut un des plus grands Princes de son siécle. Les Turcs n'ont point d'Empereur dont la mémoire leur soit plus chère. Ses victoires, ses talens, mille vertus le rendirent l'objet de la vénération des ennemis mêmes dont il triomphoit. Ce Héros si sensible à la gloire, ne put se défendre de l'être à l'amour. Mais délicat dans ses plaisirs, il sentit même au milieu de la corruption d'un serrail, que la volupté est vile sans le sentiment. Il crut l'avoir trouvé dans Roxelane jeune Italienne, amenée au serrail comme captive, tendre peut-être, mais plus artificieuse encore, ambitieuse et habile dans l'art de faire servir ses plaisirs à sa grandeur. A force de feindre le sentiment, elle amena le sensible Soliman jusqu'à fouler aux pieds la loi de l'Empire qui défendoit au Sultan de se marier. Elle monta sur le trône avec lui; ambition pardonnable si Roxelane ne se fût pas servie de son ascendant sur son Amant pour le forcer à souiller sa gloire en immolant un fils innocent! c'est cette femme que Mr. Marmontel a choisie pour en faire l'héroïne d'un de ses Contes. Mais qu'il l'a changée! d'abord d'Italienne, il l'a fait Françoise. D'une femme artificieuse et jouant le sentiment, il en a fait une coquette des cercles de Paris; enfin au lieu d'une ame dévorée d'ambition et capable des coups les plus hardis et les plus noirs pour la satisfaire, il lui a donné une tête légère, et un cœur excellent. Ces travestissemens sont-ils permis? Un Poëte, un Conteur, quelque licence qu'on leur ait donnée, peuvent-ils l'étendre sur les caractères connus? Maîtres de changer dans les faits, ont-ils le droit de peindre Lucrèce coquette, et Socrate galant? Ce sont des doutes que nous proposons à Mr. Marmontel lui-même. Quoiqu'il en soit, le Conte est très-agréable, et prêtoit au comique. Mr. Favart l'a apperçu, et s'est empressé de le faire passer sur le théâtre. Le succès a été brillant; *Les Sultanes* applaudies il y a six mois à leur naissance, viennent d'être reprises, et n'ont rien perdu de leur succès théatral, en paroissant au grand jour de l'impression.

Remembering his previous argument (XXIII, 118 ff.) that characters must be more sacred to the poet than facts, Lessing is not disposed (XXXIII, 127) to undertake any defence of Marmontel. But he observes that after all, it is a more pardonable fault (XXXIV, 1) not to give people in fiction their historical characters than to offend against probability in depicting them.[1] The character of Marmontel's Sultan is far from being consistent and credible (52 ff.).[2] Equally lacking is

[1] See below, pp. 442 ff.

[2] For the quotation in XXXIV, 56 ff. see Marmontel, *Contes Moraux*, ed. cit. i, pp. 51 f.: 'Je suis las, dit-il un jour, de ne voir ici que des machines caressantes. Ces Esclaves me font pitié. Leur molle docilité n'a rien de piquant, rien de flateur. C'est à des cœurs nourris dans le sein de la liberté, qu'il seroit doux de faire aimer l'esclavage.' For 65 ff. cp. 'Soliman qui étoit trop grand homme pour traiter en affaire d'état la police de ses plaisirs, fut curieux de voir cette jeune évaporée' (*ibid.* p. 64).

the sense of purpose ('Absicht') in the characters of Soliman and Roxelane (126). And the critic of the *Journal encyclopédique* may be right (137) in insisting that in these matters Favart is more at fault than Marmontel. The passage translated by Lessing (140 ff.) is in the original (pp. 91 f.):

La vraisemblance, indifférente peut-être dans un Conte, mais essentielle dans un drame, est ici violée partout. Le Grand Soliman y joue un rôle assez petit; on a de la peine à ne voir ce Héros que sous ce point de vue. Mais le caractère des Sultans y est encore plus manqué; on ne reconnoît point cette autorité absolue devant laquelle tout se tait. On pouvoit sans doute l'adoucir; mais il ne falloit pas la faire disparoître entièrement. Le caractère de Roxelane a fait plaisir à cause du jeu; mais la réflexion lui est-elle favorable? Ce rôle est-il vraisemblable? Elle parle au Sultan comme à un Bourgeois de Paris; elle critique tous ses usages; elle contredit tous ses goûts; elle lui dit des choses très-dures et souvent très-offensantes. Tout cela pourroit peut-être se dire; mais il falloit au moins l'adoucir dans les termes. On est revolté d'entendre une jeune Aventurière régenter le Grand Soliman, et lui apprendre l'art de regner. Le trait du mouchoir méprisé est trop fort, et celui de la pipe jettée est insupportable.

In elucidation of the last sentence Lessing refers (xxxv, 1) to the fact that these two incidents belong to Favart's version. In Marmontel's tale the Sultan sends a message by Délia, the deposed favourite, to Roxelane, inviting her to supper. The latter, however, regards the invitation as an insult, and demands of the Sultan that Délia shall be invited too, to which he agrees. She also insists that Délia shall sing to them, and presents her with a handkerchief as a compliment from the Sultan:

Roxelane parut charmée; elle demanda tout bas un mouchoir à Soliman; il lui en donna un sans se douter de son dessein. Madame, dit-elle à Délia en le lui présentant, c'est de la part du Sultan que je vous donne le mouchoir; vous l'avez bien mérité.[1]

In the play, on the other hand (Act II, sc. xiii—sc. xv in the German translation), the Sultan grows angry, takes the handkerchief back from Délia and gives it to her other rival Elmire. The incident of the pipe occurs in Act II, sc. iii, where Roxelane seizes the Sultan's pipe from his hand and throws it to the ground.

Lessing has clearly a higher opinion of Favart's comedy than the French reviewer;[2] indeed, one must add, too high an opinion. He

[1] *Contes Moraux, ed. cit.* i, pp. 76 f.
[2] It is interesting, however, to compare with Lessing's opinion of the play here his letter of November 29, 1770 to Eva König, who was then in Vienna. Favart's

claims the same right which he had claimed for Marmontel, to create consistent characters irrespective of the historical setting. Here again, may we not admit considerable justification for the contrary standpoint? Lessing remarks, in particular, that, while Marmontel is content to depict Roxelane as a mere coquette, who tantalises the Sultan until she attains her object (xxxv, 24), Favart's heroine 'scheinet die kecke Buhlerinn mehr gespielt zu haben, als zu seyn', and he quotes with approval her confession of love for him at the end (Act III, [sc. ix]; xxxv, 56 ff.). Apart from the thought which must strike every modern reader, that this is a by no means blameless descent into theatrical sentimentality, it is interesting to examine the reasons for Lessing's approval. It may merely seem a bid—and from the standpoint of the theatre no doubt a justifiable bid—for the audience's sympathy; but Lessing clothes the idea in more philosophical phrase: it is the infusion of an element of interest into the character of Roxelane, which justifies the reward she receives in being elevated to the rank of Sultana. Without the happy turn given by Favart at the end, he says (xxxvi, 1) her triumph would have been as ludicrous as that of a *Serva Padrona*; Soliman would have been no more than a 'kläglicher Pimpinello' and Roxelane a 'hässliche, verschmitzte Serbinette';[1] so too, he adds (15), without some similar concession, the story of *Die Matrone von Ephesus* is impossible on the stage.

Lessing evidently intended to return to this matter in his discussion of the representation of the play on August 24—it may be noted that St. xxxv is dated August 28. In his *Verzeichnisse der aufgeführten Dramen* he made a note to this effect: 'N.B. das Rückständige von 36.'[2] And in the *Entwürfe zu Besprechungen*[3] is the following:

71te Vorstellung. Soliman der zweyte.
Ob Favart die Veränderung aus kritischen Ursachen gemacht? Ob er es nicht blos gethan, um s. Nation zu schmeicheln? Um seine Französin nicht allein zum lebhaftesten, witzigsten, unterhaltendsten, sondern auch

comedy had just been the cause of Sonnenfels's retirement from the office of censor. 'Dem Stücke, welches ihm diese kleine Kränkung verursacht hat, bin ich selbst nicht gut. Ich würde es kaum auf einem deutschen Theater dulden, wenn Roxellane auch eine Deutsche wäre: nun aber gar in der vermeinten Hauptstadt von Deutschland—denn dafür will S[onnenfels] Wien mit aller Gewalt gehalten wissen,—den Triumph einer Französischen Stumpfnase auf die Bühne zu bringen, ist schlechterdings unerträglich. Ich will auch hoffen, dass es mehr dieser Umstand, als das Schnupftuch oder Spiegel ist, welcher die Dame oder die Damen in Wien bewogen hat, das Stück verbieten zu lassen' (*Schriften*, xvii, p. 352).

[1] See below, pp. 280 f.   [2] *Schriften*, xv, p. 51.   [3] *Ibid.* pp. 44 f.

edelsten und grossmüthigsten Mädchen zu machen? Damit man sagen müsse: es ist wahr, sie ist ein närrisches unbedachtsames Ding, aber doch zugleich das beste Herz?—So wie Boissy, im Franzosen zu London, seinen Petitmätre, am Ende doch zu einem jungen Menschen von Ehre macht; und dadurch alles das Gute was die Schilderung seiner Thorheiten stiften könnte wieder verderbt.[1] Marmontel sagt überhaupt schon von der Rolle des Petitmaitres (Poetiq. Fr. T. II, p. 395)[2] On s'amuse à recopier le Petit-Maitre, sur lequel tous les traits du ridicule sont épuisés, et dont la peinture n'est plus qu'une ecole pour les jeunes gens, qui ont quelque disposition à le devenir. Die französischen dramatischen Dichter überhaupt sind itzt die berechnendsten Schmeichler der Nation. Nur durch die Eitelkeit derselben bringen sie ihre Versuche in Schutz. Beweise hiervon an der Belagerung von Calais, und noch neuerlich an—. Gleichwohl sind wir Deutsche so gutherzige Narren ihnen diese Stücke nachzuspielen, und die kahlen Lobeserhebungen der Franzosen auf deutschen Theatern erschallen zu lassen. Unmöglich können doch bey uns ihre Tragödien von der Art gefallen; und ihre Comödien von der Art müssen vollends verunglücken. Wir haben keine Roxelanen, wir haben keine Petitmätres; wo sollen unsre Schauspieler die Muster davon gesehen haben. Kein Wunder also, dass sie diese Rollen allerzeit schlecht spielen. Und desto besser!

P. L. B. DE BELLOY

The only quite modern French tragedy which it fell to Lessing to criticise was the *Zelmire* of P. L. Buyrette de Belloy—following the error of the playbill, Lessing calls him 'Du Belloy'. I have been unable to discover the source of Lessing's information about this author (XVIII, 118). Léris notes concerning *Zelmire* (*op. cit.* p. 459) that it was a '*Trag*[édie] de M. Belloy, donnée au Thé[âtre] Fran[çais] le 6 Mai 1762, et qui a eu beaucoup de succès. C'est un sujet d'invention, mais extrêmement bien tissu, bien conduit et même neuf...' and concerning *Titus* (*ibid.* p. 430) that it was a tragedy 'donnée le 28 Février 1759, et qui n'eut que cette représentation'. Of the poet himself Léris says (*ibid.* pp. 509 f.): 'Il s'étoit destiné au Barreau que le genre dramatique lui a fait abandonner; il est Auteur de la Tragédie de *Titus*...et de celle de *Zelmire*.' Lessing probably had his information about the esteem and appreciation shown by Calais towards the

[1] Boissy's *Le François à Londres* was produced in Paris on July 3, 1727 (Léris, *op. cit.* p. 214). It was translated in the second volume of Schönemann's *Schaubühne* in 1748.

[2] For Lessing's use of this work, see also below, pp. 355, 398; cp. also p. 371, note 4. He appears to have used the edition published at Paris (Lesclapart) in two volumes in 1763.

poet (xviii, 93 ff.) from the *Journal encyclopédique* of May 15, 1765 (p. 128):[1]

> Nous avons appris avec la joie la plus vive, que le *Siège de Calais*, que M. de Belloy vient de mettre au jour, a été couronné du succès le plus éclatant. Cet Auteur s'est couvert d'une gloire immortelle, et cette ville a l'avantage de la partager avec lui....

Consideration of this patriotic enthusiasm leads Lessing to compare his own countrymen unfavourably with the French; and, as we have seen, the passage in question was probably also influenced by Klopstock's visit to Hamburg.[2]

In the same journal for July 1, 1762 (pp. 101 ff.), Lessing found a review of *Zelmire* from which he learned that:

> Cette Tragédie a eu le succès le plus brillant. Quatorze représentations consécutives, n'avoient point encore satisfait la curiosité, lorsqu'on l'a retirée.... Le sujet de cette piéce est entiérement d'imagination (pp. 122 f.).

And at the end of St. xviii and in St. xix he translates two long passages from this review. The first of them has more particular bearing on historical drama and the relation of tragedy to historical fact. I deal with it later.[3] But the second is a criticism of *Zelmire* itself. It is as follows (pp. 125 ff.):

> Un second vice de cette pièce, c'est que, comme l'Auteur en convient, Zelmire est une Tragédie d'événemens. Sans vouloir proscrire absolument ce genre (car pourquoi diminuer les sources des plaisirs?) Nous ne pouvons nous empêcher de remarquer qu'il est bien inférieur à celui des Tragédies de caractères, et qu'il demande moins de fécondité et moins de génie, malgré les apparences qui semblent décider le contraire. D'ailleurs il est bien difficile que ces incidens multipliés aient de la vraisemblance, quand on les resserre dans un espace de 24 heures; enfin il n'est guères possible que ces situations, si recherchées de nos jours, ces coups de théâtre, si chéris du Peuple des Spectateurs, puissent jamais faire illusion aux véritables Connoisseurs; et Mr. de Belloi est fait pour plaire surtout à ceux-ci. Mais il est inutile de chicaner l'Auteur sur ce point. On voit bien qu'il s'est fait cette observation à lui-même, et qu'il en a senti la justesse. Il a tout ce qu'il faut pour réussir dans les deux genres; lorsqu'il a préféré le moins bon, il est visible qu'il a cru qu'un Commençant devoit quelques sacrifices au goût de la multitude. Le plan et la texture méritent les plus grands éloges. Quelques nombreux que soient les incidens, ils sont en général amenés naturellement; ils sortent du fond de la première situation, et de

---

[1] See also the *Journal encyclopédique* of March 1, 1765, p. 152, and May 15, 1765, pp. 101 f.　　　　[2] See above, pp. 160 f.　　　　[3] See below, pp. 439 f.

celui des caractères. Voici cependant quelques endroits qui nous paroissent devoir être retouchés. La confidence du Tyran à Rhamnès n'est pas suffisamment motivée; on ne voit point assez la nécessité où se trouve Antenor de révéler ses crimes. L'arrivée d'Ilus n'est point assez préparée; et la conversion de Rhamnès est trop prompte. Jusqu'au moment où il frappe Antenor, on n'a vu en lui qu'un Complice décidé des crimes de son Maître; s'il a eu un moment de remords, ils ont été bientôt étouffés. Enfin il y a quelquefois de trop petits moyens pour de grandes choses. Par exemple, on a soin d'avertir que Polidore revenant de la bataille pour se cacher dans le tombeau, tourne le dos à Zelmire. En effet, s'il marchoit autrement, la Princesse le reconnoîtroit, et l'on seroit privé de ce beau coup de théâtre qui frappe si vivement les Spectateurs, lorsque cette tendre fille livre son père à ses Bourreaux. Cependant n'étoit-il pas naturel, nécessaire même que Polidore, en rentrant dans le tombeau, regardât Zelmire, lui fit un signe de douleur, lui dit un mot de desespoir? C'est pourtant sur ce coup de théâtre, et par conséquent sur cette façon de marcher de Polidore que sont appuyés les derniers actes. Le billet d'Azor est du même genre: si le Soldat l'apportoit avec lui dès le second acte, comme il le devoit, le Tyran étoit démasqué, et le drame fini.[1]

Thus Lessing offers no independent criticism of the play, and is apparently satisfied to endorse the judgment of the *Journal encyclopédique*. This again is a pity, for, small as we may now-a-days estimate the talent of De Belloy to have been, he was undoubtedly symptomatic of his time; his work represents a laudable attempt to put new life into the alexandrine tragedy, and to carry its development beyond the point reached by Voltaire. But the interest of Lessing, the translator of Diderot, in alexandrine tragedies of any kind was very lukewarm.

Largely as the drama of France bulks in the Hamburg repertory and in Lessing's criticism of that repertory, it can hardly be said that his account of it—when considered by itself, as in the preceding pages—leaves a very satisfactory impression. He regarded it as his chief mission to discredit the type of tragedy which is the particular glory of the French seventeenth century; and yet he has nothing to say of the greatest of its masters, Racine; his attack is limited to a demolition, in the spirit of Voltairean persiflage, of Corneille's *Rodogune*.

[1] Cp. also the report of the play from Paris in the *Bibliothek der schönen Wissenschaften*, ix (i) (1763), pp. 135 f., which was printed on the playbill (see above, pp. 74 f.).

No sooner had the French seen their theatre rise out of barbarism with Corneille (LXXXI, 39)[1] than they considered it almost perfect; and with Racine they believed it to have attained perfection. Corneille, Lessing asserts (50), did the greater harm and had the most ruinous influence on their dramatic poetry. For Racine misled only by his example; Corneille both by example and precept. He was accepted as an oracle. 'Man nenne mir das Stück des grossen Corneille, welches ich nicht besser machen wollte' (CI–CIV, 273)—thus Lessing discredits the oracle.

There are French dramas enough, he contends (LXXXI, 120), which fulfil Corneille's requirements of tragedy, but none which fulfils the Aristotelian demand that tragedy should awaken our pity and fear, as they are awakened in a number of Greek and English tragedies (132). Corneille and Racine, Crébillon and Voltaire, have little or nothing of what makes Euripides Euripides and Shakespeare Shakespeare. No nation has so deeply misunderstood the rules of ancient drama as the French (96 ff.).

Not only then have the Germans no theatre; but the nation which for a hundred years has boasted of possessing the best theatre in Europe, has none; certainly no tragic theatre. Even Voltaire had said:

Dans les beautés frapantes de notre théâtre, il y avait un autre défaut caché, dont on ne s'était pas aperçu, parce que le public ne pouvait pas avoir par lui-même des idées plus fortes que celles de ces grands maîtres. Ce défaut ne fut relevé que par Saint-Evremont; il dit *que nos piéces ne font pas une impression assez forte; que ce qui doit former la pitié, fait tout au plus de la tendresse; que l'émotion tient lieu de saisissement, l'étonnement de l'horreur; qu'il manque à nos sentimens quelque chose d'assez profond.* Il faut avouer que Saint-Evremont a mis le doigt dans la playe secrette du théâtre Français: on dira tant qu'on voudra que *Saint-Evremont* est l'auteur de la pitoyable comédie de *Sirpolitik*, et de celle des opéra, que ses petits vers de société sont ce que

---

[1] The phrase, as C. B. Boxberger has shown (*Einzelheiten über Voltaire bei Lessing*, ed. cit. p. 31), is from Voltaire's *Vie de Molière* (*Contes de Guillaume Vadé*, ed. cit. p. 309): 'Pierre Corneille tira le théâtre de la barbarie et de l'avilissement, vers l'année 1630.' And Lessing may also have had in mind the letter of Algarotti prefixed to Voltaire's *La Mort de César* (*Œuvres Complètes*, Paris, 1877–85, iii, pp. 312 ff.). (The French version of this letter, containing the following passage, which is not in the original Italian, appeared for the first time in the edition of 1736): 'Il faudrait ignorer qu'il y a une langue française et un théâtre, pour ne pas savoir à quel degré de perfection Corneille et Racine ont porté l'art dramatique; il semblait qu'après ces grands hommes il ne restait plus rien à souhaiter, et que tâcher de les imiter était tout ce que l'on pouvait faire de mieux' (*ibid*. p. 312).

nous avons de plus plat en ce genre, que c'était un petit faiseur de phrases; mais on peut être totalement dépourvu de génie, et avoir beaucoup d'esprit et de goût. Certainement son goût était très-fin, quand il trouvait ainsi la raison de la langueur de la plupart de nos piéces. Il nous a presque toujours manqué un degré de chaleur; nous avions tout le reste. L'origine de cette langueur, de cette faiblesse monotone, venait en partie de ce petit esprit de galanterie, si cher alors aux courtisans et aux femmes, qui a transformé le théatre en conversations de *Clélie*. Les autres tragédies étaient quelquefois de longs raisonnemens politiques, qui ont gaté *Sertorius*, qui ont rendu *Othon* si froid, et *Suréna* et *Attila* si mauvais. Mais une autre raison empêchait encor qu'on ne déployat un grand patétique sur la scène, et que l'action ne fût vraiment tragique; c'était la construction du théatre, et la mesquinerie du spectacle.... Que pouvait-on faire sur une vingtaine de planches chargées de spectateurs? quelle pompe, quel appareil pouvait parler aux yeux? quelle grande action théatrale pouvait être executée? quelle liberté pouvait avoir l'imagination du poëte? Les piéces devaient être composées de longs récits; c'était des conversations, plutôt qu'une action. Chaque comédien voulait briller par un long monologue; ils rebutaient une piéce qui n'en avait point.... Cette forme excluait toute action théatrale, toutes grandes expressions des passions, ces tableaux frappans des infortunes humaines, ces traits terribles et perçans qui arrachent le cœur; on le touchait, et il falait le déchirer.[1]

Lessing's particular mode of attack thus takes its stand, less on the canons of realism and common sense, than on the refutation of the supercilious and complacent belief of the French (as expressed, for instance, by Voltaire in his Dissertation prefixed to *Sémiramis*) that they had enormously improved upon the crudities of Greek drama. He defends the art of Greek tragedy as a nobler and finer thing than the baroque art of French pseudo-classicism. In so far Lessing represents a healthy reaction—that 'return to the Greeks' which, together with Winckelmann, he had the honour of inaugurating in Germany; his criticism was thus a factor of the first importance in the literary movement of his time. This enormous service may outweigh many deficiencies; but if we wish to regard the criticism of the *Hamburgische Dramaturgie* from an absolute standpoint, we must admit that it does not exonerate Lessing from the lack of impersonal fairness and historical

---

[1] *Des divers changemens arrivés à l'art tragique* in *Contes de Guillaume Vadé, ed. cit.* pp. 204 ff. The passage in St Évremond (which Voltaire does not quote word for word) is to be found in his essay *Sur les Auteurs Tragiques* (1677; *Œuvres*, ed. R. de Planhol, Paris, 1927, i, p. 196); *Sir Politick Would-be, ibid.* ii, pp. 221 ff.; *Les Opéra, ibid.* ii, pp. 137 ff. Of the latter there was a German version in Gottsched's *Deutsche Schaubühne, ed. cit.* ii, pp. 77 ff.

perspective, of ability to take account of and make the right allowance for the ideals and conventions of a particular age.

On other older writers, such as Quinault and Regnard, Lessing is content to quote French opinion; and of Destouches, Marivaux and Nivelle de la Chaussée at a later time—writers who had been living influences in his own experience and might well have tempted him to express opinions—he has little to say of his own. He reserves his main attack for Voltaire; and unfair as may be his brilliant hoisting of Voltaire 'with his own petard', when he turns on him that raillery which the French poet had, with still greater injustice, turned on the Greeks and on Shakespeare, we have to admit that there emerges from the pages of his work a dramatic, living image of Voltaire, which has something of the virtue of a creation. Voltaire stands out as the most interesting personality in the pages of the *Dramaturgie*; how far Lessing's portrait is a true one, how far a caricature inspired by personal animosity, the reader will have had little difficulty in discerning.

On the quite modern drama of France Lessing's criticism is still more disappointing. For here, too, he had a mission. If he believed that pseudo-classicism had to go, it was because he saw the salvation of the modern drama of Europe in that new art for which Diderot had been largely responsible in France. But alas, of Diderot, on whom no one in Germany was better able to speak with authority than Lessing at that time, he has practically nothing to say. If only *Der Hausvater* had appeared on the Hamburg repertory at an earlier date, it might have been different. The one serious modern French tragedy which Lessing had occasion to discuss, De Belloy's *Zelmire*, did not suggest to him the possibility of analysing the movement of ideas in France; perhaps, indeed, he was so averse to the alexandrine tragedy in any form that he refused to accept such an augury for developments in the new generation of French dramatists—or, for that matter, in Voltaire himself.

In the end, Lessing was more interested in questions of theory, in the technique of dramatic art, in the relations of different versions of the same theme, in translations and adaptations, than in the concrete question of the intrinsic values of individual plays. The problem of æsthetic value *per se* was always a subordinate one.

CHAPTER VII

THE ENGLISH DRAMA

No play was performed on the Hamburg stage in the period covered by Lessing's *Hamburgische Dramaturgie* which was not of German or French origin. Thus the present and succeeding chapters of this part are not concerned, as are their predecessors, with actual theatre criticism by Lessing; it may be a convenience, however, to the student of Lessing's work to have collected together under the headings of English, Italian, Spanish and Classical drama, such opinions and judgments as he expressed on the dramatic writers of these literatures.

SHAKESPEARE

On no aspect of Lessing's critical activity has opinion been so much at variance as on his attitude to Shakespeare. Among the older critics there was a tendency to lay excessive weight on his significance as a prophet of our English poet; this was regarded as the touchstone of his fair-mindedness and universality; and the *Hamburgische Dramaturgie* was held up as a milestone in the appreciation of Shakespeare on the continent—as of course in a large measure it was. This was the first time that a classically minded critic pinning his faith to Aristotle—no irresponsible rebel or unbalanced enthusiast—had broken a lance for Shakespeare; Lessing's defence of the English poet penetrated to circles that had hitherto only seen him with Voltairean eyes. This was the invaluable contribution which Lessing made to the appreciation of Shakespeare. Nothing that he said made a deeper impression on the world than his paradoxical assertion in the *Litteraturbriefe* (see below, p. 247, and cp. *Dramaturgie*, LXXXI, 140) that Shakespeare was a more faithful observer of the laws of Aristotle than Corneille. It was perhaps the most widely influential of all Lessing's critical dogmas; it was the greatest argument for the much debated validity of Shakespeare which the eighteenth century had to offer; and it enthroned Aristotle as a law-giver for all time, and not for Greek drama alone. But the mental attitude involved in this brave assertion in respect of Shakespeare must not be overlooked. If Lessing found him worthy of a place beside Sophocles, it was because he found it possible to fit him into Aristotle's theoretical conception of tragic poetry; in other words, he would admit Shakespeare to the number of the great immortals because he could be proved to be a good Aristotelian; the case is not, as we should prefer to put it now-a-days, that Aristotle is a universal theorist of tragedy because his definition of it is wide enough to include Shakespeare. Lessing's claim for Shakespeare's essential obedience to the Aristotelian law is rather an intuition than a reasoned conclusion. He is not prepared—even in his discussion of *Richard III*, where the reader most feels the need of it—to defend his view by logical argument. In the end, we have to accept his belief less as a tribute to Aristotle than as a proof of his own sensitive judgment on dramatic poetry.

The facts of Lessing's interest in Shakespeare prior to the *Dramaturgie* may be briefly recapitulated here.[1] The earliest mention of him in Lessing's writings is to be found in the preface to the *Beyträge zur Historie und Aufnahme des Theaters*, where, with obviously no knowledge that went beyond the translation of *Julius Caesar*, by Caspar Wilhelm von Borck (1741),[2] he brackets Shakespeare with Restoration and more recent English dramatists:

> Shakespear, Dryden, Wicherley, Vanbrugh, Cibber, Congreve sind Dichter, die man fast bey uns nur dem Namen nach kennet, und gleichwohl verdienen sie unsere Hochachtung sowohl als die gepriesenen französischen Dichter....Das ist gewiss, wollte der Deutsche in der dramatischen Poesie seinem eignen Naturelle folgen, so würde unsre Schaubühne mehr der englischen als französischen gleichen.[3]

In the *Theatralische Bibliothek*, as has been seen,[4] Lessing translated a considerable part of Dryden's *Essay of Dramatic Poesy*. His version of the famous passage on Shakespeare is as follows:

> Shakespear...war von allen neuern, und vielleicht auch alten Dichtern derjenige, der den ausgebreitesten, uneingeschränktesten Geist hatte. Alle

---

[1] Cp. M. Joachimi-Dege, *Deutsche Shakespeare-Probleme im 18. Jahrhundert und im Zeitalter der Romantik*, Leipzig, 1907, pp. 19 ff.; F. Gundolf, *Shakespeare und der deutsche Geist*, Berlin, 1920, pp. 105 ff.; A. Böhtlingk, *Lessing und Shakespeare (Shakespeare und unsere Klassiker* I), Leipzig, 1909 (unsatisfactory and misleading); F. W. Meisnest, *Lessing und Shakespeare* in *Publications of the Modern Language Association of America*, xix (1904), pp. 234 ff.; G. Kettner, *Lessing und Shakespeare* in *Neue Jahrbücher für das klassische Altertum, Geschichte und deutsche Literatur und für Pädagogik*, xix (1907), pp. 267 ff.

[2] Lessing's dramatic fragment *Samuel Henzi* (1749) may show some slight influence of *Julius Caesar*. (E. Schmidt, *Lessing*, 4th ed. Berlin, 1923, i, p. 210, and H. Hettner, *Geschichte der deutschen Literatur im 18. Jahrhundert*, Braunschweig, 1893–4, ii, p. 455, suggest that Lessing was influenced rather by Otway's *Venice Preserv'd*.)

[3] *Schriften*, iv, pp. 52 f. See above, pp. 96 f.   [4] See above, pp. 113 f.

Bilder der Natur waren ihm stets gegenwärtig, und er schilderte sie nicht sowohl mühsam als glücklich; er mag beschreiben was er will, man sieht es nicht bloss, man fühlt es so gar. Die ihm Schuld geben, dass es ihm an Gelehrsamkeit gefehlt habe, erheben ihn um so viel mehr; er war gelehrt, ohne es geworden zu seyn; er brauchte nicht die Brillen der Bücher, um in der Natur zu lesen; er blickte in sich selbst, und da fand er sie.[1]

The high claim made by Dryden for Shakespeare, and his criticism of Corneille, probably alone emboldened Lessing to write the seventeenth of the *Litteraturbriefe* (February 16, 1759). This letter—which anticipated by a year a similar claim for the superiority of Shakespeare to Corneille published in the *Journal encyclopédique*[2]—is the most daring appreciation of Shakespeare to be found in any German writer before the 'Sturm und Drang'. There is, indeed, nothing in Lessing's later writings which goes beyond the claims he makes here:

Wenn man die Meisterstücke des Shakespear, mit einigen bescheidenen Veränderungen, unsern Deutschen übersetzt hätte, ich weiss gewiss, es würde von bessern Folgen gewesen seyn, als dass man sie mit dem Corneille und Racine so bekannt gemacht hat....Auch nach den Mustern der Alten die Sache zu entscheiden, ist Shakespear ein weit grösserer tragischer Dichter als Corneille; obgleich dieser die Alten sehr wohl, und jener fast gar nicht gekannt hat. Corneille kömmt ihnen in der mechanischen Einrichtung, und Shakespear in dem Wesentlichen näher. Der Engländer erreicht den Zweck der Tragödie fast immer, so sonderbare und ihm eigene Wege er auch wählet; und der Franzose erreicht ihn fast niemals, ob er gleich die gebahnten Wege der Alten betritt.[3]

Shakespeare has no place in his controversy with Mendelssohn and Nicolai on the nature of tragedy, a controversy which took place at a time when Lessing was most actively interested in dramatic theory. In the *Laokoon*, however, our poet is quoted to illustrate Lessing's views on the æsthetic use of the ugly and the repulsive.[4]

It might thus be expected that the *Dramaturgie* would give Lessing his opportunity. But what strikes the modern reader is not that he takes advantage of this opportunity; but how little he has to say, and how much he has left unsaid.

First we may pass in review what the *Dramaturgie* contains on the

---

[1] *Schriften*, vi, p. 288.
[2] *Parallèle entre Shakespear et Corneille traduit de l'Anglois*, October 15, 1760, pp. 100 ff.
[3] *Schriften*, viii, p. 43.   [4] *Schriften*, ix, pp. 141 ff.

subject of Shakespeare. Since Lessing's appeal for a translation of the poet in the *Litteraturbriefe*, this hope had been realised. Between 1762 and 1766 Wieland had published in eight volumes *Shakespears theatralische Werke* (Zürich, 1762–66, containing twenty-two plays), and in St. xv (64), while discussing *Zayre*, Lessing breaks a lance for this translation, which had been badly handled by the critics:[1] 'Ich hätte grosse Lust, sehr viel Gutes davon zu sagen. Nicht, um diesen gelehrten Männern zu widersprechen; nicht, um die Fehler zu vertheidigen, die sie darinn bemerkt haben: sondern, weil ich glaube, dass man von diesen Fehlern kein solches Aufheben hätte machen sollen.' And in St. lxix (69 ff.) he quotes a long passage from Wieland's *Agathon*[2] in defence of the mingling of the comic and the tragic in Shakespeare—this poet who (in Wieland's words) 'unter allen Dichtern seit Homer...die Menschen, vom Könige bis zum Bettler, und von Julius Cäsar bis zu Jak Falstaff am besten gekannt, und mit einer Art von unbegreiflicher Intuition durch und durch gesehen hat'.[3]

[1] The reviews which Lessing had in mind were probably that by Weisse in the *Bibliothek der schönen Wissenschaften*, ix (ii) (1763), pp. 257 ff., and that of vols. iv and v of the translation in the *Allgemeine deutsche Bibliothek*, i (i) (1766), p. 300; possibly also H. W. von Gerstenberg's in the *Briefe über die Merkwürdigkeiten der Litteratur*, xiv–xviii, in 1766 (*Deutsche Litteraturdenkmale des 18. u. 19. Jahrhunderts*, xxix; see especially pp. 110 ff. and p. 166). Cp. E. Stadler, *Wielands Shakespeare* (*Quellen und Forschungen*, cvii), Strassburg, 1910, pp. 78 ff. Lessing may have been thinking of Wieland's translation when he wrote (xix, 97) of the 'Zwitterton...der aus den prosaischen Übersetzungen englischer Dichter entstanden ist, in welchen der Gebrauch der kühnsten Tropen und Figuren, ausser einer gebundenen cadensirten Wortfügung, uns an Besoffene denken lässt, die ohne Musik tanzen'.

[2] *Agathon*, which Lessing describes (lxix, 139, 154) as 'unstreitig unter die vortrefflichsten [Werke] unsers Jahrhunderts...der erste und einzige Roman für den denkenden Kopf, von klassischem Geschmacke', appeared in two volumes in 1766–67. His defence of it seems to have been called forth by a review in the *Deutsche Bibliothek*, i (iii) (1768), pp. 11 ff. (see esp. pp. 45 ff.).

[3] Wieland wrote in part ironically, perhaps to defend the lack of plan in his own novel. Lessing might more effectively have quoted Gerstenberg's introduction to his translation *Die Braut, eine Tragödie, von Beaumont und Fletcher. Nebst kritischen und biographischen Abhandlungen über die vier grössten Dichter des ältern brittischen Theaters*, Copenhagen and Leipzig, 1765, pp. 10 f.: '[Der Dichter muss] niemals bey der Absicht stehen bleiben, das menschliche Leben zu malen, sondern es so zu malen, dass der Zuschauer hingerissen werde, zu glauben, er sehe das wahre Werk der Natur, indem die blosse Vorstellung desselben alle Wirkungen auf seine Gesinnungen und Leidenschaften äussert, welche die Natur selbst nicht anders hätte hervorbringen können, als wofern sie in ein dem Zwecke des Dichters untergeordnetes Ganze wäre concentrirt worden. Diess heisst das Pathos in einen Plan ordnen...' (cp. Kettner, *Lessing und Shakespeare*, pp. 280 f.).

In St. LXXXI (137) Shakespeare is coupled with the ancients against the French dramatists: 'ihr Corneille und Racine, ihr Crebillon und Voltaire [haben] von dem wenig oder gar nichts, was den Sophokles zum Sophokles, den Euripides zum Euripides, den Shakespear zum Shakespear macht.'[1] Later on (XCIII, 115 ff.), Lessing quotes in translation a passage from Hurd in praise of the powerfully drawn characters of Shakespeare's comedies[2]—in which, for the rest, he seems to have taken small interest.

The one play of the Hamburg repertory which might have given Lessing an opportunity of speaking at length on Shakespeare was Weisse's *Richard der Dritte*, but there is very little about Shakespeare's tragedy in his comments, unless we may say that much of Lessing's criticism of Weisse has also relevance to the English dramatist. To Weisse's remark in his prefatory note that it might be a merit to plagiarise Shakespeare,[3] Lessing retorts (LXXIII, 81 ff.):

Vorausgesetzt, dass man eines [ein Plagium] an ihm begehen kann. Aber was man von dem Homer gesagt hat, es lasse sich dem Herkules eher seine Keule, als ihm ein Vers abringen, das lässt sich vollkommen auch vom Shakespear sagen. Auf die geringste von seinen Schönheiten ist ein Stämpel gedruckt, welcher gleich der ganzen Welt zuruft: ich bin Shakespears! Und wehe der fremden Schönheit, die das Herz hat, sich neben ihr zu stellen!

Shakespear will studiert, nicht geplündert seyn. Haben wir Genie, so muss uns Shakespear das seyn, was dem Landschaftsmahler die Camera obscura ist: er sehe fleissig hinein, um zu lernen, wie sich die Natur in allen Fällen auf Eine Fläche projektiret; aber er borge nichts daraus.

Ich wüsste auch wirklich in dem ganzen Stücke des Shakespears keine einzige Scene, sogar keine einzige Tirade, die Herr Weiss so hätte brauchen können, wie sie dort ist. Alle, auch die kleinsten Theile beym Shakespear, sind nach den grossen Maassen des historischen Schauspiels zugeschnitten,

---

[1] Young had drawn a parallel between Shakespeare and the ancients; he said: 'Shakespeare is not their Son but Brother; their Equal, and that in spite of all his faults' (*Conjectures on Original Composition, in a letter to the Author of Sir Charles Grandison*, London, 1759, p. 78; in the German translation, *Gedanken über die Original-Werke*, Leipzig, 2nd ed. 1761, p. 67: 'Shakespeare ist nicht ihr Abkömmling, sondern ihr Bruder; und bey allen seinen Fehlern, dennoch ihnen gleich'). In a comment on Euripides in the *Philologischer Nachlass* Lessing writes: 'Man sagt so viel von den Fehlern des Shakespear. Man nenne mir nur Einen, der diesem das Gewicht halte. Von Shakespears Fehlern getraue ich mir fast immer einen Grund angeben zu können. Er begeht sie, um die Hauptsache zu befördern, und die Zuschauer desto lebhafter zu rühren' (*Schriften*, xv, p. 428).

[2] The English text of the whole quotation from Hurd will be found below, pp. 403 ff. [3] See above, p. 152.

und dieses verhält sich zu der Tragödie französischen Geschmacks, ungefehr wie ein weitläuftiges Frescogemählde[1] gegen ein Miniaturbildchen für einen Ring. Was kann man zu diesem aus jenem nehmen, als etwa ein Gesicht, eine einzelne Figur, höchstens eine kleine Gruppe, die man sodann als ein eigenes Ganze ausführen muss? Eben so würden aus einzeln Gedanken beim Shakespear ganze Scenen, und aus einzeln Scenen ganze Aufzüge werden müssen. Denn wenn man den Ermel aus dem Kleide eines Riesen für einen Zwerg recht nutzen will, so muss man ihm nicht wieder einen Ermel, sondern einen ganzen Rock daraus machen.

And he regrets (113) that Weisse had not known *Richard III* when he wrote his own tragedy,[2] for it would have been a mirror in which to see his own faults.

Lessing's argument here about the impossibility of deriving advantage from Shakespeare by imitating him is surely open to question; at the least, it is not clear what he exactly means. He had obviously in mind, however, the following passage from Mendelssohn's review of Wieland's *Clementina von Porretta* in the *Litteraturbriefe*:[3]

Die Einheit der Zeit hat unter der Menge von Begebenheiten [in *Lear*] etwas gelitten, aber wer achtet dieser, wenn das Gemüth ernsthafter beschäftiget, und in beständigen Leidenschaften herumgetrieben wird? Ich gieng also zum Shakespear, um mich Raths zu erholen; allein aller Muth sank mir, als ich dieses vortrefliche Trauerspiel noch einmal las. Was hilft mir der Bogen des Ulysses, wenn ich ihn nicht spannen kann?— Shakespear ist der einzige dramatische Dichter, der es wagen kann, in dem Othello die Eifersucht, und in dem Lear die Raserey, in dem Angesichte des Zuschauers entstehen, wachsen, und bis auf den Gipfel gedeihen zu lassen, ohne sich sogar der Zwischenscenen zu bedienen, um dem Fortgange des Affects einen Ruck zu geben, dem der Zuschauer nicht mit den Augen folgen kann. Wer ist aber kühn genug einem Herkules seine Keule,[4] oder einem Shakespear seine dramatische Kunstgriffe zu entwenden?

[1] Kettner (*loc. cit.* p. 282) recalls Gerstenberg's comparison (*Briefe über Merkwürdigkeiten der Litteratur*, xviii): Wenn er [der Dichter] seine Charaktere nicht gut anzuordnen, ihnen nicht durch die Abstechung eine pittoreske Wirkung zu geben...wenn er die Geschichte nicht mit den stärksten Fresco-Zügen zu treffen weiss, wenn die Zeichnung der Umrisse nicht das Leben selbst athmet: wie will er uns verargen, wenn wir gähnen?' (*Deutsche Litteraturdenkmale*, xxix, p. 160.)

[2] See above, p. 152.

[3] *Litteraturbriefe*, No. cxxiii (Beschluss), August 28, 1760, *ed. cit.* vii, pp. 130 f.; *Gesammelte Schriften, ed. cit.* iv, 2, p. 149.

[4] Tib. Cl. Donatus in his *Vita Virgilii*, 64, makes Vergil answer the charge of borrowing from Homer with the words: 'Cur non illi quoque eadem furta tentarent? Verum intellecturos facilius esse Herculi clavam, quam Homero versum surripere' (cp. Cosack, *op. cit.* p. 340). The passage is quoted in the *Bibliothek der schönen Wissenschaften*, iv (i) 1758, p. 523.

A penetrating appreciation of Shakespeare is to be found in St. xi (76), where the ghost in Voltaire's *Sémiramis* is compared with that in *Hamlet*. This justification of Shakespeare's handling of the supernatural is, in fact, one of the most memorable parts of Lessing's work. The general aspect of the introduction of the supernatural into dramatic poetry I deal with in a later chapter;[1] here it is only a question of Shakespeare's employment of it in *Hamlet*. The comparison of the ghosts in *Sémiramis* and *Hamlet* had been suggested by Voltaire himself, who had defended his own introduction of one (xi, 5) on the ground that all antiquity believed in the existence of ghosts. Moreover he had said:

Les Anglais ne croyent pas assurément plus que les Romains aux revenans; cependant ils voyent tous les jours avec plaisir dans la Tragédie d'*Hamlet*, l'ombre d'un Roi qui paraît sur le Théâtre dans une occasion à peu près semblable à celle où l'on a vû à Paris le spectre de *Ninus*.[2]

The comparison had been frequently discussed before Lessing's time. M. C. Curtius, for instance, had dealt with it in his *Critische Abhandlungen und Gedichte*, Hanover, 1760, and, like Lessing, had disapproved of Voltaire and approved of Shakespeare: the ghost in *Hamlet*, he wrote (*Abhandlung vom Erhabenen in der Dichtkunst*, p. 24), 'hat sonst so viele Schönheiten, dass man dem Dichter für seine Abweichung von den gewöhnlichen Regeln danket'.

As will be seen, Lessing's attitude to the employment of the supernatural had probably been influenced by Du Bos.[3] This source of terror and pathos is by no means closed, he says (xi, 44), to the real poet; for, however sceptically the ordinary man may express himself about ghosts, the seed of a belief in the supernatural is implanted in us all. We may believe what we like in ordinary life, but the poet must have it in his power to make us believe in the theatre what he wishes us to believe (76 ff.):

So ein Dichter ist Shakespear, und Shakespear fast einzig und allein. Vor seinem Gespenste im Hamlet richten sich die Haare zu Berge, sie mögen ein gläubiges oder ungläubiges Gehirn bedecken....Shakespears Gespenst kömmt wirklich aus jener Welt; so dünkt uns. Denn es kömmt zu der feyerlichen Stunde, in der schaudernden Stille der Nacht, in der vollen Begleitung aller der düstern, geheimnissvollen Nebenbegriffe, wenn und mit welchen wir, von der Amme an, Gespenster zu erwarten und zu denken gewohnt sind....Beym Shakespear ist es der einzige Hamlet, mit

---

[1] See below, pp. 445 ff.
[2] *Œuvres, ed. cit.* ix, p. 26. See below, p. 446.
[3] See below, pp. 446 f.

dem sich das Gespenst einlässt;[1] in der Scene, wo die Mutter dabei ist, wird es von der Mutter weder gesehen noch gehört. Alle unsere Beobachtung geht also auf ihn, und je mehr Merkmale eines von Schauder und Schrecken zerrütteten Gemüths wir an ihm entdecken, desto bereitwilliger sind wir, die Erscheinung, welche diese Zerrüttung in ihm verursacht, für eben das zu halten, wofür er sie hält. Das Gespenst wirket auf uns, mehr durch ihn, als durch sich selbst. Der Eindruck, den es auf ihn macht, gehet in uns über, und die Wirkung ist zu augenscheinlich und zu stark, als dass wir an der ausserordentlichen Ursache zweifeln sollten.

Again, Lessing no doubt remembered Mendelssohn's review of J. Adolf Schlegel's translation of Batteux in the *Litteraturbriefe*:

Je grösser die Gewalt ist, mit welcher der Dichter durch die Poesie in unsere Einbildungskraft würkt, desto mehr äusserliche Action kann er sich erlauben, ohne der Poesie Abbruch zu thun, desto mehr muss er anwenden, wenn er die Täuschungen seiner Poesie mächtig genug unterstützen will. Sie kennen den Shakespear. Sie wissen wie eigenmächtig er die Phantasie der Zuschauer gleichsam tyrannisirt, und wie leicht er sie, fast spielend, aus einer Leidenschaft, aus einer Illusion in die andere wirft. Aber wie viel Ungereimtheiten, wie viel mit den Regeln streitendes übersiehet man ihm auch in der äusserlichen Action, und wie wenig merkts der Zuschauer, dessen ganze Aufmerksamkeit auf eine andere Seite beschäftiget ist!... Wer ist in England noch der incredulus gewesen, der an der Erscheinung des Geists im Hamlet gezweiffelt hätte?...Wer das Gemüth so zu erhitzen, und in einen solchen Taumel von Leidenschaften zu stürzen weis, als Shakespear, der hat die Achtsamkeit seines Zuschauers gleichsam gefesselt, und kann es wagen, vor dessen geblendeten Augen die abendtheurlichsten Handlungen vorgehen zu lassen, ohne zu befahren, dass solches den Betrug stöhren werde. Ein nicht so grosser Geist aber, der uns auf der Bühne noch Sinne und Bewusstseyn lässt, ist alle Augenblick in Gefahr, Ungläubige anzutreffen....[2]

In another review—of Klopstock's *Der Tod Adams*—Mendelssohn refers to the 'panischen Schrecken, den die Engländer dem Geiste im Hamlet nachzurühmen pflegen'.[3] Behind these passages stands, doubtless, the passage in the *Spectator*, No. xliv; I quote it in Frau Gottsched's translation:[4]

Die Erscheinung eines Geistes im Hamlet ist ein Meisterstück in seiner Art, und mit allen Umständen begleitet, welche entweder Aufmerksamkeit, oder Grausen hervor bringen können. Das Gemüth des Zuschauers ist durch die vorhergehenden Reden vortrefflich vorbereitet, dasselbe zu

---

[1] This, of course, is not the case in the opening scene.

[2] *Litteraturbriefe*, No. lxxxiv, February 14, 1760, *ed. cit.* v, pp. 111 f.; *Gesammelte Schriften*, *ed. cit.* iv, 2, pp. 16 f.

[3] *Bibliothek der schönen Wissenschaften*, ii (i) (1757), p. 219 (quoted by L. Goldstein, *op. cit.* p. 178).   [4] *Der Zuschauer* (2nd ed.), Leipzig, 1750, i, pp. 209 f.

empfangen. Sein stummes Bezeigen bey seinem ersten Auftritte rührt die Einbildungskraft überaus sehr: aber je öfter es hernach wiederkömmt, desto schrecklicher wird es. Wer kann wohl die Rede, ohne Zittern, lesen, womit es der junge Hamlet anredet.... Ich finde keinen Fehler in oberwähnten Kunstgriffen, wenn sie nur geschicklich angebracht werden, und von gehörigen Gedanken und Worten begleitet, zum Vorscheine kommen.

It is significant that both these discussions of Shakespeare by Lessing were to some extent suggested by Mendelssohn; among Lessing's many intellectual debts to his friend, his sympathetic appreciation of Shakespeare may well have been one.

The other references to Shakespeare in the *Dramaturgie* are slight and sporadic. In St. v (55) Hamlet's instruction to the actors (Act III, sc. ii: 'Speak the speech, I pray you,' etc.) is quoted, apparently in Lessing's own translation.[1] The claim is made for Shakespeare (47) that he had reflected the more deeply on this art 'because he had much less genius for it'.[2] Rowe, whose biography of Shakespeare was used and partly translated by Wieland, seems to have been responsible for the opinion that he was an indifferent actor; or Lessing may have drawn his information from Baker's *Companion to the Playhouse*.[3] In St. VII (72, 85), Quin's acting as Falstaff,[4] and as the king in *Hamlet*, is mentioned; and also Garrick's performance in *Hamlet*, with a quotation (89) of the familiar passage in *Tom Jones* descriptive of Partridge's visit to the play.[5]

---

[1] See below, p. 481.

[2] Pope, in the preface to his edition of Shakespeare, had found a reason for the poet's lapses from good taste in the fact that he was an actor (*Works of Shakespear*, ed. Pope and Warburton, London, 1747, i, p. xxxiv). This preface appeared in Wieland's translation (cp. *Wielands Gesammelte Schriften*, ed. E. Stadler, IIte Abt., i (Berlin, 1909), p. 4).

[3] [D. E. Baker], *Companion to the Playhouse*, London, 1764, ii (art. Shakespeare): 'His first Admission into the Play-house was suitable to his Appearance; a Stranger, and ignorant of the Art, he was glad to be taken into the Company in a very mean Rank; nor did his Performance recommend him to any distinguished Notice. —The Part of an under Actor neither engaged nor deserved his Attention.' (See also R. Farmer, *Essay on the Learning of Shakespeare*, Cambridge, 1767, p. 37, and cp. *Shakespears theatralische Werke* in *Wielands Gesammelte Schriften, ed. cit.* IIte Abt., iii, p. 563. Petersen (*ed. cit.* p. 184) also refers to J. E. Schmidt, *Shakespeares Dramen und sein Schauspielerberuf*, Berlin, 1914.)

[4] Falstaff is mentioned again in St. LXIX, 72 together with *Julius Caesar*; *Othello* in St. LXXIV, 123—both in quotations.

[5] Lessing quotes from the *Historie des menschlichen Herzens, nach den Abwechselungen der Tugenden und Laster in den sonderbaren Begebenheiten Thomas Jones, eines Fündlings, Moralisch und satyrisch beschrieben. Aus dem Englischen.* Hamburg, 1750–55 (reprinted 1758–59), Bk. xvi, ch. v (Teil vi, pp. 42 f. in ed. of 1758–59). There is a

In St. xv (29) after quoting Sainte Albine's statement: 'Die Liebe selbst hat Voltairen die Zayre diktirt', Lessing contravenes it by reference to *Romeo and Juliet* (see above, p. 209); and he proceeds (48) to compare *Zayre* with its alleged model, *Othello*. Compared with Shakespeare's Moor, he asserts, Voltaire's hero is but a figure without life.[1]

There is thus no systematic criticism of Shakespeare in the *Dramaturgie*, and no comprehensive statement of Lessing's opinion of him. But of Shakespeare's genius Lessing had no doubts, even if he considered that genius an untutored one. The primitiveness of Shakespeare's art was an eighteenth-century dogma beyond which even Lessing could not advance. But this very quality made him the more apt an example with which to confront the vaunted masters of the modern French theatre, who were, in Lessing's view, far inferior to him in the faithful reproduction of nature and life. The great virtues of Shakespeare for Lessing were his realism—producing a complete illusion in the spectator—and his power of 'moving' us, of fulfilling the sole end of tragedy, which is to arouse 'Mitleid', or compassion.[2]

BEN JONSON

The only other older English dramatist who receives any attention in the *Dramaturgie* is Ben Jonson, and that chiefly in respect of the meaning of the English word 'humour'.[3] In the long extracts translated from Hurd (xcii, 35–xcv, 80) mention is made of *Every Man out of his Humour* (xciii, 46 ff.), and this gives Lessing occasion for a note of more than a page on the meaning of the title. He claims to have been the first to render 'humour' by 'Laune' (93), presumably in his translation of Dryden's *Essay of Dramatic Poesy* in his *Theatralische*

reference to 'der Barbier, Partridge im Tom Jones, wenn er den Hamlet zum erstenmale vorstellen sieht,' in the *Litteraturbriefe*, No. ccv, December 24, 1761, *ed. cit.* xii, p. 347.

[1] Lessing may have remembered Gerstenberg's comparison of Young's *Revenge* with *Othello* (*Briefe über Merkwürdigkeiten der Litteratur*, xv, *ed. cit.* p. 115): 'Young betrachtete die Natur des Eifersüchtigen von einer Seite, von der sie dem Herzen Schauder, Entsetzen und Mitleiden abdringen sollte.—Schakespear bemühte sich, ihre feinsten Nuancen zu entwickeln, und ihre verborgenste Mechanik aufzudecken' (quoted by Kettner, *loc. cit.* p. 287).

[2] See Kettner, *loc. cit.* p. 285.

[3] Ben Jonson's name is also mentioned xv, 135; lix, 119; Randolph's *Muses Looking-Glasse* is referred to in xciii, 79 (in a quotation from Hurd). On Daniel's *Philotas*, see below, p. 263.

Bibliothek: 'Ich erinnere zugleich, dass ich H u m o r, wo ich das Wort übersetzen will, durch L a u n e gebe, weil ich nicht glaube, dass man ein bequemers in der ganzen deutschen Sprache finden wird.'[1] He now withdraws this rendering as inadequate. 'Laune' can become 'Humor'; except, however, in this particular case, 'humour' is never 'Laune'. He had been misled (xciii, 99) by the fact that the French 'humeur' was rendered by 'Laune'. In Voltaire's 'Lettre à Mr. l'Abbé d'Olivet' of August 20, 1761, published in the *Journal encyclopédique* of October 1 of the same year, he no doubt read the following passage (pp. 116 f.):

Ils [les Anglais] ont un terme pour signifier cette plaisanterie, ce vrai comique, cette gaité, cette urbanité, ces saillies, qui échappent à un homme sans qu'il s'en doute; et ils rendent cette idée par le mot *humeur, humour,* qu'ils prononcent *yumor;* ils croyent qu'ils ont seuls cette humeur, et que les autres Nations n'ont point de terme pour exprimer ce caractère d'esprit.[2]

Jonson's two plays, *Every Man in his Humour* and *Every Man out of his Humour*, which Lessing evidently had before him, drew his attention to the different significance of the word, and he quotes lines 111–20 from the Induction to the latter (52 ff.). 'I have', he says (89), 'industriously collected examples which I should like to be able to arrange in order, simply to correct an error which has become fairly general.' Of this collection we have no trace, however, except a single note on Xenophon's *Cyropædia* in his *Philologischer Nachlass*:

Der Charakter des Artabazus hat mich nicht wenig befremdet, weil ich mir nichts weniger vermuthete, als bey einem Alten einen Charakter anzutreffen, der vollkommen das Individuelle hat, was die Engländer Humor nennen.[3]

The chief English source of Lessing's remarks (63 ff.) on humour as 'affectation', on the impossibility of true humour as a subject of comedy, on the absence of any trace of 'humour' in classical drama (although it is present now and then in the ancient historians and orators, when historical truth or the explanation of a certain fact demands this exact description καθ' ἕκαστον (84 ff.)), would seem to be Dryden.[4]

[1] *Theatralische Bibliothek*, iv, p. 122; *Schriften*, vi, p. 291.
[2] Voltaire's interest in the word was probably awakened by the Abbé le Blanc's *Lettres d'un François*, La Haye, 1745 (see letter xii, vol. i, pp. 114 ff.).
[3] *Schriften*, xv, pp. 430 f.
[4] Cp. Dryden's Essay in Lessing's translation (*Theatralische Bibliothek*, iv, pp. 122 ff.; *Schriften*, vi, pp. 291 ff.): 'Die Alten hatten in ihren Lustspielen sehr wenig

ENGLISH DRAMA AT THE BEGINNING OF THE EIGHTEENTH CENTURY

Lessing had had the intention of dealing with the life of Dryden in his *Theatralische Bibliothek*,[1] but beyond a few introductory words to the *Versuch über die dramatische Poesie*, this plan did not materialise. In the *Dramaturgie* Dryden is mentioned (VII, 126) as a master in the art of writing epilogues; and again (XV, 135) as one of the English poets who put rhyming verses at the end of their acts. His *All for Love* is referred to in the passage which Lessing translates here (96) from Voltaire's second 'Lettre à M. Fakener', prefixed to his *Zayre*:

> Vous aviez une coûtume à laquelle Mr. *Addisson*, le plus sage de vos Ecrivains, s'est asservi lui-même; tant l'usage tient lieu de raison et de loi. Cette coûtume peu raisonnable était de finir chaque Acte par des vers d'un goût différent du reste de la piéce, et ces vers devaient nécessairement renfermer une comparaison. *Phèdre* en sortant du Théâtre se comparait poëtiquement à une biche, *Caton* à un rocher, *Cléopatre* à des enfans qui pleurent jusqu'à ce qu'ils soient endormis.
>
> Le Traducteur de *Zayre* est le premier qui ait osé maintenir les droits de la Nature contre un goût si éloigné d'elle. Il a proscrit cet usage; il a senti que la passion doit parler un langage vrai, et que le Poëte doit se cacher toujours pour ne laisser paraître que le Héros.[2]

In this statement Lessing finds three 'untruths'. It is true that the English poets from Shakespeare on, and perhaps farther back, end their blank verse acts with a couple of rhymed lines; but that these always contain similes is false. Secondly, every act of Hill's *Zara* ends with rhymed verses, although they do not contain similes; and lastly, there is no evidence that Hill set an example that was followed in

davon'; and 'Bey den Engländern aber ist es ganz anders, die unter H u m o r irgend eine ausschweifende Gewohnheit, Leidenschaft oder Neigung verstehen, die... einer Person eigenthümlich ist, und durch deren Seltsamkeit sie sich sogleich von allen übrigen Menschen unterscheidet' (pp. 122, 123 f.; *Schriften*, vi, pp. 291 f.).

[1] See above, pp. 107, 113 f.

[2] *Œuvres, ed. cit.* viii, pp. 21 f. The source of Voltaire's information is unknown. The plays which he mentions can hardly be other than *Phædra and Hippolitus* by Edmund Smith, *Cato* by Addison and *All for Love* by Dryden. But if so, the statement seems only correct of the last: Act III of *All for Love* closes, as Cosack has pointed out (*op. cit.* p. 111), with the words:

> 'There I till death will his unkindness weep,
> As harmless infants moan themselves asleep.'

In the other two plays, similes in rhymed verse occur at the end of Acts I, II and III, but in no case do they correspond to Voltaire's description.

England. Where Lessing's superior knowledge came from it is difficult to say; he may have based his statement on the fact that final rhymed lines (but usually more than two) occur in the plays of some of the English dramatists to whom he alludes in the *Dramaturgie*—Otway, Lee, Addison, Rowe, or James Thomson.

For Addison Lessing expresses a temperate admiration. He is 'ein guter Kopf' (xvii, 76), although not, as Voltaire's reference to him might appear to suggest, the 'wisest' of English poets (xv, 112). Sagacity, however, Lessing is willing to grant him—a sagacity which might well endear him to the French (xv, 118). It is this quality which (in spite of the fact that he is not by nature a dramatist) enables him to write plays that have some—though not the highest—dramatic virtues (xvii, 76 ff.). But even twenty Addisons, Lessing adds (xvii, 81), could not make the conventional regularity of French drama acceptable to English taste: 'Begnüge sich damit, wer keine höhere Schönheiten kennet!' In the same section (xvii, 5 ff.) Lessing begins a discussion of Gresset's *Sidnei* by objecting to the idea that this piece would be more popular in London than in Paris. He finds the play un-English: Sidnei does not act quickly enough, he philosophises too much before taking a decisive step, too little afterwards; his remorse is too much like timorousness and that his French servant should so mislead him might well be considered a disgrace to him. But such considerations, Lessing continues, would not affect the reception of *Sidnei* in Germany: 'wir mögen eine Raserey gern mit ein wenig Philosophie bemänteln' (14).

There are one or two allusions in the *Dramaturgie* to continental criticisms of the mixture of comic and serious elements in English drama. While Lessing quotes with approval Thomson's condemnation of the comic epilogues appended to English tragedies,[1] he breaks a lance for Banks's introduction of a box on the ear in *Essex*,[2] and to the imagined reproach: 'wie englisch, wie unanständig!' he retorts by pointing to *Le Cid*.

In a discussion of Colman's adaptation of Voltaire's *L'Écossaise*,[3] Lessing notes the fact that this adaptation has not enough action to please English critics, who prefer Colman's other plays (xii, 112). He is quick to seize on the differences between English and German taste. The English favour a complicated plot; Germans prefer a simpler dramatic action, which can be grasped more easily; while

---

[1] See below, pp. 261 f. [2] See below, pp. 267 f.
[3] See below, pp. 259 f.

the English have to add episodes to French pieces to make them acceptable, Germans have to strip English plays of these. The best English comedies, those of a Congreve or a Wycherley—it will be noticed that Shakespeare (in whose comedies Lessing, like most of his contemporaries, took little interest) is not included here—are instanced (XII, 131) as plays which would be intolerable on the German stage without the excision of their all too luxuriant growths.[1] English tragedies, on the other hand—and again he is thinking, not of Shakespeare, but of *The Merchant of London*, *The Gamester*, *Venice Preserv'd*, *The Orphan*—are not so difficult to accept; they are less complicated, and some have been successful in Germany even without alteration.

AARON HILL

Voltaire's *Zayre* was translated into English by Aaron Hill, 'himself a dramatic poet, not of the worst kind' (xv, 87).[2] The performance of this translation at Drury Lane (xvi, 1 ff.) is discussed by Voltaire in his second *Lettre à M. Fakener*:

L'art de déclamer était chez vous un peu hors de la nature; la plûpart de vos Acteurs tragiques s'exprimaient souvent plus en Poëtes saisis d'enthousiasme, qu'en hommes que la passion inspire. Beaucoup de Comédiens avaient encor outré ce défaut; ils déclamaient des vers ampoulés, avec une fureur et une impétuosité, qui est au beau naturel, ce que des convulsions sont à l'égard d'une démarche noble et aisée.[3]

Voltaire had also referred to the actors at this performance (xvi, 24):

Une nouveauté qui va paraître plus singulière aux Français, c'est qu'un Gentilhomme de votre pays, qui a de la fortune et de la considération, n'a pas dédaigné de jouer sur votre Théâtre le rôle d'*Orosmane*. C'était un spectacle assez intéressant de voir les deux principaux personnages remplis, l'un par un homme de condition, et l'autre par une jeune Actrice de dix-huit ans, qui n'avait pas encor récité un vers en sa vie. Cet exemple d'un Citoyen, qui a fait usage de son talent pour la déclamation, n'est pas le premier parmi vous. Tout ce qu'il y a de surprenant en cela, c'est que

---

[1] Lessing is perhaps thinking here of his own experiments in translating Wycherley and Congreve in earlier years; *The Country Wife* and *The Double Dealer* attracted his interest then. See E. Schmidt, *ed. cit.* i, pp. 127 f.

[2] Aaron Hill (1685–1750) was manager of Drury Lane in 1709. He wrote some sixteen plays, of which four were adaptations of tragedies by Voltaire. See H. L. Bruce, *Voltaire on the English stage*, Berkeley, Cal., 1918 (University of California Publications in Modern Philology, VIII, i), pp. 23 ff.

[3] *Œuvres, ed. cit.* viii, p. 19.

nous nous en étonnions. Nous devrions faire réflexion, que toutes les choses de ce monde dépendent de l'usage et de l'opinion. La Cour de France a dansé sur le Théâtre avec les Acteurs de l'Opéra; et on n'a rien trouvé en cela d'étrange, sinon que la mode de ces divertissemens ait fini. Pourquoi sera-t-il plus étonnant de réciter que de danser en public? Y a-t-il d'autre différence entre ces deux Arts, sinon que l'un est autant au-dessus de l'autre, que les talens où l'esprit à quelque part sont au-dessus de ceux du corps?[1]

Lessing supplements this information (xvi, 6 ff.) by turning to Hill's *Dramatic Works*, London, 1760.[2] Here he found (ii, p. 26):

Thus, *confirmed* in my sentiments, I ventured on the *cast* of two *capital* characters, into hands, *not disabled*, by custom, and obstinate prejudice, from pursuing the *plain track*, of NATURE. It was easy to induce OSMAN (as he is a relation of my own, and *but too fond* of the amusement) to make trial, *how far* his delight, in an art, I shall never allow him to *practise*, might enable him to supply *one* part of the proof, that, to *imitate Nature*, we must proceed, *upon natural principles*. At the same time, it happened, that Mrs CIBBER[3] was, fortunately, inclinable to exert her inimitable talent, in *additional* aid of my purpose, with view to *continue* the *practice* of a profession, for which, her *person*, her *voice*, the unaffected *sensibility* of her *heart*, (and, her *face*, so finely dispos'd, for *assuming*, and *expressing*, the PASSIONS) have, so naturally, qualify'd her.

GEORGE COLMAN

Voltaire, as we have seen,[4] had given out his *Écossaise* as a translation from 'the English of Hume'—not the historian and philosopher, but 'another of this name who had made a name with the tragedy *Douglas*' (xii, 66). *L'Écossaise* was translated into English in 1760; and again in 1767 it was adapted for the English stage, under the title of *The English Merchant*, by George Colman the elder (1732–94), whom Lessing characterises (90) as 'unquestionably now their best comic

---

[1] *Ibid.* pp. 20 f. Voltaire published in the first edition an *Épitre à Mlle. Gossin*, a young actress who had represented Zaïre with great success.

[2] Not to the separate edition of *The Tragedy of Zara*, London, 1736. This inference may be drawn from the four lines which Lessing quotes from Hill's prologue (xv, 81); in the original edition the reading is 'his tragic pile', not 'this tragic pile'.

[3] Mrs Cibber was not, as Lessing says (xvi, 17), the wife of Colley Cibber, but of his son Theophilus. It may be added that Hill's nephew, who played 'Osman', was severely handled by the critics and abandoned his part to a professional actor. Cp. H. L. Bruce, *op. cit.* p. 25.

[4] See above, p. 226.

poet'.[1] He then turns to Colman's translation and to the English criticisms of it, in order to show how indifferently Voltaire had succeeded in reproducing English conditions. He quotes (93–112) arguments drawn from the *Monthly Review* of March, 1767:[2]

Monsieur de Voltaire, though he lived some time in England, has forgot, or knowingly neglected, our customs; and has introduced his Heroine in *L'Ecossaise*, lodging at a Coffee-house. There are many other oversights in his play, which our English Author has altered with great judgment. Among the many changes he has made with success, the addition of literary conceit, to the pride and insolence of *Lady Alton*, has raised her character to a pitch of ridicule, which is wanted in the original, and naturally accounts for the mischievous alliance between her and *Spatter*. The worthy Mrs. *Goodman* is very judiciously put in the place of *Fabrice*, the master of Voltaire's *Coffee-house*; and her being settled so well, and properly, by the benevolence of *Freeport*, connects and brings together the *Dramatis Personæ*, much more easily and naturally than in the original French. . . . [Mr Colman's] diction is pure, spirited and unaffected, or, in one word, *natural*; his wit and sentiments are always subordinate to the characters; without which indeed both would be impertinent.

Lessing also refers (113) to Colman's other pieces, of which *The Jealous Wife* ' was formerly seen here in the Ackermann theatre'.[3]

JAMES THOMSON

James Thomson, for whose dramatic work Lessing had so strangely warm an admiration, receives some attention in connexion with the question of prologues and epilogues (VII, 66). In Lessing's translation

[1] Cp. Diderot's comment in his *Réflexions sur Térence*: 'M. Colman, le meilleur auteur comique que l'Angleterre ait aujourd'hui, a donné, il y a quelques années, une très-bonne traduction de Térence' (*Œuvres Complètes, ed. cit.* v, p. 237. There would seem to be some confusion as to the date (1762) under which the *Réflexions* are here printed, since Colman's translation of Terence appeared in 1765. See below, p. 319).

[2] Vol. xxxvi, pp. 224 f., 229.

[3] *The Jealous Wife* (1761) was translated by J. J. C. Bode: *Die eifersüchtige Ehefrau*, ein Lustspiel in fünf Aufzügen. Aus dem Englischen durch B**. Hamburg, 1764. It was produced by Ackermann in Hamburg in 1765 (F. L. W. Meyer, *op. cit.* ii, 2, p. 54) and under the present management was revived on September 2, 7, November 9, 1768, January 23, and February 28, 1769. Cp. J. Wihan, *J. J. Ch. Bode als Vermittler englischer Geisteswerke in Deutschland* (Prager Deutsche Studien, III), Prague, 1906, pp. 25 ff. (where an earlier edition, published at Hamburg in 1762, is mentioned as being inaccessible to the author). A copy of the 1764 edition is in the British Museum.

of the Life of Thomson from Th. Cibber's *Lives of the Poets of Great
Britain and Ireland*, published in the *Theatralische Bibliothek*, there is
a passage referring to the posthumous production of Thomson's
Coriolanus[1]:

Der Prologus war von dem Herrn George Lyttleton verfertiget
worden, und von dem Herrn Quin wurde er gehalten, welches einen sehr
glücklichen Eindruck auf die Zuhörer machte. Herr Quin war ein
besond[r]er Freund des Herrn Thomson gewesen, und als er folgende
Zeilen, die an und für sich selbst sehr zärtlich sind, aussprach, stellten sich
seiner Einbildungskraft auf einmal alle Annehmlichkeiten des mit ihm
lange gepflogenen Umganges dar, und wahrhafte Thränen flossen über
seine Wangen.

> He lov'd his friends (forgive this gushing tear:
> Alas! I feel i [*sic*] am no actor here)
> He lov'd his friends with such a warmth of heart,
> So clear of int'rest, so devoid of art,
> Such generous freedom, such unshaken zeal,
> No words can speak it, but our tears may tell.

This passage seems to have made an impression on Lessing, for he
returns to it in his preface to the translation of Thomson's dramas
published in 1756.[2] There is also an apparent echo of it in the Epilogue
to the opening performance in Hamburg (VI, 132). It might be added
that Lessing's discussion of Prologue and Epilogue as they are to be
found in English plays (VII, 99 ff.) gives the impression of being in the
main a deduction from his reading of those attached to Thomson's
dramas.[3] The reference here (119) is to the sentiments expressed in
the Epilogue to *Agamemnon*:

> Our bard, to modern epilogue a foe,
> Thinks such mean mirth but deadens generous woe;
> Dispels in idle air the moral sigh,
> And wipes the tender tear from pity's eye:
> No more with social warmth the bosom burns;
> But all th'unfeeling selfish man returns.[4]

and in that to *Tancred and Sigismunda*:

> Hence with your flippant epilogue, that tries
> To wipe the virtuous tear from British eyes;

---

[1] *Theatralische Bibliothek*, i, p. 112; *Schriften*, vi, pp. 67 f. See above, pp. 108 f.
[2] *Schriften*, vii, pp. 70 f.
[3] See below, p. 464.
[4] James Thomson, *Works*, London, 1750, iii, p. 205.

That dares my moral, tragic scene profane,
With strains—at best, unsuiting, light and vain.
Hence from the pure unsully'd beams that play
In yon fair eyes where virtue shines—Away![1]

Lessing's knowledge of the tragedy *Creusa* (xlix, 66), by William Whitehead (1715–85), which was produced at Drury Lane on April 20, 1754, may have come from a criticism and analysis of the play in the *Monthly Review* of May, 1754:[2]

In his prologue mr. Whitehead ridicules his good friends the antients, and the more modern *French* poets, for their awkward methods of introducing their plays to the audiences; being obliged, either in their prologues, by supernatural powers, to let them into the opening of the fable, or by tragic relations to a confidante, to repeat a story they were acquainted with before.

But there was also a French criticism of the play (including a summary of the Prologue) in the *Journal étranger* of March, 1755,[3] and a German one, with a summary of the plot, in *Das Neueste aus der anmuthigen Gelehrsamkeit*.[4] In the *Geschichte der englischen Schaubühne* Nicolai mentions Whithead [sic] among the chief living writers, whom he does not discuss.[5]

JOHN BANKS

There remains only to be considered the large section of the *Dramaturgie* devoted to *The Unhappy Favourite, or The Earl of Essex*, by John Banks, and other dramas on the same theme. The discussion, which takes its start from Thomas Corneille's *Comte d'Essex*, is not prompted by any special admiration for the English play, but rather by a desire to show its superiority to the French one.

The discussion is initiated in St. liv (4 ff.):

Da die Engländer von je her so gern domestica facta[6] auf ihre Bühne gebracht haben, so kann man leicht vermuthen, dass es ihnen auch an

---

[1] *Works, ed. cit.* iv, pp. 201 f.　　　[2] *Monthly Review*, May, 1754, x, pp. 374 ff.
[3] *Journal étranger*, March, 1755, pp. 137 ff.
[4] *Das Neueste aus der anmuthigen Gelehrsamkeit*, Leipzig, 1756, i, pp. 34 ff., ii, pp. 111 ff.　　　[5] *Theatralische Bibliothek*, iv, p. 49.
[6] 'Domestica facta' is from Horace, *De arte poetica*, l. 287:
'Nec minimum meruere decus vestigia Graeca
Ausi deserere et celebrare domestica facta.'
There is a note in Lessing's *Verzeichnisse der aufgeführten Dramen* (*Schriften*, xv, p. 52):
'Canut. Schlegels Hang domestica facta zu wählen. Hord [sic], p. 211, n. 286.'

Trauerspielen über diesen Gegenstand nicht fehlen wird. Das älteste ist das von Joh. Banks, unter dem Titel, der unglückliche Liebling, oder Graf von Essex. Es kam 1682 aufs Theater, und erhielt allgemeinen Beyfall. Damals aber hatten die Franzosen schon drei Essexe: des Calprenede von 1638; des Boyer von 1678, und des jüngern Corneille, von eben diesem Jahre.[1] Wollten indess die Engländer, dass ihnen die Franzosen auch hierinn nicht möchten zuvorgekommen seyn, so würden sie sich vielleicht auf Daniels Philotas beziehen können; ein Trauerspiel von 1611, in welchem man die Geschichte und den Charakter des Grafen, unter fremden Namen, zu finden glaubte.[2]

Banks scheinet keinen von seinen französischen Vorgängern gekannt zu haben. Er ist aber einer Novelle gefolgt, die den Titel, Geheime Geschichte der Königinn Elisabeth und des Grafen von Essex, führet, wo er den ganzen Stoff sich so in die Hände gearbeitet fand, dass er ihn blos zu dialogiren, ihm blos die äussere dramatische Form zu ertheilen brauchte.[3]

Lessing gives as the source of his knowledge Cibber's *Lives of the Poets* (London, 1753), vol. i, p. 147. Here he found, in the Life of Samuel Daniel:

6. The Tragedy of Philotas, 1611, 8vo. It is dedicated to the Prince, afterwards King Charles I. This play met with some opposition, because it was reported that the character of Philotas was drawn for the unfortunate earl of Essex, which obliged the author to vindicate himself from this charge, in an apology printed at the end of the play; both this play and that of Cleopatra, are written after the manner of the ancients, with a chorus between each act.

A note which is to be found in Lessing's *Entwürfe zu Besprechungen* may have been the basis for the present discussion of Banks:

Von Banks seinem Essex, der von 1682 ist, und also nach des Corneille seinem heraus gekommen. Er scheint aber das Werk des Franzosen nicht gekant zu haben. Er hat sich genau an die historischen Umstände gehalten, und ob sein Stück gleich in Ansehung der Einrichtung und des Ausdrukes

[1] Lessing's information concerning the three French Essex dramas comes from Léris (see above, p. 182).

[2] There is no foundation for the suggestion that Daniel's *Philotas* was based on the story of the Earl of Essex. Cp. R. Schiedermair, *Der Graf von Essex in der Literatur* (Diss. München), Kaiserslautern, 1908, p. 38.

[3] It might be mentioned that there is a brief note based upon Cibber in Nicolai's *Geschichte der englischen Schaubühne* in the *Theatralische Bibliothek* (iv, p. 42): 'John Banks; Verfasser von verschiednen Tragödien, die von keinem grossen poetischen Genie zeigen, aber doch nicht selten Thränen erregt haben, welches besonders von seinem Grafen von Essex und Anna Bullen zu sagen ist. Er lebte noch im Jahr 1706.'

sehr mittelmässig ist, so hat er doch die Kunst gehabt, sehr interessante Situationes anzubringen, welche gemacht dass sich das Stück lange auf dem Theater erhalten.[1]

Lessing now proceeds (LIV, 18–LV, 41) to give in translation 'the story in which Banks found his material so ready to his hand that he only needed to turn it into dialogue and give it dramatic form'. He found it, as he states in a footnote (LIV, 47), in *A Companion to the Theatre, or a View of our most celebrated Dramatic Pieces: in which the Plan, Characters and Incidents of each are particularly explained*, 2 vols. London, 1747 (ii, pp. 99 ff.). I reprint the English original in full:

THE EARL OF ESSEX: OR, THE UNHAPPY FAVOURITE. A TRAGEDY.

BY MR BANKS

The Author is indebted for the Conduct of this Play to a Novel, intitled, *The Secret History of Queen* Elizabeth *and the Earl of* Essex;[2] and happy he was to have so popular a Subject modell'd to his Hands in that interesting Manner we find it.

To heighten our Compassion for the unhappy Earl, and justify the Queen's vehement Affection for him, he is represented as possest of all those eminent Qualities which compose a Hero; and to be a faultless Character requires only to have had a greater Command over his Passions. *Burleigh*, first Minister to the Queen, jealous of her Glory, and envious of the Favours heap'd on *Essex*, is continually labouring to render him suspected. Sir *Walter Raleigh*, no less his Enemy, joins his Endeavours for the same End, and both are abetted by the malicious Countess of *Nottingham*, who, having been passionately in Love with *Essex*, and rejected by him, seeks to ruin what she can't enjoy. The Impetuosity of the Earl's Temper gave them but too great an Opportunity, and they accomplish'd their Ends in the following Manner.

A Rebellion breaking out in *Ireland*, headed by *Tyronne*, a very valiant Man, *Essex*, as being Lord-Lieutenant of that Kingdom, and Captain-General of all her Majesty's Forces both by Sea and Land, marched with a powerful Army against him; after some slight Skirmishes, the Earl's

---

[1] *Schriften*, xv, p. 47.

[2] This novel appeared in London (*ca.* 1650) as *History of the most renowned Queen Elizabeth and her Great Favourite, the Earl of Essex*. In two parts: a romance. In an edition of 1689 (Bentley's Modern Novels, 1, 1692) the title is *The Secret History of the most renowned Queen Elizabeth and the Earl of Essex*, by a person of quality. See R. Schiedermair, *op. cit.* pp. 30 ff. There were many editions, and the work appeared in French in 1678, and in German in 1687, 1731, 1742, 1743 and 1787. Schiedermair compares Banks's drama briefly with this work; it is evident that Banks drew on other sources—e.g. the novel makes no mention of the historical box on the ear.

Troops being much harassed, and the Enemy posted very advantageously, he yielded to a Parley, which being very private, was represented to the Queen as derogatory to her Honour, and as if the Earl was not free from some clandestine Designs. *Burleigh* and *Raleigh*, with some other Members of both Houses, petition her for Leave to impeach him of High Treason, which she not only refuses, but is extremely incensed that such a Motion has been made, repeats the former Services the Earl has done the Nation, and reproaches them with Malice, Envy, and Ingratitude: The Earl of *Southampton*, a very sincere friend of *Essex*, urges every Thing he can in his Behalf, and extols the Queen's Justice in protecting him; so that for that Time his Enemies are put to Silence.

The Queen however, not satisfied with his Behaviour, sends Orders to him to repair his past Conduct, and not quit *Ireland* till the Rebels are totally subdued, and all Things quieted; but the Earl hearing of the Accusations which had been brought against him, was too impatient to be clear'd; and having engaged *Tyronne* to lay down his Arms, came over in spite of the Queen's positive Command to the contrary. His cruel Foes rejoiced; all his Friends were alarmed at this imprudent step; the Countess of *Rutland*, to whom he was privately married, trembled for the Consequence; and the Queen herself was beyond Measure afflicted to find that his rash Proceeding now left her no Pretence to espouse his Cause, without manifesting a Tenderness which she was desirous of concealing from the whole World. The Consideration of her Dignity, heighten'd by her native Haughtiness, and the secret Love she bears him, occasion cruel Conflicts in her Breast; long she debates within herself, whether she shall obey the Dictates of the *one*, and send the audacious Man to the Tower, or comply with the soft Impulse of the *other*, and admit the beloved Criminal to justify himself before her: The latter, after much Struggling, gets the better, but not without some Restrictions; she resolves to see him, but to receive him in such a Manner as shall leave him no Room to hope she will easily pardon his offences.

Burleigh, *Raleigh*, and *Nottingham* are present at this Interview, on the latter of which she leans, and seems busy in Discourse, without once looking on the Earl; and, after suffering him to kneel some Time, quits the Room, sternly commanding all who have Loyalty to follow her, and leave the Traitor to himself. None dare to disobey, even *Southampton* goes, but soon returns, and, with the disconsolate *Rutland*, bewail his Misfortunes. Immediately after *Burleigh* and *Raleigh* are sent to demand his Staff of Offices, which he refuses to resign to any but the Queen herself; and both he and *Southampton* treat those Ministers with Contempt.

The Queen being presently informed of this Behaviour, is highly incens'd, yet still divided in her Thoughts; she cannot brook the Railings of *Nottingham* against him, and the Praises bestowed on him by the unwary *Rutland* make her yet more uneasy, by the Discovery that she loves him: She, however, at last, commands he shall be brought into her Presence: he attempts to vindicate his Conduct, but the Reasons he gives seem too weak to convince her Judgment of his Innocence. She pardons him to satisfy the secret Affection she has for him; but deprives him of all his Honours in Consideration of what she thought owing to herself as Queen. Here the Earl is no longer able to restrain the Impetuosity of his Nature, he throws his Staff at her Feet, accompanied with some Expressions, that sound like Reproaches; on which the Queen, inflamed with Wrath, gives him a Blow. He lays his Hand on his Sword, and it is in vain that *Southampton* conjures him to be more moderate; he goes on repeating his Services, and accusing *Burleigh*, *Raleigh*, and even her Majesty, of Injustice. She leaves him in the utmost Rage, and none remain with him but *Southampton*, who in this Exigence will not forsake him.

Grown desperate with his Misfortunes, he runs head-long into the City, proclaims his Wrongs, and inveighs against the Ministry. All this is told with Aggravations to the Queen, who orders the two Earls to be seized. They are pursued and taken, and sent close Prisoners to the Tower, there to wait their Trial. But the Queen, in spite of all can be said to her, will needs see *Essex* before he goes, and fearing his Crimes were too flagrant to escape Sentence, in order to save his Life, gives him a Ring, with a solemn Promise, that whenever he sends that, to grant him in Return whatever he shall ask.

As she expected, he was found guilty by the Law, and condemned to lose his Head; as was also his Friend *Southampton*. Her Majesty knew that by her Prerogative she had a Right to pardon him; but then she thought such a Grace would too much betray a Weakness unworthy of a Queen, and waited till he should send the Ring, and beg his Life. Impatient till she knows him secure she sends *Nottingham* to him, who pretending the greatest Compassion for him, is intrusted by him with this precious Pledge of Safety, and with it a Petition to the Queen for Mercy. She had now all she wish'd in her Possession, and a full Opportunity to revenge the Contempt he had shewn her Charms. Instead of bearing his Message to the Queen, she represents him as insolent, disdaining to receive any Favour from her; and daring all that her Power and Indignation can inflict: To heighten her Displeasure against him, an unlucky Accident contributes: His Wife hearing he was condemn'd to die, quite desperate with Grief, flies to the Queen, reveals the Secret of their Marriage, and begs her Husband's Life.

Never did publick Indignation, or secret Despair, rise to a greater Height than in the Behaviour, and Breast of this Princess; she spurns the Countess from her, and gives Orders that the Sentence past on *Essex* shall be immediately executed. The malicious *Nottingham*, who now engrosses her Ear, persuades her to pardon the Earl of *Southampton*, not out of any real Pity for that Nobleman, but because she imagines *Essex* will feel the Severity of his own Doom more deeply, in seeing that Mercy which is denied to himself bestowed on his Friend. To imbitter Death the more, she also intreats his unhappy Wife may be permitted to see him as he is conducting [*sic*] to the Block; to both these the Queen consents, but unhappily for the cruel Adviser, the Earl then gives a Letter to his Wife to be delivered to the

Queen, who being at that Time in the Tower, receives it, soon after the Earl is carried off; and finding by it that the Earl had sent the Ring, and beg'd his Life by *Nottingham,* sends to forbid the Execution; but *Burleigh* and *Raleigh,* who were intrusted with the fatal Orders, took so much Care they should not be delayed, that the Earl was dead before the Arrival of this second Message. The Queen is grieved beyond Measure, banishes the treacherous *Nottingham,* for ever from her Presence, and is much displeased with all who had shewn themselves Enemies to the unfortunate Earl.

It must be confessed there is something in this Play capable of raising Compassion in the most insensible Hearts; but then it is wholly owing to the Story; for the Diction is every where very bad, and in some Places so low, that it even becomes unnatural, and shews our Author little acquainted with Courts, when he puts into the Mouth of the prime Nobility such Language as a civil Coster-monger would blush to use. And I think there cannot be a greater Proof of the little Encouragement this Age affords to Merit, than that no Gentleman possest of a true Genius and Spirit of Poetry, thinks it worth his Attention to adorn so celebrated a Part of History with that Dignity of Expression befitting Tragedy in general, but more particularly where the Characters are perhaps the greatest the World ever produced.

As will be seen from a comparison of the above with Lessing's version of it, he frequently expands the text slightly in order to bring it into closer parallelism with Banks's play. This is particularly noticeable in the passage (LIV, 119): 'er wirft den Stab...' ('He throws his Staff at her Feet...'); the following four lines of Lessing's version are only represented in the original by the words: 'He lays his hand on his sword.' The statement in LIV (142 ff.) ('Doch indess...') and the last sentence of St. LIV are Lessing's additions, as well as the references to the acts of the play. On the other hand, after 'das Äusserste ankommen zu lassen' (LV, 18) Lessing omits a passage of some length in the English narrative.

From his comparison of Banks's play with the romance Lessing concludes (LV, 42) that the former is superior in respect of 'nature, truth and consistency' to the drama of Corneille. Banks has kept more faithfully to history, where he found, although not at the points where he utilises them, the box on the ear—not explicitly described in the romance—and the episode of the ring. As far as the latter is concerned, Lessing thinks that Banks has not availed himself of it to the best advantage; he would have preferred to see the queen forget all about the ring, and to receive it unexpectedly and too late, after she had been convinced of the earl's comparative innocence. Much more successful (91) is Banks's introduction of the box on the ear, which inevitably recalls to Lessing the famous scene in *Le Cid*.[1] In *The Earl of Essex*, the incident is, of course, much more serious, as the blow is administered by the queen (LVI, 106). Banks's handling of it has, on the whole, Lessing's approval. For a historical account of the episode Lessing turns again (126) to Hume's *History of England*.[2] In respect of this affair with the queen, Banks has depicted his Essex, Lessing thinks (LVII, 8), too realistically, too much 'nach dem Leben'. He is too much of a boaster—indeed, quite as much a Gascon as the Essex of the Gascon Calprenède; at one time too mean-spirited and obsequious, at another over-bold towards the queen. Much better is the treatment of Elizabeth, in Lessing's view (LVII, 20); he considers that Banks is more successful than Corneille in this, and by way of illustration, he quotes, in translation, a scene from Act III of the play.

I subjoin the original of this scene (LVII, 50–LVIII, 130); as will be seen, it is of particular interest to compare it with Lessing's version. Among the many editions of Banks's drama it is difficult to decide which Lessing possessed, the English quotation in the note (LVII, 26 ff.) being the only clue. I have selected that of 1712: *The Unhappy Favourite: or, The Earl of Essex*. A Tragedy acted at the Theatre Royal, by their Majesties Servants. Written by John Banks...London, 1712 (pp. 25 ff.):

> *Queen.* ...Where hast thou been?
> I thought, dear *Nottingham*, I'd been alone.
> *Nottingham.* Pardon this bold Intrusion, but my Duty
> Urges me farther—On my Knees I first
> Beg Pardon that I am so bold to ask it,
> Then, that you wou'd disclose what 'tis afflicts you;
> Something hangs heavy on your Royal Mind,
> Or else I fear you are not well.
> *Queen.* Rise, prithee—
> I am in health and thank thee for thy Love,
> Only a little troubled at my People.
> I have reign'd long, and they're grown weary of me;
> New Crowns are like new Garlands, fresh and lovely;
> My Royal Sun declines towards its West,
> They're hot, and tyr'd beneath its Autumn Beams—
> Tell me, what says the World of *Essex* coming?
> *Not.* Much do they blame him for't, but think him brave.
> *Queen.* What, when the Traytor serv'd me thus!
> *Not.* Indeed it was not well.

[1] See above, pp. 174 f.
[2] For the passages in question see above, pp. 185, 187.

Queen. Not well, and was that all?

Not. It was a very bold and heinous Fault.

Queen. I [*sic*] was it not? And such a base Contempt,
As he deserves to die for; less than that
Has cost a hundred nearer Favourites Heads...

....

Not. Most true—can *Essex* than [*sic*] be thought so guilty,
And not deserve to die?

Queen. To die! to wrack,
And as his Treasons are the worst of all Mens,
So I will have him plagu'd above the rest,
His Limbs cut off, and plac'd to th' highest View,
Not on low Bridges, Gates, and Walls of Towns,
But on vast Pinacles that touch the Sky,
Where all that pass may in Derision say,
Lo, there is *Essex*, proud, ingrateful *Essex*!
Essex that brav'd the Justice of his Queen—
Is not that well? Why dost not speak?
And help the Queen to rail against this Man.

Not. Since you will give me leave I will be plain,
And tell your Majesty what all the World
Says of that proud ingrateful Man.

Queen. Do so. Prithee what says the World of him and me?

Not. Of you they speak no worse than of dead Saints,
And worship you no less than as their God,
Than Peace, than Wealth, or their Eternal Hopes;
Yet do they often wish with kindest Tears,
Sprung from the purest Love, that you wou'd be pleas'd
To heal their Grievances on *Essex* charg'd,
And not protect the Traytor by your Power,
But give him up to Justice and to Shame
For a Revenge of all your Wrongs, and theirs.

Queen. What would they then prescribe me Rules to Govern?

Not. No more but with Submission as to Heaven;
But upon *Essex* they unload Reproaches,
And give him this bad Character:
They say he is a Person (bating his Treasons)
That in his Noblest, best Array of Parts,
He scarcely has enough to make him pass,
For a brave Man, nor yet a Hypocrite,
And that he wears his Greatness and his Honours
Foolish and Proud as Lacquies wear gay Liveries:
Valiant they will admit he is, but then
Like Beasts precipitately Rash and Brutish,
Which is no more commendable in him
Than in a Bear, a Leopard, or a Wolf.

He never yet had Courage over Fortune,
And which to shew his natural Pride the more,
He roars and staggers under small Affronts.
And can no more endure the Pain than Hell;
Then he's as Covetous, and more Ambitious
Than that first Fiend that sow'd the Vice in Heav'n,
And therefore was Dethron'd and Tumbl'd thence;
And so they wish that *Essex* too may fall.

 Queen. Enough, thou'st rail'd thy self quite out of Breath;
I'll hear no more—Blisters upon her Tongue.   [*Aside.*
'Tis baseness tho' in thee but to repeat,
What the rude World maliciously has said;
Nor dare the vilest of the Rabble think,
Much less prophanely speak such horrid Treasons—
Yet 'tis not what they say, but what you'd have 'em.

 Not. Did not your Majesty command me to speak?

 Queen. I did, but then I saw thee on a sudden,
Settle thy Senses all in eager Postures,
Thy Lips, thy Speech, and Hands were all prepar'd,
A joyful Red painted thy envious Cheeks,
Malicious Flames flasht in a Moment from
Thy Eyes like Lightning from thy o'er-charg'd Soul,
And fir'd thy Breast, which like a hard ramm'd Piece,
Discharg'd unmannerly upon my Face.

 Not. Pardon bright Queen, most Royal and belov'd,
The manner of expressing of my Duty;
But you your self began and taught me first.

 Queen. I am his Queen, and therefore may have leave;
May not my self have Privilege to mould
The Thing I made, and use it as I please?
Besides he has committed Monstrous Crimes
Against my Person, and has urg'd me far
Beyond the Power of mortal Suffering.
Me he has wrong'd, but thee he never wrong'd.
What has poor *Essex* done to thee? Thou hast
No Crown that he cou'd hope to gain,
No Laws to break, no Subjects to molest,
Nor Throne that he cou'd be ambitious of—
What Pleasure cou'dst thou take to see
A drowning Man Knock'd on the Head, and yet
Not wish to save the miserable Wretch!

 Not. I was to blame.

 Queen. No more—
Thou seest the Queen, the World, and Destiny
It self against this one bad Man, and him
Thou canst not Pity nor Excuse.

Not. Madam—

Queen. Be gone, I do forgive thee; and bid *Rutland*
Come to me straight. [*Exit* Nottingham.

....

[St. LVIII] *Enter the Countess of* Essex.

Queen. How now my *Rutland*? I did send for you—
I have observ'd you have been sad of late.
Why wearest thou black so long? And why that Cloud,
That mourning Cloud about thy lovely Eyes?
Come I will find a noble Husband for thee.

C. Ess. Ah! mighty Princess, most ador'd of Queens!
Your Royal Goodness ought to blush, when it
Descends to Care for such a Wretch as I am.

Queen. Why say'st thou so? I love thee well, indeed
I do, and thou shalt find by this 'tis Truth—
Injurious *Nottingham*, and I had some
Dispute, and it was about my Lord of *Essex*—

C. Ess. Ha! [*Aside.*

Queen. So much that she displeas'd me strangely,
And I did send her from my sight in Anger.

C. Ess. O that dear Name o' th' sudden how it starts me!
Makes every Vein within me leave its Channel,
To run, and to protect my feeble Heart;
And now my Blood as soon retreats again   *Aside.*
To croud with Blushes full my guilty Cheeks—
Alass. I fear.

Queen. Thou blushest at my Story!

C. Ess. Not I my Gracious Mistress, but my Eyes
And Cheeks, fir'd and amaz'd with Joy turn'd red
At such a Grace that you were pleas'd to shew me.

Queen. I'll tell the[e] then, and ask thee thy Advice;
There is no doubt, dear *Rutland*, but thou hear'st
The daily Clamours that my People vent
Against the most unhappy Earl of *Essex*,
The Treasons that they would Impeach him of,
And which is worse, this day he is arriv'd
Against my strict Commands, and left Affairs
In *Ireland* desperate, headless, and undone.

C. Ess. Might I presume to tell my Humble Mind,
Such Clamours very often are design'd
More by the Peoples Hate than any Crimes
In those they would accuse.

Queen. Thou speak'st my Sense:
But oh! dear *Rutland*, he has been too [*sic*] blame—
Lend me thy Breast to lean upon—O 'tis

A heavy Yoke they wou'd impose on me
Their Queen, and I am weary of the Load,
And want a Friend like thee to lull my Sorrows.
　　C. Ess. Behold these Tears sprung from fierce Pain and Joy,
To see your wond'rous Grief, your wond'rous Pity.
O that kind Heav'n would but instruct my Thoughts,
And teach my Tongue such softning, healing Words,
That it might Charm your Soul, and cure your Breast
For ever.
　　Queen. Thou art my better Angel then,
And sent to give me everlasting Quiet—
Say, Is't not pity that so brave a Man,
And one that once was reckon'd as a God,
That he should be the Author of such Treasons!
That he, that was like *Cæsar*, and so great,
Has had the Power to make and unmake Kings,
Shou'd stoop to gain a petty Throne from me?
　　C. Ess. I can't believe 'tis in his Soul to think,
Much less to act a Treason against you,
Your Majesty, whom I have heard him so
Commend, that Angels Words did never flow
With so much Eloquence, so rare, so sweet,
That nothing but the Subject cou'd deserve.
　　Queen. Hast thou then heard him talk of me?
　　C. Ess. I have,
And of so much Excellence, as if
He meant to make a rare Encomium on
The World, the Stars, or what is brighter, Heav'n.
She is, said he, the Goddess of her Sex,
So far beyond all Woman kind beside,
That what in them is most ador'd, and lov'd,
Their Beauties, Parts and other Ornaments,
Are but in her the Foils to greater Lustre,
And all Perfections else, how rare soever,
Are in her Person but as lesser Gleams,
And infinite Beams that usher still the Sun,
But scarce are visible amidst her other Brightness.
And then she is so good, it might be said,
That whilst she lives, a Goddess reigns in *England*;
For all her Laws are register'd in Heaven,
And copy'd thence by Her—But then he cry'd,
With a deep Sigh fetch'd from his Loyal Heart,
Well may the World bewail that time at last,
When so much Goodness shall on Earth be mortal,
And wretched *England* break its stubborn Heart.
　　Queen. Did he say all this?

C. Ess. All this! nay more,
A thousand times as much, I never saw him
But his Discourse was still in praise of you;
Nothing but Raptures fell from *Essex* Tongue:
And all was still the same, and all was you.

Queen. Such Words spoke Loyalty enough.

C. Ess. Then does
Your Majesty believe that he can be
A Traytor?

Queen. No, yet he has broke the Laws,
And I for Shame no longer can protect him;
Nay, durst not see him.

C. Ess. What, not see him, say you!
By that bright Star of Mercy in your Soul,
And listening through your Eyes, let me intreat;
'Tis good, 'tis God-like, and like *England*'s Queen;
Like only her to pity the distress'd—
Will you not grant that he shall see you once?

Queen. What he
That did defy my absolute Commands,
And brings himself audaciously before me!

C. Ess. Impute it not to that, but to his Danger,
That hearing what proceedings here had past
Against his Credit and his Life, he comes
Loyal, tho' unadvised, to clear himself.

Queen. Well, I will see him then, and see him straight—
Indeed my *Rutland* I would fain believe
That he is honest still, as he is brave.

C. Ess. O nourish that most kind Belief, 'tis sprung
From Justice in your Royal Soul—Honest!
By your bright Majesty, he is faithful still,
The pure and Virgin Light is less untainted;
The glorious Body of the Sun breeds Gnats,
Insects that Molests [*sic*] its curious Beams;
The Moon has Spots upon her Chrystal Face,
But in his Soul are none—And for his Valour,
The Christian World records its wondrous Story,
Baseness can never mingle with such Courage.
Remember what a Scourge he was to Rebels,
And made your Majesty ador'd in *Spain*
More than their King, that brib'd you with his *Indies*,
And made himself so dreadful to their Fears,
His very Name put Armies to the Rout;
It was enough to say here's *Essex* come;
And Nurses still'd their Children with the Fright.

Queen. Ha! she's concern'd, Transported!

RL

18

I'll try thee farther—Then he has a Person!

   C. Ess. I [*sic*], in his Person, there you summ up all.

Ah! Loveliest Queen, did you e're see the like!

The Limbs of *Mars*, and awful Front of *Jove*,

With such an Harmony of Parts as put

To blush the Beauties of his Daughter *Venus*.

A Pattern for the Gods to make a perfect Man by,

And *Michael Angelo* to frame a Statue

To be ador'd th[r]ough all the wondring World.

   Queen. I can endure no more—Hold *Rutland*,

Thy Eyes are moist, thy Senses in a Hurry,

Thy Words come crouding one upon another.

Is it real Passion, or extorted?

Is it for *Essex* sake, or for thy Queen's

That makes this furious Transport in thy Mind?

She loves him—Ah, 'tis so—What have I done?

Conjur'd another Storm to rack my Rest?

Thus is my Mind with Quiet never blest,

But like a loaded Bark finds no Repose,

When 'tis becalm'd, nor when the Weather blows.

Enter Burleigh, *Countess of* Nottingham, Rawleigh,
Lords, Attendants and Guards.

   Burl. May't please your Majesty the Earl of *Essex*

Return'd by your Command, intreats to kneel

Before you.

   Queen. Now hold my Treacherous Heart,

Guard well the Breach that this proud Man has made—   *Aside.*

Rutland, we must defer this Subject till

Some other Time—Come hither *Nottingham*.

Lessing concludes his translation with the remark (LVIII, 144): 'I, for my part, would rather have merely conceived these scenes than have composed the whole *Essex* of Corneille.'

In St. LIX, however, he criticises the style of Banks's play, which, he says, must not be judged by his translation. 'Er ist zugleich so gemein und so kostbar, so kriechend und so hochtrabend, und das nicht von Person zu Person, sondern ganz durchaus, dass er zum Muster dieser Art von Misshelligkeit dienen kann' (LIX, 3). This judgment was, no doubt, influenced by what Lessing read in *The Companion to the Theatre*.[1] And from *The Companion to the Playhouse* he quotes in his *Collectanea* (*Schriften*, xv, p. 150): 'His Verse is not

---

[1] *Ed. cit.* ii, p. 105. The passage which Lessing quotes in his note (LIX, 109) will be found in full on p. 267 above.

Poetry, but Prose run mad.'[1] Cibber, it might be added, had also said of Banks in his *Lives of the Poets* (*ed. cit.* iii, p. 174):

> Mr Banks's genius was wholly turned for tragedy; his language is certainly unpoetical, and his numbers unharmonious; but he seems not to have been ignorant of the dramatic art: For in all his plays he has very forcibly rouzed the passions, kept the scene busy, and never suffered his characters to languish.

Prosy and uninspired as Banks's verse often is, there is in all these strictures a certain element of unfairness; even his imitations of Miltonic phrases[2] are not always blameworthy.

Lessing's translation, it will be seen, is extremely free; and it seems prompted by a desire to substantiate the English criticisms he had read. Banks's verse is turned into the baldest prose of the 'bürgerliches Trauerspiel',[3] and Lessing allows himself unjustifiable liberties of curtailment. He has guarded, he says (LIX, 9), rather against the bombastic than against the trite. This is only too true; Banks's triteness becomes in Lessing's hands considerably more trite; and the injustice done to such poetry as the play contains is serious. If the phrases which Lessing quotes (LIX, 60 ff.) as examples of Banks's lack of poetic sense are compared with the original text, it will be seen that practically in every case the blame is to be laid at Lessing's door; the words he complains of are gratuitous additions of his own! One trembles to think how even Shakespeare would appear if translated in this fashion.

In St. LIX (117, 127) Lessing mentions three other dramatists, whose plays on the subject of Essex are, however, merely adaptations from that of Banks: Henry Jones, James Ralph and Henry Brook [*sic*].[4] He does not know their works, and his information about them

---

[1] *Companion to the Playhouse, ed. cit.* ii, v.s. Banks.

[2] For examples of Miltonic influence on Banks see R. Schiedermair, *op. cit.* pp. 39 ff.

[3] Karl Lessing wrote on February 3, 1772 to his brother (*Schriften*, xx, p. 127): 'In Deiner Emilia Galotti herrscht ein Ton, den ich in keiner Tragödie, so viel ich deren gelesen, gefunden habe; ein Ton, der nicht das Trauerspiel erniedrigt, sondern nur so herunterstimmt, dass es ganz natürlich wird, und desto leichter Eingang in unsere Empfindungen erhält. Ich besinne mich wohl, dass Du in Deiner Dramaturgie aus dem Bankschen Trauerspiele Elisabeth oder Essex einige Scenen in eine solche Sprache übersetzt hast; aber wer diese Scenen im Originale suchen will, (denn ich habe es gelesen)—der muss seyn, was Du bist.'

[4] It is interesting to note that a play entitled *Die Gunst der Fürsten, oder Elisabeth und Essex* 'nach dem Englischen der Herren Banks, Brooke, Jones, und Ralph,

comes only from 'gelehrten Tagebüchern'. In the *Monthly Review* for March, 1753, where '*The Earl of Essex*, a Tragedy...by mr. Henry Jones' is reviewed, he read:

This play has had a considerable run, and was performed with universal applause. 'Tis written on *Banks's* plan, but somewhat varied in the conduct, and much improved in diction. The notice taken by several judicious critics of the happy conduct of *Banks's* scenery, (who all, however, unanimously decry his writing) has tempted others to adopt this subject, besides mr. *Jones*; viz. mr. *James Ralph* and mr. *Henry Brooke*, author of *Gustavus Vasa*; and those who have seen them, generally allow the superiority in point of merit to mr. *Jones's* performance. Mr. *Brooke's*, indeed, has not yet appeared in print, tho' frequently acted in *Ireland*.

Our author, who gained great reputation by his poems, printed by subscription a few years ago, is peculiarly entitled to the notice and encouragement of the public, as he appears to be a man of extraordinary genius; and whose personal merit also joins to render him worthy of that patronage and favour he has met with, and which has deservedly raised him from the obscurity of a mechanical employment, as little suited to mr. *Jones's* natural talents, as the same calling was to his great predecessor, *Ben. Johnson*.[1]

After giving a specimen of the play, the critic quotes the Epilogue in which Jones is described as an 'Irish Bricklayer' and 'Old Ben' is mentioned, 'who chang'd (like him) the trowel for the pen' (cp. LIX, 119).

In Lessing's *Entwürfe zu Besprechungen* we find the following note:

1753 liess Jones seinen Essex spielen (S. Cibbers Lifes III, p. 175). Er wollte Banks Stük regelmässiger machen, und machte es frostiger. Aber sein Styl ist besser, und seine Sprache poetischer.[2]

The criticism by Cibber to which Lessing refers is the following, which occurs in the Life of Banks:

We cannot but acknowledge, that Mr Jones has improved the story, and heightened the incident in the last act, which renders the whole more moving....Mr Jones in his language (in this piece) does not affect being very poetical;—nor is his versification always mellifluent, as in his other

vom Herrn Professor Schmidt' was performed in Vienna on April 30, 1778. The playbill on which this statement of joint authorship occurs is preserved in the Theatersammlung of the Nationalbibliothek, Vienna.

[1] *Monthly Review*, March, 1753, viii, pp. 225 f. Lessing himself gives the reference in his repertory list (where 'Johnson' is a slip for 'Jones' (*Schriften*, xv, p. 49)).

[2] *Schriften*, xv, p. 47.

writings;—but it is well adapted for speaking: The design is well conducted, the story rises regularly, the business is not suspended, and the characters are well sustained.

Under the heading 'Unstudirte Dichter' Lessing noted further: 'Heinrich Jones, der Verfasser des neuen Essex war ein Maurer.'[1]

Lessing's information about Brooke comes from an article in the *Journal encyclopédique* of March 1, 1761 (pp. 117 f.), to which his attention may have been drawn by a reference in the *Bibliothek der schönen Wissenschaften*.[2] In continuation of the passage just quoted from the *Entwürfe zu Besprechungen* he notes:

1761 kam Brooks seiner heraus. Er suchte das Beste von seinen beiden Vorgängern zu nutzen, (indem er sich über den Vorwurf des Plagii weg-setzte) und ihre Fehler zu vermeiden. Man sagt er habe das Feuer und das Pathetische des Banks mit der schönen Poesie des Jones zu verbinden gewusst. Brook war schon durch einen Gustav Wasa bekannt, der aber in London nicht gespielt werden durfte, weil man verschiedne Züge wider das Gouvernement darinn zu finden glaubte. Brook hat den Charakter des Essex veredelt, und ihn in der letzten Scene gegen die Königin nicht so kochend sprechen lassen.[3]

Then follow the French quotation given in the *Dramaturgie* (note to LIX, 133), and the words: 'Desto schlimmer für die Franzosen!' The passage from the *Journal encyclopédique* which is the source of all this is in full (pp. 119 f.):

Dans le tems que Mr. Jones faisoit jouer sa Tragédie sur le Théâtre de Londres, Mr. Brooke publioit la sienne du même sujet en Irlande, où il jouissoit déjà d'une certaine réputation qu'il s'étoit acquise par sa Tragédie de Gustave Vasa dont on n'avoit pas voulu permettre la représentation à Londres, parcequ'on prétendoit qu'il y avoit quelques traits contre le gouvernement; ce qui fait bien voir qu'en Angleterre, comme ailleurs, on n'est pas aussi libre qu'on le pense, du moins lorsqu'il s'agit de certains objets. Quoiqu'il en soit, sa Tragédie du Comte d'Essex se joue à présent à Londres avec le plus grand succès. Si l'Auteur de cette nouvelle Tragédie a trouvé l'art de conserver dans cette piéce toutes les beautés qui avoient frappé dans les deux autres, sans s'embarrasser de l'imputation de plagiat, très ridicule en ce cas: il a eu aussi assez de goût pour en éviter les défauts. Il a sçu réunir très-heureusement le feu et le pathétique de Mr. Banks à la belle Poésie de Mr. Jones, et il a répandu sur le tout une liberté et une

[1] *Schriften*, xv, p. 60.
[2] viii (i) (1762), pp. 167 f. Perhaps this notice may have been by Lessing himself. The spelling 'Brook' is that of the *Bibliothek*.
[3] *Schriften*, xv, p. 47.

noblesse de sentimens qu'il ne doit qu'à lui même: ses caractères sont beaucoup mieux finis, et surtout ceux d'Elizabeth, et du Comte d'Essex, qui sont ici bien supérieurs à ceux que les deux premiers tragiques en ont tracé. On sent bien qu'il n'étoit pas possible que Mr. Brooke s'écartât, ni même qu'il altérât les situations principales qui forment l'intérêt et le nœud de l'action. Cependant il n'a pas laissé d'y faire deux ou trois petits changemens qui ont paru assez heureux; par exemple, il s'est gardé de presenter le Comte d'Essex trop rampant dans sa derniere scène avec la Reine, défaut dans lequel étoient tombés ses Prédecesseurs; et il a mis une certaine dignité dans son emportement, qui s'accorde assés avec la hauteur de son caractère. Mr. Brooke a aussi fait tomber en démence...(here follows the quotation in Lessing's note to LIX, 133).

CHAPTER VIII

Luigi Riccoboni's *Histoire du Théâtre italien* (2 vols. Paris, 1728–31), the greater part of which Lessing had translated in his *Theatralische Bibliothek*, still remained in 1767 his chief source of information concerning the dramatic literature of Italy. When he speaks (XLI, 1) of the state of Italian drama at the beginning of the eighteenth century, he is obviously relying on this work.[1] In St. IX (125) he refers his readers directly to Riccoboni's commendation of Cecchi's comedy *La Dote*, based on Plautus's *Trinummus*, as one of the best of the old Italian comedies. Of this piece Riccoboni had given a lengthy analysis,[2] summing up his opinion of it in the words: 'Suivant ma façon de penser, je trouve cette piece très-bonne. Elle est assez intriguée, assez intéressante, et assez comique même pour amuser d'honnêtes gens.'[3] To Riccoboni Lessing turned again, as will be seen, for information about Maffei's *Merope*.

Another Italian work which Lessing possessed was the *Biblioteca teatrale italiana* of Ottaviano Diodati (1762–65), which, as we have seen, had some share, with Leone Allacci's *Drammaturgia*, in defining the general character of Lessing's journal.[4] But apart from its 'Trattato di Drammaturgia', Diodati's work is merely a collection of plays. Here Lessing found an Italian translation of *Mélanide* (VIII, 24; Diodati, ii, pp. 199 ff.), which he considered much worse than the German translation, and one of *L'Écossaise*[5] (XII, 137; Diodati, i, pp. 180 ff.). There is also in this collection a reprint of the 1730 edition of Maffei's *Merope* (ix, pp. 7 ff.).

When it is remembered how deeply Lessing was interested in Goldoni at an earlier period of his life, the references to that writer in the *Dramaturgie* seem disappointingly meagre.[6] The repertory list

---

[1] See especially vol. i, chaps. vii and viii (*Theatralische Bibliothek*, ii, pp. 195 ff.).

[2] *Histoire du Théâtre italien, ed. cit.* ii, pp. 227 ff.

[3] *Ibid.* p. 257.

[4] See above, p. 122.

[5] Cosack (*op. cit.* p. 79) states that this translation was 'by Gabrielli'.

[6] In 1755 and 1756 he began translating Goldoni's *L'Erede fortunata* (*Schriften*, iii, pp. 336 ff.). *Minna von Barnhelm* shows traces of the influence of *La Locandiera* and possibly *Gli Innamorati*. In the *Bibliothek der schönen Wissenschaften*, vols. ii–iv,

for the first period of the 'Enterprise' gave him no opportunity of criticising any play by Goldoni, although after Lessing's time the Hamburg theatre, drawing on Ackermann's former repertory, played no less than five of the comedies.[1] Goldoni is only mentioned twice in the *Dramaturgie*. In St. xii (70) a similarity is suggested between Frélon in Voltaire's *L'Écossaise* and Don Marzio in Goldoni's *La Bottega del Caffè* (1750);[2] and in St. ci–civ (70) it is stated that Goldoni enriched the Italian theatre with thirteen plays in one year. This information comes from Goldoni's own play, *Il teatro comico*; but 'dreyzehn' should be 'sechzehn'.[3]

In St. xvi (40) there is a reference to the translation of *Zayre* by Gasparo Gozzi, elder brother of Carlo Gozzi. Lessing quotes the close of Gozzi's 'very exact and very pretty' translation[4] to show the divergence of Italian and French taste. The Frenchman gives Orosmane only a few words to say after he has stabbed himself: Gozzi makes him deliver a long tirade. In a preface to the Italian translation it is stated: 'Egli è il vero, che l'Autore professa d' avervi fatto diversi cambiamenti; i quali furono giustificati dall' accoglienza ch' ebbe questa Tragedia in tutte le rappresentazioni.'[5]

In St. xxxvi (4), in connexion with Favart's *Soliman II*, Lessing refers to an Italian Intermezzo, *La Serva padrona*.[6] An Italian Intermezzo of this title, for which Pergolesi composed the music in 1733, was long popular, and had been adapted, or parodied, for the French

---

1757–59, there appeared a series of articles on Bettinelli's edition of Goldoni, signed 'C' (C. F. Nicolai?). Cp. L. Mathar, *Carlo Goldoni auf dem deutschen Theater des 18. Jahrhunderts*, Montjoie, 1910 (and especially pp. 14 ff., 21 ff., 64, 84 ff.) and E. Maddalena, *Lessing e Goldoni*, in *Giornale storico della letteratura italiana*, xlvii (1906), pp. 193 ff. A German translation of Goldoni's comedies began to appear in 1767 (*Sämmtliche Lustspiele*, Leipzig, 1767–77).

[1] See above, p. 45.

[2] See above, p. 227. For a comparison of these two characters, and an account of Goldoni's later version of *L'Écossaise*, cp. P. Toldo, *Attinenze fra il Teatro comico di Voltaire e quello del Goldoni*, in *Giornale storico della letteratura italiana*, xxxi (1898), pp. 351 ff.

[3] Act i, sc. ii; *Opere Complete di Carlo Goldoni*, edite dal Municipio di Venezia, Venice, 1909, iv, pp. 21 f. Cp. also *Mémoires de M. Goldoni*, Paris, 1787, ii, pp. 44, 46. The number is given as sixteen in the *Bibliothek der schönen Wissenschaften*, ii (ii) (1758), p. 305): 'Rosaura, welche spröde thun will, sagt; sie wisse nicht warum sie eben zum erstenmale bey ihrer Ankunft in Venedig diese kleine Farce spielen sollten, da doch, eben der Verfasser derselben in einem Jahre sechzehn neue Stücke gemacht habe, von welchen sie ja eines spielen könnten'.

[4] *Opere in versi e in prosa*, Venice, 1758, iii, pp. 62 f.

[5] *Ibid.* p. [iii].   [6] See above, p. 238.

theatre as *La Servante Maîtresse* by N. Baurans in 1754;[1] but this does not seem to be the piece Lessing has in mind.[2] Schütze mentions *La Serva padrona* as having been performed in Hamburg in 1749, and later refers also to an Intermezzo *Pimpinon und Vespette*.[3] In 1766 we find a *Serva padrona* in Ackermann's repertory, when his daughter Dorothea played 'Serpilla'; and in 1769 Schröder played 'Vespone' in this Intermezzo.[4] Minor, following a suggestion made by Redlich, believed that he had identified the piece which Lessing had in mind as *Die ungleiche Heyrath, oder das Herrsch-süchtige Cammermädgen*; but the characters whom Lessing calls Pimpinello and Serbinetta are here Pimpinone and Vespetta.[5] It is tempting to assume that the names in the *Dramaturgie* are due to a slip in Lessing's memory.

SCIPIONE MAFFEI

The main points of contact between the *Dramaturgie* and Italian literature are to be found in St. XXXVII–L, where Lessing compares Voltaire's *Mérope* with Maffei's tragedy on the same theme. As the general conclusions of this comparison are more relevant to Voltaire than to Maffei, I have already dealt with them to a great extent in the second chapter of this part.[6] There remain to be considered the sources of Lessing's knowledge of Maffei, and his own and Voltaire's criticism of the Italian *Merope*.

Lessing appears to have possessed more than one edition of Maffei's tragedy. He certainly had that in the *Teatro del Sig. Marchese Scipione Maffei*, edited by G. C. Becelli, Verona, 1730 (L, 4), and he must have consulted one or more of the later editions (XLIII, 22)—possibly that published at Livorno in 1763.[7] He was under the impression that the

[1] See Léris, *op. cit.* p. 404.

[2] Nor does *La Serva padrona*, a prose comedy in three acts by Jacopo-Angelo Nelli, published at Lucca in 1731. (Cp. G. Radiciotti, *G. B. Pergolesi*, Rome, 1910, pp. 28 f., and E. Faustini-Fasini, *G. B. Pergolesi attraverso i suoi biografi e le sue opere*, Milan [1900], pp. 21 f.) Still another comedy with the same title, by G. B. Fagiuoli, published at Cremona in 1727, shows no correspondence in the names of the characters.

[3] *Hamburgische Theatergeschichte*, ed. cit. pp. 81, 308.

[4] F. L. W. Meyer, *op. cit.* ii, 2, pp. 125, 145.

[5] Cp. *Lessing's Werke*, Hempel ed., xx, 2, p. 3, and J. Minor, *C. F. Weisse*, Innsbruck, 1880, pp. 134 ff.

[6] See above, pp. 214 ff.

[7] He had also, as we have seen above (p. 279) the edition (of the text of 1730) in Diodati's *Biblioteca teatrale italiana*, ix (1764).

1730 edition contained the text of the original edition (Venice, 1714), and that the later texts represented the results of the author's revision (XLIII, 22). As a matter of fact, the reverse may well have been the case: for while the 1730 edition is, in some respects at least, a revised text, some of those published at later dates contain earlier unrevised wordings.[1] The occasion of Lessing's statement is a passage of arms with Voltaire with reference to the text of a dialogue in Act III, sc. iv of the Italian play (XLIII, 6 ff.). Voltaire had stated—the passage is quoted below (p. 290)—that in the first edition of *Merope* Egisto said to his mother: 'Ah Polidore, mon père', for which Maffei subsequently substituted 'un défaut encor plus grand'—'Egiste lui dit, que son père est un vieillard; et à ce mot de vieillard la Reine s'attendrit.' Voltaire thus knew two editions of *Merope*; certainly the first of 1714, and probably that of 1745; in the former the reading is 'Ah Polidoro', in the latter 'Ah padre mio...Bisogna credere a i vecchi'—followed by Merope's words: 'Un vecchio è il padre tuo?' Lessing, however, was clearly unaware of the irregularities in the variants of the later texts when he said: 'Es ist wahr, in der ersten Ausgabe nennt Aegisth den Polydor seinen Vater; aber in den nachherigen Ausgaben ist von gar keinem Vater mehr die Rede'; for the readings of the original edition and the edition of 1730 are as follows:

First edition (1714)		Second edition (1730)	
Egi.	Ah Polidoro!	*Egi.*	Fatal Messenia!
Tu mel dicesti un dì, ch' io mi guardassi		Mel disse il padre mio, ch' io mi guardassi	
Dal por già mai ne la Messenia il piede.		Dal por già' mai nella Messenia il piede.	
Mer. Polidoro! Chi sei?		*Mer.* Nella Messenia? e perchè mai?	
Egi.	Creder bisogna	*Egi.*	Bisogna
A i vecchi.		Credere a i vecchi.	
Mer.	Di', qual Polidoro è questi?	*Mer.*	Dì, come si noma Il padre tuo? dì tosto.

---

[1] Cp. G. Hartmann, *Merope im italienischen und französischen Drama*, Erlangen and Leipzig, 1892, pp. 55 f., where reference is made to the Turin edition of 1765 as containing the earlier reading of the passage in Act III, sc. iv, criticised by Voltaire. The text of this edition, however, does not correspond with Lessing's quotations. Where he quotes Maffei's text (XLII, 42, 83; XLIII, 37, 133; XLVI, 73, 94, 140) he cites the form of the edition of 1730, except in the notes XLIII, 133, where the form corresponds to that of the 1763 edition. (These latter passages are disfigured by wrong accentuation, which has been perpetuated by Muncker.)

	Egi.	L' infelice
	Chiamasi Polidoro.	
	Mer.	Polidoro!
Dal capo a i piè m' è corso un gelo,	Dal capo a i piè m' è corso un gelo,	
Euriso,	Euriso,	
Che instupidita m' ha.	Che instupidita m' ha.[1]	

From the editions of *Merope* came practically all Lessing's knowledge of Maffei.[2] The poet's own 'Proemio' (ed. of 1763, p. xci) gave him the personal details of Maffei's youth (XLII, 6):

L'Autore della presente Tragedia all' anno dell' età sua trentesimo ottavo arrivato era, senza avere a metter mano in Tragica Poesia pensato pure un momento già mai: anzi ogni specie di Componimento, siccome all' arte Poetica fin da fanciullo fortemente inclinato; negli anni suoi giovanili tentato avea, fuorchè questa.

And Becelli, after quoting the testimony of writers who had marvelled that Maffei, engrossed in graver studies, should have succeeded as a dramatic poet (ed. of 1730, pp. xxi, xxvi), adds:

E per verità a nissun genere di studio il nostro Autore ha pensato meno, che a questo, anzi quanto ne sia stato lontano dalle sue edizioni delle Complessioni di Cassidorio...da quanto contra il Pfaff, e contra il Basnage ha scritto,[3] e dalla Storia de' Diplomi, e dall' altre opere si può arguire: ed è notissimo, come questi componimenti per occasioni nate, e per compiacere a Compagnie nobili, e ad onestissime conversazioni da lui speditamente fatti furono....Si sa da molti, che meno di due mesi l' Autore v' impiegò....

From Becelli's introduction to the edition of 1730 Lessing also

---

[1] In the edition published at Venice in 1747, the text of which is in the main that of 1714, Maffei states expressly (pp. 118 f.): 'Nelle prime Edizioni diceva Egisto: *ah Polidoro, Tu mel dicesti un dì* etc. E Merope: *Polidoro! Chi sei?*...Gli Amici dell' Autore vollero, ch' Ei levasse tal nome da quel sito, dicendo non esser naturale, che un Figliuolo in vece di dire, *ah Padre,* lo chiami per nome. Si ha però in altre Edizioni: *Mel disse il Padre mio....*'

[2] There was a brief biography of Maffei in German in Jakob Brucker's *Bilder-sal heutiges Tages lebender...Schrifft-steller,* ii (Augsburg, 1742), but Lessing is hardly likely to have seen this work.

[3] Maffei's controversy with C. M. Pfaff is to be found in letters to the Abate Bacchini in the *Giornale de' Letterati d' Italia,* xvi (1713), pp. 226 ff. and xxvi (1716), pp. 51 ff. (cp. also F. Doro, *Bibliografia Maffeiana* in *Studi Maffeiani* (*Appendice*), Turin, 1909, p. 12); it concerned the genuineness of some newly discovered fragments attributed by Pfaff to Irenæus. Basnage is referred to in the same correspondence.

draws his statements at the beginning of St. XLI. Becelli writes (pp. viii ff.):

Cominciando dalla Tragedia, si può dire essere stata questa la più fortunata, che sulle Scene si vedesse. Mentre ancora lavoravasi, avendone il Sig. Abate Giuseppe Signoretti Piemontese mandati i due primi Atti a Roma al Sig. Leonardo Adami, quell' ammirabil giovane, nominato trà primi Letterati d' Italia dal Sig. Alberto Fabrizio nel tredicesimo tomo della sua Biblioteca Greca, questo distico nella risposta gli mandò:

> *Cedite Romani Scriptores, cedite Graii,*
> *Nescio quid majus nascitur Œdipode.*

ch' è imitazione di quel di Properzio [*Eleg.*, ii, 34, ll. 65 f.] riferito da Donato nella vita di Virgilio, e fatto sopra l' Eneide appena cominciata, qual diceva:

> *Nescio quid majus nascitur Iliade.*

... Ma perchè il vero paragone delle Tragedie è il recitarle in un Pubblico frequente, e numeroso, ricorderò, come rappresentata questa in Venezia l' anno 1714. quando il nome di Tragedia sulla publica Scena era da grandissimo tempo andato in disuso, e in total dimenticanza; e quando si disperava che in stagione d' allegria giugnesse pure il popolo a soffrire una favola ignuda d' amori, e tanto grave, e patetica, così smisurato favore incontrò, che convenne seguitare a farla quasi tutto il carnevale con folla sempre maggiore di sceltissima udienza, onde i Teatri di Musica quasi abbandonati restarono, e conveniva che nel recitare più e più volte gli Attori si soffermassero, interrotti dal commovimento, e dagli applausi.... Al Pastorfido hanno resa testimonianza le molte edizioni, e le varie traduzioni: molto più alla Merope, perchè in sedici anni sopra trenta ristampe fatte se ne sono, e fuor d' Italia in Vienna, in Parigi, in Londra; ed è stata tradotta in Francese, in Inglese, e in Tedesco: e si stamperà forse con quelle traduzioni appresso, acciò a forastieri anche per la lingua servir possa.[1] In Francese, oltre la traduzione stampata dal Sig. Freret in prosa, un' altra ve n' è di bravo Poeta Tragico in versi.

Lessing, however, also consulted Riccoboni, where he found (*Histoire du Théâtre italien, ed. cit.* i, p. 82):

---

[1] The French translation by Fréret appeared in Paris in 1718; and there was another by Du Bourg, published in 1743; Riccoboni had already included one in his *Nouveau Théâtre italien*; a German translation (in prose) appeared at Vienna in 1724, and there was another by F. Molter (*Deutsche Schaubühne zu Wienn*, iii, Vienna, 1752); there was an English one by William Ayre, London, 1740. Cp. *Œuvres Complètes de Voltaire*, Paris, 1877–85, iv, p. 179; cp. also F. Doro, *op. cit.* pp. 11 f. The edition of Maffei's tragedy published at Verona in 1745 included the translations of Fréret and Ayre.

Je donnai la *Merope* du même Marquis *Maffei*; on ne sçauroit exprimer le bruit qu'elle fit et les applaudissemens qu'elle reçût; il s'en fit quatre Editions dans la même année.[1]

Lessing recalls the fact (XL, 75) that two Italian dramatists of the sixteenth century had treated the story of Cresphontes and Merope: G. B. Liviera and P. Torelli. In his Dedication 'all' Altezza Serenissima di Rinaldo I. Duca di Modena', Maffei had said:

Mi perdoni V. A. questo breve svagamento, e ritornando al proposito, Gio: Batista Liviera, che stampò nel 1588. una Tragedia su questo Soggetto, prese nell' essenziale la constituzione da Igino. Il Conte Pomponio Torelli, che ne publicò un' altra nel 1598,[2] seguì parimente la traccia stessa: così questi Poeti rinovarono in parte Euripide senza saperlo.[3]... And also: Altri però si pensava, che mio intento fosse d' andar seguendo le vestigia di quella, e di rappresentarla quanto è possibile; talchè io potessi poi intitolar la mia *Indovinamento sopra Euripide*, come l' insigne Matematico Vincenzio Viviani intitolò *Indovinamento sopra Apollonio Pergeo* il suo *Trattato de' Massimi e de' Minimi*. Ma io tutto all' incontro nella mia tessitura ho anzi cercato d' allontanarmene; e ciò sì per fare una Tragedia nuova, sì per non creder vietato il tentare qualche cosa di più.[4]

This is followed by the passage quoted by Lessing in his foot-note (XXXIX, 112 ff.).

The situation of a mother who loves her son so deeply as to commit a terrible crime in order to avenge him suggested to Maffei (XL, 85) the idea of making his tragedy one of maternal love, to the exclusion of any other motive (cp. Dedication, ed. of 1730, p. xxxix):[5]

...onde cercai di condurmi per affatto diversa strada; singolarmente facendo, che il giovane non venisse in Messenia per far la sua vendetta, ma fosse ignoto a se stesso, e ci capitasse a caso; e facendo, che non sia creduto

---

[1] Lessing's translation, *Theatralische Bibliothek*, ii, pp. 206 f. See also Léris' notice quoted above, p. 212. In a review of a translation of an Italian tragedy *Rutzvanscad, il Giovine*, in Gottsched's *Neuer Büchersaal der schönen Wissenschaften und freyen Künste*, i (1745), pp. 116 ff., mention is made of Maffei's *Merope* and its popularity, as shown by the number of editions and translations (pp. 118, 134).

[2] This date should be 1589. 1598 was the date of the second edition. Cp. T. Copelli, *Il Teatro di Scipione Maffei*, Parma, 1907, pp. 103–7. Lessing could also have found the titles of the tragedies by Liviera and Torelli in Allacci's *Drammaturgia*, Venice, 1755, cols. 228, 525 f.

[3] Ed. of 1730, p. xxxviii; the passage occurs, with slight verbal alterations, in the ed. of 1763, pp. xxvii f.

[4] Ed. of 1730, pp. xxxvi f.; with slight verbal differences in the ed. of 1763, pp. xxv f.   [5] Ed. of 1763, p. xxviii.

da Merope uccisor del suo figlio per affermarlo lui, ma per combinazione d' accidenti: lasciando l' idea principale, ch' io mi son prefissa, cioè di dipingere una Madre, il che ad essi non cadde in animo.

And he modified his plot accordingly.

Lessing admits (XLII, 1) that the Italian *Merope* has its faults. Maffei is no poet; he approaches his theme as an imitator and a moralist; he has more fancy than poetry; in short, he is a 'Litterator' and 'Versificateur', rather than a genius and a poet.[1] As a versifier (28) he shows too great fondness for descriptions and similes; Lessing instances Egisto's circumstantial description of his fight with the robbers in Act I, sc. iii. He describes happenings, such as the fall of a heavy body into water, with tedious detail; a man being tried for his life could not be expected to be so 'childishly accurate'. As a 'Litterator' (57), he has too much respect for the simplicity of the Greek stage, and shows too close an observance of Greek customs. Our emotions are not roused by a form strange to our own age. He is too fond of imitating fine passages in the ancients, without due regard to their appropriateness to a dramatic work. A Nestor in the epic is all very well; in tragedy he is intolerable. Here Lessing had in mind the following passage from Maffei's 'Proemio':

Concorrevano altre ragioni ancora. Si ha da Plutarco; e da Igino, che colui dal quale fu Merope trattenuta, e che avea nodrito Cresfonte; era un Vecchio. È noto, che il rappresentare i costumi delle età è uno de' migliori fonti della perfetta Poesia. *Ætatis cuiusque notandi sunt tibi mores.* Ma delle età niuna è atta ad essere imitata con maggior grazia, più a lungo, e in più modi della vecchiezza. In Teatro si può quasi dire, che fino allora niun l' avea fatto: perchè Vecchi sono introdotti da Eschilo ne' Persiani, e nelle Supplici, da Euripide nell' Elena, nell' Ione, e nell' Ifigenia in Aulide; ma non posero studio per dipingergli come vecchi: così de' Moderni può dirsi. Molti e bellissimi tratti ne ha bensì il Nestore d' Omero.[2]

Lessing also quotes (85) a passage from Maffei's Dedication, in which the latter states that he had not sought to incorporate in his play fragmentary lines of the play of Euripides.

There are times, however, Lessing says (77), when we could wish that Maffei had had a better memory, as when Ismene speaks of a theatre (Act IV, sc. vii) before theatres existed.[3] He objects to this,

---

[1] See below, p. 453.

[2] This passage is not in the edition of 1730; it occurs in the edition of 1763 on pp. xcv f.

[3] It might be noted that Lessing allows himself a similar anachronism in his own *Nathan der Weise* (Act IV, sc. ii, ll. 2522 f.).

not merely as an anachronism, but as one that is destructive of the illusion. One would hardly expect it, he says, of a poet who in his preface excuses himself for having used the name Messene (Messenia), at a time when no town of Messene yet existed:

La Città di Messene è assai credibile, che in que' tempi non vi fosse ancora, non essendo nominato da Omero; con tutto ciò in antichità così remota, ed oscura ho stimato meglio di porre in essa l'azione, e di ritenere un nome già noto, e di miglior suono.[1]

The genesis of Voltaire's *Mérope* and its debt to Maffei have already been discussed in my chapter on Lessing's criticism of the French drama (pp. 211 ff.). Here we have to turn to the controversy in which Voltaire became involved with the Italian Marchese. In his dedication to Maffei, Voltaire had instanced (cp. XLI, 87) the garrulousness of Polidoro[2]:

Dans votre quatriéme Acte, le vieillard *Polidore* demande à un homme de la Cour de *Mérope*, qui il est? Je suis *Eurises* le fils de *Nicandre*, répond-il. *Polidore* alors en parlant de *Nicandre*, s'exprime comme le *Nestor* d'*Homère*:

> ...*Egli era umano*
> *E liberal; quando appariva, tutti*
> *Faceangli onor; io mi ricordo ancora*
> *Di quanto ei festeggiò con bella pompa*
> *Le sue nozze con Silvia, ch'era figlia*
> *D'Olimpia e di Glicon fratel d'Ipparco....*
>
> [Act IV, sc. iv.]

...Et dans un autre endroit, le même vieillard, invité d'aller voir la cérémonie du mariage de la Reine, répond:

> *Oh curioso*
> *Punto io non son, passò stagione. Assai*
> *Veduti ho sacrificii, io mi ricordo*
> *Di quello ancora quando il Rè Cresfonte*
> *Incominciò à regnar. Quella fù pompa.*
> *Ora più non si fanno a questi tempi*
> *Di cotaï sacrificj. Più di cento*
> *Fur le bestie svenate. I Sacerdoti*
> *Risplendean tutti, ed ove ti volgessi*
> *Altro non si vedea che argento ed oro.*
>
> [Act v, sc. v.]

[1] Ed. of 1730, p. xxxv; ed. of 1763, pp. xxiv f.
[2] *Œuvres, ed. cit.* viii, pp. 228 ff.

...Tous ces traits sont naïfs: tout y est convenable à ceux que vous introduisez sur la scène, et aux mœurs que vous leur donnez. Ces familiarités naturelles eussent été, à ce que je croi, bien reçues dans Athènes; mais Paris, et notre Parterre, veulent une autre espèce de simplicité....

Vous avez pû, dans votre Tragédie, traduire cette élégante et simple comparaison de *Virgile*:

> *Qualis populea mœrens Philomela sub umbra,*
> *Amissos queritur fœtus.*[1]

Si je prenais une telle liberté, on me renverrait au Poëme épique, tant nous avons affaire à un Maître dur, qui est le public.

> *Nescis, heu nescis nostræ fastidia Romæ:* [...]
> *Et pueri nasum Rhinocerontis habent.*[2]

Les Anglais ont la coutume de finir presque tous leurs Actes par une comparaison; mais nous exigeons, dans une Tragédie, que ce soit les Héros qui parlent, et non le Poëte; et notre public pense que dans une grande crise d'affaires, dans un conseil, dans une passion violente, dans un danger pressant, les Princes, les Ministres ne font point de comparaisons poëtiques.

Lessing omits the reference to English usage, which he had already discussed (xv, 96 ff.). The passage in Maffei's drama to which Voltaire refers is spoken by Polifonte in Act III, sc. i:

> Or freme, ed urla, or d' una in altra stanza
> Sen va gemendo, e chiama il figlio a nome:
> Qual Rondine talor, che ritornando
> Non vede i parti, e trova rotto il nido;
> Ch' alto stridendo gli s' aggira intorno,
> E parte, e riede, e di querele assorda.

Maffei, in his reply to Voltaire, denied his indebtedness to Virgil (ed. of 1763, p. 451):

Dicesi, che ho tradotta quella di Virgilio dell' usignolo: ma veramente non è così. Virgilio dice solamente con eleganza ammirabile, che quell' uccello si duole, e flebilmente canta la notte:

> *Flet noctem, ramoque sedens miserabile carmen*
> *Integrat, et mæstis late loca quæstibus implet.*[3]

---

[1] *Georgics*, iv, 511 f.

[2] The passage occurs in the Epigram of Martial numbered i, iii in most modern editions, and runs thus:

> 'Nescis, heu nescis dominæ fastidia Romæ...
> ...Et pueri nasum Rhinocerotis habent.'

[3] In Virgil (*Georgics*, iv, 514 f.) the passage refers to Orpheus's grief for Eurydice; in Maffei Polifonte is describing Merope's grief for her son.

Ma io rappresento ciò che la rondine fa, tornando al nido, nell' atto di trovarlo disfatto:

> *Ch' alto stridendo gli s'aggira intorno,*
> *E parte, e riede, e di querele assorda:*

onde vi assicuro, che non Virgilio, ma una rondine ebbi in mente, che mi era occorso di veder poco innanzi fare appunto così.

Lessing refers (XLI, 135) to Voltaire's further criticism, which is as follows:

Comment pourrais-je encor faire parler souvent ensemble des personnages subalternes? Ils servent chez vous à préparer des scènes intéressantes entre les principaux Acteurs; ce sont les avenuës d'un beau Palais: mais notre public impatient veut entrer tout d'un coup dans le Palais. Il faut donc se plier au goût d'une Nation, d'autant plus difficile, qu'elle est depuis longtems rassasiée de chefs-d'œuvres.[1]

When Lessing sums up Voltaire's letter in his witty 'paraphrase' (XLI, 144): 'Mein Herr Marquis, Ihr Stück hat sehr, sehr viel kalte, langweilige, unnütze Scenen', he is no doubt reading more malice into Voltaire than the latter felt. The letter is not necessarily 'Persifflage' (159).[2]

What followed Voltaire's dedication? A letter, says Lessing (XLI, 38), from a fictitious personage, 'de la Lindelle', to Voltaire; to this Voltaire replies, but 'Dieser ganzen Correspondenz mit sich selbst, dünkt mich, fehlt das interessanteste Stück; die Antwort des Maffei' (XLII, 142). As we have seen, however, Maffei did reply at once to Voltaire's dedicatory letter.[3]

Lessing now turns to Lindelle's systematic attack on the Italian *Merope* (XLII, 113 ff.). Lindelle, he admits, is not always wrong in his criticism; but he is intent on trampling Maffei underfoot, on destroying him; and to this end he distorts the truth. Voltaire indeed seems to have had some perception of this (138). In point of fact, Voltaire closed the controversy with a short 'Réponse à M. de la Lindelle', in which he reproached his man of straw for not having pointed out the merits of Maffei.

Lindelle's attack did not mince words:

L'intérêt de *Mérope* est tout autrement touchant que celui de la Tragédie d'*Athalie*; mais il paraît que Mr. *Maffei* s'est contenté de ce que présente naturellement son sujet, et qu'il n'y a mis aucun art théatral....

[1] *Œuvres, ed. cit.* viii, p. 231.
[2] Lessing's quotation 'Desinit in piscem mulier formosa superne' (XLI, 158) is, of course, from Horace's *Ars poetica*, l. 4 (Desinat in piscem mulier formosa superne).
[3] See above, pp. 216 f.

Nulle vraisemblance, nulle dignité, nulle bienséance, nul art dans le
Dialogue...cela serait sifflé à Paris par les moins connaisseurs....Ces
scènes froides et indécentes, qui ne sont imaginées que pour remplir un
Acte, ne seraient pas souffertes sur un Théâtre Tragique regulier. Vous
vous êtes contenté, Monsieur, de remarquer modestement une de ces scènes,
dans laquelle la suivante de *Mérope* prie le Tyran de ne pas presser les nôces;
parce que, dit-elle, sa Maîtresse a *un assaut de fièvre*: et moi, Monsieur, je
vous dis hardiment, au nom de tous les connaisseurs, qu'un tel dialogue, et
une telle réponse, ne sont dignes que du Théâtre d'*Arlequin*.[1]

And Lessing quotes its conclusion (XLII, 119):

En un mot, Monsieur, l'ouvrage de *Maffei* est un très beau sujet, et une
très mauvaise piéce. Tout le monde convient à Paris, que la représentation
n'en serait pas achevée, et tous les gens sensés d'Italie en font très peu de cas.
C'est très vainement, que l'Auteur dans ses voyages n'a rien négligé pour
engager les plus mauvais Ecrivains à traduire sa Tragédie: il lui était bien
plus aisé de payer un Traducteur que de rendre sa piéce bonne.[2]

Lessing contends that in almost all points Lindelle's censure has
to be palliated; Maffei may have made mistakes, but they are not
always as absurd as Lindelle would make them out to be (XLIII, 4).
And he instances the case, which has already been quoted, where
Maffei's texts show different readings, and where, in his opinion, the
argument is false:

Egiste, qui a été annoncé comme un voleur, et qui a dit, qu'on l'avait
voulu voler lui-même, est encor pris pour un voleur une seconde fois; il
est mené devant la Reine malgré le Roi, qui pourtant prend sa défense.
La Reine le lie à une colomne, le veut tuer avec un dard, et avant de le
tuer elle l'interroge. *Egiste* lui dit, que son père est un vieillard; et à ce
mot de vieillard la Reine s'attendrit. Voilà-t-il pas une bonne raison, de
changer d'avis, et de soupçonner, qu'*Egiste* pourrait bien être son fils?
Voilà-t-il pas un indice bien marqué? Est-il donc si étrange qu'un jeune
homme ait un père âgé. *Maffei* a substitué cette faute, et ce manque d'art
et de génie, à une autre faute plus grossière qu'il avait faite dans la première
édition. *Egiste* disait à la Reine: *Ah! Polidore, mon père*.[3] Et ce *Polidore*
était en effet l'homme à qui *Mérope* avait confié *Egiste*. Au nom de *Polidore*,
la Reine ne devait plus douter qu'*Egiste* ne fût son fils; la piéce était finie.
Ce défaut a été ôté; mais on y a substitué un défaut encor plus grand.[4]

---

[1] *Œuvres, ed. cit.* viii, pp. 236 ff.　　　　　　　　　　[2] *Ibid.* p. 241.

[3] The exact form of this quotation does not correspond to those in the editions
of 1714, 1730, 1745, and is not quoted in the variants given in the edition of 1747
(pp. 49 f.).

[4] *Œuvres, ed. cit.* viii, p. 238. See above, p. 282.

Lessing's defence of Maffei against Voltaire's pedantic objection is reasonable, provided that the essential artificiality of the situation is accepted. It does not matter very much which of the readings we choose. Lessing sums up by saying (63) that it is not so serious that Merope should come a second time to murder her son, as that the poet should use the motive of chance so freely as to allow it to occur twice in the play.

To illustrate obvious and intentional 'falsifications' by Lindelle, Lessing quotes (83) from the following passage:

Le quatriéme Acte commence encor par une scène froide et inutile entre le Tyran et la suivante: ensuite cette suivante rencontre le jeune *Egiste*, je ne sai comment, et lui persuade de se reposer dans le vestibule, afin que, quand il sera endormi, la Reine puisse le tuer tout à son aise. En effet il s'endort comme il l'a promis. Belle intrigue! et la Reine vient pour la seconde fois une hache à la main pour tuer le jeune homme qui dormait exprès. Cette situation répétée deux fois est le comble de la stérilité, comme le sommeil du jeune homme est le comble du ridicule. Mr. *Maffei* prétend qu'il y a beaucoup de génie et de varieté dans cette situation répétée; parce que la première fois la Reine arrive avec un dard, et la seconde fois avec une hache: quel effort de génie!

Enfin le vieillard *Polidore* arrive tout à propos, et empêche la Reine de faire le coup: on croirait que ce beau moment devrait faire naître mille incidens intéressans entre la mère et le fils, entre eux deux et le Tyran. Rien de tout cela; *Egiste* s'enfuit, et ne voit point sa mère; il n'a aucune scène avec elle; ce qui est encor un défaut de génie insupportable. *Mérope* demande au vieillard, quelle récompense il veut; et ce vieux fou la prie de le rajeunir. Voilà à quoi passe son tems une Reine qui devrait courir après son fils. Tout cela est bas, déplacé et ridicule au dernier point.[1]

So much for Lindelle's misrepresentations. In St. xliv Lessing turns to his criticisms; but as his argument is of the *tu quoque* kind, directed to showing that Voltaire was equally at fault, that he even aggravated Maffei's pseudo-classic artificialities, I have dealt with this criticism above in connexion with the French play.[2]

The commentators on the *Hamburgische Dramaturgie* are unanimous in discovering another reference to Maffei in that work. In St. xxxii (111) Lessing says: 'Hernach lebte, zu Anfange des itzigen Jahrhunderts, irgendwo in Italien, ein Pedant, der hatte den Kopf von den Trauerspielen der Griechen und seiner Landesleute des sechszehnten Seculi voll, und der fand an der Rodogune gleichfals vieles

---

[1] *Œuvres, ed. cit.* viii, pp. 239 f.   [2] See above, pp. 217 ff.

auszusetzen.' On the ground that Maffei wrote *Osservazioni sopra la Rodoguna* in 1700 (*Rime e Prose*, Venice, 1718),[1] this sentence has been held to refer to him. But it is far from likely that Lessing would describe a well-known writer, intimately associated with Verona and then little more than ten years dead—Maffei was born in 1675 and died in 1755—as having 'lived somewhere in Italy at the beginning of the century'; nor was there any ground for saying that Maffei's head was 'full of the tragedies of the Greeks', although he did edit some plays by his countrymen of the sixteenth century. The word 'pedant', moreover, seems inapplicable to a writer of whom it is said (XLII, 6) that he had 'in his youth much inclination for poetry', and that he wrote with great ease 'in all the different styles of the most famous poets of his country'. The reference here is not to Maffei, but to Count Pietro dei Conti di Calepio, the unnamed author of the *Paragone della Poesia tragica d'Italia con quella di Francia*, published by Bodmer at Zürich in 1732. In this little volume there is much about Greek and early Italian drama, and *Rodogune* is severely handled.[2]

[1] Cp. F. Doro, *op. cit.* pp. 8, 13. I. Pindemonte, *Elogi de' Letterati*, Verona, 1825–26, i, p. 249, cites the identical edition of 1719 (pp. 165 ff.).

[2] See my note in the *Modern Language Review*, xiii (1918), pp. 482 ff. On the possible influence of Calepio on Lessing's dramatic theory see below, pp. 365, 366, note 3, 367, 420.

CHAPTER IX

THE SPANISH DRAMA

In early days Lessing had turned with some zeal to the study of Spanish.[1] In a letter to his father of November 2, 1750, he wrote:

Auf das Spanische habe ich eine Zeit her sehr viel Fleiss verwendet, und ich glaube meine Mühe nicht umsonst angewendet zu haben. Da es eine Sprache ist, die eben in Deutschland so sehr nicht bekannt ist, so glaube ich, dass sie mir mit der Zeit nützliche Dienste leisten soll.[2]

And his first two dramaturgic journals and a number of book reviews bear witness to a growing interest in Spanish literature.

In the preface to the *Beyträge zur Historie und Aufnahme des Theaters* he states:

Wir werden besonders unser Augenmerk auf das englische und spanische Theater richten....Eben so ist es mit dem Lopez de Vega, Augustin Moreto, Antonio de Mendosa, Francisco de Rojas, Fernando de Zarate, Juan Perez de Montalvan, Antonio de Azevedo, Francisco Gonsalez de Bustos und andern. Diese sind alle Männer, die zwar eben so grosse Fehler als Schönheiten haben, von denen aber ein vernünftiger Nachahmer sich sehr vieles zu Nutze machen kann.[3]

Whence Lessing derived this extraordinary list of authors—of whom several are quite unknown or unrecognisable, and amongst whom Calderón is not mentioned—is still an enigma. There is nothing further about Spanish drama in the *Beyträge*, but in his *Theatralische Bibliothek* Lessing devoted a section to an *Auszug aus dem Trauerspiele Virginia des Don Augustino de Montiano y Luyando*. Here he wrote:

Die Schriften der Spanier sind diejenigen, welche unter allen ausländischen Schriften am wenigsten unter uns bekannt werden. Kaum dass man einige ihrer jetztlebenden Gelehrten in Deutschland dem Namen nach kennt, deren nähere Bekanntschaft uns einen ganz andern Begrif von der Spanischen Litteratur machen würde, als man gemeiniglich davon zu haben pflegt. Ich schmeichle mir, dass schon die gegenwärtige Nachricht

[1] The entire subject of Lessing's knowledge of Spanish and Spanish literature has been exhaustively investigated by C. Pitollet, *Contributions à l'étude de l'Hispanisme de G. E. Lessing*, Paris, 1909; and there is little to add to the results of Pitollet's research. Cp. also B. A. Wagner, *Zu Lessings spanischen Studien*, Berlin, 1883.

[2] *Schriften*, xvii, p. 22. Cp. Karl Lessing, *G. E. Lessings Leben*, Berlin, 1793–95, i, pp. 110 f.   [3] *Schriften*, iv, p. 52. See Pitollet, *op. cit.* pp. 72 ff.

ihn um ein grosses erhöhen wird, und dass meine Leser erfreut seyn werden, den grössten tragischen Dichter kennen zu lernen, den jezt Spanien aufweisen und ihn seinen Nachbarn entgegen stellen kann. Es ist dieses Don Augustino de Montiano y Luyando, von dessen Lebensumständen ich, ohne weitre Vorrede, einige Nachricht ertheilen will, ehe ich von einem der vorzüglichsten seiner Werke einen umständlichen Auszug vorlege.[1]

The section was merely translated from the French version of A. d'Hermilly, *Dissertation sur les Tragédies Espagnoles, Traduites de l'Espagnol de Don Augustin de Montiano y Luyando*, 2 vols. Paris, 1754.[2] Lessing's attention had been drawn to this work by a review in the *Journal des Sçavans* (April, 1751) a large part of which he had translated in the *Critische Nachrichten* of June of that year.[3] Later, in the *Dramaturgie* (LXVIII, 100), Lessing repudiated his all too favourable opinion of Montiano: 'Wir sind mit den dramatischen Werken der Spanier so wenig bekannt; ich wüsste kein einziges, welches man uns übersetzt, oder auch nur Auszugsweise mitgetheilet hätte. Denn die Virginia des Augustino de Montiano y Luyando ist zwar spanisch geschrieben; aber kein spanisches Stück: ein blosser Versuch in der correcten Manier der Franzosen, regelmässig aber frostig.'

In the interval Lessing's knowledge of Spanish drama had obviously widened. What he must have read in Cronegk's little essay on *Die spanische Bühne*, printed at the end of the first volume of the latter's *Schriften* (Leipzig, 1765–66, pp. 389 ff.), could not but have stimulated his curiosity:

Es ist zu beklagen, dass wir in Deutschland so wenig Gelegenheit haben, mit den neuen Stücken, die in Spanien heraus kommen, bekannt zu werden. Die Virginia und der Ataulpho sind fast die letztern, von denen wir etwas wissen; und wie weit müssen es die Spanier nicht gebracht haben, wenn sie diesen Meistern gefolget sind? Da ich von der neuen spanisch. Bühne meinen Lesern nichts besonders sagen kann: so glaube ich, dass es vielleicht einigen unter ihnen nicht unangenehm seyn wird, wenn ich ihnen einen Begriff von der alten spanischen Bühne zu geben unternehme: denn auch diese Nachrichten, die man von den ältesten Schriftstellern in dieser Sprache geben kann, sind fast in Deutschland neu; und ich weiss nicht, warum die Bewunderer der französ. und italien. Dichter nicht die Quelle zu erforschen suchen, aus welcher diese so vieles geschöpft, und diejenigen Schriftsteller ganz vergessen, die nebst den Alten die einzigen Lehrmeister eines Corneille und Moliere, und so vieler andern grossen Geister waren.

---

[1] *Theatralische Bibliothek*, i, p. 117; *Schriften*, vi, p. 70.
[2] See especially preface to vol. i, pp. xxv ff.
[3] *Schriften*, iv, pp. 225 f. Cp. also Pitollet, *op. cit.* pp. 84 ff.

Lessing probably only knew Montiano's second tragedy *Ataulpho* (1753) (LXVIII, 127) from a review in the *Journal étranger* of June, 1755.[1]

It is, however, generally conceded that the main stimulus to Lessing's interest in Spanish was his friendship with J. A. Dieze, a native of Hamburg and professor in the university of Göttingen. In 1768 Dieze made a translation of the *Origenes de la Poesía Castellana* by Luis José Velazquez de Velasco, Malaga, 1754 (*Geschichte der spanischen Dichtkunst*, Göttingen, with the date 1769); and it is tempting to look to this work as one of Lessing's sources of information about the literature of Spain. The German version, however, does not seem to have appeared until late in 1768, and a letter from Lessing is preserved, dated January 5, 1769, in which he thanks Dieze for the copy of the book which the latter had sent him.[2] But Lessing, no doubt, learned a good deal from his friend in personal intercourse and possibly in correspondence. His change of view in respect of Montiano may have been due, as Pitollet suggests, to information which reached him in this way. In his translation of Velazquez, Dieze states his own opinion of Montiano in the following note (*ed. cit.* p. 373):

> Was seine beyden Trauerspiele anbetrift, so haben sie wohl unstreitig das Verdienst, die regelmässigsten zu seyn, die die Spanier haben. Aber weder die genaue Beobachtung der Regeln, die Aristoteles und seine Nachfolger vorgeschrieben haben, noch die sehr schöne Versification, haben diese Stücke so interessant machen können, als viele sind, in denen die Regeln nicht so ängstlich beobachtet worden. Sie sind ganz nach französischem Schnitte, und fehlt ihnen selbst im Styl das Eigenthümliche und nationale der Spanier. Sie haben auch die Originalstücke bey ihnen noch nicht ganz verdrängen können, daher auch noch nicht viele Nachahmer dieses Geschmacks aufgestanden sind.

It is hardly likely that Lessing knew the original work of Velazquez, except through extracts in the *Journal étranger* of 1755.[3] What he has to say on Spanish drama in the *Hamburgische Dramaturgie* concerns in the main the Spanish *Essex*,[4] which interested him from the point of

---

[1] Vol. ii of June, 1755, pp. 108 ff.

[2] *Schriften*, xvii, pp. 280 ff. Unfortunately other letters from Lessing to Dieze were destroyed at the siege of Mainz in 1793 (cp. *G. E. Lessings Sämmtliche Schriften*, Berlin, 1771–94, xxix, p. 486, note by Eschenburg). See also Pitollet, *op. cit.* p. 198.

[3] From February, 1755 to July, 1755 the journal printed a series of articles summarising the contents of Velazquez' *Origenes de la Poesía Castellana*. For observations on Montiano see especially the first number of June, 1755, pp. 91 ff.

[4] See below, pp. 300 ff

view of its subject more than from any other. Modifying his previous praise of Montiano, he adds (LXVIII, 129) that he still prefers to turn to Lope and Calderón. He also proceeds to make some general statements on Spanish drama which hardly seem based on any extensive knowledge. After analysing the Spanish *Essex*, he concludes (LXVIII, 132) that the genuine Spanish pieces are wholly in the manner of this play. In condemning the 'Künsteleyen' of the dialogue in Act 1, sc. xii (LXII, 120), Lessing had already compared the Spanish dramas with the German 'Staats- und Heldenactionen' ['Haupt- und Staats-aktionen'], an association which was suggested in Löwen's *Geschichte des deutschen Theaters*:

Die ernsthaften Stücke, welche Velthem spielte, waren spanische geradebrechte Uebersetzungen, die unter dem lächerlichen Titel der Haupt- und Staatsaktionen die Stelle des Trauerspiels vertraten.[1]

The characterisation of Spanish plays which follows later (LXVIII, 135): 'Eine ganz eigne Fabel; eine sehr sinnreiche Verwicklung; sehr viele, und sonderbare, und immer neue Theaterstreiche; die aus-gespartesten Situationen; meistens sehr wohl angelegte und bis ans Ende erhaltene Charaktere; nicht selten viel Würde und Stärke im Ausdrucke', would appear to come from Du Perron de Castera, *Extraits de plusieurs pieces du Théatre espagnol; avec des Réflexions, et la Traduction des endroits les plus remarquables* (2 vols. Amsterdam and Paris, 1738):[2]

Toutes ces oppositions de génie, ces differences prodigieuses de notre Scene et du Theatre des Espagnols, ne doivent pas nous faire imaginer que leurs Pieces n'ont aucun mérite. On y trouve beaucoup d'invention, des sentimens nobles et pleins de délicatesse, des caracteres marqués avec force et soutenus avec dignité, des situations heureuses, des surprises bien

---

[1] Reprint, ed. Stümcke, p. 15. In a note Löwen refers to Gottsched as his authority (cp. *Nöthiger Vorrath*, i, pp. 52 f., under the date 1520). Cp. Schröter and Thiele, *ed. cit.* pp. 360 f. These latter critics also refer (p. 361) to the following from Nicolai's *Beschreibung einer Reise durch Deutschland und die Schweiz im Jahre 1781*, iv (Berlin, 1784), p. 566: 'Mein sel. Freund Lessing besass, aus dem Nachlass der berühmten Neuberinn, eine Anzahl dieser Ludovicischen Stücke. Es waren darinn nach damaliger Art, zum Extemporiren, nur die Folge und der Inhalt der Auftritte angezeiget, und nur wenige Hauptscenen waren ganz ausgeschrieben....Ich erinnere mich besonders noch des Grafen von Essex, des Kromwell, und des Königs von Böhmen.' The 'Haupt- und Staatsaktionen', however, were in the main developed in Germany, though subject to foreign influences.

[2] Vol. i, pp. 8 ff. Cp. also B. A. Wagner, *op. cit.* pp. 12 f.; A. Sauer in *Viertel-jahrschrift für Litteraturgeschichte*, i (1888), p. 24, and Pitollet, *op. cit.* pp. 181 ff.

ménagées,[1] un grand fonds de Comique, un feu d'intérêt qui ne laisse point languir le Spectateur.

Voilà les beautés que nous offrent presque toutes les Comédies de Lopès de Véga, de Don Guillen, de Don Pedro Calderon et d'autres Poëtes illustres qui font honneur à l'Espagne.... Ainsi la connoissance du Théatre Espagnol n'est point indifferente pour les Belles-Lettres, on peut en tirer d'excellens sujets qui auront pour nous les graces de la nouveauté. Il ne faut qu'adopter l'invention, simplifier les matieres, *élaguer* les avantures, saisir les images, presser les mouvemens et relever quelquefois le Comique, cette espece d'imitation pratiquée avec goût pourroit nous procurer des copies qui vaudroient des Originaux.

Pitollet also suggests (pp. 182 f.)—but this appears more doubtful— that the following passage from Lesage's *Théâtre espagnol*,[2] the substance of which also appears in Goujet's *Bibliothèque françoise*,[3] may have been in Lessing's mind:

Ce n'est pas tout, les Pieces Espagnoles sont remplies de contre-temps ingenieux, de contrarietés dans les desseins des Acteurs, et de mille jeux de Theatre qui reveillent à tout moment l'attention du spectateur. Enfin leurs intrigues ont presque toutes du merveilleux; mais ce merveilleux ne donne pas dans le fabuleux et le romanesque, et comme ils le ramenent toûjours au vraysemblable par les regles de l'art, il fait un admirable effet sur la Scene. Nos François ne connoissent point ces beautés, il ne paroît pas du moins qu'ils les ayent assés recherchées dans les Pieces qu'ils n'ont pas copiées ou imitées des Espagnols.

Again, the description of 'Cosme, dieser spanische Hanswurst' (LXVIII, 152 ff.) may have been suggested, according to Pitollet (p. 216), by Du Perron (*op. cit.* i, p. 4):

Outre cela dans les Pieces Espagnoles, souvent le tragique le plus relevé se trouve confondu avec le burlesque; souvent un Bouffon qu'ils nomment *le Laquais gracieux*, ou bien quelqu'autre Personnage de même étoffe, prend la liberté d'interrompre les Heros et les Rois au milieu des situations les plus touchantes; pareille indécence nous révolteroit. Elle révoltoit aussi Philippe II. Ce Prince, au rapport de Lopès de Véga, ne voyoit jamais sans dégoût la majesté des grands Rôles avilie par un badinage si déplacé, et certainement il avoit raison.

Spanish dramas, Lessing says (LXII, 141), have only three acts,

---

[1] Pitollet (*op. cit.* p. 182) points to this term as the original of Lessing's 'aus-gespart', a technical term still used in water-colour painting.

[2] *Théâtre espagnol*, La Haye, 1700, Preface, pp. [iii] f.

[3] *Bibliothèque françoise*, viii (Paris, 1755), chap. xiv, pp. 159 f.

which are called 'Jornadas, Tagewerke'.[1] The oldest pieces had four. Virves was the first to reduce this number to three; and Lope de Vega followed him. We learn this, he adds, from a passage in Lope's *Arte nuevo de hazer Comedias en este tiempo*, which is appended to his *Rimas*. Lessing quotes, in a note, the lines in question (215–21). To this statement he finds Cervantes opposed, that writer claiming in the preface to his comedies[2] to have reduced the Spanish tragedy from five acts to three. The source of this information was perhaps a review of Velazquez' *Origenes de la Poesía Castellana* in the *Journal étranger* of May, 1755, where the following statement is made (pp. 73 f.):

Cervantes, dans le Prologue de ces huit Comédies, se vante d'avoir été le premier qui divisa la Comédie en trois journées, et qui fit voir pour la premiere fois cette division sur le Théâtre, dans sa Comédie de la *Bataille Navale*; mais Naharro avoit déja donné ce nom à ses Actes. On voit par là combien *Lopé de Vega* s'est trompé, en attribuant cette invention à *Christophe de Virves*, quand il dit:

> El Capitan Virves, insigne ingegno,
> Puso en tres Actos la Comedia, que antes,
> Andaba en quatro, como pies de nino.

Le Capitaine *Virves*, célebre par son esprit, ne donna à la Comédie que trois Actes, au lieu de quatre, avec lesquels elle se présentoit autrefois, semblable à un enfant qui marche à *quatre pattes*.

Only three lines of the passage from Lope are quoted in the *Journal étranger*; thus Lessing evidently turned to the original (1609), of which he may have had the edition of 1623.[3]

The redondilla, which is introduced into Act II of the Spanish *Essex*, and which Lessing quotes, gives occasion for a note of explana-

---

[1] Pitollet (*op. cit.* p. 203) points out that 'jornada' means 'Tagereise' rather than 'Tagewerk'; but Lessing may be translating 'journée' from the French.

[2] *Comedias y Entremeses* de Miguel de Cervantes Saavedra, Madrid, 1749, i, p. [lxx] (p. [iii] of the 1615 ed. of which this is a reprint), *Prologo al Lector*: 'Donde me atreví à reducir las Comedias à tres jornadas, de cinco que tenian.'

[3] In the 1609 edition, the lines are on pp. 205 f. Cp. a letter from Meinhard to Nicolai of December 17, 1765: 'An Herrn Lessing werde ich nächstens die Poesien des Lope de Vega zurücksenden. Dürfte ich bitten, ihn zu fragen, ob er etwas von Spanischen Büchern aus der Auction für mich übrig hat?' (Danzel and Guhrauer, *op. cit.* ii, p. 654.) Lessing had also a French translation of Lope's *Arte nuevo* (cp. *Chefs-d'œuvre des Théâtres étrangers*, xii (Théâtre Espagnol, i), Paris, 1822, pp. lxix ff. and especially p. lxxv). Cp. further A. Morel-Fatio, *L'Arte nuevo de Hazer Comedias en este Tiempo de Lope de Vega* in *Bulletin hispanique*, Annales de la Faculté des Lettres de Bordeaux, iii (1901), p. 393. See also below, p. 395.

tion (LXIII, 103).[1] In connexion with this, he observes that the Spaniards have a kind of poem called 'Glossa' [*sic*] in which lines from the text ('Mote' or 'Letra') are elaborated. But all 'Glossas', he says, need not be as symmetrical as that in the *Conde de Sex*. These 'Glossas' are only to be found in the older Spanish poetry; after Boscan and Garcilasso they fell into disuse. The source of this information seems to have been again the chapter in Goujet's *Bibliothèque françoise*,[2] where C. Lancelot's [de Trigny's] *Nouvelle méthode pour apprendre...la langue espagnole* (Paris, 1660) is discussed. Here Goujet, drawing from Lancelot, makes the following statements about 'la Glose':

[Les Gloses sont] ces piéces où l'on prend d'abord 'quelque mot ou quelque sentence', sur laquelle on fait ensuite 'des vers ausquels ce mot et cette sentence servent de reprise'.

Les Espagnols ont été longtems sans connoître d'autre forme de poësie, que celle dont je viens de parler....Dans la suite Jean Boscan et Garcilasso de la Véga, morts avant le milieu du seiziéme siecle, introduisirent dans leur langue la forme de la poësie Italienne qu'ils connurent par la communication qu'ils eurent avec les meilleurs Poëtes Italiens de leur tems dans les voyages qu'ils firent à Naples....[3]

Elle n'y a pas suivi la regle la plus ordinaire de cette ancienne poësie Espagnole, de répéter chaque vers du *Texte* dans son ordre, à la fin de chaque stance de la Glose; dans celle-ci [*la Glose de Sainte Thérese*] il n'y a que le dernier vers du texte qui serve de reprise....[4]

In St. LXIX Lessing returns to Lope de Vega's *Arte nuevo*. He gives a paraphrase (18 ff.) of lines 157–80, and quotes the original text in his note. But the paraphrase appears to be in the main a translation of a French version of the poem. As Pitollet has shown (p. 203), this translation is not, as Lessing stated,[5] in the *Nouveau Recueil des Pièces fugitives d'Histoire, de Littérature etc.* of Archimbaud (Paris, 1717) but in the *Pièces fugitives d'histoire et de littérature anciennes et modernes*, edited by Flachat de Saint-Sauveur (pseudonym of the Abbé A. de Tricaud),

---

[1] The redondilla is in general a four-lined strophe, usually rhyming *a b b a*. Cp. Petersen, *ed. cit.* p. 235, and C. Lancelot [de Trigny], *Nouvelle méthode pour apprendre...la langue espagnole*, 2nd ed., Paris, 1665, pp. 91 ff.

[2] *Ed. cit.* viii, pp. 152 ff.

[3] *Ibid.* p. 152. The words enclosed in quotation marks occur in Lancelot, *ed. cit.* p. 103.

[4] Goujet, *op. cit.* p. 155.

[5] In his notes *Zur Gelehrten-Geschichte und Literatur* (*Schriften*, xvi, p. 238): 'Lope de Vega's Kunst, neue Komödien zu machen. Dieses Werkchen, woraus ich in der Dramaturgie eine Stelle übersetzt habe, hat der Abt Archimbaud, Französisch übersetzt, seinen Pieces fugitives, Part. II, p. 248. mit eingerückt.'

ii (Paris, 1704), pp. 248 ff. The translation is entitled *Nouvelle Pratique de Théatre, accommodée à l'usage présent d'Espagne, adressée à l'Académie de Madrid et traduite de l'espagnol de Lopez de Vega* (par l'Abbé de Charnes).[1] The passage which Lessing quotes is as follows in the French version :

Il faut donc choisir un sujet, et les régles me pardonneront si je dis qu'il n'importe pas que ce soit l'action de quelque Roi: Quoi qu'il soit vrai, comme on me l'a dit, que Philippe le Prudent, Roi de notre Espagne et notre Souverain, voyant paroître un Roi dans nos Comédies, ne pouvoit pas s'en accommoder; soit que ce fût un effet de son bon goût pour le vrai, soit qu'il trouvât mauvais de voir la Majesté Royale avilie parmi le menu peuple. Ce qui est en effet en revenir à l'ancienne Comédie, dans laquelle Plaute mettoit les Divinitez; Jupiter, par exemple, dans son Amphitrion. Dieu sçait aussi la peine que j'ai de l'approuver, aprés ce que Plutarque, parlant de Menandre, a dit contre cette Comédie ancienne: Mais puis que nous nous éloignons des régles, et que nous les méprisons si fort en Espagne, Messieurs les Doctes n'ont qu'à prendre patience et se taire. Il faut donc sans difficulté mêler le Tragique avec le Comique; Térence avec Seneque formeront une espèce de Urinotaure; une partie de la piéce sera serieuse et l'autre burlesque. Cette varieté plaît infiniment; Et en effet, n'est-elle pas fondée sur la nature, qui n'est belle que par cette diversité?[2]

In a letter to Dieze of January 5, 1769 which has already been quoted, Lessing mentions that he has collected 'eine ansehnliche Menge' of Spanish comedies :

Denn selten ist ein Hamburger, der sich zu Cadix bereichert, wieder zurückgekommen, ohne ein Paar Komödien mitzubringen. Von einer habe ich in dem 60sten bis 69sten Stücke meiner Dramaturgie einen weitläuftigen Auszug geliefert; und ich möchte wohl wissen, ob Ihnen diese unter dem Namen des Verfassers irgendwo vorgekommen?[3]

Dieze was evidently unable to supply the information. And Lessing had forgotten, when he was writing his *Dramaturgie*, that d'Hermilly, in his translation of Montiano's *Dissertation*[4], had attributed the play to 'Philippe IV. Roi d'Espagne'.[5] It was left to A. F. von Schack, in his *Geschichte der dramatischen Litteratur und Kunst in Spanien*, to establish

---

[1] It has been reprinted by Pitollet in the *Siècle*, Nos. 16, 17, 18, November, 1906.

[2] *Pièces fugitives, ed. cit.* ii, pp. 255 f. (A copy of this work is in the Bayerische Staatsbibliothek, Munich.)

[3] *Schriften*, xvii, p. 281.

[4] Lessing refers to this translation in the *Theatralische Bibliothek* (i, p. 121; *Schriften*, vi, p. 72).

[5] Cp. Pitollet, *op. cit.* p. 170.

the fact that the author of *Dar la vida por su Dama ó El Conde de Sex*;
'da un Ingenio de esta Corte', was Antonio Coello, who died in
1652.[1]

The edition which Lessing possessed he found (LX, 2) in 'einer
Sammlung von Komödien, die Joseph Padrino zu Sevilien gedruckt
hat, und in der er das vier und siebzigste Stück ist'. This was the
tenth edition of the play.[2]

Beyond a few corrections in Lessing's Spanish quotations, resulting
from a collation with the edition which Lessing had before him, I am
able to offer little more than a résumé of the data and criticism of
Pitollet and other commentators. This will be found in the Appendix
below.

APPENDIX

References are to the reprint of *La Tragedia mas lastimosa de amor. Dar la
vida por su Dama ó El Conde de Sex* in Brockhaus's Coleccion de Autores
Españoles xxvii (Leipzig, 1870), pp. 165 ff., where the acts are divided into
scenes and the lines are numbered, unfortunately with some misprints.
The correct numbers are quoted here in square brackets, where they differ
from those in the reprint.

Hamburgische Dramaturgie	*El Conde de Sex*
LX, 18. 'Essex kömmt von seiner Expedition wider die Spanier zurück.'	Essex's return from his expedition and his vision of the half-masked lady are narrated in the course of conversation between him and his servant Cosme, Act I, sc. iii. In scene i the attempt on the queen's life, which is frustrated by Essex, takes place, and in scene ii the queen, wearing a half mask, thanks Essex, with the gift of a scarf to bind up his injured hand.
LX, 41. 'Las dos columnas bellas etc.'	The quotation is from Act I, sc. iii, ll. 154–61.

[1] *Geschichte der dramatischen Litteratur und Kunst in Spanien*, Berlin, 1845–46, iii,
pp. 4 f., 407, and *Nachträge* (Frankfurt, 1854), p. 102. Cp. also Cosack, *op. cit.*
p. 307.
[2] There are two MSS. in the Biblioteca Nacional of Madrid. See Emilio Cotarelo
y Mori, *Don Antonio Coello y Ochoa*, Madrid, 1919, pp. 26, 28, 30.

Hamburgische Dramaturgie	*El Conde de Sex*
LX, 47. 'er kann nicht begreifen' is a mistranslation.	'juzgué' ('methought', 'it seemed to me'), Act I, sc. iii, l. 185.
LX, 49. 'Basalt.' The translation is erroneous; the word means 'jet' (Schröter and Thiele, *ed. cit.* p. 353, and Petersen, *ed. cit.* p. 232). Possibly Lessing was misled by his dictionary.	'azabache', Act I, sc. iii, l. 189.
LX, 58. 'Sie...knüpft ihre Schärpe los, und giebt sie ihm.... Zugleich, sagt sie, soll diese Schärpe dienen, mich Euch zu seiner Zeit zu erkennen zu geben....'	'Aquesa banda Señal para hacer buscaros Serà...', Act I, sc. ii, ll. 53–5.
LX, 66. 'Diese Hand, sagt er, war dem klaren Wasser so ähnlich....'	Act I, sc. iii, ll. 196–203. The correct translation would be: 'For that which she drank resembled her hands so much that I feared in sudden apprehension—and not without reason—that she might drink a part of her hand' (Pitollet, *op. cit.* p. 24 and Cosack, *op. cit.* pp. 308 f.).
LX, 77. 'Yo, que al principio vi, ciego, y turbado....'	The passage is in Act I, sc. iii, ll. 182–9.
LX, 100. 'Aus diesem Zuge, kann man leicht auf das Übrige schliessen.' Pitollet takes exception to Lessing's inference here (*op. cit.* p. 25) and also to the later one, LX, 132 ('Man erwartet, dass der Herzog auf diesen Einwurf die Lauterkeit seiner Absichten betheuern werde...') as unjustifiable.	
LX, 110. 'Ruido de armas en la Quinta....' 'Cosme, que ha...' and 'La Muger del hortelano....'	The passages are in Act I, sc. i, ll. 9–14, I, iii, ll. 65–6, and I, iii, ll. 243–4.
LX, 149. 'Te hice dueño de mi honor.'	Act I, sc. vii, l. 312 [412]: 'I make thee master of my honour.'

Hamburgische Dramaturgie	*El Conde de Sex*
LXI, 14. 'Sie hatte an ihren Oheim geschrieben....' Lessing repeats this erroneous translation of 'primo' in LXI, 28.	Act I, sc. vii, ll. 429–33 [529–33]: 'Y hasta Roberto, mi primo, Por pariente de mi padre, Que no por otro delito, Huyó del riesgo, y sin esto [estado, 1638] Vive en Escocia escondido.' 'And until Robert my cousin, on account of his being a kinsman of my father, and for no other crime, should flee the danger and unconditionally live concealed in Scotland.'
LXI, 23. 'Bien podré seguramente ....'	Act I, sc. vii, ll. 340–3 [440–3].
LXI, 47–62 and 83–94. 'Ay tal traicion! vive el Cielo....'	From Act I, sc. vii, ll. 506–33 [606-33].
LXI, 95. 'Si estàs consultando, Conde....'	From Act I, sc. vii, ll. 552–6 [652-6].
LXI, 115. 'Wer darf das sagen?'	Act I, sc. viii, ll. 629–32 [729–32]. To illustrate the lack of accuracy in Lessing's rendering, Pitollet points to this passage (*op. cit.* pp. 26 f.). Lessing gives a loose translation.
LXI, 116. 'Por vida del Rey mi hermano....'	From Act I, sc. viii, ll. 608–15; 619–57 [708–15; 719–57].
LXII, 16. 'Miradlo mejor, dexad ....'	From Act I, sc. viii, ll. 692–7 [792-7].
LXII, 22. 'No he de responder al Duque....'	From Act I, sc. viii, ll. 706–11 [806-11].
LXII, 51. 'Y pues son dos los culpados....'	From Act I, sc. ix, ll. 733–7 [833–7].
LXII, 56. 'Y es gran materia....'	From Act I, sc. ix, ll. 747–55 [847-55].
LXII, 47 and 61 ff. 'Ausserordentliche Verbrechen werden besser verschwiegen, als bestraft....'	The literal translation of ll. 752–5 [852–5] is 'And thus secrecy should investigate enormous crimes, since, more than the punishment, the sin itself brings exemplary chastisement.'

Hamburgische Dramaturgie	*El Conde de Sex*
LXII, 94. 'Que ya solo con miraros ....'	From Act I, sc. xi, ll. 763–4 [863–4].
LXII, 96. 'No bastaba, amor tyranno....'	From Act I, sc. xi, ll. 809–12 [909–12].
LXII, 123. 'Loco Amor—....'	From Act I, sc. xii, ll. 876–89 [976–89].
LXIII, 29. 'Er kann kein Geheimniss eine Stunde bewahren....'	This is a paraphrase of the passages quoted in the notes (LXIII, 41 ff.) from Act II, sc. iii, ll. 975–81 [1075–81] and 990–3 [1090–3], also of ll. 987–9 [1087–9].
LXIII, 73. 'Ya se me viene a la boca....'	From Act II, sc. iv, ll. 1015–18, 1025–7, 1043–9 [1115–18, 1125–7, 1143–9].
LXIII, 87. 'Es hombre al fin, y ay de aquella....'	From Act II, sc. v, ll. 1054–6 [1154–6].
LXIII, 110. 'Abate, abate las alas ....'	From Act II, sc. vii, ll. 1078–87 [1178–87].
LXIII, 131. 'Eine Liebe, sagt sie unter andern, die man verschweigt, kann nicht gross seyn....' Pitollet (*op. cit.* p. 28) and Petersen (*ed. cit.* p. 237) point out that 'die man verschweigt' should be 'die nicht belohnt wird'.	Paraphrased from the passage in Act II, sc. vii, ll. 1192–1201 [1292–1301]: 'No puede haber grande amor Sin ser pagado; y por eso Fingió allá la antigüedad, Que hasta que creciese Anteo, Que es el recíproco, nunca Crecia Cupido; luego Si no decís vuestro amor, Nunca lo sabrá el sujeto; Sin saberlo no os tendrá Recíproco amor, es cierto....'
LXIII, 132. 'Mote. Si acaso mis desvarios....'	From Act II, sc. vii, ll. 1118–21 [1218–21] and 1143–81 [1243–81].
LXIV, 25–9, 46–57. 'El mas verdadero amor....'	From Act II, sc. vii, ll. 1210–16, 1252–9 [1310–16, 1352–9] and 1264–5 [1364–5].
LXIV, 58–66 and 76–106. 'Por no morir de mal....'	From Act II, sc. vii, viii and ix, ll. 1286–1324 [1386–1424].

Hamburgische Dramaturgie	*El Conde de Sex*
LXIV, 117 ff. 'Essex. Wenn denn also....'	The passage is as follows (Act II, sc. ix, ll. 1312 ff. [1412 ff.]: 'Conde. Segun lo que dijo Vuestra Alteza aquí, y supuesto Que cuesta cara la dicha Que se compra con el miedo, Quiero morir noblemente.'
LXIV, 122 ff. 'Essex. Weil ich hoffe....'	'Conde. ¿Qué espero? ¿Si á vuestra Alteza (¿qué dudo?) Le declarase su afecto Algun amor....'
LXIV, 126. 'Wissen Sie, wer ich bin? Und wer Sie sind?' This is not literally translated.	Act II, sc. ix, ll. 1322 f. [1422 f.]: '¿Quien soy yo? Decid quien soy....'
LXIV, 140. '...No me veais....'	From Act II, sc. ix, ll. 1356–9 [1456–9].
LXV, 3. '...Ya estoi resuelta....'	From Act II, sc. xii, ll. 1435–53 [1535–53].
LXV, 39. 'Le llamé una noche obscura....'	From Act II, sc. xii, ll. 1518–25 [1618–25].
LXV, 50 and 69. 'Die Königinn. Eifersucht?—Nein....' 'Este es zelo, Blanca....' The whole of the passage is very loosely translated.	The Queen's speech is Act II, sc. xii, ll. 1580 ff. [1680 ff.]. Lessing selects ll. 1580–96 [1680–96], 1602–3 [1702–3], 1616–19 [1716–19], 1622–3 [1722–3] for translation.
LXV, 95. 'Dieser Zug ist vortrefflich....' Schröter and Thiele (ed. cit. p. 371) suggest a resemblance here to the first scene of Emilia Galotti, where a petition with the signature 'Emilia' recalls to the prince his love.	Refers to Act II, sc. xvi, where the Queen finds among the petitions presented to her one from a Count Felix, and comments on the coincidence which recalls her thoughts to the tangled situation.
LXV, 153. 'Conde, vos traidor?....' This is also loosely translated.	From Act II, sc. xvii, ll. 1766–93 [1866–93].
LXVI, 13. 'No pudo ser que mintiera....'	From Act III, sc. i, ll. 1880–94 [1980–94].
LXVI, 57. 'Que escucho? Señores mios....' Lessing only offers a paraphrase of the original.	From Act III, sc. iii, ll. 2111–15, 2127–38.

Hamburgische Dramaturgie	*El Conde de Sex*
LXVI, 112–39 and 159–70. 'Solo el descargo que tengo....'	From Act III, sc. vi, ll. 2242–58, 2260–84.
LXVII, 15. '"Keinen Traum" fährt die Königinn fort....'	From Act III, sc. viii, l. 2415. The Spanish word is 'sombra' (shadow).
LXVII, 27. 'El Conde me diò la vida....'	From Act III, sc. viii, ll. 2393–2400.
LXVII, 57. 'Ingeniosa mi fortuna ....'	From Act III, sc. viii, ll. 2475–81.
LXVII, 64. 'Pues si esto ha de ser ....'	From Act III, sc. viii, ll. 2510–20.
LXVII, 96. 'Morirè yo consolado ....'	Act III, sc. viii, ll. 2531–43. 'Ya moriré consolado.'
LXVII, 133. 'Luego esta, que assi camino....'	From Act III, sc. viii, ll. 2567–79.
LXVII, 146. Vil instrumento De mi vida, y de mi infamia ....' Much of Lessing's translation is only a paraphrase.	From Act III, sc. viii, ll. 2590–8.
LXVIII, 44. 'Hasta que el tronco cadaver Le sirva de muda lengua.' Lessing translates 'mit stummer Zunge Treue und Gehorsam zurufe' (cp. Petersen, *ed. cit.* p. 239).	From Act III, sc. x, ll. 2701–2. Literally 'serve as a mute tongue'.
LXVIII, 46. 'Y assi al salon de palacio.' This also is loosely rendered.	From Act III, sc. x, ll. 2703–20.
LXVIII, 83. 'Blanca en el ultimo trance....'	From Act III, sc. x, ll. 2739–63.

CHAPTER X

THE DRAMA OF ANTIQUITY

Apart from Lessing's treatment of Aristotle, his discussion of the literatures of antiquity is meagre.[1] An index to the *Hamburgische Dramaturgie* may contain many names of Greek and Latin writers; but for the most part, these owe their presence there to passing references and quotations. One would hardly look to this work to obtain an idea of Lessing's classical scholarship or of his attitude to antiquity—Aristotle, of course, always excepted. But it is something of a defect, if we remember that one of the main theses of the *Dramaturgie* is to prove the immeasurable inferiority of French classic tragedy to that of the Greeks, that Lessing should have taken so little opportunity to justify the supremacy of the latter, and notably of Sophocles. The only classical dramatist who is dealt with in any detail is Terence; here alone Lessing comes to grips with problems of scholarship.

Of the Greek writers, we find references to and quotations from Homer,[2] Pindar,[3] Plato[4] and Plutarch,[5] and a few mentions of historical writers;[6] but Lessing's discussions of Greek literature are restricted to the Greek dramatists and Aristotle.

It is, as I have said, a recurrent theme of the *Dramaturgie* that the tragedy of the Greeks fulfils those conditions of real tragic poetry

---

[1] See on this subject the excellent treatise of J. Kont, *Lessing et l'Antiquité*, 2 vols. Paris, 1894–99.

[2] [XXI, 117]; XXXVI, 116, 120; XLII, 59, 92; [LXIX, 70]; LXXIII, 82; XCI, 21. (I enclose in square brackets references occurring in quotations from other writers.) For 'Wir...vergessen, dass Homer...entzücket' (XXXVI, 119) cp. Madame Dacier, *L'Iliade d'Homere, traduite en François, avec des Remarques*, Paris, 1711, i, p. 31: 'Cette ignorance, où l'on est sur le pays, sur la vie et sur le nom mesme d'Homere, prouve admirablement la verité de ce que dit l'Empereur Marc Aurele, qu'un homme inconnu peut estre un homme divin'...and *ibid.* p. 29: 'Dion Chrysostome, admirant cette modestie, l'oppose à la vanité de ces escrivains qui mettent leur nom au commencement, à la fin, et dans le cours mesme de leurs ouvrages...'; on Homer's Μαργείτης as an 'erdichteter Name' derived from μαργής (XCI, 20), see Pauly, *Real-Encyclopädie der classischen Altertumswissenschaft* (Neue Bearbeitung), XIV, ii, 1708, and VIII, ii, 2152 ff. Cp. also H. Stephanus, *Lexicon Græcolatinum*, [Lyons], 1607 (1005, under μαργός, etc.).   [3] XXXIV, 21.

[4] XCI, 95; [XCIV, 46].   [5] XXXVII, 41, 65; XXXIX, 27, [42]; XCVI, 52.

[6] XXIX, 63; XXXII, 15; XXXIX, 83; XC, 123.

which French tragedy fails to fulfil. The interest of the Hamburg audience in 'maxims' reminds Lessing (II, 115) of the Attic stage, where a Euripides could win fame and a Socrates be amongst his audience; but alas, he comments, there was only one Athens where the moral sense of the people was so delicate that actors and poets could be repudiated for impure morals. While discussing Voltaire's *Sémiramis* (x, 89 ff.) he holds up to ridicule, as we have seen, the French writer's condescending patronage of the Greek theatre and his belief that the ancients might have learned from the French.[1] And again, still more emphatically, in St. LXXXI (139), Lessing couples Greek tragedy with that of Shakespeare—surely strange bedfellows—and denies that any French tragedy excites pity 'in the degree in which tragedy should excite it, in that degree which I know from various Greek and English pieces that it can excite it'. He is convinced (137) that 'their Corneille and Racine, their Crébillon and Voltaire have little or nothing of that which makes Sophocles Sophocles, Euripides Euripides, Shakespeare Shakespeare'.

At the beginning of St. XXXII Lessing writes of the origins of Greek tragedy. Thespis, he asserts, quoting as his authority the life of Solon by Diogenes Laertius, 'had no interest in historical correctness'. In this account Lessing read that 'Solon forbade Thespis to prepare and perform tragedies, saying that the untrue had no utility. When Peisistratos wounded himself, he said that this was a result of it.'[2] This is drawn from a note by Curtius in his *Aristoteles Dichtkunst*:

Thespis liess zuerst eine Person zwischen den Chören reden, welche erdichtete Begebenheiten oder Fabeln vorstellete: Dass es erdichtete und nicht wahre Begebenheiten waren, erhellet aus Solons Verbot an Thespis, zu Athen Tragödien zu spielen, um nicht die Athenienser zur Unwahrheit anzuführen (Diogenes Laert. in Solone Lib. i. Segm. 59).[3]

[1] See above, p. 221.

[2] Diogenes Laertius, *De vitis, dogmatibus et apophthegmatibus clarorum virorum*, Liber i, Segm. 59–60, Amsterdam, 1692, pp. 37 f. Cp. also Lessing's note to Plutarch's *Life of Solon* (*Anmerkungen über alte Schriftsteller, Schriften*, xv, pp. 432 f.): 'Vom Thespis heisst es daselbst: ἀρχομένων δὲ τῶν περὶ Θέσπιν ἤδη τὴν τραγῳδίαν κινεῖν etc. Kind übersetzt: Thespis fing damals an mit seinen Trauerspielen herumzuziehen. Aber ist es denn nicht weit vernünftiger, κινεῖν in der Bedeutung für mutare zu nehmen? κινεῖν τοὺς νόμους ist so viel als μεταβάλλειν, ändern. Und das that Thesphis wirklich: er änderte die Tragödie, und machte etwas ganz anderes daraus, als sie war.—Aus derselben Stelle sehen wir auch, dass Thespis sich nicht sehr an die historische Wahrheit gebunden haben muss. Denn das war eben das, was dem Solon missfiel.'

[3] *Aristoteles Dichtkunst*, ins Deutsche übersetzet...von Michael Conrad Curtius, Hanover, 1753, p. 101 (note to chap. iv).

GREEK TRAGEDY

Of the three great tragic dramatists of Greece, Euripides alone receives any considerable measure of attention in the *Dramaturgie*. To Aeschylus Lessing makes only one unfortunate reference (xcvii, 48), where he cites that poet's 'Perserinnen' as a proof of the lack of 'Costume' in the Greek poets.[1] Sophocles fares a little better, but when Greek tragedy is mentioned, his name is usually coupled with that of Euripides. Six years before the *Dramaturgie*, it will be remembered, Lessing had written a learned *Leben Sophocles*, and the *Philoctetes* is discussed in the *Laokoon* (iv). Now the name of Sophocles occurs for the most part in quotations from other writers.[2] The only time when Lessing ventures an independent judgment here is in a note to xciv, 92 (102 ff.) where he gives his approval to Hurd's interpretation of the Aristotelian Σοφοκλῆς ἔφη αὐτὸς μὲν οἵους δεῖ ποιεῖν, Εὐριπίδης [the original reading: Heinsius was responsible for the modern Εὐριπίδην] δὲ οἷοί εἰσιν (chap. xxv, 1460 b), as meaning that Sophocles strove to present through his characters an abstract generalisation of humanity rather than to portray perfect individuals (which had been Dacier's interpretation of the passage).[3]

Aristotle had described Euripides as τραγικώτατος τῶν ποιητῶν (*Poetics*, xiii, 1453 a), the most tragic of tragic poets (xlviii, 110; xlix, 71). But Lessing is not convinced that his true reason for this praise was the fact that the majority of the dramas end tragically. Lessing may have remembered Dacier's conjecture (*Poétique d'Aristote*, *ed. cit.* pp. 204 f.):

Mais ce qui marque extrêmement l'esprit tragique d'Euripide, c'est que dans la plûpart de ces dernieres pieces, dont la fin est heureuse, il ne laisse pas d'exciter la terreur et la compassion, et l'on peut dire que la constitution en est tragique, il n'y a que la fin qui gâte tout.

When Lessing recalls (xlix, 84) that Socrates was the teacher and friend of Euripides, but that many believe the poet may have owed

[1] It is some exoneration that Lessing took this over from D'Aubignac (*Pratique du Théâtre*, Amsterdam, 1715, i, p. 148); although it had been corrected by Ménage (cp. *ibid.* ii, p. 49) and by Dacier (*Poétique d'Aristote*, ed. cit. p. 173).

[2] [xxix, 111]; [xxxi, 121]; xxxviii, 101; lxxxi, 139; [xciv, 73, 104 ff.]; [xcv, 75]. To the first of these quotations, recording Corneille's assertion that we should now give Sophocles' *Trachiniæ* the title *The Dying Hercules*, Lessing adds a comment on the choice of titles by the ancients. (See below, p. 467.)

[3] The passages quoted by Lessing from Dacier will be found in *Poétique d'Aristote*, *ed. cit.* pp. 442 and 458.

nothing more to him than the moral sentiments with which he so
liberally bestrews his plays,[1] he may have been thinking of Sebastiano
Pauli's *Ragionamento* attached to Maffei's *Merope*:

> ...a' suoi tempi la Filosofia non era uscita dalle private case alla pubblica
> luce: laddove a que' d' Euripide era stata da Socrate tratta a pubblico
> uso nel Liceo, e nell' Accademia, donde la scienza col suo lume anche sugli
> occhi del popolo tralucea. Sicchè trovando alle Sentenze gli orecchi
> popolari meglio disposti; prese ad usarle con assai minor risparmio di
> Sofocle.[2]

In St. xxxvii–xlix, in connexion with *Merope*, the ancient sources
of the fable and the utilisation of these by Euripides are discussed at
some length. Lessing prepares the way for his comparison of the
dramas of Maffei and Voltaire by investigating the 'historical facts'
on which *Merope* is based (xxxvii, 9 ff.). Maffei himself is the source
of his information. That writer, in the Dedication of his drama, stated
the matter as follows:

> Che qualche tempo dopo la presa di Troja gli Eraclidi, cioè a dire i
> discendenti d' Ercole, s' impadronissero della Messenia: che questa Pro-
> vincia toccasse poi a Cresfonte nelle sorti, che si gettarono: che questi
> avesse Merope in moglie, e che essendo favorevole alla plebe, fosse
> da' potenti ucciso insieme co' suoi figliuoli, trattone l' ultimo, che riuscì
> valorosissimo, e fece poi la vendetta del padre, si ha da Pausania. Che
> ucciso Cresfonte con due fanciulli, occupasse il Regno Polifonte, nato
> parimente del sangue degli Eraclidi, che costui forzasse Merope a divenir
> sua moglie; che il terzo figlio, trafugato già dalla madre, uccidesse il
> Tiranno, e ricuperasse il Regno, si ha da Apollodoro. Che a Merope
> facesse un Vecchio riconoscere il figliuolo, mentr' ella stava per ucciderlo,
> e che il giovane uccidesse Polifonte nell' atto del sagrificio, si ha da Igino.
> Il nome per altro di questo giovane diversamente si referisce.[3]

It would have been surprising had the ancients not availed themselves of so excellent a subject. Lessing continues (38) to follow
Maffei:

> Parla di essa Aristotele nella Poetica, dove trattando de' modi di ben
> compor la Favola, dà per esempio dell' ottimo il Cresfonte d' Euripide, in
> cui l' atrocità veniva dal Riconoscimento impedita....[For Aristotle's

---

[1] Cp. Lessing's *Philologischer Nachlass* (*Schriften*, xv, p. 428): 'Dass Euripides zur
Unzeit moralisirt, ist bekannt genug, und das will ich ihm als einem Freunde des
Sokrates vergeben.' Cp. St. ii, 115.

[2] Ed. of 1763, p. lxix.

[3] Ed. of 1730, pp. xxxiv f.; ed. of 1763, pp. xxiii f.

argument see below, pp. 385 f.]...Non ho alterati già...certi punti principali della tradizione, come l' uccision di Polifonte nel Sagrificio, e l'eccesso della Madre contra il Figliuolo non conosciuto: il che avrei avuto scrupolo di non ritenere esattamente, facendoci fede Plutarco di quanto effetto facesse anticamente negli spettatori con queste parole: *Considera quella Merope che alzata la Scure sta per ferire il Figliuolo, ch' ella crede l' uccisor di lui, e dice: Io ti darò morte con questo colpo. Quanta commozione non eccita nel Teatro, stando ognuno intento, e temendo, ch' ella non prevenga il Vecchio, che l' impedisce, e non ferisca il Giovinetto?*[1]

The fragment quoted by Plutarch in his *De esu carnium oratio*, ii (*Moralia*, 998 E)—the reference is given in a note to Maffei's Dedication in the edition of 1763[2]—was not included (XXXVII, 47) in Joshua Barnes's edition of Euripides (Cambridge, 1694); but Schröter and Thiele point out (*ed. cit.* p. 224) that just before Lessing wrote, the Dutch scholar L. C. Valckenaer had included it in his *Diatribe in Euripidis perditorum dramatum reliquias* (Leyden, 1767, p. 181 c). Aristotle does not attribute the *Cresphontes* he mentions to Euripides; but Cicero, in the *Tusculanæ Disputationes* (i, 48, referred to by Barnes, Pt. ii, p. 476) uses the words 'qua est sententia in Cresphonte usus Euripides'; and both Dacier (*ed. cit.* p. 220) and Curtius (*ed. cit.* p. 30), in their translations of Aristotle, insert Euripides's name.

In the letter prefixed to Voltaire's *Mérope* Tournemine had written:

Aristote, ce sage législateur du Théâtre, a mis ce sujet au premier rang des sujets tragiques. *Euripide* l'avait traité, et nous apprenons d'*Aristote*, que toutes les fois qu'on représentait sur le Théâtre de l'ingénieuse *Athènes* le *Cresfonte* d'*Euripide*, ce peuple, accoûtumé aux chefs-d'œuvres tragiques, était frappé, saisi, transporté d'une émotion extraordinaire.[3]

But, after translating this passage, Lessing points out that these are mere fine phrases without much truth in them (XXXVII, 63). Tournemine's second statement rests on a confusion between Aristotle and Plutarch; and his first on a misunderstanding of Aristotle. And to the problem raised by this misunderstanding Lessing now turns. I deal with it below (pp. 385 ff.). The upshot, as far as Euripides is concerned, is the conclusion (XXXIX, 3) that *Merope* cannot be regarded as a perfect dramatic fable.

Voltaire himself makes statements similar to those of Tournemine —that Aristotle held the recognition in *Merope* to be the most

---

[1] Ed. of 1730, pp. xxxvi ff.; ed. of 1763, pp. xxv ff.
[2] P. xxix.　　　　　　　　　　[3] *Œuvres, ed. cit.* viii, p. 2

interesting moment in the Greek theatre, and that Plutarch had described the play as the most touching of all the works of Euripides —in his 'Lettre à M. Maffei'.[1] This passage Lessing quotes in a foot-note (xxxix, 39 ff.). He questions Voltaire's interpretation of Aristotle's words: the latter, he contends, only mentions *Merope* as an example of one kind of interesting moment; and, moreover, he does not mention *Merope* alone; he adds the *Iphigeneia* and *Helle*.[2] And who shall say that *Cresphontes* and *Helle* did not end unhappily, that is, in the manner which made Euripides the most tragic of all the tragic poets?

What, Lessing continues (74 ff.), was the theme of *Cresphontes*? The few fragments that have been preserved[3] throw no light on the plot of the drama. At most, a passage quoted by Barnes from Polybius[4]—an appeal to the goddess of peace—would imply that the Messenian state was not yet restored to order. In drawing inferences from the other passages (86) and in commenting on the difficulty

---

[1] *Œuvres, ed. cit.* viii, pp. 218 f.

[2] Dacier (*Poétique d'Aristote, ed. cit.* p. 238) attributed *Helle* to Euripides: 'Je croy que c'étoit encore une piece d'Euripide. Je n'en sçay pas le sujet, je sçay seulement que Phryxus et sa sœur Hellé étoient enfans d'Athamas et de Nephelé.' Valckenaer was also of this opinion. There would appear, however, to be no evidence to support it. (See Pauly, *Real-Encyclopädie der classischen Altertumswissenschaft* (Neue Bearbeitung), VIII, i (1912), 162.)

[3] In Barnes's edition, Part ii, p. 476. Dacier had referred to one of these (cp. Lessing's note, XXXIX, 80) in the *Poétique d'Aristote* (*ed. cit.* p. 237): 'Je me souviens d'en avoir lû quelque-part un fragment qui merite d'être raporté pour la beauté du sens qu'il renferme. C'est Merope qui parle de la mort de son mary et de ses enfans, et qui dit

$$αἱ \ τύχαι \ δέ \ με$$
$$μισθὸν \ λαβοῦσαι \ τῶν \ ἐμῶν \ τὰ \ φίλτατα$$
$$σοφὸν \ ἔθηκαν,$$

La fortune m'a enseigné à être sage, en prenant pour sa peine ce que j'avois de plus cher.' Dacier does not know where these lines come from. Lessing found the reference to Plutarch (*De capienda ex inimicis utilitate, Moralia*, 90 A) in a note to Maffei's dedication (ed. of 1763, p. xxviii).

[4] Polybius, *Historia*, xii, 26:

$$ὁμογνωμονεῖν \ δὲ \ τῷ \ ποιητῇ \ καὶ \ τὸν \ Εὐριπίδην \ ἐν \ οἷς \ φησιν,$$
$$εἰρήνα \ βαθύπλουτε,$$
$$καλλίστα \ μακάρων \ θεῶν,$$
$$ζῆλός \ μοι \ σέθεν, \ ὡς \ χρονίζεις.$$
$$δέδοικα \ δὲ \ μὴ \ πρὶν \ ὑπερβάλῃ \ με \ γῆρας,$$
$$πρὶν \ σὰν \ χαρίεσσαν \ προσιδεῖν \ ὥραν$$
$$καὶ \ καλλιχόρους \ ἀοιδὰς$$
$$φιλοστεφάνους \ τε \ κώμους.$$

caused by the title (92) Lessing would seem to have been influenced by the following observations in Orsi's 'Avvertimento' to Maffei's *Merope* (ed. of 1763, pp. xxxv f.):

Ciò stante, parmi, che io possa così discorrere: se l' ultimo Figliuolo di Merope, sottratto alla crudeltà di Polifonte, e lunga pezza occulto da lei tenuto, comparisce nella Tragedia d' Euripide, e sconosciuto alla Madre, corre pericolo di perir per sua mano; come mai nel giro della Tragedia stessa (che a una giornata, o poco più dee esser ristretto) potea vedersi il padre di lui Cresfonte tanto prima dal Tiranno estinto? Non altramente da quello che si è supposto, star poteva la Favola d' Euripide:...Un altro dubbio potrebbe mettersi in campo, siccome fu già promosso dal Castel-vetro: ed è, se la Tragedia d' Euripide fosse veramente intitolata Cresfonte: *perciocchè* (così va speculando quel sottil Critico) *non si potè far Tragedia, nella quale Merope fosse per uccidere il Figliuolo nominato Cresfonte: conciossi cosa chè essa non venisse a quest' atto, se non molti anni dopo la morte di Cresfonte*: e tanto in tale difficoltà s' innoltra, che arriva a temer mendo nel testo Aristotelico, nel quale secondo lui *vuole essere scritto* ἐν τῷ τελεφόντῃ. Vi ha di più chi al Figliuolo avanzato dal primo letto di Merope applica altro nome, che quello di Telefonte, al dir già allegato Colonna: *solus autem ex Cresphontis filiis Æpytus, sive, ut alii dicunt, Telephon natu minimus superstes fuit....*

And further on (ed. of 1763, pp. xxxvii f.):

...e lo stesso Castelvetro si dispone alla fine ad ammettere, come ci verisimilmente esser possa, col soggiugnere: *o è da dire, che il Figliuolo di Cresfonte scampato, avesse, secondo alcuni Autori il nome paterno Cresfonte, dal quale fosse dinominata la Tragedia allegata qui da Aristotile.* Il perchè opportunata-mente fa il Sig. Marchese Maffei, che nella prima Scena manifestante tutto l'Antifatto, così rimproveri Polifonte a Merope.

> Che il terzo figlio, in cui del Padre il nome
> Ti piacque rinnovar, tu trafugasti.

But have we ever heard of tragedies (xxxix, 100) which are named after personages who do not appear in them?[1] Corneille and Dacier get over this difficulty by assuming that the son's name was also Cresphontes.[2]

---

[1] On Lessing's views on the titles of plays, see below, pp. 467 f.

[2] Dacier cites the words quoted in Lessing's note (110) as if they were Corneille's (*Poétique d'Aristote*, ed. cit. p. 232): 'M. Corneille est d'un sentiment tout opposé... La raison de cela est, dit-il, que dans la troisiéme [manière], *Une mere qui va tuer son fils, comme Merope va tuer Cresphonte, et une sœur qui va sacrifier son frere, comme Iphigenie, les regardent, ou comme indifferens, ou comme ennemis, jusqu'à ce qu'ils son reconnus....'* In fact the words do not appear in Corneille's *Discours de la Tragédie*

Maffei believed that Euripides had found the plan of his *Cresphontes* in Hyginus's 184th fable. The passage, which Lessing quotes in his foot-note (112), is from the Dedication. It begins:

> Potrebbe qui richiedermi V.A. qual certezza possa aver io d' essermene allontanato: e poichè tanti Poeti si sono augurati in vano di poter sapere, in qual modo conducesse Euripide questa Favola, come io pretenda ora d' averlo scoperto. Al che risponderò, come questa scoperta penso io d' aver fatta....[1]

Whether the 184th fable of Hyginus represents the material from which Euripides constructed his tragedy, or is merely an abstract of that tragedy, it is, at least, a story suitable for tragic treatment; and in its simplicity stands much nearer to the ancient plan than all the modern *Meropes* (XL, 3). Lessing lays Hyginus's fable before his readers,[2] and in a note (43) points out that in Scheffer's edition of Hyginus, Hamburg, 1674 [pp. 154 f.], Fable 184, entitled *Pentheus et Agave*, begins with a passage dealing with these personages which belongs properly to No. 137 (entitled *Merope*):

> Pentheus Echionis et Agaves filius, Liberum negavit deum esse, nec mysteria ejus accipere voluit. Ob hoc eum Agave mater cum sororibus Ino et Autonoe, per insaniam à Libero objectam membratim laniavit. Agave ut suæ mentis compos facta est, et vidit se Liberi impulsu tantum scelus admisisse, profugit ab Thebis, atque errabunda in Illyriæ fines devenit, ad Licotersen regem, quam Licoterses excepit. Cum qua Polyphontes, occiso Cresphonte, regnum occupavit. filium autem ejus infantem Merope mater, quem ex Cresphonte habebat, absconse ad hospitem in Ætoliam mandavit....

(*Œuvres de Pierre Corneille*, ed. Marty-Laveaux, Paris, 1862, i, pp. 67–70) where Corneille mentions Aristotle's examples 'de Mérope dans *Cresphonte* et de *Hellé*, dont nous ne connoissons ni l'un ni l'autre' (pp. 67 f.).... 'Cependant je pense être bien fondé sur l'expérience à douter...si celle qu'il tient la plus belle n'est point la moindre. La raison est que celle-ci ne peut exciter de pitié. Un père y veut perdre son fils sans le connoître, et ne le regarde que comme indifférent, et peut-être comme ennemi...et quand cette reconnoissance arrive, elle ne produit qu'un sentiment de conjouissance...' (pp. 69 f.).

[1] Ed. of 1730, p. xxxvii; ed. of 1763, p. xxvi. The Reinesio to whom reference is made in Maffei (ed. of 1730, p. xxxvii; ed. of 1763, p. xxvii) was Thomas Reinesius, born at Gotha in 1587, died 1667. The reference (cp. Schröter and Thiele, *ed. cit.* p. 236) is to Reinesius, *Variarum lectionum libri III*, Altenburg, 1640, pp. 372 ff.

[2] Weisse prefixed a translation of Hyginus's fable to his tragedy *Atreus und Thyest* (mentioned by Lessing, XXXIX, 127). On Hyginus see also J. Brock, *Hygins Fabeln in der deutschen Literatur*, Munich, 1913 (and especially p. 102).

The separation which has been made by subsequent editors was indicated by Maffei in his *Proemio*:

In queste Favole il medesimo [Aristotele] avea osservato altresì, che ci si ha interamente la condotta del Cresfonte, sol che si congiungano i tre versi della 137. mal dati nella Stampa come Favola intera, con la 184. principiando alle parole *Cum qua*, e lasciando quanto precede, che appartiene ad un' altra, di che parimente sembra non si accorgesse il Munckero.[1]

Here Lessing takes leave of Euripides, but in St. xlviii (93) he returns to him, and defends his use of prologues.[2]

One other small point may be added here in connexion with Greek tragedy. In St. xviii (55) Lessing makes a reference (from Horace's *Ars poetica*, 220 ff.) to the peculiar form of drama into which the Greeks introduced 'Satyri'. He probably had in mind the following note in Dacier's *Poétique d'Aristote* (*ed. cit.* p. 52):

Quand Aristote dit que la Tragedie retint long-temps le style burlesque des pieces satyriques d'où elle étoit sortie, on se tromperoit infiniment si l'on pensoit qu'il eût voulu parler des Tragedies satyriques. Car ces Tragedies succederent au contraire à la veritable Tragedie. Et le style de ces pieces n'étoit nullement burlesque, mais moitié serieux et moitié plaisant; c'étoit un mélange agreable du Tragique et du Comique, comme cela a été expliqué assez au long, dans les remarques sur l'art Poëtique d'Horace.

GREEK COMEDY

The references to Aristophanes in the *Hamburgische Dramaturgie* are almost exclusively to be found in notes to St. xc and xci; but they are passing allusions, for the most part in quotations, and call for little comment.

Lessing refers (xc, 86) to the name which Aristophanes gives to one of his characters in *The Clouds* as an illustration of his thesis that Greek comedy did not make use of real names, but only of names which represented types: even when the Greek writer calls a character 'Socrates' (xci, 2), he does not mean that individual philosopher, but all Sophists.[3] But Aristophanes would not let himself be deprived of the honour (42) of having been the first to attack the great men of the state—here Lessing quotes two lines from the *Irene* (ll. 750 f.)—

---

[1] Ed. of 1763, p. xcvi.   [2] See below, pp. 465 f.

[3] The illustration may have been suggested by the account in Fabricius, *Bibliotheca Græca*, ii, xxi (3rd ed., i, Hamburg, 1718, pp. 706 f.). Cosack (*op. cit.* p. 404) points out that the ultimate source of the illustration is Ælianus, *Varia Historia*, ii, cap. xiii. (This reference is given by Fabricius, *loc. cit.*)

'he might rather have regarded this as his particular privilege. He was highly jealous when he saw that many other poets whom he despised imitated him in this.' Lessing disputes (49 ff.) Dacier's interpretation of Aristotle's observation as meaning that the poets of the old comedy did not invent at all.[1] One has only to look into Aristophanes to find this disproved; indeed, if Aristotle had believed that these poets did not invent, would he not have excluded them from the class of poets altogether?

The edition of Aristophanes which Lessing possessed was *Aristophanis Comœdiæ undecim, Græce et Latine*, edited by Ludolph Kusterus [Küster], Amsterdam, 1710.[2] Here he found (p. xiv) the quotation from the life of Aristophanes concerning the Κώκαλος which he cites in a note (xc, 131).

The new Greek comedy, and especially the work of Menander, receives fuller consideration, but again, less for its own sake than by way of elucidation of Terence's sources and Terence's art. The edition which Lessing had at hand was *Menandri et Philemonis Reliquiæ*, edited by H. Grotius and J. Le Clerc, Amsterdam, 1709; he expressly refers to this edition in a foot-note (xci, 103).[3]

In St. LXXXVII–LXXXVIII (50), where Lessing points out that if Terence is to be censured for his *Heautontimorumenos*, the blame should really fall on Menander, he speaks of Menander's 'hundred and more pieces' (102) and quotes (59): ὦ Μένανδρε καὶ βίε, πότερος ἄρ' ὑμῶν πότερον ἐμιμήσατο;—'Menander and life, which of you has imitated the other?' For this information he appears to have been again indebted to Fabricius, *Bibliotheca Græca* (II, xxii, *ed. cit.* i, p. 768): 'Et Menander Byzantius apud Scholiasten Hermogenis, pag. 38. dubium esse ait utrum vita Menandrum, an Menander vitam expresserit ac depinxerit.'[4]

---

[1] *Poétique d'Aristote, ed. cit.* pp. 64 f.

[2] Lessing quotes this edition in his *Leben Sophocles* (*Schriften*, viii, pp. 307 f., 339 f.).

[3] The note on Ktesippos cited by Lessing is as follows (*Menandri et Philemonis Reliquiæ, ed. cit.* p. 137): 'Filius Chabriæ, ut diximus, clarissimi Atheniensium ducis, sed patri dissimillimus.... "*Ctessipus, Chabriæ filius, ad tantum luxum devenit, ut etiam monumenti patris, in quod Athenienses mille drachmas absumserant, lapides venderet, in voluptates suas.*" Verba sunt Athenæi, lib. vi, p. 165. Hinc videmus cur dicat hic senex luxuriosus, se lapides ipsos comesturum.'

[4] Fabricius then quotes the sentence in the original (but in the form πότερος... πρότερον); it was written by the grammarian Aristophanes of Byzantium (born *ca.* 260 B.C.).

In St. xc (105) he returns to the new comedy, disputing Hurd's claim for Menander as its founder; and in the following section he has still more to say on the relations of the old Aristophanic comedy to that of Menander and Philemon. Again his authorities are the works I have cited.

Beyond these, Dacier is quoted as authoritative on such questions and on Aristotle's comment upon them. Apart from the passages where the French critic is actually quoted, it might be noticed that Dacier refers to the difference in comic manner between the old and the new comedy, citing Menander and Terence as examples of a 'ridicule leger et gracieux' (*Poétique d'Aristote, ed. cit.* p. 61), and to the custom of using fictitious names in comedy (pp. 140 f.).

Menander is mentioned again in St. xcvi, where Lessing cites Plutarch's statement (51) that his early pieces are not to be compared with his later ones; from these, he adds, we might infer what he might have done had he lived longer. And yet he wrote a hundred and five pieces, and died at fifty-two. The passage from Plutarch's ἐπιτομὴ τῆς συγκρίσεως Ἀριστοφάνους καὶ Μενάνδρου is to be found on p. 1568 (*not* p. 1588) of the edition which Lessing quotes (63): *Plutarchi Chæronensis quæ extant opera, cum Latine interpretatione*, edited by Henricus Stephanus, Geneva, 1572 (*Variorum Plutarchi Scriptorum* iii). It is as follows: Εἰ οὖν πρὸς τὰ πρῶτα τῶν Μενάνδρου δραμάτων τὰ μέσα καὶ τὰ τελευταῖα παραβάλοι τις, ἐξ αὐτῶν ἐπιγνώσεται, ὅσα ἔμελλεν, εἰ ἐπεβίω, καὶ τούτοις ἕτερα προσθήσειν.

The statement about Menander's life Lessing probably found in Fabricius, *Bibliotheca Græca*, II, xxii (*ed. cit.* i, pp. 767 f.): 'Menander... cv. dramatum auctor, octiesque victor....Natus est Olympiade cix. anno 3, mortuus sive in Piræeo portu submersus, sive alio fato extinctus ...Olympiade cxxii....ætatis LII.'

NARRATIVE LITERATURE

A late Greek romance of which Lessing is reminded by the plot of *Mérope* (xlvii, 79) is the novel of Chariton, edited by D'Orville. This work appeared at Amsterdam in 1750 with the title *Charitonis Aphrodisiensis de Chærea et Callirrhœ amatoriarum Narrationum libri viii, græce et latine*, J. Ph. D'Orville publicavit, Animadversionesque adjecit. (The passage referred to appears in vol. i, p. 38 of this edition.) The work had been translated into German as: *Charitons Liebesgeschichte des Chäreas und der Callirhoe, aus dem Griechischen übersetzt*, Leipzig, 1753 [by Chr. G. Heyne]. The German version was reviewed, in all probability by Lessing himself, in the *Vossische Zeitung* (St. 28) of March 6, 1753.[1] The source of what Lessing has to say in the *Dramaturgie*, however, is less likely to have been the book itself than the very detailed account of a French edition given in the *Journal étranger* of December, 1755 (ii, pp. 3 ff.). In the novel Callirrhœ is the wife of Chæreas, who in a fit of jealousy strikes her down. She is thought to be dead and is laid in a vault outside the gates of Syracuse. Pirates hear that her valuable jewels have been buried with her; they break into the vault and find her still alive. They carry her off to Miletos, where her purchaser, Dionysius, falls in love with her. She is much troubled as to whether she should poison herself or become his wife. But as she knows she is to bear Chæreas's child, she ultimately decides, for its sake, to marry Dionysius. After the marriage has taken place, she undergoes a series of adventures, while Chæreas on his side experiences equally strange vicissitudes in his search for Callirrhœ after her abduction is discovered; but after many trials the lovers are finally re-united.[2]

TERENCE

Apart from passing references in earlier sections,[3] Terence is first discussed in the *Dramaturgie* in St. LXX–LXXIII; and then in LXXXVI–LXXXVIII, XC, and XCVII–C. The occasion is provided in the first instance by the representation of the German version of the *Adelphi*, *Die Brüder*, by Romanus. Lessing begins by pointing out (LXX, 106) that 'it has been said that Molière also drew from this source, namely, in his *École des Maris*'; he then turns to Voltaire's *Vie de Molière, avec de petits Sommaires de ses pièces* (1739, but reprinted in *Contes de Guillaume Vadé*, which Lessing had at hand).[4] Here he found the passage which he translates at the end of St. LXX (133).[5]

The comparison with Molière may have been suggested to Lessing

---

[1] E. Consentius, *Lessing und die Vossische Zeitung*, Leipzig, 1902, pp. 44 f., questions Lessing's authorship of this review and would prefer to attribute it to Naumann; but his arguments are not very cogent.

[2] For a fuller account see E. Rohde, *Der griechische Roman und seine Vorläufer*, Leipzig, 1876, pp. 485 ff.

[3] XXI, 49; [LXIX, 31].   [4] See above, pp. 177 ff.

[5] See above, p. 180, where the passage is given in the original.

by George Colman's work, *The Comedies of Terence*, translated into familiar Blank Verse, London, 1765 (2nd ed. 2 vols. London, 1768). In a note to the final line of the *Adelphi* Colman quotes in English this same passage from Voltaire, and adds (ed. of 1765, pp. 422 f.):

It is impossible for any reader, who is come fresh from the perusal of the Brothers of Terence, and the Ecole des Maris of Moliere to acquiesce in the above decision, and I would venture to appeal from Mons. Voltaire to any member of the French academy for a reversal of it. The reputation of Moliere has taken too deep root to be rendered more flourishing by blasting that of Terence; nor can such an attempt ever be made with a worse grace than when the imitation is blindly preferred to the original. Moliere, so far from having taken only the idea of his piece from the Brothers, has translated some passages almost literally, and the latter part of the second scene of the Ecole des Maris is a very close imitation of one in the fourth act of the Brothers. In point of fable, I make no scruple to prefer the piece of Terence to that of Moliere. The intrigue of the four first acts of the Brothers is more artfully conducted than that of any other of Terence's pieces. . . . I cannot think the fable of the Ecole des Maris quite so happy. In Terence we see a good-humoured uncle adopting one of his nephews, while the other remains under the tuition of the severe father. This is natural enough; but in Moliere we have two young women left by their father's will as the intended wives of their antiquated guardians. Is there not some absurdity in such an idea? . . . If it [intrigue] be the Dramatick Narration of a story, so laid out as to produce pleasant situations, I will not scruple to pronounce, that there is more intrigue in the Brothers than in the Ecole des Maris.

In St. LXXI Lessing takes Voltaire to task for his views on Terence; he cannot have read the Latin author since he left the Jesuit College Louis le Grand.[1] In Act III (sc. iv, 39 f.) Pamphila does not, as Voltaire suggests, appear on the stage (8); only her voice is heard.[2] But Voltaire falls into a more serious error (16) when he writes of the character of Demea. Lessing maintains that this character is not suddenly changed in the course of the play; he holds with Colman

[1] Voltaire was at the College from 1704 to 1711. Schröter and Thiele note (*ed. cit.* p. 395) that the reading of Terence was then forbidden in Jesuit schools.

[2] Cp. Diderot, *De la poésie dramatique* (*Œuvres complètes, ed. cit.* vii, p. 373; Lessing's translation, ii, p. 423): 'Terence a exposé l'enfant nouveau-né sur la scène. Il a fait plus. Il a fait entendre du dedans de la maison, la plainte de la femme dans les douleurs qui le mettent au monde. Cela est beau, et cela ne vous plairait pas.' The birth on the stage is in Terence's *Hecyra*.

that the apparent change is only intentional dissimulation.[1] The English author had written (*The Comedies of Terence, ed. cit.* p. 423):

> ...the particular objection made by Mons. de Voltaire to the catastrophe is founded on a mistake: the complaisance, gaiety, and liberality of Demea being merely assumed; and his aukwardness in affecting those qualities full as comick as the admired catastrophe of the Ecole des Maris.

Lessing observes that this ability to dissimulate on the part of Demea is carefully suggested by Terence in his drawing of the character. In support of this thesis he quotes (LXXI, 21, 52) the commentator on Terence, Ælius Donatus: 'But through the whole piece Micio remains gentle, Demea cruel, Leno miserly, etc.',[2] and: 'Here Terence shows that Demea has rather pretended to change his manners than actually changed them.' Donatus, Lessing thinks (LXXII, 86), might with advantage be studied by young actors: 'he is so admirably rich in remarks which may form our taste that he is able, more than any one else, to unveil the most hidden beauties of his author' (75 ff.).

Donatus's commentaries were included in several of the older editions of the poet, notably in that 'in usum...Delphini' by N. Camus, Paris, 1675, which Lessing apparently used when he was occupied with the *Beyträge*, and in the edition of Westerhov, published at the Hague in 1726.[3] Lessing mentions (73) the unreliability of the texts of Donatus, and in his *Collectanea* (*Schriften*, xv, p. 205) we find:

> Ich habe in der Dramaturgie gesagt, wie viel ich auf ihn halte. Es wäre nur zu wünschen, dass wir ihn lauter und rein hätten. So aber wie wir ihn itzt haben, ist nicht allein vieles verderbt, sondern auch vieles mit eingeflossen, welches vom Donatus gewiss nicht ist.

When Donatus wrote (79) Terence was still being played on the Roman stage; he could thus observe the gestures of the actors—this

---

[1] In connexion with Lessing's criticism of the play, it may be pointed out that 'Vetter' (LXXI, 34) should be 'Bruder'; it is in Romanus's play that the two 'brothers' are cousins. See XCVII, 69 ff. The scene which Lessing numbers Act v, sc. iv (37) is so indicated in most of the older editions (Camus, Westerhov, Bentley); others, and also Mad. Dacier's translation, number Demea's monologue Act v, sc. ii; and Colman opens the fifth act with it.

[2] Donatus, *Commentum Terenti* (Teubner ed. Leipzig, 1905, ii, p. 8).

[3] The text of Terence which Lessing quotes corresponds more closely to that in the edition of Westerhov; in this edition also the comment of Donatus quoted by Lessing (LXXI, 52) is printed at the end of the scene (i, p. 858).

was a matter the importance of which had been impressed upon
Lessing by Diderot. The latter, in the section on 'Pantomime' in his
De la poésie dramatique, had given examples from Terence.[1] Lessing
complains (93) that later interpreters of Terence have taken so little
advantage of Donatus's commentary: in his view, neither Madame
Dacier nor J. S. Patzke paid sufficient attention to it. The former's
translation, *Les Comédies de Terence, traduites en François, avec des Re-
marques, par Madame Dacier*, first appeared in Paris in 1688; whether
Lessing knew the later corrected edition of 1747 (Amsterdam and
Leipzig) 'enrichie des différentes Leçons de Mr *Bentlei*, de *Donat*, de
Faern, et d'autres' is doubtful; there was also an edition of Madame
Dacier's work published at Frankfurt and Leipzig in 1733, and a
Leipzig one of 1754. Lessing dismisses her version as 'watery and
stiff'; and Patzke's German translation (Halle, 1753), which
included Madame Dacier's *Remarks*, he considers to be lacking in
comic language (96)—a criticism which is borne out by the short
specimen which Lessing gives (note, 103 ff.).[2]

Romanus, Lessing continues (110), follows Voltaire's false interpretation—it might be more correct to say that he followed the French

[1] Cp. especially *Œuvres complètes, ed. cit.* vii, pp. 378 ff.; also p. 385 (Lessing's
translation, ii, pp. 438 ff.; and p. 458): 'J'avoue cependant que, si la pantomime
était portée sur la scène à un haut point de perfection, on pourrait souvent se
dispenser de l'écrire: et c'est la raison peut-être pour laquelle les Anciens ne l'ont
pas fait.'

[2] In a review of Patzke's *Freundschaftliche Briefe* (Frankfurt and Leipzig, 1754)
in the *Berlinische privilegirte Zeitung* of July 27, 1754, which is attributed to Lessing
(*Schriften*, v, p. 420) the following reference occurs: 'Man kennet den Herrn P a t z k e
schon längst als einen sehr guten Dichter, und weiss, dass ihm muntre, witzige und
empfindungsreiche Gedanken nicht schwer fallen. Man kennt ihn aber auch als
den glücklichen Übersetzer des Terenz, und kann sich leicht einbilden, dass er
diesem Muster die edle Einfalt des Ausdrucks werde abgelernt haben.' (Cp.
Schröter and Thiele, *ed. cit.* p. 402.)

The passages from Terence in Lessing's notes (LXXI, 61 ff., 63 ff.) are in English
as follows (I quote the translation of J. Sargeaunt in the Loeb Classical Library):
Act v, sc. iv, 5 f.: 'The hard life which up to now I have lived, now that my race
is almost run I renounce.' Act v, sc. ix, 27 ff.: '*Micio.* What's the meaning of this?
What has brought about this sudden change in your ways? What's the whim of it?
What's this sudden openness of hand? *Demea.* I will tell you. I did it to show that
what our boys account your good nature and pleasant ways doesn't spring from
sincerity, no, nor from justice and goodness, but from complaisance, from indulgence,
from an open hand, Micio. Now if the reason why my life is odious to you,
Aeschinus, and to your brother is that I do not at once wholly fall in with all your
desires, right or wrong, I wash my hands of it. Squander, spend, indulge every
caprice.'

play which suggested his own, Baron's *École des Pères*—and brings about a complete change of character in Demea at the close.[1] The question as to why Romanus's close should please his audience so much is one which Lessing reserves until he has occasion to notice the next performance; and, as we have seen, he was obliged to insert a performance of *Die Brüder* on the fifty-second evening (July 28) in order to give himself the opportunity of rounding off his discussion.

In St. LXXXVII–LXXXVIII Lessing again returns to Terence. He discusses (50 ff.) his debt to Menander, and this leads to a very long and learned note (61) on which I offer the following commentary. The lines which he quotes (62, 84, 91–3, 96–7, 110–13) from the Prologue to the *Heautontimorumenos* in this note are in translation (Sargeaunt) as follows:

> We are about to produce a fresh comedy from a fresh Greek source, the Self-Tormentor. It has been changed from a single into a double plot. [I have told you it is a new play....As to the...rumours]...that he has combined many Greek plays and written few Latin ones, he doesn't deny having done this: he declares he does not repent and will do it again. He has the precedent of good writers, whose example he considers himself entitled to follow.

Madame Dacier's commentary on the conversion of the single into the double plot had been:

> *Duplex quæ ex argumento facta est simplici.*] *Avec cette différence, que le sujet est double, quoi qu'il ne soit que simple dans l'original.* Ce passage a exercé inutilement tous ceux qui ont travaillé sur *Terence*; jusques là que *Jule Scaliger* a cru que ce Poëte appelloit cette Comedie *double*, parce qu'elle fut jouée à deux fois, les deux premiers Actes furent jouez le soir, et les trois autres le lendemain matin; et qu'ainsi c'étoit comme deux Pieces au lieu d'une. Mais cette explication est insoûtenable en toutes manieres. *Terence*

---

[1] Colman had commented (*ed. cit.* p. 423) on Baron's play: 'The piece opens with a very elegant, though pretty close version, of the first act of the Brothers; but on the whole I think this attempt less happy than his first....Telamon and Alcée are drawn with neither the strength nor delicacy of Micio and Demea; and the old man's change of character in the fifth act is neither rejected nor retained, but rather mangled and deformed. On the whole, it were to be wished, that Baron had adhered still more closely to Terence, or, like Moliere, deviated still further from him: for, as the play now stands, his attention to the Roman poet seems to have thrown a constraint on his genius, and taken off the air of an original; while his alterations have rendered the Ecole des Péres but a lame imitation, and imperfect image of the Brothers of Terence.'

veut dire que n'ayant pris de *Menandre* qu'un sujet simple, un Vieillard, un jeune homme amoureux, une Maîtresse, etc. il en a fait un sujet double, en y mettant deux Vieillards, deux jeunes hommes amoureux, deux Maîtresses, etc. C'est pourquoi il ajoûte, *novam esse ostendi; elle peut passer pour nouvelle.* C'est la veritable explication; ainsi il n'est pas necessaire de corriger *simplex quæ ex argumento facta est duplici.* Car si *Terence* avoit pris ce double sujet de *Menandre*, sa Piece n'auroit eu que ce qu'on voyoit dans celle du Poëte Grec; et par conséquent il n'auroit pû ajoûter, *novam esse ostendi*, car il n'y auroit eu rien de nouveau.[1]

Madame Dacier translates lines 5–6 of the Prologue: 'Je dois aujourd'hui représenter l'Heauton-timorumenos, qui est une Piece tirée toute entiere d'une seule Comedie Greque, avec cette difference, que le sujet est double, quoiqu'il ne soit que simple dans l'original.'[2]

Lessing quotes a comment on this same passage (LXXXVII–VIII, 64) by the 'new English translator of Terence, Colman'.[3] Colman's entire note (*ed. cit.* p. 213) runs as follows:

This passage has greatly perplexed the Commentators. Julius Scaliger was of opinion that Terence called this comedy *Duplex*, double, because it was acted at two different times: the *two first Acts* at the close of the evening, and the remaining *three* on the following morning; and that it therefore served as two distinct pieces. But this conjecture is not admissible: Terence only meant to say that he had doubled the characters; instead of *one old man, one young gallant, one mistress*, as in Menander, he had *two old men* etc. he therefore adds very properly, *novam esse ostendi*,—*That our Comedy is* NEW,—which certainly could not have been implied, had the characters been the same in the Greek poet. DACIER.

Lessing also refers to the comments of Barlandus and Ascensius on the disputed passage. The former published *Terentii Sex Comœdiæ* with commentaries at Louvain in 1530, the latter a quarto edition of Terence at Paris in 1499.[4]

As for Scaliger's 'ridiculous' interpretation (79)—the reference is

---

[1] *Les Comédies de Terence*, 4th ed. Amsterdam, 1706, ii, pp. 8 f.

[2] *Ibid.* p. 9 (also quoted by Cosack, *op. cit.* p. 391).

[3] See above, p. 260, note 1.

[4] The source of Lessing's information is doubtful; but the edition by Barlandus of 1530 is listed by Westerhov (*ed. cit.* i, p. lxxx) in his catalogue of editions of Terence; also one published in 1504 with notes by Ascensius (*ibid.*). Barlandus is mentioned in a list of commentators in the *Præfatio* (*ibid.* p. [xix]). There is also a reference to Hadrianus Barlandus in the section on Terence in Fabricius, *Bibliotheca latina* (5th edition, Hamburg, 1721–2, ii, p. 46). Adrian Barlandus lived from 1488 to (*ca.*) 1542; Jodocus Badius Ascensius from 1462 to 1535 (see Cosack, *op. cit.* p. 392).

to Scaliger's *Poetices*, vi, 3—Richard Bentley had already held him up to ridicule:

An, ut Julius Scaliger, *quia acta est Ludis Megalensibus; dimidium ejus vesperi: nox autem transacta ludis: alterum dimidium reliquum sub lucem: una igitur quasi duæ?* Scilicet, quia in Fabulæ argumento nox intercedit; ideo in agendo quoque? Commentum tanto viro indignum; et hoc solum tamen verum esse alii Docto persuasissimum est. Quid? An primo diluculo jejunus et semisomnus populus ad alterum dimidium redibat? Singuli qui heri spectabant, cras mane; ne alius priorem, alius posteriorem partem? Ubi demum vivimus?[1]

Faernus's note on Eugraphius (80) is as follows:[2]

Duplici prius erat in libro Bembino, postea mutatum in *simplici*. sed si *duplici* legas, hic erit sensus: duo adulescentes in hac fabula introducti, cum sua uterque amica, patre, servo, argumentum duplex efficiunt, atque ita duplicem comœdiam, ut sunt omnes Terentianæ, excepta Hecyra. Eugraphius tamen legit *simplici*; cujus hæc expositio est in totum hunc locum: *Ex integra Græca. Quoniam Andria ex duabus comœdiis videtur esse confecta, quippe Andria et Perinthia, quod quidem Terentio adversarius crimini dederat; ideo hic ex integra, inquit, comœdia integram comœdiam acturus sum, ne videatur ab altero facta, aut ipse alteram tetigisse. Sed unam comœdiam et integram ad Latinum sermonem interpretatione mutasse. denique ideo adjecit, duplex quæ ex argumento facta est simplici; ut simplex argumentum sit, duplex comœdia: dum et Latina eadem et Græca est. novam esse ostendi: propterea quod Græce tantum acta est, Latine autem nunc primum in scenam procedit. idcirco dicitur nova.*

Johannes Eugraphius was a commentator on Terence who lived in the tenth century.[3] Lessing writes erroneously 'Faerne' for 'Faerno' —he was an Italian, Gabriello Faerno, who died in 1561—but the source of his information was probably Madame Dacier, who Gallicised the name. Faerno's commentary on Terence was published by P. Victorius at Florence in 1565.

No doubt, the controversy of Ménage with d'Aubignac—printed with the latter's *Pratique du Théâtre*, and familiar to Lessing since the days of his *Beyträge zur Historie und Aufnahme des Theaters*[4]—had also been consulted by him on this point. Ménage heads his 'Seconde

---

[1] *P. Terentii Afri Comœdiæ*, Amsterdam, 1727, pp. 162 f.

[2] Cp. *ibid.* p. 162; also *Gabrielis Faerni Emendationes in Sex Fabulas Terentii*, Florence, 1565, p. 76.

[3] Cp. Cosack, *op. cit.* p. 392, and J. A. Fabricius, *Bibliotheca latina*, ed. cit. i, p. 30.

[4] Cp. *Beyträge*, iii, pp. 407 ff.; *Schriften*, iv, pp. 158 ff.

Partie' with the words: 'Il n'y a point de vuide dans l'Héauton-timoruménos de Térence. Explication de ce vers du Prologue de cette Comédie, Duplex quæ ex argumento facta est simplici....'[1] Ménage discusses Scaliger's theory at length and then continues:

> Mais d'ailleurs, ce n'est pas comme Scaliger l'explique, qu'il faut entendre ce vers du Prologue de notre Comédie. *Duplex, quæ ex argumento facta est simplici*: puisque, selon cette explication, on pourroit aussi appeller *doubles* toutes les Comédies dont la représentation seroit divisée par quelques jeux, ou par quelqu'autre intermède. Eugraphius, qui est aujourd'hui le plus ancien Interprete que nous ayions sur cette Comédie, le Commentaire de Donat sur cette Comédie aiant été perdu, dit qu'elle est appellée *double*, parce qu'elle a été faite en deux langues: en Grec, par Ménandre, et en Latin, par Térence. Fabrice croit qu'elle a été ainsi appellée, à cause des deux jours qu'elle contient. Ces deux interprétations ne me semblent pas meilleures que celle de Scaliger....[2]

In connexion with Lessing's statement of the indebtedness of Terence to Menander in his *Andria, Eunuchus* and *Adelphi* (103), it may be noted that the debt is acknowledged by the poet himself in his prologues to the first and second of these plays.[3]

The upshot of Lessing's long note is that he proposes to read 'simplex' for 'duplex' in the line: 'Duplex quæ ex argumento facta est simplici', and to interpret it as meaning nothing more than that his play is just as simple as Menander's;[4] and that the line 'Ex integra Græca integram Comœdiam' means that he has taken the whole piece from a single piece of Menander's.[5] But why should Terence then have described his comedy as 'nova'? This Lessing would explain as meaning merely a play new to the Romans. Lessing's

---

[1] *Pratique du Théâtre*, ed. cit. ii, p. 145. [2] *Ibid.* p. 148.

[3] Cp. also Fabricius, *Bibliotheca latina, ed. cit.* i, p. 28 (note): 'In Andria duas imitatus est *Menandri* Andriam et Perinthiam, in Evnucho Colacem Menandri, Evnuchum et Phasma: in Adelphis, Menandri ἀδελφοὺς et Diphili συναπο-θνήσκοντας.'

[4] The reading which Lessing quotes (84), 'Duplex...duplici'—that of the Codex Bembo—is accepted by Guyet; 'Simplex...duplici' (86) by Faber and Bentley.

[5] Faernus's note on the old gloss on the word 'integra' ('a nullo tacta') (125) is as follows: 'In libro Bembino, ut per omnes alias comœdias antiquissima manu glossemata ex Donato in margine ascripta sunt, ad locorum quæ incidunt exposi-tionem, ita in hanc ipsam Heautontimorumenon multa visuntur, quæ Donati similiter putamus esse, cujus in hanc fabulam commentarii interciderunt. Sed sive Donati sint, sive cujuspiam alius, optime certe et eruditissima sunt. quorum aliqua ponere non gravabimur, ut in hunc locum, *Ex integra Græca, A nullo tacta*' (ed. Bentley, p. 162. Cp. also Faernus, *Emendationes, ed. cit.* p. 76).

suggested emendation 'simplex' has not proved acceptable; the line remains: 'Duplex quæ ex argumento facta est simplici.'[1]

The fact that even 'the most fruitful head', such as Menander, cannot go on indefinitely creating new characters, but must occasionally degenerate into caricature, brings Lessing back (141 ff.) to a passage in Diderot to which he had already referred earlier in the section (33). Diderot is discussing the following extract from Horace's *Satires* (I, ii, 12–22):

> Fufidius vappæ famam timet ac nebulonis,
> dives agris, dives positis in fenore nummis:
> quinas hic capiti mercedes exsecat; atque
> quanto perditior quisque est, tanto acrius urget;
> nomina sectatur, modo sumpta veste virili
> sub patribus duris, tironum. 'Maxime' quis non,
> 'Iuppiter!' exclamat simul atque audivit? 'At in se
> pro quæstu sumptum facit.' Hic, vix credere possis
> quam sibi non sit amicus, ita ut pater ille, Terenti
> fabula quem miserum gnato vixisse fugato
> inducit, non se pejus cruciaverit atque hic.

On this he comments:

C'est dans la satire première ou seconde du premier livre, où il se propose de montrer que, pour éviter un excès, les fous se précipitent dans l'excès opposé. Fufidius, dit-il, craint de passer pour dissipateur. Savez-vous ce qu'il fait? Il prête à cinq pour cent par mois, et se paye d'avance. Plus un homme est obéré, plus il exige: il sait par cœur le nom de tous les enfants de famille qui commencent à aller dans le monde, et qui ont des pères durs.[2] Mais vous croiriez peut-être que cet homme dépense à proportion de son revenu; erreur. Il est son plus cruel ennemi; et ce père de la comédie, qui se punit de l'évasion de son fils, ne se tourmente pas plus méchamment: *Non se pejus cruciaverit.*[3]

---

[1] The dispute about the originality of the *Eunuchus* before the Ædiles (165) is referred to in the prologue to that play (ll. 22 ff.):
> 'Magistratus quom ibi adesset, occeptast agi.
> Exclamat furem, non poetam fabulam
> dedisse et nil dedisse verborum tamen:
> Colacem esse Nævi et Plauti veterem fabulam;
> parasiti personam inde ablatam et militis.'

In English (Sargeaunt): 'On a person of authority being present, a rehearsal began. He cries out that the author is a thief, not a playwright, "and yet", says he, "he doesn't take us in". There is an old play of Nævius and Plautus called "The Flatterer"; that is where he has got his parasite from and his captain.'

[2] Schröter and Thiele (*ed. cit.* p. 516) note Diderot's wrong translation of 'Nomina sectatur'.

[3] *Troisième Entretien sur le Fils Naturel, Œuvres complètes, ed. cit.* vii, p. 139.

Menedemus, concludes Lessing (213), Terence's self-tormentor, does not take up so hard an attitude from grief;[1] the reason why he denies himself every outlay, however small, is because he wishes to assure his absent son a more comfortable existence, since he has compelled him for the present to adopt so uncomfortable a mode of living. Hundreds of fathers might do this, and Diderot, in regarding him as a comic character, forgets the difference between modern and ancient conditions; it was not strange in the ancient world that a well-to-do man should take to agricultural work.

Lessing returns in St. xcvi to the *Brüder* of Romanus, and that play nominally occupies the pages of the *Dramaturgie* to St. c. What he has to say here, however, is less concerned with criticism of Terence than with demonstrating the disadvantages which the German playwright has incurred by departing from his Roman model. Æschinus and Ctesipho in Terence (xcvii, 70) are brothers, both sons of Demea; the former has only been adopted by Micio. In Romanus, however, only the two old men are brothers, and the young men are in reality cousins. In this way the German piece becomes more a 'school for fathers' (81)—actual fathers, not those who have voluntarily taken upon themselves a father's duty. 'Learn', says Terence (Act i, sc. 2, l. 45), 'to be a father from those who really know what it is to be one.' Very good! But by removing the tie between Æschinus and Ctesipho and between them and Demea, the machinery of the play falls to pieces (87). What deep interest can Demea have in Æschinus, a young man who is only his nephew?

The position of Demea in Terence's comedy (119), where Æschinus is the actual son of Demea, and Micio has only adopted him, is much more satisfactory; for Demea has necessarily a natural and continued interest in the young man. And the Roman Micio has more right (121) to say to Demea: 'you have handed over your son to me, reserve your interest for the one that is left to you'; 'your looking after both is as good as asking back the son you gave me' (Act i, sc. 2, ll. 51 f.). This threat brings Demea to silence; but it does not destroy his paternal interest in Æschinus.

---

[1] The passage which Lessing quotes from Cicero (204) is from the *Tusculanæ Disputationes*, iii, xxvii. Lessing's attention was probably drawn to it by Fabricius, who, under 'Heautontimorumenos' (*Bibliotheca latina, ed. cit.* ii, p. 32 [where the reference is given as iii, 28]) has a reference to this passage. In the *Collectanea*, under 'Komische Süjets' (*Schriften*, xv, p. 280) is the entry: 'Aus der Stelle des Cicero von der Traurigkeit, die ich in dem zweyten Bande der Dramaturgie angeführt habe.'

The relationship of the two young men also is unsatisfactory in the German play (xcviii, 1) because of the fact that they are not actually brothers; there is no justification for the brotherly affection which is expressed in Terence's play: 'It's his doing', says Ctesipho (Act ii, sc. 3, ll. 8 ff.) 'that I'm now alive. A pearl of a man! Why, he sacrificed all his interests to mine: the hard words, the disrepute, my trouble and offence, he took them all on himself.' It is difficult to believe that one cousin would do this for another. The whole episode of the slave girl (38): Æschinus's abduction of her from the slave-dealer, his bringing her to Micio's house, and Micio's purchase of her—all for Ctesipho who is desperately in love with her—is much more natural in Terence. The Ctesipho of the German play is merely a libertine for whom there is no excuse. And this brings Lessing to a consideration of the apparent need for a modern comedy-writer to wind up his piece either with the punishment of evil-doing or the conversion of the evil-doer (xcix, 10). Terence has no such need to put his Ctesipho to shame at the end of the play; and Micio by Demea's manœuvre (44) is brought to see that one can be excessively open-handed ('What's the whim of it? What's this sudden openness of hand', Act v, sc. 9, l. 28), while Micio in turn induces Demea to see the unreasonableness of his own harshness.[1]

In St. xcix (54) Lessing turns once more to a question of scholarly elucidation of Terence. The latter states that he combined an episode from a piece by Diphilus with the *Adelphi* of Menander. This episode is the violent abduction of the slave-girl Psaltria; and the piece by Diphilus was entitled 'Linked in Death' (59 ff.). In the Prologue to the *Adelphi* we are told: '"Linked in Death" is a comedy by Diphilus.

---

[1] Lessing's further quotations from Terence in St. xcviii (47 ff.) are in Sargeaunt's translation as follows: (Act ii, sc. 4, ll. 8 ff.) 'What pains me is that on this side the discovery was so late and things were almost come to pass where the best will of the whole world couldn't have helped you. *Cte.* I was too modest. *Aes.* Folly, dear boy, not modesty. A trifle like that almost make you flee the country? Scandalous! God forbid such a thing!'; (61 f.—Act iii, sc. 3, ll. 14 f.): 'The coins he counted down on the spot, and gave me a couple of sovereigns besides for an entertainment'; (116 f.—Act iv, sc. 1, ll. 2 f.): 'I hope to heaven he is! Short of hurting his health I should like him to get so tired out that for the next three days he couldn't get out of bed'; (129 ff.—Act iv, sc. 1, ll. 11 ff.): 'There'll be a volley of questions where I've been: "I haven't had a sight of you all day." What's to be my answer? *Syrus.* Nothing occur to you? *Cte.* Nothing at all. *Syrus.* The more good for nothing you! Is there no dependant, acquaintance, family friend? *Cte.* There are: what follows? *Syrus.* So that you had business with them? *Cte.* When I hadn't? Not to be said!'

...In the Greek play there is a young man who in the first act carries off a girl from a slave-dealer....Our playwright has introduced [this incident]...into his "Adelphi".' Diphilus seems to have depicted two lovers who preferred to die together rather than be separated. This decision Terence has softened to a wish on the part of the lover to leave father and fatherland and follow the girl. Donatus says this expressly: 'Menander stated that he wanted to die, Terence that he wanted to flee.' (Cp. *Commentum Terenti, ed. cit.* ii, p. 62.) But ought not Donatus to have said Diphilus instead of Menander? Lessing thinks that he should have done so, and adduces in support of his argument a quotation from the '*Sylloge v. Miscellanea*' of Peter Nannius, or Pieter Nannink, a professor of Latin at Louvain (Συμμίκτων, *sive Miscellaneorum decas una*, Louvain, 1548, lib. ii, pp. 53 f.). The passage quoted by Lessing (79) is in English:

I ask, let the accurate reader see, whether instead of Menander one should not read Diphilus. Certainly either the whole comedy, or a part of that argument, which is here in question, is taken over literally from Diphilus....[1] Now since the comedy of Diphilus takes its name from the idea of dying together, and in it the young man is said to have wished to die, while Terence has changed this into a wish to flee: from all this I am led to think, that that imitation was borrowed from Diphilus, not from Menander, and that the title συναποθνήσκοντες was derived from the desire to die with the girl.

But there must have been in Menander some further intrigue (87) in which Æschinus took Ctesipho's part, and thus made him suspect to his own mistress; and this suspicion would hasten their union. What this complication was it is difficult to guess; but it must have taken place just before the opening of the piece, as in Terence's play. It was necessary, to explain why Demea came to town and also to explain his quarrel with his brother (98). Lessing quotes a passage here from Terence: 'Of his old doings I say nothing: what is his last outrage? ...Broken a door-lock, forced his way into a strange house....All the town is crying out at it as a most scandalous business. Man after man, Micio, has told me of it in the streets, it's on everybody's lips.'[2] Our author, Lessing continues, has turned this violent abduction into a small fight. But what this was all about, and what the town was

---

[1] After *translata est* (xcix, 82), Nannius proceeds: 'Sic enim fatetur, Terentius in suo prologo. Synapothniscontes Diphili est comœdia....' Reference is made to Nannius (*Misc.* i, iv, and ii, iii) in Fabricius, *Bibliotheca latina, ed. cit.* ii, p. 32.

[2] Act i, sc. 2, ll. 6 ff. (Sargeaunt).

talking about remains undisclosed in the play. The loss of Menander's works is an immeasurable loss for our understanding of Terence.

Finally in St. c, Lessing considers the conclusion of the *Adelphi*, in which the old bachelor Micio is coupled off with the old woman Sostrata. Critics have severely reproached Terence for the improbability of this episode.[1] But who is to be blamed for it? Terence or Menander? Colman puts the greater blame on Menander (c, 100), although Donatus says expressly: 'With Menander the old man is not burdened by a marriage; here Terence is εὑρετικῶς.'[2] Colman, after quoting the words of Donatus, goes on to say (*ed. cit.* p. 415):

It is surprising that none of the criticks on this passage have taken notice of this observation of Donatus, especially as our loss of Menander makes it rather curious. It is plain that Terence in the plan of this last act followed Menander: and in the present circumstance though he has adopted the absurdity of marrying Micio to the old lady, yet we learn from Donatus that he rather improved on his original by making Micio express a repugnance to such a match, which it seems he did not in the play of Menander.

Lessing endeavours (124) to smooth out the difficulty by suggesting that the words 'de nuptiis gravari' are susceptible of the interpretation 'the old man is not aggravated with marriage'. Needless to say this attempt at word-twisting has found no favour. But his entire argument in this section loses any validity it might have had by the justifiable rejection, on the part of later critics, of his own and Nannius's conjecture that Donatus had written by a slip of the pen 'Diphilus' for 'Menander'.

PLAUTUS

Plautus, who had been the particular object of Lessing's interest in his first dramaturgic journal,[3] has little place in the *Dramaturgie*. Reference is made to the *Trinummus* of Plautus in connexion with Lessing's own play *Der Schatz* (ix, 102). The Latin playwright himself says in his Prologue that he was not the inventor of this excellent subject; and in his *Beyträge* Lessing had already written: 'Er hat es

[1] Madame Dacier, for instance, had said (*ed. cit.* ii, pp. 460 f.): 'Il paroît ridicule que *Terence* fasse consentir ainci *Micion* à se marier à soixante et cinq ans, et l'on ne peut pas dire que cela ne soit au moins fort outré. Mais ce Poëte a voulu faire voir par là le défaut de ces bontez sotes et excessives, elles portent toûjours ceux qui les ont à faire des sottises dont il faut qu'ils se repentent nécessairement.'

[2] *Commentum Terenti, ed. cit.* ii, p. 176.　　　　[3] See above, pp. 98 ff.

aus dem Griechischen des Philemo erborgt, bey dem es einen weit
anständigern Titel hat, nämlich: Der Schatz.'[1] Lessing's interest in
the titles of plays[2] leads him (XXI, 30 ff.) to mention Plautus's *Miles
gloriosus* and *Truculentus*. He states with complete confidence that
Plautus can only have called the first piece *Gloriosus*, 'miles' being
an addition by a grammarian. He suggests that the latter may
have had in mind a passage in Cicero's *De Officiis*, i, xxxviii: this
runs: 'Deforme etiam est de se ipsum prædicare falsa præsertim
et cum irrisione audientium imitari "militem gloriosum".' And he
quotes Plautus's words from Act II (sc. i, ll. 8 f.). A comment in the
introduction to the *Miles gloriosus* in Taubmann's edition of Plautus
([Wittenberg, 1605], p. 654) may here be noticed:

> Nomen huic Fabulæ est, *Miles Gloriosus*: de personâ et re factum nam
> *gloriosus* gloriatorem significat, qui est ἀλαζὼ, ostentator et vanus. Tale
> autem est genus hoc militare hominum, qualis et Terentianus Thraso
> [in *Eunuchus*] producitur, et alii â Plauto alibi.[3]

Earlier in his work (IX, 136) Lessing had noted that Plautus called
his play, not the *Treasure*, as Philemon had called his, but *Trinummus*,
'den Dreyling'. The habit of giving to his plays titles dependent on
minor circumstances, he observes (137), was Plautus's 'eigene
Manier'.

This practically exhausts Lessing's use of Latin literature in the
Dramaturgie. Seneca's name occurs only once, and that in a quotation;[4] Virgil's twice, once in a quotation;[5] and Horace is quoted three
times.[6] Hurd's commentaries on Horace are discussed and quoted,[7]
but not in respect of Horace or his opinions.

NARRATIVE LITERATURE

In discussing the relations of narrative to dramatic literature Lessing
takes up (XXXVI, 15) the example of Petronius Arbiter's satire *Matrona*

---

[1] *Beyträge*, i, p. 51; *Schriften*, iv, p. 81. Plautus gives this information in his
Prologue.   [2] See below, pp. 467 f.

[3] J. Kont, *Lessing et l'Antiquité, ed. cit.* i, p. 77, points out that Lessing's view on
the title of the play has been accepted by Fleckeisen (*Rheinisches Museum für
Philologie*, N.F. xiv (1859), pp. 628 f.), but opposed by Ritschl (*Parerga zu Plautus
und Terenz*, Leipzig, 1845, i, p. 132; Preface to *Stichus in Plauti Comœdiæ* (ed.
F. Ritschl, ii (Bonn, 1850), p. xviii) and by Riese (*Rheinisches Museum*, N.F. xxii
(1867), pp. 303 f.).

[4] [LXIX, 30.]   [5] I, 29; [XLI, 99].

[6] XVIII, 110, 115; XLI, 158; LIX, 14.   [7] XCII, 8 ff.; XCIII, XCIV, XCV.

Ephesi.[1] His interest in this theme goes back to his earliest period, when he planned a comedy on it in rivalry with his friend C. F. Weisse, whose one-act drama *Die Matrone von Ephesus* was produced in 1748.[2] At the present time in Hamburg Lessing took up his early sketch, his interest in it being perhaps awakened by Pfeffel's version[3] of Houdar de la Motte's one-act comedy (1702), to which he refers here (20). Lessing could learn of other French dramatic versions from Léris (*op. cit.* pp. 169, 284 f.); and in his *Entwürfe zu Besprechungen* (*Schriften*, xv, p. 45) he notes from Cibber's *Lives of the Poets*: 'Die Ephesian Matron von Ogilby v. Cibb. Vol. ii. p. 267. a Poem. Die Ephes. Matr. von Char. Johnson ibid. Vol. v. p. 342. a Farce.' The substance of this old story is that a widow saves a soldier who makes love to her by allowing him to put on the cross the dead body of the husband whom she is mourning, in place of that of the malefactor whose body is stolen. Lycas, in the tale of Petronius, is one of the guests at the banquet; the passage which Lessing quotes (47) is in English: 'If the Emperor had been just, he must have had the body of the master of the house brought back to the tomb and the woman crucified.'[4] Cosack notes (*op. cit.* pp. 217 f.) that Lessing, in telling the story, modifies the close; in his version it is not the widow who proposes to put her husband's body in place of the malefactor's; moreover, the expedient proves in the end to be unnecessary, as the news concerning the removal of the malefactor's body turns out to be false.[5] This may have all been suggested to Lessing by an article on a Chinese tale in the *Journal étranger*, December 1755 (i, pp. 176 ff.), where the reviewer compares the Chinese story with that of the Matron of Ephesus,[6] quoting the comment of Lycas. In spite of his promise here (56) and the note in the *Entwürfe zu Besprechungen*, Lessing does not return to the subject.

---

[1] *Satyricon quæ supersunt,* ed. P. Burmannus, 2nd ed. Amsterdam, 1743, i, pp. 659 ff.; Lessing refers to this edition in his *Collectanea* (*Schriften*, xv, p. 349).

[2] Weisse himself describes this play in the preface to *Beytrag zum deutschen Theater,* ii (2te verbesserte und vermehrte Auflage, Leipzig, 1767) as 'des Verfassers allererster theatralischer Versuch und eine wahre Schulübung'.

[3] *Die Matrone von Ephes,* aus dem Französischen des Herrn La Motte übersetzt, Frankfurt and Leipzig, 1766.   [4] *Satyricon, ed. cit.* i, p. 676.

[5] In his own plan for a drama on this subject (*Die Matrone von Ephesus, Schriften,* iii, pp. 439 ff.) Lessing avoids the difficulty by making the theft of the corpse a jest of the servant Dromo; by means of this device the widow is brought to make confession of the plot (cp. also Petersen, *ed. cit.* p. 215).

[6] See pp. 214 ff. The comment of Lycas is quoted on p. 217.

Part III

LESSING'S DRAMATIC THEORY

CHAPTER XI

THE SOURCES OF LESSING'S AESTHETIC THEORY

To speak of philosophical or aesthetic bases for Lessing's dramatic theory is a little misleading, for Lessing was neither a philosopher nor an aesthetician in any systematic sense of these words.[1] He had grown up in the Leibnitz-Wolffian atmosphere of Germany in the first half of the eighteenth century, and in his early years he accepted the philosophy of the 'Aufklärung' as a matter of course. Its conception of the moral fabric of the world was deeply ingrained in him; and its rationalisation of religious belief was easily brought into harmony with the orthodoxy of his childhood. The Leibnitzian conception of a 'pre-established harmony' throwing a bridge between matter and spirit, was, no doubt, an entirely satisfying explanation for him. The complacent self-assuredness of the 'Aufklärer' closed the door for him on further futile speculation. In later life, when Lessing's rationalism was tempered by English deism, and when his acquaintance with the thought of Spinoza opened up spiritual vistas unknown in the Leibnitzian faith, his philosophy does form an important factor in his interpretation of religion; but with his reflexions and speculations in the aesthetic field it has little to do. It has been suggested that Lessing's Leibnitzian optimism placed obstacles in the way of a free and unshackled attitude to the problem of the tragic, and that an intense preoccupation with Leibnitz in his Breslau years reacted on the view of tragedy set forth in the *Dramaturgie*;[2] but apart

---

[1] On Lessing's philosophy see C. Schrempf, *Lessing als Philosoph*, 3rd ed. Stuttgart, 1921; also the introduction to the anthology *Lessings Philosophie* (*Philosophische Bibliothek*, cxix), Leipzig, 1909, by Paul Lorentz. Particularly enlightening is the work by R. Sommer, *Grundzüge einer Geschichte der deutschen Psychologie und Ästhetik von Wolff-Baumgarten bis Kant-Schiller*, Würzburg, 1892 (pp. 176 ff.), a book unfortunately long out of print.

[2] J. Clivio, *Lessing und das Problem der Tragödie*, Zürich and Leipzig, 1928, pp. 66 ff. (see esp. p. 96).

from the question whether Lessing did study Leibnitz so assiduously in Breslau as is assumed, it seems to me that this study did not affect his tragic theory, if only because there is little essential difference in Lessing's attitude to that problem in 1767 and ten years before. If his eyes were always blinkered by the rationalistic insistence on the moral purpose of literature, this was too much flesh and bone of his age to require any particular philosophic explanation.

And if his philosophy plays so small a part in his theory of the drama, it is almost an anachronism to expect, before aesthetic thought had had time to crystallise out of the Baumgarten system, that Lessing should have been guided by systematic aesthetic considerations. It is true that, like all his younger contemporaries in Leipzig, he turned away from the narrow Wolffianism of Gottsched to the somewhat freer outlook of Bodmer and Breitinger, and found more satisfaction in Du Bos' *Réflexions critiques sur la Poësie et sur la Peinture* than in Gottsched's *Critische Dichtkunst*; but this was the veriest ruffling of the surface of aesthetic speculation.

The truth is that Lessing's approach to the problems of the drama —as to that of the delimitation of the arts in his *Laokoon*—was always an empiric one, neither speculative nor metaphysical. His interest began with his ambition to become himself a dramatist; his theories of drama were the outcome of purely practical considerations of ways and means. Moreover—as will, I think, be abundantly evident from the following pages—he approached his problems in an eclectic way, not as an original thinker. His industrious reading brought him face to face with a considerable body of literature on the nature and function of dramatic poetry, and he made it his business to pick and choose what was congenial to him.

From Lessing's two journals, the *Beyträge zur Historie und Aufnahme des Theaters* and the *Theatralische Bibliothek*, inferences have already been drawn in the first part of this volume concerning his interest in dramatic theory down to about the year 1758.[1] But, as we have seen, the harvest is not encouraging. In the earlier journal, where Lessing was still a docile disciple of Gottsched, the chief contribution of this kind apart from the Plautus essays is the translation of Corneille's *Trois Discours*, which, it will be remembered, I have claimed for Lessing himself. The *Theatralische Bibliothek* contains several items which have bearing on dramatic theory: Gellert's and Chassiron's disquisitions on the 'comédie larmoyante', Dryden's

[1] See above, pp. 114 f.

Essay of Dramatic Poesy, and the final volume of Du Bos' *Réflexions* containing his treatise on the theatrical representations of the ancients. Apart from these, Lessing contributed in the summer of 1751 an article to *Das Neueste aus dem Reiche des Witzes*, which deals with two writers who were to be of the first importance for his subsequent critical theory; he reviews here[1] the German translation of Batteux' *Les Beaux-Arts réduits à un même principe* by Johann Adolf Schlegel, Leipzig, 1751 (erroneously attributing the translation to Gellert), together with another and unsatisfactory version by Philipp E. Bertram (Gotha, 1751). He then passes to Diderot's *Lettre sur les sourds et muets*, which had been evoked by Batteux' treatise. A third book which is discussed in the same article, La Mettrie's *L'Art de jouir*, is mainly occupied with that writer's travesty of Haller's poem *Doris*, and does not concern us here.

This little essay might fairly be claimed as Lessing's first step on the path which ultimately led him to the *Hamburgische Dramaturgie*. The opening paragraph is his first pronouncement on the 'rules'; Batteux suggested to him that they were not the stable and unchangeable foundations of poetic composition on which the older critics had insisted. He says:

Die Regeln in den schönen Künsten sind aus den Beobachtungen entstanden, welche man über die Wercke derselben gemacht hat. Diese Beobachtungen haben sich von Zeit zu Zeit vermehret, und vermehren sich noch, so oft ein Genie, welches niemals seinen Vorgängern ganz folgt, einen neuen Weg einschlägt, oder den schon bekannten über die alten Grenzen hinausbähnet. Wie unzehlig muss also nicht die Menge der Regeln sein; denn allen diesen Beobachtungen kan man eine Art der Allgemeinheit geben, das ist, man kan sie zu Regeln machen. Wie unnütz aber müssen sie uns nothwendig durch eben diese Menge werden, wenn man sie nicht durch die Zurückführung auf allgemeine Sätze einfacher und weniger machen kan.[2]

Batteux' attempt to demonstrate the 'Einschränckung der schönen Künste auf einen eintzigen Grundsatz'—namely, the imitation of nature—had Lessing's approval. Diderot's letter also gave him much to think of: notably, the limitations of the French language for artistic expression, and the significance of gesture in the art of the actor. In 1755 Batteux re-published his treatise (with additions) as *Principes de la Littérature*[3] and Lessing's friend Karl Wilhelm Ramler published,

---

[1] *Schriften*, iv, pp. 413 ff. [2] *Ibid.* pp. 413 f.
[3] This was expanded into five volumes in 1764, under the same title.

in 1756–58, a translation of this larger treatise; a second edition of this translation appeared in 1762–63, and a sixth and last in 1802. In his *Abhandlung von dem Wesen der Fabel* (1759) Lessing, it may be added, again refers to Batteux with all respect, although maintaining his own theory of the fable against him.[1] Batteux' aesthetic theory remained, as will be seen from the following pages, an important and even a basic factor in his views on tragedy.

Another French work with which Lessing was doubtless early familiar was Hédelin d'Aubignac's *Pratique du Théâtre*. This 'ouvrage très-nécessaire à ceux qui veulent s'appliquer à la Composition des Poëmes Dramatiques, qui les récitent en public, ou qui prennent plaisir d'en voir les réprésentations' (as it is described on its title-page) originally appeared in Paris in 1657, and Lessing probably had in his possession the Amsterdam edition of 1715. This work—then nearly a hundred years old—still possessed for the Lessing of the *Dramaturgie* a certain canonical value.

With Aristotle's *Poetics* he had, no doubt, made acquaintance at an early date in Dacier's translation,[2] but his first close study of it probably dated from the appearance of a German translation by M. C. Curtius in 1753, which first brought that work home to the German reading world.[3] One cannot but notice how sparse are the references to Aristotle in Lessing's early writings.[4]

---

[1] *Schriften*, vii, pp. 433 ff. See also *Litteraturbriefe*, No. lxx, November 23, 1759, *ed. cit.* iv, pp. 329 ff.; *Schriften*, viii, pp. 186 ff. Cp. M. Schenker, *Charles Batteux und seine Nachahmungstheorie in Deutschland*, Leipzig, 1909, pp. 137 ff.

[2] In his *Theatralische Bibliothek* (*Schriften*, vi, p. 32) Lessing quotes the Paris edition of 1692. R. Petsch, *Lessings Briefwechsel mit Mendelssohn und Nicolai über das Trauerspiel* (Philosophische Bibliothek, cxxi), Leipzig, 1910, p. xv (note), mentions that Dacier's work appeared anonymously; but there were two editions in 1692, an anonymous quarto one, and a duodecimo one with Dacier's name. It is the latter to which Lessing refers in the *Theatralische Bibliothek*. There was also an Amsterdam edition of 1733.

[3] When Gottsched planned his *Deutsche Schaubühne* in 1740, he had contemplated opening its first volume with 'Die Dichtkunst Aristotels...ins Deutsche übersetzt, und mit Anmerkungen versehen von Herrn Prof. Gottscheden' ('Nachricht von der unter der Presse befindlichen deutschen Schaubühne' in the *Beyträge zur critischen Historie* etc., St. xxiii, 1740, p. 525). And in the preface to the first volume of the *Schaubühne* (1742, p. 7) he said: 'Die Übersetzung...ist längst von mir verfertiget worden; indem ich vor zwölf Jahren schon, gleich nach dem Antritte meines poetischen Lehramtes darüber öffentlich gelesen, und dadurch die Regeln der guten Schaubühne in Deutschland zuerst bekannt zu machen gesuchet.' Lessing refers to this promised translation in his review of Curtius.

[4] Aristotle's name only occurs four times in the *Beyträge*, each time in the *Critik über die Gefangnen des Plautus* (*Schriften*, iv, pp. 136, 154, 159 (in quotation), 160).

In reviewing the translation of the *Poetics* by Curtius in the *Berlinische privilegirte Zeitung* of 1753 he says:

[Aristoteles] herrscht.. in dem Reiche des Geschmacks unter den Dichtern und Rednern eben so unumschränkt, als ehedem unter seinen Peripatetikern. Seine Dichtkunst, oder vielmehr das Fragment derselben, ist der Quell aus welchem alle Horaze, alle Boileaus, alle Hedelins, alle Bodmers, bis so gar auf die Gottschede, ihre Fluren bewässert haben.[1]

In all probability then, Aristotle's *Poetics* meant Curtius's translation for Lessing down to the time of the correspondence with Mendelssohn and Nicolai in 1756–57, and even, for that matter, until the *Dramaturgie* was fairly well advanced. We have no ground for supposing that Lessing made any study of the Greek text until then.[2] Later in this chapter I deal with Lessing's attitude to Aristotle in the *Dramaturgie* and the sources of knowledge on which he relied.

In 1753 an event occurred which was of the first importance for Lessing's aesthetic speculation and which marked a turning-point in his intellectual development. In that year he made the acquaintance of Moses Mendelssohn.[3] I doubt whether even yet the full extent of his debt to Mendelssohn has been recognised. It is certainly no exaggeration to say that the latter contributed more to the moulding of Lessing's mind than any other of his friends; and if, in his later life, it was his conscious intention to raise a monument to Mendelssohn in *Nathan der Weise*, it was the just repayment of a great debt. The acquaintance seems to have been brought about by A. S. Gumpertz in 1753. The first visible effect of it is to be seen in Lessing's defence of his own drama *Die Juden* against Michaelis in the *Theatralische Bibliothek* in 1754; and in 1755 Mendelssohn and Lessing were associated in the essay *Pope ein Metaphysiker!* From that year onwards their correspondence was considerable. It was Mendelssohn who

---

[1] *Schriften*, v, pp. 194 f.

[2] G. G. Fülleborn reported to Lessing's brother (K. G. Lessing, *G. E. Lessings Leben, ed. cit.* iii, pp. vii f.) that among papers 'aus Lessings Jugendzeit' he found 'hin und wieder auf einzelnen Blättern Perioden aus Aristoteles Poetik übersetzt, welche er [Lessing] in der Folge weit richtiger und Deutscher in seiner Dramaturgie gegeben hat'. But these papers have disappeared, and it is impossible to say whether, as Muncker suggests (*Schriften*, xiv, p. 164), they belonged to a period before the publication of Curtius's book or subsequent to it, or, for that matter, whether they may not have been merely excerpts from the German translation.

[3] Cp. L. Goldstein, *Moses Mendelssohn und die deutsche Ästhetik*, Königsberg, 1904 (especially pp. 187 ff.), where Lessing's dependence on Mendelssohn, more particularly in the *Laokoon*, is discussed.

turned Lessing's mind to philosophical questions with his first publications, *Philosophische Gespräche* and *Briefe über die Empfindungen*, both of which appeared in 1755. Mendelssohn interested him in the writings of the English moralists, in Shaftesbury, Hutcheson, and Burke, with the consequence that Lessing published in 1756 a translation of Hutcheson's *Elements of Moral Philosophy* as *Sittenlehre der Vernunft*, and planned a translation of Burke's *Enquiry into the Origin of our Ideas of the Sublime and Beautiful*. In the new field of aesthetics opened up by Baumgarten and Georg Friedrich Meier in Halle, he read the latter's *Anfangsgründe aller schönen Wissenschaften* (Halle, 1748–50; 2nd ed. 1754–59) of which there are echoes in the correspondence with Mendelssohn and Nicolai on tragedy;[1] and the study of the theory of laughter to which Mendelssohn refers in a letter to Lessing in 1755[2] would perhaps have owed something to Meier's early *Gedanken von Scherzen* (Halle, 1744), as well as to Hutcheson's *Reflections upon Laughter*. In matters of literary criticism it has already been shown in these pages how much reliance Lessing placed on judgments by Mendelssohn in articles contributed by him to the *Briefe, die neueste Litteratur betreffend*.

In 1756 Nicolai planned a new journal, *Bibliothek der schönen Wissenschaften und der freyen Künste*, and offered as a prize for the best German tragedy the sum of fifty talers. In order to facilitate the work of the young dramatists whom he hoped to encourage, he himself wrote for the first number of his journal an *Abhandlung vom Trauerspiele*; and on August 31—the first number of the *Bibliothek* did not appear until the following year—he wrote to Lessing, who had already set out on his European tour with Gottfried Winkler, giving him a brief account of the contents of his essay. This formed the starting-point for a correspondence of the three friends, Lessing, Mendelssohn and Nicolai, on the nature of tragedy, which continued at intervals until the spring of the following year.[3] Lessing's share in it consisted of eight letters written between November 13, 1756 and April 2, 1757.

[1] Cp. especially *Anfangsgründe*, I (1748), vii (*Von dem sinlichen Leben der Gedanken*), §§ 192 ff. and Lessing's definition of 'Leidenschaften'.

[2] Letter to Lessing, November 19, 1755 (*Mendelssohns Gesammelte Schriften, ed. cit.* v, p. 11).

[3] The *Abhandlung* is reprinted in *Lessings Jugendfreunde*, ed. by J. Minor in Kürschner's *Deutsche National-litteratur*, lxxii, [1883]; and the correspondence will be found in *Schriften*, xvii, pp. 63 ff., and xix, pp. 40 ff. A convenient edition of *Abhandlung* and correspondence has been published by R. Petsch (see above, p. 336, note 2).

Nicolai's essay set out to bore the plank where it was thickest. He contrasts Aristotle's statement that the object of tragedy is 'to purify us by means of terror and pity from the errors of the passions represented' with Corneille's assertion that the writer of tragedies has merely in view the production of pleasure. Aristotle, he holds, says too much, Corneille not enough; and he himself proposes as a definition of the object of tragedy 'the stirring up in us of violent passions'. This is an amplification of Corneille's demand in the light of Du Bos' doctrine that the source of pleasure is the occupation of the mind, and that nothing occupies it more effectually than strong passions. Or it may be regarded as a curtailment of Aristotle's definition by removing from it the insistence on a cathartic purpose.

Although Nicolai thus rejects Aristotle's theory that tragedy 'purifies', he examines the various interpretations of that theory which have been offered. There is the view put forward by Brumoy, that the purification consists in hardening the audience against evils by familiarising them with such things.[1] But this view he considers to conflict with Aristotle's statement that the object of tragedy is to stir up and not to damp passions. Nicolai maintains that the purpose of tragedy is not at all essential to its definition; he hints, indeed, that it may have been inserted in the definition by Aristotle merely to appease Plato: it is what Corneille called a 'beautiful thought'[2] and nothing more. Thus he endorses the view held by Curtius, that Aristotle is guilty of inconsistency in asserting that there can be tragedy without morals and at the same time requiring tragedy to purify passions: there can be no passions to purify if there are no morals.[3] Purification of passions may or may not be included in the definition; but tragedy must have a moral end. The theatre, as

---

[1] *Théâtre des Grecs*, Paris, 1730, i, p. liii. Lessing, finding in Curtius's *Abhandlung von der Absicht des Trauerspiels* a translation of some lines of Timocles, with a reference to Athenæus, vi, cap. i, p. 223, suggested them to Nicolai as older evidence of this theory than that afforded by Brumoy. It is Athenæus who refers to Stobæus (whom Lessing cites as having quoted the lines of Timocles. Cp. Lessing's letter of April 2, 1757, Petsch, *op. cit.* p. 106). The original source of the reference is probably Robortello, *Aristotelis de Arte Poetica*, Florence, 1548, pp. 53 f. J. Bernays, in *Rheinisches Museum für Philologie*, N.F. xxxiv (1879), pp. 615 f., traces Lessing's quotation to *Comicorum Græcorum Sententiæ...ab H. Stephano redditæ* [Paris], 1569, p. 450 (where the passage in question is headed *Ex Timocle*).

[2] *Discours de la Tragédie*, *Œuvres*, ed. Marty-Laveau, Paris, 1862, i, p. 58.

[3] Cp. *Aristoteles Dichtkunst, ins Deutsche übersetzet, mit Anmerkungen und besondern Abhandlungen versehen*, von Michael Conrad Curtius, Hanover, 1753, pp. 123 f.

Mendelssohn had said, may have its own morality,[1] but this morality must not be in conflict with real morality.

The action, the essential part of tragedy, must have tragic greatness; it must be uninterrupted, not complicated, and it must possess unity. This leads to a discussion of the particular unities on which the French insisted. Nicolai pleads for a relaxation of the classic rule, which has the disadvantage of excluding from tragedy subjects otherwise eminently suitable. 'Die einzige Pflicht des Dichters wird also nur seyn, sich der Einheit der Zeit und des Orts, so viel möglich, zu nähern, und wenn er um grösserer Schönheiten willen davon abweichen muss, es so einzurichten, dass die Abweichung dem Zuschauer nicht sehr merklich werde.'[2] On this point Nicolai is in agreement with the views—not, however, published until some years later—of Johann Elias Schlegel. Nor does Lessing seem to differ very much from him. At least he does not revert to this matter in his reply.

Nicolai now proceeds to deal with admiration as a tragic 'passion', and he divides tragedies into three categories: (1) those which merely awaken terror and pity, that is, tragedies of common life, and dramas such as *Medea*, *Thyestes*, *Mérope* and *Zayre* in which the interest is of a similar kind; (2) heroic tragedies such as *Cato* and *Brutus*, in which by means of terror and pity admiration is awakened; and (3) mixed tragedies, in which the terror and pity are tempered by the introduction of characters who awaken our admiration, such being *Iphigeneia in Aulis*, *Le Comte d'Essex* and *Athalie*. He rejects a suggested fourth class in which admiration is awakened without the assistance of terror and pity, an example being Schlegel's *Canut*.

The correspondence of the three friends which followed this pronouncement deals only with a small part of Nicolai's programme; there is nothing in it about the unities or the different kinds of tragic plot. It is restricted, in fact, to a discussion of the legitimate tragic 'passions' and the purpose of tragedy. As these questions recur in the *Hamburgische Dramaturgie*, and as Lessing's views remained substantially those which he held in 1756–57, it will be more convenient to deal with them in later chapters.

Such then is Lessing's occupation with drama and dramatic theory down to the year 1758.

In the following year he published his first considerable treatise on literary aesthetics, the *Abhandlung von dem Wesen der Fabel* which

[1] Cp. *Briefe über die Empfindungen*, xiii, *Gesammelte Schriften, ed. cit.* i, p. 157.
[2] Petsch, *op. cit.* p. 15.

accompanied his own collection of fables. This has, however, few points of contact with drama; and beyond the fact that it affords evidence of his continued interest in Batteux, it is of little importance in the present connexion.[1] But at the same time Lessing was engaged on an undertaking of much greater relevance and importance for his future work: a translation of Diderot's *Le Fils naturel* and *Le père de famille* with their accompanying 'Entretiens'. The two plays had appeared in Paris respectively in 1757 and 1758; Lessing's translation was published in 1760, and was followed by a second edition in 1781.[2]

Diderot, the Frenchman of his generation with whom Lessing stood in most sympathetic relation, was the greatest force in the ultimate crystallisation of his ideas on the nature, function and presentation of the drama. Even now, strange to say, there is no adequate study of the relations of Lessing and Diderot, or, for that matter, of Diderot's share in the evolution of German ideas.[3] It is, however, a difficult problem, for the ramifications of Diderot's influence on Lessing are many and subtle. In the following pages I have attempted, in matters of detail, to evaluate that influence as far as it is apparent in the ideas of the *Hamburgische Dramaturgie*.

In 1759 there appeared in England a work which had a more revolutionary influence on the literature of Germany than perhaps any other of the century, the *Conjectures on Original Composition* of Edward Young. It was at once translated—indeed twice—into German: as a separate pamphlet: *Gedanken über die Original-Werke in einem Schreiben des D. Youngs an den Verfasser des Grandison*. Aus dem Englischen, Leipzig, 1760 (signed v. T. [Hans Ernst von Teubern]), and in the second and third parts of the *Freymüthige Briefe über die neuesten Werke aus den Wissenschaften in und ausser Deutschland* (signed '*G.**').[4] Here a new and kindling conception of poetic genius was enunciated, which could not but have a profound influence on

---

[1] See above, p. 336.

[2] The edition of Lessing's works in Kürschner's *Deutsche National-litteratur* (vol. lxv) reprints in its entirety his translation, as does also the latest edition in the *Goldene Klassiker Bibliothek*, Berlin [1925–9].

[3] See however R. Dikenmann, *Beiträge zum Thema Diderot und Lessing*, Diss. Zürich, 1915; E. Schmidt, *Diderot und Lessing* in *Die Gegenwart*, xxi (1882), Nos. 9 (pp. 133–6), 10 (pp. 153–5); and the slight introduction in C. Flaischlen, *O. H. von Gemmingen mit einer Vorstudie über Diderot als Dramatiker*, Diss. Zürich, 1890.

[4] There is a convenient reprint of v. Teubern's translation, ed. by K. Jahn, in the series *Kleine Texte für theologische und philologische Vorlesungen und Übungen*, lx, Bonn, 1910.

Lessing's mind. It led him to think carefully on the nature of genius, which had been explained so simply by the older theorists.

There is no ground for believing that during his sojourn in Breslau Lessing concerned himself seriously with problems of dramatic theory. His aesthetic interests centred in the problems of the *Laokoon*, and although these have obvious relevance to the tendency of the *Dramaturgie* to define the various fields of dramatic poetry and theatrical representation, *Laokoon* does not come very much into question in this volume. But the waning interest in dramatic theory was balanced by his preoccupation, during the later years in Breslau, with his great comedy *Minna von Barnhelm.*

It was, however, in these years that some important works in the field of dramatic aesthetics appeared, which have left their traces on Lessing's work. For the first time Johann Elias Schlegel—then fifteen years dead—became a force in the practical problems of creating a German national theatre, through the publication (in the third volume of his collected works in 1764) of his theoretical treatises. Indeed, we might say that the whole scheme of a national theatre in Hamburg might have remained rudimentary and impracticable, without Schlegel's clear and concrete plans for the erection of such an institution in the Danish capital.[1] In 1762 there appeared also Home's *Elements of Criticism*—in its German translation entitled *Grundsätze der Critik* (1763–66)—a work which materially furthered Lessing's movement towards naturalism and the English standpoint in the art of the drama. Lastly mention should be made of Marmontel's *Poétique françoise* (2 vols. Paris, 1763), a work which as I have shown elsewhere[2] had a marked influence in formulating one of the central dogmas of the *Laokoon.* Lessing turns to it again in his *Dramaturgie.*[3]

LESSING AND ARISTOTLE

Anticipating conclusions to which the present investigations lead, I would say at once that a common view of the *Hamburgische Dramaturgie* as a treatise essentially concerned with the *Poetics* of Aristotle is hardly in accordance with fact; Aristotle is certainly not, as Gotschlich claimed,[4] the pivot on which Lessing's journal turns. In

[1] See also above, pp. 19 f., 24.
[2] *Modern Language Review*, vi (1911), pp. 216 ff.
[3] See below, pp. 355 (note 11), 398; cp. also pp. 371 f.
[4] E. Gotschlich, *Lessings Aristotelische Studien*, Berlin, 1876, pp. 16, 129 and *passim.*

the early moulding of his theoretical views on the drama Aristotle appears to have played a very small part. As we have seen, he is practically ignored in the *Beyträge* and the *Theatralische Bibliothek*, as far as any personal views of Lessing are concerned. In his *Leben Sophocles* of 1760, it is true, Lessing cites a passage in the original Greek;[1] but I doubt whether much weight can be attached to this. There is, in fact, no evidence of his making any systematic study of the *Poetics* until he was well advanced in the *Dramaturgie*, in 1768. At the time of his correspondence with Mendelssohn and Nicolai in 1756–57, indeed, he showed some interest in Aristotle's views of the drama. Gotschlich infers from Lessing's discussions of the meaning of φόβος in his letter to Nicolai of April 2, 1757, that he turned in that year from the translation of Curtius to the Greek text of Aristotle.[2] In view of the fact, however, that his substitution of 'fear' for 'terror' as an interpretation of the word was not necessarily a conclusion of his own,[3] Gotschlich's argument does not carry much conviction—particularly as the single word φόβος is the only ground offered us from the correspondence as proof of Lessing's study of the Greek text. The most cursory reader of the *Hamburgische Dramaturgie* is obliged to admit that Lessing's interest in Aristotle was slow to awaken. Throughout the first thirty-six sections his name is only mentioned three times; on the first occasion, a reference to the actual text of the *Poetics* is not necessarily implied, on the second the sentence containing the name is interrupted, and on the third, it occurs in a passage translated from Corneille.[4] In fact, all that Lessing has to say, prior to St. xxxvii, concerning the nature and function of tragedy, is sporadic, and merely echoes ideas which he had expressed on the subject at an earlier stage of his studies.[5] In St. xxxvii, however, he plunges unexpectedly into a problem of Aristotelian exegesis suggested by a remark of Tournemine's, in connexion with Voltaire's *Mérope*, on the best form of tragic plot; and in the next section he follows this up with a discussion of the meaning of certain technical terms used by Aristotle. This is far, however, from being a beginning to a systematic consideration of Aristotle's opinions on tragedy, for

---

[1] See below, p. 345, note 1.

[2] Gotschlich, *op. cit.* p. 4.

[3] See below, pp. 354 ff.

[4] xix, 15 ('Nun hat es Aristoteles längst entschieden, wie weit sich der tragische Dichter um die historische Wahrheit zu bekümmern habe'); xxii, 57; xxxi, 127.

[5] For example, i, 115; ii, 43; xii, 19; xxxv, 93.

after St. xxxix his name is only mentioned four times[1] until St. lxxiv. Moreover, in St. xliv, xlv and xlvi Lessing discusses the Unities with reference to the views of D'Aubignac and Corneille, but, strange to say, without any specific reference to Aristotle.

With St. lxxiv, published at the end of March, 1768, Lessing settles down for the first time to a serious examination of the *Poetics*. As a first step, he puts himself right with regard to the translation of $\phi\acute{o}\beta os$; it must be translated 'Furcht', not 'Schrecken'. Surely there could be no more convincing proof of Lessing's indifference to Aristotle throughout three-quarters of the *Dramaturgie* than the fact that he had continued to write 'Schrecken' until in the seventy-fourth section he suddenly remembered how, in 1757, he had already corrected Nicolai on this very point! On November 5, 1768 we find him writing to Mendelssohn: 'Ich gehe in allem Ernst mit einem neuen Commentar über die Dichtkunst des Aristoteles, wenigstens desjenigen Theils, der die Tragödie angeht, schwanger.'[2] When this letter was written, eighty-two parts of the *Dramaturgie* were published, and the greater part of the remainder, promised already for the middle of May, 1768, was in type, and out of Lessing's hands. Serious as all this interest in Aristotle no doubt was, the failure of the theatre (which Lessing had long foreseen) damped his ardour in the matter; new interests—connected with his quarrel with Klotz—supervened, and the promise was never fulfilled.

In the *Dramaturgie* Lessing makes the statement that before any one can understand the Aristotelian *Poetics* properly, he must have studied every other work of Aristotle: 'I should counsel any one who wants to give us a new commentary on his *Poetics* which shall leave that of Dacier far behind it, above all things to read the works of the philosopher from beginning to end.'[3] From this the inference has been drawn that Lessing himself had done so[4]—I doubt, however,

---

[1] xlvii, 29; xlix, 78; l, 21; lxx, 126.

[2] *Schriften*, xvii, p. 270. Also *Dramaturgie*, ci–civ, 218: 'Ich habe von dem Entstehen, von der Grundlage der Dichtkunst dieses Philosophen, meine eigene Gedanken, die ich hier ohne Weitläuftigkeit nicht äussern könnte.' In lxxxiii (23) he refers to 'eine andere Gelegenheit' when he will deal more fully with the interpretation of Aristotle.

[3] lxxv, 25. He had written similarly ten years before to Nicolai (*Schriften*, xvii, p. 98): 'Ich kann mir nicht einbilden, dass einer, der dieses zweyte Buch [der Rhetorik] und die ganze aristotelische Sittenlehre an den Nicomachus nicht gelesen hat, die Dichtkunst dieses Weltweisen verstehen könne.'

[4] Gotschlich, *op. cit.* p. 5.

if it is a correct deduction: there is, at least, no ground for believing that Lessing was intimately familiar with any work of Aristotle's except the *Poetics*. A survey of his writings reveals frequent references to the *Nicomachean Ethics*, the *Politics* and *Rhetoric*, as well as to the *Poetics*: but in the majority of instances these references are vaguely general, or based on second-hand sources.[1] It is difficult even to say with confidence what edition of Aristotle—of the works in general, or the *Poetics* in particular—Lessing possessed. The forms of the Greek text quoted in his works make it probable that he used one of the Du Val editions[2] which enjoyed a wide currency in the eighteenth century.[3]

Of all Lessing's guides to the interpretation of Aristotle, the most important was Dacier's translation and commentary which appeared in 1692 under the full title: *La Poétique d'Aristote, contenant les Regles les plus exactes pour juger du Poëme Heroïque, et des Pieces de Theatre, la Tragedie et la Comedie*. Traduite en François, avec des Remarques Critiques sur tout l'Ouvrage. Par Mr Dacier, Paris, 1692. By making the *Poetics* thus universally accessible to the Europe of his time, Dacier re-opened the problem of Aristotle's authority as a lawgiver amongst

[1] The *Nicomachean Ethics* is mentioned in the letter to Nicolai just quoted, in the preface to the translation of Hutcheson (*Schriften*, vii, p. 64), and in the *Dramaturgie*, xc, 115 (note); the *Politics* in the *Leben Sophocles* (*Schriften*, viii, p. 312) and with a special reference to H. Conring's edition (1656) in *Laokoon*, ii (*Schriften*, ix, p. 11); the *Rhetoric* in the review of Curtius (*Schriften*, v, p. 194), in the letter to Nicolai of April 2, 1757 (*Schriften*, xvii, p. 98), in the *Abhandlung von dem Wesen der Fabel*, both in the original and in translation (*Schriften*, vii, pp. 424, 440, 444 f.), in a quotation from himself in the *Litteraturbriefe*, lxx (*Schriften*, viii, p. 188), and in the *Dramaturgie*, LXXV, 40; LXXVII, 93; LXXIX, 29 (and note). In his note to LXXV, 66 (72) Lessing quotes the edition of the *Rhetoric* by Æmilius Portus, Speyer, 1598, but he does not draw his text from this edition; nor does the passage quoted in a note to LXXVII (100) correspond with Portus; and the latter numbers his chapters differently. In LXX, 127, however, he quotes from Portus's commentary on the *Rhetoric* (ii, p. 3): 'Solet autem quaerere pugnam in suis libris Aristoteles....Atque hoc facit non temere, et casu, sed certa ratione atque consilio: nam labefactatis aliorum opinionibus....' The *Poetics* is discussed in the review of Curtius (*Schriften*, v, pp. 194 f.), in the correspondence of 1757, especially in the letter to Nicolai which has been referred to of April 2, 1757; it is quoted both in Greek and in the translation of Dacier in the *Leben Sophocles* (*Schriften*, viii, pp. 351 f.) and in *Laokoon* (*Schriften*, ix, pp. 4, 140, 144). Lastly the Aristotelian treatise *De incessu animalium* is referred to, as cited by Erasmus, in the materials for *Laokoon* (*Schriften*, xiv, p. 420).

[2] *Aristotelis Opera omnia quæ extant, Græce et Latine*, edited by Du Val, appeared at Paris in 1619, 1629, 1639, 1654.

[3] Some clue to Lessing's Aristotelian literature is to be found in his discussion (LXXVI, 94) of the meaning of the word φιλάνθρωπον. See below, pp. 361 f.

poets and men of letters who had no particular classical scholarship. His purpose was not merely to familiarise the modern world with Aristotle's treatise; he also hoped to assist in counteracting 'le desordre où nôtre théatre est tombé depuis quelque temps'.[1] He advanced the movement with which Lessing, too, was identified, whereby critical opinion found its way back from the baroque pseudo-classicism of the seventeenth century to a true, or, at least, a truer classicism. The method, moreover, which Dacier followed in his interpretation of Aristotle was also Lessing's, and the French critic approached his task with no contemptible equipment of learning, both classical and modern. Amongst his predecessors, he pinned his faith in the main to Victorius, 'le plus sçavant, le plus exact et le plus sage', of Aristotle's interpreters,[2] and his own commentary is, in many respects, a polemic against the more arbitrary, if often more ingenious, deductions of Castelvetro. Of other critics, Dacier speaks with most respect of Le Bossu, and finds much to approve of in D'Aubignac's *Pratique du Théâtre*.[3]

Dacier's attitude towards Aristotle foreshadows—in fact, one might say frankly it suggested—Lessing's. He has the same confident faith in the immutability of Aristotle's authority. The rules of poetry, he maintains, 'sont si certainement celles qu'Aristote nous donne, qu'il est impossible d'y réussir par un autre chemin', and he compares the laws that Aristotle established with those of nature, not of men.[4] Lessing repeatedly expresses a similar unwavering faith in Aristotle. 'Eines offenbaren Widerspruchs', he says (xxxviii, 13), 'macht sich ein Aristoteles nicht leicht schuldig. Wo ich dergleichen bey so einem Manne zu finden glaube, setze ich das grössere Misstrauen lieber in meinen, als in seinen Verstand.'[5] And again (lxxiv, 3): 'Aristoteles

---

[1] Preface, *ed. cit.* p. [iii].

[2] *Poétique d'Aristote, ed. cit.* p. [xxiv]; but cp. also pp. 45, 53, 95, 266, etc. Lessing mentions Victorius (xxxvii, 107), but only in a quotation from Dacier; there is no reason to infer that Lessing himself consulted Victorius, whose commentary on the *Poetics* appeared at Florence in 1560.

[3] *Ibid.* pp. [xxv f.]; in his commentary he quotes Le Bossu very frequently (pp. 111, 246, 251, 266, 304, etc.); for criticisms of D'Aubignac, cp. pp. 168, 170.

[4] *Ibid.* pp. [iii, x]. Corneille, too, had said of Aristotle's precepts that they were 'de tous les temps et de tous les peuples' (*Avertissement* to *Le Cid, Œuvres, ed. cit.* iii, p. 85). This implicit faith in Aristotle would appear to have been first expressed by Scaliger.

[5] Curtius, too (*op. cit.* p. 213), had said: 'Die genaue Überlegung, womit Aristoteles schrieb, erlaubet nicht, einem so grossen Manne einen Widerspruch beyzumessen.'

würde ihn [den Charakter des Richards] schlechterdings verworfen haben; zwar mit dem Ansehen des Aristoteles wollte ich bald fertig werden, wenn ich es nur auch mit seinen Gründen zu werden wüsste.'[1] And in the famous passage at the close of the *Dramaturgie* he goes so far as to declare that the *Poetics* 'is as unerring a work as the elements of Euclid still are' (CI–CIV, 222):

> Ihre Grundsätze sind eben so wahr und gewiss, nur freylich nicht so fasslich, und daher mehr der Chicane ausgesetzt, als alles, was diese enthalten. Besonders getraue ich mir von der Tragödie, als über die uns die Zeit so ziemlich alles daraus gönnen wollen, unwidersprechlich zu beweisen, dass sie sich von der Richtschnur des Aristoteles keinen Schritt entfernen kann, ohne sich eben so weit von ihrer Vollkommenheit zu entfernen.[2]

It is Dacier's mission as well as Lessing's to uphold Aristotle in the face of modern detractors and perverters of his views: and an immediate model for Lessing's anti-Cornelian polemic is to be found in Dacier's sharp attacks on Corneille for his 'accommodating' interpretation of the *Poetics*.[3] But Lessing went a step further than his predecessor and defended Aristotle's opinion in passages where to Dacier he seemed to have nodded.[4] Lastly, Lessing's insistence on interpreting Aristotle by Aristotle was a principle extensively applied by Dacier.[5] Against all this is to be set the fact that he does

---

[1] Both these passages recall Batteux (*Principes de la littérature*, v, Pt. ii, chap. iv, Paris ed. of 1764, iii, p. 97): 'Quand un homme, tel qu'Aristote, a prononcé avec assurance et sans intérêt, sur des matieres qui sont véritablement du ressort de l'esprit humain, il faut tenter toutes sortes de voies pour l'expliquer; ou avoir des démonstrations rigoureuses, pour le condamner.'

[2] Petersen (*ed. cit.* p. 266) draws attention to two parallel comparisons of Aristotle with Euclid in reviews in the *Critische Nachrichten* of 1751, which have been ascribed to Lessing: 'Die Geometrie und Poesie haben ganz verschiedene Regeln, und derjenige, welcher den Homer nach dem Euklides beurtheilen wolte, würde eben so abgeschmackt handeln, als der, welcher den Euklides nach dem Homer beurtheilte'; and '...dass man also hier [in Euclid] die logischen Regeln beysammen antrift, deren Nutzen und Wahrheit so zu reden die Erfahrung vieler Jahrhunderte bestätiget hat; eben wie die Vorschriften in des Aristoteles Poetik von den Mustern hergenommen sind, deren Schönheit eine allgemeine Empfindung erkennet hatte' (*Schriften*, iv, pp. 217, 240).

[3] *Poétique d'Aristote, ed. cit.* pp. [xxviii], 80, 192 f., 228 f., 233 f., etc.

[4] XXXVII, 110, 129; LXXVI, 1.

[5] Dacier refers especially frequently to the *Rhetoric* (*ed. cit.* pp. 5, 37, 100, 189, 329, 340, 364, 366 f., etc.). But such cross-references were general even in the early Italian editions; they go back, in fact, in the majority of cases, to that most industrious of Aristotle's commentators, Robortello.

not speak very kindly of Dacier; he calls him a 'Pedant' and, with obvious irony, 'der ehrliche Dacier'; and when he quotes him, it is usually to refute his opinion. But this was an ungenerous trait in Lessing's mentality—his way, perhaps, of interpreting the Quixotian version of the old tag, 'Amicus Plato, sed magis amica veritas'— against which we have to be constantly on our guard if we would estimate fairly his intellectual debts. It is his attitude, for example, to Gottsched, to his old friend Weisse, to Spence in the *Laokoon*, and to many another. There is no question but that his debt to Dacier is great; indeed, it is hardly a paradox to say that, without the French work, we might never have had Lessing's Aristotelian interpretation at all.

The German translation of Aristotle's *Poetics* by Michael Conrad Curtius—*Aristoteles Dichtkunst, ins Deutsche übersetzet, mit Anmerkungen, und besondern Abhandlungen, versehen*—appeared at Hanover in 1753, and, as we have seen, was briefly reviewed by Lessing on August 23 of the same year. The form and general character of Curtius's work were clearly suggested by Dacier's; but it is not by any means a mere copy of the French work. It had benefited, moreover, by the development of critical ideas during the fifty years that lay between the two translations. Curtius is even more interested than Dacier had been in contemporary literature and in the newest theories of his day: indeed, his familiarity with such things is greater than his Greek learning. His opinions are in general less original, being often an echo of Dacier's; and they are not always logically consistent. Dacier was an 'ancient' of the famous controversy; Curtius endeavours to reconcile the 'ancient' standpoint with that of the 'moderns'. He holds loyally to Aristotle, but is in sympathy with the new conception of poetry as a 'vollkommen sinnliche Rede' (enunciated by Baumgarten and Meier) without recognising the difficulties which the new theory put in the way of a wholehearted acceptance of Aristotle. For that matter, he apparently does not recognise the damaging effect of the new aesthetics on Gottschedian classicism. Thus Curtius often flounders helplessly between conflicting opinions; he is ready to accept both Bodmer and Gottsched as authorities, even in matters where they are obviously at variance. He looks up to Corneille and Voltaire as masters of modern tragedy, but he also mentions twice (pp. 114, 115) the name of Shakespeare, whose *Julius Caesar* he knew from von Borck's translation; in one passage (p. 115) he even calls him 'der englische grosse Shakespear'. Needless to say, this does not mean that he was prepared to defend a form of drama so irregular and so flagrantly in conflict with the classic rules as Shakespeare's!

In the *Dramaturgie* Lessing frequently quotes Curtius's translation; usually, it is true, with the object of contradicting it;[1] and when he cites Aristotle in German, his translation, although not drawn from Curtius, shows a considerable dependence upon him.[2]

Lessing's interpretation of Aristotelian problems is dealt with in the chapters that follow; but it may be said at once here that he arrived at no new discovery and stated no conclusion in his Aristotelian criticism that was new or unknown in his day; and where he did attempt to initiate new interpretations of the Aristotelian text, these have proved, almost without exception, unacceptable to later scholarship. But what he did achieve was to provide extraordinarily brilliant and convincing settings for the views he maintained on the wider aspects of Aristotelian doctrine; here lie his mastery and his strength, not in the novelty or correctness of his views. His interpretation of Aristotle is incomplete and often inconclusive; it will be seen how tantalisingly he has relegated crucial questions, just when a solution seemed within reach, to the unwritten commentary on the *Poetics*, which, as the *Dramaturgie* drew to a close, had a foremost place in his plans. Had the commentary been written, we have every reason for believing that it would, in Lessing's own phrase, have 'left Dacier's far behind' (LXXV, 27). Of the unfulfilled promises of Lessing's intellectual life, the failure to redeem this one is surely the most regrettable.

In considering the sources which Lessing had at hand in writing his *Hamburgische Dramaturgie* we have to remember that to a certain degree the invitation to act as critical adviser to the Hamburg Theatre took him by surprise, and found him unprepared. He had to resume a line of thought which had been virtually broken since his correspondence on tragedy with Mendelssohn and Nicolai some ten years before, or at least since his pre-occupation with Diderot in 1759–60. He himself confessed frankly, as we have seen, that his love for the

---

[1] XXXVIII, 2; LXXVI, 97; LXXVII, 66; LXXVIII, note to 143; XC, 11. Perhaps Mendelssohn was responsible for freeing Lessing from Curtius's leading-strings: that critic published in the *Litteraturbriefe*, No. cxlvi, February 19, and No. cxlvii, February 26, 1761 (*ed. cit.* ix, pp. 58 ff.) a review of Curtius's *Critische Abhandlungen und Gedichte* (Hanover, 1760), in which he did not conceal his low opinion of the author. [2] See below, pp. 385 ff.

theatre had died down.[1] There is thus no reason to infer that his standpoint in matters of dramatic theory when he began his work in Hamburg differed materially from that which he had maintained in the earlier correspondence. Moreover, he had not—as was obviously the case when he was writing *Laokoon*—a large library at his disposal. When he set out for Hamburg he gathered together from his collection such books as he thought might be useful for his new undertaking—notably all his own earlier writings, including the *Litteraturbriefe*, and works of reference such as those of Léris and Parfaict—and left the remainder to be sold by auction. Thus his library in Hamburg was comparatively limited; and it is scarcely to be thought that the resources of Hamburg could have materially added to it.

[1] Cp. his letter to Gleim of February 1, 1767; see above, p. 117, note 1.

CHAPTER XII

THEORY OF TRAGEDY

THE DEFINITION OF TRAGEDY

'It is beyond dispute', says Lessing (LXXVII, 30), 'that Aristotle did not intend to give any strict logical definition of Tragedy. For, without limiting himself to its merely essential characteristics, he introduced various fortuitous ones because the usage of his time had rendered them necessary. Apart from these, however, and after the others had been reduced by linking them up with one another, a perfectly exact explanation remains, namely that Tragedy, in one word, is a poem that excites pity. In respect of its genus it is the imitation of an action, like the epic and comedy; but, in respect of its species, it is the imitation of an action that is worthy of our pity. From these two ideas all its rules may be completely deduced; and even its dramatic form is defined by them.'

Aristotle's definition occurs in the sixth chapter of his *Poetics*; and in the text of the editions of Du Val—or indeed, in any text available to the eighteenth century—it is as follows (1449 b):

ἔστιν οὖν τραγῳδία μίμησις πράξεως σπουδαίας καὶ τελείας μέγεθος ἐχούσης, ἡδυσμένῳ λόγῳ χωρὶς ἑκάστῳ τῶν εἰδῶν ἐν τοῖς μορίοις, δρώντων ἀλλὰ οὐ δι' ἀπαγγελίας, δι' ἐλέου καὶ φόβου περαίνουσα τὴν τῶν τοιούτων παθημάτων κάθαρσιν.

This had been rendered by Dacier (*ed. cit.* pp. 72 f.):

La Tragedie est donc une imitation d'une action grave, entiere, et qui a une juste grandeur: Dont le style est agreablement assaisonné, mais differemment dans toutes ses parties, et qui, sans le secours de la narration, par le moyen de la compassion et de la terreur, acheve de purger en nous ces sortes de passions, et toutes les autres semblables.

And Curtius, obviously following Dacier, gave the Germans of his time the definition in the form in which they knew it (*op. cit.* pp. 11 f.):

Das Trauerspiel ist nämlich die Nachahmung einer ernsthaften, vollständigen, und eine Grösse habenden Handlung, durch einen mit fremdem Schmucke versehenen Ausdruck, dessen sämtliche Theile aber besonders wirken: welche ferner, nicht durch die Erzählung des Dichters, sondern (durch Vorstellung der Handlungen selbst) uns, vermittelst des Schreckens und Mitleidens, von den Fehlern der vorgestellten Leidenschaften reiniget.

Both translators, Lessing observes (LXXVII, 60), had recognised the difficulty caused by the little word ἀλλά, and they had endeavoured either to gloss it over, or, by expansion, to explain it. Lessing, however, in his firm faith that the writings of Aristotle are as unassailable as those of Euclid (CI–CIV, 222), endeavours to justify Aristotle's apparent refusal to allow that the narrative form is capable of awakening the kind of pity required by tragedy, and quotes (LXXVII, 100) the following passage from chapter viii of the second book of the *Rhetoric* (his 'neuntes Kapitel' is evidently a slip):[1]

> And as sufferings are objects of compassion if they are apparently close at hand, whereas, if they occurred ten thousand years ago or will occur ten thousand years hence, the anticipation or remembrance of them, as the case may be, either excites no compassion at all in us or excites it in a much smaller degree, it necessarily follows that orators are more successful in arousing compassion, if they aid the effect of their words by their gestures, tones, habiliments and dramatic action of any kind.

This, however, is surely a specious argument, for the great narrative poet is quite as able as the dramatist—Homer is as well able as Sophocles—to make past events take on the vivid semblance of being present. But the whole discussion falls to the ground with the now accepted conclusion that the word ἀλλά is an unjustified interpolation of the Aldine text.

PITY AND FEAR

The real difficulties of the Aristotelian definition of Tragedy lie in the last words: δι' ἐλέου καὶ φόβου περαίνουσα τὴν τῶν τοιούτων παθημάτων κάθαρσιν. What is the precise meaning of ἔλεος and φόβος? How are we to understand κάθαρσις? What is the end or purpose of Tragedy? These are the debatable questions on which the burning controversies of Aristotelian interpretation have always turned, and Lessing's contribution to them forms a pivotal part of his dramatic theory.

Throughout the first part of the *Hamburgische Dramaturgie* Aristotle's

---

[1] I quote from the translation of J. E. C. Welldon, London, 1886, pp. 152 f.

ἔλεος and φόβος are translated by Lessing 'Mitleid' and 'Schrecken'.[1] But in St. LXXIV (49, 62), when discussing Weisse's *Richard der Dritte*, he corrects 'Schrecken' to 'Furcht', and throughout the remainder of the work Aristotle's phrase appears as 'Mitleid und Furcht'.[2] The correction was probably prompted by consideration of the character of Richard III. Such an unmitigated villain as he is represented to be can only awaken in us 'Schrecken', that is to say (LXXIV, 30) 'das Erstaunen über unbegreifliche Missethaten, das Entsetzen über Bosheiten, die unsern Begriff übersteigen...'. This is not one of the legitimate purposes of Tragedy; indeed, the poets of antiquity attempted to minimise it by attributing responsibility for monstrous crime to fate or an avenging god rather than to the man himself. It is the kind of 'terror' in which Crébillon, 'der Schreckliche', indulges. But, Lessing argues (LXXIV, 49), Aristotle does not say 'Schrecken':

> Das Wort, welches Aristoteles braucht, heisst Furcht: Mitleid und Furcht, sagt er, soll die Tragödie erregen; nicht, Mitleid und Schrecken. Es ist wahr, das Schrecken ist eine Gattung der Furcht; es ist eine plötzliche, überraschende Furcht.

As I have already suggested,[3] it is difficult to reconcile Lessing's late discovery of this in the seventy-fourth section, dating from 1768, with the fact that as far back as April 2, 1757 he had written to Nicolai:[4]

> Furcht und Mitleiden. Können Sie mir nicht sagen, warum so wohl Dacier als Curtius, Schrecken und Furcht für gleich bedeutende Worte nehmen? Warum sie das aristotelische φόβος, welches der Grieche durchgängig braucht, bald durch das eine, bald durch das andre übersetzen? Es sind doch wohl zwey verschiedne Dinge, Furcht und Schrecken? Und wie, wenn sich das ganze Schrecken, wovon man nach den falsch verstandenen aristotelischen Begriffen bisher so viel geschwatzt, auf weiter nichts, als auf diese schwankende Übersetzung gründete? Lesen Sie, bitte ich, das zweyte und achte Hauptstück des zweyten Buchs der aristotelischen Rhetorik: denn das muss ich Ihnen beyläufig sagen, ich kann mir nicht einbilden, dass einer, der dieses zweyte Buch und die ganze aristotelische Sittenlehre an den Nicomachus nicht gelesen hat, die Dichtkunst dieses

---

[1] XXXII, 31, 56, 57, 73; XXXVII, 72; XXXVIII, 64, 120; XLVII, 140; XLIX, 52; LI, 130; LXXIV, 6. Also in Lessing's earlier writings; *Theatralische Bibliothek* (*Schriften*, vi, p. 6); *Das Theater des Herrn Diderot*, Berlin, 1760, i, pp. 235, 282 (unchanged in the edition of 1781).

[2] E.g. LXXIV, 49 ff.; LXXV, 17 ff.; LXXX, 102.

[3] See above, p. 344.

[4] *Schriften*, xvii, pp. 97 f.; Petsch, *op. cit.* pp. 104 f.

Weltweisen verstehen könne. Aristoteles erklärt das Wort φόβος, welches Herr Curtius am öftersten Schrecken, Dacier aber bald *terreur*, bald *crainte* übersetzt, durch die Unlust über ein bevorstehendes Übel, und sagt, alles dasjenige erwecke in uns Furcht, was, wenn wir es an andern sehen, Mitleiden erwecke, und alles dasjenige erwecke Mitleiden, was, wenn es uns selbst bevorstehe, Furcht erwecken müsse. Dem zu Folge kann also die Furcht, nach der Meynung des Aristoteles, keine unmittelbare Wirkung des Trauerspiels seyn, sondern sie muss weiter nichts als eine reflectirte Idee seyn. Aristoteles würde bloss gesagt haben: das Trauerspiel soll unsre Leidenschaften durch das Mitleiden reinigen, wenn er nicht zugleich auch das Mittel hätte angeben wollen, wie diese Reinigung durch das Mitleiden möglich werde; und dieserwegen setzte er noch die Furcht hinzu, welche er für dieses Mittel hielt. Jenes hat seine Richtigkeit; dieses aber ist falsch. Das Mitleiden reiniget unsre Leidenschaften, aber nicht vermittelst der Furcht, auf welchen Einfall den Aristoteles sein falscher Begriff von dem Mitleiden gebracht hat. Hiervon können Sie sich mit Herrn Moses weiter unterreden; denn in diesem Puncte, so viel ich weiss, sind wir einig. Nun behalten Sie, durch die ganze Dichtkunst des Aristoteles, überall wo Sie Schrecken finden, diese Erklärung der Furcht in Gedanken, (denn Furcht muss es überall heissen, und nicht Schrecken), und sagen mir alsdann, was Sie von der Lehre des Aristoteles dünkt.

This letter not merely anticipates Lessing's substitution in the *Dramaturgie* of 'Furcht' for 'Schrecken', but even the reference to the *Rhetoric* (LXXV, 38) in elucidation of Aristotle's conception of φόβος is repeated in the later work in terms which (apart from the alteration of the number of a chapter) distinctly recall the letter. It would thus seem likely that Lessing now turned to his old letters to Mendelssohn and Nicolai, which (it will be remembered) he had asked to have sent back to him.[1] The further inference is hardly to be avoided, that until now he had entirely forgotten his previous insistence that 'Furcht' should be substituted for 'Schrecken'.

Lessing was not the first critic to insist upon a discrimination between 'terror' and 'fear'. The practice of his predecessors in interpreting Aristotle's words is worth recording. Heinsius—to go no further back—in his Latin version of the *Poetics* had accepted Victorius's 'misericordia et metus', but in his *De Tragœdiæ constitutione*, which profoundly influenced the eighteenth-century interpretation of the Aristotelian theory, he wrote 'Affectus proprii illius sunt duo: Misericordia, et Horror', and again, 'terrorem...ac miseri-

---

[1] Letter to Nicolai of April 17, 1757 (*Schriften*, xvii, p. 102).

cordiam'.[1] Corneille wrote 'crainte', but he clearly meant 'terreur'.[2] Boileau translated φόβος by 'terreur'.[3] Dacier used 'terreur', but in his notes to Aristotle's thirteenth chapter he several times substituted 'crainte'.[4] Brumoy, too, wrote both 'terreur' and 'crainte'; mainly, however, the latter, and he would seem to give it the significance claimed for it by Lessing.[5] The older German writers invariably translated 'Schrecken und Mitleiden'.[6] As the eighteenth century moved on, the word 'terreur' established itself more firmly in France. It will be found, for instance, in Du Bos' *Réflexions critiques sur la poësie et sur la peinture*,[7] in Batteux' *Les Beaux-arts réduits à un même principe*, and in the enlarged form of that treatise, *Principes de la littérature*;[8] and the German translators of these works render 'terreur' by 'Schrecken'.[9] Both Rousseau and Diderot use 'terreur'.[10] Marmontel in his *Poétique françoise*, a work with which Lessing was familiar, translated the phrase in Aristotle's definition: 'la terreur et la pitié'; but in the text of his work he also wrote: 'la crainte et la pitié.'[11]

[1] *Aristotelis de poetica*, Leyden, 1611, p. 11; *De Tragœdiæ constitutione*, Leyden, 1643, pp. 10, 19 f. It might be noted in this connexion that La Mesnardière, in his *Poétique* (Paris, 1640, pp. 22 ff.), discussed at great length the difference between 'horror' and 'terror'.

[2] *Trois discours* (*Œuvres, ed. cit.* i, pp. 22, 52 ff.). The translation in Lessing's *Beyträge zur Historie und Aufnahme des Theaters*, ii (pp. 211 ff.), follows Corneille with 'Furcht'.   [3] *L'Art poétique*, iii, 18.

[4] *Poétique d'Aristote, ed. cit.* 'terreur', pp. 73, 81 f., 185, 187, 197, etc.; 'crainte', pp. 185, 186, 188 ff.

[5] *Théâtre des Grecs*, Paris, 1730, i, pp. li, liii, lv. Cp. especially p. li: 'D'où il arrive que la crainte nous est plus naturelle, et nous donne des secousses plus fréquentes que toute autre passion, par le sentiment intime et experimental qui nous avertit toujours que les maux assiégent de toutes parts la vie humaine.'

[6] For instance, Gottsched, *Critische Dichtkunst*, 2nd ed. Leipzig, 1737, p. 675; Breitinger, *Critische Dichtkunst*, Zürich, 1740, i, p. 69; Curtius's translation of Aristotle, *ed. cit.* pp. 25, 26, 28, 185 and *passim*. Cp. Mendelssohn, *Briefe über die Empfindungen* and *Rhapsodie* (*Gesammelte Schriften, ed. cit.* i, pp. 173, 249).

[7] Cp. Pt. i, Sections xiv and xv (Paris edition of 1755, i, pp. 106, 110).

[8] *Principes de la littérature*, Paris, 1764, iii, pp. 72 f., 76, 81 f., etc.

[9] It is, however, interesting to note that Ramler, the translator of Batteux, who did not hesitate to bring Batteux up to date or occasionally impute to him views which he could not possibly have held, changed 'Schrecken' to 'Furcht' in editions of the work published subsequently to Lessing's *Dramaturgie* (e.g. 3rd ed. Leipzig, 1769, ii, pp. 273, 274, 277, etc.).

[10] Rousseau, *Lettre à M. D'Alembert*, Amsterdam, 1758, p. 30; Diderot, *Le fils naturel, Second et Troisième Entretiens, Œuvres Complètes, ed. cit.* vii, pp. 116, 135. (Lessing's translation, i, pp. 235, 282.)

[11] *Poétique françoise*, Paris, 1763, ii, pp. 95, 96, 97, 98, 128 f., etc. Lessing quotes

Lessing had, however, an immediate predecessor for his argument in Louis Racine, who wrote, in the *Traité de la poésie dramatique ancienne et moderne* appended to his commentary to his father's works (1752):[1]

Nous sommes depuis long-temps en usage de rendre ce mot φόβος par celui de *terreur*; cependant la terreur est un trouble de l'âme fort différent de celui qui cause la crainte, et φόβος ne signifie que crainte. L'auteur de l'argument qui est à la tête de l'Agamemnon d'Eschyle, pour dire que le discours de Cassandre excite la terreur et la pitié, emploie ces deux mots ἔκπληξιν καὶ οἶκτον. *Metus* est le mot dont les interprètes latins d'Aristote se servent ordinairement. Castelvetro s'est servi d'*ispavento*, et non de *terrore*; un commentateur espagnol se sert du mot *miedo*, qui veut dire crainte; enfin Corneille, dans son Discours sur la Tragédie, nommant les deux passions qui en sont l'âme, suivant Aristote, nomme toujours *la pitié et la crainte*.

Lessing may have read Racine's book; but it should be noted that the passage in question is commented on prominently in a review of the book in the *Mercure de France* of January, 1751 (pp. 75 ff.); and we know that Lessing possessed a set of this periodical down to the year 1758.[2]

When Lessing first interested himself in the meaning of φόβος, and before he had reason to doubt the correctness of its translation as 'Schrecken', he accepted Mendelssohn's definition of the word. In his letter to Nicolai of November [13], 1756, he wrote: 'Das Schrecken in der Tragödie ist weiter nichts als die plötzliche Überraschung des Mitleides, ich mag den Gegenstand meines Mitleids kennen oder nicht';[3] which is clearly Mendelssohn's 'dasjenige, was in den Trauerspielen unter dem Namen des Schreckens bekannt ist, ist nichts als ein Mitleiden, das uns schnell überrascht; denn die Gefahr droht niemals uns selbst, sondern unserm Nebenmenschen, den wir

from this work in his *Laokoon*, xvii (*Schriften*, ix, pp. 106 f.; see my note in *Modern Language Review*, vi, 1911, pp. 216 ff.), and seems to have it in mind in the *Dramaturgie*, xiv, 43. There is also a reference to Marmontel's book in Lessing's notes for subsequent use in the *Dramaturgie* (*Schriften*, xv, p. 44).

[1] Louis Racine, *Œuvres*, Paris, 1808, vi, pp. 379 f. Attention has already been drawn to this by J. Meyer in an article on *Lessing und die Franzosen* in *Alemannia*, xvii (1889), pp. 157 ff.

[2] See letter to Gleim, February 1, 1767 (*Schriften*, xvii, p. 229; cp. also in the same volume, pp. 238, 251, 253, 268, 311). Lessing refers repeatedly to the *Mercure* in his *Collectanea* (*Schriften*, xv, pp. 193, 224, 283, 302, 318); also in *Laokoon*, iv (*Schriften*, ix, p. 28). [3] *Schriften*, xvii, p. 65; Petsch, *op. cit.* p. 53.

bedauern.'[1] It is the first shock which we feel when misfortune suddenly befalls anyone, and which has, as its consequence, the awakening of our pity. But with the more careful consideration of Aristotle's words—which would appear to have taken place between November 13, 1756 and April 2, 1757—Lessing was obliged to discard the word 'Schrecken'. Aristotle defines his φόβος as an emotion awakened by a misfortune overtaking a person like ourselves (περὶ τὸν ὅμοιον). This is not the terror which is awakened in us by an unmitigated villain such as Richard III, whom we could never regard as a person like ourselves; it is the fear which we as spectators have, lest we might possibly meet with a similar fate—a fear for ourselves. Or in Lessing's own words in the *Dramaturgie* (LXXV, 18): '[Aristoteles] Furcht ist durchaus nicht die Furcht, welche uns das bevorstehende Übel eines andern, für diesen andern, erweckt, sondern es ist die Furcht, welche aus unserer Ähnlichkeit mit der leidenden Person für uns selbst entspringt...diese Furcht ist das auf uns selbst bezogene Mitleid.'

To illustrate the confusion caused by misunderstanding of the word φόβος, Lessing quotes (LXXIV, 65) a passage from a work entitled *Komisches Theater*, von S., Breslau, 1759 (Vorrede, p. 35).[2] This writer, using the word 'Schrecken', points out that Aristotle is wrong in limiting it to 'unsers gleichen'—or rather that the limitation is unnecessary, for we can be equally affected by this emotion in witnessing a monster of wickedness fall into misfortune; in fact this

---

[1] *Briefe über die Empfindungen* (*Gesammelte Schriften, ed. cit.* i, p. 173).

[2] The passage (with slight verbal differences) actually occurs on pp. 35 f. 'S.', according to F. von Blankenburg, *Litterarische Zusätze zu J. G. Sulzers Allgemeiner Theorie der schönen Künste*, i (Leipzig, 1796), p. 248, is Straube, presumably G. B. Straube, who had objected to comedies in rhymed verse in Gottsched's *Beyträge zur critischen Historie* etc. (xxiii, 1740), while the author of the three 'Abhandlungen' which precede the comedies in the *Komisches Theater* was J. P. Schrader. Cosack, on the other hand (*op. cit.* p. 343), says that 'S.' is Chr. Ernst Schenk, a statement supported by the entry in Kayser, *Bücher-Lexicon*, vi, *Schauspiele* (Leipzig, 1836), p. 100. The volume is the subject of a review of some length—which Schröter and Thiele (*ed. cit.* p. 417) claim, not very convincingly, for Lessing himself—in the *Bibliothek der schönen Wissenschaften*, v, 2 (1759), pp. 335 ff. The critic here has no very high opinion of the introductory 'Abhandlungen': 'Die Folge...ist, dass der Verfasser bekannte Dinge, die Aristoteles, Hedelin, Batteux, der Verfasser der Briefe über die Empfindung, und andere, schon vor ihm und besser gesagt hatten, auf eine veränderte Art einmal sagt, oder wo er ja etwas neues hinzusetzet, sich mehrentheils irrt. Unter der Larve eines theatralischen Metaphysikers streut er seinen Lesern nur Staub in die Augen.'

limited 'Schrecken' is a kind of 'Mitleid' and need not have been mentioned at all. And from Mendelssohn's *Rhapsodie oder Zusätze zu den Briefen über die Empfindungen* (1761)[1] Lessing quotes another long passage in which Mendelssohn elaborates his conception of 'Mitleid', also coming to the conclusion that 'theatralisches Schrecken' is 'Mitleiden'. Lessing accepts these views as incontrovertibly correct as far as they go; but he is not prepared to admit that Aristotle is wrong.

In his letter to Nicolai of April 1757, claiming 'Furcht' as the correct equivalent for φόβος, Lessing had, as we have seen, referred his friend to 'das zweyte und achte Stück des zweyten Buchs der aristotelischen Rhetorik'; in the *Dramaturgie* (LXXV, 39) he repeats the reference,[2] and in a way which shows that he had the old correspondence before him. Aristotle, he affirms, must always be explained from himself. In chapter v of book ii of the *Rhetoric* Aristotle defines 'fear' as 'a species of pain or disturbance arising from an impression of

---

[1] In a later edition of the *Rhapsodie* (in the new edition of his *Philosophische Schriften*, 1771) Mendelssohn defended his original view against Lessing's attempt to vindicate Aristotle. Aristotle, he says, was of the opinion 'dass wir bei einer jeden tragischen Vorstellung Rücksicht auf uns selbst nehmen. Allein ich für meinen Theil leugne diese Rücksicht auf uns selbst. Wenigstens ist sie nicht nothwendig, wenn wir mit andern sympathisiren sollen. Wie oft ist der Bemitleidete nicht in solchen Umständen, in welche wir schlechterdings nie gerathen können? Dass wir leichter zum Mitleiden bewegt werden, wenn wir in ähnlichen Umständen sind, ein ähnliches Unglück ausgestanden oder zu befürchten haben, kann zwar nicht geleugnet werden. Allein dieses kömmt nicht, wie Aristoteles zu glauben scheint, aus eigensüchtiger Furcht; denn die Eigensucht ist es gewiss nicht, die unser Herz dem Mitleiden aufschliesst. Es ist vielmehr das lebhaftere Selbstgefühl eines ähnlichen Übels, das unser Mitleiden schärft, indem es uns den Leidenden als desto bedauernswerther betrachten lässt' (*Gesammelte Schriften, ed. cit.* i, p. 250).

[2] To Nicolai he quoted chapters ii and viii, but in the *Dramaturgie*, v and viii. 'Stl.' in his criticism in Klotz's *Deutsche Bibliothek* (iv (1769), p. 502) reprimanded him for this inaccuracy: 'Die Erklärung dieser Furcht steht nicht im fünften und achten, sondern im zehnten, eilften und zwanzigsten Kapitel des zweyten Buchs von Aristoteles Rhetorik. Einem Manne, der anderer Scribenten Allegate mit so grossem Geschrey berichtigt, kann man diesen Dienst ja auch thun.' This seems, however, to be a question of different editions. Lessing's statement (LXXV, 41) that Aristotle's interpreters had not referred to the *Rhetoric* is wrong. Robortello had done so (pp. 151 ff. of his edition), and Heinsius, *De tragœdiæ constitutione* (*ed. cit.* pp. 71 f., 74); also Dacier (*ed. cit.* p. 189) and L. Racine (*Œuvres, ed. cit.* vi, p. 389). In view of this there is no reason, here at least, to claim Heinsius's treatise as a source of Lessing's opinion, as does M. Zerbst (*Ein Vorläufer Lessings in der Aristoteles-interpretation*, Jena, 1887, pp. 27 f.).

impending evil which is destructive or painful in its nature'; and in chapter viii 'pity' as 'a sort of pain at an evident evil of a destructive or painful kind in the case of somebody who does not deserve it, the evil being one to which we may naturally expect ourselves or some one of our own friends to be liable, and this at a time when it appears to be near at hand'. And later in chapter viii:

Again, we experience a feeling of compassion, when the danger *which threatens others* approaches ourselves. We compassionate those who are like ourselves in age, character, habit of mind, reputation or family, as in all these cases there appears to be a greater probability of the same misfortune happening to ourselves *as to them*; for in regard to compassion again it is a general principle to be observed that whatever moves us to fear, when it affects ourselves, moves us to compassion, when it affects other people.[1]

The sentence quoted by Lessing in the original in his note (LXXV, 72)[2] is from chapter v of book ii: 'generally speaking too, a thing is formidable to us, if it excites compassion when it happens or threatens to happen to others.'[3]

Thus, Lessing concludes (LXXV, 96), Aristotle's conception of pity necessarily includes fear, for nothing excites our pity save that which at the same time can awaken our fear. Why he found it necessary to mention fear at all is a question to which I return immediately. Meanwhile, it might be noted that this Aristotelian definition of tragic fear as a fear for ourselves was more generally held than the contrary opinion maintained by Mendelssohn. It is implicit, for instance, in Batteux' statement:

La pitié émeut nos entrailles, parce que nous voyons notre semblable malheureux. La terreur nous resserre le cœur, parce que nous craignons pour nous le malheur que nous voyons dans les autres: mais cette crainte est mêlée d'une certaine douceur qui vient de la comparaison secréte que nous faisons de notre état avec celui du malheureux qui souffre.[4]

---

[1] My quotations are again from J. E. C. Welldon's translation, London, 1886, pp. 133, 149, 152.

[2] The comment of Portus (*Aristotelis…Rhetoricæ, libri III*, Speyer, 1598, II, x, p. 213) criticised here by Lessing runs in English: 'Finally, to speak simply, things are to be feared which, when they have come into the power of others, or are about to come (Lessing would read 'when they have happened, or are about to happen'), are to be pitied.'

[3] Welldon's translation, p. 136.

[4] *Principes de la littérature*, v, ii, chap. iii (*ed. cit.* iii, pp. 73 f.); Ramler's translation (Leipzig, 1762), ii, p. 273.

Brumoy, too, wrote:

La pitié qui n'est qu'un secret repli sur nous à la vûë des maux d'autrui, dont nous pouvons être également les victimes, a une liaison si étroite avec la crainte, que ces deux passions sont inséparables dans les hommes, que le besoin mutuel oblige de vivre dans la societé civile....La crainte en un mot, et la pitié qui l'accompagne presque toujours, sont les premiers fruits de l'amour de nous-mêmes, parce qu'elles ont pour objet direct le mal present que nous voulons fuir sur toutes choses.[1]

But what if Aristotle's conception of ἔλεος were wrong? In the correspondence of 1756–57, when Lessing's views on the subject were those of Mendelssohn, he frankly stated that Aristotle was wrong. In his letter of December 18, 1756, he speaks of Mendelssohn's 'better notion' of 'Mitleid' (*i.e.* better than Aristotle's).[2] This notion is stated in the 'Beschluss' of the *Briefe über die Empfindungen* thus:

Allein was ist das Mitleiden? Ist es nicht selbst eine Vermischung von angenehmen und unangenehmen Empfindungen?... [Diese Gemüths-bewegung] ist nichts, als die Liebe zu einem Gegenstande mit dem Begriffe eines Unglücks, eines physikalischen Übels verbunden, das ihm unver-schuldet zugestossen.[3]

The limitations of Aristotle's false idea of pity, Lessing goes on to say,[4] are clearly seen when Aristotle declares in his thirteenth chapter that the misfortunes of a too virtuous hero do not induce 'Mitleid' in us, but 'Entsetzen und Abscheu'. According to the better modern conception of 'Mitleid', they produce in us on the contrary 'Mitleid' of the highest kind; and if Aristotle's statement were true, then 'Entsetzen und Abscheu' would be equivalent to 'Mitleid'—but of course they are not so equivalent. Thus Aristotle is clearly wrong.

By the time Lessing came to write his *Laokoon*, an English thinker, Adam Smith, had given him occasion once more to reflect on the nature of 'Mitleid'; and the views which he expresses on the subject in section iv of the *Laokoon* are drawn exclusively from the first chapter of Smith's *Theory of Moral Sentiments* (London, 1759, 2nd ed. 1761). This writer's discussion of the nature of sympathy and his condemnation of Greek tragedy for attempting 'to excite compassion,

---

[1] *Théâtre des Grecs, ed. cit.* i, pp. li, lv.
[2] *Schriften,* xvii, p. 85; Petsch, *op. cit.* p. 87.
[3] *Gesammelte Schriften, ed. cit.* i, p. 173.
[4] Cp. also *Schriften,* xvii, p. 98; Petsch, *op. cit.* p. 105.

by the representation of...bodily pain',[1] might have called forth further speculation on Lessing's part on the subject of sympathy in tragedy; but *Laokoon* afforded no opportunity of pursuing the matter. In the *Dramaturgie* (LXXIV, 102) he quotes a long passage containing Mendelssohn's definition of pity, but in the more elaborated form which Mendelssohn had given to it in his *Rhapsodie über die Empfindungen*, published in 1761 in his *Philosophische Schriften*.[2] Referring here to what he had formerly written in the last part of his *Briefe über die Empfindungen* 'über die vermischten Empfindungen, die von Lust und Unlust zusammengesetzt sind', Mendelssohn insists that pity is a mixed feeling, a combination of love for an object and displeasure at the misfortune which overtakes it. But there can be many kinds of pity: pitying fear, pitying terror.... Why should not all kinds of unpleasant feelings, fear, terror, anger, jealousy, desire for vengeance, even envy, not spring from pity?[3] Lessing does not see how anyone— even Aristotle—could disagree with this definition of 'Mitleid' (LXXV, 1). How then is Aristotle's credit to be saved? Lessing discovers the means in a passage which he quotes (LXXVI, 86) from the thirteenth chapter of the *Poetics*. Aristotle there says that a bad man must not be seen passing from misery to happiness, for this is the most untragic form possible; it has not one of the requisites of Tragedy; it does not appeal to the human feeling in us ($\phi\iota\lambda\acute{a}\nu\theta\rho\omega\pi\text{o}\nu$) nor does it call forth pity or fear. Nor, on the other hand, should an extremely bad man be seen falling from happiness into misery. Such a story may arouse the human feeling in us, but it will not move us to either pity or fear.

In this 'Philanthropie'—that is to say, disinterested, 'unfearing' sympathy for our fellowmen[4]—Lessing finds the solution to his

[1] Pt. I, ii (4th ed. London, 1774, p. 44). Cp. also p. 43: 'Pain never calls forth any very lively sympathy unless it is accompanied with danger. We sympathize with the fear, though not with the agony of the sufferer. Fear, however, is a passion derived altogether from the imagination, which represents, with an uncertainty and fluctuation that increases our anxiety, not what we really feel, but what we may hereafter possibly suffer.'

[2] Lessing also refers to this work in his *Laokoon* (xxiii, *Schriften*, ix, p. 139). The passage quoted will be found in Mendelssohn's *Gesammelte Schriften, ed. cit.* i, pp. 248 ff.

[3] Cp. *Philosophische Schriften*, Berlin, 1777, ii, pp. 28 ff.; *Gesammelte Schriften, ed. cit.* i, pp. 248 f.

[4] Lessing passes in review (LXXVI, 94) the various translations of $\phi\iota\lambda\acute{a}\nu\theta\rho\omega\pi\text{o}\nu$ by the commentators. The ordinary Latin translation—that of Du Val—is 'hominibus gratum' (this would appear to go back to Victorius, from whom it was

difficulty of 1756, when he spoke of Aristotle's 'false notion' of 'Mitleid'—false in so far as it prevented the application of the word 'Mitleid' to the feelings awakened in us alike by the just retribution befalling an utterly evil person and the sufferings of a too perfect character. He quotes (LXXVI, 105) Curtius's limitation of the compassionate feeling for the vicious person to cases where his suffering befalls him when he is innocent (*ed. cit.* p. 191); but as Mendelssohn had shown in a graphic passage, which Lessing quotes (117) (it is the 'Beschluss' to the *Briefe über die Empfindungen, Gesammelte Schriften, ed. cit.* i, p. 174), such limitation is not feasible. We do suffer with the evil person under all circumstances. Aristotle, he asserts (LXXVI, 72): 'betrachtet das Mitleid nach seinen primitiven Regungen, er betrachtet es blos als Affekt.... Mitleidige Regungen, ohne Furcht für uns selbst, nennt er Philanthropie: und nur den stärkern Regungen dieser Art, welche mit Furcht für uns selbst verknüpft sind, giebt er den Namen des Mitleids.' The excessively evil person may be beyond the pale of our pity and yet arouse in us this 'Philanthropie'. So, too, may be the too virtuous hero, by whose undeserved sufferings we (who do

adopted by Antonio Riccoboni); the French '[ce qui] peut faire quelque plaisir' (Dacier, p. 181); the German 'was Vergnügen machen kann' (cp. Curtius, p. 25); Goulston, on the other hand, whom Lessing holds to be alone correct, translates it by 'quod humanitatis sensu tangat' (*Aristotelis de Poetica liber, Latine conversus et analytica methodo illustratus*, London, 1623, p. 27). Daniel Heinsius has been suggested as Lessing's source here, as in one passage of his translation of the *Poetics* he renders the Greek word by 'aliquid gratum hominibus' (*De Tragœdiæ constitutione, ed. cit.* p. 269); but the fact that Lessing does not refer to the more picturesque interpretation which Heinsius also gives, 'communi lege ac vinculo humanitatis' (*ibid.*; cp. also *Aristotelis de Poetica Liber*, Leyden, 1611, p. 28)—an interpretation which surely might have appealed to him, as he seems to have approved of it later— does not lend support to the view that he consulted Heinsius when he was writing this section. That Lessing was at a later date familiar with Heinsius is to be seen from a letter to Eschenburg of April 25, 1772, concerning the latter's translation of Hurd's *Commentary* on Horace's *Epistles* (*Schriften*, xviii, p. 37): 'Ich wünschte, dass Sie aus der Erklärung des Aristotelischen φιλανθρωπον das Wort Pflicht- mässig wegliessen. Sie scheinen es aus dem lege der Heinsiusschen Umschreibung genommen zu haben, wo es aber nicht absolute stehet, sondern auf humanitatis geht, und so viel als vinculo humanitatis seyn soll. Das Pflichtmässige wäre, meiner Meinung nach, gerade wieder das φιλανθρωπον. Denn es wäre ohnstreitig unsere Pflicht, uns über das Unglück eines Bösewichts zu freuen: wenn Pflicht das heisst, was dem positiven Gesetze gemäss ist. Aber dieser Pflicht ungeachtet, können wir ihn nicht ganz ohne Mitleid lassen, weil dieser Bösewicht doch ein Mensch ist.' But I can find no certain evidence that Heinsius's *De Tragœdiæ constitutione* was one of Lessing's direct sources when he was engaged on the *Dramaturgie*. (See above, p. 358, note 2.)

not feel ourselves perfect) are not moved, and in consequence are not tempted to put ourselves in the place of the sufferer. 'We are right', he adds (140), 'when we include "Philanthropie" under the name of pity. But Aristotle was also not wrong when he gave it a special name, in order, as we have said, to distinguish it from the highest degree of compassionate feeling, in which, by the addition of a probable fear for ourselves, it becomes an active emotion.' As will be seen, Lessing returns to these 'philanthropischen Gefühle' for an explanation of τῶν τοιούτων παθημάτων in the definition of tragedy.

As early as his letter of November [13], 1756, Lessing had expressed the opinion that the only emotion which it is the business of tragedy to awaken in the spectator is pity. 'Kurz, ich finde keine einzige Leidenschaft, die das Trauerspiel in dem Zuschauer rege macht, als das Mitleiden.'[1] He does not, however, deny that it may also awaken both 'Schrecken' and 'Bewunderung'; but 'diese sind keine Leidenschaften, nach meinem Verstande'. He objects, as we have seen, to the inclusion of 'Schrecken', because he had learned from Mendelssohn that this was a mere modification of 'Mitleid'. But then comes the question, if 'Schrecken' is only a form of 'Mitleid' why should Aristotle have expressly mentioned it? Mendelssohn was frankly of opinion that it ought not to have been mentioned, and proposed the substitution of 'Bewunderung'. In April, 1757, when Lessing discovered that he ought to have written 'Furcht', not 'Schrecken', he still had difficulty in explaining its presence in the definition. 'Die Furcht', he said, '...[kann] keine unmittelbare Wirkung des Trauerspiels seyn, sondern sie muss weiter nichts als eine reflectirte Idee seyn'; the only reason he can see for any mention of it by Aristotle is that it was in his opinion the means whereby pity brought about the catharsis. But if this was Aristotle's opinion, he was wrong. 'Das Mitleiden reiniget unsre Leidenschaften, aber nicht vermittelst der Furcht, auf welchen Einfall den Aristoteles sein falscher Begriff von dem Mitleiden gebracht hat.'[2] In the *Dramaturgie*, however, Lessing returns to the matter with increased respect for the infallibility of Aristotle. 'Aristoteles würde nicht sagen, Mitleiden und Furcht; wenn er unter der Furcht weiter nichts als eine blosse Modification des Mitleids verstünde' (LXXIV, 99). This great 'economist of words' might just as well have said: 'die Tragödie soll durch Erregung des Mitleids die Reinigung unserer Leidenschaft bewirken' (LXXVII, 6).

[1] *Schriften*, xvii, p. 65; Petsch, *op. cit.* p. 52.
[2] *Schriften*, xvii, p. 98; Petsch, *op. cit.* p. 105.

The reason which Lessing now offers for Aristotle's mention of fear is that, although it is superfluous in so far as it is included in pity, he wished also to indicate what passions in us tragedy is to purify; and of these fear is one. Fear may be a necessary ingredient of pity, but the converse is not true: when the tragedy is over, our pity ceases, but the fear (for ourselves) remains, and helps to complete the purification of that emotion in us. Thus Lessing returns after all—although with a different justification for Aristotle's mention of 'fear'—to his first conviction that the business of tragedy is to awaken pity and pity only: 'die Tragödie...[ist] ein Gedicht, welches Mitleid erreget' (LXXVII, 36).

Having arrived at these conclusions on the nature of pity and fear as tragic effects, Lessing does not miss the opportunity of attacking Corneille for his 'accommodation' of the Aristotelian definition to his own needs (LXXV, 121).[1] In his *Discours de la Tragédie* Corneille had argued, in order to justify his own 'martyr tragedy' *Polyeucte*, that Aristotle's use of the disjunctive—'*neither* fear *nor* pity'—implied that it was sufficient for the purpose of tragedy if only one of these were present:

Cependant, quelque difficulté qu'il y aye à trouver cette purgation effective et sensible des passions par le moyen de la pitié et de la crainte, il est aisé de nous accommoder avec Aristote. Nous n'avons qu'à dire que par cette façon de s'énoncer il n'a pas entendu que ces deux moyens y servissent toujours ensemble; et qu'il suffit selon lui de l'un des deux pour faire cette purgation, avec cette différence toutefois, que la pitié n'y peut arriver sans la crainte, et que la crainte peut y parvenir sans la pitié.... Cette explication se trouvera autorisée par Aristote même, si nous voulons bien peser la raison qu'il rend de l'exclusion de ces événements qu'il désapprouve dans la tragédie. Il ne dit jamais: *Celui-là n'y est pas propre, parce qu'il n'excite que de la pitié et ne fait point naître de crainte; et cet autre n'y est pas supportable, parce qu'il n'excite que de la crainte, et ne fait point naître de pitié;* mais il les rebute, *parce*, dit-il, *qu'ils n'excitent ni pitié ni crainte*, et nous donne à connoître par là que c'est par le manque de l'une et de l'autre qu'ils ne lui plaisent pas, et que s'ils produisoient l'une des deux, il ne leur refuseroit point son suffrage.[2]

[1] Lessing is wrong in his statement in a note to St. LXXV (109) that Corneille had written all his plays before he turned his attention to Aristotle. He may have been misled by Corneille's mention of his 'cinquante ans de travail' in the first *Discours*. But see above, p. 102.

[2] *Œuvres*, ed. cit. i, pp. 60 f. The translation in the *Dramaturgie* is (in all but a few words) that of the *Beyträge* (ii, pp. 221 ff.), which, it will be remembered, I have claimed for Lessing himself.

Dacier had overlooked this very vulnerable aspect of Corneille's theory (LXXVI, 1); and Lessing's attention may possibly have been drawn to it by Calepio's *Paragone della poesia tragica d'Italia con quella di Francia*.[1] Calepio had stated here (Capo i, art. i, pp. 5 f.):

[Cornelio] affetta in sembianza di seguire i precetti, che lasciocci Aristotele, e nel mostrar l'utile, che la tragedia ha per proprio fine, allega (*Note*: Discor. 2) que testi, che stabiliscono consister la perfezione della favola tragica nel muover la compassione, ed il timore per mezzo d'un attore illustre, che cada per qualche errore di felicità in miseria: ma poi veggendo poco corrispondere a tal regola molte delle sue tragedie s'ingegna con sue nuove interpretrazioni di far servire i precetti del greco maestro al sostenimento delle medesime; però soggiunge egli, che Aristotele non giudicando essenziali alla favola tragica le sentenze ed i discorsi instruttivi, nè potendo rinvenire altra ferma utilità, volle sostituirne una la qual non è forse se non imaginaria; perciocche il purgamento delle sopradette passioni non pare che segua nelle tragedie stesse, ove si ritrovano le condizioni che richiede quel Filosofo. Quindi conchiude che la più tolerabile spiegazione che si possa dare a' passi della sua poetica, si è il dire, ch' egli non intenda esser necessarie amendue le commozioni, e che l' una possa bastar senza l' altra.

ADMIRATION

In the *Dramaturgie* Lessing avoided a controversy on which he had had something to say in 1756, namely, how far 'admiration' ('Bewunderung') is an emotion legitimately called forth by tragedy. The matter is only touched on in passing: 'Wenn heldenmüthige Gesinnungen Bewunderung erregen sollen: so muss der Dichter nicht zu verschwenderisch damit umgehen; denn was man öfters, was man an mehrern sieht, höret man auf zu bewundern' (1, 89); and again (LXXV, 49): 'ich möchte wohl hören, was sie [Aristotle's commentators] aus ihrem Kopfe antworten würden, wenn man sie fragte: warum z. E. die Tragödie nicht eben so wohl Mitleid und Bewunderung,[2] als Mitleid und Furcht, erregen könne und dürfe?'

[1] See especially Letters i and ii. (Bodmer's correspondence with Calepio was published later, in his *Critische Briefe* (1746).) For other evidence of Lessing's probable familiarity with Calepio's treatise see pp. 172, 292; see also below, pp. 366 (note 3), 367, 420. In his review of F. Braitmaier, *Geschichte der poetischen Theorie und Kritik* (Frauenfeld, 1888), in the *Anzeiger für deutsches Altertum*, xvii (1891), pp. 55 ff., O. F. Walzel discusses the influence of the *Paragone* on Lessing.

[2] This was what Mendelssohn demanded (see below, p. 367). Vossius in *Poeticarum Institutionum libri tres*, II, cap. xiii, § 19 (Amsterdam, 1647, ii, p. 64) was apparently the first to suggest the addition of τὸ θαυμαστόν to the effects of tragedy; he was, no doubt, influenced by Corneille. Cp. C. Arnaud, *Étude sur la Vie et les Œuvres de l'Abbé d'Aubignac et sur les théories dramatiques au* xviie *siècle*, Paris, 1887, pp. 154 f.

In his *Abhandlung vom Trauerspiele* Nicolai had said of Corneille's
'heroic tragedies', which excite admiration without terror and pity:
'Wir glauben,...dass eine solche Gattung, wo nicht unmöglich,
dennoch sehr schwer auszuführen, und deswegen gar nicht anzurathen
sey.'[1] Lessing, in his letter of November, 1756, did not object to the
inclusion of admiration, but he insisted on the subordination of both
admiration and terror to pity—since the real purpose of tragedy is
to awaken pity, whereas terror and admiration are, in his view, 'der
Anfang und das Ende des Mitleids'.[2] He expressed himself still more
emphatically a little farther on in the same letter:

> Die Bewunderung...ist das entbehrlich gewordene Mitleid. Da aber
> das Mitleid das Hauptwerk ist, so muss es folglich so selten als möglich
> entbehrlich werden; der Dichter muss seinen Held nicht zu sehr, nicht
> zu anhaltend der blossen Bewunderung aussetzen, und Cato als ein Stoiker
> ist mir ein schlechter tragischer Held. Der bewunderte Held ist der
> Vorwurf der Epopee; der bedauerte des Trauerspiels.[3]

The last distinction is one that is repeatedly insisted on by Batteux.[4]
Finally, in his letter of December 18, 1756, Lessing stated his view
in its most complete form, namely, that admiration in tragedy must
only be an element in pity, pity itself being an emotion made up of
admiration and pain:

> Die Bewunderung findet also in dem Trauerspiele nicht als ein besonderer
> Affekt Statt, sondern blos als die eine Hälfte des Mitleids. Und in dieser
> Betrachtung habe ich auch Recht gehabt, sie nicht als einen besondern
> Affekt, sondern nur nach ihrem Verhältnisse gegen das Mitleiden zu
> erklären. Und in diesem Verhältnisse, sage ich noch, soll sie der Ruhe-
> punkt des Mitleidens seyn.[5]

---

[1] Petsch, *op. cit.* p. 20.　　　　[2] *Schriften*, xvii, p. 66; Petsch, *op. cit.* p. 53.

[3] *Schriften*, xvii, p. 68; Petsch, *op. cit.* p. 56. Petsch draws attention (p. xxi) to
the fact that Lessing's phrases echo the comment of the German translator of
Le Bossu (*Abhandlung vom Heldengedicht* nach der neusten französischen Ausgabe
übersetzet und mit einigen critischen Anmerkungen begleitet von D. Johann
Heinrich Z***. Nebst einer Vorrede Hrn. Georg Friedr. Meiers, Halle, 1753; see
especially pp. 316 f.) which Lessing had reviewed (*Schriften*, v, pp. 193 f.). Calepio
had maintained in his correspondence with Bodmer (*Briefwechsel von der Natur des
poetischen Geschmackes*, Zürich, 1736, p. 103) that Cato was not suited to be a tragic
hero.

[4] See especially *Principes de la littérature*, iv, ch. v, and v, ii, ch. iii (*ed. cit.* ii,
pp. 198 f., iii, p. 72).

[5] *Schriften*, xvii, p. 80; Petsch, *op. cit.* p. 81. 'Ruhepunkt des Mitleidens' is
Mendelssohn's phrase in the letter to which Lessing's is a reply (cp. *Schriften*, xix,
pp. 56 f.; Petsch, *op. cit.* pp. 76, 78).

Mendelssohn and Nicolai, on the other hand, came to an agreement:

dass sowohl Bewunderung als Mitleiden den moralischen Geschmack beschäftigen können, und ich wünsche mit dem Hrn. Nikolai, dass man künftig statt Schrecken und Mitleiden, Bewunderung und Mitleiden setzen möchte, weil das Schrecken blos eine besondre Modifikation des Mitleidens ist.[1]

But Mendelssohn also realised that 'Bewunderung ohne Mitleiden, ohne Schrecken ist für die Dichtkunst überhaupt, und um so viel mehr für das Theater, ein gar zu kalter Affect'.[2]

Walzel is inclined to see here the influence of Calepio, who in his *Paragone* (cap. ii, art. i) had insisted on the subordination of admiration because it introduced into tragedy an untragic moral purpose.[3] But the matter had been put quite trenchantly enough by Dacier, who held that Aristotle would have excluded Corneille's *Nicomède* from his tragedies, since the poet here

n'a travaillé qu'à exciter l'admiration dans l'ame du spectateur, et...en s'éloignant des préceptes d'Aristote, a crû trouver une maniere nouvelle de purger les passions;...Mais ce n'est nullement le but de la Tragedie, de purger les passions par l'admiration, qui est une passion trop douce pour produire un si grand effet; elle n'employe que la crainte et la pitié, et laisse regner l'admiration dans le Poëme Epique auquel elle est plus propre et plus necessaire, et où elle a plus de temps pour agir sur les habitudes et sur les mœurs.[4]

The question of admiration is largely bound up with that of the kinds of characters appropriate to tragedy; and to this I return later.[5] Meanwhile, it is clear that Lessing's views on the subject had undergone no material change between his correspondence of 1756–57 and the *Dramaturgie*; that is to say, he still considered that 'Bewunderung' might be an element in tragic effect, but it must be strictly subordinate

---

[1] *Schriften*, xix, pp. 83 f.; Petsch, *op. cit.* p. 119.

[2] The statement occurs in a review of Wieland's *Clementina von Porretta* in the *Litteraturbriefe* (No. cxxiii, August 21, 1760; *Gesammelte Schriften, ed. cit.* iv, 2, p. 146). Lessing echoes this opinion in *Laokoon* (i, *Schriften*, ix, p. 10): 'Sieht man ihn sein Elend mit grosser Seele ertragen, so wird diese grosse Seele zwar unsere Bewunderung erwecken, aber die Bewunderung ist ein kalter Affekt, dessen unthätiges Staunen jede andere wärmere Leidenschaft, so wie jede andere deutliche Vorstellung, ausschliesset.'

[3] *Anzeiger für deutsches Altertum*, xvii (1891), pp. 55 ff. (esp. pp. 66 ff.).

[4] *Poétique d'Aristote, ed. cit.* p. 148. Cp. also Dacier's note to chap. xiii (pp. 185 ff.).

[5] See below, pp. 415 ff., 423 f.

and sparingly used; for as he had written to Mendelssohn in December, 1756, 'just in the proportion in which admiration on the one hand increases, pity on the other decreases'.[1]

THE PURPOSE OF TRAGEDY AND THE KATHARSIS

Thus from the first Lessing was emphatically of the opinion that the end or purpose of tragedy is to awaken pity. Nicolai had proposed in his *Abhandlung vom Trauerspiele* to substitute for 'den Satz... den man dem Aristoteles so oft nachgesprochen hat, es sey der Zweck des Trauerspiels die Leidenschaften zu reinigen oder die Sitten zu bilden' another, namely, 'de[r] Zweck des Trauerspiels [sey] die Erregung der Leidenschaften'.[2] Lessing replied cautiously; he admitted the practical disadvantage of a utilitarian doctrine of tragedy—'das Trauerspiel soll bessern'; and he recognised at least that Nicolai's definition would produce good tragedies; but he was not satisfied that Nicolai was justified in throwing over the old theory. One aspect of it represents the means, the other the end; both are necessary. He wrote:

Das meiste wird darauf ankommen: was das Trauerspiel für Leidenschaften erregt. In seinen Personen kann es alle mögliche Leidenschaften wirken lassen, die sich zu der Würde des Stoffes schicken. Aber werden auch zugleich alle diese Leidenschaften in den Zuschauern rege? Wird er freudig? wird er verliebt? wird er zornig? wird er rachsüchtig? Ich frage nicht, ob ihn der Poet so weit bringt, dass er diese Leidenschaften in der spielenden Person billiget, sondern ob er ihn so weit bringt, dass er diese Leidenschaften selbst fühlt, und nicht blos fühlt, ein andrer fühle sie?[3]

This recalls the implications of an argument used by Batteux:

Elles [*i.e.* passions, such as anger, envy, cruelty, despair, etc.] peuvent se trouver dans les acteurs; mais ce ne doit être que pour en produire d'autres, différentes d'elles, dans les spectateurs. Car il faut observer que les sentimens ne sont pas les mêmes dans les uns et dans les autres: l'orgueil dans les acteurs produit l'envie dans les spectateurs: la

---

[1] *Schriften*, xvii, p. 81; Petsch, *op. cit.* p. 83.

[2] Letter of August 31, 1756 (*Schriften*, xix, p. 40; Petsch, *op. cit.* p. 47); cp. also *Abhandlung*, Petsch, *op. cit.* p. 5. Nicolai's view agrees with that of Mendelssohn in his *Briefe über die Empfindungen*, xiii (*Gesammelte Schriften, ed. cit.* i, pp. 157 f.): 'Der Zweck des Trauerspiels ist, Leidenschaft zu erregen; und das schwärzeste Laster, das zu diesem Endzwecke leitet, ist auf der Schaubühne willkommen.'

[3] *Schriften*, xvii, p. 65; Petsch, *op. cit.* p. 52.

cruauté produit l'horreur, la douleur la compassion, la perfidie l'indignation; ainsi du reste. Le sceau qui caractérise la Tragédie est donc l'espéce du sentiment, non qu'elle contient, mais qu'elle produit.[1]

And Batteux' conclusion is that the only passions which tragedy awakens in the spectator are 'la terreur et la pitié'. With this, too, Lessing agreed, or would have agreed, had not Mendelssohn's more comprehensive definition of 'Mitleid' absolved him from the necessity of mentioning 'Schrecken'. But in any case, it was the awakening of pity on which Batteux laid emphasis: 'Vous avez l'idée d'une Tragédie parfaite. Il n'y a point de doute que ce ne soit celle qui touche le plus vivement, et le plus long-temps le Spectateur.'[2] Thus Lessing concluded in 1756, as later in his *Dramaturgie*, that the essential purpose of tragedy was to awaken 'Mitleid'. 'Das Trauerspiel soll so viel Mitleid erwecken, als es nur immer kann.'[3]

When Lessing insists that the object of tragedy is to awaken our pity—to move us—he is expressing a conviction that had been strengthened in him by his predilection, practical as well as theoretical, for the 'bürgerliches Trauerspiel'. This same conviction is expressed in the preface which he wrote to the volume of *Des Herrn Jacob Thomson sämtliche Trauerspiele* (1756), where he says that he would rather be the author of *The Merchant of London* than of *Der sterbende Cato*:

Denn warum? Bey einer einzigen Vorstellung des erstern sind, auch von den Unempfindlichsten, mehr Thränen vergossen worden, als bey allen möglichen Vorstellungen des andern, auch von den Empfindlichsten, nicht können vergossen werden. Und nur diese Thränen des Mitleids, und der sich fühlenden Menschlichkeit, sind die Absicht des Trauerspiels, oder es kann gar keine haben.[4]

And some years later, in the famous seventeenth *Litteraturbrief* (February, 1759), in which he places Shakespeare above the French classics, he states that his tragic quality is the 'Gewalt über unsere Leidenschaften';[5] the more Shakespeare moves us, the greater he is. Finally, it is unnecessary to point out where the sympathies of the translator of Diderot were likely to lie in this matter.

[1] *Principes de la littérature*, v, ii, ch. iii (*ed. cit.* iii, pp. 74 f.).
[2] *Principes de la littérature*, i, ii, ch. viii (*ed. cit.* i, pp. 120 f.).
[3] *Schriften*, xvii, p. 67; Petsch, *op. cit.* p. 55. See also above, p. 363.
[4] *Schriften*, vii, p. 68. Even in the *Dramaturgie* we still hear of the 'angenehmen [Thränen], die das Trauerspiel erregen will' (i, 115).
[5] *Schriften*, viii, p. 43.

In all this it is noticeable that Lessing has very little to say concerning a function of tragedy on which Corneille had laid emphasis, namely that of affording pleasure to the spectator. Towards the end of the letter to Nicolai of November, 1756, in which he discusses the part of pity in tragedy, we find, however:

Beyder Nutzen, des Trauerspiels sowohl als des Lustspiels, ist von dem Vergnügen unzertrennlich; denn die ganze Hälfte des Mitleids und des Lachens ist Vergnügen, und es ist grosser Vortheil für den dramatischen Dichter, dass er weder nützlich, noch angenehm, eines ohne das andere seyn kann.[1]

And in the *Dramaturgie* (in a passage quoted below[2]) he does speak once of 'the pleasure which a true and lively depiction of manners and characters affords' (xxxv, 97). That it is one of the functions of art to give pleasure was perhaps too obvious a commonplace to require particular emphasis.[3]

On the other hand, it will have been noticed that Lessing was more inclined than his two friends to insist on the moral purpose of tragedy. It is true that he agrees with Batteux[4] in thinking that it is not necessary for tragedy to embody a 'moralische Lehre' (xii, 19):

Ich will nicht sagen, dass es ein Fehler ist, wenn der dramatische Dichter seine Fabel so einrichtet, dass sie zur Erläuterung oder Bestätigung irgend einer grossen moralischen Wahrheit dienen kann. Aber ich darf sagen, dass diese Einrichtung der Fabel nichts weniger als nothwendig ist.[5]

And again, when with reference to his own *Abhandlung von dem Wesen der Fabel*, he compares the drama with the fable (xxxv, 93), he writes:

Das Drama hingegen macht auf eine einzige, bestimmte, aus seiner Fabel fliessende Lehre, keinen Anspruch; es gehet entweder auf die

---

[1] *Schriften*, xvii, p. 67; Petsch, *op. cit.* pp. 54 f.   [2] See below, p. 371.

[3] In *Laokoon*, ii (*Schriften*, ix, p. 13) we find: 'Der Endzweck der Künste hingegen ist Vergnügen; und das Vergnügen ist entbehrlich. Also darf es allerdings von dem Gesetzgeber abhangen, welche Art von Vergnügen, und in welchem Maasse er jede Art desselben verstatten will.'

[4] Cp. *Principes de la littérature, ed. cit.* iii, p. 88: 'Nous pouvons cependant dire en général que ce n'est point une maxime comme dans l'Apologue, ni aucune leçon d'instruction, qui s'adresse d'abord à l'esprit pour être ensuite appliquée à la conduite. Si on veut que la Tragédie soit une leçon d'instruction, j'ose dire qu'on va contre son objet.'

[5] Curtius, in his *Abhandlung von der Absicht des Trauerspiels* (*Aristoteles Dichtkunst, ed. cit.* p. 392) had also said: 'Es ist deswegen nicht nothwendig, dass ein jedes Trauerspiel nur eine moralische Wahrheit in sich fasse. Man hat zu geschwinde von der Einheit der Handlung auf die Einheit der Moral geschlossen.'

Leidenschaften, welche der Verlauf und die Glücksveränderungen seiner Fabel anzufachen, und zu unterhalten vermögend sind, oder auf das Vergnügen, welches eine wahre und lebhafte Schilderung der Sitten und Charaktere gewähret.

This view Lessing had already expressed forcibly and unambiguously in his article on Seneca in the *Theatralische Bibliothek* many years before:

Eigentlich halte ich es eben für keine Nothwendigkeit, dass aus der Fabel eines Trauerspiels eine gute Lehre fliessen müsse, wenn uns nur einzelne Stellen von nützlichen Wahrheiten unterrichten. Allein so viel wird doch wenigstens nothwendig seyn, dass man auch keine böse Lehre daraus folgern könne....Alles, was man also zur Entschuldigung dieser beyden alten Muster anführen kann, ist dieses, dass sie es für ganz unnöthig gehalten haben, an die Moral des Ganzen zu denken, und dass sie ihre Tragödien nicht so gemacht haben, wie sie uns eine sogenannte critische Dichtkunst zu machen lehret. Erst eine Wahrheit sich vorzustellen, und hernach eine Begebenheit dazu zu suchen, oder zu erdichten, war die Art ihres Verfahrens gar nicht.[1]

No great weight need be attached to isolated dicta at the beginning of the *Dramaturgie*, such as that the dramatist 'wenn er sich zu dem Pöbel herablässt, lässt sich nur darum zu ihm herab, um ihn zu erleuchten und zu bessern' (i, 136), and that 'das Theater die Schule der moralischen Welt seyn soll' (ii, 8);[2] but in St. LXXVII (143) he expresses himself emphatically: 'Bessern sollen uns alle Gattungen der Poesie: es ist kläglich, wenn man dieses erst beweisen muss; noch kläglicher ist es, wenn es Dichter giebt, die selbst daran zweifeln.'

Lessing has often been reproached for this insistence on the moral purpose of poetry; but unfairly, for the conception of an amoral aestheticism was virtually unknown to the eighteenth century. Even Corneille, who insisted that the primary object of tragedy was to give pleasure, had much to say about its 'utilité';[3] and later eighteenth-century theory in France, from Voltaire to Marmontel[4] and Diderot,

---

[1] *Schriften*, vi, pp. 196 f.

[2] Cp. Voltaire's 'la véritable Tragédie est l'école de la vertu' (*Dissertation* prefixed to *Sémiramis*, *Œuvres, ed. cit.* ix, p. 31), and Dacier's 'leur Theatre étoit une école où la vertu étoit souvent mieux enseignée que dans les écoles des Philosophes' (*Poétique d'Aristote, ed. cit.* Preface, p. [xxiii]).

[3] For him, as for Lessing, the 'purification' effected by tragedy implies the moral improvement of the spectator. Cp. Arnaud, *op. cit.* p. 212.

[4] 'La Tragédie', says Marmontel (*Poétique françoise, ed. cit.* ii, pp. 99 f.), 'peut avoir deux fins, l'une prochaine, et l'autre éloignée. La première est de plaire en

laid increasing emphasis on the moral end of tragedy.[1] Neither Mendelssohn nor Nicolai, in spite of an apparently exclusive insistence that tragedy should only 'awaken passions', was at variance with Lessing on the question of ultimate moral betterment. They recognised, as clearly as Diderot, that the more the feelings of the spectator were harrowed, the greater the moral effect was likely to be. It was merely a question of keeping distinct the two issues.[2]

What then is the process whereby pity achieves its end in tragedy? In other words, what is Lessing's interpretation of the Aristotelian κάθαρσις? The eighteenth century had before it a choice between a medical and a religious interpretation. According to the former, the Aristotelian purging is analogous to the medical use of the term. This is the generally accepted view to-day, first convincingly established by Jakob Bernays in 1857.[3] Bernays was under the impression that his interpretation was new. Not only, however, had he an immediate German predecessor in Heinrich Weil,[4] but, as Spingarn has shown, similar views are to be found in Minturno's *De Poeta* (1559) and *L' Arte poetica* (1563); and from Minturno the interpretation passed to Milton (preface to *Samson Agonistes*, 1671).[5] But there is more to be said than this: the interpretation was generally familiar to the whole eighteenth century. It is quite unequivocally expressed by Dacier:

intéressant, et celle-là est indispensable: la seconde d'instruire et de corriger, et celle-ci, quoique moins essentielle au Poëme, en fait l'excellence et le prix.' And again (p. 145): 'Le but de la Tragédie est, selon nous, de corriger les mœurs en les imitant, par une action qui serve d'exemple.'

[1] This has been clearly brought out by F. Gaiffe, *Le drame en France au XVIIIe siècle*, Paris, 1910 (see especially pp. 78 ff.).

[2] Cp. Nicolai, *Abhandlung vom Trauerspiele* (Petsch, *op. cit.* p. 11): 'Doch folget hieraus nicht, dass das Trauerspiel gar nichts zur Verbesserung der Leidenschaften beytragen, und also gar keinen moralischen Nutzen haben könne; man muss nur diesen entfernten Nutzen des Trauerspiels nicht zu weit ausdehnen und zum Hauptzwecke desselben machen.'

[3] *Grundzüge der verlorenen Abhandlung des Aristoteles über Wirkung der Tragödie*, Breslau, 1857; reprinted in *Zwei Abhandlungen über die Aristotelische Theorie des Dramas*, Berlin, 1880.

[4] H. Weil, *Über die Wirkung der Tragödie nach Aristoteles* (*Verhandlungen der 10. Versammlung deutscher Philologen, Schulmänner und Orientalisten in Basel*, Basel, 1848 (see *Beilage*, pp. 131 ff.)).

[5] See J. E. Spingarn, *Literary Criticism in the Renaissance*, 2nd ed. New York, 1908, pp. 79 ff. Cp. Minturno, *De Poeta*, Venice, 1559, i, pp. 61 f., 63 f. and *L'Arte poetica*, Venice, 1563, ii, p. 77; cp. also I. Bywater, *Aristotle on the Art of Poetry*, Oxford, 1909, pp. 152 ff., and *Journal of Philology*, xxvii, No. 54 (1900), pp. 267 ff.

On peut comparer en cette occasion Platon et Aristote à deux Medecins, dont l'un condamneroit une medecine, et l'autre l'approuveroit....La Tragedie est donc une veritable medecine, qui purge les passions, puisqu'elle apprend à l'ambitieux, à moderer son ambition; à l'impie, à craindre les Dieux; à l'emporté, à retenir sa colere, et ainsi du reste. Mais c'est une medecine agreable, qui ne fait son effet que par le plaisir.[1]

This alone was sufficient to give the medical interpretation general currency in Europe.[2] The religious interpretation would appear to go back to Lambin, a French commentator on Aristotle in the sixteenth century, who translated κάθαρσις 'lustratio seu expiatio', and saw in it a kind of religious purification, a cleansing from spiritual dross.[3] Lambin's interpretation reappears in Heinsius.

Generally speaking, however, the eighteenth century was not interested in the original meaning or implication of κάθαρσις, but was content to accept it in a figurative sense as 'moral purification'. There were two views on the question of the method by which such purification might be achieved. One of these was that the fear and pity engendered by tragedy render us so familiar with these emotions that we cease to shrink from them; that is to say, tragedy works ethically by moderating, damping, or rendering less acute the spectator's emotions. The other maintained that tragic pity and fear excite instead of damping our emotions, and thus by making our souls more sensitive, render us more ready to extend our sympathies and our fears; in other words, they make us more humane. The former of these views comes down from the Italian commentators Robortello, Vettori and Castelvetro; Nicolai mentions it in his *Abhandlung*, quoting Brumoy's authority in support of it;[4] and it is also Dacier's view. The second interpretation seems to be due to Heinsius. In his *De Tragœdiæ constitutione* he says:

De affectibus autem, ita judicabat Aristoteles. Nec virtutes eos neque vitia esse. Cæterum, habitum quendam, quatenus et quando, gaudendum, dolendum, commiserandum, cæterique, è præscripto rationis, admittendi essent, comparare virum sapientem posse....Talem è Tragœdiæ repræsentatione nasci....Ad talem autem habitum reduci posse affectus, multa sunt quæ docent...iisque actionibus horrorem pariter et miserationem

[1] *Poétique d'Aristote, ed. cit.* p. 83.

[2] Louis Racine compares such explanations of the cathartic action of tragedy to inoculation for small-pox (*Œuvres, ed. cit.* vi, p. 395).

[3] Cp. J. H. Reinkens, *Aristoteles über Kunst, besonders über Tragödie*, Vienna, 1870, p. 85.

[4] See above, p. 339, and note 1.

mouet. Quæ eosdem in humano animo affectus mitigant aut sedant. et si
recte adhibeantur, defectum quoque eorum atque excessum expiant ac
purgant. mediocritatem vero, quod hic primum est, relinquunt.[1]

This view was espoused by Batteux in France; and from Batteux it
passed to Lessing. In his first letter to Nicolai Lessing says:

> Wenn es also wahr ist, dass die ganze Kunst des tragischen Dichters auf
> die sichere Erregung und Dauer des einzigen Mitleidens geht, so sage ich
> nunmehr, die Bestimmung der Tragödie ist diese: sie soll unsre Fähig-
> keit, Mitleid zu fühlen, erweitern.

And in that to Mendelssohn of December 18, 1756:

> Das Trauerspiel soll das Mitleiden nur überhaupt üben, und nicht uns
> in diesem oder jenem Falle zum Mitleiden bestimmen....Ich lasse mich
> zum Mitleiden im Trauerspiele bewegen, um eine Fertigkeit im Mitleiden
> zu bekommen...ohne Zweifel [ist] derjenige der beste Mensch...der die
> grösste Fertigkeit im Mitleiden hat.[2]

These thoughts finally reappear in the *Dramaturgie* in the statement
(LXXVIII, 116): 'diese Reinigung [beruhet] in nichts anders...als in
der Verwandlung der Leidenschaften in tugendhafte Fertigkeiten.'
Lessing's opinion would appear to come directly from Batteux. In
his chapter 'Qu'elle [*sic*] peut être la fin morale de la Tragédie'
Batteux writes:

> On ne peut guéres disconvenir, je crois, que la Tragédie ne soit générale-
> ment parlant, un exercice de l'ame par des émotions tristes. Il n'est point
> de Tragédie qui ne s'annonce ainsi dès le premier vers. Les émotions
> répétées, doivent, comme tous les autres actes de l'ame, se changer en
> habitude, et l'effet de cette habitude, vertu ou non, ce que je n'examine
> pas encore, doit être nécessairement de rendre notre ame plus aisée à
> remuer et moins facile à abbatre par le malheur: toute habitude ayant
> pour effet essentiel de rendre plus facile l'exercice de la faculté qui est
> exercée, et d'accoutumer l'ame à l'objet qui l'exerce.

And a few pages later he adds:

> Mais pour que la Tragédie produisît ces utiles effets, il falloit que la
> terreur et la pitié fussent des passions vertueuses, et qu'elles ne missent pas
> un mal à la place d'un autre mal.[3]

---

[1] *Ed. cit.* pp. 11 f., 13, 19. Cp. also M. Zerbst, *op. cit.* pp. 49 f.

[2] *Schriften*, xvii, pp. 66, 83; Petsch, *op. cit.* pp. 54, 84 f.

[3] *Principes de la littérature*, v, ii, chap. iv (*ed. cit.* iii, pp. 92, 96). Ramler had
translated 'Les émotions répétées...habitude' in the edition of 1769 (ii, p. 291;
the chapter is omitted in the edition of 1762–63): 'Wiederholte Bewegungen

Lessing, however, was not content with the phrase 'Verwandlung in tugendhafte Fertigkeiten'; he sought an explanation of the process by which the 'Verwandlung' was effected. All Dacier could tell him in this matter was contained in the statement that the 'Peripateticiens' regarded the expression 'purger les passions' as equivalent to 'emporter l'excez [des passions] par où elles péchent, et les reduire à une juste moderation'.[1] Here again, Batteux was more explicit:

Purger la terreur et la pitié, je crois que c'est les purifier, c'est-à-dire, leur ôter ce qu'elles peuvent avoir ou de trop ou d'étranger, qui les empêcheroit d'être aussi profitables qu'elles le seroient sans cela. On conçoit bien que la *pitié* et la *terreur* même peuvent être utiles à l'humanité; mais comment l'une et l'autre peuvent-elles cesser de l'être, faute d'être purifiées, ou *purgées*, puisque c'est le terme d'Aristote?...Il faut donc que la terreur et la pitié, pour en faire deux vertus secourables, soient sans mélange et sans excès. Si la terreur est mêlée d'horreur, elle effarouche l'ame, plutôt qu'elle ne l'affermit; si la pitié est mêlée de foiblesse, elle dégénere en pusillanimité. Si elles sont l'une et l'autre en-deçà d'un certain point, elles ne font qu'effleurer l'ame sans la remuer; si elles sont au-delà, elles l'emportent au loin, ou la pétrifient. Il falloit donc les réduire à leur point juste, les épurer, les dégager de tout ce qui pouvoit altérer leur nature, pour les rendre vraiment utiles à l'humanité.[2]

müssen, wie alle übrigen Beschäfftigungen der Seele, sich in Fertigkeiten verwandeln.' Batteux' theory is also enunciated by Curtius in his *Abhandlung von der Absicht des Trauerspiels* (*Aristoteles Dichtkunst*, ed. cit. p. 390): 'Wenn das Unglück eines Fremden auf der Bühne uns lebhaft rühret, so wird das Mitleiden und Erbarmen zu einer Fertigkeit der Seelen, und der Menschenfreund in den Logen und dem Parterre, bey dem die auf der Bühne vorgestellte Begebenheiten das Gefühl der Menschlichkeit rege gemacht haben, wird auch in den Handlungen seines Lebens sich als ein Menschenfreund erweisen.' Another work might be quoted, Home's *Elements of Criticism*, which was also familiar to Lessing in the German translation (*Grundsätze der Critik*, Leipzig, 1763–66, iii, pp. 272 f.): 'Ein pathetisches Werk, es mag episch oder dramatisch seyn, wirkt zu einer Fertigkeit in der Tugend, indem es Bewegungen erregt, die gute Handlungen hervorbringen, oder uns von denen abwenden, die lasterhaft und unregelmässig sind. Durch die häufigen Gemählde von menschlichem Elend macht es die Seele menschlicher, und stärkt uns, unsre eignen Unglücksfälle zu ertragen.' Mendelssohn provided a definition of 'Fertigkeit' in his *Von der Herrschaft über die Neigungen*, which he sent to Lessing in manuscript in January, 1757 (cp. *Schriften*, xix, p. 64; Petsch, *op. cit.* p. 95). He says: 'Durch die Übung (welche mit der Gewohnheit einerlei Wirkung hat) wird eine jede Fähigkeit in unserer Seele zu einer Fertigkeit. Eine Fertigkeit besteht in einem Vermögen, etwas so geschwind zu verrichten, dass wir uns nicht mehr alles dessen bewusst bleiben, was wir dabei vorgenommen' (*Gesammelte Schriften*, ed. cit. iv, 1, p. 41, also Petsch, *op. cit.* p. 131).

[1] *Poétique d'Aristote*, ed. cit. p. 81.
[2] *Principes de la littérature*, ed. cit. iii, pp. 97 f., 100.

Lessing recalls (LXXVIII, 118) the Aristotelian theory—which lies behind Batteux' statement—that virtue consists in the avoidance of the extremes of passion. It is to be found in book ii of the *Nicomachean Ethics*.[1] And he may also have remembered what Rapin had written on this particular point. In his *Réflexions sur la Poétique d'Aristote et sur les ouvrages des Poètes anciens et modernes* (Paris, 1674) that writer had advanced the following argument:

...Elle [la Tragédie] rend l'homme modeste, en luy representant des Grands humiliés; et elle le rend sensible et pitoyable, en luy faisant voir sur le theatre les étranges accidens de la vie et les disgraces impreveües, ausquelles sont sujettes les personnes les plus importantes. Mais parce que l'homme est naturellement timide, et compatissant, il peut tomber dans une autre extremité, d'estre ou trop craintif, ou trop pitoyable: la trop grande crainte peut diminuer la fermeté de l'ame, et la trop grande compassion peut diminuer l'équité. La Tragedie s'occupe à regler ces deux foiblesses: elle fait qu'on s'apprivoise aux disgraces, en les voyant si frequentes dans les personnes les plus considerables: et qu'on cesse de craindre les accidens ordinaires, quand on en voit arriver de si extraordinaires aux Grands. Mais comme la fin de la Tragedie est d'apprendre aux hommes à ne pas craindre trop foiblement des disgraces communes, et à menager leur crainte: elle fait estat aussi de leur apprendre à menager leur compassion, pour des sujets qui la meritent. Car il y a de l'injustice d'estre touché des malheurs de ceux, qui meritent d'estre miserables.[2]

---

[1] Cp. especially chap. vi: 'Virtue therefore, since like nature it is more exact and better than any art, must also aim at the mean—virtue of course meaning moral virtue or excellence; for it has to do with passions and actions, and it is these that admit of excess and deficiency and the mean. For instance, it is possible to feel fear, confidence, desire, anger, pity, and generally to be affected pleasantly and painfully, either too much or too little, in either case wrongly; but to be thus affected at the right times, and on the right occasions, and towards the right persons, and with the right object, and in the right fashion, is the mean course and the best course, and these are characteristics of virtue. And in the same way our outward acts also admit of excess and deficiency, and the mean or due amount. Virtue, then, has to deal with feelings or passions and with outward acts, in which excess is wrong and deficiency also is blamed, but the mean amount is praised and is right—both of which are characteristics of virtue' (translation of F. H. Peters, London, 1881, pp. 45 f.).

[2] R. Rapin, *Réflexions*, Paris, 1674, pp. 169 ff. (*Œuvres*, Amsterdam, 1709, ii, pp. 159 f.). I am indebted for this reference to G. Kettner (*Zu Lessings Hamburgischer Dramaturgie*, in *Zeitschrift für deutsche Philologie*, xxx (1898), pp. 237 ff.), who points out that Lessing shows a familiarity with Rapin in his *Critische Briefe* (1753), xvi (*Schriften*, v, p. 80) and in his *Anmerkungen über das Epigramm* (*Schriften*, xi, p. 249). Louis Racine had also quoted Rapin's views in his *Traité de la poésie dramatique* (*Œuvres*, ed. cit. vi, p. 393).

Corneille, Lessing recalls (LXXVIII, 17), had dealt with the Aristotelian κάθαρσις in his second discourse (*De la Tragédie*). He quotes (LXXVIII, 22) Corneille's interpretation of Aristotle's dictum that 'pity demands some one who suffers undeservedly while fear requires one of our like'—in the main the translation is that of the *Beyträge*.[1] The original is as follows:

Ainsi la pitié embrasse l'intérêt de la personne que nous voyons souffrir, la crainte qui la suit regarde le nôtre, et ce passage seul nous donne assez d'ouverture pour trouver la manière dont se fait la purgation des passions dans la tragédie. La pitié d'un malheur où nous voyons tomber nos semblables nous porte à la crainte d'un pareil pour nous; cette crainte, au désir de l'éviter; et ce désir, à purger, modérer, rectifier, et même déraciner en nous la passion qui plonge à nos yeux dans ce malheur les personnes que nous plaignons, par cette raison commune, mais naturelle et indubitable, que pour éviter l'effet il faut retrancher la cause.[2]

The logical inference from this reasoning, Lessing points out (30), would be that Aristotle meant tragedy to cure by purification all manner of 'passions' or emotions—curiosity, envy, ambition, etc.— but not the two essential ones, pity and fear. Fear would be merely an instrument in the process of purification. He observes that Dacier at least saw the purification of pity and fear to be essential, and translates a passage, the full text of which is in the original:

Voyons presentement comment elle [la tragedie] excite en nous la terreur et la compassion pour les purger; cela n'est pas bien difficile. Elle les excite en nous mettant devant les yeux les malheurs, que nos semblables se sont attirez par des fautes involontaires, et elle les purge, en nous rendant ces mêmes malheurs familiers, car elle nous apprend par là à ne les pas trop craindre, et à n'en être pas trop touchez quand ils arrivent veritablement....Voilà donc le premier effet de la Tragedie, elle purge la terreur et la compassion par elles-mêmes. C'est déja un assez grand bien qu'elle fait aux hommes, puisqu'elle les prépare à supporter courageusement tous les accidens les plus fâcheux, et qu'elle dispose les plus miserables à se trouver heureux, en comparant leurs malheurs avec ceux que la Tragedie leur represente; En quelque état qu'un homme puisse être, quand il verra un Edipe, un Philoctete, un Oreste, il ne pourra s'empêcher de trouver ses maux legers auprés des leurs. Mais la Tragedie n'en demeure pas là. En purgeant la terreur et la compassion, elle purge en même temps toutes les autres passions qui pourroient nous précipiter dans la même misere, car en étalant les fautes qui ont attiré sur ces malheureux les peines qu'ils souffrent, elle nous apprend à nous tenir sur nos gardes pour n'y pas tomber,

[1] Cp. *Beyträge*, ii, pp. 212 f. See also above, pp. 102, 364, note 2.
[2] *Discours de la tragédie, Œuvres, ed. cit.* i, p. 53.

et à purger et moderer la passion qui a été la seule cause de leur perte. Par exemple, il n'y a personne qui en voyant l'Edipe de Sophocle, n'apprenne à corriger en soy la temerité et l'aveugle curiosité, car ce sont les seules causes de ses malheurs, et non pas ses crimes. Voilà quelle est la pensée d'Aristote, et quel est le but de la Tragedie.[1]

This, however, says no more (LXXVIII, 100) than that pity purifies our fear, that is to say, it is only one of the four possible consequences of Aristotle's statement: the purification of pity by pity, of fear by fear, of fear by pity and of pity by fear. And his successors have not advanced the matter; they—and Lessing here instances Curtius[2]— have drawn into the definition of the purpose of tragedy a general instruction in moral virtue which, after all, is common to all kinds of literature.

Lessing, however, finds himself confronted by a difficulty: in stating the emotions which tragedy purifies Aristotle does not say τῶν τούτων παθημάτων, but τῶν τοιούτων παθημάτων. This had given —and still gives—trouble to the commentators. Robortello, for instance, restricted the phrase to fear and pity; so, too, did Castelvetro; while Maffei, in the preface to his *Merope*, proposed the omission of τοιούτων altogether from the definition.[3] Corneille held that 'all passions' could be cured by the pity and fear excited by tragedy; such was also Dacier's view, but he qualifies his statement. He translates the text: 'achève de purger en nous ces sortes de passions, et toutes les autres semblables', but in his note he enlarges and distinguishes between two functions. The first is that tragedy 'purge la terreur et la compassion par elles-mêmes'. In the second place, he emphasises the purging of other passions:

En purgeant la terreur et la compassion, elle purge en même temps toutes les autres passions qui pourroient nous précipiter dans la même misère, car en étalant les fautes qui ont attiré sur ces malheureux les peines qu'ils souffrent, elle nous apprend à nous tenir sur nos gardes pour n'y pas tomber, et à purger et modérer la passion qui a été la seule cause de leur perte.

Here, again, Lessing agrees with Batteux: he says (LXXVII, 124): 'Das τοιουτων bezieht sich lediglich auf das vorhergehende Mitleid

---

[1] *Poétique d'Aristote, ed. cit.* pp. 81 f.

[2] Cp. *op. cit.* p. 396: '...dass dadurch die Triebe der Menschlichkeit gepflanzet, erwecket und unterhalten, die Liebe zur Tugend und der Hass des Lasters gewirket, und die Leidenschaften verbessert werden.'

[3] Cp. *Proemio*, ed. of 1763, p. xciv.

und Furcht', at the same time admitting the possibility of a further purgation (137): 'Zwar können sich in der Tragödie auch zur Reinigung der andern Leidenschaften, nützliche Lehren und Bey-spiele finden.' Batteux' words are as follows:

Aristote dans la définition même qu'il donne de la Tragédie, nous dit que ce poëme est fait pour *purger la terreur et la pitié qu'elle produit.* [And in a note: Il faut faire attention à la lettre du texte. Corneille s'y est trompé, lorsqu'il a dit (Disc. 2) que la pitié purgeoit les passions qui causent les malheurs. C'est la pitié même qui est purgée.][1]...Il est certain que la terreur et la pitié sont l'effet de la Tragédie; il est certain encore que la terreur et la pitié tragique peuvent être utiles à l'homme dans le sens que nous venons de dire; c'est où je m'arrête. J'ajouterai pourtant que tous les autres effets qu'elle peut produire, toutes les vues politiques qu'on lui donne quelquefois, toutes les allégories, toutes les allusions qu'on peut y trouver, toutes les maximes, toutes les belles sentences, n'y sont, comme dans l'Épopée, que des finesses de l'artiste, et non l'objet de l'art. Une Tragédie avec ces beautés, ou sans elles, n'en sera ni plus ni moins une Tragédie, si elle exerce l'ame au malheur, et qu'elle le conduise par dégré aux deux passions que nous avons dites, et dont on peut faire deux vertus.[2]

As we should expect in view of his attitude to Aristotle, Lessing feels that the τοιούτων must be accounted for in some way. He could not be expected to agree with the common modern acceptance of the word as practically equivalent to τούτων—an equivalence, however, which is by no means beyond question.[3] So he ingeniously interprets the 'like' passions as the 'philanthropische Gefühle',[4] which formed a constituent of his own and Mendelssohn's definition of 'Mitleid', but were excluded from Aristotle's ἔλεος. I am doubtful whether Lessing put forward this very questionable explanation with much conviction, or, indeed, as anything more than an attempt to justify the word in the interest of Aristotle's infallibility. At least, a little

---

[1] *Principes de la littérature, ed. cit.* iii, pp. 96 f.

[2] *Ibid.* pp. 100 f.

[3] Cp. for instance Bywater, *ed. cit.* p. 152: 'τῶν τοιούτων παθημάτων, therefore, is a general expression for this whole group of disturbing emotions (enthusiasm, pity, fear etc.) instead of being, as is so often thought, either limited to the two emotions (pity and fear) which appear in the context, or applying to the emotions in general.'

[4] Petersen (*ed. cit.* p. 247) quotes Lessing's letter to Eschenburg of April 25, 1772 (*Schriften*, xviii, p. 37): 'Ich wünschte, dass Sie aus der Erklärung des Aristotelischen φιλάνθρωπον das Wort Pflichtmässig wegliessen...Das Pflicht-mässige wäre, meiner Meinung nach, gerade wieder das φιλάνθρωπον....' See above, p. 361, note 4.

later (LXXVIII, 70) he states quite unambiguously that the purgation is strictly limited to fear and pity. '[Aristoteles], um es abermals und abermals zu sagen, hat an keine andere Leidenschaften gedacht, welche das Mitleid und die Furcht der Tragödie reinigen solle, als an unser Mitleid und unsere Furcht selbst.'

THE UNITIES

In sections XLIV-XLVI of the *Dramaturgie*, in connexion with the *Merope* dramas of Maffei and Voltaire, Lessing discusses the unities of time, place and action—without, as we have seen, mentioning Aristotle's name. In respect of matter and argument he has nothing to add to a controversy that was by no means new,[1] and were it not for the trenchant and brilliant expression he gives to his views, his discussion

---

[1] The validity of the unities of time and place, for which claims had been made, on insufficient grounds, by the early Italian critics, and notably by Castelvetro, was questioned long before the seventeenth century was out. Cp. H. Breitinger, *Les unités d'Aristote avant le Cid de Corneille*, 2nd ed. Geneva, 1895; J. Ebner, *Beitrag zu einer Geschichte der dramatischen Einheiten in Italien*, Erlangen, 1898 (*Münchener Beiträge zur romanischen und englischen Philologie*, xv, esp. pp. 59 ff.); J. E. Spingarn, *History of Literary Criticism in the Renaissance*, 2nd ed. New York, 1908, pp. 89 ff. In France, as early as 1628, François Ogier, in his preface to Schélandre's *Tyr et Sidon* (Paris, 1628), had opposed the unity of time on the ground that it caused too great a number of coincidences, and made it necessary for the poet to narrate, instead of representing, interesting and vivid scenes; and early in the eighteenth century the Abbé Vatry had argued against the unity of time (*Histoire de l'Académie des Inscriptions*, vii, pp. 182 ff.). But it was Houdar de la Motte who, in his *Premier Discours sur la Tragédie, à l'occasion des Machabées* (1721), emboldened eighteenth-century dramatists to disregard the unities in practice. 'Loin que l'unité de lieu soit essentielle,' he wrote (*Œuvres*, Paris, 1754, iv, pp. 38 ff.), 'elle prend ordinairement beaucoup sur la vraisemblance. Il n'est pas naturel que toutes les parties d'une action se passent dans un même apartement.... Je dispenserois donc en bien des rencontres les Auteurs dramatiques de cette unité forcée, qui coûte souvent au Spectateur des parties de l'action qu'il voudroit voir, et ausquelles on ne peut supléer que par des recits toujours moins frapans que l'action même. L'unité de tems n'est pas plus raisonnable, sur tout si on la pousse à la rigueur comme l'unité de lieu: car en ce cas il ne faudroit prendre pour l'action que le tems de la représentation même; et cela par les mêmes principes, sur lesquels on prétend établir l'unité de lieu.... Je ne prétens donc pas anéantir ces regles; je veux dire seulement qu'il ne faudroit pas s'y attacher avec assez de superstition, pour ne les pas sacrifier dans le besoin à des beautés plus essentielles.' There is, of course, no need to claim, as E. Asplin has claimed (*Lamottes Afhandlingar om Tragedin, granskada och jemförda med Lessing*, in *Acta Soc. Scientiarum Fennicae*, xvi (Helsingfors, 1888), pp. 141 ff.), that Lessing was immediately indebted to La Motte.

might well date from the days before he was immediately interested in Aristotle.[1]

He discusses first the unity of place and quotes with approval (XLIV, 62) a lengthy passage from Johann Elias Schlegel's *Gedanken zur Aufnahme des dänischen Theaters*; it opens with the significant statement, which Lessing made his own: 'Die Wahrheit zu gestehen, beobachten die Engländer, die sich keiner Einheit des Ortes rühmen, dieselbe grossentheils viel besser, als die Franzosen, die sich damit viel wissen, dass sie die Regeln des Aristoteles so genau beobachten.'[2] There is, however, no reason to suppose that Lessing would not also have subscribed to Schlegel's final reservation:

Ich will hierdurch die Gewohnheit, die Einheit der Zeit und des Ortes zu beobachten, keinesweges in Verachtung bringen; sondern ich sage es bloss, um einer jeden Regel ihren rechten Werth zu bestimmen, damit man nicht fortfahre, wie viele thun, nach der äusserlichen Form der Schauspiele, ihre innerliche Schönheit zu schätzen.[3]

Schlegel had recommended his readers to turn to D'Aubignac's *Pratique du Théâtre* for an authoritative explanation of the unities,[4] and to that treatise, then nearly a hundred and ten years old, Lessing also had recourse. D'Aubignac, he found, demanded that the scene should not be greater than the 'espace dans lequel une vüe commune peut voir un homme marcher, encore qu'on ne le puisse pas bien reconnoître...'; and to support this, he put forward the following argument:

---

[1] Lessing had translated Dryden's observations on the unities in his *Theatralische Bibliothek*: 'Vors erste aber erlauben Sie mir zu sagen, dass die Einheit des Orts, sie [die Alten] mögen sie noch so sehr beobachtet haben, doch niemals eine von ihren Regeln gewesen ist; wir finden sie weder bey dem Aristoteles, noch Horaz, noch bey sonst einem, der von der Kunst geschrieben, und sie ist nur erst neuerlich von den Franzosen zu einer Vorschrift der Bühne gemacht worden. Die Einheit der Zeit hat selbst Terenz, der doch ihr bester und regelmässigster komischer Dichter ist, vernachlässiget.' (*Schriften*, vi, p. 262.)

[2] J. E. Schlegel, *Werke, ed. cit.* iii, p. 294: 'Climenens' in the passage quoted (96) is an obvious misprint, in the edition of Schlegel's works, for 'Celimenens'.

[3] *Ibid.* p. 295.

[4] 'Wer eine ausführliche Erklärung derselben verlangt, kann sie nirgends vollkommener und mit mehrerm Verstande abgehandelt finden, als in Hedelins theatralischer Dichtkunst, einem sehr guten Buche, welches zu einer gründlichen Kenntniss des Theaters vorzügliche Dienste leistet' (*Werke, ed. cit.* iii, p. 293). Elsewhere (*ibid.* p. 21) Schlegel speaks of D'Aubignac as a critic 'welchen man in den Regeln der Schaubühne auch für einen Aristoteles gelten lassen muss'.

Si le Poëte representoit par son Theatre tous les endroits ensemble d'un Palais, ou tous les quartiers d'une Ville, ou bien toutes les Provinces d'un Etat, il devroit faire voir alors aux Spectateurs, non seulement toutes les choses generalement qui se sont faites dans son histoire; mais encore tout ce qui s'est fait dans le reste du Palais, et dans toute la Ville, ou dans tout cet Etat.[1]

And Lessing recalls (XLIV, 82) how Corneille had said: 'J'accorderois très-volontiers que ce qu'on feroit passer en une seule ville auroit l'unité de lieu', but with the proviso that the scene should not be changed in the course of the same act.[2] With this view of Corneille's Lessing is evidently in agreement (III).

Lessing's main quarrel, however, is with the unity of time.[3] Already in his study of Plautus in the *Beyträge* he had pleaded for a certain amount of freedom in this matter.[4] Here he showed that the journey which Philocrates makes in the *Captivi* might have been completed within twenty-four hours; but, he continued, even if this were not credible, it was a 'Vergehen, das er [Plautus] mit hundert alten und neuen Dichtern gemein hat'. Moreover 'Zuschauer, welche keine Kunstrichter sind...lassen sich von der Hitze der Handlung fort-reissen, und ich bin gewiss, die meisten Römer werden diese Übereilung des Plautus nicht bemerkt, wenigstens nicht angemerkt haben.'[5] Corneille was willing, as a result of his own practical experience, to extend the time of a dramatic action from twelve or twenty-four hours to thirty;[6] his argument indeed went further:

La représentation dure deux heures, et ressembleroit parfaitement, si l'action qu'elle représente n'en demandoit pas davantage pour sa réalité. Ainsi ne nous arrêtons point ni aux douze, ni aux vingt-quatre heures; mais resserrons l'action du poëme dans la moindre durée qu'il nous sera possible, afin que sa représentation ressemble mieux et soit plus parfaite.[7]

This, as Lessing would have agreed, is not unreasonable; but in connexion with *Mérope* he shows the absurdity (XLV, I) of crowding together eventful happenings merely in order to keep within the rule.

---

[1] *Pratique du Théâtre*, ii, chap. vi (Amsterdam ed. of 1715, i, p. 93).
[2] *Discours des Trois Unités, Œuvres, ed. cit.* i, pp. 119 f.
[3] He did not find a strict unity of time unreasonable, however, in criticising Heufeld's *Julie* (IX, 36). He mentions this unity again in enumerating a French critic's objections to Zelmire (XIX, 43).
[4] *Beyträge*, iv, pp. 583 ff.; *Schriften*, iv, pp. 187 ff.
[5] *Schriften*, iv, p. 188.
[6] *Discours des Trois Unités, Œuvres, ed. cit.* i, pp. 111 f.
[7] *Ibid.* p. 113.

Corneille had shown, in a somewhat similar way, how unnatural this is in the *Agamemnon* of Aeschylus and *The Suppliant Women* of Euripides. One is tempted, however, to think of Scudéry's ironical criticism of *Le Cid* in 1637:

Mais faire arriuer en vingt-quatre heures la mort d'un pere, et les promesses de mariage de sa fille, auec celuy qui l'a tué; et non pas encor sans le conoistre; non pas dans une rencontre innopinée; mais dans un duel dont il estoit l'appellant; c'est (comme a dit bien agreablement un de mes Amis) ce qui loing d'estre bon dans les vingt-quatre heures, ne seroit pas suportable dans les vingt-quatre ans. Et par consequent (ie le redis encor une fois) la regle de la vray semblance n'est point observée, quoy qu'elle soit absolument necessaire. Et veritablement toutes ces belles actions que fit le Cid en plusieurs années, sont tellement assemblees par force en cette Piece, pour la mettre dans les vingt-quatre heures, que les Personnages y semblent des Dieux de machine, qui tombent du Ciel en terre: car enfin, dans le court espace d'un iour naturel, on eslit un Gouuerneur au Prince de Castille; il se fait une querelle et un combat, entre Dom Diegue et le Comte, autre combat de Rodrigue et du Comte; un autre de Rodrigue contre les Mores; un autre contre Dom Sanche; et le mariage se conclut, entre Rodrigue et Chimene; ie vous laisse à iueger, si ne voila pas un iour bien employé, et si l'on n'auroit pas grand tort d'accuser tous ces personn[a]ges de parresse? il est du subiet du Poeme Dramatique, comme de tous les corps Phisiques, qui pour estre parfaicts, demandent une certaine grandeur, qui ne soit ny trop vaste, ny trop resserree.[1]

It is very doubtful whether Lessing was familiar with this passage; but it is precisely the kind of criticism which he himself uses so effectively and so brilliantly. He sums up the whole matter here in one pregnant sentence (XLV, 60): 'Denn was er [Voltaire] an Einem Tage thun lässt, kann zwar an Einem Tage gethan werden, aber kein vernünftiger Mensch wird es an Einem Tage thun.'

Lessing points out (XLVI, 4) that the unities of time and place were a natural consequence of the unbroken presence of the chorus on the Greek stage. Castelvetro seems to have been the first to make this observation; but the fact is mentioned more than once by D'Aubignac, and it is discussed by Home in his *Elements of Criticism*.[2] Any breach of the unities within the act was prevented in French drama by the

---

[1] *Observations sur le Cid*, Paris, 1637, pp. 16 ff.
[2] Cp. *Pratique du Théâtre*, ii, chap. vi, vii (*ed. cit.* i, pp. 87, 109 f.); Home, *Elements of Criticism*, chap. xxiii (Edinburgh, 1762, iii, pp. 270 ff.; German translation, *ed. cit.* iii, pp. 326 ff.).

rule of 'liaison'. This had been stated by Corneille (xlv, 88) to be not a rule, but an ornament:

La liaison des scènes qui unit toutes les actions particulières de chaque acte l'une avec l'autre,...est un grand ornement dans un poëme, et qui sert beaucoup à former une continuité d'action par la continuité de la représentation; mais enfin ce n'est qu'un ornement et non pas une régle.[1]

But in a note on this passage Voltaire commented: 'Cet ornement de la tragédie est devenu une règle, parce qu'on a senti combien il étoit devenu nécessaire.'[2]

In the end, Lessing maintains (xlvi, 4), the only unity that matters is the unity of action: 'Die Einheit der Handlung war das erste dramatische Gesetz der Alten.'[3] But into a discussion of the nature of this unity he does not enter.

In these sections dealing with the unities, Lessing is not so much concerned with pleading for an English freedom from their restrictions as in showing how Voltaire, in his *Mérope*, sins against the Cornelian canon while professing to observe it. He changes the scene within the act; he crowds so many happenings into his play as to reduce the

---

[1] *Discours des Trois Unités, Œuvres, ed. cit.* i, p. 101. Cp. D'Aubignac, *Pratique du Théâtre*, iv, chap. i (*ed. cit.* i, pp. 252 f.): 'Il faut sçavoir, Que tous les Acteurs qui paroissent au Theatre, ne doivent jamais entrer sur la Scéne sans une raison qui les oblige à se trouver en ce moment plûtôt dans ce lieu-là qu'ailleurs; autrement ils n'y doivent pas venir, et en beaucoup d'Acteurs il ne sera pas vraisemblable qu'ils y soient venus....Il en doit être de même de la sortie des Acteurs; car s'ils ne quittent le lieu de la Scéne avec raison, il sera vraisemblable qu'ils y devoient demeurer encore: de sorte qu'il faut toûjours qu'ils se retirent, ou pour quelque affaire qui les oblige de se trouver ailleurs, ou par quelque consideration qui ne leur permette pas de s'arrêter davantage dans le lieu de la Scéne.' It has been observed that Lessing himself in his own dramas shows a fondness for closing acts and scenes with 'Kommen Sie' (K. Heinemann, *Vorhang und Drama*, in *Die Grenzboten*, March, 1890, Nos. x, xi (esp. xi, pp. 521 f.); quoted by Petersen, *ed. cit.* p. 222).

[2] See *Œuvres Complètes de Voltaire*, Paris, 1877–85, xxxii, p. 364.

[3] D'Aubignac devotes the third chapter of his second book to the unity of action. Nicolai had said of it in his *Abhandlung* (Petsch, *op. cit.* p. 14): 'Wenn also endlich die Handlung eines Trauerspiels so wohl von fremden Handlungen ununterbrochen fortdauert, als auch von ihren eigenen Nebenhandlungen nicht verwirrt oder undeutlich gemacht wird, so wird sie die Eigenschaft haben, die die Kunstrichter schon längstens unter dem Namen der E i n h e i t anbefohlen haben; eine Eigenschaft, die einem jeden dramatischen Stücke, das vollkommen schön seyn soll, unentbehrlich ist; denn an einem dramatischen Stücke, dem die Einheit der Handlung fehlt, können zwar wohl einzelne Stellen, aber unmöglich das G a n z e, Beyfall verdienen.'

unity of time to an absurdity; and while reproving Maffei for not providing satisfactory motives for his 'liaisons', he himself provides inadequate ones. But these observations belong to a criticism of the plays in question rather than to dramatic theory, and have already been considered.[1] In spite of his brave words (XLVI, 57): 'Möchten meinetwegen Voltairens und Maffeis Merope acht Tage dauern, und an sieben Orten in Griechenland spielen! Möchten sie aber auch nur die Schönheiten haben, die mich diese Pedanterieen vergessen machen!' there is no reason to infer that Lessing's own convictions went far beyond those expressed by Nicolai in his *Abhandlung von dem Trauerspiele*:

Die einzige Pflicht des Dichters wird also nur seyn, sich der Einheit der Zeit und des Orts, so viel möglich, zu nähern, und wenn er um grösserer Schönheiten willen davon abweichen muss, es so einzurichten, dass die Abweichung dem Zuschauer nicht sehr merklich werde.[2]

One can hardly think that the author of *Minna von Barnhelm*, and later of *Emilia Galotti* and *Nathan der Weise*, would really approve, any more than Nicolai, of what the latter called '[die üble] Gewohnheit der meisten Engländer, den Schauplatz ohne Noth alle Augenblicke verändern [zu lassen]'.[3]

THE BEST FORM OF TRAGIC PLOT

The 'best form of tragic plot' is discussed in St. XXXVII, again in connexion with *Mérope*, the play which was so fruitful in suggesting theoretical speculations. Aristotle, Lessing tells us (70), investigates in the fourteenth chapter of his *Poetics* the question of the precise kind of events by which terror and pity are excited. Lessing does not quote Aristotle in Curtius's translation, but his phraseology shows an unmistakable similarity with that of his predecessor. Curtius translates the passage in question as follows:

Nothwendiger Weise müssen alle Begebenheiten zwischen Freunden, Feinden, oder gleichgültigen Personen vorgehen. Ein Feind, der seinen Feind tödtet, erwecket weder bey Ausübung noch Beschliessung der Handlung, ein Mitleiden, ausser demjenigen, was mit Vollbringung des Unglücks verknüpfet ist: und auf gleiche Weise verhält es sich mit gleichgültigen Personen. Wenn aber dergleichen Unglück sich zwischen Freunden

[1] See above, p. 218.   [2] Petsch, *op. cit.* p. 15.
[3] *Ibid.* p. 17.

zuträgt, wenn ein Bruder den andern, der Sohn den Vater, die Mutter den Sohn, der Sohn die Mutter ermordet, oder ermorden will, oder eine andere ähnliche Handlung vornimmt; so sind dieses Begebenheiten, die man für das Trauerspiel aufsuchen muss.[1]

The difficulty with which the commentators on Aristotle had been confronted—attention was first drawn to it by Castelvetro—was to reconcile the preference which Aristotle expressed here for a tragic plot in which the tragic issue is prevented by a timely recognition, with the statement in chapter xiii that a good tragic plot should not end happily. In presenting the problem (xxxvii, 70 ff.) Lessing draws upon Curtius:

Die ganze Ordnung, nach welcher Aristoteles die tragischen Handlungen zählet, ist folgende; von unten auf ist die erste oder unvollkommenste Gattung, wenn man wissentlich ein Verbrechen begehen will, es aber nicht ins Werk richtet: die zweyte, wenn man es wissentlich wirklich begeht: die dritte, wenn man es unwissentlich begeht, aber hernach erkennet: die vierte, wenn man es unwissend begehen will, aber vorher erkennet. Dieses scheint einer andern Stelle des Aristoteles zu widersprechen. Dieser Kunstrichter hat oben im 13. Cap. fest gesetzt, dass ein gutes Trauerspiel sich vielmehr mit dem Unglücke als Glücke der handelnden Personen endigen müsse. Hier aber zieht er die vierte Gattung, wo das Verbrechen nicht begangen wird, und das Stück einen glücklichen Ausgang hat, der dritten vor, worinn der Ausgang unglücklich ist. Die genaue Überlegung, womit Aristoteles schrieb, erlaubet nicht, einem so grossen Manne einen Widerspruch beyzumessen. Dacier hat schon gesuchet, den Aristoteles zu rechtfertigen, allein seine Gründe

---

[1] *Aristoteles Dichtkunst, ed. cit.* pp. 28 f. Cp. also the phraseology in St. xxxviii: for πράξεως μίμησις (Dacier's 'imitation d'une action') both Curtius and Lessing write 'Nachahmung einer Handlung'; for σύνθεσις πραγμάτων ('composition des choses'), 'Verknüpfung von Begebenheiten'; for μῦθος ἁπλοῦς and μῦθος πεπλεγμένος ('fable simple', 'fable implexe'), 'einfache Fabeln' and 'verwickelte (in Curtius sometimes also 'zusammengesetzte') Fabeln'; ἀναγνωρισμός ('reconnoissance'), 'Erkennung' (Curtius also occasionally 'Erkenntniss'); περιπέτεια ('peripétie' or 'changement de fortune'; Batteux' 'péripétie' or 'révolution') appears in Curtius as 'Peripetie', 'Glückswechsel' or 'Glücksänderung', which is also Nicolai's word; Ramler writes 'Glücksveränderung' and Lessing 'Glückswechsel'. Finally, πάθος, which under French influence ('passion') Curtius had translated 'Leidenschaft', Lessing translates, if only here, 'Leiden'. Dacier, it may be noted, apologised for his use of the word 'passion' (p. 164): 'Je sçay bien que le mot *passion*, n'est François, en ce sens, que dans les choses de la Religion, et que par tout ailleurs, il signifie les sentimens, ou pour mieux dire, les maladies de l'ame; mais il n'y en a point qui explique si bien ce qu'Aristote a voulu dire.' Lessing's indebtedness to Curtius is further to be seen in the fact that, in enumerating the different kinds of plot here, he follows the order in which Curtius states them.

scheinen nicht zureichend. Er will; Aristoteles rede hier nicht von der Tragödie und ihren Handlungen überhaupt, sondern zeige nur, auf was für Art ein Dichter sich der Verbrechen in bekannten Fabeln bedienen müsse.[1]

And now Lessing turns (107) to the text of Dacier:

Le Sçavant Victorius est le seul qui l'ayt veuë; mais comme il n'a pas connu de quoy il s'agissoit dans ce Chapitre, et que ce n'est que par-là qu'on peut la résoudre, il n'a pas seulement tenté de l'éclaircir....Ils [les commentateurs] ont tous crû qu'Aristote parloit icy de la constitution des fables en general, mais il ne travaille qu'à enseigner, comment on doit se conduire dans les actions atroces pour ne pas changer les fables, et pour s'en servir comme il faut; voilà le dessein de tout ce Chapitre. Par exemple, je veux traiter le meurtre de Clytemnestre par Oreste; Aristote me donne icy un plan des quatre differentes maniéres[2] dont les actions atroces peuvent se passer. Je dois voir celle qui m'accommode. La premiere ne convient point, parce qu'elle est trop horrible. La quatriéme ne convient pas non plus, parce qu'elle est imparfaite et atroce sans passion, et que d'ailleurs elle détruit la fable. La troisiéme qui seroit la plus propre, est encore inutile, parce qu'elle sauveroit Clytemnestre qui doit necessairement mourir par les mains de son fils. Il n'y a donc que la seconde dont je puisse me servir.[3]

The only explanation which Curtius can offer (xxxviii, 7) of Aristotle's apparent self-contradiction is that the philosopher was here less careful than usual.

Lessing's interpretation (xxxviii, 80) is that Aristotle is considering each of the ingredients of a tragic plot on its own merits.[4] The best περιπέτεια is where there is a change from better to worse; whereas the best form of 'suffering' is where the persons concerned do not know one another, and the recognition comes in time to prevent the carrying out of the fatal act. He holds that there is no contradiction, for Aristotle is speaking of two different aspects of the matter. This

---

[1] *Aristoteles Dichtkunst, ed. cit.* p. 213.

[2] Cp. Corneille, *Discours de la Tragédie* (*Œuvres, ed. cit.* i, p. 67): 'La diverse combinaison de ces deux manières d'agir forme quatre sortes de tragédies.' Aristotle virtually only discusses three.

[3] *Poétique d'Aristote, ed. cit.* pp. 235 f.

[4] With Dacier, Lessing holds (60) that 'passion' is the most important ingredient. Cp. *Poétique d'Aristote, ed. cit.* p. 164: 'La passion est encore plus essencielle au sujet, que la reconnoissance et la péripetie, puisqu'il y a des sujets simples, c'est-à-dire, qui n'ont ny péripetie, ny reconnoissance, et qui ont la passion, comme l'Ajax de Sophocle, l'Hecube d'Euripide.'

explanation, however, has met with no greater acceptance than Dacier's; and it is doubtful whether the most modern interpreters of Aristotle have come any nearer to justifying what in the end has to be frankly recognised as an inconsistency.[1]

---

[1] See, for instance, Bywater's note (*Aristotle on the Art of Poetry, ed. cit.* p. 225): 'In chap. 13 Aristotle was thinking only of the emotional effect of tragedy as produced by the most obvious means; here he comes to see that the same effect may be produced in a finer form without their aid. It is his somewhat tardy recognition of the necessity of avoiding τὸ μιαρόν that has caused this change of view.'

CHAPTER XIII

COMEDY AND OTHER FORMS OF DRAMA

COMEDY

On the subject of Comedy Lessing, like Aristotle, has little to say, and that little is of small importance. Moreover, since most of his observations are in the earlier sections of the *Dramaturgie*, they are if anything more a reproduction of traditional opinion than what he has to say on Tragedy.

The 'purpose' and 'use' of Comedy are dealt with in St. xxvIII and xxIX in connexion with Regnard's *Der Zerstreute* (xxvIII, 114): 'Die Komödie [sagt man] müsse sich nur mit Fehlern abgeben, die sich verbessern lassen. Wer aber von Natur zerstreut sey, der lasse sich durch Spöttereyen eben so wenig bessern, als ein Hinkender.' This, as we have seen,[1] is only a translation of a passage quoted by the brothers Parfaict from the *Lettres d'un François* of the Abbé Leblanc: 'La Comédie ne doit jou[e]r que les défauts qu'elle peut corriger. Les Plaisanteries que l'on fera sur un Boiteux, lui aideront aussi-tôt à marcher droit, que la Pièce de Re[g]nard corrigera un Homme qui est né Distrait.' But Lessing questions the Frenchman's contention that a 'distrait' is not a fair theme for comedy; and even if this were right, why, he asks (133), should comedy be restricted to moral errors and rectifiable bad habits?

He then proceeds (xxIX, 4) to define the 'use' of comedy. Its true general use lies in laughter itself; in developing our faculty of perceiving the ridiculous. In his letter to Nicolai of November [13], 1756, he had already advanced this argument:

[Die Komödie] soll uns zur Fertigkeit verhelfen, alle Arten des Lächerlichen leicht wahrzunehmen. Wer diese Fertigkeit besitzt, wird in seinem Betragen alle Arten des Lächerlichen zu vermeiden suchen, und eben dadurch der wohlgezogenste und gesittetste Mensch werden. Und so ist auch die Nützlichkeit der Komödie gerettet.[2]

---

[1] See above, pp. 192 f., and cp. *Lettres d'un François* (Lettre xi), La Haye, 1745, i, p. 88.

[2] *Schriften*, xvii, p. 66; Petsch, *op. cit.* p. 54. Curtius in his *Abhandlung von den Personen und Vorwürfen der Comödie* (*Aristoteles Dichtkunst*, ed. cit. p. 397) claimed that everyone was agreed 'dass die Vorstellung und Verbesserung des Lächerlichen in

The distinction which Lessing draws in considering the French criticism of *Le Distrait*: 'Die Komödie will durch Lachen bessern; aber nicht eben durch Verlachen', was not foreign to the older definitions.[1] Batteux, for instance, says:

Il faut observer que tout ridicule n'est pas risible. Il y a un ridicule qui nous ennuie, qui est maussade.... Celui qui se montre sur la scène comique est toujours agréable, délicat: et ne nous cause aucune inquiétude secrète.[2]

Bishop Hurd, too, held, in opposition to the general sentiment, that ridicule is not of the essence of comedy; but I am doubtful whether Lessing knew Hurd's book[3] at this stage.

Lessing recalls (xxviii, 140) that Rousseau (in his *Lettre à M. D'Alembert* of March 20, 1758) had complained that Molière makes us laugh at his misanthrope, who is really the honourable man of the piece: 'Vous ne sauriez me nier deux choses: l'une, qu'Alceste dans cette Piece est un homme droit, sincere, estimable, un véritable homme de bien; l'autre, que l'Auteur lui donne un personnage ridicule.'[4] To this D'Alembert replied: 'Quoique le Misantrope divertisse les spectateurs, il n'est pas pour cela ridicule à leurs yeux: il n'est personne au-contraire qui ne l'estime, qui ne soit porté même

den menschlichen Handlungen der Endzweck des Lustspiels sey'. Petersen (*ed. cit.* p. 210) notes that in the Plautus essay in his *Beyträge*, Lessing stated the purpose of comedy to be 'Die Sitten der Zuschauer zu bilden und zu bessern' (*Beyträge*, iv, pp. 588 f.), while in the *Theatralische Bibliothek* (*Schriften*, vi, p. 52) he concluded that it is a function of true comedy to move us to laughter.

[1] Lessing's distinction between 'Lachen' and 'Verlachen' is at bottom that which Quintilian establishes between 'risus' and 'derisus' (*Inst.* vi, iii); and Home (*Elements of Criticism*, chap. vii, *ed. cit.* i, p. 341) had distinguished between 'risible' and 'ridiculous'. Cp. the German translation, *Grundsätze der Critik, ed. cit.* i, p. 415: 'Ein lächerlicher Gegenstand ist bloss lustig; ein belachenswerther ist zugleich lustig und verächtlich. Der erste wirkt eine Bewegung zum Lachen, die ganz ergetzend ist; die Bewegung, die der zweyte erregt, wird durch die Bewegung der Verachtung bestimmt, und die vermischte Bewegung, die daher entspringt, und theils ergetzend, theils verdrüsslich ist, kann man die Bewegung des Belachenswerthen nennen.' In 1755, Lessing had a plan for writing an *Abhandlung vom Lachen*. Cp. his letter to Mendelssohn of [October], 1755 (*Schriften*, xvii, p. 45, note 2; cp. also xix, p. 20), and those of August [23], and September 14, 1757 (*Schriften*, xvii, pp. 118, 120).

[2] *Principes de la littérature, ed. cit.* iii, p. 190.

[3] Cp. *Dissertation concerning the Provinces of the several Species of the Drama*, in *Q. Horatii Flacci Epistolæ ad Pisones et Augustum, with an English Commentary and Notes*, 3rd ed. Cambridge, 1757, i, p. 279; cp. also pp. 270 f., 273, 276. See also below, pp. 392, 402 ff.

[4] *Lettre à M. D'Alembert*, Amsterdam, 1758, p. 55.

à l'aimer et à le plaindre.'[1] The argument depends on the definition of 'das Lächerliche'. This Lessing deals with in St. xxvIII. He does not, however, accept Aristotle's definition (*Poetics*, chap. v), which according to Batteux, is as follows:

tout défaut qui cause difformité sans douleur, et qui ne menace personne de destruction, pas même celui en qui se trouve le défaut. Car s'il menaçoit de destruction, il ne pourroit faire rire que ceux qui n'ont pas le cœur bon. Un retour secret sur eux-mêmes leur feroit trouver plus de charmes dans la compassion.[2]

Nor does he take up the polemic into which Corneille had entered, in his first *Discours*, against Aristotle's definition. He sets up, however, a new definition of 'das Lächerliche' (135): 'Jede Ungereimtheit, jeder Kontrast von Mangel und Realität, ist lächerlich', which is a modification of what he had already stated in the *Laokoon*: 'Hässlichkeit ist Unvollkommenheit, und zu dem Lächerlichen wird ein Contrast von Vollkommenheiten und Unvollkommenheiten erfodert.'[3] This in turn comes from Mendelssohn, and is rooted in the Wolff-Baumgarten aesthetic theory. In his *Rhapsodie über die Empfindungen* Mendelssohn had written:

[Das Lachen] gründet sich...sowohl als das Weinen, auf einen Kontrast zwischen einer Vollkommenheit und Unvollkommenheit. Nur dass dieser Kontrast von keiner Wichtigkeit sein und uns nicht sehr nahe angehen muss, wenn er lächerlich sein soll. Die Thorheiten der Menschen, die wichtige Folgen haben, erregen mitleidige Zähren; die aber ohne Gefahr sind, machen sie bloss lächerlich. Man nennt einen solchen Kontrast eine Ungereimtheit, und sagt daher, ein jedes Lächerliche setze eine Ungereimtheit zum voraus. Ein jeder Mangel der Übereinstimmung zwischen Mittel und Absicht, Ursache und Wirkung, zwischen dem Charakter eines Menschen und seinem Betragen, zwischen den Gedanken und der Art, wie sie ausgedrückt werden; überhaupt ein jeder Gegensatz des Grossen, Ehrwürdigen, Prächtigen und Vielbedeutenden, neben dem Geringschätzigen, Verächtlichen und Kleinen, dessen Folgen uns in keine Verlegenheit setzen, ist lächerlich.[4]

In discussing Romanus's modernisation of Terence's *Adelphi*, Lessing touches upon the question of depicting foreign manners in comedy (xcvi, 126). Is there any necessity, he asks, for the dramatist

---

[1] *Mélanges de Littérature, d'Histoire et de Philosophie* (nouvelle éd.), Amsterdam, 1759, ii, p. 422.
[2] *Principes de la littérature, ed. cit.* iii, pp. 188 f.
[3] *Laokoon*, xxiii (*Schriften*, ix, p. 139).   [4] *Gesammelte Schriften, ed. cit.* i, p. 256 f.

to be exact and naturalistic in this respect? And he quotes with approval (140) Pope's view that this is not called for in comedy to the degree that is required in tragedy. In point of fact the passage is not Pope's but is, as M. Bernays discovered,[1] in Warburton's commentary on Pope's imitation of Horace's Epistle. Lessing did not find it here, however, but in Hurd's *Dissertation concerning the Provinces of the several Species of the Drama* in his edition of Horace's *Epistolæ ad Pisones et Augustum* (*ed. cit.* i, pp. 268 f.), where the passage is quoted:

Comedy succeeds best when the scene is laid *at home*, tragedy for the most part when *abroad*. 'This appears at first sight whimsical and capricious, but has its foundation in nature. What we chiefly seek in comedy is a true image of life and *manners*, but we are not easily brought to think we have it given us, when dressed in foreign modes and fashions. And yet a good writer must follow his scene, and observe decorum. On the contrary, 'tis the action in tragedy which most engages our attention. But to fit a domestick occurrence for the stage, we must take greater liberties with the action than a well-known story will allow.' (*Pope's Works*, vol. iv, p. 185.)

To Lessing's views on the kind of characters demanded by comedy and the relation in which these stand to the characters of tragedy, and to his opinions on rhymed comedy, I return later.[2]

TRAGI-COMEDY

In his *Beschluss der Critik über die Gefangnen des Plautus* in the *Beyträge*, Lessing had discussed Plautus's use of the word 'Tragico-comœdia' at some length:

Dass die Alten in der That, diejenigen Stücke, worinne Leute von Stande vorkamen, ob gleich ihr Inhalt vollkommen komisch war, gleichwohl nicht Komödien genennt, ist aus dem Vorredner des Amphitruo deutlich zu beweisen.... Es würde sich nicht schicken, spricht Plautus, wenn ich dieses Stück, worinne Götter und vornehme Leute (denn so ist das Wort Reges hier zu übersetzen) vorkommen, eine Komödie nennen wollte; es würde sich aber auch nicht schicken, wenn ich ihm den Namen einer Tragödie beylegte, weil auch Personen vom geringen Stande darinne auftreten, ich will es also, um weder auf der einen noch auf der andern Seite zu verstossen, eine Tragikomödie nennen. Wie sehr weicht folglich die Bedeutung, die wir jetzo diesem Worte geben, von der ab, welche die Alten damit zu

---

[1] Cp. G. Witkowski in *Euphorion*, vi (1899), pp. 338 f.
[2] See below, pp. 400 ff., 461 ff.

verbinden pflegten. Ich will aber damit nicht sagen, als ob die Neuern nicht Grund gehabt hätten in Benennung ihrer Stücke mehr auf den Inhalt als die Personen zu sehen; sondern ich will nur zeigen, dass die Alten Leute von Stande und wichtigen Bedienungen durchaus aus ihren Lustspielen ausgeschlossen, und sich die niedrigsten Sorten von Menschen darinne aufzuführen begnügt haben.[1]

D'Aubignac also paraphrases the passage from Plautus and adds:

Après ces paroles fort intelligibles, je ne puis comprendre comment on s'est avisé de dire, que Plaute avoit emploié ce mot de Tragi-Comédie comme nous, car il n'y pensa jamais: c'est une raillerie qu'il fait dans son Prologue, en joignant les noms de ces deux Poëmes, comme il en avoit mêlé les Personnages.[2]

In the *Dramaturgie*, Lessing is led to discuss Tragi-Comedy (LV, 91) by a reference to the box on the ear administered to Essex by Elizabeth in Banks's *Earl of Essex*. Voltaire had commented on the famous and much criticised scene in *Le Cid*, in a passage of which I have already quoted the beginning (see above, p. 174):

On ne donnerait pas aujourd'hui un souflet sur la joue d'un héros. Les acteurs mêmes sont très-embarrassés à donner ce souflet, ils font le semblant. Cela n'est plus même soufert dans la comédie; et c'est le seul exemple qu'on en ait sur le théatre tragique. Il est à croire que c'est une des raisons qui firent intituler *le Cid* tragi-comédie. Presque toutes les piéces de *Scudéri* et de *Boisrobert* avaient été des tragi-comédies. On avait cru longtems en France qu'on ne pouvait suporter le tragique continu sans mêlange d'aucune familiarité. Le mot de *tragi-comédie* est très-ancien: *Plaute* l'employe pour désigner son *Amphitrion*, parce que si l'avanture de *Sosie*[3] est comique, *Amphitrion* est très-sérieusement afligé.[4]

But Voltaire is wrong, Lessing says (LV, 113), in his statement that *Le Cid* is the only tragedy which contains a box on the ears; and his definition of Tragi-Comedy is incorrect. Lessing himself would define it as 'die Vorstellung einer wichtigen Handlung unter vornehmen Personen, die einen vergnügten Ausgang hat'. This was practically

---

[1] *Beyträge*, iv, pp. 575 f.; *Schriften*, iv, p. 182 (note).

[2] *Pratique du Théâtre*, ii, chap. x (*ed. cit.* i, pp. 136 f.).

[3] For Lessing's form 'Sosias' cp. Krüger's reference to 'Sosias' quoted below, p. 425. The form *Sosia* is found in a list of Schröder's rôles (cp. F. L. W. Meyer, *op. cit.* i, p. 153).

[4] *Commentaires sur Corneille*, ed. *cit.* i, pp. 190 f.

D'Aubignac's definition, as it was stated in a passage preceding that which Lessing quotes in his note (132):

Mais ce que nous avons fait sans fondement, est que nous avons ôté le nom de *Tragédie* aux Piéces de Theatre dont la Catastrophe est heureuse, encore que le Sujet et les personnes soient Tragiques, c'est à dire heroïques, pour leur donner celui de *Tragi-Comedies*.[1]

And the brothers Parfaict had defined it similarly,[2] in a passage from which Lessing also makes a quotation (137). He denies, however, their claim that Garnier's *Bradamante* was the first tragi-comedy (LV, 143): 'ich kenne eine Menge weit frühere spanische und italienische Stücke, die diesen Titel führen.' Lessing, however, seems to have dated Garnier's play 1682 instead of 1582,[3] and he could certainly find several Italian tragi-comedies in Riccoboni's list before the former date, if not before the latter; while Montiano in his account of Spanish tragedies[4] deals with Spanish tragi-comedies from *La Celestina* (1499) onwards. In St. LXVIII (153) Lessing comments on the mingling of comic and tragic elements which is characteristic of Spanish drama, and adds: 'ich bin weit entfernt, diese zu verthei-

---

[1] *Pratique du Théâtre*, ii, chap. x (*ed. cit.* i, p. 133). Petersen (*ed. cit.* p. 229) refers to a letter written by Lessing to Gerstenberg on February 25, 1768, in which he says: '...obgleich eine Tragödie eben so wohl einen glücklichen, als einen unglücklichen Ausgang haben kann, so sehen wir es doch gleich aus der ersten Anlage, welchen von beyden sie haben wird' (*Schriften*, xvii, pp. 247 f.).

[2] *Op. cit.* iii, pp. 454 f. I am doubtful whether, as Cosack suggests (*op. cit.* p. 298), Lessing had in mind the following passage in Hurd's *Dissertation concerning the Provinces of the several Species of the Drama* when he wrote the last fourteen lines of St. LV: '*The representation of high life* cannot, without offence to probability, be made *ridiculous*, or consequently be admitted into comedy under this view. And therefore PLAUTUS, when he thought fit to introduce these *reverend personages* on the comic stage in his AMPHITRUO, though he employed them in no very serious matters, was yet obliged to apologize for this impropriety in calling his play a *Tragicomedy*. What he says upon the occasion, though delivered with an air of pleasantry, is according to the laws of just criticism.

"Faciam ut commista sit TRAGICOCOMŒDIA.
Nam me perpetuo facere, ut sit Cŏmœdia
REGES QUO VENIANT ET DII, non par arbitror.
Quid igitur? Quoniam hic SERVOS QUOQUE PARTES HABET,
Faciam sit, proinde ut dixi, TRAGICOCOMŒDIA."'

(*Q.Horatii Flacci Epistolæ ad Pisones et Augustum, ed. cit.* i, pp. 257 f.) It may be noted that Lessing does not quote the Latin text in the form given by Hurd; nor does he use his own earlier form in the *Beyträge* (iv, p. 576).

[3] See *Hamburgische Dramaturgie*, Hamburg [1769], ii, p. 24.

[4] Translated by d'Hermilly as *Dissertation sur les Tragédies espagnoles*, Paris, 1754, i, pp. 97 ff. See above, pp. 109, 294, 300.

digen.' He recalls (LXIX, 1) that Lope de Vega, while deploring this 'Zwitterton', had perforce to conform to the dramatic tradition of his country and employ it. But he recalls also (34) the opinion expressed by Lope, in his poem *Arte nuevo*, that nature herself demonstrates to us this diversity, from which she derives some of her beauties. He seizes on the implication of this statement: if it be true— and he is inclined to grant it—then Lope has done more than he set out to do: he has shown that the defect he endeavoured to gloss over is no defect at all: 'denn nichts kann ein Fehler seyn, was eine Nachahmung der Natur ist' (67).

After quoting a long passage concerning Shakespeare from Wieland's *Agathon*, Lessing makes his own appeal (LXX, 60) for a type of drama in which the farcical and the interesting are mingled. 'Es ist wahr, und auch nicht wahr, dass die komische Tragödie, gothischer Erfindung,[1] die Natur getreu nachahmet; sie ahmet sie nur in einer Helfte getreu nach, und vernachlässiget die andere Helfte gänzlich; sie ahmet die Natur der Erscheinungen nach, ohne im geringsten auf die Natur unserer Empfindungen und Seelenkräfte dabey zu achten.'[2] In nature (66) everything is linked up with everything else.

'DAS WEINERLICHE LUSTSPIEL'

In considering Nivelle de la Chaussée's *Mélanide* (VIII, 4), Lessing remembered Voltaire's words in his preface to *Nanine*: 'ce genre de comédie...qu'on appelle par dérision *Comédie larmoyante*,'[3] and describes the play as being 'von der rührenden Gattung, der man den spöttischen Beynamen, der Weinerlichen, gegeben'. Many such pieces, he contends, are more than merely 'weinerlich', if the term be taken in the sense of bringing us near to tears; they cause the sensitive soul to pour out floods of tears; they are more tragic than the mass of French tragedies of the traditional kind. In the *Thea-*

---

[1] Petersen (*ed. cit.* pp. 239 f.) points out that the term 'Mischspiel' (LXX, 3) (cp. LXX, 43 'das gothische Mischspiel') was used by Kaspar Stieler as an equivalent of 'Tragico-Comœdia' (*Deutscher Sprachschatz*, Nürnberg, 1691, 2088 under 'Spiel'); and that Lessing may have found examples of 'Mischspiele' in Gottsched's *Nöthiger Vorrath* (Leipzig, 1757–65, i, pp. 218, 243, 248, ii, pp. 255, 258).

[2] L. Goldstein (*op. cit.* p. 210 and pp. 45 f.) points out the similarity between this view and Mendelssohn's notion of 'idealische Schönheit' in the *Hauptgrundsätze der schönen Künste und Wissenschaften* (*Gesammelte Schriften*, ed. cit. i, pp. 288 f.).

[3] *Œuvres*, ed. cit. x, p. 373.

tralische Bibliothek he had claimed that he was the first[1]—presumably in his brief notice of Frau Gottsched's translation of *Cénie* in the *Berlinische privilegirte Zeitung* of May 24, 1753[2]—to use the German expression 'weinerliches Lustspiel'.

Nanine itself was produced in Hamburg on June 1, and Lessing describes it as a comedy of this type (xxi, 90). But what he has to say here is no more than a paraphrase and translation from Voltaire, who had written in the preface to *Nanine*:

> La Comédie encor une fois peut donc se passionner, s'emporter, attendrir, pourvu qu'ensuite elle fasse rire les honnêtes gens. Si elle manquait de comique, si elle n'était que larmoyante, c'est alors qu'elle serait un genre très-vicieux, et très-désagréable. On avoue, qu'il est rare de faire passer les spectateurs insensiblement de l'attendrissement au rire. Mais ce passage, tout difficile qu'il est de le saisir dans une Comédie, n'en est pas moins naturel aux hommes. On a déjà remarqué ailleurs,[3] que rien n'est plus ordinaire que des avantures qui affligent l'ame, et dont certaines circonstances inspirent ensuite une gaieté passagère....*Homère* représente même les Dieux rians de la mauvaise grace de *Vulcain*, dans le tems qu'ils décident du destin du Monde. *Hector* sourit de la peur de son fils *Astyanax*, tandis qu'*Andromaque* répand des larmes.[4] On voit souvent jusques dans l'horreur des batailles, des incendies, de tous les désastres qui nous affligent, qu'une naïveté, un bon mot, excitent le rire jusques dans le sein de la désolation et de la pitié. On défendit à un Régiment, dans la bataille de Spire,[5] de faire quartier; un Officier Allemand demande la vie à l'un des nôtres, qui lui répond: *Monsieur, demandez-moi toute autre chose, mais pour la vie il n'y a pas moyen.* Cette naïveté passe aussi-tôt de bouche en bouche, et on rit au milieu du carnage. A combien plus forte raison le rire peut-il succéder dans la Comédie à des sentimens touchans? Ne s'attendrit-on pas avec *Alcmène*? Ne rit-on pas avec *Sosie*?[6] Quel misérable et vain travail, de disputer contre l'expérience![7]

For the intervening passage (99 ff.) Lessing took the hint in Voltaire's own cross-reference and turned to the preface to his *Enfant prodigue*:

> Si la Comédie doit être la représentation des mœurs, cette piéce semble être assez de ce caractère. On y voit un mélange de sérieux et de plaisanterie, de comique et de touchant. C'est ainsi que la vie des hommes est bigarrée; souvent même une seule avanture produit tous ces contrastes. Rien n'est si commun qu'une maison dans laquelle un père gronde, une fille occupée

---

[1] *Schriften*, vi, p. 7. [2] *Schriften*, v, p. 168. See above, pp. 229 f.
[3] The reference is to the preface to *L'enfant prodigue, Œuvres, ed. cit.* x, pp. 83 f.
[4] *Iliad*, i, 599 ff., vi, 466 ff. [5] November 15, 1703.
[6] This is of course a reference to Molière's *Amphitryon*.
[7] *Œuvres, ed. cit.* x, pp. 379 f.

de sa passion pleure; le fils se moque des deux: et quelques parens prennent différemment part à la scène. On raille très-souvent dans une chambre de ce qui attendrit dans la chambre voisine; et la même personne a quelquefois ri et pleuré de la même chose dans le même quart-d'heure.

Une Dame très-respectable étant un jour au chevet d'une de ses filles qui était en danger de mort, entourée de toute sa famille, s'écriait en fondant en larmes: *Mon* Dieu, *rendez la moi, et prenez tous mes autres enfans!* Un homme, qui avait épousé une de ses filles, s'approcha d'elle, et la tirant par la manche: *Madame*, dit-il, *les gendres en sont-ils?* Le sang froid et le comique avec lequel il prononça ces paroles, fit un tel effet sur cette Dame affligée, qu'elle sortit en éclatant de rire; tout le monde la suivit en riant, et la malade ayant sû de quoi il était question, se mit à rire plus fort que les autres.[1]

'DAS BÜRGERLICHE TRAUERSPIEL'

It is particularly to be regretted that Lessing had so very little to say on the subject of the type of drama which he himself, with his *Miss Sara Sampson*, had been mainly instrumental in acclimatising in Germany. Even in the *Theatralische Bibliothek*, when this form of tragedy was of immediate interest to him, he was content to let others speak for him. On July 20, 1756, he wrote to Nicolai, who was busy with his *Abhandlung vom Trauerspiele*: 'Ich habe eine Menge unordentlicher Gedanken über das bürgerliche Trauerspiel aufgesetzt, die Sie vielleicht zu der bewussten Abhandlung brauchen können.'[2] But unfortunately we have no trace of these.

In connexion with the performance of *Miss Sara Sampson* on May 6, 1767, Lessing contented himself with quoting two French opinions on the 'tragédie bourgeoise'. The first of these (xiv, 5) is paraphrased from a review of the French translation of his play in the *Journal étranger* for December, 1761 (pp. 5 ff.):

Les noms des Rois et des Héros sont imposans sur le théâtre; mais tout ce qui impose n'intéresse pas. En fait de revers, il est vrai, l'élévation des personnages contribue au pathétique. Belizaire mendiant excitera la pitié bien plus qu'un homme de la lie du peuple; mais en général, plus les personnages sont près de nous, plus leur situation nous intéresse. Il est dans l'homme de ne s'affecter que de ce qui arrive à ses semblables: or les

---

[1] *Œuvres, ed. cit.* x, pp. 83 f. (A note in the edition of Voltaire's complete works published at Paris, 1877–85, iii (Théâtre ii), p. 443, explains that the lady in the anecdote was the Maréchale de Noailles, her daughter Madame de Gondrin, and the husband of the other daughter the Duc de la Vallière.)

[2] *Schriften*, xvii, p. 59.

Rois ne sont nos semblables que par les sentimens de la nature et par ce
mêlange de biens et de maux qui confondent toutes les conditions en une
seule, qui est celle de l'homme.

The second is a quotation (XIV, 15) from Marmontel's *Poétique
françoise*:

C'est faire injure au cœur humain et méconnoître la Nature, que de
croire qu'elle ait besoin de titres pour nous émouvoir et nous attendrir.
Les noms sacrés d'ami, de pere, d'amant, d'époux, de fils, de mere, d'homme
enfin: voilà les qualités pathétiques: leurs droits ne prescriront jamais.
Qu'importe quel est le rang, le nom, la naissance du malheureux, que sa
complaisance pour d'indignes amis, et la séduction de l'exemple, ont
engagé dans les piéges du jeu, qui a ruiné sa fortune et son honneur, et qui
gémit dans les prisons, dévoré de remords et de honte? Si vous demandez
quel il est; je vous répons: Il fut homme de bien, et pour son supplice il
est époux et pere; sa femme, qu'il aime et dont il est aimé, languit, réduite
à l'extrême indigence, et ne peut donner que des larmes à ses enfans qui
demandent du pain. Cherchez dans l'histoire des héros une situation plus
touchante, plus morale, en un mot plus tragique; et au moment où ce
malheureux s'empoisonne, au moment, où après s'être empoisonné, il
apprend que le ciel venoit à son secours; dans ce moment douloureux et
terrible, où à l'horreur de mourir se joint le regret d'avoir pu vivre heureux;
dites-moi ce qui manque à ce sujet pour être digne de la Tragédie? Le
merveilleux, me direz-vous. Hé, ne le voyez-vous pas ce merveilleux dans
le passage rapide de l'honneur à l'opprobre, de l'innocence au crime, du
doux repos au desespoir, en un mot, dans l'excès du malheur attiré par
une foiblesse.[1]

In criticising Banks's *Earl of Essex* Lessing makes some remarks on
style in tragedy (LIX, 1) which have a bearing on the 'bürgerliches
Trauerspiel'. In Banks's play he found a strange combination of
rhetoric and everyday speech, and as will be remembered, he defends
his own reprehensible manner of translating it into realistic prose.[2]
In support of this he calls to his aid Diderot (17) who in the second
of the *Entretiens sur le Fils naturel* had condemned the conventional
language so commonly used in tragedy:

[DORVAL] se promenant à pas comptés sur la scène, et battant nos oreilles
de ce qu'Horace appelle...*Ampullas, et sesquipedalia verba*, (De Arte poetica,
v. 97) 'des sentences, des bouteilles soufflées, des mots longs d'un pied et
demi'.

Nous n'avons rien épargné pour corrompre le genre dramatique. Nous
avons conservé des anciens l'emphase de la versification qui convenait tant

---

[1] *Poétique françoise, ed. cit.* ii, p. 147 ff.   [2] See above, pp. 274 f.

à des langues à quantité forte et à accent marqué, à des théâtres spacieux, à une déclamation notée et accompagnée d'instruments; et nous avons abandonné la simplicité de l'intrigue et du dialogue, et la vérité des tableaux.[1]

Lessing maintains emphatically (28) that in this matter we should not allow ourselves to be guided by the practice of the ancients, which was conditioned by the fact that the people spoke in public places surrounded by a curious crowd; they were obliged to choose and measure their words. The moderns have dispensed with the chorus: the action takes place within four walls; thus the whole manner of tragedy must change. It is not difficult to read into this argument a plea for the 'bürgerliches Trauerspiel'.

[1] *Œuvres complètes*, *ed. cit.* vii, p. 121 (Lessing's translation, *ed. cit.* i, pp. 247 f.).

CHAPTER XIV

CHARACTERS IN DRAMA

CHARACTERS IN TRAGEDY AND COMEDY

A significant contrast is drawn in St. LI (124 ff.) between comedy and
tragedy in respect of the relative importance of character and situation: '...in der Komödie [sind] die Charaktere das Hauptwerk, die
Situationen aber nur die Mittel...jene sich äussern zu lassen....
Umgekehrt ist es in der Tragödie, wo die Charaktere weniger wesent-
lich sind, und Schrecken und Mitleid vornehmlich aus der Situation
entspringt.' Similar situations, Lessing concludes, will thus produce
similar tragedies, but not similar comedies; whereas similar characters
are likely to produce comedies (but not tragedies) which resemble
each other.[1] This argument might well have led directly to a discussion of types of character in drama; but it is not until a later
section of the *Dramaturgie* (LXXXVII–LXXXVIII) that Lessing turns to
this question, and considers how far a discrimination may be made
between the types which are suitable for tragedy and for comedy.
His analysis is based on a discussion of Diderot's practice in his *Fils
naturel* and of the views which he expresses in the third *Entretien* on
that play. Diderot (LXXXVII–VIII, 33) had said:

Le genre comique est des espèces, et le genre tragique est des individus.
Je m'explique. Le héros d'une tragédie est tel ou tel homme: c'est ou
Régulus, ou Brutus, ou Caton; et ce n'est point un autre. Le principal
personnage d'une comédie doit au contraire représenter un grand nombre
d'hommes. Si, par hasard, on lui donnait une physionomie si particulière,
qu'il n'y eût dans la société qu'un seul individu qui lui ressemblât, la
comédie retournerait à son enfance, et degénérerait en satire....Dans
le genre sérieux, les caractères seront souvent aussi généraux que dans le
genre comique; mais ils seront toujours moins individuels que dans le
genre tragique.[2]

---

[1] Petersen (*ed. cit.* p. 226) refers to Lessing's correspondence with Mendelssohn
(cp. letter of December 18, 1756), when Lessing had insisted that in tragedy, by
contrast with the epic, the misfortunes of the hero must be a consequence of his
character (*Schriften*, xvii, p. 87; Petsch, *op. cit.* p. 89).

[2] *Troisième Entretien sur le Fils naturel, Œuvres complètes*, ed. cit. vii, pp. 138 ff.;
the last sentence is quoted by Lessing later in the same section (272).

Diderot's statement, however, Lessing says (LXXXIX, 1), is put forward without any proof. Can it be that he believes that the historical characters who appear in tragedy are identical with these characters as history depicts them? This would be in flagrant contradiction of what Aristotle says in his ninth chapter; and Lessing quotes an extract (21) in a translation which he claims as his own (53).[1] Aristotle, he sums up (59), makes no difference, in respect of their universal nature, between the characters of tragedy and those of comedy; in this 'generalisation' alone lies the reason why poetry is more philosophic, and in consequence more instructive, than history. If, as Diderot says, a 'particular' character in comedy would throw the *genre* back into its infancy, this is surely equally true of tragedy.

The interpreters of Aristotle have moreover failed to understand (83) what the critic means when he says that by the names attached to his characters the poet aims at generalising them. Here Lessing quotes the translations of both Dacier and Curtius.[2] The notes which both translators append to the passage—and Curtius practically repeats what Dacier says—give further proof of this misunderstanding. Curtius says (*ed. cit.* pp. 150 f.):

Man möchte einwerfen, dass die Dichter, eben sowohl, als die Geschichtschreiber, nur besondere Begebenheiten beschrieben, weil Oedipus, Ulysses, Phormio etc. nur besondere Personen sind. Allein schon oben ist gezeiget, dass in den epischen und dramatischen Gedichten nicht eigentlich Personen, sondern Handlungen, und in den Handlungen Charaktere vorgestellet werden. Die Reden und Handlungen müssen vollkommen mit dem Charakter übereinstimmen, und folglich allen Personen von gleichem Charakter zukommen. Dieses ist das Allgemeine, welches Aristoteles versteht. So, wie Achilles bey dem Homer spricht, würde ein Conde, ein zwölfter Karl, unter gleichen Umständen gleichfalls geredet haben, und wozu sich ein Leonidas entschliesst, das würde auch eines Decius, Fabricius oder Catons Entschluss gewesen seyn. Man muss daher den Charakter von der Person unterscheiden, oder vielmehr, man muss die Begebenheiten, die jemand, zu Folge seines Charakters, treffen, von den Begegnissen unterscheiden, die bloss Wirkungen des Zufalles sind. Jene gehören zu dem Allgemeinen, und können in der Dichtkunst Statt finden, diese zu dem Besondern, und gehören für die Historie. Dass Alcibiades sich den Hass des Volkes zuzog, dass er wider sein undankbares Vaterland fochte, hernach aber sich wieder auf desselben Seite schlug, dieses waren

---

[1] It is, however, interesting to compare Curtius's version, *ed. cit.* pp. 19 f. See above, pp. 385 f. (and note to p. 386).

[2] Cp. Dacier, *ed. cit.* p. 132; Curtius, *ed. cit.* p. 19.

Folgen seines Charakters, und jedermann von seinem Charakter und
Umständen würde ein gleiches gethan und gelitten haben. Dass aber die
Niederwerfung der Säulen des Merkurs ihn verjagte, und andere dergleichen
Umstände, sind persönliche Zufälle. Jenes war etwas allgemeines, dieses
gehöret unter das Besondere.

Both Curtius and Dacier miss the fact that, according to Aristotle,
the giving of names to characters—not the lack of these names—
emphasises the general or universal in them. Nor do they, of course,
attempt to explain how this generalisation is effected. Both, Lessing
points out (xc, 17), make Aristotle merely assert that the comic poets
did not write like the iambic—that is, the satiric—poets;[1] that they
did not keep to the particular, but aimed at creating universal
characters, to whom they gave any names they pleased ('willkührliche
Namen', 'tels noms qu'il leur plaît'). But where is Aristotle's οὕτω?[2]
His meaning must be that the comic poets aimed *in this wise* (*i.e.* by
giving them arbitrarily chosen names) at endowing their characters
with a universal significance. Lessing's conclusion is thus that Aristotle is right and Diderot wrong (xci, 131): 'Die Charaktere der
Tragödie müssen eben so allgemein seyn, als die Charaktere der
Komödie.'

He now turns (xcii, 1) to another 'no less excellent critic...who
has thrown most light on this matter'—Richard Hurd, whose edition
of Horace's *Epistolæ ad Pisones et Augustum* Lessing had before him.[3]
Hurd, like Diderot, appears to contradict Aristotle, and yet he does
not actually do so.[4] Sections xcii to xcv are largely taken up with

---

[1] Dacier in his note to this passage (*ed. cit.* p. 141) had explained: 'Le Grec dit,
et ne font pas, comme les faiseurs d'iambes, c'est-à-dire, (comme je l'ay expliqué),
comme les Poëtes satyriques; Car le vers ïambe étoit consacré à la médisance et à la
satyre.' Cp. xviii, 55 and see above, p. 315.

[2] Concerning the practice of the comedy writers of giving their characters names
which indicate their characters Lessing quotes (xc, 46) the commentary on Terence
of Ælius Donatus. See also above, p. 315.

[3] Richard Hurd, *Q. Horatii Flacci Epistolæ ad Pisones et Augustum, with an English
Commentary and Notes; to which are added Critical Dissertations,* 3 vols. London, 1749.
Lessing used the third edition published at Cambridge in 2 vols. in 1757. Hurd
was born in 1720 and died in 1808.

[4] J. J. Eschenburg took the hint thrown out by Lessing that this work should be
translated, and in 1772 published: *Horazens Episteln an die Pisonen und an den
Augustus, mit Kommentar und Anmerkungen nebst einigen kritischen Abhandlungen.* Aus
dem Englischen übersetzt und mit eigenen Anmerkungen begleitet, Leipzig, 1772.
As Cosack notes (*op. cit.* p. 413) he took over verbatim the passages translated by
Lessing, as well as Lessing's long note (xciii, 47).

extracts in German translation from the *Dissertation concerning the Provinces of the several Species of the Drama* in this work. I give the passages in the original text (3rd ed. Cambridge, 1757, i, pp. 262 ff.):

[XCII, 35 ff.] The same genius in the two dramas is observable, in their draught of *characters*. Comedy makes all its Characters *general*, Tragedy, *particular*. The *Avare* of Moliere is not so properly the picture of a *covetous man*, as of *covetousness* itself. Racine's *Nero*,[1] on the other hand, is not a picture of *cruelty*, but of a *cruel man*.

Yet here it will be proper to guard against two mistakes, which the principles now delivered may be thought to countenance.

The *first* is with regard to *tragic* characters, which I say are *particular*. My meaning is, they are *more* particular than those of comedy. That is, the *end* of tragedy does not require or permit the poet to draw together so many of those characteristic circumstances which shew the manners, as Comedy. For in the former of these dramas, no more of *character* is shewn, than what the course of the action necessarily calls forth. Whereas, all or most of the features, by which it is usually distinguished, are sought out and industriously displayed in the *latter*.

The case is much the same as in *portrait painting*; where, if a great master be required to draw a *particular face*, he gives the very lineaments he finds in it; yet so far resembling to what he observes of the same turn in other faces, as not to affect any minute circumstance of peculiarity. But if the same artist were to design a *head* in general, he would assemble together all the customary traits and features, any where observable through the species, which should best express the idea, whatever it was, he had conceived in his own mind and wanted to exhibit in the picture.

There is much the same difference between the two sorts of *dramatic* portraits. Whence it appears that in calling the tragic character *particular*, I suppose it is only *less representative* of the kind than the comic; not that the draught of so much character as it is concerned to represent should not be *general*: the contrary of which I have asserted and explained at large elsewhere [*Notes on the A. P. ver.* 317].[2]

Next, I have said, the characters of just comedy are *general*. And this I explain by the instance of the *Avare* of Moliere, which conforms more to the idea of *avarice*, than to that of the real *avaricious man*. But here again, the reader will not understand me, as saying this in the strict sense of the words. I even think Moliere faulty in the instance given; though, with some necessary explanation, it may well enough serve to express my meaning.

The view of the comic scene being to delineate characters, this end, I suppose, will be attained most perfectly, by making those characters as *universal* as possible. For thus the person shewn in the drama being the representative of all characters of the same kind, furnishes in the highest

---

[1] In *Britannicus*.   [2] See below, pp. 405 ff.

degree the entertainment of *humour*. But then this universality must be such as agrees not to our idea of the *possible* effects of the character as conceived in the abstract, but to the *actual* exertion of its powers which experience justifies, and common life allows. Moliere, and before him Plautus, had offended in this; that for a picture of the *avaritious man,* they presented us with a fantastic unpleasing draught of the *passion of avarice.* I call this a *fantastic* draught, because it hath no archetype in nature. And it is, farther, an *unpleasing* one, for being the delineation of a *simple passion unmixed,* it wanted all those

> —Lights and shades, whose well accorded strife
> Gives all the strength and colour of our life.

These *lights and shades* (as the poet finely calls the intermixture of many passions which, with the *leading* or principal one, form the human character) must be blended together in every picture of dramatic manners; because the avowed business of the drama is to image real life. Yet the draught of the *leading* passion must be as general as this *strife* in nature permits, in order to express the intended character more perfectly.

[St. xciii] All which again is easily illustrated in the instance of painting. In *portraits of character,* as we may well call those that give a picture of the *manners,* the artist, if he be of real ability, will not go to work on the possibility of an abstract idea. All he intends, is to shew that some one quality *predominates*: and this he images strongly, and by such signatures as are most conspicuous in the operation of the *leading passion.* And when he hath done this, we may, in common speech or in compliment, if we please, to his art, say of such a portrait that it images to us not the *man* but the *passion*; just as the antients observed of the famous statue of Apollodorus by Silarion, that it expressed not the angry *Apollodorus,* but his passion of *anger* (Note: *Non hominem ex ære fecit, sed iracundiam* Plin. xxxiv. 8). But by this must be understood only that he has well expressed the leading parts of the designed character. For the rest he treats his *subject* as he would any other; that is, he represents the *concomitant affections,* or considers merely that general symmetry and proportion which are expected in a human figure. And this is to copy nature which affords no specimen of a man turned all into a single passion. No metamorphosis could be more strange or incredible. Yet portraits of this vicious taste are the admiration of common starers, who, if they find a picture of a *miser* for instance (as there is no commoner subject of moral portraits) in a collection, where every muscle is strained, and feature hardened into the expression of this idea, never fail to profess their wonder and approbation of it.—On this idea of excellence, Le Brun's book of the Passions[1] must be said to contain a set of the justest *moral portraits*: And the Characters of Theophrastus might be recommended, in a *dramatic* view, as preferable to those of Terence.

[1] Charles Le Brun, *Conférences sur l'expression des différents caractères des passions,* Paris, 1667. (This work had appeared in an English translation by J. Williams, London, 1734.)

The virtuosi in the fine arts would certainly laugh at the former of these judgments. But the latter, I suspect, will not be thought so extraordinary. At least if one may guess from the practice of some of our best comic writers, and the success which such plays have commonly met with. It were easy to instance in almost all plays of character. But if the reader would see the extravagance of building dramatic manners on abstract ideas, in its full light, he needs only turn to B. Johnson's *Every man out of his humour*;[1] which under the name of a *play of character* is in fact, an unnatural, and, as the painters call it, *hard* delineation of a group of *simply existing passions*, wholly chimerical, and unlike to any thing we observe in the commerce of real life. Yet this comedy has always had its admirers. And *Randolph* in particular, was so taken with the design, that he seems to have formed his *muse's looking-glass* in express imitation of it.[2]

Shakespeare, we may observe, is in this as in all the other more essential beauties of the drama, a perfect model. If the discerning reader peruse attentively his comedies with this view he will find his *best-marked* characters discoursing through a great deal of their *parts*, just like any other, and only expressing their essential and leading qualities occasionally, and as circumstances concur to give an easy exposition to them. This singular excellence of his comedy, was the effect of his copying faithfully after nature, and of the force and vivacity of his genius which made him attentive to what the progress of the scene successively presented to him: whilst *imitation* and *inferior talents* occasion little writers to wind themselves up into the habit of attending perpetually to their main view, and a solicitude to keep their favourite characters in constant play and agitation. Tho' in this illiberal exercise of their wit, they may be said to use the *persons of their drama* as a certain facetious sort do their *acquaintance*, whom they urge and teize with their civilities, not to give them a reasonable share in the conversation, but to force them to play *tricks* for the diversion of the company.

In St. xciv and xcv Lessing translates (xciv, 8 ff.) Hurd's comment on ll. 317 f. of the *Ars poetica*:

> Respicere exemplar vitæ morumque jubebo
> Doctum imitatorem, et vivas hinc ducere voces.[3]

The English text is as follows (*ed. cit.* i, pp. 220 ff.):

Truth, in poetry, means such an expression, as conforms to the general nature of things; *falshood*, that, which however suitable to the particular instance in view, doth yet not correspond to such *general nature*. To attain

---

[1] On Lessing's long note on Ben Jonson (xciii, 47) see above, pp. 254 f.

[2] Thomas Randolph, *The Muse's Looking-Glasse*, Oxford, 1638.

[3] 'I shall bid thee regard the example of life and manners, that thou mayst be a skilful imitator and deduce living words from them.' Hurd reads '*veras*' in his text and note (ed. of 1757, i, pp. 23, 220), and Lessing quotes the line in this form (xcii, 101).

to this *truth* of expression in dramatic poetry two things are prescribed: 1. A diligent study of the Socratic philosophy; and 2. A masterly knowledge and comprehension of human life. The *first*, because it is the peculiar distinction of this school *ad veritatem vitæ propius accedere* [Cic. de Or. i. 51]. And the *latter*, as rendering the imitation more universally striking. This will be understood by reflecting that *truth* may be followed too closely in works of imitation, as is evident in two respects. For, 1. the artist, when he would give a Copy of nature, may confine himself too scrupulously to the exhibition of *particulars*, and so fail of representing the general idea of the *kind*. Or, 2. in applying himself to give the *general* idea, he may collect it from an enlarged view of *real* life, whereas it were still better taken from the nobler conception of it as subsisting only in the *mind*. This last is the kind of censure we pass upon the *Flemish* school of painting, which takes its model from real nature, and not, as the *Italian*, from the contemplative idea of beauty. (Note: In conformity with the *Antique*. *Nec enim Phidias, cum faceret Jovis formam aut Minervæ, contemplabatur aliquem e quo similitudinem duceret: sed ipsius in mente incidebat* species pulchritudinis eximia quædam, *quam intuens in eaque defixus ad illius similitudinem artem et manum dirigebat* [Cic. Orat. 2]). The *former* corresponds to that other fault objected also to the Flemish masters, which consists in their copying from particular odd and grotesque nature in contra-distinction to general and graceful nature.

We see then that in deviating from particular and partial, the poet more faithfully imitates *universal*, truth. And thus an answer occurs to that refined argument, which Plato invented and urged, with much seeming complacency, against poetry. It is, that *poetical imitation is at a great distance from truth*. 'Poetical expression, says the Philosopher, is the copy of the poet's own conceptions; the poet's conception, of things; and things, of the standing archetype, as existing in the divine mind. Thus the poet's expression, is a copy at third hand, from the primary, original truth.' (Plat. De rep. L. x.) Now the diligent study of this rule of the poet obviates this reasoning at once. For, by abstracting from existences all that peculiarly respects and discriminates the *individual*, the poet's conception, as it were neglecting the intermediate particular objects, catches, as far as may be, and reflects the divine archetypal idea, and so becomes itself the copy or image of truth. Hence too we are taught the force of that unusual encomium on poetry by the great critic, *that it is something more severe and philosophical than history*, φιλοσοφώτερον καὶ σπουδαιότερον ποίησις ἱστορίας ἐστίν. The reason follows, which is now very intelligible; ἡ μὲν γὰρ ποίησις μᾶλλον τὰ καθόλου,[1] ἡ δ' ἱστορία τὰ καθ' ἕκαστον λέγει. [περ. ποιητ. κ. θ.] And this will further explain an essential difference, as we are told, between the two great rivals of the Greek stage. Sophocles, in return to such as objected a want of truth in his characters, used to plead, *that he drew men such as they ought to be, Euripides such as they were.* Σοφοκλῆς ἔφη, αὐτὸς μὲν οἵους δεῖ ποιεῖν,

---

[1] Lessing returns to this point in St. xcv (125). See below, p. 409.

Εὐριπίδης δὲ οἷοί εἰσι. [περ. ποιητ. κ. κε.] The meaning of which is, Sophocles, from his more extended commer[c]e with mankind, had enlarged and widened the narrow, partial conception, arising from the contemplation of *particular* characters, into a complete comprehension of the *kind*. Whereas the philosophic Euripides, having been mostly conversant in the academy, when he came to look into life, keeping his eye too intent on single, really existing personages, sunk the *kind* in the *individual*; and so painted his characters naturally indeed, and *truly*, with regard to the objects in view, but sometimes without that general and universally striking likeness, which is demanded to the full exhibition of poetic truth.

But here an objection meets us, which must not be overlooked. It will be said, 'that philosophic speculations are more likely to render men's views *abstract* and *general* than to confine them to *individuals*. This latter is a fault arising from the *small number* of objects men happen to contemplate: and may be removed not only by taking a view of many *particulars*, which is knowledge of the world; but also by reflecting on the *general nature* of men, as it appears in good books of morality. For the writers of such books form their *general* notion of human nature from an extensive experience (either their own, or that of others) without which their writings are of no value.' The answer, I think, is this. *By reflecting on the general nature of man* the philosopher learns, what is the tenor of action arising from the predominancy of certain qualities or properties: *i.e.* in general, what that conduct is, which the imputed character requires. But to perceive clearly and certainly, how far, and with what degree of strength this or that character will, on particular occasions, most probably shew itself, this is the fruit only of a knowledge of the world. Instances of a want of this knowledge cannot be supposed frequent in such a writer, as Euripides; nor, when they occur, so glaring as to strike a common reader. They are niceties, which can only be discerned by the true critic; and even to *him*, at this distance of time, from an ignorance of the Greek manners, that may possibly appear a fault, which is a real beauty. It would therefore be dangerous to think of pointing out the places, which Aristotle might believe liable to this censure in Euripides. I will however presume to mention one, which, if not justly criticized, will, at least, serve to illustrate my meaning.

[St. xcv] The story of his *Electra* is well known. The poet had to paint, in the character of this princess, a virtuous, but fierce, resentful woman; stung by a sense of personal ill treatment; and instigated to the revenge of a father's death, by still stronger motives. A disposition of this warm temperament, it might be concluded by the philosopher in his closet, would be prompt to shew itself. *Electra*, would, on any proper occasion, be ready to avow her resentment, as well as to forward the execution of her purpose. But to what lengths would this *resentment* go? *i.e.* what degree of fierceness might *Electra* express, without affording occasion to a person widely skilled in mankind, and the operation of the passions, to say, 'this is improbable?' Here abstract theories will be of little service. Even a moderate acquaintance with real life will be unable to direct us. Many

individuals may have fallen under observation, that will justify the poet in
carrying the expression of such a *resentment* to any extreme. History would,
perhaps, furnish examples, in which a virtuous resentment hath been
carried even farther than is here represented by the poet. What way then
of determining the precise bounds and limits of it? Only by observing in
numerous instances, *i.e.* from a large extensive knowledge of practical life,
how far it usually, in such characters, and under such circumstances,
prevails. Hence a difference of representation will arise in proportion to
the extent of that *knowledge*. Let us now see, how the character before us,
hath, in fact, been managed by Euripides.

In that fine scene, which passes between Electra and Orestes, whom as
yet she suspects not to be her brother, the conversation very naturally
turns upon Electra's distresses, and the author of them, Clytæmnestra, as
well as on her hopes of deliverance from them by means of Orestes. The
dialogue upon this proceeds:

Or. What then of Orestes, were he to return to this Argos?

El. Ah! wherefore that question, when there is no prospect of his
return at all?

Or. But supposing he should return, how would he go about to revenge
the death of his father?

El. In the same way, in which that father suffered from the daring
attempts of his enemies.

Or. And could you then dare to undertake with him the murder of your
mother?

El. Yes, with that very steel, with which she murdered my father.

Or. And am I at liberty to relate this to your brother, as your fixed
resolution?

El. I desire only to live, till I have murdered my mother. The Greek
is still stronger:

May I die, as soon as I have murdered my mother![1] Now that this last sentence
is absolutely unnatural, will not be pretended. There have been doubtless
many examples, under the like circumstances, of an expression of revenge
carried thus far. Yet, I think, we can hardly help being a little shocked at
the fierceness of *this* expression. At least *Sophocles* has not thought fit to
carry it to that extreme. In him, *Electra* contents herself with saying to
Orestes, on a similar occasion:

'The conduct of this affair now rests upon you. Only let me observe this
to you, that had I been left alone, I would not have failed in one of these
two purposes, either to deliver myself gloriously, or to perish gloriously.'[2]

Whether this representation of Sophocles be not more agreeable to *truth*,
as collected from wide observation, *i.e.* from human nature at large, than

[1] Lessing inserts here (xcv, 55) the Greek line: θάνοιμι μητρὸς αἷμ' ἐπισφάξασ'
ἐμῆς.

[2] Hurd's quotations are from Euripides's *Electra*, ll. 274 ff.; from that of Sophocles,
ll. 1318 ff.

that of Euripides, the capable reader will judge. If it be, the reason I suppose to have been, *that Sophocles painted his characters, such, as, from attending to numerous instances of the same kind, he would conclude they ought to be; Euripides, such, as a narrower sphere of observation had persuaded him they were.*[1]

Lessing now sums up (xcv, 86) the conclusions he wishes to draw from this long extract. Hurd, like Diderot (86), shows that 'particular' characters belong to tragedy, 'universal' only to comedy; but Hurd argues that this does not contradict Aristotle's demand for the 'universal' in all poetic characters. The tragic character, Hurd says, must admittedly be particular, or less universal than the comic; that is, it must less obviously represent the 'kind' to which it belongs; at the same time, whatever the poet finds it appropriate to let us see of the tragic character must be envisaged in the light of the universal, as Aristotle requires.

An apparent inconsistency between Diderot's view and those of Hurd and Aristotle is explained by the fact that they use the expression 'allgemein'—'général' or 'universal'—in two different senses. Where Diderot and Hurd refuse its application to tragic characters, they are not thinking of 'universal' as Hurd uses it when he is applying it to such characters. In the first case it means a composite or 'overladen' character combining the elements of many individuals, the personified idea of a character rather than a characterised person; in the second sense it means no more than that the character strikes a certain average of the features observable in many individuals: it is an 'ordinary' character, not in the sense that the character is *per se* ordinary, but that the degree and proportion in which the person is characterised is ordinary.[2]

Lessing approves (xcv, 125) Hurd's interpretation of Aristotle's καθόλου as 'general' in the second sense. But if Aristotle demands this kind of universality in both tragic and comic characters, how can they at the same time be overladen *and* ordinary? Even if they are not as overladen as are Ben Jonson's characters, would they not still be more extraordinary than is consistent with Aristotle's demand for universality? With this point of interrogation Lessing breaks off:

[1] In St. xciv (102, note) Lessing expresses his preference for Hurd's interpretation of Aristotle's statement that Sophocles depicted men as they should be, while Euripides drew them as they were, as compared with Dacier's explanation of the same passage. (Cp. Hurd, *ed. cit.* i, p. 222, and *Poétique d'Aristote, ed. cit.* pp. 457 f.)

[2] The passage from Hurd to which Lessing refers in his note (xcv, 102) is to be found *ed. cit.* i, pp. 222 f.

what he offers, he says apologetically (141), is not logical conclusions but only 'fermenta cognitionis'.[1]

The whole argument is obviously one that has little interest for us to-day; no one would now seriously discriminate between tragedy and comedy in respect of the kind of character which may be introduced. At most we may say that Aristotle's distinction is clear and comprehensible enough, while the attempts of Diderot and Hurd (and we might add, of Lessing himself) to justify the Greek writer are rendered futile and nugatory by the disappearance of the distinction between tragedy and comedy in this respect.

Lessing had dealt more specifically with the characters of comedy in the sections immediately preceding those which have just been discussed. He recalls (LXXXVI, 1) Diderot's assertion concerning comic characters in the third *Entretien sur le Fils naturel*:

[MOI.]...Il n'y a, dans la nature humaine, qu'une douzaine, tout au plus, de caractères vraiment comiques et marqués de grands traits.

[DORVAL.] Je le pense.

[MOI.] Les petites différences qui se remarquent dans les caractères des hommes, ne peuvent être maniées aussi heureusement que les caractères tranchés.

[DORVAL.] Je le pense. Mais savez-vous ce qui s'ensuit de là?...Que ce ne sont plus, à proprement parler, les caractères qu'il faut mettre sur la scène, mais les conditions. Jusqu'à présent, dans la comédie, le caractère a été l'objet principal, et la condition n'a été que l'accessoire; il faut que la condition devienne aujourd'hui l'objet principal, et que le caractère ne soit que l'accessoire. C'est du caractère qu'on tirait toute l'intrigue. On cherchait en général les circonstances qui le faisaient sortir, et l'on enchaînait ces circonstances. C'est la condition, ses devoirs, ses avantages, ses embarras, qui doivent servir de base à l'ouvrage. Il me semble que cette source est plus féconde, plus étendue et plus utile que celle des caractères.[2]

To this Palissot had replied (23) in his *Petites lettres sur de grands Philosophes* (ii, *Le Fils naturel*):

Non, Madame, non. Les caractères ne sont point aussi épuisés qu'il le dit. Ecoutez parler Moliere lui-même dans une de ses Comédies. Voici comme il répond à quelqu'un qui pensait, comme M. Diderot, que les sources du comique allaient lui manquer. Remarquez combien ce grand homme était loin de deviner les Comédies de condition. [Palissot then

---

[1] See above, p. 130, note 1.

[2] *Œuvres complètes, ed. cit.* vii, pp. 149 f.; Lessing's translation, i, pp. 321 f.

quotes in his text the passage from *L'Impromptu de Versailles* which Lessing reproduces in his note.]...Je croirais en trouver encore un [sujet de Comédie] dans ce vers du *Méchant*:

Des protégés si bas, des protecteurs si bêtes.

L'homme déplacé; l'homme fin, dont la finesse échoue toujours contre la naïveté d'un homme simple; le faux Philosophe; l'homme singulier, manqué par Destouches; le Tartuffe de société, comme on a fait celui de religion: voilà, ce me semble, des sujets qui n'attendent que des hommes, et qui valent bien le *Frere*, la *Sœur*, l'*Epoux* etc.[1]

Even, Palissot says (46), if there are so few comic characters, would the factors of rank or profession ease the situation? He argues against Diderot's whole theory of 'conditions':

Une idée qui est entierement de l'Auteur, mais qui est bien aussi la chose la plus singuliere que l'on ait dite, c'est ce qu'il appelle des Comédies de *Condition*. Jusqu'à présent on a fait, dit-il, des pieces de caractères, et les caractères sont épuisés. Nous avons des financiers dans nos Comédies, mais le financier n'est pas fait....En vérité je ne sais plus de quel nom appeller ce délire d'imagination. Si je choisis un de ces sujets, le Magistrat, par exemple, il faudra bien que je lui donne un caractère: il sera triste ou gai, grave ou frivole, affable ou brusque, et ce sera ce caractère qui en fera un personnage réel, qui le tirera de la classe des abstractions métaphysiques. Voilà donc le caractère qui redevient la base de l'intrigue et de la morale de la piece, et la condition qui n'est plus que l'accessoire.[2]

A man's position in life or society is thus only an accidental factor. Diderot might answer that only a certain type of character is consistent with a certain profession: a judge, for instance, must necessarily be serious and suave. But here (88) he approaches the rock of the 'perfect' character. Mendelssohn had discussed the question of the perfect character, not merely in the passage which occurs in his criticism of *Codrus* and which has already been quoted,[3] but also in an article in the *Litteraturbriefe*, No. lxvi, of November 8, 1759.[4] The

---

[1] *Théâtre et Œuvres diverses*, London and Paris, 1763, ii, pp. 153 ff. This edition had been noticed in the *Bibliothek der schönen Wissenschaften*, x (i), 1763, pp. 180 ff. Charles Palissot de Montenoy (1730–1814) was involved in a bitter feud with Diderot and the Encyclopaedists, against whom the *Petites lettres* were directed. The passage quoted from Molière's *Impromptu de Versailles* (50) is from sc. iv, not iii. *Le Méchant* is a comedy by Gresset, and the line quoted is from Act ii, sc. iii; *L'homme singulier* is a comedy by Destouches.

[2] *Théâtre et Œuvres diverses*, ed. cit. ii, pp. 151 f.

[3] See above, pp. 146 f.

[4] *Gesammelte Schriften*, ed. cit. iv, 1, pp. 579 ff.

ancients, he said here, do not scruple to hold up perfect characters to mortals for imitation (p. 581):

Aber sie hätten mehr als stoisch gesinnt seyn müssen, wenn sie ihren vollkommenen Weisen für alles in allem, und sogar für die geschickteste dramatische Person gehalten hätten. Ich weiss kein einziges dramatisches Stück von den Alten, in welchem vollkommen tugendhafte Personen vorkommen sollten.

Lessing rightly thinks that Diderot has not sufficiently avoided the difficulty (97), and instances an observation made by him on the characters of Demea and Micio in Terence's *Adelphi*. If the characters, Lessing argues, must always be completely suited to the rank or profession of the person, where would comedy be?

CONSISTENCY AND PURPOSE IN CHARACTER

In connexion with Favart's *Soliman II*, Lessing considers the qualities of character-drawing which may be expected from the poet of genius (XXXIV, 43), and selects two essentials: 'Übereinstimmung', consistency, and 'Absicht', purpose. The former of these requires that the personages of a drama should be presented with uniformity and harmony; they may express themselves with greater or less emphasis as circumstances may dictate; but such expression should never be of a kind that will turn black into white.[1] And in an earlier passage, where he is discussing Corneille's attitude to history in his *Comte d'Essex* (XXXII, 40),[2] he insists that it is not enough for the poet to base his characters merely on the testimony of history; he must endeavour to present the occurrences which set them in action as a natural chain of cause and effect, and so to colour and regulate the emotions of the characters that they appear to arise in the most natural way and take their natural course. A person in a drama must not act or speak in a way which would leave the impression on the ordinary intelligence that a man of his character would be unlikely to behave thus; in other words, he must not fall out of his rôle. If the poet achieves this end he cannot altogether fail. And still more emphatically Lessing insists in his criticism of *Mérope* (XLVI, 61):

---

[1] It had been the criticism (XXXIV, 136) of the *Journal encyclopédique* that this 'Wahrscheinlichkeit' was lacking in the characters of *Soliman II*. See above, pp. 236 f.   [2] See below, pp. 440 f.

'Die strengste Regelmässigkeit kann den kleinsten Fehler in den Charakteren nicht aufwiegen.'

This demand had also been emphasised by Lessing's predecessors. Johann Elias Schlegel, for instance, had said in his *Gedanken zur Aufnahme des dänischen Theaters*:

Sowohl in der Wahl, Verschiedenheit und Feinigkeit, als auch der genauen Bestimmung der Charaktere, zeiget sich besonders die Grösse des Meisters....Je grösser der Meister ist, desto mehr wird man den Charakter der Person, die er vorstellt, fast aus jedem Worte erkennen. In ihren Leidenschaften, in ihren Entschlüssen, in ihren vernünftigsten Reden, und so gar in ihren Complimenten wird sie ihre schwache Seite verrathen.... So bald ein Poet sich bemüht, seine Charaktere vom Anfange bis zu Ende wohl auszudrücken, so wird auch sein Ausdruck schön seyn. Und der geringste Fehler im Ausdrucke wird auch ein Fehler im Charakter seyn.[1]

But Shaftesbury had already formulated this requirement. In discussing dialogue, in his *Advice to an Author* (1710) he wrote:

Nor is it enough that the persons introduced speak pertinent and good sense at every turn. It must be seen from what bottom they speak; from what principle, what stock or fund of knowledge they drew; and what kind or species of understanding they possess. For the understanding here must have its mark, its characteristic note, by which it may be distinguished. It must be such and such an understanding; as when we say, for instance, such or such a face; since Nature has characterised tempers and minds as peculiarly as faces. And for an artist who draws naturally, 'tis not enough to show us merely faces which may be called men's: every face must be a certain man's. Now as a painter who draws battles or other actions of Christians, Turks, Indians, or any distinct and peculiar people, must of necessity draw the several figures of his piece in their proper and real proportions, gestures, habits, arms, at least with as fair resemblance as possible, so in the same manner that writer, whoever he be, among us moderns, who shall venture to bring his fellow-moderns into dialogue, must introduce them in their proper manners, genius, behaviour and humour.[2]

Elsewhere in the *Dramaturgie*, in different connexions, Lessing emphasises the need for naturalness in character-drawing. His discussion of Clorinde's sudden conversion to Christianity in Cronegk's *Olint und Sophronia* (II, 1) leads him to insist that all that appertains to a dramatic character must arise from the most natural causes. Miracles may be tolerated in the physical world; but in the moral

---

[1] *Werke, ed. cit.* iii, pp. 288 ff.
[2] *Characteristics*, ed. J. M. Robertson, London, 1900, i, pp. 132 f.

world everything must take its proper course.[1] The motive of every decision (9), of every change of thought or opinion, must be minutely weighed in the light of the character of the personage, and such motives must never lead to consequences for which they cannot in the strictest truth be held responsible. So, too, Diderot had said:

Il arrive quelquefois à l'ordre naturel des choses, d'enchaîner des incidents extraordinaires. C'est le même ordre qui distingue le merveilleux du miraculeux. Les cas rares sont merveilleux; les cas naturellement impossibles sont miraculeux: l'art dramatique rejette les miracles.[2]

It is the function of the theatre, Lessing affirms (II, 8), to be the school of the moral world.[3]

The test of consistency in character-drawing must be, of course, what the characters say. But dramatists may put into the mouths of their tragic characters maxims or moral sentiments which are too often the 'langweiligen Ausbeugungen eines verlegenen Dichters' (II, 96).[4] These sentiments must in any case correspond (123) with the character of the speaker. They need not have the stamp of absolute truth; it is enough if they are poetically true. Lessing sees that a certain limit must be set to the naturalness of dramatic characters; their poetic reality can only approximate to absolute truth. He takes umbrage (108) at the line in Cronegk's play: 'Der Himmel kann verzeihn, allein ein Priester nicht'—which presumably the poet regarded as natural and consistent with the character of Ismenor—on the ground that, although Ismenor may be a cruel priest, all priests are not Ismenors (137). He objects to the utterance of such wrong sentiments from the stage. Is it surprising, he asks (146), that there should in return be priests who attack the theatre as 'die grade Heerstrasse zur Hölle!'[5]

---

[1] Du Bos argues on somewhat similar lines in discussing 'la vraisemblance en Poësie': '...Je n'entends pas ici par impossible ce qui est au-dessus des forces humaines, mais ce qui paroît impossible, même en se prétant à toutes les suppositions que le Poëte sçauroit faire' (*Refléxions, ed. cit.* i, p. 228).

[2] *Œuvres complètes, ed. cit.* vii, p. 329 (Lessing's translation, *ed. cit.* ii, p. 293).

[3] But see also above, pp. 370 ff.

[4] Cp. D'Aubignac, *Pratique du Théâtre*, iv, chap. v (*ed. cit.* i, p. 295): 'Premierement, ces Maximes generales, ou Lieux-communs, doivent être attachées au Sujet, et appliquées par plusieurs circonstances aux Personnages et aux affaires du Theatre; en sorte qu'il semble que celui qui parle, ait plus presens à l'esprit les interêts du Theatre, que ces belles veritez.'

[5] There appeared in London in 1767 an anonymous pamphlet of 43 pp., entitled *The Stage the High Road to Hell*, which was noticed in the *Monthly Review*, xxxvi (1767),

The other essential of dramatic characters mentioned by Lessing in St. XXXIV is 'Absicht', or purpose. As purposive action (100) distinguishes man from other living creatures, so to create and imitate with purpose distinguishes the writer of genius from the minor verse-writer.. In his *Betrachtungen über die Quellen und Verbindungen* Mendelssohn had said: 'Das Genie erfordert eine Vollkommenheit aller Seelenkräfte, und eine Übereinstimmung derselben zu einem einzigen Endzwecke.'[1] Lessing's conception of 'Absicht' here does not, however, correspond with the wider aesthetic conception of Mendelssohn's 'Endzweck', but solely with moral purpose, that is, the inculcation of love for the good and the proper, and a hatred for the bad and the ridiculous.[2]

THE HERO OF TRAGEDY

Lessing devotes considerable space to discussion of the kind of hero suitable for tragedy. The matter arises in St. LXXIV, in connexion with Weisse's *Richard III*, a play which offends seriously against the Aristotelian canon that the hero of tragedy must neither be a wholly virtuous man nor a complete villain. As we have seen, this led Lessing to define, as a preliminary step, the meaning of ἔλεος and φόβος. In St. LXXIX he returns to *Richard III* and condemns in his most vigorous and trenchant manner the introduction into tragedy of an unmitigatedly bad character. The fullest discussion of the character of the tragic hero, is, however, reserved for St. LXXXII and LXXXIII, where it resolves itself into a polemic against Corneille.

Lessing recalls (LXXXII, 1) Aristotle's statement in chapter xiii of his *Poetics* that an entirely good man cannot be allowed to end unhappily in tragedy without any fault of his own, for this would be odious to us. The word used is μιαρόν, which Lessing translates 'grässlich' and Curtius by the words 'würde Abscheu erwecken'. Corneille had translated it 'tout à fait injuste', adding: 'Quelques interprètes poussent la force de ce mot grec μιαρόν, qu'il fait servir

---

p. 326; xxxvii (1767), p. 64. In reviewing the *Neue Lustspiele* of J. L. Schlosser, who was a clergyman, a critic in the *Deutsche Bibliothek*, ii (vii), 1768, p. 391—possibly remembering this passage of Lessing's—wrote: 'Gewiss, nicht wenig Muth wird dazu erfordert, einen Weg zu betreten, den die meisten Hoch- und Wohlerwürdigen Confratres für die HEERSTRASSE ZUR HÖLLE ausschrein.'

[1] *Bibliothek der schönen Wissenschaften*, i (ii), 1757, p. 238. This essay was published later as *Abhandlung über die Hauptgrundsätze der schönen Wissenschaften und Künste*. The above passage is quoted by L. Goldstein, *op. cit.* p. 15.

[2] Cp. also above, pp. 370 ff.

d'épithète à cet événement, jusqu'à le rendre par celui d'*abominable*.'[1] Lessing's criticism of Corneille's interpretation of μιαρόν savours somewhat of hair-splitting. Aristotle had said (25) that a misfortune of this kind is odious or abominable in its very nature, and consequently untragic; while Corneille argues that it is only untragic in so far as it may appear to us to be abominable; that it is consequently legitimate to introduce such a motive into tragedy if the poet is able to avoid giving the beholder the impression that it is abominable.

Lessing's criticism that Corneille is merely twisting Aristotle's doctrine to justify his own tragedies (32) is, however, entirely pertinent. Corneille says in his *Discours de la Tragédie*:

Il ne veut point qu'un homme tout à fait innocent tombe dans l'infortune, parce que, cela étant abominable, il excite plus d'indignation contre celui qui le persécute que de pitié pour son malheur; il ne veut pas non plus qu'un très-méchant y tombe, parce qu'il ne peut donner de pitié par un malheur qu'il mérite, ni en faire craindre un pareil à des spectateurs qui ne lui ressemblent pas; mais quand ces deux raisons cessent, en sorte qu'un homme de bien qui souffre excite plus de pitié pour lui que d'indignation contre celui qui le fait souffrir, ou que la punition d'un grand crime peut corriger en nous quelque imperfection qui a du rapport avec lui, j'estime qu'il ne faut point faire de difficulté d'exposer sur la scène des hommes très-vertueux ou très-méchants dans le malheur. En voici deux ou trois manières, que peut-être Aristote n'a su prévoir, parce qu'on n'en voyait pas d'exemples sur les théâtres de son temps.

La première est, quand un homme très-vertueux est persécuté par un très-méchant, et qu'il échappe du péril où le méchant demeure enveloppé, comme dans *Rodogune* et dans *Héraclius*, qu'on n'auroit pu souffrir si Antiochus et Rodogune eussent péri dans la première, et Héraclius, Pulchérie et Martian dans l'autre, et que Cléopatre et Phocas y eussent triomphé. Leur malheur y donne une pitié qui n'est point étouffée par l'aversion qu'on a pour ceux qui les tyrannisent, parce qu'on espère toujours que quelque heureuse révolution les empêchera de succomber....[2]

To this Lessing replies (56) that whereas Corneille pretended that Aristotle had forgotten this kind of plot (of which the *Odyssey* is an example), in point of fact he regarded it as more suitable for comedy than for tragedy. The passage which he has in mind is the following:

After this comes the construction of Plot which some rank first, one with a double story (like the *Odyssey*) and an opposite issue for the good and the bad personages. It is ranked as first only through the weakness of the

---

[1] *Discours de la Tragédie, Œuvres, ed. cit.* i, pp. 55 f.
[2] *Œuvres, ed. cit.* i, pp. 63 f. Cp. the version in the *Beyträge*, ii, pp. 224 f.

audiences; the poets merely follow their public, writing as its wishes dictate. But the pleasure here is not that of Tragedy. It belongs rather to Comedy, where the bitterest enemies in the piece (e.g., Orestes and Aegisthus) walk off good friends at the end, with no slaying of any one by any one.[1]

Lessing then quotes (67) Corneille's description of the second 'manière', which in the original is as follows:

Il peut arriver d'ailleurs qu'un homme très-vertueux soit persécuté, et périsse même par les ordres d'un autre, qui ne soit pas assez méchant pour attirer trop d'indignation sur lui, et qui montre plus de foiblesse que de crime dans la persécution qu'il lui fait. Si Félix fait périr son gendre Polyeucte, ce n'est pas par cette haine enragée contre les chrétiens, qui nous le rendroit exécrable, mais seulement par une lâche timidité, qui n'ose le sauver en présence de Sévère, dont il craint la haine et la vengeance après les mépris qu'il en a faits durant son peu de fortune. On prend bien quelque aversion pour lui, on désapprouve sa manière d'agir; mais cette aversion ne l'emporte pas sur la pitié qu'on a de Polyeucte, et n'empêche pas que sa conversion miraculeuse, à la fin de la pièce, ne le réconcilie pleinement avec l'auditoire.[2]

Again, Aristotle had said in the same chapter:

The second [form of plot—i.e., the passing of a bad man from misery to happiness] is the most untragic that can be; it has no one of the requisites of Tragedy; it does not appeal either to the human feeling in us, or to our pity, or to our fears.[3]

Here Corneille's comment is:

Le malheur d'un homme fort méchant n'excite ni pitié, ni crainte, parce qu'il n'est pas digne de la première, et que les spectateurs ne sont pas méchants comme lui pour concevoir l'autre à la vue de sa punition; mais il seroit à propos de mettre quelque distinction entre les crimes. Il en est dont les honnêtes gens sont capables par une violence de passion, dont le mauvais succès peut faire effet dans l'âme de l'auditeur. Un honnête homme ne va pas voler au coin d'un bois, ni faire un assassinat de sang-froid; mais s'il est bien amoureux, il peut faire une supercherie à son rival, il peut s'emporter de colère et tuer dans un premier mouvement, et l'ambition le peut engager dans un crime ou dans une action blâmable. Il est peu de mères qui voulussent assassiner ou empoisonner leurs enfants de peur de leur rendre leur bien, comme Cléopatre dans *Rodogune*; mais il en est assez qui prennent goût à en jouir, et ne s'en dessaisissent qu'à regret et le plus tard qu'il leur est possible. Bien qu'elles ne soient pas

---

[1] Chap. xiii, 1453a; Bywater, *ed. cit.* p. 37.
[2] *Œuvres, ed. cit.* i, p. 64; cp. *Beyträge*, ii, pp. 225 f.
[3] Bywater, *ed. cit.* p. 35.

capables d'une action si noire et si dénaturée que celle de cette reine de Syrie, elles ont en elles quelque teinture du principe qui l'y porta, et la vue de la juste punition qu'elle en reçoit leur peut faire craindre, non pas un pareil malheur, mais une infortune proportionnée à ce qu'elles sont capables de commettre. Il en est ainsi de quelques autres crimes qui ne sont pas de la portée de nos auditeurs.[1]

Lessing disposes of the fallacy of Corneille's argument (111) by recalling his proof that fear and pity in tragedy are inseparable.

Corneille would justify the introduction of wholly evil personages as the chief characters in tragedy, not merely as subsidiary and unimportant ones. Du Bos, on the other hand, in his chapter 'Des personnages de Scélérats qu'on peut introduire dans les Tragédies', writes:

Il ne faut point encore que le principal intérêt de la piéce tombe sur les personnages de scélérats. Le personnage d'un scélérat ne doit point être capable d'intéresser par lui-même; ainsi le spectateur ne sçauroit prendre part à ses aventures, qu'autant que ces aventures seront les incidens d'un événement où des personnages d'un autre caractere auront un grand intérêt. Qui fait une grande attention à la mort de Narcisse dans Britannicus?[2]

To this Lessing adds that if so little importance is attached to such subsidiary characters, the less they are introduced the better.

The foremost quality which Aristotle demands of the characters of tragedy (chap. xv) is that they should be 'good' ($\chi\rho\eta\sigma\tau\acute{a}$). Again Corneille is obliged to put an 'accommodating' interpretation on this statement if his own tragedies are not to be condemned as transgressing the Aristotelian canon. Lessing quotes his argument (LXXXIII, 3):

Je ne puis comprendre comment on a voulu entendre par ce mot de bonnes, qu'il faut qu'elles soient vertueuses. La plupart des poëmes, tant anciens que modernes, demeureroient en un pitoyable état, si l'on en retranchoit tout ce qui s'y rencontre de personnages méchants, ou vicieux, ou tachés de quelque foiblesse qui s'accorde mal avec la vertu.... Il faut donc trouver une bonté compatible avec ces sortes de mœurs; et s'il m'est permis de dire mes conjectures sur ce qu'Aristote nous demande par là, je crois que c'est le caractère brillant et élevé d'une habitude vertueuse ou criminelle, selon qu'elle est propre et convenable à la personne qu'on introduit. Cléopatre, dans *Rodogune*, est très-méchante; il n'y a point de parricide qui lui fasse horreur, pourvu qu'il la puisse conserver sur un trône qu'elle préfère à toutes choses, tant son attachement à la domination

---

[1] *Œuvres, ed. cit.* i, pp. 59 f.; cp. *Beyträge*, ii, pp. 220 f.

[2] *Réflexions critiques sur la Poësie et sur la Peinture*, 6th ed. Paris, 1755, i, p. 112.

est violent; mais tous ses crimes sont accompagnés d'une grandeur d'âme qui a quelque chose de si haut, qu'en même temps qu'on déteste ses actions, on admire la source dont elles partent. J'ose dire la même chose du *Menteur*. Il est hors de doute que c'est une habitude vicieuse que de mentir; mais il débite ses menteries avec une telle présence d'esprit et tant de vivacité, que cette imperfection a bonne grâce en sa personne, et fait confesser aux spectateurs que le talent de mentir ainsi est un vice dont les sots ne sont point capables.[1]

Lessing, who maintains that Aristotle's word can only imply 'moral goodness' (13), holds that Corneille's interpretation will only lead to the negation of all truth, illusion and moral value in tragedy; with his own firm conviction of the moral purpose of tragic drama, he emphasises particularly this evil effect of Corneille's misinterpretation. As he admits (60), Corneille had already been attacked on this vulnerable point. Dacier in his anti-Cornelian criticism had seized upon it, though on different grounds; indeed, Lessing's indebtedness to Dacier here is obvious. In his note to the passage in Aristotle, Dacier says:

Dans tout ce Livre il n'y a rien de plus clairement expliqué que cette premiere condition des mœurs, *qu'elles soient bonnes*. Cependant on s'y est trompé, car on a crû qu'Aristote veut qu'elles soient vertueuses. M. Corneille a solidement réfuté cette explication, qui condamneroit également tous les Poëmes anciens, tant les Poëmes Epiques que les Tragiques, où l'on voit beaucoup de personnages vicieux, et il a fort bien vû qu'il falloit chercher une bonté qui fût compatible avec les mœurs moralement mauvaises, et avec celles qui sont moralement bonnes; mais c'est cela même qu'il n'a pû trouver, l'explication qu'il donne à ces paroles d'Aristote, n'étant pas meilleure que l'autre; *Pour moy*, dit il, *je croy que c'est le caractére brillant et élevé d'une habitude vertueuse ou criminelle, selon qu'elle est propre et convenable à la personne qu'on introduit*; mais outre que cette explication condamneroit encore beaucoup de caractéres que les anciens Poëtes ont faits, et qui n'ont ny cette grandeur d'ame, ny cette élevation que M. Corneille demande, il est certain que cette qualité ne conviendroit pas toûjours avec les deux autres, qui sont la ressemblance et la convenance....Ce qu'Aristote dit, *que les mœurs doivent être bonnes*, c'est ce qu'Horace traduit, *notandi sunt tibi mores*, comme je l'ay expliqué, c'est-à-dire, *qu'il faut que les mœurs soient bien marquées*, soit qu'on introduise un personnage moralement vicieux, ou un personnage moralement bon....L'Auteur du Traité du Poëme Epique a admirablement traité toute cette matiere, on ne peut rien voir de plus judicieux, que tout ce qu'il en a écrit, aussi a-t-il toûjours pris Aristote pour guide.[2]

---

[1] *Discours du poème dramatique, Œuvres, ed. cit.* i, pp. 31 f.; cp. *Beyträge*, i, pp. 74 f.
[2] *Poétique d'Aristote, ed. cit.* pp. 245 f.

The views of Le Bossu to which Dacier refers will be found in chapters iv–vi of the fourth book of his *Traité du Poème épique* (Paris, 1675). Here the critic insists on a distinction between 'bonté morale' and 'bonté poétique', and considers the mark of poetic goodness to be that 'les mœurs [soient] bien exprimées'.[1] The portrait of a vicious man can equally well show this poetic goodness: 'Elle ne consiste que dans l'addresse du Poëte à bien faire connoître les inclinations de ceux qu'il fait parler, et qu'il fait agir dans son Poëme.'[2] Brumoy, in his *Discours sur l'origine de la Tragédie*, mentions two interpretations of Aristotle's statement: that goodness signifies a 'probité commune' (the quality in a character which lays claim to our sympathy), or—and here he observes that the passage is ambiguous—that 'les mœurs soient bien marquées' (Dacier's phrase).[3] Lessing's German predecessor Curtius accepts the view expressed by Corneille, Dacier and Le Bossu that Aristotle cannot have meant moral goodness; and he mentions Vossius and Calepio as upholders of a contrary opinion.[4] It has already been seen that Lessing had read Calepio's *Paragone* with sympathetic interest, and knew Bodmer's *Critische Briefe*, and he may again have been influenced by Calepio here;[5] but Batteux had put the matter cogently enough. After condemning Corneille's pronouncement, Batteux proceeds:

D'autres enfin pensent que la bonté dont il s'agit ici est une bonté légale, c'est-à-dire, la conformité des mœurs avec la loi naturelle, qui commande la vertu et proscrit le vice. Le terme d'Aristote semble signifier particulierement cette espèce de bonté. C'est une certaine droiture d'ame, qui porte l'homme à l'équité, et à la bienveillance: mais droiture qui peut se rencontrer avec des fautes considérables, même avec des crimes, pourvû que ce soit des crimes où l'on tombe par imprudence, par foiblesse, par emportement. Il n'y a pas un héros d'Homère qui soit méchant ou vicieux par caractère ou par principe. Cependant il n'y en a pas un qui n'ait quelque défaut.... Qu'en général les personnages poëtiques soient bons, mais d'une bonté qui souffre quelque écart ou quelque excès passager, dans le genre de la vertu qui fait la base des mœurs.[6]

---

[1] *Traité du Poëme épique*, Paris, 1675, ii, pp. 32, 35.

[2] *Ibid.* ii, p. 35.

[3] *Théâtre des Grecs*, ed. cit. i, p. lxxxvi.

[4] *Aristoteles Dichtkunst*, ed. cit. p. 219. Cp. also Vossius, *Poeticarum Institutionum libri tres*, 1, cap. v, § 3, ed. cit. i, pp. 52 f.

[5] See above, p. 365; and cp. Calepio, *Paragone*, cap. 1, 2 (*ed. cit.* pp. 9 ff.); Bodmer, *Critische Briefe*, Zürich, 1746, p. 48.

[6] *Principes de la littérature*, ed. cit. ii, pp. 275 f., 277 f.

Another critic of Aristotle with whose work Lessing was familiar, Marmontel, had stated the position perhaps still more acceptably. Marmontel speaks of 'une bonté morale, c'est-à-dire, un fond de bonté naturelle qui perce à travers les erreurs, les foiblesses, les passions'.[1] And he emphasises the fact that Aristotle is only concerned with the chief character in the drama—'le personnage intéressant'. He would have him endowed with a mixture of virtues and vices; he wished him to be unfortunate by reason of a fault which any of us might commit; but in order to accommodate his theory to the practice of the Greek theatre he imagined the solution—which is no true solution—of an involuntary fault.[2]

It is to be regretted that at this point Lessing abruptly breaks off his discussion (LXXXIII, 74), presumably reserving a statement of his considered views for the commentary on Aristotle which he hoped to write. He himself no doubt felt that his 'schlechterdings eine moralische Güte' could not stand without some more weighty support; and his hint that the justification must depend on the nature of the προαίρεσις or intention is vague and obscure. He may have hoped for more light on this point after he had made a thorough study of the Aristotelian *Ethics* and *Rhetoric*.

'CHRISTIAN' TRAGEDY

If Weisse's *Richard III*, in Lessing's view, sinned against Aristotle's precepts by introducing a hero who was unmitigatedly bad, Corneille with his martyr-tragedy *Polyeucte* sinned in the opposite direction by writing a tragedy with a wholly blameless hero. Lessing is led to speak of *Polyeucte* at the very beginning of the *Dramaturgie* (II, 35), since the first play of the repertory, *Olint und Sophronia*, was a 'Christian tragedy' of the same class. Beyond pointing out that the Christian with his 'tranquil placidity' and his 'unchangeable meekness' is not well adapted to the purpose of tragedy—the purification of passions by passions—Lessing has nothing to say here of the theoretical aspects of this type of play.[3] He merely recommends the

---

[1] *Poétique Françoise*, ed. cit. ii, p. 179.

[2] Marmontel, *Poétique Françoise*, ed. cit. ii, p. 181: 'Ce personnage étoit le seul qu'il eût en vûe; et en effet, voulant qu'il fût malheureux par une faute involontaire, il n'avoit pas besoin de lui opposer des méchans: les dieux et les destins en tenoient lieu dans les sujets conduits par la fatalité.'

[3] See above, pp. 365 ff., for Lessing's earlier views on 'admiration' as a tragic effect.

dramatist to avoid the martyrs who figure in Christian tragedies, or, if he cannot avoid them altogether, to see that the motives which lead them to seek death are of the strongest; to the theatre he offers the advice (II, 52): 'Better leave all the Christian tragedies that have so far been written unperformed.' Similarly, Curtius—who, however, defended Corneille—recognised the unsuitability of martyrs as subjects for modern tragedies (*ed. cit.* pp. 187 f.):

...die christlichen Märtyrer können also, überhaupt betrachtet, ohngeachtet der Regel des Aristoteles, Vorwürfe der Tragödie seyn, wenn nicht einige andere Betrachtungen, in Ansehung der Sitten, und Denkungsart des itzigen Jahrhunderts, uns anriethen, dieselbe zwar nicht von der Bühne zu verbannen, aber doch auch nicht oft aufzuführen.

The admissibility of martyr tragedies was a frequent theme of discussion among the critics of the time. Saint-Évremond, for instance, in his essay *De la Tragédie ancienne et moderne* (1672), had already put the matter in a form which suggests Lessing's criticism:

L'esprit de nôtre Religion est directement opposé à celui de la Tragédie. L'humilité et la patience de nos Saints sont trop contraires aux vertus des Heros que demande le Théatre. Quel zele, quelle force, le Ciel n'inspire-t-il pas à Néarque et à Polyeucte; et que ne font pas ces nouveaux Chrétiens pour répondre à ces heureuses inspirations?...Polyeucte a plus d'envie de mourir pour Dieu, que les autres hommes n'en ont de vivre pour eux. Néanmoins ce qui eût fait un beau Sermon, faisoit une misérable Tragédie, si les entretiens de Pauline et de Sévère, animés d'autres sentimens et d'autres passions, n'eussent conservé à l'Auteur la réputation que les Vertus Chrétiennes de nos Martyrs lui eussent ôtée. Le Théatre perd tout son agrément dans la représentation des choses saintes, et les choses saintes perdent beaucoup de la religieuse opinion qu'on leur doit, quand on les représente sur le Théatre.[1]

Possibly Lessing had this passage in mind, but it is hardly likely.[2] A. G. Kästner, again, had published, in Schwabe's *Belustigungen des Verstandes und des Witzes* for August, 1742,[3] *Gedanken über die christlichen Tragödien*: but this essay hardly touches upon the particular points in which Lessing is interested. Mendelssohn, on the other hand, repeatedly expressed, with reference to Shaftesbury, his objection to 'perfect characters'. He was inclined, however, to make one

---

[1] *Œuvres*, Amsterdam, 1739, iii, pp. 175 f.
[2] Saint-Évremond is mentioned by Lessing in St. LXXX (53) as author of the comedies *Sir Politick Would-be* and *Les Opéra*, but only in a quotation from Voltaire.
[3] 2nd ed. Leipzig, 1744, pp. 116 ff.

exception: 'Ich weiss nur einen Fall, da die vollkommenen Charaktere auf der Bühne erträglich sind; dieser ist: wenn die tugendhaften Personen unglücklich werden, wenn sie durch ihre Tugend selbst einen Raub des Neides und der Verfolgung abgeben, und mit ihrem Schicksale in einem beständigen Kampfe leben müssen. Alsdann erregen sie unser Mitleid; und schlagen desto tiefere Wunden in unser Gemüth, je mehr Liebe, Hochachtung und Bewunderung sie sich durch ihre moralische Vollkommenheit erworben. Sobald der Tugendhafte aber das Unglück überkommt, wird er gleichgültig.'[1] But if outside suggestion is to be sought for Lessing's criticism of the 'Christian' hero of tragedy, I do not think that we need look beyond Dacier. After justifying Aristotle in his exclusion from tragedy of the misfortunes of a very virtuous man, he proceeds—the passage is in his first note to Aristotle's thirteenth chapter:

M. Corneille voyant que cette maxime bannit les Martyrs du Theatre, cherche des autoritez pour défendre son Polyeucte, par d'autres endroits que par ses grands succez, et il trouve enfin un Minturnus qui examine dans son Traité du Poëte, Si la Passion de Jesus-Christ et les Martyres des Saints, doivent être exclus du Theatre, à cause de leur vertu, et qui décide en sa faveur.... Le succez justifie assez le Poëte; mais je ne sçay s'il seroit aisé de justifier ce succez. Je ne parle icy que du sujet dont peu de gens jugent, car d'ailleurs c'est peut-être la piece de M. Corneille la mieux conduite, elle est pleine de beaux sentimens et a de parfaitement beaux caractéres, où les mœurs sont marquées admirablement. Il n'y a personne qui ne s'interesse pour Pauline et pour Severe, et qui ne soit touché de leur malheur, et c'est ce qui fait réussir la piece; mais ce sujet n'est nullement propre au Theatre, qui ne doit exposer ny le bonheur ny le malheur d'un homme tres vertueux. De quelque maniére qu'on regarde le martyre, ou comme un mal ou comme un bien, il ne peut exciter, ny la pitié ny la crainte, et par consequent il ne purgera pas les passions, ce qui est l'unique but de la Tragedie, comme on l'a déja vû. Cette regle d'Aristote fait encore le procez à beaucoup d'autres pieces qui n'ont pas laissé de plaire, mais elles ont plû par d'autres endroits que par le sujet, et par des endroits qui étant conformes aux regles, ont toute la beauté qu'ils peuvent avoir.[2]

It might be added that Lessing had already expressed himself unequivocally on *Polyeucte* in his letter to Mendelssohn of December 18, 1756:[3]

In eben dem Verhältnisse, in welchem die Bewunderung auf der einen Seite zunimmt, nimmt das Mitleiden auf der andern ab. Aus diesem

---

[1] *Gesammelte Schriften, ed. cit.* iv, 2, p. 146; cp. also iv, 1, pp. 496, 579 ff. and iv, 2, pp. 237 f. [2] *Poétique d'Aristote, ed. cit.* p. 186.
[3] *Schriften,* xvii, pp. 81 f.; Petsch, *op. cit.* p. 83.

Grunde halte ich den Polyeukt des Corneille für tadelhaft; ob er gleich wegen ganz anderer Schönheiten niemals aufhören wird zu gefallen. Polyeukt strebt ein Märtyrer zu werden; er sehnet sich nach Tod und Martern; er betrachtet sie als den ersten Schritt in ein überschwenglich seliges Leben; ich bewundere den frommen Enthusiasten, aber ich müsste befürchten, seinen Geist in dem Schoosse der ewigen Glückseligkeit zu erzürnen, wenn ich Mitleid mit ihm haben wollte.

THE HARLEQUIN

The formal expulsion of the Harlequin from German tragedy in 1737 by Karoline Neuber 'sub Auspiciis Sr. Magnificenz, des Herrn Prof. Gottscheds' (XVIII, 22) was an incident of considerable importance in the rise of the German theatre to literary recognition.[1] But Lessing points out that it was something of an exaggeration to say that the Harlequin had been 'banished'; he only appeared (26) under a new name as 'Hännschen' or 'Peter'.[2] In point of fact, Karoline Neuber's

[1] See above, pp. 7 f.

[2] Two comedies by Marivaux in the Hamburg repertory of Lessing's time, *Die falschen Vertraulichkeiten*—which gives occasion for the present discussion—and *Der unvermuthete Ausgang*, have a 'Peter' in the German versions; a servant of this name also appears in Destouches' *Gespenst mit der Trommel* and in Lessing's own *Die alte Jungfer* (cp. Petersen, *ed. cit.* p. 199). In the German translations of Delisle's *Le Faucon* and *Timon* (XVIII, 43), which had been in Schönemann's repertory since 1747 and were printed in his *Schaubühne* (vols. ii and iii; see H. Devrient, *op. cit.* pp. 128 f.), the Harlequin appears. For references to these two plays cp. Lessing's *Theatralische Bibliothek* (*Schriften*, vi, p. 334; cp. also v, p. 151). 'Hännschen' (XVIII, 30) is the name of 'Lisanders Bedienter' in the version of L'Affichard's *La Famille*, which was played on the same evening as *Die falschen Vertraulichkeiten*. F. L. Schröder as a young man excelled in rôles of this kind: '...als Schauspieler gefiel Schröder ungemein, und ward, nach dem Bedienten des Bramarbas... überall Peter genannt' (Meyer, *op. cit.* i, p. 116). In the list of Schröder's rôles, 'Peter' occurs in Holberg's *Bramarbas* and in Löwen's *Der Liebhaber von Ohngefähr*; 'Johann' (or 'Hans') in Lessing's *Freygeist*, Weisse's *Die Poeten nach der Mode* and *Die Haushälterinn*, Marivaux' *Der Bauer mit der Erbschaft*, Schlegel's *Der Geheimnissvolle*, as well as in other comedies of later date (cp. Meyer, *op. cit.* ii, 2, pp. 139 ff.). Cp. also an article by Mylius, *Von der nöthigen Wahrscheinlichkeit bey Vorstellung der Schauspiele* in Gottsched's *Beyträge zur critischen Historie der deutschen Sprache, Poesie und Beredsamkeit*, St. xxx (1743), pp. 312 f. 'Was soll ich aber von dem in etlichen Schauspielen vorkommenden Peter, oder dem sogenannten Crispin sagen? Was sind diese doch für Geschöpfe? Und in welcher möglichen Welt gehören sie zu Hause? Sie sollen Diener vorstellen: aber welcher Herr ist so thöricht, dass er seinen Diener eine solche närrische Librey giebt? Und was sind die zwo hölzernen Degen, die Peter in der Tasche führt, für unwahrscheinliche Dinge? In Wahrheit, so abgeschmackt jemals Harlekin und Skaramutz gewesen, so ungereimt sind auch Peter und Crispin.' Cp. also P. Schlenther, *Frau Gottsched und die bürgerliche Komödie*, Berlin, 1886, pp. 110 f.

aim had been rather to reform him, to free him from his licentious ribaldry and incongruous impromptu jesting.[1] In his earlier attacks on Gottsched Lessing had stigmatised this reform as retrograde: 'Er liess den Harlequin feyerlich vom Theater vertreiben, welches selbst die grösste Harlequinade war, die jemals gespielt worden.'[2] But this is what Gottsched had to say in the *Critische Dichtkunst* about Harlequin:

Die Kleidungen der Personen müssen nach ihrem Character und Stande eingerichtet seyn: Nur der Harlekin hat hier, ich weis nicht warum, eine Ausnahme. Er soll zuweilen einen Herrendiener bedeuten: Allein, welcher Herr würde sich nicht schämen, seinem Kerle eine so buntscheckigte Lieberey zu geben? Der Scapin hat eine spanische Tracht; und das kann man in einem spanischen Stücke schon gelten lassen; allein bey uns schickt sichs nicht. Den Scaramutz, Pantalon, Anselmo, Doctor und Capitain, Pierrot und Mezetin, und wie die närrischen Personen der italienischen Comödien mehr heissen, können wir auch entbehren. Denn warum soll man immer bey einerley Personen bleiben? Die Namen dörfen auch in einer Comödie nicht aus der Historie genommen werden. So bald die Personen neue Charactere haben, müssen sie auch neue Namen bekommen: Um die Verwirrung zu vermeiden, die sonst bey dem Zuschauer vieler Comödien entstehen könnte.[3]

When Lessing suggests that the parasite of ancient drama was only a Harlequin under another name (52), he is repeating an idea which had been expressed in the *Critik über die Gefangnen des Plautus*,[4] the immediate source being probably the preface to Krüger's translation of Marivaux: 'Wer mir aber diese Art der Arlequine aus dem Grunde verwirft, weil Plautus und Terentius ihre Sosias nicht Arlequins genannt haben...der wird es mir nicht verargen, wenn ich ihn auf folgende Art einem Geizhalse an die Seite setze.'[5] But Lessing's criticism was in substance prompted, as he implies (58), by Justus Möser's little book: *Harlekin, oder Vertheidigung des Groteske-Komischen*,

---

[1] See above, pp. 7 f.; and cp. F. J. von Reden-Esbeck, *Caroline Neuber*, Leipzig, 1881, p. 211; W. Creizenach, *Zur Entstehungsgeschichte des neuern Lustspiels*, Halle, 1879, pp. 18 ff.; G. Waniek, *Gottsched und die deutsche Litteratur seiner Zeit*, Leipzig, 1897, pp. 341 ff., and Petersen's note, *ed. cit.* p. 199.

[2] *Litteraturbriefe*, No. xvii, February 16, 1759; *Schriften*, viii, p. 42.

[3] *Critische Dichtkunst*, ed. of 1737, pp. 708 f.

[4] *Beyträge*, iv, p. 588.

[5] *Sammlung einiger Lustspiele aus dem Französischen des Herrn von Marivaux übersetzt.* Hanover, 1747–49, i, pp. 3–4. This quotation was transcribed by the kindness of the authorities of the Universitäts-Bibliothek, Marburg, which possesses a copy of the translation. Cp. also W. Wittekindt, *J. C. Krüger*, Berlin, 1898, pp. 105 ff. (where the general argument of the Preface is summarised).

published in 1761.[1] The following extracts from this work are elucidatory for Lessing's text:

Ich [Harlekin] schmeichle mir, in der besten komischen Welt ein nothwendiger und angenehmer Bürger zu seyn; und hoffentlich wird man mich auch nicht aus einer andern Welt verbannen, worin so viele Thoren zum grössten Dienst der Weisen geduldet....An dem Titel Komödie, ist mir ohnedem wenig gelegen....Meine komischen Vorstellungen mögen künftig immer Harlekinaden heissen, und meinen Namen, so wie ehemaals eine Pflanzstadt ihren Stifter, verewigen. Vielleicht ist es mir auch weit rühmlicher, ein eignes Thier in meiner Art zu bleiben, als wie der Löwe zum Katzengeschlecht gezählt zu werden. Diese meine aufrichtige und jedem Redner gegen seine...kritische Obrigkeit wohlanständige Demuth erlaubet mir aber nicht, denen zu schmeicheln, welche die komischen Vorstellungen blos auf die eigentliche Komödie und höchstens auf das rührende oder sogenannte weinerliche Lustspiel einschränken wollen. Die Sphäre des menschlichen Vergnügens lässt sich noch immer erweitern.... Wenn ich also auch gleich kein Redner für meine eigne Sache wäre: so würde mich dennoch ein blosses warum nicht? womit Fontenelle so viele unentdeckte Welten bevölkert, von der Möglichkeit mehrerer komischen Arten überzeugen. Ich will hier nicht untersuchen, ob die fürchterlichen Alten eine andre Art, als die Terenzische, gekannt haben. Sonst liesse sich vielleicht aus einigen Scenen des Aristophanes und Plautus zeigen, dass diese grossen Meister, eben wie Terenz und Moliere, von meinen Vorfahren manche schöne Stellung geborgt, und solche mit ihren geschickten Pinseln originalisirt hätten. Vernünftige Leser werden mir ohnedem glauben, dass den Satyren, diesen ersten Schauspielern der Griechen, der Bocksfuss nicht edler, als mir mein buntschäckigtes Kleid gestanden, wozu alle Stände in der Welt, sowohl geist- als weltliche, ihre Läppchen hergegeben haben.[2]

It may be recalled that in the review of Möser's book which appeared in 1761 in the *Litteraturbriefe*, the following passage occurs:

Und nun; ehe sie es sich versehen, giebt Harlekin Hr. Lessingen einen Schlag, tritt gleich darauf vor ihn hin, und macht ihm eine tiefe Verbeugung. „Herrr Lessing, spricht er, ein Mann, der Einsicht genug besitzet, um dermaleins mein Lobredner zu werden, würde mir vielleicht

---

[1] J. Möser, *Sämmtliche Werke*, herausg. von B. R. Abeken, Berlin, 1842–43, ix, pp. 63 ff. The little book on the Harlequin had been reviewed in the *Bibliothek der schönen Wissenschaften*, vii (ii), 1762, pp. 334 ff., and in the *Litteraturbriefe*, Nos. cciv–ccvi, December 17–31, 1761, *ed. cit.* xii, pp. 331 ff.; also in the French *Journal encyclopédique*, vii, October 15, 1762, pp. 47 ff.

[2] *Harlekin, oder Vertheidigung des Groteske-Komischen*, 2nd ed. Bremen, 1777, pp. 13 ff.

hier einwenden, dass die Übertreibung der Gestalten ein sicheres Mittel
sey, seinen Endzweck zu verfehlen, indem die Zuschauer dadurch ver-
führet würden, zu glauben, dass sie weit über das ausschweifende lächerliche der Thorheit erhaben wären. Allein meine gelehrten Feinde urtheilen hier abermal nach ihrer gebesserten Empfindung, und denken
nicht, dass mancher einen Geruch kaum empfinde, welcher dem andern
schon die schwersten Kopfschmertzen verursachet. Sie erwägen nicht,
dass es hinter ihnen noch ansehnliche Classen von Thoren gebe, für deren
Empfindungen sie nicht bürgen können." Deucht Ihnen nicht, dass
Harlekin Recht habe?[1]

[1] *Litteraturbriefe*, No. ccv, December 24, 1761, *ed. cit.* xii, pp. 345 f. The quotation
is from *Harlekin, oder Vertheidigung des Groteske-Komischen, ed. cit.* pp. 46 f. In this
(revised) edition of 1777 Möser added the following footnote to this passage:
'Herr Lessing hat mich in seiner Dramaturgie aufgefodert, ihm diese Vermuthung
zu erweisen. Ich kann aber weiter nichts sagen, als dass ich etwas, das mich zu
dieser Vermuthung berechtigte, in den von ihm mit beförderten Beyträgen zur
Historie und Aufnahme des Theaters, wovon im Jahr 1750. vier Stück zum
Vorschein kamen, gelesen zu haben glaubte; beym Nachschlagen finde ich aber,
dass ich mich geirret habe.'

CHAPTER XV

IMITATION AND ILLUSION

IMITATION

Fundamental for the aesthetics of the eighteenth century was the dictum that art is an 'imitation' of reality. This was the 'même principe' to which Batteux had led back all literary art.[1] D'Aubignac had dealt with it in book ii, chapter ii of his *Pratique du Théâtre*;[2] Madame Dacier had assumed it in the preface to her translation of the *Odyssey*;[3] Du Bos had devoted sections xxviii and xxix of his first volume to 'la vraisemblance en Poësie' and to the question 'si les Poëtes Tragiques sont obligés de se conformer à ce que la Géographie, l'Histoire et la Chronologie nous apprennent positivement';[4] Gottsched had stated the principle of imitation,[5] Breitinger had given considerable space to it in his *Critische Dichtkunst*,[6] and Johann Elias Schlegel had written a long essay *Von der Nachahmung*.[7] The principle is assumed, of course, in all eighteenth-century commentaries on the *Poetics* and discussions of Aristotle's theory.

How is the artist to imitate nature and life? Is his imitation what we should now call a photographic process—or, as it would have been described in the eighteenth century, the way of the *camera obscura* (LXXIII, 90)—or is it governed by certain laws and limitations which the artist must observe? The ancients had accepted the fundamental principle of imitation; but they had only touched the fringe of the problem of the means. From Horace had come down a dogma enshrined in the words 'ut pictura poesis', which by unconsidered application—such, at least, was Lessing's view—had injuriously affected both poetry and painting; and he wrote his *Laokoon* to prove its dangers. The problem of that treatise had been to determine the

---

[1] Cp. *Principes de la littérature, ed. cit.* i, pp. 4 ff., 17 ff. (and *passim*).

[2] *Pratique du Théâtre, ed. cit.* i, pp. 66 ff.

[3] *L'Odyssée d'Homère*, traduite en François, avec des Remarques. Par Madame Dacier, Paris, 1716, i, pp. viii, xxvi f., lii ff. (and *passim*).

[4] *Réflexions critiques sur la Poësie et sur la Peinture, ed. cit.* i, pp. 227, 233.

[5] *Critische Dichtkunst, ed. cit.* pp. 89 f., 136 (and *passim*).

[6] *Critische Dichtkunst*, Zürich, 1740, i, pp. 7, 53–77 (and *passim*).

[7] *Werke, ed. cit.* iii, pp. 107 ff.

conditions which govern the pictorial and plastic artist on the one hand, and the poet on the other. Similarly, in the *Dramaturgie*, Lessing is not concerned with the general question whether art is or is not an imitation—perhaps because the proposition was so clearly established as to need no asseveration. Here he applies his analytic method to the drama, discriminating between the different modes of dramatic imitation. But in contrast to *Laokoon*, the *Dramaturgie* shows a tendency on Lessing's part to discover community of purpose in the various kinds of dramatic composition. He finds common ground in Sophocles and Shakespeare; he insists that former reasons for discriminating between the characters of tragedy and comedy have little justification; and he confesses to a certain personal sympathy with the mixed forms of drama. Caught up by the new demand for a greater truth to nature and life, he applied this criterion to the drama of the past and of his own day. His clear, logical mind, together with his predilection for the new English tragedy of common life, made him lay stress on truth to reality—on a closer imitation of reality than was to be found in the older poets. We have already seen the effect of this in his critical approach to dramas concerned with contemporary life. Here Lessing is quite definitely a realist: he maintains that this kind of drama, if it is to enlist the sympathies of the audience, must be 'true'.[1] Such plays are criticised unfavourably when they do not represent life as it is, or appears to be.[2] This principle governs many of the judgments of the *Dramaturgie*.

Thus, although the word 'Nachahmung' does not occur frequently in this work, and although Lessing made no pretence of investigating its scope as Schlegel had done—rather he accepted Batteux' doctrine as an established matter of fact—much of the concrete criticism of plays in the *Dramaturgie* consists in applying the measuring-tape of 'reality'; in judging dramas by their greater or less approximation to truth in their imitation.[3] But what is this 'truth'? Scrutinised more closely, the imitation of reality is seen to be something other than the simple transference of life to the theatre. To begin with, if a dramatic action had to be kept always within the three hours' traffic of the stage which it would occupy in reality—had to present, as was sometimes proclaimed, a slice of life exactly as it was lived— this would curtail enormously the scope and power of the drama as an art.[4] Moreover, what purpose would be served if it succeeded in

[1] Cp. xxii, 6; xcvii, 23, 60. [2] Cp. xii, 93.
[3] Cp. xlii, 22. [4] Cp. lxx, 78.

thus identifying itself with actuality? That a drama should be 'true', of course, does not imply merely the presentation of a meaningless slice of life, but also the use of such a presentation to express a higher truth, an interpretation of the ways of man to man and God to man. Lessing does not lose sight of this, although he has little to say of it in criticising the drama of contemporary life. What is required in the theatre is that the spectator should be deceived—not of course unwillingly—into the belief that he is witnessing reality in the presenting of a case that is not 'real'. Success depends thus on something quite other than the reproduction of reality; it depends on illusion—an illusion whereby the spectator is led to believe that he is witnessing something actual. It behoves us therefore to look at what Lessing meant by illusion.

ILLUSION

The attitude of the dramatist towards facts was a question which had exercised the minds of many theorists of the drama. How far must a dramatic work be true, how far might it be invented, and merely an illusion? Lessing discusses on more occasions than one the nature of such illusion, or 'Täuschung'. In the period of his correspondence with Mendelssohn and Nicolai on tragedy he had refused to countenance the idea that illusion is essential to the aesthetic effect.[1] To Mendelssohn he wrote on December 18, 1756:

Wenn Sie Ihre Gedanken von der Illusion mit dem Hrn. Nicolai aufs Reine bringen werden, so vergessen Sie ja nicht, dass die ganze Lehre von der Illusion eigentlich den dramatischen Dichter nichts angeht, und die Vorstellung seines Stücks das Werk einer andern Kunst, als der Dichtkunst, ist. Das Trauerspiel muss auch ohne Vorstellung und Akteurs seine völlige Stärke behalten; und diese bey dem Leser zu äussern, braucht sie nicht mehr Illusion als jede andre Geschichte.[2]

But by the time he came to write *Laokoon*, where he had necessarily much to say on illusion, he had thought more deeply on the subject; and in the *Dramaturgie* he has plainly accepted Mendelssohn's views.

---

[1] In this connexion cp. Du Bos, *Réflexions critiques sur la Poësie et sur la Peinture*, i, section xliii: 'Que le plaisir que nous avons au Théâtre, n'est point produit par l'illusion' (*ed. cit.* i, pp. 411 ff.).

[2] *Schriften*, xvii, p. 87; Petsch, *op. cit.* p. 90. Cp. also *Schriften*, xvii, pp. 90 f., 96; Petsch, *op. cit.* pp. 99 f., 103.

In the passages where he discusses or refers to illusion,[1] there is no essential disparity between his standpoint and that of his friend.

In the first section (23) he analyses the art of the dramatist, who instead of describing passions must make them arise before the eyes of the spectator in 'such illusory continuity' that the latter must sympathise, whether he will or no. In St. v (72), however, he reminds us that the actor must not carry the appearance of actuality to the extreme of illusion (78), and in St. ix (65) he expresses a warning against carrying pantomime to such revolting lengths of realism as the display of blood. Similarly in *Laokoon* he had written: 'Hierzu füge man, dass der Schauspieler die Vorstellung des körperlichen Schmerzes schwerlich oder gar nicht bis zur Illusion treiben kann.'[2] Any exaggeration of gesture or action, in fact, is apt to disillusion the spectator (LVI, 82). In like manner, Lessing deprecates the bad custom, still known in the French provinces, of admitting spectators to the stage, on the ground that all illusion is thereby destroyed (x, 141). In the eleventh section, a more important statement of the dramatist's purpose (35) arises from the discussion of ghosts upon the stage: 'er will uns täuschen, und durch die Täuschung rühren... ohne Täuschung [können] wir unmöglich sympathisiren.' Whatever we may think in ordinary life—if the poet has the power of convincing us, we believe in the theatre what he wants us to believe (73). Nevertheless, Lessing quotes (XIX, 43), and accepts, the comment made on *Zelmire* by a French reviewer that the action of that play is a tissue of coincidences, compressed into twenty-four hours and 'aller Illusion unfähig'. Illusion is vital to tragedy: 'Der tragische Dichter sollte alles vermeiden, was die Zuschauer an ihre Illusion erinnern kann; denn sobald sie daran erinnert sind, so ist sie weg' (XLII, 103); comedy, on the other hand (109), need not produce so great a degree of illusion for the attainment of its purpose. But in either case the illusion is stronger than that of a mere narrative (XXXV, 144); for this reason our interest in the characters of drama is incomparably greater. It is interesting to note Lessing's argument that indigenous customs, by the fact of their familiarity, assist in the creation of illusion both in tragedy and comedy. Characteristically, Lessing fits his disparaging comment on Voltaire's acceptance of his call before the curtain into the general theory of illusion (XXXVI,

---

[1] Cp. I, 23; V, 77; X, 141; XI, 35, 74; XIX, 43; XXXV, 144; XXXVI, 124; XLII, 103; LVI, 84; XCVII, 28, 34.   [2] See below, p. 485.

124): 'Die Täuschung muss sehr schwach seyn, man muss wenig
Natur, aber desto mehr Künsteley empfinden, wenn man so neugierig
nach dem Künstler ist.'

It is of some interest to compare with these observations of Lessing
the following opinions expressed by Mendelssohn. The most complete
statement which the latter has left us of his theory is to be found in
the *Rhapsodie oder Zusätze zu den Briefen über die Empfindungen*:

> Es ist wahr, die sinnliche Erkenntniss und Begehrungskräfte der Seele
> werden durch die Kunst getäuscht, und die Einbildungskraft so mit
> fortgerissen, dass wir zuweilen aller Zeichen der Nachahmung vergessen,
> und die wahre Natur zu sehen wähnen. Allein dieser Zauber dauert nur
> so lange, als nöthig ist, unserm Begriffe von dem Gegenstande das gehörige
> Leben und Feuer zu geben. Wir haben uns gewöhnt, zu unserm grössern
> Vergnügen, die Aufmerksamkeit von allem, was die Täuschung stören
> könnte, abzulenken, und nur auf das zu richten, wodurch sie unterhalten
> wird. Sobald aber die Beziehung auf den Gegenstand unangenehm zu
> werden anfängt; so erinnern uns tausend in die Augen fallende Umstände,
> dass wir eine blosse Nachahmung vor uns sehen. Hierzu kömmt, dass die
> mannigfaltigen Schönheiten, womit die Vorstellung durch die Kunst aus-
> geziert wird, die angenehme Empfindung verstärken und die unange-
> nehme Beziehung auf den Gegenstand mildern helfen.[1]

Moreover, in the section 'Von der Illusion' in his *Von der Herrschaft
über die Neigungen* (which, although it was not published until 1831,
Lessing had an opportunity of reading in 1757) he wrote:

> Soll eine Nachahmung schön seyn, so muss sie uns ästhetisch illudiren;
> die obern Seelenkräfte aber müssen überzeugt seyn, dass es eine Nachah-
> mung, und nicht die Natur selbst sei.[2]

With this may be compared the following passage in Mendelssohn's
essay *Über die Hauptgrundsätze der schönen Künste und Wissenschaften*
(which appeared in the *Philosophische Schriften* of 1761):

> Die Gegenstände [der künstlerischen Vorstellung] können entweder in
> der Natur anzutreffen, oder erdichtet seyn. In beeden Fällen muss der Aus-
> druck, dessen sich die Kunst bedienet, unsere Sinne täuschen. Das heisst,
> wir müssen eine solche Menge von Merkmalen auf einmal warnehmen,
> dass wir die Sache selbst uns lebhafter vorstellen, als die ausdrückenden

---

[1] *Philosophische Schriften* (verbesserte Auflage), Berlin, 1777, ii, pp. 20 f.; *Gesammelte Schriften*, ed. cit. i, pp. 244 f. The passage is quoted by Goldstein, *op. cit.* p. 132.
[2] *Gesammelte Schriften*, iv, 1, p. 44. Cp. Petsch, *op. cit.* p. 134. Cp. also J. Heinemann, *Moses Mendelssohn. Sammlung theils noch ungedruckter, theils in andern Schriften
zerstreuter Aufsätze und Briefe von ihm, an und über ihn*, Leipzig, 1831, p. 55.

Zeichen, und zwar um so viel lebhaffter, dass unsere Sinne, wenigstens einen Augenblick, die Sachen selbst vor sich zu sehen glauben. Dieses ist der höchste Grad der anschauenden Erkenntnis, den man die ästhetische Illusion nennet. Man siehet hieraus, dass in dem Falle, wann die Gegenstände in der Natur anzutreffen sind, der Ausdruck auch getreu seyn müsse, dass heisst, er muss uns alle Theile des Gegenstandes so abbilden, wie wir sie an ihm selbst vermittelst der Sinne wargenommen haben würden. Die Abbildung eines Gegenstandes, die mit allen seinen Theilen genau übereinstimmt, wird eine Nachahmung genannt; daher ist die Nachahmung in diesem Falle eine nothwendige Eigenschaft der schönen Künste und Wissenschaften.[1]

In the *Dramaturgie*, Lessing appeals more than once to the authority of Diderot when he is advocating naturalism in the drama—that is, an illusion that shall succeed in illuding. In sections LXXXIV and LXXXV he adduces a long extract from *Les bijoux indiscrets*, a satiric romance, ascribed to Diderot, which was published anonymously in 1748.[2] This romance was translated into German,[3] and in a recent reprint Lessing's possible authorship of this translation is discussed.[4] But even if this conjecture (based on the identity of the preface to the translation with Lessing's account of *Les bijoux indiscrets* in the *Dramaturgie* (LXXXIV)) is on the whole unlikely, the extract quoted in the *Dramaturgie* bears a considerable resemblance to this translation. It is from chapter v of the second volume of the novel[5] in the original text, which runs as follows:

---

[1] This passage is quoted by Goldstein, *op. cit.* p. 130, who notes that it was inserted by Mendelssohn in the second version of the essay in the *Philosophische Schriften* (Berlin, 1761, ii, pp. 77 f.). It is quoted above from the edition published separately as *Abhandlung über die Hauptgrundsätze der schönen Wissenschaften und Künste*, [Berlin], 1771 (pp. 10 f.); but it does not appear in the 1777 edition of the *Philosophische Schriften*, where a further revision was made.

[2] *Les bijoux indiscrets*. Au Monomotapa [Paris, 1748]. Cp. *Œuvres Complètes de Diderot, ed. cit.* iv, pp. 135 f.

[3] *Die Verräther*. Nach Diderot. Monomotapa. A translation with this title, by F. L. W. Meyer, is recorded in Kayser, *Vollständiges Bücher-Lexicon* (vi, Leipzig, 1836, s. *Romane*, p. 31) as having been published at Braunschweig in 1793; cp. also K. Rosenkranz, *Diderots Leben und Werke*, Leipzig, 1866 (i, pp. xviii, 61), who gives the date as 1792.

[4] *Die geschwätzigen Kleinode*, München, 1921, pp. viii ff. Erich Schmidt asserts that the style of the extract in the *Dramaturgie* shows that Lessing used an early version of his own (*Diderot und Lessing* in *Die Gegenwart*, xxi, 1882, No. 9, p. 135).

[5] *Les Bijoux indiscrets*. Au Monomotapa [Paris, 1748], ii, pp. 43 ff.; cp. *Œuvres Complètes, ed. cit.* iv, pp. 282 ff. (chap. xxxviii).

Je crois, monsieur, que vous vous trompez, répondit Ricaric à Sélim.[1]
L'académie est encore le sanctuaire du bon goût; et ses beaux jours ne
nous offrent ni philosophes, ni poëtes, auxquels nous n'en ayions aujour-
d'hui à opposer. Notre théatre passoit, et peut passer encore pour le premier
théatre de l'Afrique. Quel ouvrage que le Tamerlan de Tuxigraphe![2]
C'est le pathétique d'Eurisopé et l'élévation d'Azophe.[3] C'est l'antiquité
toute pure.

J'ai vu, dit la favorite, la premiere représentation de Tamerlan, et j'ai
trouvé, comme vous, l'ouvrage conduit, le dialogue élégant, et les con-
venances bien observées.

Quelle différence, madame, interrompit Ricaric, entre un auteur tel que
Tuxigraphe, nourri de la lecture des anciens, et la plupart de nos modernes!

Mais ces modernes, dit Sélim, que vous frondez ici tout à votre aise, ne
sont pas aussi méprisables que vous le prétendez. Quoi donc! ne leur
trouvez-vous pas du génie, de l'invention, du feu, des détails, des caracteres,
des tirades? Et que m'importe à moi des regles, pourvu qu'on me plaise?
Ce ne sont assurément ni les observations du sage Almudir et du savant
Abaldok,[4] ni la poétique du docte Farcadin,[5] que je n'ai jamais lues, qui
me font admirer les pieces d'Aboulcazem, de Mubardar, d'Albaboukre,[6]
et de tant d'autres Sarrazins. Y a-t-il d'autre regle que l'imitation de la
nature? et n'avons-nous pas les mêmes yeux que ceux qui l'ont étudiée?

La nature, répondit Ricaric, nous offre à chaque instant des faces
différentes. Toutes sont vraies, mais toutes ne sont pas également belles.
C'est dans ces ouvrages dont il ne paroît pas que vous fassiez grand cas,
qu'il faut apprendre à choisir. Ce sont les recueils de leurs expériences et
de celles qu'on avoit faites avant eux. Quelque esprit que l'on ait, on
n'apperçoit les choses que les unes après les autres; et un seul homme ne
peut se flatter de voir dans le court espace de sa vie, tout ce qu'on avoit
découvert dans les siecles qui l'ont précédé. Autrement il faudroit avancer
qu'une seule science pourroit devoir sa naissance, ses progrès et toute sa
perfection à une seule tête; ce qui est contre l'expérience.

Monsieur Ricaric, repliqua Sélim, il ne s'ensuit autre chose de votre
raisonnement, sinon que les modernes jouissant des trésors amassés jusqu'à
leur tems, doivent être plus riches que les anciens; ou, si cette comparaison
vous déplaît, que, montés sur les épaules de ces colosses, ils doivent voir
plus loin qu'eux. En effet, qu'est-ce que leur physique, leur astronomie,
leur navigation, leur méchanique, leurs calculs, en comparaison des

[1] Sélim has been identified with the Maréchal de Richelieu, and Ricaric
with La Motte. The Emperor Mangogul is Louis XV; the favourite Mirzoza
probably Madame de Pompadour (cp. *Œuvres Complètes*, ed. cit. iv, pp. 137 f.,
p. 280).

[2] Variously identified with Lanone's *Mahomet le Second*, Voltaire's *Mahomet*, and
Marmontel's *Denys le Tyran*.

[3] Probably Euripides and Sophocles (cp. *Œuvres Complètes*, ed. cit. iv, p. 283).

[4] Perhaps Fontenelle and La Motte or D'Aubignac.

[5] Boileau.   [6] Corneille, Racine and probably Crébillon.

nôtres? Et pourquoi notre éloquence et notre poésie n'auroient-elles pas aussi la supériorité?

Sélim, répondit la sultane, Ricaric vous déduira quelques jours les raisons de cette différence. Il vous dira pourquoi nos tragédies sont inférieures à celles des anciens; pour moi, je me chargerai volontiers de vous montrer que cela est. Je ne vous accuserai point, continua-t-elle, de n'avoir pas lu les anciens. Vous avez l'esprit trop orné, pour que leur théatre vous soit inconnu. Or, mettez à part certaines idées relatives à leurs usages, à leur[s] mœurs et à leur religion, et qui ne vous choquent que parce que les conjonctures ont changé, et convenez que leurs sujets sont nobles, bien choisis, intéressans; que l'action se développe comme d'elle-même; que leur dialogue est simple et fort voisin du naturel; que les dénouemens n'y sont pas forcés; et que l'intérêt n'y est point partagé, ni l'action surchargée par des épisodes. Transportez-vous en idée dans l'isle d'Alindala;[1] examinez tout ce qui s'y passe; écoutez tout ce qui s'y dit, depuis le moment que le jeune Ibrahim et le rusé Forfanti y sont descendus; approchez-vous de la caverne du malheureux Polipsile; ne perdez pas un mot de ses plaintes, et dites-moi, si rien vous tire de l'illusion. Citez-moi une piece moderne qui puisse supporter le même examen, et prétendre au même degré de perfection, et je me tiens pour vaincue.

De par Brama! s'écria le sultan en bâillant, madame a fait une dissertation académique.

Je n'entends point les regles, continua la favorite, et moins encore les mots savans dans lesquels on les a conçues; mais je sais qu'il n'y a que le vrai qui plaise et qui touche. Je sais encore que la perfection d'un spectacle consiste dans l'imitation si exacte d'une action, que le spectateur trompé sans interruption, s'imagine assister à l'action même. Or, y a-t-il quelque chose qui ressemble à cela dans ces tragédies que vous nous vantez?

En admirez-vous la conduite? Elle est ordinairement si compliquée, que ce seroit un miracle qu'il se fût passé tant de choses en si peu de tems. La ruine ou la conservation d'un empire, le mariage d'une princesse, la perte d'un prince, tout cela s'exécute en un tour de main. S'agit-il d'une conspiration? on l'ébauche au premier acte; elle est liée, affermie au second; toutes les mesures sont prises, tous les obstacles levés, les conspirateurs disposés au troisieme, il y aura incessamment une révolte, un combat, peut-être une bataille rangée; et vous appellerez cela, conduite, intérêt, chaleur, vraisemblance! Je ne vous le pardonnerois jamais, à vous qui n'ignorez pas ce qu'il en coûte quelquefois pour mettre à fin une misérable intrigue, et combien la plus petite affaire de politique, absorbe de tems en démarches, en pour-parlers, et en déliberations.

Il est vrai, madame, répondit Sélim, que nos pieces sont un peu chargées, mais c'est un mal nécessaire; sans le secours des épisodes, on se morfondroit.

---

[1] Obviously the *Philoctetes* of Sophocles is the drama meant; thus Alindala is Lemnos; Ibrahim, Forfanti and Polipsile respectively Neoptolemos, Odysseus and Philoctetes.

C'est-à-dire, que pour donner de l'ame à la représentation d'un fait, il ne faut le rendre ni tel qu'il est, ni tel qu'il doit être. Cela est du dernier ridicule, à moins qu'il ne soit plus absurde encore de faire jouer à des violons des arrêtes-vives [ariettes vives] et des sonates de mouvement, tandis que les esprits sont imbus qu'un prince est sur le point de perdre sa maîtresse, son trône et la vie.

Madame, vous avez raison, dit Mangogul; ce sont des airs lugubres qu'il faut alors, et je vais vous en ordonner. Mangogul se leva, sortit, et la conversation continua entre Sélim, Ricaric et la favorite.

Au moins, madame, repliqua Sélim, vous ne nierez pas que, si les épisodes nous tirent de l'illusion, le dialogue nous y ramene. Je ne vois personne qui l'entende comme nos tragiques.

Personne n'y entend donc rien, reprit Mirzoza. L'emphase, l'esprit et le papillotage qui y régnent, sont à mille lieues de la nature. C'est en vain que l'auteur cherche à se dérober; mes yeux percent, et je l'apperçois sans cesse derriére ses personnages. Cinna, Sertorius, Maxime, Emilie[1] sont à tout moment les sarbacanes de Corneille. Ce n'est pas ainsi qu'on s'entretient dans nos anciens Sarrazins. Mr. Ricaric vous en traduira, si vous voulez, quelques morceaux; et vous entendrez la pure nature s'exprimer par leur bouche. Je dirois volontiers aux modernes: "Messieurs, au lieu de donner à tout propos de l'esprit à vos personnages, placez-les dans des conjunctures qui leur en donnent."

Après ce que madame vient de prononcer de la conduite et du dialogue de nos drames, il n'y a pas apparence, dit Sélim, qu'elle fasse grace aux dénouemens.

Non, sans doute, reprit la favorite; il y en a cent mauvais pour un bon. L'un n'est point amené; l'autre est miraculeux. Un auteur est-il embarrassé d'un personnage qu'il a traîné de scenes en scenes pendant cinq actes? il vous le dépêche d'un coup de poignard: tout le monde se met à pleurer; et moi, je ris comme une folle. Et puis a-t-on jamais parlé, comme nous déclamons? Les princes et les rois marchent-ils autrement qu'un homme qui marche bien? Ont-ils jamais gesticulé comme des possédés ou des furieux? Les princesses poussent-elles en parlant des sifflemens aigus? On suppose que nous avons porté la tragédie à un haut degré de perfection; et moi je tiens presque pour démontré, que de tous les genres d'ouvrages de littérature auxquels les Africains se sont appliqués dans ces derniers siecles, c'est le plus imparfait.

La favorite en étoit là de sa sortie contre nos pieces de théatre, lorsque Mangogul rentra. "Madame, lui dit-il, vous m'obligerez de continuer: j'ai, comme vous voyez, des secrets pour abréger une poétique, quand je la trouve longue."

Je suppose, continua la favorite, un nouveau débarqué d'Angot[2] qui n'ait jamais entendu parler de spectacles, mais qui ne manque ni de sens

---

[1] Cinna, Maxime and Emilie in Corneille's *Cinna*; Sertorius in the tragedy of that name. [2] Perhaps England.

ni d'usage; qui connoisse un peu la cour des princes, les maneges des courtisans, les jalousies des ministres, et les tracasseries des femmes, et à qui je dise en confidence: "Mon ami, il se fait dans le serrail des mouve-mens terribles. Le prince, mécontent de son fils, en qui il soupçonne de la passion pour la Manimonbanda,[1] est homme à tirer de tous les deux la vengeance la plus cruelle; cette aventure aura, selon toutes les apparences, des suites fâcheuses.[2] Si vous voulez, je vous rendrai témoin de tout ce qui se passera." Il accepte ma proposition, et je le mene dans une loge grillée, d'où il voit le théatre, qu'il prend pour le palais du sultan. Croyez-vous que, malgré tout le sérieux que j'affecterois, l'illusion de cet homme durât un instant? Ne conviendrez-vous pas au contraire qu'à la démarche empesée des acteurs, à la bizarrerie de leurs vêtemens, à l'extravagance de leurs gestes, à l'emphase d'un langage singulier, rimé, cadencé, et à mille autres dissonances qui le frapperont, il doit m'éclater au nez dès la premiere scene, et me déclarer ou que je me joue de lui, ou que le prince et toute sa cour extravaguent?

Je vous avoue, dit Sélim, que cette supposition me frappe; mais ne pourroit-on pas vous observer qu'on se rend au spectacle avec la persuasion que c'est l'imitation d'un événement, et non l'événement même qu'on y verra?

Et cette persuasion, reprit Mirzoza, doit-elle empêcher qu'on n'y repré-sente l'événement de la maniere la plus naturelle?

DRAMA AND HISTORY

The problems of imitation and illusion assume a more complicated form in the case of dramas dealing with historical themes. Here there can be little question of deceiving the spectator by realism into thinking that he is viewing an actual happening. Nor is it always possible, Lessing argues, for the dramatist to be 'true' to history, concerning which we are often so ill-informed (XIX, 23); and even if it were possible, it would not always be desirable. The dramatic poet is no historian (XI, 29); he does not describe what has happened or what is believed to have happened; he reconstructs the course of events before our eyes—not merely for the sake of historical truth, but with a higher purpose.[3] In St. XIX, during the discussion of

---

[1] Probably Marie, the wife of Louis XV (cp. *Œuvres Complètes*, *ed. cit.* iv, p. 138).
[2] The situation resembles that of Racine's *Phèdre*, Act iv.
[3] Cp. on this subject D'Aubignac, *Pratique du Théâtre*, ii, chap. i (*ed. cit.* i, p. 58):
'[Les Poëtes] prennent de l'Histoire ce qui leur est propre, et y changent le reste pour en faire leurs Poëmes, et c'est une pensée bien ridicule d'aller au Theatre apprendre l'Histoire. La Scene ne donne point les choses comme elles ont été, mais comme elles devoient être....'

De Belloy's *Zelmire*, Lessing reminds his readers (15) that Aristotle
had decided long ago how far the poet had to concern himself with
history: he asks no more from it than will provide him with a suitable
plot in which he can embody his purpose. Aristotle's statement[1] had,
in fact, left no room for any ambiguity of interpretation. Batteux had
already made this clear:

Aristote compare la Poësie avec l'Histoire. Leur différence, selon lui,
n'est point dans la forme ni dans le style, mais dans le fonds des choses.
Mais comment y est-elle? L'Histoire peint ce qui a été fait: la Poësie, ce
qui a pu être fait. L'une est liée au vrai, elle ne crée ni actions, ni acteurs.
L'autre n'est tenue qu'au vraisemblable: elle invente: elle imagine à son
gré: elle peint de tête. L'Historien donne des exemples tels qu'ils sont,
souvent imparfaits. Le Poëte les donne tels qu'ils doivent être. Et c'est
pour cela que, selon le même Philosophe, la Poësie est une leçon bien plus
instructive que l'Histoire.[2]

And Dacier had remarked in a note to his *Poétique d'Aristote*:

L'Historien ne fait pas sa matière, il ne dit que ce qu'il sçait, et on n'en
demande pas d'avantage, pourvû qu'il s'attache uniquement à la verité.
Il n'en est pas de même du Poëte, comme c'est luy qui est l'Auteur de sa
matiére, il ne suit que la necessité ou la vray-semblance, c'est-à-dire, que
tout ce qu'il dit a pû ou dû arriver, comme il le dit, et si quelquefois il tire
quelque chose de l'Histoire, ce n'est qu'autant que l'Histoire peut l'accommoder, et qu'elle luy fournit des sujets, comme il auroit pû les feindre, car
autrement il y change tout ce qui ne l'accommode pas.[3]

---

[1] Chap. ix of the *Poetics*; Lessing's own translation will be found in St. LXXXIX
(21 ff.).

[2] *Principes de la littérature*, i, i, chap. iii (*ed. cit.* i, pp. 28 f.). In another passage, in
the section on the epic, iv, chap. i (*ed. cit.* ii, pp. 179 f.), we find: 'L'Histoire est
consacrée à la vérité. C'est un témoin qui dépose, qui présente les faits tels qu'ils
sont, sans les altérer, ni les embellir. L'Epopée au contraire ne vit que de men-
songes: elle invente tout ce qu'elle raconte, et ne connoît d'autres bornes que celles
de la possibilité.... L'Histoire présente les faits sans songer à plaire par la singularité
des causes, ou des moyens. C'est le portrait des temps et des hommes; par conséquent
l'image de l'inconstance et du caprice, de mille variations, qui semblent l'ouvrage
du hazard et de la fortune. L'Epopée ne raconte qu'une action, et non plusieurs.
Cette action est essentiellement intéressante: ses parties sont concertées: ses causes
sont vraisemblables: ses acteurs ont des caractères marqués, des mœurs soutenues:
c'est un tout, entier, proportionné, ordonné, parfaitement lié dans toutes ses
parties....'

[3] *Ed. cit.* pp. 136 f. Curtius virtually repeats this note (*op. cit.* pp. 148 f.). Cp.
also the section 'Du plan de la Tragédie' in Diderot, *De la poésie dramatique* (*Œuvres
complètes*, *ed. cit.* vii, pp. 327 ff.; Lessing's translation, *ed. cit.* ii, pp. 289 ff.).

If, Lessing continues (xix, 21), the historical facts happen to suit the poet's purpose, he will use them with satisfaction, but it is not necessary for him to search for facts, or to be bound by them; it will avail him little to turn to his history books.[1] Lessing's statement of the case here was occasioned by the review of De Belloy's *Zelmire* in the *Journal encyclopédique* for July 1, 1762 (pp. 101 ff.), where the critic had expressed a predilection for historical tragedy. He had written (pp. 123 f.):

Nous aimerions bien mieux un sujet historique. Les annales du monde si fécondes en crimes fameux, sont un champ inépuisable pour Melpomène. La Tragédie n'est faite que pour proposer à l'admiration et à l'imitation des Citoyens, les actions des grands hommes. C'est en même tems payer le tribut que la postérité doit à leurs mânes, et embraser nos Contemporains de la noble ardeur de les suivre. Ainsi pensoient les Grecs; ainsi ont pensé presque toujours nos illustres modernes. Qu'on ne dise point que *Zaïre*, *Alzire* et *Mahomet*, sont des sujets de pure fiction. Les noms des deux premières pièces sont imaginés; mais le fond des faits est historique. Il y a eu en effet des Croisades, où les Chrétiens et les Ottomans tantôt vaincus, tantôt vainqueurs, se sont haïs et égorgés pour la gloire d'un Dieu leur pere commun. La conquête du Pérou a réellement fait naître ces contrastes si heureux et si sublimes des mœurs des Européans et des Americains, du Fanatisme et de la véritable Religion. Pour la Tragédie de *Mahomet*, elle est le précis, osons le dire, l'esprit de toute la vie de ce fourbe; elle est encore le fanatisme mis en action, et la plus belle, la plus philosophique peinture qui fut jamais de ce dangereux monstre.

And in the same journal for May 15, 1765, with reference to *Le Siège de Calais*, the view had been expressed:

M. de B[elloy] assure, avec raison, que c'est en excitant la vénération de la France pour les Grands hommes qu'elle a produits, qu'on parviendra à inspirer à la nation une estime et un respect pour elle même, qui seuls peuvent la rendre ce qu'elle a été autrefois. C'est par là que les tragiques Grecs entretenoient le patriotisme et l'amour de la liberté dans l'ame de leurs Spectateurs; ils n'alloient chercher leurs sujets que dans leur histoire....[2]

[1] C. B. Boxberger, *Einzelheiten über Voltaire bei Lessing*, Dresden, 1879, p. 29, suggests that possibly Lessing was here thinking of a remark in Voltaire's *Dissertation* prefixed to *Sémiramis* (see *Œuvres, ed. cit.* ix, p. 18): '...un sujet de pure invention, et un sujet vrai, mais ignoré, sont absolument la même chose pour les spectateurs; et comme notre scène embrasse des sujets de tous les tems et de tous les pays, il faudrait qu'un spectateur allât consulter tous les livres, avant qu'il sût si ce qu'on lui représente est fabuleux ou historique: il ne prend pas assurément cette peine.'

[2] *Journal encyclopédique*, May 15, 1765, p. 100.

This argument Lessing cannot accept (XIX, 32): the purpose of the theatre is not to perpetuate the memory of great men. In the theatre we are not to learn what this or that individual has done in the past, but what every individual of a certain character in certain given circumstances will do. The purpose of tragedy (37) is, as Aristotle had said in the ninth chapter of the *Poetics*, much more philosophical than the purpose of history. Moreover, he argues in a later section (XXXII, 2), it is a mistake to think that the tragedy of Greece was invented to revive the memory of great and strange events; that its business was to step in the footsteps of history, and look neither to right nor left. Thespis was quite unconcerned with historical accuracy.

Lessing's criticism of Thomas Corneille's *Graf von Essex* (XXII–XXV) is almost exclusively concerned with this question of the attitude of the tragic poet to history; and we have seen how he waxes indignant over Voltaire's carping criticism of the poet for his lack of historical accuracy.[1] Corneille's ignorance of history, he argues, is really of no importance; his tragedy is not one whit better or worse as a tragedy because he has used historical names. Why, Lessing asks (XXIII, 118), does a poet use real names at all for his characters? Does he choose them because the characters which history associates with these names correspond to the needs of his story? Does the story come first or do the characters? If it is the characters who come first, the attitude of the poet to historical truth is clear: he may depart from the actual facts of history as widely as he likes. 'Nur die Charaktere sind ihm heilig; diese zu verstärken, diese in ihrem besten Lichte zu zeigen, ist alles, was er von dem Seinigen dabey hinzuthun darf; die

---

[1] See above, pp. 183 ff. and cp. below, p. 444. Lessing is, however, unjust to Voltaire's criticism of Corneille; for Voltaire was no stickler for absolute historical accuracy on the part of the poet. He demanded adherence to the events of history in a case such as that of the Comte d'Essex, where the facts—this at least was his contention—were too well known to be violated with impunity. Cp. *Théâtre de Pierre Corneille, avec des Commentaires*, ed. cit. x, p. 259: 'Il n'est pas permis de falsifier à ce point une histoire si récente, et de traiter avec tant d'indignité des hommes de la plus grande naissance et du plus grand mérite...'; but also *ibid.* pp. 262 f.: 'On demande jusqu'à quel point il est permis de falsifier l'histoire dans un poëme? Je ne crois pas qu'on puisse changer sans déplaire, les faits ni même les caractères connus du public.... Mais quand les événemens qu'on traite sont ignorés d'une nation, l'auteur en est absolument le maître. Presque personne en France du tems de *Thomas Corneille* n'était instruit de l'histoire d'Angleterre; aujourd'hui un poëte devrait être plus circonspect.'

geringste wesentliche Veränderung würde die Ursache aufheben, warum sie diese und nicht andere Namen führen.'[1]

Some years previously Lessing had expressed a similar opinion in a review in the *Litteraturbriefe*:

Der Dichter ist Herr über die Geschichte; und er kann die Begebenheiten so nahe zusammen rücken, als er will....Ich meinte, nur der Verfasser der Parisischen Bluthochzeit [Gottsched] stehe in dem schülerhaften Wahne, dass der Dichter an einer Begebenheit, die er auf die tragische Bühne bringen wolle, weiter nichts ändern dürfte, als was mit den Einheiten nicht bestehen wolle, übrigens aber genau bey den Charakteren, wie sie die Geschichte von seinen Helden entwirft, bleiben müsse.[2]

The question of the use of historical names is discussed by Aristotle in his ninth chapter (Lessing quotes the passage in St. LXXXIX (43 ff.) with reference to Diderot's view of the alleged difference between the characters of tragedy and comedy). As Petersen has pointed out (*ed. cit.* p. 205), Lessing inclines not a little in St. XXIII to the notorious recipe for writing tragedy in the following passage of Gottsched's *Critische Dichtkunst* (ed. of 1737, p. 674):

Der Poet wählet sich einen moralischen Lehrsatz, den er seinen Zuschauern auf eine sinnliche Art einprägen will. Dazu ersinnt er sich eine allgemeine Fabel, daraus die Wahrheit eines Satzes erhellet. Hiernächst sucht er in der Historie solche berühmte Leute, denen etwas ähnliches begegnet ist: Und von diesen entlehnet er die Namen, für die Personen seiner Fabel, um derselben also ein Ansehen zu geben. Er erdenket sodann alle Umstände dazu, um die Hauptfabel recht wahrscheinlich zu machen, und das werden die Zwischenfabeln, oder Episodia genannt. Dieses theilt er dann in fünf Stücke ein, die ungefehr gleich gross sind, und ordnet sie so, dass natürlicher Weise das letztere aus dem vorhergehenden fliesset: Bekümmert sich aber weiter nicht, ob alles in der Historie so und nicht anders geheissen haben.

Lessing returns to this matter of names a few pages later: in St. XXIV (59) he insists that tragedy is not history in dialogue: for the purposes of tragedy history is nothing more than a storehouse of

---

[1] A critic in the *Journal encyclopédique* for July 15, 1764, reviewing Voltaire's edition of Corneille, had said with reference to *Le Comte d'Essex* (pp. 36 f.): 'Conservés l'unité dans le caractère, mais variés le par mille nuances, tantôt par des soupçons, par des craintes, par des espérances, par des réconciliations et des ruptures, tantôt par un incident qui donne à tout une face nouvelle.'

[2] *Litteraturbriefe*, No. lxiii, October 18, 1759, *ed. cit.* iv, pp. 246, 250; *Schriften*, viii, pp. 168, 170; also referred to by Petersen, *ed. cit.* p. 206.

names with which we are wont to associate certain characters. If the poet finds in history circumstances suitable for the adornment or individualisation of his theme, let him by all means make use of them. But this should no more be regarded as a merit than should the ignoring of the facts of history be regarded as a crime. On another occasion (LVII, 9) Lessing finds that Banks in his *Earl of Essex* has kept too closely to history: 'Ein Charakter, der sich so leicht vergisst, ist kein Charakter, und eben daher der dramatischen Nachahmung unwürdig. In der Geschichte kann man dergleichen Widersprüche mit sich selbst, für Verstellung halten, weil wir in der Geschichte doch selten das Innerste des Herzens kennen lernen: aber in dem Drama werden wir mit dem Helden allzuvertraut, als dass wir nicht gleich wissen sollten, ob seine Gesinnungen wirklich mit den Handlungen, die wir ihm nicht zugetrauet hätten, übereinstimmen, oder nicht. Ja, sie mögen es, oder sie mögen es nicht: der tragische Dichter kann ihn in beiden Fällen nicht recht nutzen. Ohne Verstellung fällt der Charakter weg; bey der Verstellung die Würde desselben.'

Lessing's dictum that characters must be much more sacred to the poet than facts is further developed in St. XXXIII, where Favart's *Soliman II* is compared with the tale by Marmontel of which it is a dramatisation. The French reviewer of Favart's play in the *Journal encyclopédique* of January 15, 1762 had asked (p. 80): 'Un Poëte, un Conteur, quelque licence qu'on leur ait donnée, peuvent-ils l'étendre sur les caractères connus? Maîtres de changer dans les faits, ont-ils le droit de peindre Lucrèce coquette, et Socrate galant?' Lessing agrees that Marmontel (and, in consequence Favart, who adopts his faults, but for different reasons) can hardly be defended (XXXIV, 24 ff., 136 ff.): instead of making the facts of the story appear as naturally resulting from the characters, both writers reverse the process. Characters are 'more sacred' than the actions in which they are involved, first, because if the characters are thoroughly understood, their actions—the facts—cannot be very different, whether in history or in fiction; while on the other hand, the same kind of fact or action can be deduced from different characters. Secondly, we learn nothing from a mere statement of facts, but only from our knowledge that such and such characters under such and such circumstances do or think certain things—must indeed do or think them. The poet has thus to make his choice between the different kinds of actions for which a given character under given circumstances is responsible, whether they be provided by history or be merely in accordance with the moral purpose of his fiction. If he choose other than historical characters, he should avoid giving them historical names; it is better to attribute the known facts to quite unknown persons than to impose on known persons characters, actions or motives which may not have been theirs. The facts then are merely adventitious and accidental; they may be common to different persons; but the characters are essential; they brook no contradiction or inconsistency (XXXIII, 159).

This statement receives considerable elucidation from a passage in Johann Elias Schlegel's *Vergleichung Shakespears und Andreas Gryphs*,[1] which Lessing may well have had in mind:

Man kann den Charakter einer Person, die in der Historie bekannt ist, zwar in etwas ändern, und entweder höher treiben, oder etwas weniger von seinen Tugenden und Lastern in ihm abbilden, als die Geschichte ihm zuschreibt. Aber wenn man weiter gehen wollte, so würde man mit seiner Menschenmacherey mehr zum Romanenschreiber, als zum Dichter, werden, und es würde lächerlich seyn, so oft einem ein Fehler vorgeworfen wird, den man wider den Charakter begangen hat, sich damit zu entschuldigen, dass man seine Menschen selber macht. Man wird mir erlauben, dass ich, um den Werth dieser grossen Tugend des Shakespear recht ins Licht zu setzen, eine Ausschweifung auf andre Nationen mache, welche sich zuweilen nicht undeutlich zu rühmen scheinen, dass ihre theatralischen Personen zwar die Namen der historischen Personen führen, aber von denselben ganz unterschieden sind. Denn sind es Namen, die in der Historie bekannt sind; so wird einem Zuschauer, der nicht ungelehrt ist, indem er diesen Namen hört, auch dieser Charakter beyfallen. Und an statt, dass er ein Vergnügen über die Aehnlichkeit, die der nachgeahmte Held mit dem wahren hat, empfinden sollte; so wird er ein Misvergnügen über die Unähnlichkeit empfinden. Dieses wird nicht so leicht geschehen, wenn der Charakter in den Hauptumständen ähnlich, und nur in Nebenumständen verändert wird. Man pflegt, auch von den grössten Helden, nur ihre Haupttugenden und ihre Hauptlaster im Gedächtnisse zu behalten. Unähnlichkeiten, die nicht merklich sind, sind in Absicht auf unsre Empfindung keine Unähnlichkeiten. Dennoch ist es nicht zu läugnen, dass ein Charakter, welcher auch die kleinsten Züge des historischen nachmalet, deswegen hoch zu schätzen sey, weil er auch die genauesten Kenner der Geschichte, welche die Aehnlichkeit am besten beurtheilen können, befriedigen wird. Hingegen wird ein selbstgemachter Held den grössten Vortheil darinnen haben, dass die Züge desselben viel verwegner scheinen. Aber je künstlicher die Bildung seines Charakters ist, desto gefährlicher wird sie auch seyn; weil man leicht Dinge, die nicht seyn können, malen wird, wenn man Dinge malt, die nicht sind. Man findet die Gemüthsbewegungen viel heftiger und ausgedrückter in den Gesichtern abgebildet,

[1] *Werke, ed. cit.* iii, pp. 48 ff.

die der Maler selbst gedichtet hat. Ein Contrefey, welches nach einem Menschen gemacht ist, zeiget hingegen mehrentheils Gelassenheit, oder doch nur gelinde Gemüthsbewegungen. Es ist also eine erlaubte Kühnheit, seine Helden selbst zu machen, wenn sie nur die Geschichte nicht offenbar Lügen strafen. Es ist keine Kunst, seiner Einbildung den Zügel schiessen zu lassen, und sein Hirngespinst alsdann unter dem ersten Namen zu verkaufen, der einem in den Mund kömmt. Und es ist eine lobenswürdige Mühsamkeit, die innersten Winkel der Geschichte zu durchstören, und den alten Helden wieder lebendig zu machen. Wer das erste thut, der wird leicht unwahrscheinlich; wer das andre thut, ist es schon; und wer den dritten Weg erwählet, der ist sicher, es nicht leicht zu werden.

It is not historical truth, Lessing argues (xix, 28) that makes a poetic theme or a fiction credible, but its 'inner verisimilitude';[1] and again we are reminded of Aristotle's statement that the purpose of tragedy is more philosophical than that of history. In his vigorous defence of Corneille against Voltaire (xxxi, 136) Lessing gives trenchant expression to his conviction: 'Allerdings durfte Corneille mit den historischen Umständen nach Gutdünken verfahren. Er durfte, z. E. Rodogunen so jung annehmen, als er wollte; und Voltaire hat sehr Unrecht, wenn er auch hier wiederum aus der Geschichte nachrechnet, dass Rodogune so jung nicht könne gewesen seyn; sie habe den Demetrius geheyrathet, als die beiden Prinzen... noch in ihrer Kindheit gewesen wären. Was geht das dem Dichter an? Seine Rodogune hat den Demetrius gar nicht geheyrathet; sie war sehr jung, als sie der Vater heyrathen wollte... Voltaire ist mit seiner historischen Controlle ganz unleidlich. Wenn er doch lieber die Data in seiner allgemeinen Weltgeschichte dafür verificiren wollte!'

In the further discussion of *Rodogune* Lessing deals (xxxii, 37) with the poet's attitude to the improbable in history. If he be a true poet, he will make it his business to convert the improbable into the probable by arranging the events and moulding the characters in such a way that what happens not only may, but must happen. If he follow this course, he cannot fail. As Johann Elias Schlegel had said: 'So bald ein Poet sich bemüht, seine Charaktere vom Anfange bis zu Ende

---

[1] Curtius in his *Abhandlung von der Wahrscheinlichkeit* (*Aristoteles Dichtkunst, ed. cit.* p. 401) had defined this: 'Die innerliche Wahrscheinlichkeit beruhet auf den Gründen, welche die Sache wirklich in sich hat. Je stärker diese Gründe sind, desto näher gränzet der Satz an die Wahrheit, und desto grösser, ist die innerliche Wahrscheinlichkeit.'

wohl auszudrücken, so wird auch sein Ausdruck schön seyn.'[1] He
need have no fear of failing to fill his five acts; on the contrary, they
may prove too short for all they must contain. On the other hand
(68), the inferior poet rejoices in improbabilities of plot—as does
Corneille in *Rodogune*; he heaps improbability upon improbability,
and in a few weeks his tragedy is finished, to be read or forgotten,
to be admired or buried; 'denn "et habent sua fata libelli"'.[2] It is
characteristic of Lessing's whole attitude to the problems of imitation
and illusion that his inveterate antagonism to the *tragédie classique*
should be based, not on a dislike of offences against historical accuracy,
but on the conviction that a type of tragedy governed by artificial
laws and restrictions offends against the ordinary human sense of how
things happen in the world. He defends Thomas Corneille, as we
have seen, against Voltaire's trivial hunt for historical errors in *Le
Comte d'Essex*; and the lack of historical truth in *Rodogune* does not
disturb him. But tragedies of this kind, he contends, cannot successfully create illusion. Events are absurdly crowded together to satisfy
meaningless unities of time and place; the poet offers us a complicated
and obviously manufactured intrigue which goes beyond all reasonable
probability.

THE SUPERNATURAL IN DRAMA

Consideration of the dramatist's attitude to history leads to another
of the problems of imitation and illusion: the poet's attitude to the
supernatural. The student of older *artes poeticæ* is accustomed to the
large amount of space devoted to 'le merveilleux'—its legitimacy and
its poetic function. Batteux, for instance, states that whereas history
is 'le récit véritable d'actions naturelles', the epic is distinguished
from it by being 'le récit poëtique d'une action merveilleuse'.[3] From
the preliminary invocation to the muse of the poet onwards, the
supernatural was regarded as a peculiar adjunct of the epic. But
Lessing is not concerned with such wider questions; the problem

---

[1] *Gedanken zur Aufnahme des dänischen Theaters* (*Werke*, ed. cit. iii, p. 291).

[2] Cosack points out (*op. cit.* p. 205) that this is a reminiscence of Voltaire's letter
to Maffei (Preface to *Mérope*, *Œuvres*, ed. cit. viii, pp. 220 f.): '...cependant elle
[*Amasis*, by de la Grange] n'eut pas d'abord un succès éclatant, *et habent sua fata
libelli*.' The original passage—it is from Terentianus Maurus—has no 'et'; it
reads 'pro captu lectoris habent sua fata libelli' (l. 1286; *Terentiani Mauri De litteris
syllabis et metris liber*, ed. C. Lachmannus, Berlin, 1836, p. 44).

[3] *Principes de la littérature*, ed. cit. ii, p. 181.

arises in connexion with a concrete case—Voltaire's *Sémiramis*. In his preface to this play, in which he brought a ghost upon the stage, Voltaire raised the general question. He defended his ghost (XI, 5) not as a poetic expedient, but on historical grounds; for all antiquity, he said, believed in the existence of ghosts (*Œuvres, ed. cit.* ix, pp. 25 f.) :

> ...on disait et on écrivait de tous côtés, que l'on ne croit plus aux revenans, et que les apparitions des morts ne peuvent être que puériles aux yeux d'une Nation éclairée. Quoi! toute l'Antiquité aura cru ces prodiges, et il ne sera pas permis de se conformer à l'Antiquité? Quoi! notre Religion aura consacré ces coups extraordinaires de la Providence, et il serait ridicule de les renouveller?
>
> Les Romains Philosophes ne croyaient pas aux revenans du tems des Empereurs, et cependant le jeune *Pompée* évoque une ombre dans la *Pharsale*. Les Anglais ne croyent pas assurément plus que les Romains aux revenans; cependant ils voyent tous les jours avec plaisir dans la Tragédie d'*Hamlet*, l'ombre d'un Roi qui paraît sur le Théâtre dans une occasion à peu près semblable à celle où l'on a vû à Paris le spectre de *Ninus*.

The question of the admissibility of ghosts in tragedies had also been discussed by Curtius in his *Critische Abhandlungen und Gedichte* (Hanover, 1760). Curtius does not approve of Voltaire; he says:

> Die Dichter des Alterthums folgeten den Vorurtheilen, und der Denkungsart ihrer Zeiten: was ist billiger, als dass sich unsere Dichter nach den Vorurtheilen des Alters und der Nation richten, in welchem, und für welche sie schreiben.

And, like Lessing, he makes an exception in the case of the ghost in *Hamlet*, because 'diese Erscheinung aber hat sonst so viele Schönheiten, dass man dem Dichter für seine Abweichung von den gewöhnlichen Regeln danket'.[1]

Lessing admits (XI, 22) that the ancients believed in ghosts, and that the Greek dramatists had consequently a right to introduce them; but has the modern dramatist the same right, he asks, when he takes his themes from those more superstitious times? This is the claim which Du Bos makes in a section '*De la vraisemblance en Poësie*':

---

[1] *Ed. cit.* pp. 23, 24. The critic of Curtius's book in the *Bibliothek der schönen Wissenschaften*, vii (i), 1761, p. 106, defended both *Hamlet* and *Sémiramis*: 'Die Umstände aber, mit denen sie im Hammlet und in der Semiramis begleitet ist, sind so beschaffen, dass gewiss noch kein vernünftiger Mensch in dem Augenblicke der Vorstellung, seine Vernunft um Rath gefragt, ob es Gespenster gäbe.'

Un fait vraisemblable est un fait possible dans les circonstances où on le fait arriver....Comme le Poëte est en droit d'exiger de nous que nous trouvions possible tout ce qui paraissoit possible dans les tems où il met sa scène, et où il transporte en quelque façon ses lecteurs, nous ne pouvons point, par exemple, l'accuser de manquer à la vraisemblance, en supposant que Diane enleve Iphigénie pour la transporter dans la Tauride, dans le moment qu'on alloit sacrifier cette Princesse. L'événement étoit possible, suivant la théologie des Grecs de ce tems-là.

But Du Bos also recognised the difficulties of employing the supernatural; for he goes on:

Après cela, que des personnes plus hardies que moi, osent marquer les bornes entre la vraisemblance et le merveilleux, par rapport à chaque genre de Poësie, par rapport au tems où l'on suppose que l'événement est arrivé; enfin par rapport à la credulité, plus ou moins grande, de ceux pour qui le Poëme est composé: Il me paroît trop difficile de placer ces bornes....Il ne me paroît donc pas possible d'enseigner l'art de concilier le vraisemblable et le merveilleux. Cet art n'est qu'à la portée de ceux qui sont nés Poëtes et grands Poëtes. C'est à eux qu'il est réservé de faire une alliance du merveilleux et du vraisemblable, où l'un et l'autre ne perdent pas leurs droits.[1]

Lessing, rejecting in the main the argument of historical justification, stresses these poetic possibilities. The true poet (xi, 67) has full liberty to draw on this source of terror and pathos, if he can only develop the seed of belief in the supernatural which is implanted in us all—if he can, in fact, create illusion. So Shakespeare is exalted, at the expense of Voltaire (76), because Shakespeare, in *Hamlet*, introduces his ghost in the right way. As has already been pointed out, Lessing is rather less than fair to Voltaire in the comparison.[2]

In his approach to this problem Lessing was again clearly influenced by Mendelssohn. The latter had written in the *Litteraturbriefe*:

Je grösser die Gewalt ist, mit welcher der Dichter durch die Poesie in unsere Einbildungskraft würkt, desto mehr äusserliche Action kann er sich erlauben, ohne der Poesie Abbruch zu thun, desto mehr muss er anwenden, wenn er die Täuschungen seiner Poesie mächtig genug unterstützen will. Sie kennen den Shakespear. Sie wissen wie eigenmächtig er die Phantasie der Zuschauer gleichsam tyrannisirt, und wie leicht er sie, fast spielend aus einer Leidenschaft, aus einer Illusion in die andere wirft. Aber wie viel Ungereimtheiten, wie viel mit den Regeln streitendes übersiehet man ihm auch in der äusserlichen Action, und wie wenig

---

[1] *Réflexions critiques sur la Poësie et sur la Peinture*, i, xxviii (*ed. cit.* i, pp. 228 ff.).
[2] See above, pp. 224 f.

merkts der Zuschauer, dessen ganze Aufmerksamkeit auf eine andere Seite beschäftiget ist!...Wer ist in England noch der *incredulus*[1] gewesen, der an der Erscheinung des Geists im Hamlet gezweiffelt hätte?...Wer das Gemüth so zu erhitzen, und in einen solchen Taumel von Leidenschaften zu stürzen weis, als Shakespear, der hat die Achtsamkeit seines Zuschauers gleichsam gefesselt, und kann es wagen, vor dessen geblendeten Augen die abendtheuerlichsten Handlungen vorgehen zu lassen, ohne zu befahren, dass solches den Betrug stöhren werde. Ein nicht so grosser Geist aber, der uns auf der Bühne noch Sinne und Bewusstseyn lässt, ist alle Augenblick in Gefahr Ungläubige anzutreffen....[2]

The root of the matter, both for Mendelssohn and for Lessing, is thus the creation of poetic illusion.

[1] A reference to Horace, *De Arte Poetica*, 188.

[2] *Litteraturbriefe*, No. lxxxiv, February 14, 1760, *ed. cit.* v, pp. 111 f.; *Gesammelte Schriften, ed. cit.* iv, 2, pp. 16 f. Cp. Goldstein, *op. cit.* p. 181.

CHAPTER XVI

GENIUS AND GOOD TASTE. SOME POINTS OF FORM AND TECHNIQUE

GENIUS

An adequate history of the word 'genius' has not yet been written.[1] But it would cover a very important section of the aesthetics of the eighteenth century; it would have to deal with the interpretations of the idea that came down from antiquity and the 'génie' of the first French translators of the *Arabian Nights*, through the contrast of 'wit' and 'genius' in Warton's Essay on Pope, to the conception of creative genius in Shaftesbury and Young, and the aesthetic anarchism of the German 'Geniezeit'. Lessing, standing as he did between the rationalistic era and the individualist revolt which swept across Germany before he died, had some part in the development of the idea.

The word 'Genie' occurs with considerable frequency in the *Hamburgische Dramaturgie*; it is used, in the double sense which German, in common with other European languages, permits, for the quality of genius[2] and the possessor of that quality.[3]

The first thing which Lessing postulates of genius is the power of achieving its end (I, 26) 'ohne es zu wissen, ohne es sich langweilig zu erklären'. This spontaneity of genius had been emphasised by Du Bos; in a passage which is quoted by Mendelssohn in a review of Sulzer's treatise on genius in the *Litteraturbriefe*,[4] he had said:

On appelle génie, l'aptitude qu'un homme a reçu de la nature, pour faire bien et facilement certaines choses, que les autres ne sçauroient faire que très-mal, même en prenant beaucoup de peine. Nous apprenons à faire les choses pour lesquelles nous avons du génie, avec autant de facilité que nous en avons à parler notre langue naturelle.[5]

---

[1] See H. Wolf, *Versuch einer Geschichte des Geniebegriffs in der deutschen Ästhetik des 18. Jahrhunderts*, i (Von Gottsched bis auf Lessing), Heidelberg, 1923.

[2] E.g., II, 49; V, 52; [VI, 32]; XII, 101; XVIII, 101; XXVI, 127; XXX, 51, 66; XXXII, 60; XXXIV, 6; XXXVI, 127; XLII, 9; [XLIII, 14]; XLIV, 68; LIX, 122.

[3] E.g., I, 26; VII, 15; XI, 46; XIV, 48; XVIII, 126; XXX, 38, 41, 42, 64; XXXIII, 102; XXXIV, 33, 35, 44, 47, 102, 109; XLII, 12, 26.

[4] *Litteraturbriefe*, No. xcii, April 3, 1760; *Gesammelte Schriften*, ed. cit. iv, 2, p. 47.

[5] *Réflexions critiques sur la Poësie et sur la Peinture*, ii, i (*ed. cit.* ii, p. 6).

R L

And to this might be added a passage from a later article in the *Litteraturbriefe*:

> Warum wird einem Genie sein ihm angemessenes Geschäft leicht? Weil die Thätigkeit seiner Seelenkraft sich grade bey diesem Gegenstande am wirksamsten erzeigt; weil alle andre Federn der Kraft so gesetzt und gespannt sind, dass sie harmonisch zu einem gemeinschaftlichen Zwecke wirken; weil diese grössere Thätigkeit, diese Harmonie, die Seele nach wenigen Versuchen schnell zu einer Fertigkeit erhebt, in dieser ihr allein recht natürlichen Richtung zu wirken.[1]

In the first section of the *Dramaturgie* Lessing goes on to contrast (28) the genius with the wit ('der witzige Kopf'):[2] genius achieves 'what the mere wit tortures himself in vain to imitate'. And in St. xxx (38) he discusses the superiority of genius. For a genius, he says, there is nothing lacking for a tragic drama in the facts concerning *Rodogune*; for a bungler ('Stümper') everything. 'Da ist keine Liebe, da ist keine Verwicklung, keine Erkennung, kein unerwarteter wunderbarer Zwischenfall; alles geht seinen natürlichen Gang.'

It is a distinctive characteristic of genius that it works in harmony with nature (41). The natural course of things acts as a stimulus to genius; it scares the inferior poet. Genius can only concern itself with happenings which are based on one another, with chains of causes and effects. To trace the latter to the former, to weigh the effect with its cause, to exclude the fortuitous, to make everything that takes place happen in such a way that it could not happen in any other way: this is the task of genius, if it is working in the field of history to transmute the treasures of memory into nourishment for the mind.[3] On the other hand, the 'wit' is not interested in the interdependence of happenings, but merely asks whether they are similar or dissimilar; if he attempts works which should be reserved for genius alone, he dwells on events which have nothing more in common than simultaneity. To link these events with one another, to weave their threads together and confuse them, so that we are unable to keep them apart and are plunged from one surprise into another: this (56) is all that mere wit can do. This is perhaps Lessing's most important pro-

---

[1] *Litteraturbriefe*, No. cccxvii, March 7, 1765, *ed. cit.* xxii, p. 27.
[2] This phrase occurs again in x, 28; xxiv, 24; xxx, 64; xxxii, 69; lxxxiv, 40.
[3] Cp. also lxxix, 66 ff. for a similar description of the poet's function.

nouncement on the nature of genius; it is at all events the one in which, as far as I can see, he is least specifically indebted to suggestion from outside.

Later in the *Dramaturgie* (LXX, 66) Lessing returns to this question of the attitude of genius towards the process of nature: 'In der Natur ist alles mit allem verbunden.... Um endliche Geister an dem Genusse desselben Antheil nehmen zu lassen, mussten diese das Vermögen erhalten, ihr Schranken zu geben, die sie nicht hat; das Vermögen abzusondern, und ihre Aufmerksamkeit nach Gutdünken lenken zu können.... Die Bestimmung der Kunst ist, uns in dem Reiche des Schönen dieser Absonderung zu überheben, uns die Fixirung unserer Aufmerksamkeit zu erleichtern.' This is an essential opinion of Mendelssohn's. The latter's most complete statement of it is to be found in *Über die Hauptgrundsätze der schönen Künste und Wissenschaften*:

Man sieht hieraus, in welchem Falle es der Kunst zukomme, die Natur zu verlassen, und die Gegenstände nicht völlig so nachzubilden, wie sie im Urbilde anzutreffen sind. Die Natur hat einen unermesslichen Plan. Die Mannigfaltigkeit desselben erstreckt sich vom unendlich Kleinen bis ins unendlich Grosse, und seine Einheit ist über alles Erstaunen hinweg. Die Schönheit der äusserlichen Formen überhaupt, ist nur ein sehr geringer Theil von ihren Absichten, und sie hat dieselbe zuweilen grössern Absichten nachsetzen müssen. Ist es also wohl möglich, dass der eingeschränkte Raum, welchen wir von der Natur betrachten können, dass dieser Raum in so fern er uns in die Sinne fällt, alle Eigenschaften der idealischen Schönheit erschöpfen sollte?
Der menschliche Künstler hingegen wählt sich einen Umfang, der seinen Kräften angemessen ist. Seine Absichten sind so eingeschränkt, als seine Fähigkeiten. Sein ganzer Endzweck ist, die Schönheiten, die in die menschliche Sinne fallen, in einem eingeschränkten Bezirke vorzustellen. Er wird also den idealischen Schönheiten näher kommen können, als die Natur in diesem oder jenem Theile gekommen ist, weil ihn keine höheren Absichten zu Abweichungen veranlassen. Was sie in verschiedenen Gegenständen zerstreuet hat, versammelt er in einem einzigen Gesichtspunkte, bildet sich ein Ganzes daraus, und bemühet sich, es so vorzustellen, wie es die Natur vorgestellt haben würde, wenn die Schönheit dieses begränzten Gegenstandes ihre einzige Absicht gewesen wäre. Nichts anders als dieses bedeuten die gewöhnlichen Ausdrücke der Künstler: die Natur verschönern, die schöne Natur nachahmen u.s.w. Sie wollen einen gewissen Gegenstand so abbilden, wie ihn Gott geschaffen haben würde, wenn die sinnliche Schönheit sein höchster Endzweck gewesen wäre, und ihn also keine wichtigeren Endzwecke zu Abweichungen hätten veranlassen können. Dieses ist die vollkommenste idealische Schönheit, die in der

Natur nirgend anders, als im Ganzen anzutreffen, und in den Werken der Kunst vielleicht nie völlig zu erreichen ist.

Der Künstler muss sich also über die gemeine Natur erheben, und weil die Schönheit sein einziger Endzweck ist; so steht es ihm frey, dieselbe allenthalben in seinen Werken zu koncentriren, damit sie uns stärker rühre.[1]

The result of Lessing's discussion of genius in St. xxx is the conclusion that Corneille, in his handling of the theme of *Rodogune*, has shown himself not a genius, but a 'witziger Kopf' (63): 'Das Genie liebt Einfalt; der Witz, Verwicklung.' So, too, Diderot had insisted on simplicity as characteristic of the work of genius: 'O mon ami, que la simplicité est belle!'[2]

The contrast of genius and wit was of English origin. Gustav Kettner is doubtless correct in tracing it to Joseph Warton's Essay on the *Genius and Writings of Pope*, which had been translated into German in 1763 in the sixth part of the *Sammlung vermischter Schriften zur Beförderung der schönen Wissenschaften und der freyen Künste* (pp. 1 ff.).[3] Warton's *Essay* was also reviewed at length by Mendelssohn in the *Bibliothek der schönen Wissenschaften*,[4] and it is quoted by Lessing himself in the *Litteraturbriefe*.[5] The passage in Warton which has some bearing on the present question is the following (it occurs on p. 2 of the 1763 version, but I quote from the translation in Mendelssohn's article, which was no doubt Lessing's immediate source):[6]

In der Zueignungsschrift an Dr. Young sagt unser Verfasser: „Ich habe Hochachtung für das Andenken eines Pope, ich verehre seine Talente; aber ich glaube nicht, dass er die Vollkommenheit in seiner Kunst erreicht habe.... Man giebt, wie es scheinet, auf den Unterschied nicht genug Achtung zwischen einem witzigen Kopfe, einem sinnreichen Schriftsteller, (a man of sense) und einem wahren Dichter."

---

[1] *Philosophische Schriften*, Berlin, 1777, ii, pp. 114 ff.; *Gesammelte Schriften, ed. cit.* i, pp. 288 f. (The passage occurs, in slightly different forms, in the earliest version of the essay (see above, p. 415, note 1), and in the separate edition of 1771, pp. 14 ff.)

[2] *De la poésie dramatique, Œuvres complètes, ed. cit.* vii, p. 339; Lessing's translation, ii, p. 324.

[3] Cp. G. Kettner, *Lessing und Shakespeare*, in *Neue Jahrbücher für das klassische Altertum, Geschichte und deutsche Literatur und für Pädagogik*, xix, 1907, p. 272.

[4] iv (i), 1758, pp. 500 ff. and iv (ii), 1759, pp. 627 ff.; *Gesammelte Schriften, ed. cit.* iv, 1, pp. 388 ff.

[5] *Litteraturbriefe*, No. ciii, May 8, 1760; *Schriften*, viii, p. 230.

[6] *Bibliothek der schönen Wissenschaften*, iv (i), 1758, p. 502; *Gesammelte Schriften, ed. cit.* iv, 1, p. 389.

A little later in the *Dramaturgie* Lessing contrasts the genius with the 'kleine Künstler' (xxxiv, 101): 'Mit Absicht dichten, mit Absicht nachahmen, ist das, was das Genie von den kleinen Künstlern unterscheidet.' Here he may possibly have been thinking of Mendelssohn's dictum in his *Betrachtungen über die Quellen und Verbindungen der schönen Künste und Wissenschaften*: 'Das Genie erfordert eine Vollkommenheit aller Seelenkräfte, und eine Übereinstimmung derselben zu einem einzigen Endzwecke.'[1] Again, in his discussion of Maffei (xlii, 6 ff.), Lessing contrasts 'das Genie und der Dichter' with the 'Litterator' and 'Versificateur'. On this contrast, a passage from a review by Lessing in the *Litteraturbriefe* of May 8, 1760,[2] may supply a commentary:

Ich habe gezweifelt, ob man dem Herrn Cramer ein poetisches Genie zugestehen könne. Ich habe aber mit Vergnügen bekannt, dass er der vortrefflichste Versificateur ist. Ich nehme beyde Ausdrücke so, wie sie die feinsten Kunstrichter der Engländer und Franzosen nehmen. "Ein poetisches Genie, sagt einer von den ersten (*Note*: Der Verfasser des Essay on the Writings and Genius of Pope. S. 111), den ich eben vor mir liegen habe, "ist so ausserordentlich selten, that no cou[n]try in the succession of many ages has produced above three or four persons that deserve the title. The *man of rhymes* may be easily found; but the genuine poet, of a lively plastic imagination, the true *Maker* or *Creator*, is so uncommon a prodigy....Ist denn ein Versificateur nichts als ein Reimer? Kann man der vortrefflichste Versificateur seyn, ohne ein Mann von vielem Witze, von vielem Verstande, von vielem Geschmacke zu seyn? Diderot, der neueste, und unter den neuen unstreitig der beste französische Kunstrichter, verbindet keinen geringern Begrif mit dem Namen eines Versificateurs. Quelle difference entre le Versificateur et le Poete! Cependant *ne croyez pas que je méprise le premier: son talent est rare....*[3]

Genius must create; indeed, it may create a world entirely its own —a world different from ours, in which causes and effects (xxxiv, 30) may indeed follow another order but yet move equally towards a general effect of good: 'in short, the world of a genius, who—if I may be permitted to designate the nameless Creator by his noblest work— who, I say, in order to imitate the highest genius in little, transposes, interchanges, diminishes, intensifies...and thereby creates a whole of his own which embodies his own purposes.' Above all, Lessing lays

---

[1] *Bibliothek der schönen Wissenschaften*, i (ii), 1757, p. 238. See above, p. 415.

[2] *Litteraturbriefe*, No. ciii, *ed. cit.* vi, pp. 297 ff.; *Schriften*, viii, pp. 229 f.

[3] The passage from Diderot is in *De la poésie dramatique*, *Œuvres complètes*, *ed. cit.* vii, p. 332; Lessing's translation, ii, pp. 303 f.

stress on this quality of purpose in the work of genius.[1] He may possibly have remembered Sulzer's statement of the matter in his *Untersuchung des Genies*:[2]

Ist Witz erforderlich, in den Werken des Genies alles, was mit einem Vorwurfe in Beziehung steht, zu entdecken; so muss man auch nothwendig noch eine andere Fähigkeit damit verbinden, nämlich die Gründlichkeit des Urtheils, um die Grössen solcher Beziehungen zu schätzen. Man erlaube mir diesen Ausdruck, der zwar ein wenig zu geometrisch ist, sich aber gut hieher zu schicken scheint. Ich erkläre mich deutlicher. Ein Ding ist gemeiniglich mit unzähligen andern verbunden; die Bande aber, die sie mit einander vereinigen, sind nicht alle gleich stark. Eins ist unmittelbarer und wesentlicher mit einer Sache verbunden, als das andere... Nun ist es klar, dass das Urtheil über diese Grössen der Beziehung eine sehr wesentliche Eigenschaft des Genies ist. Diese Eigenschaft bringt in den Werken des Genies das hervor, was das schätzbarste ist. Die Gründlichkeit, Ordnung und Schönheit des Plans und der Anordnung eines Werks; die Wirksamkeit der Mittel; die Richtigkeit und Leichtigkeit der Verbindungen; die Subordination der Theile, welche den gleichen Fortgang hervorbringt, den Geist in einer beständigen, aber mannigfaltigen Beschäftigung erhält, und die grossen wesentlichen Schönheiten sowohl als die geringern und untergeordneten gleich angenehm und nothwendig macht; sind Folgen dieser Eigenschaft. Durch sie erhält jede Sache und jeder besondere Zug seinen gehörigen Platz, um die Wirkung des Ganzen fühlbarer zu machen. Durch sie endlich kann man in seinen Werken zu der edlen Einfalt gelangen, welche alles überflüssige verwirft, und nur wenige Mittel braucht, die grossen Wirkungen hervorzubringen, die für einige Werke der grössten Genies des Alterthums unsere Bewunderung erwecken.[3]

Another characteristic, or rather privilege, of genius is to be able to commit mistakes. 'It is vouchsafed to genius (xxxiv, 6) to ignore thousands of things which every schoolboy knows; not the acquired stores of memory, but what he is able to bring forth from himself, from his own feelings, constitutes his wealth;[4] what he may have

[1] See above, pp. 415, 450.

[2] I quote this article as it was translated from the French in the *Sammlung vermischter Schriften zur Beförderung der schönen Wissenschaften und der freyen Künste* in 1762 (v, i, pp. 137 ff. The passage quoted occurs on pp. 146 f.). The idea may perhaps be traced to Shaftesbury.

[3] Cp. also Mendelssohn's review of Sulzer's treatise cited below, p. 455.

[4] Here Lessing refers to Pindar's ode, *Olymp.* II, 94: σοφὸς ὁ πολλὰ εἰδὼς φυᾷ. μαθόντες δὲ λάβροι παγγλωσσίᾳ, κόρακες ὥς, ἄκραντα γαρύετον Διὸς πρὸς ὄρνιχα θεῖον. 'Wise is he who knows many things through himself. The learners chatter boldly and unceasingly like ravens against the divine bird of Zeus.'

heard or read either he has forgotten again, or he is content to ignore it except in so far as it may suit his plan. He thus transgresses, sometimes from self-assurance, sometimes from pride, sometimes intentionally and sometimes not, and so frequently, so crudely, that we other good people cannot be enough surprised.'

This aspect of genius may have been suggested to Lessing by Mendelssohn, who in a review of Sulzer's treatise on genius[1] had quoted a passage from the Abbé Trublet expressing a similar idea:

Der Abt Trublet hat hiervon einige sehr artige Gedanken. „Wie kömmts, fragt er, dass in manchem Werke, sehr matte Stellen und grobe Fehler, neben sehr grosse Schönheiten anzutreffen sind?—Die Antwort ist leicht. Der Verfasser war ein Genie. Dieselbe Ursache erzeuget seine Fehler und seine Schönheiten. Man kann ihm das Talent, jene zu vermeiden, nicht geben, ohne ihm das wichtigere Talent, diese hervorzubringen, zu benehmen. Was er von Seiten der Kunst und des Geschmackes gewinnen würde, das würde er von Seiten der Einbildungskraft und des Genies, wieder verlieren.—Wenn ein Werk ohne Fehler möglich wäre; so müsste es einen mittelmässigen Menschen zum Verfasser haben.“[2]

And in another review—of Flögel's *Vermischte Beyträge zur Philosophie und den schönen Wissenschaften* (Breslau, 1762) which may also have been written by Mendelssohn—we find:

Warum sind viele Genies in fremden Fächern ausser dem ihrigen oft so stumpf, den Dummköpfen so ähnlich?—Ihre Seele lebt nur in der Richtung, wohin sich ihre Thätigkeit äussert, in allen andern Richtungen ist sie gleichsam todt. . . . Wie geht es sonst zu, dass man manche Genies gekannt hat, (und wie viele unterdruckte bleiben uns unbekannt!) die in dem Fache, dahinein sie gezwungen worden, elende Stümper waren, und nun auf einmal ihr rechtes Feld finden, und sich als Meister darin zeigen?[3]

For the development of aesthetic theory, however, perhaps the most significant claim for genius which Lessing makes is that it may rise superior to rules. In St. VII (15) he says: 'Das Genie lacht über alle die Grenzscheidungen der Kritik'; in St. XI (45) he refers to 'Beyspiele. . .wo das Genie aller unserer Philosophie trotzet'; and in

---

[1] *Analyse du Génie*, published in *Histoire de l'Académie Royale des Sciences et Belles Lettres, Année 1757* (Berlin, 1759, pp. 392 ff.).

[2] *Litteraturbriefe*, No. xcii, April 3, 1760, *ed. cit.* vi, p. 223; *Gesammelte Schriften, ed. cit.* iv, 2, p. 51. The original of the passage translated will be found in Abbé N. C. J. Trublet, *Essais sur divers sujets de littérature et de morale*, Paris, 1754–60, iii (1754), pp. 131 f.

[3] *Litteraturbriefe*, No. cccxvii, March 7, 1765, *ed. cit.* xxii, pp. 27 f.

St. xxxiii (100) he speaks contemptuously of 'alle die mechanischen Gesetze, mit denen sich kahle Kunstrichter herumschlagen, und deren Beobachtung sie lieber, dem Genie zum Trotze, zur einzigen Quelle der Vollkommenheit eines Drama machen möchten'.

This privilege of genius, which had been warmly defended by Mendelssohn, had been given general currency by Young's *Conjectures on Original Composition*. Here the critic had boldly asserted:

For unprescribed Beauties, and unexampled Excellence, which are Characteristics of *Genius*, lie without the Pale of *Learning's* Authorities, and Laws; which Pale, Genius must leap to come at them.[1]

But even before Young, Trublet had insisted that genius should be free from the tyranny of rules. In the *Essais sur divers sujets* he had written:

Les regles qui sont un secours pour les esprits médiocres, sont quelquefois un obstacle pour les génies supérieurs. Nous devons les regles aux premiers ouvrages, et ceux-ci au génie seul. Nous devons les seconds ouvrages, en partie aux premiers, en partie aux regles, mais en plus grande partie encore au génie. Un homme ordinaire fait un ouvrage conforme aux regles conues. Un grand homme en fait un qui donne lieu à de nouvelles regles.[2]

It is probable that Trublet helped to mould the opinions of Mendelssohn—and possibly also those of Young; we find Mendelssohn, before he could have known Young's essay, writing in the *Bibliothek der schönen Wissenschaften*:

Der Kunstrichter hat sich...für dem sehr schädlichen Vorurtheile zu hüten, als wenn die Regeln des Ganzen allezeit das vornehmste wären. Hat der Dichter Genie genug, die Fehler der Anlage durch die Gewalt der Leidenschaften, die er erregt, unserer Bemerkung zu entziehen; so macht sich der Kunstrichter lächerlich, wenn er seine Empfindungen verläugnet, und nach Regeln urtheilet, über die sich der Dichter weit hinweg gesetzt hat. Es ist hier der Ort nicht, diese Materie auszuführen. Unsers Wissens haben die Kunstrichter noch sehr wenig daran gedacht, die Grenzen der Regeln und des Genies aus einander zu setzen.[3]

---

[1] *Conjectures on Original Composition, in a Letter to the Author of Sir Charles Grandison*, London, 1759, pp. 27 f.; for the German translation, see *Gedanken über die Originalwerke*, Leipzig, 1760, reprint by K. Jahn, Bonn, 1910, pp. 15 f.

[2] *Essais sur divers sujets de littérature et de morale*, ed. cit. iii, pp. 138 f.

[3] *Bibliothek der schönen Wissenschaften*, iv (ii), 1759, p. 786; *Gesammelte Schriften*, ed. cit. iv, 1, p. 485.

And again in the sixtieth *Litteraturbrief* he writes:

> Der Herr Professor Sulzer sagt irgendwo: ,,Wenn in der Republik der Gelehrten Gesetze könnten gegeben werden, so sollte dieses eines der ersten seyn; dass sich niemand unterstehen sollte ein Schriftsteller zu werden, der nicht die vornehmsten griechische und lateinische Schriften der Alten, mit Fleiss, und zu wiederholten malen durchgelesen." Mich wunderts, dass dieser warhaftig denkende Kopf, gegen die sich selbst bildende Genies hat so unbillig seyn können. Sein Gesetz hätte uns ja um alle Werke des Schakespears bringen können! Wenn es möglich wäre, so sollte man lieber den Leuten, die nicht selbst denken, das Schriftsteller-handwerk legen, und wenn sie auch die Alten mit noch so viel Fleiss durchgelesen hätten! Das Genie kann den Mangel der Exempel ersetzen, aber der Mangel des Genies ist unersetzlich.[1]

Still another passage might be quoted from a later review in the *Litteraturbriefe*:

> Young sagt: die Regeln sind Krücken, welche nur der Kranke gebraucht, der Gesunde hingegen wegwirft.—Wenn nun diese Vergleichung gleich nicht völlig richtig seyn solte, so ist es doch gewiss, dass nichts schädlicher ist, als Regeln die das Genie einschränken, und es so zu sagen, hindern auf seine eigene Füsse zu treten. Nirgend sind solche Regeln häufiger als in Systemen, die Leute von seichter Einsicht bauen. Weil sie selbst nicht weit sehen, so sind ihre vornehmste Satzungen, Verbote an alle die nach ihnen folgen, auch nicht weiter zu sehen. So sind viele Regeln beschaffen, durch welche Hedelin und sein treuer Abschreiber Gottsched,—zwey Leute, welche beyde mit gleich schlechtem Erfolge für die Schaubühne gearbeitet haben—die dramatische Schriftsteller gern fesseln, und sie zwingen möchten, nicht besser zu schreiben als sie geschrieben haben.[2]

It might be added that Lessing himself in his *Laokoon* had said of Sophocles: '. . . nur indem er sich über [die Theorie] hinwegsetzet, hat er Schönheiten erreicht, von welchen dem furchtsamen Kunstrichter, ohne dieses Beyspiel, nie träumen würde.'[3] And in St. XLVIII of the *Dramaturgie* he defends Euripides's neglect of the element of surprise in tragedy in a similar way (135): 'wenn ein Genie, höherer Absichten wegen, mehrere derselben [Gattungen] in einem und eben demselben

---

[1] *Litteraturbriefe*, No. lx, October 11, 1759; *Gesammelte Schriften, ed. cit.* iv, 1, pp. 569 f. Both this and the preceding passage are quoted by Goldstein, *op. cit.* pp. 12 ff.

[2] *Litteraturbriefe*, No. cciv, December 17, 1761, *ed. cit.* xii, p. 327. The image of the crutches is used by Lessing CI–CIV, 57. See above, pp. 131 f.

[3] *Laokoon*, iv; *Schriften*, ix, p. 24. Cp. G. Kettner, *Lessing und Shakespeare*, in *Neue Jahrbücher für das klassische Altertum* etc. xix, 1907, p. 278.

Werke zusammenfliessen lässt, so vergesse man das Lehrbuch und untersuche blos, ob es diese höhere Absichten erreicht hat.'

But in demanding for genius freedom from the shackles of the rules, Lessing did not anticipate all the consequences which his demand might bring with it. In this his position was similar to that of Voltaire —who, it will be remembered, lived to repent bitterly of his early championship of Shakespeare. The warmth of his brother Karl's admiration for *Götz von Berlichingen* found no response in Lessing;[1] and in St. XCVI of the *Dramaturgie* we find him crying a halt to those who give their approval to the lawlessness of genius—that is, to a disobedience to the traditional laws which he himself had advocated throughout his work. 'Wir haben', he says (67), '...itzt ein Geschlecht selbst von Critikern, deren beste Critik darinn besteht—alle Critik verdächtig zu machen. „Genie! Genie! schreien sie. Das Genie setzt sich über alle Regeln hinweg! Was das Genie macht, ist Regel!"' This outburst, however, may have been provoked not so much by writers who foreshadowed the coming 'Sturm und Drang' as by the misuse which critics of the Klotzian school had made of such opinions.[2]

GOOD TASTE

The activity of the genius is thus not guided by rules, but by his own taste; and the critic who judges him must possess taste. In the earlier part of the *Dramaturgie* Lessing expresses a few opinions on the subject of this 'Geschmack'. But these do not show any deeper interest or preoccupation with the question, and may well have been echoes of the *Critische Dichtkunst* of Gottsched: indeed, even for Gottsched the day of the 'buon gusto' was past—the dust of controversy which it raised had been laid. In the *Ankündigung* (55) Lessing, thinking of the public to which the theatre was to appeal, speaks of 'true taste' as being the general taste 'which is extended to beauties of every kind, but expects from none more pleasure and delight than it is in its

---

[1] Cp. letter to Karl Lessing of April 30, 1774 (*Schriften*, xviii, p. 109). It is usual also to refer to Goethe Lessing's often quoted words: 'Er füllt Därme mit Sand, und verkauft sie für Stricke. Wer? Etwa der Dichter, der den Lebenslauf eines Mannes in Dialogen bringt, und das Ding für Drama ausschreit?' (*Schriften*, xvi, p. 535).

[2] Cp. Petersen, *ed. cit.* p. 261. See also Grimm, *Deutsches Wörterbuch*, under *Genie* (especially (9) and (10), 3412–3428) for numerous examples of the use of the word by Lessing and his contemporaries.

nature to afford'. And he adds (75) that taste can be instilled into a 'man of healthy understanding simply by explaining to him why something has not given him pleasure'. This almost corresponds to Gottsched's statement: 'Man darf ihnen nur was Schönes zeigen, und sie aufmerksam darauf machen: So werden sie es gewahr.'[1] Again, at the end of St. 1 (131), where Lessing affirms that the good writer has always in view the best and most enlightened minds of his age and country, and that if he descends to the level of the 'Pöbel', it is only 'um ihn zu erleuchten und zu bessern', one thinks of Gottsched's principle:

So müssen sich denn die Poeten niemals nach dem Geschmacke der Welt, das ist, des grossen Haufens, oder des unverständigen Pöbels richten. Dieser vielköpfigte Götze urtheilt oft sehr verkehrt von Dingen. Er muss vielmehr suchen, den Geschmack seines Vaterlandes, seines Hofes, seiner Stadt zu läutern: Es wäre denn, dass dieses schon vor ihm geschehen wäre.[2]

A further parallel can be drawn between Lessing's statement in St. xix (12): 'Der wahre Kunstrichter folgert keine Regeln aus seinem Geschmacke, sondern hat seinen Geschmack nach den Regeln gebildet, welche die Natur der Sache erfodert', and Gottsched's conviction that 'Die Schönheit eines künstlichen Werkes beruht nicht auf einem leeren Dünkel; sondern sie hat ihren festen und nothwendigen Grund in der Natur der Dinge.'[3] One might also perhaps compare a passage interpolated by Ramler in the 'Vorerinnerung' to Part II of his translation of Batteux' *Principes de la Littérature*:

Man muss also diese Fragen einmal für allemal studiert und untersucht haben; man muss die Grundsätze, die daraus herfliessen, erkannt und eingesehen haben; und wenn man sie einmal wohl begriffen hat: so wird der Geschmack seinen Weg weit gewisser und zuversichtlicher gehn; ja er wird noch weiter gehn, er wird im Stande seyn, ein richterliches Urtheil zu fällen, ohne Furcht zu fehlen und in Irrthum zu gerathen.[4]

All the statements by Lessing which have been quoted above are obviously based on a traditional conception of 'taste', and take no account of the reservations which would follow from those statements about genius, and its freedom from the rules, which are made elsewhere in the *Dramaturgie*. But it will be noticed that they all occur in the earlier sections of the work.

[1] *Critische Dichtkunst*, 2nd ed. Leipzig, 1737, p. 134.
[2] *Ibid*. pp. 129 f.   [3] *Ibid*. p. 126.
[4] 2nd ed. Leipzig, 1762–63, ii, p. 7.

DRAMA AND NARRATIVE

Among what might be called the technical questions discussed in the *Dramaturgie* is the distinction between the methods of narrative and dramatic writing. To some extent the pigeon-holing process of *Laokoon* is continued here. Lessing has an opportunity of dealing with the question at the very outset of his journal, for the first play of the repertory was a dramatisation of an episode in Tasso's *Gerusalemme liberata*. He observes (1, 16 ff.) that the merely mechanical problem of inventing complications or elaborating emotions in scenes is not difficult; but to maintain the interest of the spectator, to avoid improbabilities, to transfer oneself from the standpoint of the narrator to that of the dramatic character—all this does present peculiar difficulties. Passions must not be described, but must spring into existence before our eyes, if the poet is to create that illusion which compels our sympathy. Only genius can solve this problem.

Such difficulties had already been commented upon by Mendelssohn. In discussing Wieland's *Clementina von Porretta*, and a similar plan of his own, in the *Litteraturbriefe* he had said:

Dem ersten Anblicke nach, sollte nichts leichter scheinen, als die Verwandelung einer rührenden Episode in ein bürgerliches Trauerspiel, und der Vortrag des Herrn Richardson kömmt hier diesem Betruge sehr zu Statten. Denn da er so natürlich dialogirt, und so sorgfältig die Gebehrden seiner unterredenden Personen beschreibet, so wird man verführt zu glauben, er habe nicht nur die Erfindung, sondern auch den grössten Theil der theatralischen Ausführung, bis auf die Pantomime so gar, die der Schauspieler zu beobachten hat, über sich genommen.— Dieses glaubte ich, und fing an den Plan zu entwerfen. Allein ich ward gar bald inne, dass die Dichtungsarten sich so schwehr, als die Arten der Natur, eine in die andere umschmelzen lassen. Jede hat ihre wesentliche Bestandtheile, die gleichsam in Rauch aufgehen, so bald man eine gewaltsame Verwandelung mit ihnen vornimmt.[1]

---

[1] *Litteraturbriefe*, No. cxxiii, August 21, 1760, *ed. cit.* vii, p. 114; *Gesammelte Schriften, ed. cit.* iv, 2, pp. 141 f. Cp. also Lessing's letter to Gerstenberg of February 25, 1768 (*Schriften*, xvii, p. 247) concerning the latter's dramatisation from Dante in his *Ugolino*: 'Bey dem Dante hören wir die Geschichte als geschehen: bey Ihnen sehn wir sie als geschehend. Es ist ganz etwas anders, ob ich das Schreckliche hinter mir, oder vor mir erblicke. Ganz etwas anders, ob ich höre, durch dieses Elend kam der Held durch, das überstand er: oder ob ich sehe, durch dieses soll er durch, dieses soll er überstehen. Der Unterschied der Gattung macht hier alles.' (Quoted also by Petersen, *ed. cit.* p. 178.)

Lessing returns to this matter in criticising Heufeld's dramatisation of Rousseau's *Nouvelle Héloïse*. Here the problem is clearly stated (IX, 24). We wish to see on the stage what people are, and can only learn this from what they actually do. We cannot be interested in the good qualities which are ascribed to them by others; we must be convinced of the existence of these qualities by actions, and actions such as can be concentrated in the brief duration of a play.[1] A third discussion of the problem is to be found in Lessing's comparison of Favart's *Soliman II* with the story by Marmontel on which it was based (XXXIII, 87).[2] He has nothing but praise for the skill with which Favart has accomplished the dramatisation; but he is chiefly concerned in these sections with the qualities which should distinguish dramatic characters. In St. XXXV (80) he turns to the comparison of drama and moral fable. Finally, in St. XXXVI, he discusses in passing the *Matron of Ephesus* of Petronius and its dramatisations.

DRAMAS IN VERSE AND PROSE

In his criticism of Schlegel's *Die stumme Schönheit* (XIII, 51) Lessing turns to the general question whether comedies should be written in rhymed verse or in prose. The play in question is in verse—'as fluent as it is elegant'—but Lessing considers it fortunate that Schlegel did not always carry out his theories, and that he did not write his greater comedies in verse. Schlegel's advocacy of the verse form for comedy is to be found in an article, *Schreiben über die Comödie in Versen*, published in Gottsched's *Beyträge zur critischen Historie der Deutschen Sprache* for 1740.[3] This was itself a reply to an article by G. B. Straube, *Versuch eines Beweises, dass eine gereimte Comödie nicht gut seyn könne*, which had appeared in the previous number.[4] The controversy, no doubt originally prompted by Houdar de la Motte's plea for tragedy in prose,[5] was continued in subsequent numbers of the journal. In his *Gedanken*

[1] See also above, pp. 157, 382, note 3.
[2] See above, pp. 235 ff.
[3] *Beyträge zur critischen Historie der Deutschen Sprache, Poesie und Beredsamkeit*, St. xxiv (1740), pp. 624 ff. Reprinted in Schlegel's *Werke, ed. cit.* iii (1764), pp. 65 ff., and ed. of Antoniewicz, pp. 9 ff.
[4] *Beyträge zur critischen Historie*, St. xxiii (1740), pp. 466 ff.
[5] In my *Genesis of Romantic Theory* (Cambridge, 1923, pp. 214 f.) I have shown that this plea was probably of Italian inspiration.

zur Aufnahme des dänischen Theaters, however, Schlegel expressed a somewhat modified view:

> Man hat viel eher Komödien in Versen, als in Prose, gehabt, und diese letztern sind eine ganz neue Erfindung. Nur sind der Komödie die guten Verse sehr schwer; und es ist gleichwohl besser, eine Komödie in guter Prose, als in schlechten Versen, anzuhören; denn schlechte Verse verderben den Nachdruck der Gedanken, an statt ihn zu erheben.[1]

To this view Lessing would certainly have assented. He himself refers to Houdar de la Motte's view that verse is a 'childish constraint' (xix, 105), although he does not share it. Here he is obviously drawing on Voltaire's preface to the 1730 edition of his own *Œdipe*:[2]

> Mr. *de la Motte* prétend, qu'au moins une scène de Tragédie mise en prose ne perd rien de sa grace ni de sa force. Pour le prouver il tourne en prose la première scène de *Mithridate*, et personne ne peut la lire. Il ne songe pas que le grand mérite des vers est qu'ils soient aussi naturels, aussi corrects que la prose. C'est cette extrême difficulté surmontée[3] qui charme les connaisseurs. Réduisez les vers en prose, il n'y a plus ni mérite ni plaisir.
>
> Mais, dit-il, nos voisins ne riment point dans leurs Tragédies. Cela est vrai; mais ces piéces sont en vers, parce qu'il faut de l'harmonie à tous les peuples de la Terre. Il ne s'agit donc plus que de savoir, si nos vers doivent être rimés ou non....Les Italiens et les Anglais peuvent se passer de rime, parce que leur langue a des inversions, et leur Poësie mille libertés qui nous manquent. Chaque langue a son génie déterminé par la nature de la construction de ses phrases, par la fréquence de ses voyelles ou de ses consonnes, ses inversions, ses verbes auxiliaires, etc. Le génie de notre langue est la clarté et l'élégance; nous ne permettons nulle licence à notre Poësie, qui doit marcher comme notre prose dans l'ordre précis de nos idées. Nous avons donc un besoin essentiel du retour des mêmes sons, pour que notre Poësie ne soit pas confondue avec la prose.

This was also Schlegel's argument for the use of verse.[4]

But Lessing observes (xiii, 60) that the difficulties which Schlegel clearly encountered in practice outweighed the advantages which

---

[1] *Werke, ed. cit.* iii, p. 291; ed. Antoniewicz, p. 220.

[2] *Œuvres, ed. cit.* vii, pp. 19 f. Cp. also *Œuvres complètes*, Paris, 1877–85, ii, pp. 9, 55 f. La Motte's argument is to be found in his *Quatrième Discours à l'occasion de la Tragédie d'Œdipe, Œuvres*, Paris, 1754, iv, pp. 390 ff.

[3] Cp. 'der überstandenen Schwierigkeit' (xix, 117); cp. also 'aus diesen überstiegenen Schwierigkeiten' (xiii, 63). Antoniewicz, in his Introduction to Schlegel's aesthetic writings (*ed. cit.* p. cxliv) compares Rémond de St Mard, *Œuvres*, Amsterdam, 1749, iv, p. 44; the passage is as follows: 'Après avoir ainsi rendu justice à la rime, je dis hardiment qu'elle a grand besoin du surcroît de plaisir que lui donne la convention et le mérite de la difficulté vaincue.'

[4] Cp. *Werke, ed. cit.* iii, pp. 88 ff.; cp. also Antoniewicz, *ed. cit.* p. cxliii.

seemed so irrefutable in his theory. Possibly there is an echo here of Schlegel's preface to his translation of Destouches' *Le Glorieux*:

Diejenigen kennen also die Natur der Poesie besser, welche die Comödie in Versen aus dem Grunde angreifen, dass es allzuschwer, ja gar unmöglich sey, die dialogische Art, zu reden, mit dem Zwange des Sylbenmaasses zu verbinden, ohne sie undialogisch zu machen; dass also die kleinre Anmuth, nämlich die, so das Sylbenmaas dem Werke ertheilt, der grössren Anmuth, nämlich der, welche die dialogische Art, zu reden, einem Lustspiele giebt, weichen müsse. Auf den Beweis und auf die Widerlegung dieses Grundes kömmt entweder die Verdammung oder die Lossprechung der Comödie in Versen an.[1]

Lessing's criticism of the French contempt for prose comedies (65) again recalls Schlegel's *Schreiben über die Comödie in Versen*:

Wir beobachten aber, dass...bey den Franzosen, da vorher die Unwissenheit der Komödianten, so lange der schlechte Zustand und das barbarische Alter der Komödien gedauert hatte, prosaische Komödien eingeführet, die Verse nach und nach wiederum in ihr altes Recht gesetzet worden, und wie Voltaire in der Vorrede vor seinem Brutus versichert, selbst die Lustspiele des Moliere, welche er in ungebundener Rede gemacht hatte, noch nach seinem Tode in Verse gesetzt werden müssen....[2] Die Engländer aber können hierinnen ebenfalls nichts gültiges bezeigen,[3] weil ihre Komödien auch noch nicht in dem Stande sind, dass man sie eigentlich Komödien nennen könnte....Aber, werden Sie sagen, man würde doch unrecht thun, wenn man die Deutschen in diesen Dingen nicht auch für Leute rechnen wollte, deren Urtheile von einiger Folge wären. Gleichwohl empfinden viele, theils grosse Leute, insonderheit welche sich in der Kritik umgesehen haben, bey Vorstellung unserer Komödien in Versen dieses Vergnügen nicht, und befinden es viel natürlicher, wenn eine Komödie in ungebundener Rede aufgeführet wird.[4]

But Lessing is by no means a convert to the Houdartian view of verse as a childish constraint. La Motte, he says (XIX, 110), had French verse in mind, which is only a 'titillation of the ears'; whereas German verse has more of the quality of Greek verse, which by its rhythm is able to indicate the passions it describes.

[1] Ed. Antoniewicz, pp. 164 f.; cp. also *ibid*. Introduction, pp. cxxxiii ff., and especially pp. cxl f.

[2] Voltaire, *Discours sur la Tragédie*, prefixed to *Brutus*, *Œuvres*, *ed. cit.* vii, p. 194: '...nous avons des Comédies en prose du célèbre *Molière*, que l'on a été obligé de mettre en vers après sa mort, et qui ne sont plus jouées que de cette manière nouvelle.' See above, p. 180.

[3] Lessing's statement (XIII, 68): 'Den Engländer hingegen würde eine gereimte Komödie aus dem Theater jagen' is a rather sweeping generalisation.

[4] *Werke, ed. cit.* iii, pp. 83 ff.; cp. ed. Antoniewicz, pp. 19 ff.

PROLOGUE AND EPILOGUE

The first performance of the Hamburg 'Enterprise' gave Lessing an opportunity of expressing his views on the purpose, and propriety, of providing plays with prologues and epilogues—a practice which he knew to be firmly established in England (VII, 99). But he points out that the English do not use the Prologue, as did the ancients, for the purpose of exposition;[1] nor do they imitate Plautus in using the Epilogue to provide information which could not be put into the fifth act.[2] Their prologues tell the audience about the poet or the subject of the play, and plead for indulgent criticism of the author or the actor; while their epilogues are used to point the moral of the play, or to criticise it or its performance—all this in the most humorous tone, even in the case of tragedies. Whether Lessing knew more than the prologues and epilogues of Thomson (119)[3] and some of Dryden's (126), it is difficult to decide. He would approve (121) of the adoption of prologues and epilogues for new plays in Germany; but, like Thomson, he would prefer serious epilogues—'unserm deutschen Ernste angemessener'—for tragedies.

[1] D'Aubignac, for instance, had said (*Pratique du Théâtre*, iii, chap. i, *ed. cit.* i, pp. 145 f.): 'Les premiers et les plus ordinaires Prologues de la Tragédie Grecque sont ceux que faisoit l'un des principaux Acteurs qui venoit expliquer aux Spectateurs, non pas l'Argument de la Piéce, mais tout ce qui s'étoit passé de l'histoire concernant le Theatre jusqu'au point que s'en faisoit l'ouverture et que l'action Theatrale commençoit.' Cp. *Critik über die Gefangnen des Plautus* in Lessing's *Beyträge* (iv, p. 582; *Schriften*, iv, p. 146): 'Der Prolog mag also bey den Alten ein nothwendiges Theil der Komödie seyn oder nicht....'

[2] This is characteristic of the epilogues to three of Plautus's comedies, *Casina*, *Cistellaria* and *Menechmi* (Schröter and Thiele, ed. of 1895, p. 98).

[3] Cp. the Epilogue to *Agamemnon* (*Works*, London, 1750, iii, p. 205):

> 'Our bard, to modern epilogue a foe,
> Thinks such mean mirth but deadens generous woe;
> Dispels in idle air the moral sigh,
> And wipes the tender tear from pity's eye:
> No more with social warmth the bosom burns,
> But all th'unfeeling selfish man returns.'

or that to *Tancred* and *Sigismunda* (*ibid.* iv, pp. 201 f.):

> 'Hence with your flippant epilogue, that tries
> To wipe the virtuous tear from British eyes;
> That dares my moral, tragic scene profane,
> With strains—at best, unsuiting, light and vain.
> Hence from the pure unsully'd beams that play
> In yon fair eyes where virtue shines—Away!'

D'Aubignac had censured Euripides for his use of the prologue in the following terms:

Les Tragiques Grecs, ou pour le moins Euripide (car nous n'en avons point d'autres exemples) ont fait une autre espece de Prologue bien plus vicieux, sçavoir quand ils y emploioient quelqu'un de leurs Dieux: car souvent ils faisoient que ce Dieu, qu'on presupposoit sçavoir tout, expliquoit non seulement les choses passées, mais aussi les futures; ils ne se contentoient pas d'instruire les Spectateurs de l'histoire precedente, necessaire à l'intelligence de la Piéce; mais ils en faisoient encore sçavoir le Dénoüement et toute la Catastrophe; de sorte qu'ils en prévenoient tous les evenemens: ce qui étoit un défaut très-notable du tout contraire à cette attente ou suspension qui doit toûjours regner au Theatre, et détruisant tous les agrémens d'une Piéce, qui consiste presque toûjours en la surprise et en la nouveauté.[1]

Lessing translates the latter part of this passage (XLVIII, 97) and defends Euripides on the ground that the factor of surprise did not enter into his conception of tragedy; in thus disclosing at the outset the coming events he was pursuing a higher purpose, even if that purpose be not allowed for in the text-books on tragedy.[2]

Lessing's more detailed argument in favour of the prologues to Euripides's *Ion* and *Hecuba* in the following section (XLIX, 10 ff.)— that they detract in no way from the tragic purpose of the poet and that he could with a stroke of the pen have omitted them had he thought they would do so—recalls a passage in his *Philologischer Nachlass*:

Von dem Prolog dieses Stücks [*Ion*] muss ich noch anmerken, dass das Stück ohne ihn vollkommen bestehen kann, und vollkommen verständlich ist. Warum hat ihn Euripides gleichwohl für nöthig erachtet? Wenn wir aus ihm nicht gelernt hätten, wer Ion eigentlich wäre, würde unsre Neugierde nicht weit besser unterhalten werden? Würden wir nicht weit stärker überrascht werden, wenn ihn Creusa nun endlich für ihren Sohn erkennt? Recht. Aber dafür würden wir uns auch weniger entsetzt,

---

[1] *Pratique du Théâtre*, iii, chap. i (*ed. cit.* i, p. 147).

[2] Lessing may also have had in mind the following passage from Corneille. When discussing the employment of the prologue to communicate information, the latter says (*Discours du poëme dramatique, Œuvres, ed. cit.* i, pp. 44 f.): 'Euripide en a usé assez grossièrement, en introduisant, tantôt un dieu dans une machine, par qui les spectateurs recevoient cet éclaircissement, et tantôt un de ses principaux personnages qui les en instruisoit lui-même....' And a little further on, Corneille speaks of this 'désordre d'Euripide' (p. 45). In the essay on Seneca in the *Theatralische Bibliothek* (*Schriften*, vi, p. 229) Lessing himself had admitted that such prologues had defects. (Cp. Petersen, *ed. cit.* p. 225.)

weniger für den Ion und die Creusa gezittert haben, wenn wir nicht gewusst hätten, dass diese in jenem ihren eignen Sohn umzubringen Gefahr laufe. Dem Euripides war es also weit wichtiger, und das mit Recht, das Herz des Zuschauers zu beschäftigen, als seine Neugierde.[1]

Towards the end of his long discussion of *Mérope*, Lessing had already raised the general question how far 'surprise' is a legitimate dramatic motive (XLVIII, 3);[2] and with the support of Diderot (from whose essay *De la poésie dramatique* he quotes a long passage in his own translation),[3] had asserted that the Euripidean plan, whereby all the incidents of the plot were familiar to the audience before they witnessed the play, is preferable to the modern reliance on surprise.

[1] *Schriften*, xv, p. 430.

[2] See above, p. 220.

[3] The quotation from Diderot (34 ff.) is as follows in the original (*Œuvres complètes*, ed. cit. vii, pp. 341 ff.; cp. Lessing's translation, ii, pp. 329 ff.):

'O faiseurs de règles générales, que vous ne connaissez guère l'art, et que vous avez peu de ce génie qui a produit les modèles sur lesquels vous avez établi ces règles, qu'il est le maître d'enfreindre quand il lui plaît!

On trouvera, dans mes idées, tant de paradoxes qu'on voudra, mais je persisterai à croire que, pour une occasion où il est à propos de cacher au spectateur un incident important avant qu'il ait lieu, il y en a plusieurs où l'intérêt demande le contraire.

Le poëte me ménage, par le secret, un instant de surprise; il m'eût exposé, par la confidence, à une longue inquiétude.

Je ne plaindrai qu'un instant celui qui sera frappé et accablé dans un instant. Mais que deviens-je, si le coup se fait attendre, si je vois l'orage se former sur ma tête ou sur celle d'un autre, et y demeurer longtemps suspendu?...

Que tous les personnages s'ignorent, si vous le voulez; mais que le spectateur les connaisse tous.

J'oserais presque assurer qu'un sujet où les réticences sont nécessaires, est un sujet ingrat; et qu'un plan où l'on y a recours est moins bon que si l'on eût pu s'en passer. On n'en tirera rien de bien énergique; on s'assujettira à des préparations toujours trop obscures ou trop claires. Le poëme deviendra un tissu de petites finesses, à l'aide desquelles on ne produira que de petites surprises. Mais tout ce qui concerne les personnages est-il connu? J'entrevois, dans cette supposition, la source des mouvements les plus violents....

Pourquoi certains monologues ont-ils de si grands effets? c'est qu'ils m'instruisent des desseins secrets d'un personnage; et que cette confidence me saisit à l'instant de crainte ou d'espérance.

Si l'état des personnages est inconnu, le spectateur ne pourra prendre à l'action plus d'intérêt que les personnages: mais l'intérêt doublera pour le spectateur, s'il est assez instruit, et qu'il sente que les actions et les discours seraient bien différents, si les personnages se connaissaient. C'est ainsi que vous produirez en moi une attente violente de ce qu'ils deviendront, lorsqu'ils pourront comparer ce qu'ils sont avec ce qu'ils ont fait ou voulu faire.'

THE TITLES OF PLAYS

The choice of a suitable title for a play was a matter which had considerable interest for Lessing. It is first mentioned in a mild protest (XIV, 112) against the alteration which had been made in the title of his own *Freygeist*, which in Hamburg was called *Der beschämte Freygeist*. Lessing points out with justice that Adrast is not the only character of the play who is a 'Freygeist'. But, he adds, 'was liegt an dem Titel? Genug, dass die Vorstellung alles Beyfalls würdig war.'[1] In St. IX (136) he comments on Plautus's choice of titles for his plays;[2] in XXIX (106) he quotes an extract from Corneille's apology for not giving to his tragedy of *Rodogune* the name of *Cléopâtre*.[3] He agrees (114) with Corneille's argument that the ancients regarded the title of a play as quite unimportant; 'they did not believe in the least that it must indicate the content of the drama'.[4] At the same time, he does not think that Sophocles would have called his tragedy (the *Trachiniæ*) *Deianira*. At least, he contends, the Greek poet did not choose a misleading title—one which would suggest a wrong emphasis. A similar argument is used in St. LXXXVII–LXXXVIII (5) where Lessing discusses Palissot's objection to the title of *Le Fils naturel*,[5] and Diderot's justification of his choice.

The lengthiest discussion of the use of titles, however, is to be found in the section on Voltaire's *Nanine* (XXI, 23). Lessing sets out from a criticism of that play which had appeared in *La Bigarure* and which he had already translated in his *Beyträge zur Historie und Aufnahme des Theaters*:[6]

Cette Comedie est intitulée *Nanine*, titre ridicule, et vague, qui n'annonce rien, et qui d'ailleurs ne convient nullement a une Piéce Comique, mais bien aux Tragedies; parce que ces dernieres s'annoncent toujours par

---

[1] Similarly, after recording an objection to the rendering of *Le Distrait* by *Der Zerstreute* (XXVIII, 70) he adds 'Man versteht sie [diese Worte] nunmehr, und das ist genug'.   [2] See above, p. 331.

[3] For the original passage in full see above, pp. 167 f.

[4] In a letter to his brother Karl of February 10, 1772, discussing his *Emilia Galotti*, Lessing wrote (*Schriften*, xviii, p. 18): 'Weil das Stück Emilia heisst, ist es darum mein Vorsatz gewesen, Emilien zu dem hervorstechendsten, oder auch nur zu einem hervorstechenden Charakter zu machen? Ganz und gar nicht. Die Alten nannten ihre Stücke wohl nach Personen, die gar nicht aufs Theater kamen.' In his discussion of the probable subject of Euripides's Cresphontes Lessing asks (XXXIX, 100): 'Hat man jemals gehört, dass ein Trauerspiel nach einer Person benennet worden, die gar nicht darinn vorkömmt?'   [5] See above, p. 234.

[6] *Theatralische Neuigkeiten aus Paris, Beyträge*, ii, p. 287. See above, p. 104.

le nom du Personage qui en fait le principal sujet.[1] C'est ainsi que par de simples noms un Lecteur, ou un Spectateur, connoit d'abord les Tragedies de *Mithridate, Cinna, Pompée, Polieucte, Andromaque, Phedre, Iphigenie, Britannicus,* etc. La Comédie, du moins la véritable, étant une image divertissante et risible de la vie et de la conduite des hommes, de leurs vices, de leurs défauts, de leurs imperfections et de leurs ridicules, elle doit toujours s'annoncer de même par quelqu'un de ces endroits. C'est ainsi, du moins, que l'ont pratiqué jusqu'à ce jour tous ceux qui ont réussi dans cette pénible cariere.[2]

'A title', says Lessing, 'must not be a menu.' The less it betrays of the contents of a play, the better. In discussing L'Affichard's *Ist er von Familie*, he complains (XVII, 62) that, although a title need neither give nor exhaust the contents of a piece, this one is misleading; whereas the title of Hippel's play, *Der Mann nach der Uhr* (XXII, 63) gives away too much. The ancients, Lessing contends (XXI, 27), seldom gave their comedies other than titles that meant nothing; there are hardly three or four within his knowledge which name the chief characters or betray anything of the story. And of these, one is Plautus's *Miles gloriosus*, which the author himself simply called *Gloriosus*. Even if the French dramatists have exhausted such descriptive character-titles, he argues, there is no copyright in them; and there is no real reason why a later dramatist should not write another *Misanthrope*. But *Nanine* (XXI, 72) has a sub-title, which gives additional information; this sub-title has two variants: *l'homme sans préjugé*, and *le préjugé vaincu*. Voltaire, Lessing comments, does not seem to have made up his mind; but the two variants, after all, mean very much the same thing. A comedy, he says later (XXII, 72), may very well have a double title; but in that case, each should mean something different. Hippel's *Der Mann nach der Uhr, oder der ordentliche Mann* is an example of redundancy.

TRANSLATION

As we have seen, Lessing has a good deal to say about the merits and demerits of the German translations of the French plays that appeared on the Hamburg stage. These observations I have dealt with in

---

[1] Lessing translates this sentence: '...ein lächerlicher und unbestimmter Titel, welcher nichts ankündiget, und welcher sich zwar zu Trauerspielen, aber gar nicht zu einem komischen Stück schickt; weil man die letztern allemal durch den Namen der Hauptpersonen ankündiget.' By reversing the position of 'Trauerspielen' he destroys the sense of the original. The translation of the passage is otherwise a literal one.   [2] *La Bigarure*, i (1749), No. 6, p. 55.

discussing his criticism of the plays; it only remains here to review his general opinions on the subject of translation.

With his prejudice in favour of the use of prose in the drama, it was natural that he should not approve the practice of translating French verse dramas into German verse. In dealing with *Zelmire* he asks (xix, 76): 'wer wird nicht lieber eine körnichte, wohlklingende Prosa hören wollen, als matte, geradebrechte Verse?' And he adds: 'Unter allen unsern gereimten Übersetzungen werden kaum ein halbes Dutzend seyn, die erträglich sind. Und dass man mich ja nicht bey dem Worte nehme, sie zu nennen!'

To translate good verses into good prose requires more than accuracy (viii, 27)—or, at least, something different from accuracy. Too great literalness makes for stiffness; for what is natural in one language is not so in another. The original becomes in the translation 'wässrig und schielend'. For where is the 'Versificateur' who is not obliged by the necessities of verse to say a little more than he would say in plain, straightforward prose? And under the constraint of metre and rhyme, he necessarily says things differently; he uses metaphors and similes where in prose he would be content with the simple truth. It needs some taste and courage on the part of the translator to excise the metaphors and ellipses which the writing of verse demands, but which are out of place in prose. Here, perhaps, some remarks of Mendelssohn may have had weight with Lessing. In reviewing a German translation of Pope's works (the first volume of which was published at Altona in 1758), that writer had said:

Die einzige Sorge des Uebersetzers (wenn ja übersetzt werden soll) muss also dahin gehen, den Verstand, die scharfsinnigen Sentenzen, und die philosophischen Betrachtungen seiner Urschrift beyzubehalten, und sie in einen fliessenden prosaischen Discurs zu verwandeln. Ist er aber, wie der gegenwärtige Uebersetzer der popischen Schriften, sklavisch genug, sich an die Worte der Urschrift zu binden; so wird er einen wohlgestalten Körper in eine elende Misgeburt verwandeln, der Wohlklang verschwindet, die Wiederholungen, welche in einem gereimten Gedichte angenehm sind, werden in der Uebersetzung eckelhaft, die uneigentlichen Wörter, die der grösste Dichter, wenn er reimen muss, nicht vermeiden kann, werden hier unerträglich, und jeder feurige Schwung von einem Gedanken auf den andern, der dem Dichter erlaubt ist, wird eine unverantwortliche Lücke, von welcher der Leser einer prosaischen Schrift Rechenschaft fordern wird.[1]

---

[1] *Bibliothek der schönen Wissenschaften*, iv (ii), 1759, p. 628; *Gesammelte Schriften, ed. cit.* iv, 1, pp. 411 f.

Is it really worth while, Lessing asks (XIX, 92), to expend so much trouble in putting French verse into German verse? The French poet [of *Zelmire*] (82) 'war schon nicht der grösste Versifikateur, sondern stümperte und flickte; der Deutsche war es noch weniger'. Little is gained by the production of watery, cold, correct verses, and were all the poetic ornament of the French transferred to German prose, it would hardly become poetic thereby. German verse translations, moreover, create difficulties for the actor instead of helping him. On the other hand, he refers to the mongrel tones ('Zwitterton') which are to be found in German prose translations of English plays —was Lessing thinking of Wieland's Shakespeare?—where the effect of the boldest tropes and figures, deprived of their metrical cadence, reminds one of drunken men dancing without music.[1]

---

[1] Cp. also Lessing's judgment on Banks's style, pp. 274 f. above. Petersen (*ed. cit.* pp. 201 f.) notes however that in a review [published in the *Berlinische privilegirte Zeitung* of December 19, 1752 (*Schriften*, v, pp. 17 f.)] he made severer demands, and reproached the translator of Crébillon's *Idoménée* for not having translated into rhymed verse.

CHAPTER XVII

THE ART OF THE ACTOR. MUSIC IN THE THEATRE

No aspect of the *Hamburgische Dramaturgie* falls more disappointingly short of expectations than that which is concerned with the actor's art. In his *Ankündigung* Lessing had declared (83) that one of the touchstones of a dramatic critic's capacity lay in his ability to determine what share of the success or failure of a play was to be ascribed to the poet, and what share to the actor. 'To blame the one for the shortcomings of the other means spoiling both; the former will lose courage, and the latter become self-assured. In particular, the actor has a right to look for the strictest freedom from bias. The poet can be justified at any time, for his work remains and can be laid before us again; but the art of the actor is in its effect transitory.'[1] Unfortunately the actors themselves did not see eye to eye with Lessing in this matter; and from the first, any real and honest criticism was out of the question. Susanna Mecour, as we have seen, made it a condition that she should not be criticised at all; while the chief actress of the company, Friederike Hensel, resented Lessing's criticism so emphatically that after the twenty-fifth part he decided to abandon entirely that part of his plan which was concerned with how the plays were performed. But it was also clear from the first that he must necessarily be hampered by his official connexion with the theatre; and it would be rash to describe even such criticism as he offers of the actors in the first twenty-five sections as completely unbiased; after all, those in power, and particularly Ekhof, had to be handled with kid gloves.[2]

Lessing's first interest in the actor's art was historical and theoretical

---

[1] See below, p. 482.
[2] See above, pp. 30 f., 34 ff. Petersen (*ed. cit.* p. 207) quotes from *Vierteljahrschrift für Litteraturgeschichte*, ii (1889), p. 137, a letter from Weisse to Ramler of June 20, 1797: 'als Lessing mir die ersten Bogen seiner Dramaturgie zuschickte, schrieb er mir: „Meiner Absicht nach sollten diese Blätter hauptsächlich der Kritik der Schauspieler gewiedmet seyn: ich sehe aber wohl, dass mit diesem Volke nichts anzufangen ist; sie nehmen Privaterinnerungen übel, was würden sie bey einer öffentlichen Rüge thun: ich werde es also wohl die Autoren müssen entgelten lassen."'

rather than practical.[1] He approached it as a classical scholar with
a view to winning the recognition of the University of Göttingen.
A fragment of the treatise he planned with this object in view, *Von
den Pantomimen der Alten*, has been preserved, and Muncker, who
dates it 1749–50, has shown that it is largely based on Nicholas
Calliachius's *De ludis scenicis mimorum et pantomimorum* (published in
A. H. de Sallengre's *Novus thesaurus antiquitatum romanarum*, The
Hague, 1716–19, ii, 699–768).[2] And in the third part of the
Theatralische Bibliothek (1755) he published a translation of the third
and final volume of Du Bos' *Réflexions critiques*, which deals with the
'représentations théâtrales des Anciens'.

There are a few echoes of these early studies on the theatre of the
ancients in the *Dramaturgie*, where, in particular, he occasionally
makes use of the volume of Du Bos.[3] But already in the *Beyträge* the
art of acting had been approached also from a more practical angle.
It was, indeed, an important part of the programme of that periodical.
In his preface Lessing wrote:

> Wer sieht also nicht, dass die Vorstellung ein nothwendiges Theil der
> dramatischen Poesie sey? Die Kunst dieser Vorstellung verdienet dero-
> halben unsrer Aufmerksamkeit eben sowohl, als die Kunst der Verfassung.
> Sie muss ihre Regeln haben, und diese wollen wir aufsuchen. Es sind uns
> einige neue Schriftsteller hierinne schon vorgegangen, und wir werden uns
> ihrer Arbeit auf eine erlaubte Art zu bedienen wissen. Diese Regeln
> erstrecken sich nicht allein auf die Schauspieler, sie können allen nutzen,
> welche die Beredsamkeit des Körpers brauchen.[4]

The *Beyträge* opens with a contribution by Mylius, *Versuch eines
Beweises, dass die Schauspielkunst eine freye Kunst sey*. Lessing would at
this time have had little difficulty in subscribing to Mylius's conclusion that 'Wahrscheinlichkeit' was of more importance to the actor's
success than the observance of artificial rules. The new writers whose

---

[1] See above, p. 94.

[2] *Schriften*, xiv, p. 144. Lessing also reviewed in 1749 Samuel Geissler's *Abhandlung
von den Pantomimen*. See above, p. 94; and cp. also below, pp. 479 ff.

[3] Cp. for example LXXXII, 127 ff.

[4] *Schriften*, iv, p. 54. Mylius had published earlier *Eine Abhandlung, worinnen
erwiesen wird: dass die Wahrscheinlichkeit der Vorstellung, bey den Schauspielen eben so
nöthig ist, als die innere Wahrscheinlichkeit derselben* (in Gottsched's *Beyträge zur
critischen Historie der Deutschen Sprache, Poesie und Beredsamkeit*, St. xxx (1743),
pp. 297 ff.). Cp. H. Oberländer, *Die geistige Entwicklung der deutschen Schauspielkunst
im 18. Jahrhundert*, Hamburg and Leipzig, 1898 (*Theatergeschichtliche Forschungen*, xv),
pp. 98, 206.

work the preface promised to introduce were François Riccoboni, son of a more famous father, and Sainte Albine—although room was not found for the latter until the publication of the *Theatralische Bibliothek*.

Lessing's translation of Riccoboni's *Art du Théâtre* (Paris, 1750) appears in the fourth part of the *Beyträge* as *Die Schauspielkunst*. This treatise supports the emancipation of acting from the stiff classicism of the earlier eighteenth century: Riccoboni seeks to mediate between the old tradition and the new demand for verisimilitude. The actor may indeed yield to the emotion which his part awakens in him, but he must always remain master of himself; it may be necessary for him to exaggerate a little, however, if he is to have the right effect upon his audience. Riccoboni accepts the approximation between the art of presenting tragedy and that of presenting comedy which was called for by the *comédie larmoyante*, and has much to say that is valuable on the subject of pantomimic action.

Amongst Lessing's papers is a skeleton plan of a work which was to have been entitled *Der Schauspieler: Ein Werk worinne die Grundsätze der ganzen körperlichen Beredsamkeit entwickelt werden.*[1] On the ground of its similarity to Riccoboni's book Danzel is inclined to date the plan 1750;[2] but Muncker would date it a few years later, when Lessing was engaged in translating Sainte Albine's *Le Comédien*. It may be noted in favour of the later date that the sketch of *Der Schauspieler* bears evidence of having been influenced by Hogarth's *Analysis of Beauty*, a work with which Lessing probably first became acquainted through Mylius's translation in 1754.[3] It may well be the 'kleines Werk über die körperliche Beredsamkeit' which Lessing promised the readers of his *Theatralische Bibliothek*.[4]

Rémond de Sainte Albine's *Le Comédien* was published in 1747, three years before François Riccoboni's work. But it may have only come later into Lessing's hands, even if his translation of extracts in the *Theatralische Bibliothek* was one of the contributions left over from the *Beyträge*. In many respects Sainte Albine's book represents a more advanced stage in the theory of acting than Riccoboni's. Not being an actor himself, Sainte Albine was more interested in theoretical questions. He made greater demands than Riccoboni for 'natural-

---

[1] *Schriften*, xiv, pp. 179 ff.
[2] Danzel and Guhrauer, *Lessing, ed. cit.* i, p. 185.
[3] Cp. H. Oberländer, *op. cit.* p. 99.
[4] *Theatralische Bibliothek*, i, p. 266; *Schriften*, vi, p. 152.

ness': insisted, in fact, in direct opposition to the latter, that the actor must give himself up unreservedly to the emotions which he has to represent. In the short critical introduction with which Lessing prefaced his translation he endeavoured to mediate between the two critics.[1] But between the *Theatralische Bibliothek* and the *Dramaturgie* Lessing had made the acquaintance of Diderot's *Lettre sur les sourds et muets* (published in 1751); and Diderot had been much influenced by Sainte Albine. The views which Lessing sets forth in the *Dramaturgie* are largely in agreement with Sainte Albine's; and Lessing saw the latter's theories realised in the art of Ekhof.

In the general demands which Lessing made upon the actor, towards the close of his *Ankündigung* (98), he was thinking of Sainte Albine's first chapter where the question is discussed 'S'il est vrai que d'excellens Acteurs ayent manqué d'esprit':

> Il ne suffit pas que sa figure soit propre au Théâtre, et que son visage puisse exprimer.... Non seulement il est essentiel qu'il ne fasse rien perdre aux discours de leur force ou de leur délicatesse, mais il faut qu'il leur prête toutes les graces que la déclamation et l'action peuvent leur fournir. Il ne doit pas se contenter de suivre fidélement son Auteur: il faut qu'il l'aide, et qu'il le soutienne. Il faut qu'il devienne Auteur lui-même; qu'il sache non seulement exprimer toutes les finesses d'un rôle, mais encore en ajoûter de nouvelles; non seulement exécuter, mais créer.[2]

In St. III (19) Lessing deals with the question how far an actor should 'feel' his rôle: 'How far is the actor who only understands a passage removed from one who at the same time feels it!' This requirement was emphatically stated by Sainte Albine. In his second chapter he discusses 'Ce que c'est que le *Sentiment*', a word which he defines as 'dans les Comédiens la facilité de faire succéder dans leur ame les diverses passions, dont l'homme est susceptible'. He says (p. 32): 'Il faut que l'esprit et le cœur d'une personne de Théâtre soient propres à recevoir toutes les modifications que l'Auteur veut leur donner.' And again later:

> Les Acteurs Tragiques veulent-ils nous faire illusion? Ils doivent se la faire à eux-mêmes. Il faut qu'ils s'imaginent être, qu'ils soient effectivement ce qu'ils représentent, et qu'un heureux délire leur persuade que ce sont eux qui sont trahis, persécutés. Il faut que cette erreur passe de leur esprit à leur cœur, et qu'en plusieurs occasions un malheur feint leur arrache des larmes véritables.[3]

---

[1] Cp. H. Oberländer, *op. cit.* pp. 98 ff.
[2] *Le Comédien*, Paris, 1747, pp. 21 f.
[3] *Ibid.* pp. 91 f. (part I, book II, section i, chap. iii).

Thus (III, 5) 'Alle Moral muss aus der Fülle des Herzens kommen, von der der Mund übergehet.'

Such is Sainte Albine's view, and Lessing, when he has stated it, proceeds in a long parenthesis (26–78) to modify it by maintaining that the identification of the actor with the feelings he has to express is not enough; he must have acquired the art of giving expression to them; that, in fact, this art is more essential than his subjective response to them.[1] This had been precisely his standpoint in the *Theatralische Bibliothek*:

Der Herr Remondvon Sainte Albine setzet in seinem ganzen Werke stillschweigend voraus, dass die äusserlichen Modificationen des Körpers natürliche Folgen von der innern Beschaffenheit der Seele sind, die sich von selbst ohne Mühe ergeben. Es ist zwar wahr, dass jeder Mensch ungelernt den Zustand seiner Seele durch Kennzeichen, welche in die Sinne fallen, einigermaassen ausdrücken kann, der eine durch dieses, der andre durch jenes. Allein auf dem Theater will man Gesinnungen und Leidenschaften nicht nur einigermaassen ausgedrückt sehen; nicht nur auf die unvollkommene Weise, wie sie ein einzelner Mensch, wenn er sich wirklich in eben denselben Umständen befände, vor sich ausdrücken würde; sondern man will sie auf die allervollkommenste Art ausgedrückt sehen, so wie sie nicht besser und nicht vollständiger ausgedrückt werden können. Dazu aber ist kein ander Mittel, als die besondern Arten, wie sie sich bey dem und bey jenem ausdrücken, kennen zu lernen, und eine allgemeine Art daraus zusammen zu setzen, die um so viel wahrer scheinen muss, da ein jeder etwas von der seinigen darinnen entdeckt. Kurz, ich glaube, der ganze Grundsatz unsers Verfassers ist umzukehren. Ich glaube, wenn der Schauspieler alle äusserliche Kennzeichen und Merkmale, alle Abänderungen des Körpers, von welchen man aus der Erfahrung gelernet hat, dass sie etwas gewisses ausdrücken, nachzumachen weis, so wird sich seine Seele durch den Eindruck, der durch die Sinne auf sie geschieht, von selbst in den Stand setzen, der seinen Bewegungen, Stellungen und Tönen gemäss ist. Diese nun auf eine gewisse mechanische Art zu erlernen, auf eine Art aber, die sich auf unwandelbare Regeln gründet, an deren Daseyn man durchgängig zweifelt, ist die einzige und wahre Art die Schauspielkunst zu studiren.[2]

Thus, in spite of the deepening and widening of the problem by Diderot, Lessing's standpoint in 1767 would appear to be still that of 1754.

[1] This was François Riccoboni's standpoint (*L'Art du Théâtre*, Paris 1750, pp. 36 ff.). Cp. H. Oberländer, *op. cit.* pp. 102 ff. Later, about 1774, Mendelssohn expressed his views on this subject in his *Beantwortung einiger Fragen in der Schauspielkunst* (*Gesammelte Schriften, ed. cit.* iv, 1, pp. 26 ff.).

[2] *Theatralische Bibliothek*, i, pp. 264 f.; *Schriften*, vi, pp. 151 f.

The discussion in St. v (65 ff.) whether an actor can have too much fire again goes back to Sainte Albine. Chapter iii of book i of *Le Comédien* is entitled: 'Un Comédien peut-il avoir trop de *Feu*?' The following passages have some bearing on Lessing's text:

Il est des Acteurs, qui en criant et en s'agitant beaucoup, s'efforcent de remplacer par une chaleur factice le *Feu* naturel, qui leur manque. Il en est plusieurs, à qui la foiblesse de leur constitution et de leurs organes ne permet pas d'user de cette ressource. Ces derniers, ne pouvant entreprendre d'en imposer à nos sens, se flattent d'en imposer à notre esprit, et ils prennent le parti de soûtenir que le *Feu* chez les gens de leur Art est plûtôt un défaut qu'une perfection.

Les uns sont de faux monnoyeurs qui nous donnent du cuivre pour de l'or: les autres, des foux qui prétendent nous persuader que les frimats sont des beautés de la Nature, parce qu'elle couvre de neige pendant la plus grande partie de l'année le pays qu'ils habitent.

Ne soyons point les dupes de l'artifice des premiers, ni des sophismes des seconds. Ne prenons point les cris et les contorsions d'un Comédien pour de la chaleur, ni la glace d'un autre pour de la sagesse, et bien loin d'imiter certains amateurs du Spectacle, qui recommandent soigneusement aux Débutantes dont les succès les interressent, de modérer leur *Feu*, annonçons aux personnes de Théâtre, qu'elles ne peuvent trop en avoir; que plusieurs d'entr'elles n'ont le malheur de déplaire au Public, que parce que la nature ne leur a pas accordé cette qualité, ou parce que leur timidité les empêche d'en faire usage; qu'au contraire quelques-uns des Acteurs qui sont applaudis, jouiroient d'une réputation encore plus générale et moins contestée, s'ils étoient plus animés de cette précieuse flamme, qui donne en quelque sorte la vie à l'action Théâtrale.

On ne révoquera point en doute ces propositions, lorqu'on cessera de confondre la véhémence de la déclamation avec le *Feu* du Comédien, et lorsqu'on voudra faire réflexion, que le *Feu* dans une personne de Théâtre n'est autre chose que la célérité et la vivacité, avec lesquelles toutes les parties, qui constituent l'Acteur, concourent à donner un air de verité à son action.

Ce principe posé, il est évident qu'on ne peut apporter trop de chaleur au Théâtre, puisque l'action ne peut être jamais trop vraie, et que par consequent l'impression ne peut être jamais trop promte ni trop vive, et l'expression répondre trop tôt ni trop fidélement à l'expression.

Vous serez critiqués justement, lorsque votre action ne sera pas convenable au caractere et à la situation du personnage que vous représentés, ou lorsqu'en voulant montrer du *Feu*, vous ne nous ferez voir que des mouvemens convulsifs, ou entendre que des cris importuns. Mais alors les personnes de goût, bien loin de vous accuser d'avoir trop de *Feu*, se plaindront de ce que vous n'en avez pas assez; comme au lieu de trouver avec le Public trop d'esprit à certains Auteurs, elles trouvent qu'ils en manquent.

Un Auteur dans une Comédie prête le langage d'un bel Esprit à un

Valet ou à une Suivante: il met des madrigaux ou des épigrammes dans la bouche d'un Acteur agité d'une passion violente, et l'on dit qu'il a trop d'esprit. Il seroit plus exact de dire qu'il n'a pas celui de connoître la nature, et de l'imiter. En jouant un rôle, vous vous livrerez à l'emportement dans des endroits qui n'en demandent pas; ou si votre emportement n'est pas hors de propos, il n'est pas naturel. Vous tombez dans ces fautes, non par excès, mais par défaut de chaleur. Dès lors vous ne sentez, vous n'exprimez point ce que vous devez sentir et exprimer. Ainsi ce n'est pas du *Feu*, c'est de la déraison et de la maladresse que nous appercevons en vous.[1]

Once only in his *Dramaturgie* does Lessing refer to Sainte Albine by name. It is at the end of his discussion of *Zayre* (XVI, 147), where he says that Ekhof so completely fulfils all that Sainte Albine demands of the actor that he alone might have been the model the critic had in view. Lessing had in mind, as his foot-note tells us, the tenth chapter of the Second Part of the French work, which is entitled: 'Dans lequel, aux principes déja établis sur la verité de la Récitation et de l'Action, on ajoûte quelques préceptes importans', and he was evidently thinking more particularly of the section of this chapter which deals with 'l'art de nuer les passages d'un mouvement à l'autre.' It is as follows:

La Scene sixieme du quatrieme Acte de Zaïre[2] me fournira un exemple de l'usage qu'ils doivent faire de ce talent. Dans cette Scene, l'Acteur qui joue le rôle d'Orosmane doit se rappeller, que ce Sultan s'annonce comme assez genereux, pour sacrifier sa passion, s'il découvre que Zaïre soit entrainée vers quelque autre par un penchant invincible, mais qu'il veut lire dans le cœur de cette Belle; qu'il desire que si elle lui refuse son amour, elle lui accorde sa confiance; qu'il peut consentir de n'être pas favorisé comme Amant, mais qu'il ne peut se résoudre à n'être pas distingué comme ami, et qu'il seroit plus offensé de la dissimulation que de l'indifférence.

Ces dispositions étant supposées dans Orosmane, il est évident qu'il n'écoute tout son ressentiment, que lorsqu'il croit être convaincu de l'obstination de Zaïre à le tromper par une feinte tendresse. Non seulement il ne cede qu'alors à son courroux, mais même auparavant il est un instant, dans lequel on s'imagine qu'un seul mot de la bouche de Zaïre va calmer l'orage qui gronde sur sa tête, et à cette occasion il est à propos de remarquer qu'il se fait successivement deux métamorphoses dans le cœur d'Orosmane; que d'abord il passe de la fierté à l'attendrissement, et qu'ensuite ce dernier mouvement fait place au plus violent dépit.

Il est donc à présumer que le Sultan prend d'abord le ton de Souverain,

---

[1] *Le Comédien, ed. cit.* pp. 41 ff.

[2] A note adds the comment quoted above (p. 209): 'On peut citer après Phedre une Piece que l'amour lui-même semble avoir dictée.'

non d'un Souverain irrité, (il auroit à craindre d'effrayer Zaïre, et de la détourner par là de l'aveu qu'il veut tirer d'elle) mais d'un Monarque déterminé à pardonner, pourvû qu'elle se reconnoisse coupable.

Quelque penchant qu'il ait à la clémence, il est sensible au tort prétendu de sa Maîtresse, et s'il a la force de ne pas lui montrer de ressentiment, du moins il affecte de lui parler avec froideur. Insensiblement, en la regardant, il sent son amour se rallumer, et bientôt entraîné par sa foiblesse il lui dit avec un tendre emportement,

> Ta grace est dans mon cœur. Prononce. Elle t'attend.

Ayant donné cette assurance à Zaïre, il ne doute pas qu'elle n'use avec lui de la sincerité qu'il demande. Comme les premiers discours de cette jeune Beauté ne répondent pas d'une façon précise à la question qu'il lui a faite, il demeure incertain pendant quelque tems, s'il doit ceder à l'amour ou à la haine. Sa colere se ranime, lorsqu'il entend Zaïre prononcer,

> Je jure que Zaïre, à soi-même rendue,
> Des Rois les plus puissans détesteroit la vue;
> Que tout autre après vous me seroit odieux.

Plus Zaïre met de tendresse dans son expression, plus il la soupçonne de fausseté, et plus elle lui paroît indigne de pardon. Ainsi il s'irrite plus, à mesure qu'elle se passionne davantage, et cette protestation,

> Si mon cœur fut coupable, Ingrat, c'étoit pour vous.

Cette protestation, dis-je, qui devroit désarmer un Amant moins prévenu, acheve de porter au plus haut point l'indignation d'Orosmane. Le mépris chez lui se joint à l'indignation. Il dédaigne de faire éclatter le transport qui l'agite.

Un reste d'amour vient combattre encore dans le cœur du Sultan. Il est tenté de faire un nouvel effort, pour obliger Zaïre de renoncer à sa dissimulation. Il lui adresse de nouveau la parole, et il prononce le nom de cette infortunée avec un courroux mêlé de trouble et de tendresse. Mais enfin son ressentiment l'emporte. Les preuves, qu'il croit avoir de la trahison de sa Maîtresse, se présentant à lui dans toute leur horreur, il ne voit plus en elle qu'une Parjure, qui mérite le plus cruel supplice.

L'art de passer adroitement d'un mouvement à l'autre est difficile. Il l'est sur-tout, lorsque ces mouvemens se détruisent l'un l'autre avec une extrême rapidité, ainsi que dans ces endroits de la même Tragédie de Zaïre,

> O nuit, nuit effroyable!
> Peux-tu prêter ton voile à de pareils forfaits?...[1]

Again, Lessing's description of Madame Hensel's declamation of a passage in Act III, sc. iii of *Olint und Sophronia* (IV, 116) is clearly

---

[1] *Le Comédien*, ed. cit. pp. 208 ff.

suggested, as I have already pointed out, by Sainte Albine's discussion of how Act II, sc. v of *Phèdre* should be interpreted by the actors.[1]

That Lessing should have been influenced by what Diderot has to say about the actor's art in the *Entretiens* accompanying his plays—the famous *Paradoxe sur le Comédien* was not printed until 1830—was only natural. And Diderot, as we have seen, was indebted to Sainte Albine in this matter. But there is perhaps less direct influence of Diderot on the *Dramaturgie* than might have been expected. It is chiefly to be traced in the observations on gesture and pantomime, to which Diderot attached great importance; this indeed was a subject in which Lessing had long been interested. The use of gesture ('gestus')[2] by the actor is discussed at the close of St. III and in St. IV.

In the sketch of *Der Schauspieler* Lessing had already noted for discussion: 'Die Lehre von der Bewegung der Hände hiess bey den Alten die Chironomie. Deutsch vielleicht die Hände-Sprache.' This heading was, no doubt, suggested by Du Bos' *Dissertation sur les représentations théâtrales des anciens*, translated for the *Theatralische Bibliothek*, where the sixteenth section deals with 'Des Pantomimes, ou des Acteurs qui jouoient sans parler'. In section xiii, Du Bos had said concerning 'la Saltation, ou...l'Art du Geste':

Suivant Athénée, Thélestes avoit été l'inventeur de cette espéce de jeu muet, ou de danse sans saults et sans pas élevés, et laquelle nous appellerons ici le plus souvent l'art du geste. Nous ne ferons en cela que lui donner le même nom que lui donnoient souvent les Anciens. Ils l'appelloient souvent *Chironomie*, et ce mot traduit littéralement, signifie la regle de la main.[3]

---

[1] *Le Comédien, ed. cit.* pp. 198 ff. (part II, chap. x). See above, p. 34, note 2.

[2] Batteux defines the word 'gestus' as follows (*Principes de la littérature, ed. cit.* i, p. 319): 'Nous entendons par geste, les mouvemens extérieurs et les attitudes du corps: *Gestus*, dit Ciceron, *est conformatio quædam et figura totius oris et corporis*.' At the end of his criticism of Ekhof as Dorimond in *Cenie*, Lessing quotes *Tot linguæ, quot membra viro!*—a quotation which he found in Du Bos' *Réflexions critiques sur la Poësie et sur la Peinture* (xvi, *Des Pantomimes*, 6th ed. Paris, 1755, iii, p. 265; Lessing's translation, *Theatralische Bibliothek*, iii, p. 262): 'Le Commentateur de Sidonius rapporte même à ce sujet l'Epigramme ancienne qu'on va lire, et dont on ne connoît point l'Auteur: *Tot linguæ*....Tous les membres du corps d'un Pantomime sont autant de langues, à l'aide desquelles il parle sans ouvrir la bouche.' (Also cited by Petersen, *ed. cit.* p. 203.)

[3] *Réflexions*, iii, xiii (*ed. cit.* iii, pp. 210 f.); cp. *Theatralische Bibliothek*, iii, p. 209.

And further:

Nous avons dit ci-dessus que l'art du geste étoit composé de gestes naturels et de gestes d'institution.[1] On peut bien croire que les Pantomimes se servoient des uns et des autres, et qu'ils n'avoient pas encore trop de moyens pour se faire entendre. Aussi, comme le dit Saint Augustin, tous les mouvemens d'un Pantomime signifioient quelque chose. Tous ses gestes étoient des phrases, pour ainsi dire, mais seulement pour ceux qui en avoient la clef.[2]

Lessing realised (IV, 14) that the art of the pantomime and that of the actor must be measured by different standards; a greater restraint was imposed upon the latter—or as Du Bos had put it: 'Comme les Pantomimes étoient dispensés de rien prononcer; et comme ils n'avoient que des gestes à faire, on conçoit aisément que toutes leurs démonstrations étoient plus vives, et que leur action étoit beaucoup plus animée que celle des Comédiens ordinaires.'[3] But Lessing will not countenance the actor who uses conventional and artificial gestures. It is true, he says (IV, 35), that Hogarth recommended the actor to move his arms in beautiful waving lines, but with every possible variety, and not as a constant mannerism. Hogarth's *Analysis of Beauty* (published in 1753) had been translated into German by Lessing's friend Mylius under the title of *Zergliederung der Schönheit, die schwankenden Begriffe von dem Geschmack festzusetzen* (London [and Hanover], 1754); and for the second edition (Berlin, 1754) Lessing had provided a preface. The following is the passage from the original which comes into question here:

From what has been said of habitually moving in waving lines, it may possibly be found that if stage-action, particularly the graceful, was to be studied lineally, it might be more speedily and accurately acquired by the help of the foregoing principles than the methods hitherto taken. It is known that common deportment, such as may pass for elegant and proper off the stage, would no more be thought sufficient upon it than the dialogue of common polite conversation, would be accurate or spirited enough for

---

[1] Petersen notes (*ed. cit.* p. 183) that Lessing had intended to discuss in the second part of *Laokoon* the difference between 'natürliche' and 'willkührliche' signs (the terms used by Lessing in his translation of this passage. See *Theatralische Bibliothek*, iii, p. 259). And in his *Collectanea* we find a beginning of a collection of 'die verabredeten Gebehrden und Zeichen...durch welche bey den Alten die Kunst der Pantomime sehr erleichtert wurde' (*Schriften*, xv, p. 336).

[2] *Réflexions*, iii, xvi, *ed. cit.* iii, p. 262; Lessing's translation, *Theatralische Bibliothek*, iii, p. 259. A note in the *Réflexions* (*ibid.*) adds the reference *S. Aug. de Doctr. Chr. l. 2.*   [3] *Réflexions, ed. cit.* iii, pp. 276 f.

the language of a play. So that trusting to chance only will not do. The actions of every scene ought to be as much as possible a compleat composition of well varied movements, considered as such abstractly, and apart from what may be merely relative to the sense of the words. Action consider'd with regard to assisting the authors meaning, by enforcing the sentiments or raising the passions, must be left entirely to the judgment of the performer, we only pretend to shew how the limbs may be made to have an equal readiness to move in all such directions as may be required.[1]

Löwen, in his *Kurzgefasste Grundsätze von der Beredtsamkeit des Leibes* (Hamburg, 1755), had recommended the actor to study Hogarth's work. Concerning the use of the arms and hands he says, 'diess nannte er eine Schlangenlinie oder eine wellenförmige Bewegung'.[2] Lessing, however, will have no artificial 'Portebras' of meaningless gesture (IV, 44).[3]

Lessing resists the temptation (56) of entering further into the distinction of 'bedeutend', 'mahlerisch' and 'pantomimisch' in gesture. In the *Collectanea* he speaks of these—'Mahlende und bedeutende Gebehrden und Gesten, die allgemein oder doch in gewissen Gegenden allgemein verständlich sind'—as a matter for further consideration.[4]

Hogarth had referred to 'what Shakespear calls, *continually sawing the air*',[5] and to *Hamlet* Lessing now turns in his further discussion of the performance of *Olint und Sophronia* (v, 47 ff.). He quotes Hamlet's advice to the players (but not, be it noted, in Wieland's translation):

Speak the speech, I pray you, as I pronounced it to you, trippingly on the tongue: but if you mouth it, as many of your players do, I had as lief the town-crier spoke my lines. Nor do not saw the air too much with your hand, thus, but use all gently: for in the very torrent, tempest, and, as I may say, the whirlwind of passion, you must acquire and beget a temperance that may give it smoothness.

[1] *Analysis of Beauty*, London, 1753, p. 151 (Mylius's translation, London, 1754, pp. 127 f.).

[2] The same terms are used in an interesting passage (quoted by Petersen, *ed. cit.* p. 183) from J. C. Brandes's *Lebensgeschichte* (2nd ed. Berlin, 1802, i, p. 169), in which Brandes relates how the ballet-master of Schönemann's company instructed him in deportment—among other things in the 'Schlangenlinie' or 'wellenförmige Bewegung'.

[3] I have failed to find this word in any French source. May it be a contraction of 'porte de bras'? François Riccoboni, discussing the word 'grace', says that the actor in scenes of great emotion may forget all rules of gesture and 'porter ses bras jusqu'au-dessus de sa tête' (*L'Art du Théâtre*, ed. cit. pp. 13 f.).

[4] *Schriften*, xv, p. 154.   [5] *Analysis of Beauty*, ed. cit. p. 152.

The art of the actor, Lessing says in St. v (95), stands midway between the graphic arts and poetry. It is transitory (*Ank.* 93); a 'transitory painting' (v, 97). As visible painting, beauty must be its highest law; as transitory painting, it need not always give its positions that calm which is so impressive in ancient works of art. These thoughts form one of the links between *Laokoon* and the *Dramaturgie*; in the 'Vorrede' of the earlier treatise he had quoted Simonides's statement that painting was a 'stumme Poesie'—a phrase which he uses here of acting.[1] Lessing has high praise for Ekhof's delivery of 'moral apophthegms and general sentiments, these tedious evasions of an embarrassed poet' (II, 95).[2] What is the secret of his success in delivering even the commonest of 'moral utterances'? Such sentiments must come from the heart (III, 5); they must, moreover, be well memorised, so that the actor may deliver them with complete fluency and mastery, and they may appear inspired by the immediate situation.

This matter had been under discussion ten years earlier between Lessing and Mendelssohn. On August 11, 1757, the latter expressed the opinion, in discussing the performance of *Miss Sara Sampson*, that philosophical passages were not suitable for declamation:

> Wenn die Philosophie sich in ihrer ganzen Stärke zeigt, so will sie mit einer gewissen Monotonie ausgesprochen werden, die sich auf dem Theater nicht gut ausnehmen kann.[3]

---

[1] Sainte Albine more than once compares the actor with the painter: 'Le Peintre ne peut que représenter les évenemens. Le Comédien en quelque sorte les reproduit' (*Le Comédien, ed. cit.* Introduction, pp. 14 f.); and 'Le Comédien est Peintre ainsi que le Poëte' (*ibid.* part I, chap. i, *ed. cit.* p. 24). I have not succeeded in tracing the source of the allusion to 'das Wilde eines Tempesta, das Freche eines Bernini' (v, 100). Tempesta is Antonio Tempesta of Florence (1555–1630), famous as a painter of battle pieces and as the illustrator of Tasso; Lorenzo Bernini (1598–1680) was most widely known as an architect. Lessing mentions him in his *Collectanea* (*Schriften*, xv, pp. 154 f.). An allusion to the independence and self-confidence of Bernini occurs in a review of *Mémoires de Charles Perrault*, Avignon [Paris?], 1759, in the *Bibliothek der schönen Wissenschaften*, vii (i), 1761, pp. 127 f.

[2] Cp. D'Aubignac, *Pratique du Théâtre*, iv, chap. v (*ed. cit.* i, pp. 289 f.): 'Il faut poser pour assûré, Que tous ces Discours Instructifs, sont ordinairement defectueux sur le Theatre, parce qu'ils sont de leur nature froids et languissans.' And again (p. 295): 'Premierement, ces Maximes generales, ou Lieux-communs, doivent être attachées au Sujet, et appliquées par plusieurs circonstances aux Personnages et aux affaires du Theatre; en sorte qu'il semble que celui qui parle, ait plus presens à l'esprit les interêts du Theatre, que ces belles veritez....'

[3] *Gesammelte Schriften, ed. cit.* v, p. 121; cp. *Schriften*, xix, p. 104.

To this Lessing replied on September 14:

Der Grundsatz ist richtig: der dramatische Dichter muss dem Schauspieler Gelegenheit geben, seine Kunst zu zeigen. Allein das philosophische Erhabne ist, meines Erachtens, am wenigsten dazu geschickt; denn eben so wenig Aufwand, als der Dichter, es auszudrücken, an Worten gemacht hat, muss der Schauspieler, es vorzustellen, an Geberden und Tönen machen.... Ich berufe mich, statt des besten Beweises, auf den Unterschied, der unter den Gebehrden des Schauspielers ist. Einen Theil der Gebehrden hat der Schauspieler jederzeit in seiner Gewalt; er kann sie machen, wenn er will; es sind dieses die Veränderungen derjenigen Glieder, zu deren verschiednen Modifikationen der blosse Wille hinreichend ist. Allein zu einem grossen Theil anderer, und zwar gleich zu denjenigen, aus welchen man den wahren Schauspieler am sichersten erkennt, wird mehr als sein Wille erfordert; eine gewisse Verfassung des Geistes nehmlich, auf welche diese oder jene Veränderung des Körpers von selbst, ohne sein Zuthun, erfolgt. Wer ihm also diese Verfassung am meisten erleichtert, der befördert ihm sein Spiel am meisten.[1]

In so far then as moral sentiments are general deductions, Lessing now concludes (III, 85), they must be spoken with calmness and a certain coldness; yet in so far as they are not abstract 'symbolical conclusions', but expressive of generalised feeling, a certain fire and enthusiasm are called for. The actor must vary his delivery of such sentiments as the one or the other of these considerations predominates. If the situation is calm he must put warmth and enthusiasm into his tone; if the situation is violent, the moral sentiment must have a calming effect. Ekhof—and Lessing is writing under the immediate effect of his acting in the small rôle of Evander in *Olint und Sophronia*—shows up, by his just observance of these principles, the defects of most actors who reverse the process and spoil everything by excessive gesture.

Madame Hensel's impressive acting in the death of Miss Sara Sampson[2] suggests some theoretical considerations on the representation of death in the theatre which may find a place here. Following J. Adolf Schlegel in his translation of Batteux,[3] and J. Elias

---

[1] *Schriften*, xvii, p. 121. This is also quoted by Petersen (*ed. cit.* p. 182), and by S. Rindskopf, *Der sprachliche Ausdruck der Affekte in Lessings dramatischen Werken* (Diss. Würzburg, Dresden, 1901, p. 7). This dissertation deals with Lessing's mode of indicating emotion in his dramas.

[2] See above, pp. 34 f.

[3] *Einschränkung der schönen Künste auf einen einzigen Grundsatz*, note to part II, chap. v (3rd ed. Leipzig, 1770, i, pp. 110 ff.).

Schlegel,[1] Mendelssohn had already demanded restraint in presentation:

Die äusserliche Handlung eines Sterbenden z. B. muss nur der Vorstellung, die wir vom Sterben haben, nicht widersprechen. Durch ein gelindes Hauptneigen, durch eine matte unterbrochene Stimme, kann sie der Einbildungskraft zu Hülfe kommen, die itzt in der grössten Bereitwilligkeit ist, sich betrügen zu lassen. Das Hauptwerk aber, den grössten Antheil an dem Betruge, muss sie der Poesie überlassen, die in dem Trauerspiele die herrschende Kunst ist. So bald der Sterbende röchelt, schäumt, die Augen verdrehet, und die Glieder verzuckt; so verdunkeln diese gewaltsame sinnliche Handlungen durch ihre Gegenwart alle Täuschungen der Dichtkunst.[2]

No doubt it was with a view to his description of Madame Hensel as Sara that Lessing wrote to his brother Karl, asking him to send him a medical treatise from his library: *Von dem Zupfen der Sterbenden*. 'Ich weiss nicht, wie der Verfasser heisst, auch kann ich mich auf den lateinischen Tittel nicht besinnen: Du wirst sie aber bald erkennen, und sie muss zuverlässig da seyn. Schicke mir sie gleich.'[3]

Lessing's comment on the delivery of Madame Löwen is that it shows a correct, but not too noticeable accentuation (VIII, 52). If it tends to monotony, she makes up for this by a 'delicacy' which he misses in most actors. He explains this by comparing it to that which in music is called 'Mouvement'[4]—that is, not the bar itself, but the degree of quickness or slowness with which it is played. Here Lessing appears to have had in mind a passage in Diderot's second *Entretien sur le Fils naturel*:

Dans les *cantabile*, le musicien laisse à un grand chanteur un libre exercice de son goût et de son talent; il se contente de lui marquer les intervalles

[1] *Von der Unähnlichkeit in der Nachahmung, Werke*, ed. cit. iii, pp. 174 f.

[2] *Litteraturbriefe*, No. lxxxiv, February 14, 1760, *ed. cit.* v, pp. 109 f.; *Gesammelte Schriften*, ed. cit. iv, 2, pp. 15 f.

[3] *Schriften*, xvii, p. 232. In the *Beyträge zur critischen Historie* etc., St. xv (1736), pp. 390 ff., there is an *Abhandlung von denen auf der Schaubühne sterbenden Personen; in sofern man sie nemlich vor den Augen der Zuschauer solle sterben oder ihren Tod erzählen lassen*. But it is not relevant to the present passage, though the representation of death by poison is somewhat superficially discussed (pp. 402 ff.).

[4] 'Les tons et les gestes,' Batteux had said (*Principes de la littérature, ed. cit.* i, p. 347), 'ne sont pas aussi libres dans les Arts, qu'ils le sont dans la Nature....Tout est calculé, 1° par la Mesure, qui régle la durée de chaque ton et de chaque geste; 2° par le Mouvement, qui hâte ou qui retarde cette même durée, sans augmenter ni diminuer le nombre des tons, ni celui des gestes, ni en changer la qualité....' Sainte Albine also uses the word 'mouvement' in connexion with acting.

principaux d'un beau chant. Le poëte en devrait faire autant, quand il connaît bien son acteur. Qu'est-ce qui nous affecte dans le spectacle de l'homme animé de quelque grande passion? Sont-ce ses discours? Quelquefois. Mais ce qui émeut toujours, ce sont des cris, des mots inarticulés, des voix rompues, quelques monosyllabes qui s'échappent par intervalles....C'est l'acteur qui donne au discours tout ce qu'il a d'énergie. C'est lui qui porte aux oreilles la force et la vérité de l'accent.[1]

But Lessing insists that the actors must show a certain 'decency' in representing violent scenes (IX, 65): 'Die Pantomime muss nie bis zu dem Eckelhaften getrieben werden.' Here again, not merely a passage in *Laokoon* might be quoted—'Hierzu füge man, dass der Schauspieler die Vorstellung des körperlichen Schmerzes schwerlich oder gar nicht bis zur Illusion treiben kann'[2]—but also one by Mendelssohn in the *Litteraturbriefe*, which Lessing makes use of elsewhere (V, 74; XXVII, 30). Here Mendelssohn wrote:

...die Pantomime muss sich auf der tragischen Schaubühne, sowohl als die Musik in den Schranken einer Hülfskunst halten, und sich hüten zum Nachtheil der Hauptkunst, der dramatischen Poesie, ihre Zauberkünste zu verschwenden....Solche äusserliche Handlungen nehmlich, die durch das Schreckliche, das Wunderbare, das Ungeheuere, oder das Niedrige, das ihnen, nicht als Zeichen der Gedanken, sondern blos als Pantomime anhängt, die Aufmerksamkeit der Zuschauer von der poetischen Illusion ablocken können, die müssen von der Bühne entfernt...werden.[3]

Finally, the careful actor must preserve the 'Costume' of his rôle (I, 59; cp. also XLII, 58, 61). This technical term is defined by Du Bos as follows:

La vraisemblance poëtique consiste...à observer dans son tableau ce que les Italiens appellent *il Costumé*, c'est-à-dire, à s'y conformer à ce que nous sçavons des mœurs, des habits, des bâtimens et des armes particulieres des peuples qu'on veut représenter.[4]

Lessing accepted Löwen's view of the 'Principal' or actor-manager who had degraded a free art to a handicraft (*Ank.* 30). But he was fully aware of the practical exigences of conducting a theatre; he admitted that there must be plays of a mediocre character that provided opportunities for the actors (78). He realised that if out of

[1] *Œuvres complètes, ed. cit.* vii, pp. 105 f.; Lessing's translation, *ed. cit.* i, pp. 207 f.
[2] Section iv; *Schriften*, ix, p. 24.
[3] *Litteraturbriefe*, No. lxxxiv, February 14, 1760, *ed. cit.* v, pp. 109 f.; *Gesammelte Schriften, ed. cit.* iv, 2, pp. 15 f. See also above, p. 484.
[4] *Réflexions critiques sur la Poësie et sur la Peinture*, i, xxx, *ed. cit.* i, p. 245.

four or five persons some were excellent, one must be content; the
theatre where even the candle-snuffer is a Garrick[1] (II, 89) belongs
only to the realms of the imagination.

What Lessing has to say about the employment of music in the
theatre is not of much consequence. The matter is discussed mainly
in St. XXVI–XXVII, with particular reference to the music which
Johann Friedrich Agricola[2] had written for the performance of
Semiramis.

The modern theatre orchestra, Lessing says (XXVI, 18) has taken
the place of the ancient chorus. It is hardly necessary to seek a source
for so obvious an opinion; but the following from Parfaict's *Histoire
du Théâtre françois* (*ed. cit.* iii, p. 455—this is a page from which
Lessing cites in St. LV[3]) may be quoted. The author, in discussing
the use of the chorus in old French drama, observes:

L'embarras, et la dépense de ces Chœurs les firent disparoître du
Théatre. A la place du chant, on y substitua des joueurs d'instrumens, qui
furent d'abord placés sur les ailes du Théatre, où ils exécutoient différens
airs, avant le commencement de la piéce, et de chaque Acte. Ces Sym-
phonistes, dans la suite, changerent de place, on les mit au fond des
troisiémes loges, ensuite aux secondes, et enfin à l'Hôtel, où les Comédiens
représentent actuellement, on jugea qu'ils seroient mieux entre le Théatre
et le Parterre; et l'Acteur des Chœurs qui déclamoit, fut remplacé par
les confidens ou confidentes.

Lessing then proceeds to quote *Der critische Musikus*, a journal published by Johann Adolf Scheibe (1708–76), who had been settled in
Copenhagen since 1744. Originally published in 1737, *Der critische
Musikus* appeared in a 'neue vermehrte und verbesserte Auflage' at
Leipzig in 1745. The following quotation from St. 67 (December 8,
1739, ii (Hamburg, 1740), pp. 319 ff.) will illustrate Lessing's introductory remarks (XXVI, 22):

---

[1] The esteem which Garrick enjoyed on the continent in the eighteenth century
was very high; in fact, almost mythical. In his *Laokoon* (section iv) Lessing
says (*Schriften*, ix, p. 33): 'Wenn ich fände, dass es unsere Schauspieler nicht
könnten, so müsste ich erst wissen, ob es auch ein Garrik nicht vermögend
wäre.'

[2] J. F. Agricola, born in 1720, studied music under Sebastian Bach, and became
Court composer to the theatre in Potsdam; from 1759 he was musical director to
Frederick the Great; his death took place in 1774. He was a personal friend of
Lessing. Johann Wilhelm Hertel (mentioned XXVI, 153) was born at Eisenach in
1727, and from 1757 on was Court composer in Mecklenburg. He died in 1789.

[3] See above, p. 394.

Die zwote Gattung theatralischer Sinfonien gehöret eigentlich zu den Tragödien und Comödien. Es darf sich inzwischen niemand wundern, dass ich diese Sinfonien besonders zu untersuchen, für gut befinde. Vielleicht ist noch niemand sonderlich darauf gefallen, dass es eine nothwendige Sache ist, zu den Comoedien und Tragoedien besondere Sinfonien zu verfertigen. Vielleicht kann ich mir nicht unbillig schmeicheln, dass ich der Erste bin, der dieser Sache ordentlich nachgedacht, und sie bereits durch öffentliche Proben zur Ausübung gebracht hat.... Nachdem ich aber ganz leicht einsehen konnte, dass nach der Verschiedenheit der Schauspiele, auch die Music dazu verschieden seyn müste, und dass also ein jedwedes Schauspiel seine besondere und eigene musicalische Begleitung zwischen den Aufzügen oder Handlungen erfoderte.... Diese meine Meynung überlegte ich hernach mit einigen guten Freunden, und sonderlich sprach ich mit einigen geschickten Leuten der Neuberischen Gesellschaft, und auch selbst mit der Frau Neuberin davon, die denn sämmtlich meinem Vorschlage beyfielen, und auch um eine Probe davon ersuchten. Ich entwarf also anfangs die Sinfonien zu dem vortreflichen Trauerspiele Polyeuctes, und kurz darauf auch die Sinfonien zum Trauerspiele Mithridates, die denn auch beyde im Jahre 1738 zu erst all hier und hernach auch in Leipzig und in Kiel aufgeführet worden sind.

The lengthy quotation (XXVI, 34 ff.) from *Der critische Musikus* (ii, St. 67 (Hamburg, 1740), pp. 322 ff.) does not correspond altogether with the text, there being frequent small changes and some omissions.[1]

In St. LXXX (113) Lessing has something to say on the part played by 'Verzierungen' in the theatre—a matter suggested by Aristotle's remark, in the fourteenth chapter of his *Poetics*, on the arousing of fear and pity by spectacular means. And he points to the case of Shakespeare as showing how inessential are such decorations. He quotes here from Cibber's Life of Sir William Davenant (*Lives of the Poets of Great Britain and Ireland*, ed. *cit.* ii, pp. 78 f.) a passage which is concerned with the performance of *The Siege of Rhodes* at the Duke's Theatre in 1663. Before the words at the end of the extract quoted by

---

[1] Schütze (*op. cit.* pp. 233 f.) refers to the Hamburg practice as follows: 'Scheibe machte die für die Kunst wichtige Entdeckung: dass die vor und zwischen den Stücken zu spielende Musik mit dem Inhalt der Stücke übereinstimmen, dass jedes Stück seine eigne, ihm angepasste musikalische Begleitung haben müsse. Lessing giebt in seiner Hamb. Dramaturgie (im 26. Stücke) eine Stelle aus Scheibens kritischen Musikus, die sich darauf bezieht und fügt sein Kennerurtheil hinzu. Wie wenig ist dieser lehrreiche Wink das Orchester zu verbessern in der Folge auch in Hamburg benutzt! Wie wenig hat man Poesie und Musik in nähere Verbindung zu setzen gewusst oder gewollt! Wie oft unpassende Angloisen vor Trauerspielen, Adagios vor Lustspielen geigen lassen!'

Lessing—'The spirit and judgment of the actors supplied all deficiencies, and made as some would insinuate, plays more intelligible
without scenes, than they afterwards were with them' (p. 80)—there
occurs in Cibber's text (p. 79) the sentence: 'In Shakespear's time
so undecorated were the theatres, that a blanket supplied the place
of a curtain.'

CONCLUSION

About the beginning of the present century, when Germany was overhauling her school *curricula*, a considerable controversy was stirred up in respect of the suitability of the *Hamburgische Dramaturgie* for educational purposes,[1] with the result that this work was deposed from the prominent position which it held last century in the German schools.

This is a conclusion which has generally been admitted to be reasonable. That the *Dramaturgie* is a work whose criticism is directed for the most part to long-forgotten plays, which no schoolboy could ever be expected to read, necessarily eliminates as desirable reading for schools a large part of its contents. And even its dramatic theory can only lay claim to historical interest. Lessing's interpretation of Aristotle has not stood the test of time—indeed, as we have seen, it is for the most part out of date and misleading. And his theory of tragedy, hindered by the narrow 'moral' demands of the age of enlightenment, has long faded in the light of the new aesthetic theories which have developed in Europe under Romantic stimulus in the last century and a half. Much—very much—of Lessing's treatise has gone by the board.

The value of the *Dramaturgie* may even have been further diminished in modern eyes by the foregoing investigations, which have deprived Lessing's criticism of individual plays and his dramatic theory, to a degree not hitherto suspected, of the credit of originality and initiative. Admitting, as we have always admitted, that the valuable kernel of the treatise lies in its exposition of the theory of tragedy, it is at once obvious that a periodical journal, criticising from day to day the work of a theatre dependent for the most part on mediocre plays, was the least suitable medium for the presentation of a system of dramatic aesthetics. Views expressed under journalistic pressure, on the spur of the moment and in respect of the chance occasion offered by the play under consideration, might indeed provide valuable material for a treatise on what we now call 'dramaturgy'—though Lessing hardly envisaged it as this; but they could not constitute such a treatise. The work suffers, as the *Laokoon* also had suffered, in that it

[1] Cp. F. Seiler, *Der Gegenwartswert der Hamburgischen Dramaturgie*, Berlin, 1901 (2nd ed. Berlin, 1912).

is a collection of disjointed materials; it is not the complete work that we should have liked to receive from the pen of so great a critic. Lessing's views here do not form a clearly thought-out system; indeed they are not always to be reconciled with one another. Finally, the disheartening conditions of the whole theatrical enterprise—doomed almost before ever it had begun—cast a shadow on the work which it is difficult to forget.

In the end, those who wish to maintain the lasting value of the *Dramaturgie* have been driven to the last ditch of style. In this respect, claims for 'present-day' value certainly can be made good, although I note that even here the argument has been used that it is not wise to offer Lessing to young German scholars, lest they be tempted to write as he wrote. His style is old-fashioned—but so, for that matter, is Goethe's—and cumbered, as eighteenth-century German was, with Latinisms; it indulges unnecessarily in foreign words; it is, perhaps, more French than German in its antitheses and witty persiflage. But if I may venture the opinion, I doubt whether these objections are valid—even for the school. Perhaps, indeed, just in these days when, under the influence of new literary theories, German critical writing is falling back into old failings—nebulosity, unclear thinking, the wrapping-up of thought in a deluge of words—there could be worse lessons for German style than those which Lessing has to teach. In any case the positive value of his style is not likely to escape the admiration of the foreign reader; we in England have always rejoiced in his clear-cut phrases: his precise concrete thinking: even his often misdirected persiflage.

What Lessing has to teach us may not be as original as we used to think it was; but his way of teaching has driven the lessons home as his predecessors were unable to do. Others before him had attacked the rule-bound artificiality of the *tragédie classique*, but none was able to dethrone it so effectively as he, with his brilliant reduction of the plot of *Rodogune* to absurdity; the rules had been discredited, even in France, long before Lessing—but who has put the whole problem they involve more brilliantly and cogently than he?

Again, when it comes to concrete criticisms of individual writers, he may be manifestly unfair to his great opponent Voltaire; but who can overlook the wit of the rapier thrusts with which he demolishes him? And from no work of the eighteenth century does a more vivid portrait of the greatest of Lessing's contemporaries emerge than from the *Hamburgische Dramaturgie*. Lastly, as we have seen, Lessing's

championship of the supreme master of the drama is much less than
has often been supposed; there were other critics of the eighteenth
century before him—even men such as Gerstenberg—who had a
more whole-hearted appreciation and understanding for the greatness
of Shakespeare's art and mind than he, and whose eyes were less blinkered by eighteenth-century theories and eighteenth-century morality;
but, none the less, it was Lessing who by phrases and winged words
achieved more for the growing appreciation of Shakespeare in Germany than any other before the outbreak of the *Sturm und Drang*.
The deep value of Lessing's mind as expressed in his style is certainly
not to be gainsaid.

But still, in the end, we may agree that the amount of the *Hamburgische Dramaturgie* utilisable for pedagogic purposes might be reduced to comparatively few pages. These considerations, however,
are not such as concern us here. Did we attach weight to them, they
would place an embargo on the study of all treatises of the past on
taste or aesthetics, from Aristotle onwards. As a historical document,
a compendium of aesthetic theory, the *Hamburgische Dramaturgie* is of
the first importance. For the understanding of the drama of the
eighteenth century—and that not only in Germany—its study is
obligatory. For it is, without question, the greatest treatise on the
theory of drama which that century produced. Its value in this
respect is not diminished by a weakness which has emerged more
fully in the course of this study—its lack of originality. Rather indeed
is its historical value increased: for we are able to see how a first-class
critical mind viewed the doctrines which dominated the eighteenth-
century theatre and the theoretical conceptions of the drama. It
sums up, draws together the threads, as it were, of all that the
eighteenth century thought on this subject; and pronounces judgments—often, it may be, shortsighted, but all logically justifiable—
which do not affect German drama alone. It is not merely, in all
essentials, the greatest dramaturgic text-book of its century: it represents in general the most advanced thinking which Europe had
attained at the close of the third quarter of that century. We may not
be able to learn from it much knowledge which we can apply to the
drama of to-day—though often, amidst the vagaries of the so-called
expressionist drama of the last generation, I have felt what a godsend
would have been the cold clear light of Lessing's translucent mind.
But even so, we can and do learn from it the best that the eighteenth
century thought about the drama of its own age.

BIBLIOGRAPHICAL NOTE

The following editions of Lessing's works and commentaries on the *Hamburgische Dramaturgie* have been chiefly used:

G. E. Lessing, *Sämtliche Schriften*, ed. K. Lachmann, 3rd ed. revised by F. Muncker, Stuttgart, 1886–1924 (cited throughout as *Schriften*).

Lessings sämmtliche Schriften, Berlin, 1771–94.

Lessings Werke, Berlin [1868–79] (referred to as "Hempel edition").

Lessings Werke (Goldene Klassiker-Bibliothek), ed. J. Petersen and W. v. Olshausen, Berlin [1925–9], *Anmerkungen zu Teil 1 bis 7*, containing commentary on *Hamburgische Dramaturgie* (cited as Petersen, *ed. cit.*).

Lessings Hamburgische Dramaturgie, ed. J. Petersen, Berlin [1915].

Lessings Hamburgische Dramaturgie, ed. F. Schröter and R. Thiele, Halle, 1878 (cited as Schröter and Thiele, *ed. cit.*).

W. Cosack, *Materialien zur Hamburgischen Dramaturgie*, 2nd ed., Paderborn, 1891.

Beyträge zur Historie und Aufnahme des Theaters, Stuttgart, 1750 (cited as *Beyträge*).

Theatralische Bibliothek, Berlin, 1754–8.

Briefe, die neuste Litteratur betreffend, Berlin, 1759–65 (cited as *Litteraturbriefe*).

Das Theater des Herrn Diderot, Berlin, 1760.

Lessings Briefwechsel mit Mendelssohn und Nicolai über das Trauerspiel, ed. R. Petsch (*Philosophische Bibliothek*, 121), Leipzig, 1910.

INDEX OF SPECIFIC REFERENCES TO SECTIONS
OF THE *HAMBURGISCHE DRAMATURGIE*

GENERAL INDEX

ACKERMANN, CHARLOTTE
16, 33, 38, 39, 64, 80

ACKERMANN, DOROTHEA
16, 33, 38-9, 64, 80, 85, 281

ACKERMANN, CHARLOTTE or DOROTHEA
(appearing on playbills as 'Mlle
Ackermann')
55, 58, 64, 65, 66, 68, 69, 71, 76, 77,
78, 81, 82, 91, 93, 140 (note 1)

ACKERMANN, KONRAD ERNST
9, 11, 13 (and note 1), 14, 16, 17, 18,
19, 20, 26 (and note 3), 27, 29, 32,
33, 34, 36, 38, 39, 40, 43 (note 1),
56, 58, 93, 116
as actor 13-4, 14 (note 1), 16, 33, 76,
79, 92
repertory of 14 (and note 2), 16, 48,
49, 50, 60, 63, 64, 66, 69, 73-4, 75,
76, 79, 83, 85, 86, 88, 90, 92, 234,
260 (and note 3), 280, 281
rôles of, in Lessing's time 33, 63, 64,
66, 69, 71, 73, 85
and Löwen 17-8, 19, 33, 116, 118,
159-60

ACKERMANN, MADAME
16, 27-8

ACTING, ART OF
31-2, 110, 115, 253, 320-1, 335, 431,
471-85
(See also under DIDEROT, HILL,
LESSING, F. RICCOBONI, SAINTE
ALBINE)

ACTOR, PROFESSION OF
1, 2-3, 6, 22-3, 24, 32

ACTOR-MANAGERS (See under 'PRIN-
CIPALS')

ACTORS, ENGLISH
in Germany 2, 3

ACTORS, FRENCH
in Germany 5

ADDISON, JOSEPH
71, 97 (and note 1), 256, 257
Lessing's opinion of 257
Cato 6, 256 (and note 2), 340
The Drummer 200

AESCHYLUS
286, 309, 356, 383

AGRICOLA, J. F. A.
486 (and note 2); symphony to
Semiramis 62, 486

ALEXANDRINE VERSE
Ekhof's declamation of 28, 30
Lessing's view of 241, 244
Die stumme Schönheit in 65; *Olint und
Sophronia* in 143; Pfeffel's *Der
Schatz* in 69; *Zelmire* in 241
use of, in Germany 5, 6, 7, 9, 14, 30,
47-8; in translation of *Démocrite
amoureux* 72, of *L'Aveugle clair-
voyant* 92, of *Le Comte d'Essex* 79,
of *Le Distrait* 82, of *Le Philosophe
marié* 62, of *Mérope* 86, of *Rodogune*
82, of *Sémiramis* 61, of *Zayre* 70

ALLACCI, LEONE
La Drammaturgia 120-1, 122, 279,
285 (note 2)
first modern use of word in 120

ALLGEMEINE DEUTSCHE BIBLIOTHEK
57, 82, 248 (note 1)

*ALMANACH HISTORIQUE ET CHRONO-
LOGIQUE DE TOUS LES THÉÂTRES
DE PARIS*
121

APPIANUS ALEXANDRINUS
166, 167

ARISTOPHANES
315-6, 426
edition of, used by Lessing 316 (and
note 2)

ARISTOTLE
115, 120, 153, 171, 213, 214, 245,
246, 295, 307, 311, 315, 344, 357
(note 2), 380, 381 (and notes
1 & 4), 389, 407, 409 (and note
1), 410, 421, 422, 428, 489,
491
authority of, in European criticism
345-6, 347 (and notes 1 & 2)
definition of comedy 391; Corneille
on 391

CAMBRIDGE: PRINTED BY W. LEWIS, M.A., AT THE UNIVERSITY PRESS

M